D0338484

ALSO BY ROBERT CRAWFORD

NONFICTION

The Savage and the City
in the Work of T. S. Eliot

Devolving English Literature

Identifying Poets: Self and Territory
in Twentieth-Century Poetry

The Modern Poet

Scotland's Books: The Penguin
History of Scottish Literature

The Bard: Robert Burns, A Biography

Bannockburns

On Glasgow and Edinburgh

Robert Burns and Cultural Authority
(editor)

The Scottish Invention of English
Literature (editor)

Contemporary Poetry and
Contemporary Science (editor)

POETRY

A Scottish Assembly

Sharawaggi (with W. N. Herbert)

Talkies

Masculinity

Spirit Machines

The Tip of My Tongue

Selected Poems

Apollos of the North

Full Volume

Simonides

Testament

ANTHOLOGIES

Other Tongues: Young Scottish Poets
in English, Scots and Gaelic (editor)

The Penguin Book of Poetry from
Britain and Ireland since 1945
(editor with Simon Armitage)

The New Penguin Book of Scottish
Verse (editor with Mick Imlah)

Scottish Religious Poetry
(editor with Meg Bateman and
James McGonigal)

The Book of St Andrews (editor)

Young Eliot

Young Eliot

FROM ST. LOUIS TO
THE WASTE LAND

ROBERT CRAWFORD

FARRAR, STRAUS AND GIROUX

NEW YORK

Farrar, Straus and Giroux
18 West 18th Street, New York 10011

Library of Congress Cataloging-in-Publication Data
Crawford, Robert, 1959–
    Young Eliot : from St. Louis to The Waste Land / Robert Crawford.
        pages   cm
    Includes index.
    ISBN 978-0-374-27944-8 (hardback) — ISBN 978-1-4299-5176-0 (e-book)
    1. Eliot, T. S. (Thomas Stearns), 1888–1965.   2. Poets, American—
20th century—Biography.   I. Title.

PS3509.L43 Z6545 2015
821'.912—dc23
[B]
                                                                        2014047118

for Alice

Contents

	Acknowledgements	ix
	List of Plates	xiii
	Introduction	1
1	Tom	11
2	Hi, Kid, Let's Dance	36
3	Schoolings	59
4	A Full-Fledged Harvard Man	79
5	A Rose	101
6	Secret Knowledge	122
7	Voyages	140
8	A Philosopher and Actor Falls in Love	165
9	The Oxford Year	201
10	V. S. Eliot	232
11	Observations	260
12	American	290
13	Old Man	312
14	Professional	344
15	To Lausanne	367
16	*The Waste Land*	400
	Abbreviations	425
	Notes	427
	Index	479

Acknowledgements

THIS poet has been part of my life since at least 1974 when I bought his *Complete Poems and Plays*. In private the music of his poetry captivated me, but that book was practical in public too. It was a talisman I carried in my school bag to ward off mathematics. Eliot, who studied advanced mathematics as a graduate student, might not have approved. After reading his work further while a Glasgow University undergraduate, thanks to the Carnegie Trust for the Universities of Scotland and the Snell Exhibition, I went to Balliol College, Oxford, to write a doctoral thesis on Eliot. Only one supervisor was willing to take me on. To Richard Ellmann I owe debts that cannot be repaid; to Mary Ellmann as much. I made my first Eliot-related visit to the USA in 1983, spending time in New York Public Library, at Columbia University, at Yale, and as a visiting scholar at Eliot House, Harvard, where I kipped on a sofa and played loud music in the sombre Matthiessen Room, whose curator George Abbott White was especially welcoming.

After Kim Scott Walwyn at Oxford University Press published my first book, with help from John Carey and others I worked at St Hugh's College, Oxford, then at Glasgow University. Since 1989 at the University of St Andrews I have taught Honours-level courses on Scottish literature and on T. S. Eliot, looking out the classroom window over the North Sea while reading 'Marina' or 'The Dry Salvages'. Generations of bright St Andrews undergraduates have confirmed that this was the right thing to do, and I have learned much from their comments. Among my graduate students I would like to thank especially Will Gray and Josh Richards for their insights, help and advice. Over the years all my School of English colleagues at St Andrews have contributed to my understanding of poetry in general, and of Eliot's in particular.

This book could not have been written without the award of a British Academy/Leverhulme Trust Senior Research Fellowship for the academic session 2012–13, supplemented by a semester's research leave awarded by the University of St Andrews. Lecturing to the T. S. Eliot Society in St Louis, addressing the T. S. Eliot International Summer School in London and reading 'Little Gidding' with Seamus Heaney to the T. S. Eliot Society of the UK at Little Gidding, as well as the invitation to deliver the British Academy's Warton Lecture on English Poetry in 2009, were among the immediate spurs to the writing of the book. Crucial has been the long-standing support of my shrewd, demanding editor at Jonathan Cape, Robin Robertson, who commissioned this biography; to Jonathan Galassi, my editor at Farrar, Straus & Giroux, I owe gratitude for his trust. Patient help was supplied by Clare Bullock at Cape and by Christopher Richards at FSG. My agent David Godwin and his colleagues at David Godwin Associates in London have been essential to the project, supplying characteristically deft support. For copy-editing I thank the meticulous Lin Vasey and for indexing Marian Aird.

Going way beyond the bounds of friendship, my former student Dr Richard King and Dr Stephen N. Sanfilippo (editor of *Seasongs*) ingeniously tracked down the ballad about the schooner *Lapwing* which Eliot recalled hearing as a young man: Richard and Stephen, I salute your skill and generosity, as well as the assistance of Mr William Plaskon of the Jonesport Historical Society, Maine, and Ms Susan M. Sanfilippo, Curator, Pembroke (Maine) Historical Society. Carey Karmel alerted me to the Ether Monument in Boston, and Mark Storey to Eliot's application to join the London Library. Graciously, Aisha Farr and Cliff Boehmer went out of their way to take several photographs of buildings where Eliot lived; Rachel Falconer and colleagues at the University of Lausanne sent me copies of pictures of that city taken around 1921. Late in the writing of the book Jeremy Hutchinson, Lord Hutchinson of Lullington, shared with me his mother's memoirs of Eliot and let me record a substantial interview with him at his home. That was, as I anticipated, a delight, and gave me what I never expected: the chance to chat with someone in 2013 who remembered Eliot before the publication of *The Waste Land*.

Warm thanks are due, too, to many people for advice, guided tours, winks, drinks and staunch support. Among them are Michael and Mary Alexander; Struther and Greta Arnott; David Bradshaw; Jewel Spears Brooker; John Burnside; Marilyn Butler; Peter H. Butter; Robert Christie; Tony Cuda; Robert M. Cummings; Robert Davis; Frances Dickey; Douglas Dunn; Ulla Dydo; Melanie Fathman; Graham Bruce Fletcher; Elizabeth Glass; Lyndall Gordon; John Haffenden; Jason Harding; Henry

Hart; Hugh Haughton; Seamus Heaney; Roger Highfield; Rosalind
Ingrams; Manju Jain; Iman Javadi; David Kinloch; Joan Langhorne; Sara
Lodge; Jim McCue; Arthur E. Meikle; Edward Mendelson; Elizabeth
Micakovicz; Edwin Morgan; Les Murray; Don Paterson; Diana Franzusoff
Peterson; Richard Price; Patrick Reilly; Louise Richardson; Christopher
Ricks; John A. M. Rillie; Carl Schmidt; Ronald Schuchard; Susan Sellers;
Fiona Stafford; Jayme Stayer; Archie Turnbull; Paul Turner; Clifford Tym;
Lynda Tym; Margaret Vickers; Mark Webster; Hamish Whyte.

At the Houghton Library, Harvard, thanks are due especially to Leslie
Morris, Susan Halpert and their colleagues; at the Archive Centre of King's
College, Cambridge, to Patricia McGuire and her colleagues. Other libraries
and archives to be thanked for their consistent support and helpfulness
include the Beinecke Library, Yale University, and the Sterling Memorial
Library at Yale; the Bodleian Library, Oxford; the British Library; the
Brotherton Library, University of Leeds; Glasgow University Library;
Harvard University Archives; Haverford College Library; High Wycombe
Library; the Library of Congress (not least for such digital resources as the
Chronicling America newspaper database); the London Library; Margate
Library; Marlow Library, Buckinghamshire; Merton College Library;
Missouri History Museum; the Mitchell Library, Glasgow; the National
Library of Scotland; New York Public Library, Astor, Lennox, and Tilden
Foundations; St Andrews University Library; University of Missouri
Library; Washington University, St Louis.

For permission to quote from the published and unpublished work of
T. S. Eliot I thank the Estate of T. S. Eliot and Faber and Faber Ltd;
particularly, I acknowledge their permission to quote poetry from Faber
volumes including *Collected Poems 1909–1962* by T. S. Eliot, *Inventions of the
March Hare* by T. S. Eliot (edited by Christopher Ricks), and *The Waste
Land: A Facsimile and Transcript* by T. S. Eliot (edited by Valerie Eliot); their
permission to quote prose from *Selected Prose* by T. S. Eliot (edited by Frank
Kermode), and from *The Letters of T. S. Eliot, Volumes 1 and 2* (edited by
Valerie Eliot and Hugh Haughton); also for their permission to quote from
uncollected prose, property of the Estate of T. S. Eliot, and from unpub-
lished prose, poetry, and other materials which are also property of the
Estate of T. S. Eliot. I owe a debt of gratitude to Clare Reihill and to
Emma Cheshire for their patience and attention. I am grateful also for
permission to quote in the United States and related territories excerpts
from *Inventions of the March Hare: Poems 1909–1917* by T. S. Eliot (text copyright c. 1996 by Valerie Eliot. Reprinted by permission of Houghton Mifflin
Harcourt Publishing Company; all rights reserved); also excerpts from *The
Letters of T. S. Eliot* published by Yale University Press. Other quotations

from published works in *Young Eliot* are used under the terms of fair use, and sources are cited in detail in the endnotes to this book.

For help with and/or permission to reproduce manuscript materials in their collections I am grateful to the Beinecke Rare Book and Manuscript Library, Yale University (particularly Nancy Kuhl, Curator of Poetry, Yale Collection of American Literature); to the Bodleian Library, Oxford (where Dr Judith Priestman expedited my request); to the Cambridge Historical Society of Brattle Street, Cambridge, Massachusetts (particularly Gavin W. Kleespies); to the Hayward Bequest, King's College, Cambridge, England (where, as ever, the College Archivist Patricia McGuire and her colleague Peter Monteith were especially helpful); to the Houghton Library, Harvard University (thanks again to Leslie A. Morris, Curator of Modern Books and Manuscripts, and her colleagues Susan Halpert, Christina Linklater, and Mary Haegert); to the Warden and Fellows of Merton College, Oxford, for permission to quote from College records (thanks to Dr Julia Walworth and to Julian Reid); and to other rights holders. Though permissions to reproduce photographs in this book are acknowledged separately in the list of plates, I would like to thank especially the Bertrand Russell Archive at McMaster University, Hamilton, Ontario, and Rick Stapleton, Archives and Research Collections Librarian there for generous help; also once again the Hayward Bequest, King's College, Cambridge (especially Patricia McGuire); the Houghton Library, Harvard (especially Leslie A. Morris); the National Library of Scotland (Sarah Moxey); and the Archives of Smith College (Nichole Calero).

Though the online publication of *The Complete Prose of T. S. Eliot: The Critical Edition* (the first two volumes of which are now published by Johns Hopkins University Press along with Faber and Faber) and the new edition of Eliot's collected poetry (forthcoming from Faber) were not available in time for me to consult, I would like to thank Professor Ronald Schuchard, overall editor of *The Complete Prose*, for his guidance and generous support throughout this project and over many years; and I want to thank also Jim McCue and Professor Sir Christopher Ricks, joint editors of the poetry, for exchanging intelligence as they and I were working on our respective projects – and for their sheer wisdom. Future writers on Eliot will be in these great editors' debt.

My mother and father nurtured my love of the poetry of T. S. Eliot; my wife Alice and our children, Lewis and Blyth, have sustained it, sometimes to the limit. Without them this book would not have been written. Thank you.

R.C., St Andrews, 2014

List of Plates

Frontispiece: Tom during his student years.
(Hayward Bequest, King's College, Cambridge; reproduced with the permission of King's College Archives and the T. S. Eliot Estate)

1. Henry Ware Eliot, Jr., with his baby brother Tom in St Louis around 1890. This photograph was taken by the firm of Scholten, St Louis, often regarded as the leading St Louis photographer at that time.
    (Hayward Bequest, King's College, Cambridge; reproduced with the permission of King's College Archives and the T. S. Eliot Estate)

2. Tom's father, Henry Ware Eliot, sitting on the porch of the family's summer home at Eastern Point, Gloucester, Massachusetts.
    (Hayward Bequest, King's College, Cambridge; reproduced with the permission of King's College Archives and the T. S. Eliot Estate)

3. Tom's mother, Charlotte Champe Eliot.
    (Hayward Bequest, King's College, Cambridge; reproduced with the permission of King's College Archives and the T. S. Eliot Estate)

4. Tom, sitting on the front gate of the family home at 2635 Locust Street, St Louis, with his mother and, from the left, his cousin Henrietta, his sister Marian (obscured, with her hand to her head), and his sister Margaret on the morning after the 1896 cyclone.
    (Hayward Bequest, King's College, Cambridge; reproduced with the permission of King's College Archives and the T. S. Eliot Estate)

5. 2635 Locust Street (now demolished) was screened by dense foliage in a city often loud with the sound of cicadas.
    (Hayward Bequest, King's College, Cambridge; reproduced with the permission of King's College Archives and the T. S. Eliot Estate)

6.   The hallway of 2635 Locust Street, with (on the left) the grandfather clock which Tom's father brought from Massachusetts as a present for his wife.
     (Hayward Bequest, King's College, Cambridge; reproduced with the permission of King's College Archives and the T. S. Eliot Estate)

7.   Tom, aged about four, posing for a formal photograph.
     (Houghton Library, Harvard; reproduced with the permission of the Houghton Library and the T. S. Eliot Estate)

8.   Tom, aged about six, with his nursemaid, Annie Dunne, in St Louis. Tom's brother, Henry, was a keen amateur photographer, and took many family photographs.
     (Hayward Bequest, King's College, Cambridge; reproduced with the permission of King's College Archives and the T. S. Eliot Estate)

9.   Tom, aged about seven, in St Louis. This photograph, showing the large ears which so embarrassed him, was taken by the firm of Holborn's Dainties of 2820 Washington Avenue, St Louis, a well established photographic firm.
     (Houghton Library, Harvard; reproduced with the permission of the Houghton Library and the T. S. Eliot Estate)

10. Tom, aged about ten, standing in the yard of Smith Academy, St Louis.
     (Hayward Bequest, King's College, Cambridge; reproduced with the permission of King's College Archives and the T. S. Eliot Estate)

11. The Downs, the Eliots' extensive summer house at Eastern Point, Gloucester, Massachusetts, when recently built in the 1890s.
     (Hayward Bequest, King's College, Cambridge; reproduced with the permission of King's College Archives and the T. S. Eliot Estate)

12. The view to the sea from the porch at the Eliots' Gloucester house. The family liked to gather on this verandah.
     (Hayward Bequest, King's College, Cambridge; reproduced with the permission of King's College Archives and the T. S. Eliot Estate)

13. Tom in sailor suit, sitting astride the balustrade of the porch at the Gloucester house, contemplating a model boat.
     (Hayward Bequest, King's College, Cambridge; reproduced with the permission of King's College Archives and the T. S. Eliot Estate)

14. Tom as a boy at Gloucester, learning to sail. He was taught by a retired sailor, nicknamed 'The Skipper'.

(Hayward Bequest, King's College, Cambridge; reproduced with the permission of King's College Archives and the T. S. Eliot Estate)

15. A damaged photograph of Tom, aged about eight, enjoying the company of his cousins Eleanor and Barbara Hinkley on the rocks at Eastern Point, Gloucester, where he liked to play as a boy.
    (Houghton Library, Harvard; reproduced with the permission of the Houghton Library and the T. S. Eliot Estate)

16. Tom, aged about twelve.
    (Hayward Bequest, King's College, Cambridge; reproduced with the permission of King's College Archives and the T. S. Eliot Estate)

17. Harvard Yard at the beginning of the twentieth century. This photograph appears in *The Harvard (Class) Album 1901*, edited by Carroll J. Swan and published in Cambridge, Massachusetts.
    (Private collection)

18. Tom as a thin Harvard undergraduate in 1907, wearing what look like white flannel trousers on the porch at Eastern Point, Gloucester.
    (Hayward Bequest, King's College, Cambridge; reproduced with the permission of King's College Archives and the T. S. Eliot Estate)

19. Tom as a student, sailing in the catboat *Elsa*, with family or friends.
    (Hayward Bequest, King's College, Cambridge reproduced with the permission of King's College Archives and the T. S. Eliot Estate)

20. A modern photograph of the house at 16 Ash Street, Cambridge, Massachusetts, where Tom lodged as a graduate student. His rooms were in the attic.
    (Photograph by Clifford Boehmer, reproduced with his permission)

21. Emily Hale, aged twenty-three, in 1914 (her favourite picture of herself).
    (Sophia Smith Collection, Smith College Archives; reproduced with the permission of Smith College Archives)

22. Vivien Eliot as a young woman.
    (Houghton Library, Harvard; reproduced with the Houghton Library and the T. S. Eliot Estate)

23. Vivien and Tom as a young married couple in 1916 in their flat at 18 Crawford Mansions, Marylebone, London.
    (The Eliot Estate; this photograph, which later belonged to Valerie Eliot, is reproduced with the permission of the T. S. Eliot Estate)

24. Vivien's photograph of Tom with Violet and Sydney Schiff in the living room of the house the Eliots leased with Bertrand Russell at 31 West Street, Marlow, Buckinghamshire.
    (Hayward Bequest, King's College, Cambridge; reproduced with the permission of King's College Archives and the T. S. Eliot Estate)

25. Bertrand Russell in 1916.
    (Bertrand Russell Archive, McMaster University; reproduced with the permission of the Bertrand Russell Archive at McMaster)

26. Vivien at home in the Eliots' London flat.
    (Houghton Library, Harvard; reproduced with the permission of the Houghton Library and the T. S. Eliot Estate)

27. Tom, Osbert Sitwell, young Jeremy Hutchinson, and Mary Hutchinson at West Wittering, Sussex, in July 1919.
    (The Eliot Estate; this photograph, which later belonged to Valerie Eliot, is reproduced by permission of the T. S. Eliot Estate)

28. A modern photograph of London's Clarence Gate Gardens. The Eliots' flat at number 9 was in the far block on the left, just before the church.
    (Photograph by Aisha Farr, reproduced with her permission)

29. An early twentieth-century postcard showing the Hôtel-Pension Ste-Luce (now demolished) in Lausanne, where 'What the Thunder Said' was written.
    (Private collection)

30. Vivien's summer 1920 photograph of (right to left) Violet Schiff, Tom, Sydney Schiff, Lady Tosti (widow of the composer F. P. Tosti), Wyndham Lewis, and two Italian visitors, Signor and Signora Emanueli, in the Schiffs' garden at Eastbourne. Tom is smiling directly at the photographer.
    (Hayward Bequest, King's College, Cambridge; reproduced with the permission of King's College Archives and the T. S. Eliot Estate)

31. Tom's photograph of Vivien with the same group on the same occasion.
    (Hayward Bequest, King's College, Cambridge; reproduced with the permission of King's College Archives and the T. S. Eliot Estate)

32. The title page of *The Waste Land* when first published as a book.
    (National Library of Scotland; reproduced with the permission of the Trustees of the National Library of Scotland)

Introduction

T. S. ELIOT was never young. That, at least, is the impression many readers get from his work. 'I grow old . . . I grow old . . .' complains the voice of 'The Love Song of J. Alfred Prufrock', written when the poet was at the start of his twenties. A few years later Eliot began another poem with the words 'Here I am, an old man'. Still in his early thirties when he published *The Waste Land* in 1922, he argued that the 'most important personage in the poem' was Tiresias, who has already 'foresuffered all' and appears to have lived for thousands of years.[1]

Yet Eliot knew what it meant to be young. To follow his development from early childhood enhances alike reading of his work and understanding of his life. Presenting him as shy, sometimes naïve and vulnerable, *Young Eliot* aims to unsettle common assumptions about this poet's perceived coldness. It shows how his American upbringing combined with experience of France and England to make him not only the most remarkable immigrant poet in the English language but also the most influential and resounding poetic voice of the twentieth century. His poetry embodies an almost limitless resonance.

Eliot's youth remained vital even to his 'aged eagle' tone and achievement.[2] Several people who knew him intimately recognised this. His widow Valerie, who died in 2012, maintained that there remained always a 'little boy' inside 'Tom'.[3] His nephew Graham Bruce Fletcher remembers being taken in boyhood by Uncle Tom to a London joke shop during the early 1960s to buy stink bombs, which they then let off inside the nearby Bedford Hotel, not far from Eliot's office; with a fit of hysterical giggles, Eliot put on a marked turn of speed as he and his nephew, Macavity-like, removed themselves from the scene of the crime. 'Tom' sped off twirling his walking stick, 'in the manner of Charlie Chaplin'.[4] Back home, they did not tell Valerie what they had been up to. Instead, the septuagenarian business-suited Nobel Prize winner settled down to playing with his nephew's remote-controlled toy Aston Martin James Bond car. In age, among those whom he trusted most, the poet nicknamed Old Possum retained a certain gleefulness. He remained young Eliot.

This elderly gentleman turned stink-bomber may have been making up for lost time. His own childhood had been unabashedly strict. A shy, big-eared boy whose privileged upbringing took place within earshot of one of the most seductive productions of African American culture – ragtime music – Tom Eliot in St Louis, Missouri, was not a child renowned for wild escapades. Yet just as his first book contains poems that are unsettlingly subversive – in their rhythms, images and social satire – so throughout his life, despite his po-faced, born-venerable public persona, there was an elusive, wounded and sometimes mischievous identity that remained a source of disconcerting creative energy. He once wrote of Alfred Lord Tennyson, the iconic English Victorian Poet Laureate, that he was 'the most instinctive rebel against the society in which he was the most perfect conformist'.[5] The same could be said of the author of *The Waste Land*.

Like most people to whom his poetry matters, I fell in love with the ineradicably insinuating music of Eliot's verse. More than forty years after I first read it, there are still things about the poetry that puzzle me, luring me on; but I knew from the start, and writing his biography has confirmed the conviction, that Eliot's poems work not because they are intellectual games but because they are the products of an intense emotional life fused with a preternatural mastery of the pliancy of language. Like Tennyson and a very small number of other English poets, Eliot had perfect pitch when it came to the music of words. Yet if his hearing was the source of his greatest gift, then, ironically and absurdly, from very early childhood he hated his own ears. Their large size and shape caused him acute embarrassment, deepening his boyhood shyness. What he managed to do was to turn that apparent source of affliction into his greatest artistic asset. Repeatedly, whether in the case of his shy self-consciousness, or his later sense of sexual hurt, or his experience of death, or his raw sense of having made terrible mistakes in his life, Eliot faces up to a wound, a humiliating source of pain, and, through confronting it, incorporates it into an emotionally resonant, brilliantly intelligent work of art. His poems have their sources in word-music and in such acts of moral or emotional courage as well as in sheer technical mastery. However absurd or tortured on occasion, Eliot's life and his transformation of aspects of it into verse are the work of a great poet. Coming to terms with insistent personal damage, he was able, as few have been able, to make works at once insistently new and abiding.

T. S. Eliot did not want his biography written. Much of his most intimate correspondence, including many letters to his parents and almost all of his correspondence with his first wife, was destroyed at his own request. Having managed to make lasting poetry out of his most stinging humiliations, he wished those humiliations to be afforded the grace of oblivion. Consistent with a good deal of his criticism, which stressed poetic 'impersonality', his efforts to suppress his own biography were sometimes devastatingly successful. Between the summer of 1905 (when Eliot was sixteen) and the winter of 1910 (when he was twenty-two) all that survives of his correspondence is a single postcard. This is one reason why the few biographers who have attempted to write his life tend to pass over the first twenty-one years in around twenty-one pages. I owe these biographers great debts, and believe biography affords not a reductive explanation that undoes the mystery of an author's gift, but a form of artistic narrative attention that averts caricature and illuminates both poet and poetry. Nevertheless, earlier biographies of this particular poet are misleadingly proportioned. Eliot's formative years were exactly that. Their importance is greater than most readers have realised. *Young Eliot* presents this crucial period in much more detail. 'Home is where one starts from.'[6]

Though Eliot wanted no biography written, he did grant Valerie Eliot permission to edit his letters. After he died in 1965, she worked for decades to build a superb archive of the poet's correspondence, drawing not just on carbon copies (many held in the archives of the London publishing house of Faber and Faber, of which Eliot was a director), but also on original letters which Mrs Eliot acquired, often through auction houses. Along with much of Eliot's library, this reassembled archive grew to complement the massive assemblage of Eliot materials housed now in the Houghton Library at Harvard, a collection which owes its origins to the poet's mother and brother; it complements, too, the bequest given to King's College, Cambridge, by Eliot's friend John Hayward. Other substantial hoards developed at locations from Leeds to Texas and from London to New York and New Zealand. Recognised as a figure of global importance, Eliot has long attracted ambitious manuscript collectors. When, not long after his death, some typescripts and other drafts of *The Waste Land* were revealed among the holdings of the New York Public Library, Valerie Eliot produced an impressive scholarly edition of these. In 1988 she published the first volume of her late husband's letters; a much expanded second edition of this appeared in 2009 along with the long delayed second volume. By that time, Mrs Eliot was unwell and these books were co-edited by Professor Hugh Haughton. Now Professor John

Haffenden continues to edit *The Letters of T. S. Eliot*. Several thousand pages are in print, with many thousands more yet to be published.

Pioneering Eliot biographers, including Peter Ackroyd (forbidden to quote more than a few words from Eliot's work) and Lyndall Gordon (who often resorted to paraphrase), sometimes had little to go on when they conducted their research in the 1970s and early 1980s. Today, for long periods of Eliot's life there is so much material available that almost no one will ever read through it. His collected letters and his other prose will fill many volumes, documenting some aspects of this writer's activities (such as his editorial and publishing labours) in exhaustive, exhausting detail. However, many of these letters and articles reveal little about his personal and creative experience. So, half a century after this great poet died, there is more, not less, need for the narrative work of biography.

When I first wrote on Eliot in the 1980s, my doctoral supervisor, Richard Ellmann, told me that Valerie Eliot had discussed the idea of his writing her husband's life. Eventually, Ellmann, a great biographer from a Jewish background, who had already authored a substantial account of Eliot for the *Dictionary of National Biography*, decided he did not want to go ahead. He told me that, though he had huge admiration for Eliot's work, he was put off by an anti-Semitic streak he discerned there. As far as I know, Valerie Eliot, true to her husband's wishes, blocked all would-be official biographers. Lyndall Gordon, herself of Jewish descent, wrote two insightful biographical volumes, but few others have followed. Instead, over the ensuing decades accounts as different as the 1984 play and Hollywood biopic *Tom and Viv* (which sees Eliot as a misogynistic persecutor), Anthony Julius's *T. S. Eliot, Anti-Semitism, and Literary Form* (which prosecutes relentlessly the case that the poet was anti-Semitic), and several works by James E. Miller and others that portray Eliot as a gay man in love with a French male companion, all combined to make Mrs Eliot very wary of what she regarded as exploitative biographical distortions. Resolutely, she continued to assemble an Eliot archive, and embarked on the meticulous publication of his letters, some of them both pained and painful. Latterly, she was instrumental in commissioning editors including Christopher Ricks and Ronald Schuchard to collect and reprint Eliot's work in modern annotated editions. 'It's time', Valerie Eliot is reported to have said in 2004 as her health began to fail, 'to put Tom together now . . . but I'll need some help'.[7]

This is not an official biography. Published fifty years after the poet's death, *Young Eliot* offers an account of his life and work up to and including the first appearance of what many regard as his greatest poem. In due course I hope to publish a second volume, *Eliot after 'The Waste Land'*. When I wrote *The Savage and the City in the Work of T. S. Eliot* (published in 1987), Valerie Eliot, with whom I corresponded, was generous and encouraging. She allowed me to quote from published and unpublished materials after she had read my typescript. In the 1980s she wrote me a few letters, telling me, for instance, about how, while she 'darned his socks', Eliot would read to her from Victorian poet James Thomson's despairing masterpiece, *The City of Dreadful Night*.[8] At that time I was nervous of Mrs Eliot. I knew that had she refused me permission to quote material, not just my book but my career might have been damaged. Some years later, once as a judge of the T. S. Eliot Prize for poetry and once as a poet shortlisted for it, I met her. She was politely friendly, and I found it easy to talk to her, not least because I wanted nothing from her. My wife had written a book about the English novelist Rose Macaulay, whose notoriously bad driving Mrs Eliot enjoyed recalling. She told me how 'Tom', sitting in the back seat, had urged 'Rose' to keep her eyes on the road. Like other people, I was always impressed by the way Valerie Eliot would speak of 'Tom', using his first name. It was natural for her to do so, but there was also, I think, a strategy involved. It was a way of reminding people that T. S. Eliot was a human being, rather than a remote historic monument.

Setting out Eliot's formative years in fuller detail than ever before and showing how his life conditioned the writing of his best-known poems, *Young Eliot* tries to articulate the magnitude of Eliot's achievement and the very substantial cost involved. In an age when the Eliot Estate is more open to quotation from the full range of Eliot's writings, the challenge is to select details which will humanise this dauntingly canonical poet for new generations of readers, make clear why his work matters and set out the often painful drama of the life that underpinned *The Waste Land*. The recently published volumes of *Letters* and my extensive investigations in Massachusetts, St Louis, New Haven, Cambridge, Oxford, London, Bosham and elsewhere allow me to write a more accurate and intimate account of Eliot's time in America and in England than has been possible previously. From its title onwards, this book advances a case for Eliot's early upbringing as fascinating in itself and central to his identity.

Young Eliot presents in detail the poet's childhood in St Louis – that French-named city of ragtime, racial tensions, ancient civilisations, river-boats and (in Eliot's words) the real start of 'the Wild West'.[9] Using newly available or previously ignored sources ranging from digitally searchable newspapers to annotated volumes from Eliot's personal library, and from his later letters to his father's diary and his mother's fugitive poetry, *Young Eliot* portrays an ice-cream loving and mischievous but sometimes rather priggish little boy. St Louis made Eliot. He knew that. 'For his entire life' he went on using a black-barrelled fountain pen believed to have been given to him by his mother when he left the American South in 1905; one of its two gold bands was engraved with the initials 'T.S.E.'[10] Indisputably, in the city of his birth he became 'T. S. Eliot' of 'The T. S. Eliot Co., St. Louis'.[11] Drawing on the work of local historians and on untapped archival sources, *Young Eliot* reveals not just Eliot's early physical environment but also what it meant to his imagination.

With his early teens divided between education in Missouri and summering in Gloucester, Massachusetts, a constant, deepening pleasure for this boy was his love of reading. Images from books, newspapers and shows stayed with him throughout his life, and some of his earliest literary interests – from *Cyrano de Bergerac* to Edward Lear – subtly conditioned his poetry. Though his schooling was considerably Classical, his teenage tastes in verse reacted against this. They were markedly Romantic, even if his youthful reading was unusually gendered: no *Wuthering Heights*, no *Jane Eyre*. His protested Classicism would become a familiar credo, but the young Eliot's enthusiasm for Romantic poetry was not just something to kick against in later years. Sometimes ironised, it was a lasting presence – from the Byronic epigraph in his first full-length prose book to, several decades later, his following Shelley in recreating Dantescan *terza rima* in English.

Eliot recalled himself as indecisive. Sometimes he blamed his parents. 'It is almost impossible for any of our family to make up their minds', he complained in 1920.[12] In his student days, though far from St Louis, he wrote regularly to his mother, continuing to do so for the rest of her life. Even when in 1906 the fledgling poet went to a Harvard ruled over by President Charles William Eliot, he continued within a circle where the influence of his extended family and its code of social service prevailed. Rebelling against this, Eliot conformed to it too. He exhibited a similarly conflicted stance towards the nationality of his birth and towards American literature. Just as the avant-garde French Symbolists, whose poetry fascinated the Harvard student, had learned from the Edgar Allan Poe whose work Eliot had devoured in childhood, so Eliot's great favourite Jules Laforgue was a French poet particularly influenced by American writing. Arrestingly, Eliot's student imitation of the Whitman-loving Laforgue was true to the grain of nineteenth-century American poetry, even as it seemed a shocking, Eurocentric departure.

Francophile before he ever set foot in France, young T. S. Eliot might have died in Cambridge, Massachusetts. During the early summer of 1910 he was hospitalised there with a life-threatening infection. Instead, recovered, he proceeded, as planned, to Paris, working hard to reinvent himself. Brilliant, yet still immature, he felt dogged by failure. Eliot's life was no neat progress towards literary canonisation, towards a form of sainthood or simply towards a Nobel Prize. It was much rawer than that, more jagged, frayed and damaged. An often gruelling existence nourished his poetic vitality. Some of his life's most important experiences, the ones that changed its course, were accidental. Those accidents could be disastrous.

He wrote 'The Love Song of J. Alfred Prufrock', his greatest early poem of anxious masculinity, in 1910–11. Differing in length, its opening lines are conversationally over-familiar yet also weirdly estranging in imagery. The young Eliot who went to Paris has mastered Laforgue's idiom, and then convincingly surpassed it:

Let us go then, you and I,
When the evening is spread out against the sky
Like a patient etherised upon a table . . .[13]

Even the tiniest verbal gestures here – not 'an operating table', or even 'the table', but the more mundanely domestic 'a table' – are unsettling. Yet if 'Prufrock' sounds out unmistakably the new note of modern poetry, then this poem was written alongside other, wilder, less polished works including 'The Triumph of Bullshit'. Young Eliot (who introduced the word 'bullshit' into literature) tries hard to sound shockingly knowing. Fuelled by prejudice and laddishness, his scurrilous and obscene poems too are part of his development: student attempts at writing which struggle to cover with a fabricated voice of experience the poet's own sexual shyness, cerebral sophistication and troubled sense of lack. Triumphantly, in 'The Love Song of J. Alfred Prufrock' he manages to create a male voice which is vulnerable and sexually floundering at the same time as intellectually alert. In so doing he moves beyond effortful posturing to produce a poetic masterpiece that nonetheless draws on aspects of his own psyche.

Too much writing on Eliot over the last two decades has treated him as a thinker more than a poet. True, one of the most 'heavily annotated' books in his personal library was his copy of the philosopher F. H. Bradley's *Appearance and Reality*; yet among his lifelong 'most precious' volumes were editions of Virgil and Dante – poets who, like Eliot, were nourished by philosophical thought.[14] My narrative attends to Eliot's graduate student interests in philosophy. It salutes his intellectual brilliance, detailing his work with Masaharu Anesaki on Japanese Buddhism and with Charles Lanman on Sanskrit. Yet these intellectual adventures were neither more nor less important to his creative imagination than were his death-defying youthful navigation of Mount Desert Rock and his explorations of the coast in a sailboat – dramatic and entertaining events that undergird later poems, including *The Waste Land*.

Though he seems to have had crushes on girls in childhood, the young Eliot who customarily wore a truss was sexually gauche. His first serious falling in love was with Emily Hale, a Bostonian Unitarian preacher's daughter with a mentally ill mother. Later, his disastrous marriage to the young 'pretty vivacious' Englishwoman Vivien Haigh-Wood helped hurt him into further poetry, especially that of *The Waste Land*.[15] Vivien's and his own apparently unending ill-health put them in a state of frequent personal crisis. 'Why does Tom love me?' Vivien wondered a few years after *The Waste Land* appeared. 'I love Tom in a way that destroys us both.'[16]

Young Eliot strives to strike the right balance between the outward form of living which mattered to this bankerly poet and other, sometimes wounded kinds of inner life to which readers have limited access, yet which were vital to his intimate existence and to his writing. The verse is nowhere here treated merely as a crossword puzzle or source-hunter's labyrinth. Consciously crafted artistic work, it nonetheless transmutes personal agonies, treasured images and insights. While some of it can bristle with learning, it can also scald. However much he might have resisted the idea, knowledge of his life heightens a sense of Eliot's finest work as fusing finessed artifice with unmistakable *cri de cœur*.

I cannot claim to be in sympathy with all of Eliot's ideas, and I do not attempt to disguise anti-Semitic moments in his work, or other elements of racism and sexism deeply ingrained in his society and never fully outgrown. This poet was the grandson of a preacher whom Ralph Waldo Emerson considered to be a true 'Saint'.[17] Yet, though preoccupied with sainthood and tainted mortification from at least such early poems as 'The Death of Saint Narcissus', Eliot was no saint and should not be presented as such. From boyhood onwards he had a fascination with asceticism and religious experience which became increasingly important. Still, for all he read about such experiences, he refused to fake them in himself. The young Eliot's philosophical training led to an intense scepticism and relativism; in poems, including 'The Hippopotamus', he could attack Christianity with blasphemous vigour and guile. These facets of his sometimes conflicted personality make him all the more beguilingly complex. His biography is that of a very complicated, often subtle, sometimes prickly human being, but also one whom readers can come to understand to a perhaps surprising degree. Throughout this book, rather than employing paraphrase, I have taken care to give readers frequent and direct contact with Eliot's own words, published and unpublished, and with the words of his contemporaries. The aim is to offer a close-up view and, cumulatively, through successive brushstrokes, to make a nuanced and intimate portrait.

In some ways young Eliot knew himself well. He discerns a 'Mélange Adultère de Tout' that makes a man in different places and circumstances a professor, a journalist, a banker, a philosopher, a Parisian flâneur, and also something much wilder – that insight is astute in its self-perception. Articulated in his second language, French, it may be an obliquely voiced analysis of how Eliot managed to cope. He had an acute sense of himself as multiply displaced, and wrote on the day of England's patron saint, St George's Day, in 1928:

> Some day I want to write an essay about the point of view of an American who wasn't an American, because his America ended in 1829; and who wasn't a Yankee, because he was born in the South and went to school in New England as a small boy with a nigger drawl, but who wasn't a southerner in the South because his people were northerners in a border state and looked down on all southerners and Virginians, and who so was never anything anywhere and who therefore felt himself to be more a Frenchman than an American and more an Englishman than a Frenchman and yet felt that the U.S.A. up to a hundred years ago was a family extension.[18]

This is a writer who could view himself with obsessive, complexly inflected self-consciousness. Yet it is important to see him, too, through the eyes and words of others. His most perceptive observers included Vivien Eliot, Virginia Woolf, Mary Hutchinson and Conrad Aiken. While drawing on their viewpoints, however, *Young Eliot* presents a portrait of an individual, not a panorama of his life and times; but it shows the part Eliot played in his era, from his immersion in World War I enemy debts handled by the Colonial and Foreign Department of Lloyds Bank in London to his participation in small magazines, lectures and social gatherings. Increasingly haggard and ill, he often masked his shyness and tenacious ambition with a businessman's demeanour. In writing, his unflinching examination of his own pain was both shielded and made possible by an aesthetic of impersonality. This is the man Virginia Woolf came very close to loving, and whom she was reported to have described as a poet in 'a four-piece suit'.[19]

Though he had written fragments of it before he left Harvard, in London around 1919 Eliot began to focus on *The Waste Land*. In its drama of voices fragmentation, lost or illusory love and communion with literary tradition clash jaggedly together. As Vivien made clear in her comments, the poem's pain was also bound up with the hurt of Eliot's most intimate relationship. This biography shows clearly links between Eliot's circumstances and *The Waste Land*, but refuses to reduce that artistically crafted, strenuously edited poem to a mere offshoot of personal crisis. If for Eliot in one mood *The Waste Land* represented an outburst of personal 'grumbling', offering him 'the relief of a personal and wholly insignificant grouse against life', then he understood too the way it came to be interpreted not just as a monument of the 'modernist' era but an enduring, polymorphous and profound work of art.[20] In pieces, it is the poem of a man 'going to pieces'; but it is also brilliantly pieced together by Eliot and Ezra Pound. Quickened by Joyce's *Ulysses* and by Stravinsky's *Rite of Spring*, ultimately *The Waste Land* emerges as a poem of desperation. It draws on personal experiences as diverse as its author's interrogation of anthropology and his fondness for dancing, to produce a vision of unending spiritual and physical torture. The 'Shantih', that peace with which the poem appears to conclude, is perceived, but not achieved. *The Waste Land* is a musical astonishment, one to which Woolf listened with admiration in 1922 as its maker seemed to sing it aloud.[21]

Young Eliot aims to communicate a sense of the tentativeness, the shakiness of the young poet's reputation. His work's acceptance was no foregone conclusion. Repeatedly he felt he had dried up as a poet, and feared he had wasted his life. Not marmoreal, but wounded and sometimes wounding, young T. S. Eliot may be imposingly erudite, but is also conflictedly human.

Where I have gone to the original publications to locate Eliot's prose writings, and have consulted numerous original manuscripts of poetry, prose and drama, future generations will have access to electronic editions of much of this material. Yet there will never be an absolutely definitive biography of Eliot. Each age will crave its own portrait. My aim, no small one, is to offer a convincing account of a great poet whose life was impressive, dauntingly complex and, at times, a mess. Eliot's story, like his poetry, contains deep unhappiness; but at the beginning of his life, as at its end, he was happy. To rob him of that is to distort and caricature him. To treat his life as if it was the history of a monument is wrong. In presenting a full and detailed portrait of this poet, I want to circumvent assumptions about his often defensive persona, and so, in the chapters that follow, I shall call him neither by his surname nor by his famous initials but by the name used by most of the people whom he allowed to get close to him, and by those who knew him best from the start.

I

Tom

Before he was T. S. he was Tom. That was what his prosperous parents and his four elder sisters called him. In the summer of 1890 his only brother, Henry, wrote from Boston, Massachusetts, to hard-working Papa Eliot at home in industrial St Louis, Missouri. Henry's holiday news was that baby 'Tom' (then aged two) had just been weighed: 30 pounds.[1] Henry, almost a teenager, seems not to have resented the arrival of another male Eliot. He looks happy photographed beside his alert little brother. Indeed, before long Henry, a bookish boy who liked to go to the Boston Athenaeum to look at the magazines, was taking his own photographs of Tom.

All the baby's surviving siblings were considerably older. When Tom was born, Ada was nineteen, Margaret was seventeen, Charlotte fourteen, Marion eleven and Henry nine. Ada could easily have been mistaken for his mother; she would sit beside him on the stairs at the well-appointed family home, 2635 Locust Street, St Louis, responding to him in a kind of shared vocal game. Later, she told Tom how 'When you were a tiny boy, learning to talk, you used to sound the rhythm of sentences without shaping words – the ups and downs of the thing you were trying to say. I used to answer you in kind, saying nothing yet conversing with you.'[2]

Ada left home while Tom was still little, but he always felt attuned to her. From his early years a mixture of separation and closeness characterised his sense of family. He was loved and happy. He and his mother Lottie treasured memories of his earliest infancy; in adulthood he assured her he still cherished her singing him a song, 'The Little Tailor', while the firelight made patterns on the ceiling of his childhood home.[3] Yet, years later, Tom suggested to Henry that their parents 'in spite of the strength of their affection' had been 'lonely people'.[4] A sense of familial, shared fondness, tradition and values was unusually strong among the

Eliots: Tom inherited it; but he also inherited, and worked hard to counter, a sense of isolation in himself.

When he was born in St Louis in 1888, both his parents were forty-five. Lottie — Charlotte Champe Eliot — gave birth around 7.45 a.m. on Wednesday 26 September. Anxiety mingled with jubilation. Three years earlier Lottie's daughter Theodora had been born severely deformed. Her frail physique had failed to develop. Relatives outside the immediate family worried about how Theodora had so 'wound herself' round her parents' hearts during the sixteen months of her short, stricken life, that they transferred to baby Tom a morbid sense of trepidation that later conditioned his boyhood.[5]

Few mothers in their mid-forties who had recently watched a baby die would not have worried at a subsequent birth, even if they were, like Lottie, of 'unusual character'.[6] The new baby's father Hal — Henry Ware Eliot — sent a telegram immediately to relatives in Oregon: 'Lottie and Little Thomas are well.'[7] Thomas Stearns Eliot's name was chosen with care. Stearns had been Lottie's maiden name. Having called their first son Henry Ware Eliot Junior, after his father, the couple gave their new son the first name of Hal's elder brother, the Oregon-based Reverend Thomas Lamb Eliot, a minister in the Unitarian Church that meant so much to all these Eliots.

A year or so before Tom's birth, Hal, with his customary taste for kith and kin, had subscribed to *A Sketch of the Eliot Family* (1887). He has a short entry in it as Eliot 'No. 163', and close family members feature in its 'Index of Eliots'.[8] Familiar to him and to Lottie, surnames such as Adams, Cranch, Greenleaf, Peabody, Stearns, Stetson and Thayer populate its 'Index of Other Names'. Tom, who later spotted this book in his 'father's library', grew up with a strong, sometimes constricting sense that the world, like this book's indexes, could be divided into Eliots and non-Eliots.[9] Certainly his family tree, was formidable. A distant ancestor, Andrew Eliot, had emigrated from East Coker in Somerset, England, to Beverly in Massachusetts around 1670. Through him the St Louis Eliots could claim kinship with a substantially Unitarian New England elite. The scholar Eric Sigg has pointed out that through his tangled family tree baby Tom was related, distantly, to poets John Greenleaf Whittier and James Russell Lowell; to novelists Henry Melville and Nathaniel Hawthorne; to memoirist Henry Adams; and to the second and sixth presidents of the United States, John Adams and John Quincy Adams.[10] Few squealing infants have had quite so much to live up to.

Worried or not at the time of his birth, the new baby's parents were both strong characters. They treasured their sense of familial inheritance;

yet in each there was also something unfulfilled or repressed. Active in local women's clubs and religious as well as cultural societies, Charlotte cared deeply about education and social welfare. She campaigned for the rights of children in the courts. Her passions encompassed poetry, philosophy and religion; but her own education had not included university study, and the poetry she wrote found only limited outlets, often in Unitarian journals where she had links to the editors. Educated at Washington University in St Louis, her businessman husband had been expected to follow his elder brother and their father into the Unitarian ministry. Hal's father was the Harvard-educated Reverend William Greenleaf Eliot – Eliot 'No. 161' – founder of Washington University, pillar of Unitarianism, writer, 'unflinching supporter of the temperance cause', advocate of 'woman suffrage' and 'helper of the colored race'.[11] Yet Hal had not become a minister: 'too much pudding choked the dog' as he put it; he simply 'gagged'.[12] Nevertheless, Hal, whose cursory short entry in the *Sketch of the Eliot Family* was dwarfed by the Reverend W. G.'s magisterial three pages, 'gave as a layman' to his church 'the kind of service that ministers rarely find', becoming 'a living stone of its spiritual structure and usefulness. His face bore the stamp of real spirituality.'[13] Tom was shaped by his parents' hopes and histories; what he became was guided and abraded by what they had accomplished; and, sometimes, by what they had not.

Partially deaf by the time of Tom's childhood, his father had once been an eager musician, artist and poet. Hal's *Pocket Diary and Almanac* from 1864, when he was twenty-one, records purchases of books including Thomas Hood's *Poems*. He strummed the guitar, sang, played the flute. In his diary a poem, 'Life', dated 'April 27 '64', begins, 'Must I suffer ere my spirit, / Shall attain the highest goal'. To his liking for spiritual verse, Hal added a taste for popular song. That same year, the second last of Abraham Lincoln's presidency and while the Civil War still raged, he wrote down lines from 'Lorena', a lyric of loss and regret sung by many during a time when perhaps a million Americans were killed.

> We loved each other then Lorena
> More than we ever dared to tell
> And what we might have been Lorena
> Had but our loving prospered well . . .[14]

Much later, Ezra Pound wrote of meeting in Venice a woman who remembered a young Hal Eliot in St Louis writing poetry and not appearing at all like a businessman.[15]

Hal's father was recalled as 'one of the staunchest supporters of the Union in a city in which it was doubted, for a time, whether it would go with the Union or the Rebellion'.[16] In the early 1860s, to his family's alarm, Hal had followed his elder brother Thomas in volunteering to serve on the Union side in the Hallek Guard, mustered to defend St Louis against attack by Confederate forces which had earlier been driven out of Missouri. Yet by the late 1880s when his last child was born, those days were long gone. True, Hal still enjoyed drawing humorous sketches – not least of cats – and Tom remembered in adulthood 'a wonderful set of comic animals that he drew long ago, and were kept in an album together – I think he did them for a fair'.[17] By Tom's childhood, however, Hal the clean-shaven, sometimes nervous-looking young poet had been repressed and replaced by Henry Ware Eliot, Sr, the bearded, chess-playing businessman who had moved through several commercial jobs to become a prominent figure in the management of the Hydraulic-Press Brick Company of St Louis.

Aspects of Hal's well-read, older self survived. Having studied Classics in his youth, 'Papa', as his children called him, liked to quote Latin tags around the house, peppering his conversation, Tom observed, with occasional phrases such as 'quam celerrime', and retaining into old age a taste for bow ties and ancient Greek oratory, which, in his disciplined retirement, he reread in the original. He lived surrounded by books – the Bible, Latin and Greek texts, Americana from the age of Emerson and before – and retained a love of American history and political anecdotes. Tom remembered his father advising both his sons 'not to take up his own business'.[18] To the outside world, however, Hal was not a literary man but principally a sound, successful commercial manager. He helped found a local association of building material dealers. He looked after financial matters for his extended family. He rose, eventually, to become president of his firm and a director of several other brick companies.

In Lottie Eliot the vein of poetry was not repressed. Three months pregnant with Tom, she wrote, as she often did at the advent of spring, a poem celebrating Easter. Lent and Easter were important points in the Unitarian calendar, and often involved concerts at the Eliots' church. While Lottie's verse advocates the eschewing of 'wanton pleasures', she liked to celebrate how 'Spring returns with joy and mirth'.[19] During the second year of Tom's life she wrote 'An Easter Song', and in 1891 'An Easter Hymn'.[20] Much, though not all, of her verse was religious in tenor; liking to read theology and the Bible itself before she wrote, she had a high sense of artistic mission: 'The artist's soul must expression find / And give of its riches to all mankind, / Their vision to complete.'[21] As a girl she had studied 'Mental Philosophy'; as an adult she 'sometimes read Philosophy as a preparation for writing'.[22]

Steeped in high-mindedness, Lottie Eliot's poetry invokes a divine 'Infinite Mind' (a term favoured by Unitarians). Its topics range from 'The Raising of Lazarus' and 'Force and God' (1887) to biblical paraphrases and poems dealing with episodes in the lives of saints and martyrs.[23] She transcribed in Latin and English Fortunatus' medieval hymn in honour of the Holy Cross, with its details of crucified palms and 'wound on wound'; she wrote her own verse 'Vision of St Francis' seen 'Rapt in the ecstasy of his devotion'.[24] Sometimes, as in 'Raphael's "Ste. Marguerite"', she took inspiration from paintings. Tom's mother hung reproductions of religious pictures in her bedroom alongside ancestral portraits and pictures of her children. Martyrdom and scenes of violent self-discipline fascinated her. Tom's brother Henry remembered from his earliest infancy an engraving in her room of the Emperor Theodosius and St Ambrose, about which she wrote a poem. Her accompanying prose gloss explains to less learned readers that,

> By the order of Theodosius, Emperor of the East, in reprisal for the murder of one of his generals, thousands of innocent people were slain at the circus in Thessalonica. On account of this cruel and unjustifiable deed the Emperor was refused admission to the Cathedral, by St Ambrose, Bishop of Milan, and not allowed to partake of the Communion until after eight months of penitence and humiliation.

Lottie's emperor prostrates himself before Ambrose who represents the 'Authority' of the Church:

> On the marble floor
> Kneels Theodosius to implore
> From heaven, mercy. Day by day
> Upon the ground he prostrate lay,
> Till months had passed. And many came,
> With him to weep and share his shame,
> Till fierce desires, and passions rude
> He had within his soul subdued.[25]

Fascinated by ascetic figures from the sufferings of Catholicism, Mrs Eliot was also alert to the liberal theology of Friedrich Schleiermacher and the Unitarian New England-inflected writings of Ralph Waldo Emerson and

William Ellery Channing. She published verse in the Unitarian *Christian Register*, pasting her printed poems carefully into scrapbooks. Tom's younger cousin Abigail Eliot thought his mother 'wasn't much interested in babies', but she cherished her children as well as her verse, and grew to love her poet son with particular intensity.[26] She went on writing throughout her life, but never published a book-length collection, and her poetry underwent almost no development. It was, however, hugely important to her; and in her husband, the St Louis businessman who had once written, into his own diary, verses with the epigraph 'Perfect through Suffering (Saul)', she found a staunch life's partner.[27]

Tom grew up in an idealistic, bookish household where knowledge of saints and martyrdoms was readily taken for granted, even when it came to the punchlines of old jokes. He recalled being told a political anecdote by his father, who remembered the days of the debates over slavery in 1858 between the Republican Abraham Lincoln and the Democrat Stephen Douglas, famed for his political oratory. Mr Eliot enjoyed telling his son how, after Douglas had given one of his best speeches and received thunderous applause, Lincoln then stood up, took off his coat, rolled up his cuffs and said, '"We will now proceed to stone Stephen."'[28]

Though their home was St Louis, both Lottie, who had been raised in Massachusetts, and Hal (a confirmed Republican in politics) shared a mutual pride in their New England ancestors. 'We tended to cling to places and associations as long as possible,' Tom recalled.[29] His parents had first met in St Louis, but had married in a historic house, the Old Reed home, in Lexington, Massachusetts, on 27 October 1868. As a present for Lottie's thirty-ninth birthday in 1882 Hal, who had spent most of his life in Missouri, had gone to some trouble to buy and bring to St Louis an antique grandfather clock said to have been one of a batch shipped to America from Falmouth, England, in the 1760s. Nathan Reed, soon to be part of a company of Minute Men led by Captain Parker who faced the British at the Battle of Lexington on 19 April 1775, had bought the clock in 1770. One of Lottie's distant ancestors, Samuel Dawes, had ridden at the same time as Paul Revere to warn the rebels at Lexington that the British were coming. The clock Hal presented to his wife and which was a feature of Tom's boyhood home in St Louis had stood in the old Reed home at Lexington for many decades.[30] In Tom's childhood the hall clock told not just the present-day time but the story of the American Revolution. As a boy, Tom's brother relished the heroism of Paul Revere; among Tom's earliest surviving boyhood writings is a short, illustrated account of George Washington. Like most American children, Henry and Tom learned about these national heroes at school; but, thanks to their hall clock, their books,

pictures and ancestral stories, such history was also part of the fabric of
their home. Hal passed to his younger son an edition of Jefferson's writings; and so it was that Tom came to feel that the early history of the
United States was somehow 'a family extension'.[31]

In thriving St Louis the family lived in some style. Running southwards
through the grid-planned city for well over a mile past the Eliots' house
in the direction of the Mississippi, Locust Street was named, like nearby
Olive, Pine and Chestnut Streets, after a familiar American tree. Inside
the Eliots' substantial four-storey, brick-built home with its heavy, dark
wood furniture and elaborately patterned carpets hung treasured familial
pictures. The walls of several rooms were a three-dimensional family
album. A collection of portraits belonging to Tom's parents and his grandmother Abigail Adams Eliot (*née* Cranch), who lived nearby, included
those of President John Adams and his Secretary of State John Marshall,
as well as many ancestors with the surname Eliot, Stearns, Cranch, Blood
or Dawes. Above and to the right of the fireplace in his mother's bedroom
were at least fifteen pictures, including a Madonna and child, as well as
head-and-shoulders photographic portraits. Photographed for the parental
gallery, Tom grew up among a rich clutter of familial collectanea: a bronze
Japanese vase, brass candlesticks, the gold-headed cane which had belonged
to his formidable Grandfather Eliot.

Tom had never met Grandfather Eliot, who died in 1887, but the abiding
memory of this man whom Emerson had termed the 'Saint of the West' was
felt in the family home and in the city beyond.[32] The little boy learned about
him from his Eliot grandmother, from his Aunt Rose Smith and lawyer
Uncle Ed Eliot (who lived locally) and from his own parents. Grandfather
Eliot had travelled to Europe; in the American South he had bought slaves
and set them free, even writing the biography of one, *The Story of Alexander
Archer* (1885); he had given the name of his dead daughter, Mary, to the
school that all Tom's sisters had attended – the Mary Institute, situated right
next door to 2635 Locust Street. Tom's mother had once taught there for a
year. Straight out of Harvard Divinity School, Grandfather Eliot had reached
St Louis in 1834 and founded the first Unitarian church west of the Mississippi.
Tom and his family still served and attended it. Social reformer, zealous
preacher, occasional poet and part-time professor of Philosophy at Washington
University, handsome stern-countenanced Grandfather Eliot was dead but
unavoidable: visible in a large oil portrait painted by a Cranch, his deeds
praised in a memorial tablet at his Church of the Messiah. Lottie Eliot worked
on a biography during Tom's boyhood; it was published eventually in Boston
in 1904 as *William Greenleaf Eliot: Minister, Educator, Philanthropist*, and dedicated
to Lottie's children 'lest they forget'.

There was little danger of that. A sense of this dead patriarch stayed with Tom from boyhood to old age:

I was brought up to be very much aware of him: so much so, that as a child I thought of him as still the head of the family – a ruler for whom *in absentia* my grandmother stood as viceregent. The standard of conduct was that which my grandfather had set; our moral judgments, our decisions between duty and self-indulgence, were taken as if, like Moses, he had brought down the tables of the Law, any deviation from which would be sinful.[33]

Almost suggesting ancestor-worship, this memory of childhood indicates, too, a sense of being drilled in rectitude. Propriety mattered in every word and deed. 'When I was a small boy', he recalled, 'I was reproved by my family for using the vulgar phrase "O.K."'[34] Tom grew up in a family in which to buy candy for oneself was considered 'a selfish indulgence'.[35] He knew from a very early age that his ancestry could be traced back to those Puritan Eliots who had been involved in New England's seventeenth-century witch trials. For all their more recent Unitarianism, the Eliots had inherited a witch-hanging, judgemental, Calvinist streak. In later life, even when he tried hard not to, Tom could appear a 'Puritan ascetic'.[36]

His upbringing was strict, but cosseted. The family was looked after by a team of servants. They depended not just on the productions of a cook but also on the labour of maids, a gardener and a nurse. When baby Tom was in his second year and his sister Charlotte was ill, Lottie felt 'always stirred up by the wretched kitchen girls' who seemed to cost more in wages but to skimp on their work.[37] Set back just a little behind railings from the tree-lined sidewalk, and in summer almost screened by foliage, the Eliots' house was higher than the dwelling to its right, and enjoyed some open ground towards the left, in the direction of the Mary Institute at the intersection of Locust Street and Beaumont Street. Mary Institute classes stopped in the early afternoon and the girl pupils routinely did callisthenics in the grounds, their voices and laughter drifting over the wall. When he thought they had gone, Tom might venture into the schoolyard 'which seemed to me, as a child', he wrote, 'of vast extent'. Sometimes he even went inside the school itself, wandering the corridors, inhaling the smell of chalk, ink and cedar pencils: he was always alert to smells. Alone, or occasionally with a friend from a similarly privileged, prosperous background – such as 'Tom Kick', his playmate Thomas McKittrick, Jr – he went into the gymnasium and played on swinging rings and parallel bars, or else threw Indian clubs. Playing here was exciting,

but also unnerving. He was in a space familiar to all his sisters and several
of his female cousins who had studied there, yet usually off-limits to boys.
Once, he went into the schoolyard before all the pupils had left, and saw
girls staring at him through a window. He fled. These almost fairy-tale
incursions haunted him. He also remembered early attempts in this zone
at his father's favoured game, golf.

> There was at the front of our house a sort of picket fence which
> divided our front yard from the schoolyard. This picket fence merged
> a little later as it passed the wall of the house into a high brick wall
> which concealed our back garden from the schoolyard and also
> concealed the schoolyard from our back garden. There was a door
> in this wall and there was a key to this door. Now, when the young
> ladies had left the school in the afternoon and at the end of the week,
> I had access to the schoolyard and used it for my own purposes of
> play. When the girls had left in the afternoon, the schoolyard was
> mine for a playground, first of all under the supervision of my nurse
> and later for practicing approach shots with a lofter, which was
> sometimes dangerous for the windows. They must have been very
> brief approach shots, but then I was a very small boy with a very
> small lofter, or mashie. At any rate, then, in the schoolyard I
> remember a mound on which stood a huge ailanthus tree. Oh, it
> seemed to me very big and round on this little mound.[38]

St Louis was sometimes nicknamed 'Mound City' because of the presence
of ancient Native American earthwork mounds. Tom's own mound was
a good place to play. He went with Henry to a nearby climbing frame.
In sunhat and sailor suit he threw a ball. He was photographed at the age
of seven or eight, standing beside the big ailanthus tree with Tom Kick:
two smiling, sailor-suited boys, happy to be up to mischief.

The school grounds were Edenic, but, like the rest of St Louis, literally
polluted. The exposed brick side-wall of the Eliots' house had to be washed
periodically in this big industrial city known for its smoke and dust.
Coachmen wearing dark top-hats clattered by outside along dusty Locust
Street, sometimes cracking their whips above their horses. St Louis was
proud of its wealth and style. In a metropolis with a French name and
heritage, there were external shutters to the sides of most of the windows
of the Eliot home, making it look just a little French. The front steps
took visitors up to an arched doorway, and afforded a glimpse of basement
quarters below, familiar to the family's servants, black as well as white.
Aged three, Tom played indoors with a favourite soft toy, a little dog –

probably a dachshund – with floppy ears and black, beady eyes: Toby. A few years later, sitting in his well-tailored jacket under one of the house's many pictures, Tom learned to play the baby grand piano. There were books aplenty – from a set of Dickens novels to *An Evil and Adulterous Generation* by Tom's eighteenth-century great-great-great-grandfather, the Harvard-educated Reverend Andrew Eliot of Boston. Yet Tom himself was sometimes hard to find. In a house dominated during the day by his mother and his sisters, he sometimes concealed himself from visitors. One friend of his sisters remembered him hiding away, 'pale and thin and shy', keeping out of the way of of his sisters' female guests.[39] Though he learned to manage it through formality and occasional bluster, his shyness never left him.

Like his siblings, the boy was posed to be photographed for family albums. In one early picture, taken around 1891, he is holding Toby and dressed for cold weather in an ankle-length, hooded coat trimmed with fur. In his dark gloves he looks happy, but a little bemused perhaps, clad in outdoor clothes for a studio picture. Photographed a year or so later, long hair combed over his large ears and with an enormous pale bow tied at his neck as well as a neat striped collar visible over his darker jacket, he looks every groomed inch the model child. In early infancy, as was not uncommon for boys in wealthy families, he was sometimes dressed in what looks like a skirt. Like his sisters, he always appears carefully neat. He was, after all, an Eliot.

While very conscious of their ancestry and the standards that went with it, the Eliots also cherished, from a safe distance, some more scandalous aspects of their family history. Lottie's parents were Thomas Stearns of Lunenburg, Massachusetts, and Charlotte Blood. Tom, in distant Missouri, called them Grandpa and Grandma 'Faraway'.[40] Lottie liked to claim that one of her ancestors had been a Colonel Blood who had stolen the British crown jewels, and that another was English novelist Laurence Sterne. Neither story was accurate, but in Tom's boyhood they enhanced the family's specialness, as well as reaching back not just to New England but even to Old England beyond. What small boy, however shy, would not relish being related to a jewel thief called Colonel Blood?

Special and privileged, Tom could be teased. When he was little an African American odd-job-man, Stephen Jones, one of whose tasks was to wash down the side-wall, agitated him by pretending to fall asleep beside the fire while toasting a piece of bread held between the toes of his outstretched foot. Tom would jump in alarm as Stephen pretended to wake up and murmured, 'Some nigger's foot's burnin'.'[41] Polite yet mischievous, Tom was fascinated by Stephen's family, and ready to mythologise them. Some of the land nearby had originally been 'negro quarters' back in the days of slavery, and stories of that era persisted. Tom's closeness to these African Americans as a rich white boy in 1890s St Louis is a reminder that his grandfather had stood up for the African American community, and that the Joneses, in their kindness to Tom, would have known his family's history. Tom recalled Stephen's father, the janitor of the Mary Institute, whom he called Uncle Henry. At the school Uncle Henry

> lived in a sort of basement flat under the Beaumont Street entrance. He was a romantic figure to me as a child, not only because he possessed a parrot which actually did a little talking but because he was reputed to have been a runaway slave and certainly had one mutilated ear. He is said to have been tracked by bloodhounds. But Uncle Henry Jones was a great friend of the family. In fact, his family were great friends of the family because his son Stephen, and in succession to Stephen his grandson Charlie, undertook in succession the duties of looking after the furnace, washing the sidewalk, cutting the grass, and so on — bringing in the coal and wood.[42]

Conscious from an early age of being shy with most girls, and remaining so throughout his teens, Tom in boyhood was struck by a very different attitude to sexuality that Uncle Henry represented. In later years, he was uncertain if his boyhood impressions were accurate, but they stayed with him: 'as I remember it . . . Uncle Henry had two wives, not in succession but apparently married to both of them at the same time, and . . . this was only discovered when suddenly a new Auntie was found in place of the old Auntie, and I understood that this was the first or more legitimate bride who had turned up to turn the other one out. This, at any rate, is the story which I believed, and I'm sure to me it only added to my awe and respect of Uncle Henry.'[43] Whether or not he understood quite what was going on, Tom liked this man, who lived just next door but represented a very different world from that of the much primmer, strait-laced Eliots.

Little Tom was watched over by his Irish nurse, Annie Dunne, by his pious New England mother and by other family members, but he saw and heard in St Louis aspects of very different cultures. Just two blocks from his family home, at the corner of Washington and Jefferson Avenues was Uhrig's Cave which presented 'High-class Light and Comic Opera'.[44] When ten-year-old Tom used the expression 'A Hot Time', he was surely referring to the song 'There'll Be a Hot Time in the Old Town Tonight', which became an 1890s national hit when taken up by East Coast music promoters but which had been introduced onstage as an original song just a couple of miles from the Eliot home by 'Mama Lou' (Letitia Lula Agatha Fontaine).

> There'll be girls for ev'ry body in that good, good old town,
> For dere's Miss Consola Davis an dere's Miss Gondolia Brown;
> And dere's Miss Johanna Beasly she am dressed all in red,
> I just hugged her and I kissed her and to me then she said:
>
> Please, oh please, oh, do not let me fall,
> You're all mine and I love you best of all,
> And you must be my man, or I'll have no man at all,
> There'll be a hot time in the old town tonight![45]

This was a favourite song of Mama Lou, the 'St Louis street singer and "voodoo princess"' who starred at the Castle Club in the zone of saloons, brothels and gambling dens west of Twelfth Street along Chestnut and Market Streets.[46] Later in life Tom was heard singing 'Frankie and Johnny'; another song popularised by Mama Lou, it was based on a famous St Louis murder widely reported when Tom was ten.[47] Lottie Eliot would never have allowed her sons to go to Mama Lou's Castle Club; but the boys surely heard music associated with it, even if this was mediated through St Louis's 'Hot Time Minstrels', a group of young white men who (as was then customary) sometimes 'blacked up' to perform an annual concert each year, and who starred in a 'Black Face' show along with Tom's school's Mandolin Club in 1901 when he was twelve.[48]

Growing up in the soundscape of St Louis meant inhabiting a city where the highbrow European music of Wagner was performed not far from sophisticated ragtime. Scott Joplin, who lived for some years less than a mile from the Eliots' house, published his ragtime tune 'The Entertainer' in St Louis in 1902, dedicating it to the leader of a local mandolin club. To live at the confluence of all these musics was part of St Louis's gift to Tom; it helped shape the lilt of his poetry, and contributed to his love of dancing. In London in 1917 in the context of 'a dance', someone who knew him very well wrote to a friend, saying, 'you really must try Tom's Negro rag-time. I know you'd love it.'[49]

Tom remembered his early childhood as one of only two periods in his life when he was really happy.[50] A photograph of him, aged about seven and taken in the St Louis studio of Henry Holborn at Holborn's Dainties, 2820 Washington Avenue, shows a countenance not just mischievous, but positively scheming. Perhaps he was hoping someone might buy him candy. Yet, recalled much later, a memory of a boyhood incident implies, too, that he developed a wariness towards other lads:

> When I was a very small boy, I was given a tricycle or velocipede: a beautiful shiny japanned and nickelplated affair, with brake, bell etc., and was riding it proudly up and down the pavement under the eye of my nursemaid, when an odious small boy who lived a few doors away, who wore a kind of frilly blouse, sidled up and said ingratiatingly, 'Mother says I may ride your velocipede if I let you blow my whistle'. That aroused my first disquiet with human nature . . . I would as soon have used his toothbrush as blown his whistle.[51]

As well as signalling a physical fastidiousness rarely associated with small boys, this anecdote presents a child with a certain instinct for cutting himself off from other people – certainly from those whom he disliked. The unnamed, frilly-bloused near-neighbour was no playmate: 'I didn't blow the whistle, and he didn't ride the velocipede. I never spoke to him again.'[52]

Socially, the area around the Eliots' large house in Locust Street was on the slide. When his grandfather and grandmother had moved into nearby Washington Avenue, the place had been irreproachably classy. Along the street a little, Lucas Place was the premier enclave of the city's rich. Yet ever since the construction of the great Eads Bridge over the Mississippi in 1874, it had proved difficult to escape the incursions of through-traffic, boarding-house residents and poor vagrants. By the 1880s most well-to-do white folks were leaving these once exclusive inner-city neighbourhoods for newly constructed suburban mansions further from the river. The new mansions bordered some of the most salubrious streets in early-twentieth-century America. The Eliots, however, stayed put. They wanted to remain close to Tom's elderly grandmother in Washington Avenue. Their determination cut Tom off somewhat from playmates he and his family thought suitable.

He was also set apart by an intimate secret. He had been born with a congenital double hernia, which meant that from early on he had to wear a truss. At first he took this for granted. He seems to have assumed all boys wore one; but when he realised his condition was unusual and that his parents were concerned about it, this was another aspect of his make up conducive to shyness and an awkwardness about physical rough and tumble. He and his masculinity were watched over carefully. His mother had many demands on her time, but his nurse, Annie Dunne from County Cork, regularly took him for walks. Tom was 'devoted to her' and was 'at an age when a nanny, especially to the much-the-youngest child of a large family, is more important than anybody else'. He felt intrigued when, going 'to say her prayers', Annie brought him with her on several occasions into the small Irish Catholic Church of the Immaculate Conception at the corner of Locust Street and Jefferson Avenue. Annie attended mass there. The priest, Father G. D. Power, well known in the local Irish community, had family connections to European theatre. For Tom, who 'liked it very much', this was a very different sort of religion to that practised by his Unitarian family. The Church of the Immaculate Conception had coloured statues, paper flowers, alluring lights; 'the pews had little gates that I could swing on'.[53] The Catholic, Trinitarian Annie, to whom he felt close, discussed with him the existence of God. 'I remember', he wrote in his thirties, a theological argument about God as First Cause being 'put to me, at the age of six, by a devoutly Catholic Irish nursemaid'.[54] Theological and philosophical arguments intrigued Tom from childhood, but his sense of mischief remained unsubdued. Henry photographed his little brother with Annie, around the time Tom started at his first school. Hand on hip, Annie looks impatient to get on. Tom grins at the camera, conspiratorially.

Dramatic weather – Mississippi floods, spring rain, high winds – governed the rhythms of St Louis. In summer, with temperatures routinely reaching the 90s Fahrenheit (over 32°C), many wealthy families fled the heat and spent their time in resorts further north, often in New England. The St Louis press carried advertisements for hotels in resorts including Bar Harbor, Maine, and Gloucester, Massachusetts: leisured, well-off mothers would take their children there for several months, while fathers worked on in the heat and spent a shorter time holidaying with the family.[55] The Eliots summered this way, migrating and returning according to the seasons. In winter, when Missouri thermometers dipped to near freezing, there might be snow. Tom, who had a fondness for Mississippi steamboats (but whose mother thought Mark Twain's recent *Huckleberry Finn* unsuitable reading), delighted to hear their whistles blasting on New Year's Eve: the St Louis levee was jampacked with vessels; tales were told of heroic steamboat races. Yet perhaps spring was the Mississippi's most dramatic time, bringing with it regular inundations when, after rains, what Tom saw as the memorable 'long dark river' might burst its banks.[56] In Missouri flooding could occur at almost any time of year, but most commonly around April and May. Tom recalled being taken down in flood time to the Eads Bridge just to see the power of nature. That bridge, with its massive stone pillars and monumental girder-work, still spans the river, a celebrated feat of engineering. In 1896 it was tested almost to destruction.

During that spring, not long after the *St Louis Globe-Democrat* had published verses about 'April's laughing sheen' and how 'Cold and dull as memoried pain / Drips the rain', news items began to appear about devastation caused in the Southern states by torrential rain and cyclones.[57] Almost a hundred people were killed in Texas in mid-May when a cyclone hit. In St Louis itself, however, life went on untouched by such turmoil: Buffalo Bill's Wild West show was in town, bringing a 'free street caval-cade' with '100 Indian warriors' as well as a detachment of US Cavalry commanded by Colonel W. F. Cody – Buffalo Bill himself. Accompanied by marching bands, daily shows featured such attractions as that 'peerless lady wingshot' Miss Annie Oakley, and even an exhibition herd of buffalo.[58] Tom had a taste for such things; his grandmother Eliot liked to recall how an Indian had sneaked into her kitchen and stolen a red ribbon from her hair; a treasured family possession was a photograph of a Native American, Chief Joseph, wearing a suit; Forest Park in St Louis, where there were 'Indian Mounds', was, Tom recalled, 'to me, as a child, the beginning of the Wild West'.[59] He went there to photograph 'a rather mangy buffalo' chained to a tree.[60] His lifelong interest in comings together of the supposedly 'primitive' and the modern urban has its origins in his St Louis boyhood, but in his eighth year his city was suddenly convulsed by the most spectacular event of his boyhood.

The cyclone which struck St Louis on the afternoon of Wednesday 27 May 1896 was one of the most devastating natural disasters ever to hit an American city. Though its havoc was overshadowed in popular memory by the spectacle of the 1906 San Francisco earthquake, what happened in St Louis was also apocalyptic. Some reports refer to a 'cyclone', others to a 'tornado' or 'hurricane'. For hours heavy dark clouds built up on the horizon. 'Early mutterings' gave way to damp gusts bringing a downpour of rain. Eyewitness accounts in the following day's *St Louis Globe-Democrat* detail how a great rain cloud 'came up slowly at first; from the west, beyond Forest Park. As the black rim mounted higher above the horizon, its arc embraced more territory to the north and south.' After the thunder and lightning a 'hurricane' broke over the city's western area about 5 p.m., bringing 'a deluge of rain' and for half an hour making even 'the best built structures tremble'. Then a second storm struck from the south-west, destroying large parts of the city hospital, injuring patients and passers-by, capsizing boats moored at wharves on the Mississippi, and killing more than a hundred people. Some were 'crushed beneath falling walls, hurled against the sides of buildings, struck by flying timbers, cut by the shattered glass', or 'shocked by the network of down wires' as the city's famous streetcar system was smashed. 'Flashes of lightning' lit up the carnage as night approached and hundreds of injured people struggled through the streets of a city plunged into premature darkness because its power and public transport systems had been knocked out. 'A thousand electric cars stood dark and deserted on the tracks, while men and women toiled homeward through the drenching rain. There were pale faces and sinking hearts in more St Louis homes than ever known before in the city's history.'[61]

Some of the worst devastation was by the river, where a long line of steamboats and wharf boats had been overturned, crushed, sunk, or had their superstructure torn away. One boat, swept from its wharf, was blown to the foot of Locust Street; entire structures as well as vessels were pulverised along the levee; in the city streets buildings collapsed, roofs were torn off and raging fires lit up the night sky, their flames reflected in the Mississippi beyond the wreckage of steamboats. Eventually the conflagration was put out by the sheer intensity of the rain.

Though Locust Street was some distance from the epicentre of the storm, its power was evident there as elsewhere in a large industrial city where smokestacks and church towers collapsed, and buildings on Jefferson Avenue (where Annie sometimes took Tom to her church) were destroyed. While the Eliots' own place of worship survived, its younger St Louis sibling, the Unitarian Church of the Unity at whose dedication Tom's grandfather had preached, was so badly damaged that it required rebuilding.[62] We know Tom was at home at the time of the cyclone because on the following morning he was photographed (probably by his brother) along with his mother, two of his sisters and a cousin in front of their house. Hands clenched, his mother stares resolutely straight at the camera; cousin Henrietta looks at the photographer too; but Tom, who has climbed up on to the struts of the front gate, is looking westwards along the street. So is his sister Margaret (who was particularly sensitive to the sound of thunder); Marion Eliot can hardly be seen, but she has one hand to her head. Though the people are neatly dressed, this is not a calm, carefully composed photograph, but a record of a family conscious of themselves as survivors.[63]

More than eight thousand buildings were destroyed in the cyclone, but the Eliots' house, about a mile and a half inland from the Eads Bridge, kept even its front windows intact. No doubt the family did what they could to protect the little boy not just from the storm but also from the gruesome accounts of horror that circulated afterwards. Inside 2635 Locust Street, even if the house shook, the weather made its presence felt principally as terrific sound: thunderclaps, blasts of wind, torrential deluge. Yet no one who went outdoors in St Louis in the days that followed could fail to see the desolation. 'Death and Destruction Everywhere' read one of the headlines in the *Globe-Democrat* two days later. The newspapers were full of how, just across the river, parts of East St Louis were 'one vast charnel house' where famished homeless people roamed the streets among the groans of the injured in 'a living graveyard'.[64]

Accompanying these news stories a picture of the Eads shows mangled girder-work, fallen blocks of masonry, crashed rail carriages and downed wires. Across much of the city telegraph, telephone, electricity and gas supplies remained cut off for several days. Tales circulated of children buried alive, people blown out of their houses, even of corpses being driven through the streets on coaches pulled by storm-crazed horses. Safe and surely shielded from much of this, seven-year-old Tom left no surviving account. A quarter of a century later, however, nourished by the advanced study of Sanskrit texts and Classical learning, he would produce in the astonishing soundscape of 'What the Thunder Said' the most famous thunderstorm in world poetry, part of a work, *The Waste Land*, which envisages urban destruction, with the dead walking modern city streets, rain, a great river and scenes of horror. He was by no means writing the story of the 1896 St Louis cyclone, but he knew perhaps better than any other English-language poet what an apocalyptic thunderstorm sounded like.

After the cyclonic astonishments of the natural world came the measured anticlimax of school. Annie Dunne took him to his first educational establishment, which was run by an impressive teacher. Ellen Dean Lockwood (whose name suggests her parents relished *Wuthering Heights*) was an American Unitarian who had spent time in Brazil with her husband Robert in the early 1880s. The couple returned to the States in 1884 with their baby son and set up at 3841 Delmar Avenue in St Louis a small co-educational primary school which catered especially for prosperous and distinguished families. Tom recalled it as being 'beyond Vanteventer Place', a recently built gated community that was one of the city's most select enclaves.[65] Shortly before instructing Tom and his friend Thomas McKittrick, 'Miss Lockwood', as Tom called her, had taught the withdrawn and intense nine-year-old Sara Teasdale, helping that fledgling poet overcome her shyness and giving her the confidence to proceed to the Mary Institute. Mrs Lockwood had also taught her own son, Dean; he was a Latinist by the age of ten, went on to study Classics at Harvard and became a distinguished scholar. This was the sort of educational trajectory that the Latin-quoting Hal and the educationalist Lottie Eliot wanted for their shy, bright youngest child.

Determined, but also possessing a 'lovable disposition', Mrs Lockwood had struggled for some years with curvature of the spine and showed 'unusual vitality and will power'. Lottie knew this sensitive, cosmopolitan teacher through the Church of the Messiah as well as through a local women's group, the Wednesday Club. A schooling with her was likely to make Tom suitable for admission to the Mary Institute's partner establishment, Smith Academy, where his brother Henry had been studying. At Mrs Lockwood's school Tom seems to have done well. His friend and classmate 'Tom Kick' found it hard to keep up with him. The two boys were among Ellen Lockwood's last pupils. She died young in December 1898, when Tom was in his first term at Smith Academy.[66]

Before he went there, he summered as usual for about three months in Massachusetts. Since earliest childhood he had travelled outside St Louis, sometimes considerable distances. As a baby he was taken, as he recalled, to Louisiana, though another family member recorded that his earliest travels were with his mother to Pass Christian, then a small yachting town, in Mississippi on the Gulf of Mexico. According to this account, not long after Tom's birth his sister Charlotte was ill and their mother took her there, along with Tom and Henry, to convalesce.[67] Though Tom was too young to remember, it may have been a difficult time for Lottie; she looks rather thin and tired in photographs. With a family of six, one of whom was ill in Tom's early infancy, Lottie Eliot had to face several demands. Such circumstances, and his mother's continuing commitment to social reforms in St Louis, brought Tom even closer to Annie Dunne.

The earliest holidays Tom remembered were vacations in coastal New England. From his fifth year onwards the family went to summer at the fishing and resort town of Gloucester, on the Cape Ann coast 'about forty miles north-east of Boston'.[68] To start with they stayed at the recently constructed Hawthorne Inn. Built at Wonson's Point in East Gloucester, this large establishment had a multi-storey seafront block whose verandahs and decking extended on to the rocks of the shoreline. Surrounded by a complex of other lodgings, it was strikingly literary in its nomenclature. Not only was the hotel itself named after the great early-nineteenth-century novelist of New England Puritanism, Nathaniel Hawthorne, but the surrounding buildings, such as Seven Gables and Blythedale, were named after the titles, places and people of his works.[69] Hawthorne became one of Tom's favourite novelists, an author preoccupied with 'spiritual problems', whose work he read from his early teens onwards and whom he related to his own New England ancestry as well as to a line in American writing which included Henry James and, by implication, himself.[70] In an unusual way as a young child, he had holidayed among Hawthorne's works.

It was probably at this most literary of hotels that, as very small boys sometimes do, he fell in love for the first time. 'I had my first love affair', he recalled in 1939 in a tone at once self-mocking and embarrassedly honest, 'at (as nearly as I can compute from confirmatory evidence) the age of five, with a young lady of three, at a seaside hotel. Her name was Dorothy; that is all I know. My feeling towards her was expressed entirely by bullying, teasing, and making her fetch and carry: yet I remember clearly that I pined for a bit after we were separated in the autumn.'[71] A shy, truss-wearing, youngest child in a predominantly female household, the five-year-old boy made the most of having a little girl playmate to boss around. Yet, over four decades later and half jokingly relating this experience to Dante's meeting with the child Beatrice in the *Vita Nuova*, he knew such early encounters could be important. Recalling that 'My relations with later inamoratae(?) were more distant and respectful', he mentions in the same letter being enamoured of 'a young lady with ringlets (name unknown) who took the part of the angel child who died, in a performance called "The Birds' Christmas Carol" at another seaside resort'.[72] This little girl, playing the part of Carol in a dramatisation of a once popular sentimental story by the American writer Kate Douglas Wiggins, would have been acting the part of a beautiful, suffering invalid battling with long-term illness and inspiring her loving family at Christmas before succumbing to her fatal malady. The story was a popular one (there would be a reading from it at Tom's school when he was fourteen), and dramatisations of it often involved singing and elements of dance.[73] Whether or not Tom was aware of his sister Theodora's premature death or of how in 1864 his cherished aunt Ada (after whom one of his sisters was named) had drowned aged sixteen while skating on a pond, associations between mortality, suffering and female love were part of his childhood even before (aged about eleven) he read the works of Edgar Allan Poe in which such a nexus of ideas is common.

However shy in Missouri, he enjoyed meeting little girls at Gloucester, and at least one other little boy. A series of photographs taken on the boulder-strewn shoreline and on the sand show him around 1896 in the company of his cousins Barbara and Eleanor Hinkley and Frederick Eliot. Sometimes Fred's sisters, Abigail and Martha, came too. These Massachusetts relatives were his summer playmates. Similar in age, privileged upbringing and Unitarian background, they got on well together. They dug in the sand, carefully supervised by their nannies, or sat, all smiles, in a row on a hammock; or clambered over rocks, examining rock pools. Sometimes, wearing a hat with a brim to protect him from the summer heat, Tom played on top of a big boulder where he had erected a flagpole as if it were a fort. Less than a mile away, Fort Hill Avenue led to the remains of an actual Civil War fortification which became a military campground again in the summer of 1898 during the Spanish-American War. As Tom played by his flagpole on the rocks, his ever-vigilant mother stationed herself nearby.

Gloucester was very different from St Louis. Twenty years before Tom's birth, Philadelphia-based *Lippincott's Magazine* called it 'the most extensive fishing port in the world'.[74] In the 1890s, with three centuries of documented history behind it, the place was very much a working harbour, full of local boats and gear, busy with the salting and packing of fish; but Gloucester's increasingly well appointed hotels also lured wealthy vacationers from Boston and beyond. In the late 1880s and 1890s on land sold off at Eastern Point, some wealthy men, including Tom's father, built extensive second homes in what is today an exclusive gated community.

Decades earlier, Gloucester's combination of setting and marine light had attracted American painters of the Luminist school; in 1880 Winslow Homer had created some of his finest watercolours while living in a lighthouse on a tiny rocky island in Gloucester harbour; the area continued to appeal to artists and writers. Graced by Protestant, Catholic and Unitarian churches, this place was also sanctified by art. 'It has', wrote Tom later, 'the most beautiful harbour for small ships on the whole of that coast.'[75] Though Gloucester's growing population in 1900 hovered around 25,000, the town's eminence as a locus of fishing, fish smoking, boatbuilding and heroic voyaging endured. Tom saw how 'on the long rows of drying racks that lie behind the wharves, the salt fish is dried in the sun'. He watched fishing 'schooners' as they set out 'for their cruises of several weeks'.[76] (Locals claimed to have coined the word 'schooner'.) These vessels with their huge white sails thronged Gloucester throughout Tom's boyhood; proudly he claimed he had seen the *Rob Roy* launched in 1900.

During this time, as they had done for many, many years, schooners in quest of cod, halibut, haddock and herring voyaged from Gloucester round Eastern Point at the tip of Cape Ann, then headed north up the New England coast. Small boats called dories would be lowered over the side; men on board would row out to fish for cod. Drownings were frequent. 'Between 1830 and 1897', wrote the twentieth-century Gloucester historian Joseph Garland, '668 of Gloucester's vessels never returned around Eastern Point, nor 3775 of her men'.[77] Songs and poems (including verse by Whittier) commemorated heroism and losses beyond 'the gray rocks of Cape Ann / And Gloucester's harbor-bar';[78] and in the summers of 1894 and 1895 Rudyard Kipling resided in a hotel on Eastern Point Road, absorbing local lore for his story of Gloucester fishermen, *Captains Courageous*.

Serialised in 1896–7 and published immediately afterwards in book form, this was a tale young Tom Eliot read. Opening in North Atlantic fog and drawing to a close with a litany of drowned fishermen that forms part of late May Memorial Day commemorations in Gloucester, Kipling's novel has as its hero a fifteen-year-old boy with a wealthy businessman father and 'a strict Unitarian' mother. Harvey Cheyne, Jr, is rescued from drowning and finds himself with the Gloucester fishing fleet, listening to traditional tales of 'boats smashed to splinters' and 'ships that sailed in the fog' to such locations as 'Mount Desert', Cape Breton, 'the Maine ports' and 'the ice between the mainland and Prince Edward Island'. Mixing dialect and standard English, Kipling's book was full of places Tom knew or had heard about: one character whistles a song about sailing past Eastern Point and nearby Thacher Island where in the seventeenth century twenty-one out of twenty-three members of a family had drowned. Early in the year of the publication of *Captains Courageous*, the real-life Gloucester schooner *Yosemite* was wrecked on a Newfoundland voyage, its crew either killed or marooned in a snow-storm; a few survived, swimming through icy waters, bodies of others were frozen into the rocks.[79] Such stories were part of local life in Gloucester and surrounding ports; reminders of them were unavoidable. The most famous local sailor of Tom's boyhood was Gloucesterman Howard Blackburn who had returned frostbitten and fingerless from the waters of Newfoundland after being separated from his ship, the *Grace L. Fears*, whilst fishing in a dory; Blackburn was a familiar sight on Gloucester Streets.[80] On 20 August 1901, when Tom was almost thirteen, the *Gloucester Daily Times* published an item telling how a teenager had picked up a bottle on a local beach; inside was a message from a coura-geous captain whose vessel had gone down with all hands four years earlier: 'We are sinking in the *Grace L. Fears*. Whoever finds this, hand it to my wife.'[81]

As a boy Tom was taught to swim and given sailing lessons by an old Gloucester sailor nicknamed the Skipper. Predictably, Tom's mother and sisters kept a close eye on the proceedings. The ocean was beautiful, many-voiced and potentially deadly, but 'I don't regret all the sailing that you and I and father did together, I assure you!' Tom wrote to his mother when he was in his late twenties.[82] All his life the sea fascinated him. He relished 'brilliant' tales such as those of James B. Connolly in *Out of Gloucester* (1902) which recounted the adventures of Gloucester fishermen or 'bankers' who sailed in summer aboard schooners laden with 'seines and dories' to 'the south Banks or "Georges"' and in winter to 'the Grand Banks of Newfoundland, where the codfish abound', and even as far as 'Reykyavik, Iceland'.[83] Years afterwards, in his late teens and early twenties, Tom would voyage with friends up the New England coast towards the Canadian border, on at least one occasion risking death.

Such experiences, mixed with fact and fiction he had absorbed in successive childhood summers, fuel his later writing in *The Waste Land* manuscripts about an imagined trip from Cape Ann 'to the eastern banks' in search of 'codfish' which begins in fair weather, then moves into 'gale', loss of 'dories' and a voyage 'Northward' past 'the farthest northern islands' in deafening seas, heading eventually into a hallucinatory and lethal seascape far, far from 'Home and mother': a world of 'cracked ice', 'bones' in a 'whirlpool' and 'Death by Water'.[84] Eventually, most of that material was cut from the published poem, though alert readers will spot the word 'dory' in the poet's published notes to it. From his most famous early poem, whose last words are 'we drown', through the storm-blasted seagull of 'Gerontion', the fogbound, granite-shored seascape of 'Marina' and the white sails of *Ash-Wednesday* to his extended meditation on fishermen, loss and sheer persistence in 'The Dry Salvages', Tom's poetry is suffused with material which can be linked, however indirectly, to experiences and reading associated with the New England coast. From childhood onwards, Gloucester shaped him as a poet.

Yet in the 1890s the place was changing. Tom could still explore Whittier's 'depths of Gloucester woods, / Full of plants that love the summer' and thronged with birdlife.[85] The boy from St Louis loved the 'fir trees, the bay and goldenrod, the song-sparrows, the red granite and the blue sea'.[86] Also, situated on Cape Ann where glaciation had left great outcrops of granite, Gloucester boasted nearby quarries which had supplied the stone for Brooklyn Bridge; at Eastern Point between 1894 when Tom was six and 1905 when he was seventeen, the monumental Dog Bar Breakwater, by far the most striking man-made feature of East Gloucester, was being constructed out of locally quarried grey granite. A bell was placed at its seaward end, adding its sound to the whistling buoy southwards. Named after an Eastern Point rock formation, this buoy was called Mother Ann's Cow. Gloucester was on the Boston–Maine railroad, but when Tom was very little the town still had horse-drawn trams – horsecars; the early 1890s saw these replaced by 'electrics', though they did not run as far as Eastern Point. You could take a short ferry ride across the harbour from Gloucester itself to the East Gloucester landing, and if, like Tom, you knew about boats, you could see that schooners were evolving in subtle ways: the *Rob Roy* with its spoon bow, short foremast and minimal bowsprit, was different from most earlier Gloucester vessels: supposedly a safer design. 'Since the introduction of the "knockabout rig" – the schooner with a long bow and no bowsprit – there are fewer losses at sea', Tom wrote later, 'but Gloucester has many widows, and no trip is without anxiety for those at home'.[87]

Even if he knew it was a port familiar with danger, Gloucester for him was a family refuge. Aged six or seven and clad in his sailor suit – that customary outfit – he had a fine toy sailboat. Enthusiastic about pirates, sometimes he played at sword fights using sticks, but in all his early childhood photographs at Gloucester he is, like his cousins, decorously attired. Every inch a well-cared-for small Eliot, digging in the sand with his spade, he wears dark long trousers; sitting on a verandah in his neat sailor suit holding his model boat he looks kempt, correct and engrossed.

Spending part of his summer working in St Louis, Tom's prosperous father loved Gloucester too. Built in 1896 on land which he had purchased in 1890, Henry Ware Eliot's substantial summer residence at Eastern Point, called the Downs, was very close to the shore: a three-storey detached dwelling with a verandah overlooking the sea, a very spacious family room with a great brick fireplace, and a garden path leading down to the beach. Indoors, above the upper-storey bedrooms, the Downs had plenty of attic space where the boys in the family could indulge their taste for play; a painted skull and crossbones with the word 'Blood' and the initials 'HWE' can still be seen there. Henry, Tom's brother, liked to take family photographs. Some show 1890s visits to nearby places connected to the extended Eliot family, past as well as present: to the large, well-appointed house of Thomas Heywood Blood at Sterling, Massachusetts, and to the house and gravestones of Blood's parents, Samuel (d. 1834) and Lucretia (d. 1827); to the Cushing family home at Lunenburg in the same state – Tom's sister Marion had the middle name Cushing from her ancestor Colonel Charles Cushing (1744–1809); to the house of Tom's grandfather, Thomas Stearns, at North Lexington where his parents had married.[88] This sort of delving into the New England past quickened in Tom's brother a taste for American history – in 1897 his Paul Revere essay won second prize in a competition; but such excursions also reinforced a strong sense in Tom of his extensive New England ancestry. In later years he would sometimes say that he came from St Louis, sometimes that he hailed from New England.

Being a little boy in Gloucester was not all ancestor-worship. Sometimes Tom's father took him riding in a pony and trap, played chess with him or accompanied him on the golf course. A surviving photograph shows the father playing golf, the son looking on from a safe distance. In Gloucester his parents rarely went to church, and some prohibitions were relaxed. Tom liked the 4th of July celebrations in this New England port, associating them with fireworks, a yacht race (there was a substantial yacht club at East Gloucester) and strawberry ice cream.[89] For all the hard life of those local captains courageous, Gloucester was fun. Later, the sort of experiences he had there re-emerged, transmuted into poetry: 'There might be the experience of a child of ten, a small boy peering through sea-water in a rock-pool, and finding a sea-anemone for the first time: the simple experience (not so simple, for an exceptional child, as it looks) might lie dormant in his mind for twenty years, and re-appear transformed in some verse context charged with great imaginative pressure.'[90]

Tom's father had some interest in natural science and in 1902 was elected President of the Academy of Science of St Louis which had received a splendid collection of butterflies. A 1901 photograph of one of the rooms in the Locust Street house shows a framed butterfly on the wall. In Tom's Missouri there were 'high limestone bluffs where we searched for fossil shell-fish'.[91] In Massachusetts he enjoyed gathering algae on the shore, drying them out and classifying them.[92] He had a microscope at Gloucester, watched crabs and possessed a child's interest in small creatures, such as the field mice that got inside the Downs. Aged nine, he wrote in late June from Gloucester to his father who was still in St Louis, concerned that a box of butterflies had got broken, and saying that he was hunting for birds with his sister Charlotte.[93]

These interests stayed with him. In Missouri he loved 'the flaming red cardinal birds', but, in New England, Eastern Point, a staging post for many migratory birds, was and is an ornithologist's paradise.[94] For his fourteenth birthday his mother gave him 'a much coveted birthday present', the new sixth edition of Frank M. Chapman's black-leather-bound volume whose gilded lettering read *Handbook of Birds of Eastern North America*. Lottie wrote her son's name on the flyleaf, and the date of his birthday: no 'with love', but it was a loving gift.[95] The volume included descriptions of plumage, nest and eggs, as well as accounts of 'haunts and habits'. Specialist

articles, such as that on page 400, '*Turdus aonalaschkae pallasii*' (more famil-
iarly, the hermit thrush), detailed many different aspects of bird behaviour,
not least birdsong: 'The Hermit thrush bears high distinction among our
song birds. Its notes are not remarkable for variety or volume, but in
purity and sweetness of tone and exquisite modulation they are
unequalled.'[96] Remembered and longed for, years later that bird's song
would become part of the concluding section of *The Waste Land*, heard
at that moment in 'What the Thunder Said':

Where the hermit-thrush sings in the pine trees
Drip drop drip drop drop drop drop . . .[97]

This was a cherished sound that belonged to the poet's boyhood – to the
deep part of him that was always Tom.

2

Hi, Kid, Let's Dance

For Tom, returning from Gloucester to St Louis in late summer involved a very long rail journey in the inevitable direction of the classroom. Papa headed back to the routines of his Brick Company office. Mamma committed herself again to her social causes and cultural interests, including her poetry. From early childhood Tom was aware of his mother's verse. On 17 September 1896, for instance, not long after the family returned from Gloucester, she took pride in a public reading of one of her hymn-like poems. It proclaims her characteristic high-mindedness, invoking the 'God of our fathers' and George Washington, while surveying the 'savage' past of America and a 'happy' seaside present-day where 'ships pass ceaseless by'.[1]

After a summer watching ships pass Eastern Point, the Eliots recommitted themselves to the city that was, for most of the year, their happy home. The St Louis they returned to, from that first summer in their newly completed Gloucester house, was still rebuilding after the devastation of the cyclone. Nonetheless, it was thriving. Tom stepped off the train into his hometown's monumental Union Station whose frontage extended for over six hundred feet. Opened two years earlier, this statement of municipal pride provided another opportunity for good works: a local women's philanthropic group which his mother belonged to had arranged for it to contain boxes into which travellers could post unwanted reading matter suitable for distribution to the poor.

More railroads converged on St Louis than on any other American city. Traversing Union Station's Grand Hall, travellers saw an impressive pictorial window depicting three white female figures sitting on a bench: those at either end represented New York and San Francisco; between them sat St Louis. That was how the city regarded itself, a midpoint in the mighty

36

United States. With a population of around 600,000, by 1900 St Louis was its nation's fourth largest urban settlement: 'too far north to be a Southern city, and too southern in its social characteristics to be a Northern city; with all the polish and finish of an Eastern center, and yet toned by all the warmth and spirited verve of a Western metropolis'.[2] Its French past was still discernible in local street names such as Lafayette, Chouteau and Soulard; but by the late nineteenth century German and Irish influences mixed with African American and Jewish culture. Home to the world's largest brewery, and producing everything from bricks to newspapers, St Louis saw itself as an industrial and mercantile powerhouse. It was dominated by a rich, sometimes progressive, white elite to which the Eliots belonged.

Though the 1896 cyclone destroyed some businesses, and others suffered during a serious economic depression between 1893 and 1897, rebuilding and local population growth were good for Tom's father's Hydraulic-Press Brick Company. Large urban parklands and tree-lined streets in the better-off areas might be loud with cicadas, but towards the river were rows of poorer brick houses, while tall, imposing shops and office blocks thronged the downtown area. Smokestacks belching out fumes from soft Illinois coal dominated the horizon, dirtying the pale stone of the grand domed State House building. St Louis fogs were as thick as those in some of Tom's favourite childhood reading – recently published detective stories with 'illustrations' by Sidney Paget featuring London's Sherlock Holmes.[3] 'A thick fog rolled down between the lines of dun-coloured houses, and the opposing windows loomed like dark, shapeless blurs through the heavy yellow wreaths.'[4] Many years later, Tom stated that Prufrock's 'yellow fog' was drawn from that of his industrial birthplace, but even in his childhood St Louis fog was mixed with Conan Doyle's imaginings.[5] Tom's father supported moves to improve air quality, and a smoke abatement ordinance introduced when Tom was five had some beneficial effect, but was soon ruled unconstitutional. For most of Tom's boyhood the air was generally worse than it had been in 1885 when Frenchman Charles Croonenbergh had commented that 'the pasty dust from American coal smoke falls so thick in the streets, that one is satisfied by an afternoon walk in St Louis as if one had eaten a heavy dinner . . . Everyone coughs.'[6] 'Yellow fog' and 'brown waves of fog' billow through Tom's early urban poetry, a fog coated with 'soot that falls from chimneys'.[7] The cough in 'Gerontion' is the most insistently memorable in English-language verse. Recalling St Louis as 'very smoky' – and opining that New England brought a literal 'change of climate' that did one good – in adulthood Tom suffered increasingly from lung problems; eventually he died from

emphysema.[8] Not all of that can be blamed on his later fondness for cigarettes and London.

The St Louis of his boyhood, like its great rival Chicago, was famous
for local government corruption. His Republican father signed a petition
calling for political fair play. Yet with its heritage of municipal bribery,
grime and slumminess, the place had, too, a heritage of idealist philosophy.
Owing much to German thought, this intellectual tradition regarded
reality as a mental construct. It stressed how the intellect influences society.
Passionate about Kant and Hegel, Henry C. Brokmeyer and his followers
had founded the St Louis Philosophical Society in 1866. The following
year they launched the internationally circulated *Journal of Speculative
Philosophy*. Its contributors would include Josiah Royce and William James.
The Society invited Ralph Waldo Emerson to St Louis. It developed
connections with New England Transcendentalism as well as with the
local Unitarian community. Other figures linked to this Philosophical
Society included a remarkable Scottish polymath Thomas Davidson, who
went on to write on Aristotle and, after emigrating to England, founded
what became the Fabian Society; also the Unitarian literary scholar James
Kendall Hosmer (several of whose relations were associates of Lottie Eliot),
and Susan E. Blow who, with fellow member W. T. Harris, pioneered
the kindergarten movement in America. Blow's ideas were followed
by the St Louis Wednesday Club which Lottie Eliot helped found in 1890,
and Blow was a friend and 1890s literary collaborator with Lottie's sister-
in-law, Etta Eliot.[9]

St Louis Philosophical Society members wrote and lectured on Dante,
establishing in the city what one of their leaders, Denton J. Snider, called
a 'Dante cult'. Signs of this were still apparent in Tom's boyhood when a
local hotel hosted 'An Evening with Dante'.[10] Susan Blow's 1886 *Study
of Dante* contends that 'We live in an age which is rapidly losing the
consciousness of sin. Equally alien to our feeling are the physical self-
scourgings of the medieval saint and the spiritual agony of the Puritan.'[11]
It may seem strange that this same woman pioneered children's education,
contributing to the efforts that made the St Louis school system a national
beacon, but it would not have seemed odd to Lottie Eliot as she made
poems out of scenes of ancient martyrdom while also campaigning for
children's rights.

With her love of 'Infinite Mind' and her taste for philosophy, high
educational ideals, poetry and culture, Lottie belonged to a community
where the Philosophical Society's influence was still felt. Her own intellectual loyalties lay with such St Louis women's organisations as the
Humanity Club, the Wednesday Club, the Colonial Dames of America

and, especially, the Unitarian church. Her husband, a former Sunday School superintendent at the Church of the Messiah and a member of its choir, helped Lottie preserve Tom's earliest gifts, including a christening spoon from his great-aunt Caroline.[12] For the first ten years of Tom's life the Church of the Messiah's minister was the Reverend John Snyder, William Greenleaf Eliot's successor; Snyder even set up in the church an Eliot Society, which brought together under one aegis several congregational women's groups, and whose members included Tom's elderly Grandmother Eliot. Throughout his boyhood, Tom was taken regularly to this Unitarian place of worship, one of the most important institutions of his early life.

Writing on 'Unitarianism in St Louis' in 1899, Tom's childhood minister set out 'historically' Unitarians' beliefs. According to Snyder, the earliest Christians had belonged to a 'Unitarian epoch of the church' and had followed Jesus's teaching which, true to Jewish monotheism, maintained that 'the Lord is one!' Later, 'The Christian Church only ceased to be Monotheistic when it ceased to be Jewish.' The Unitarian Snyder contended that a modern 'Tri-Unitarian' Catholic or Protestant who believes in the Three-in-One of Father, Son and Holy Ghost 'rests his case upon the forced interpretation of a few doubtful and obscure texts, which may be stretched or shrunken to fit his dogma'. Christianity had been shaped by forces as different as 'Greek mysticism' and 'Roman imperialism'. Machinations of church 'hierarchy' had led to a deadening of spirituality into a 'magical sacramentalism'. So, for Unitarians, it was the other Christian churches which had lapsed from the true faith. However much he idealised it, Snyder recognised that 'The form of the primitive church will never be restored', but he asserted that such a restoration was not even desirable since

> Its formal administrative defects have been slowly outgrown. But Unitarianism seeks to reproduce the spirit of the Apostolic Church – its democratic simplicity –, its freedom from sacerdotalism, its boundless charity, its spiritual spontaneity, its vital ethicalism. These qualities are essential and indestructible in Christianity. They will survive all future changes of forms and all the possible modifications of doctrine which larger knowledge may make necessary.[13]

Like members of his congregation including Lottie Eliot, Snyder identified the Unitarian cause with earlier medieval, Renaissance and Reformation martyrs who had suffered 'the honor of persecution'. He saw modern Unitarianism as emerging first in sixteenth-century Europe, then spreading in seventeenth-century England where, he claimed, 'Among its most illustrious advocates were John Milton and Algernon Sidney.' He stated that the first 'distinctly known' Unitarian Church in England had been established by Theophilus Lindsey in 1778. Snyder liked the roster of writers, including Coleridge, Anna Barbauld and Harriet Martineau, who had made Unitarianism such a literary faith. Boston and New England Unitarianism he saw as countering 'frantic emotionalism'. He admired Unitarianism's ideal of Christianity as 'not a scheme of salvation to be defined by dogma, but the art of living virtuously and piously'. For him 'The history of Christianity shows that if you will lift from any mind the repressive or interpretative force of a creed, leaving it free to face either the light of nature or the teachings of the Bible, it will inevitably lose the impress of orthodoxy.'[14]

This was the teaching that permeated Tom Eliot's childhood home and the Unitarian faith community in which he was brought up. His extended family – from his uncle Thomas in Portland, Oregon, to his many New England cousins – belonged to a clan who were, he joked later, 'the Borgias of Unitarianism'.[15] Uncle Tom Eliot authored *The Radical Difference Between Liberal Christianity and Orthodoxy*, published by the American Unitarian Association in Boston. The Association's future president would be young Tom's Eastern Point playmate, cousin Fred. In St Louis the family's Unitarianism was headquartered in the stone Church of the Messiah with its tall English Gothic spire on 'Piety Hill' at the corner of Locust Street and Garrison Avenue where the Reverend Snyder presided. For years Tom's mother was secretary of the Mission Free School of the Church of the Messiah. In that church building, admired for its architectural design by Boston's Peabody and Stearns, and for its memorial stained-glass windows by Scottish artist Daniel Cottier, Tom sat, sang, prayed, worshipped, fidgeted and looked around. Under the great exposed roof-beams he saw biblical stories turned into stained-glass art: Christ as the sower, the good Samaritan, the wise and foolish virgins.

Among these windows, too, were contributions linking poetry to Christianity. A memorial window to a thirteen-year-old girl who had died in 1875 alluded to Longfellow's poem 'The Reaper and the Flowers' with its white dove and angel of death; its inscription was taken from the Gospel of Luke 20:36, in the King James version: 'Neither can they die any more, for they are equal unto the angels.' Another Cottier stained-glass window showed an angel musician, but the dominant windows, facing the congregation, were, like Eliot's grandfather's theology, firmly centred on Christ and the biblical parables. Towards the end of his life, William Greenleaf Eliot had worried that the Church of the Messiah risked 'becoming less a church than a society. The religious strength less, the social greater.' His church's architecture was designed to separate the purely social aspects from the area reserved for worship. The congregation sat surrounded by rich stained-glass memorials to former members that spoke not just of the society on earth but of that in heaven and of Christ himself. It communicated through powerful imagery and structure William Greenleaf Eliot's conviction that 'the best citizen . . . receives from the community he serves far more than he can give', and it extended that sense of community to include both the traditions of the local dead and union with Christ himself.[16] Yet Snyder's creedless Unitarianism could easily become mere undogmatic politeness.

Among generations of Unitarian Eliots, Tom grew up to be the one that got away. Yet an interest in the 'primitive' roots of religion, and in tracing religion to its earliest stages that is so evident in the Reverend Snyder's thinking would be a continuing preoccupation. Tom was not reading theology in his cradle, but certainly imbibed it from boyhood. Occasionally, too, picking up books almost at random around the 'family library', quite different kinds of religion intrigued him: 'I came across, as a boy, a poem for which I have preserved a warm affection: *The Light of Asia*, by Sir Edwin Arnold. It is a long epic poem on the life of Gautama Buddha: I must have had a latent sympathy for the subject-matter, for I read it through with gusto, and more than once.'[17] In this work, subtitled *The Great Renunciation*, Edwin Arnold presented the Buddha as combining 'the intellect of a sage and the passionate devotion of a martyr'. Reading it, Tom, who would go on to study Buddhist texts at university, read about 'The Scripture' of a 'Saviour of the World' who was not Christ. He discovered, too, 'The thunder of the preaching of the word' in Buddhist beliefs, where to be 'saint-like' meant something non-Christian, something alien whose 'Wheel of perfect Law' was intriguing not least because aspects of it chimed with his parents' religion.[18]

From infancy Tom knew he belonged not just to a special family but to a community that included the dead as well as the living, and whose great exemplar was his Saviour. Issues of faith and doubt were as inescapable as his own Christian name; a fondness for church buildings was something he carried from his childhood to his old age. St Louis Unitarianism gave him much to come to terms with. Eventually he felt he had been brought up in 'a strong atmosphere of the most Liberal theology', but concluded in adulthood that soulful 'Unitarianism is a bad preparation for brass tacks like birth, copulation, death, hell, heaven and insanity.'[19] His adult poetry likes to puncture romantic illusion with a sharp application of brass tacks.

Not long after passing from the tutelage of Mrs Lockwood to the much larger educational premises of Smith Academy, ten-year-old Tom created his earliest surviving literary work. The previous term he had started at Smith, gaining entry direct to its Preparatory Department's Year 2, where he had been studying Arithmetic, Geography, Spelling, Drawing, Writing, English and French. Familiar with words such as 'comatose', and eager to write down interesting sounds including the 'Click, click, clack' of 'the telegraph', Tom clearly relished language; his studying French so early at Smith Academy was unusual, the first indication of a Francophilia that would shape his literary life.[20] Reading in English seems to have directed him towards Classical culture as well as to Nathaniel Hawthorne, whose *Tanglewood Tales* featured on the curriculum along with Charles Kingsley's *The Heroes, or Greek Fairy Tales for my Children*.[21] In both volumes Tom encountered, probably for the first time, the story of Theseus, Ariadne and the Minotaur, which would be alluded to in his poetry. Yet the *Fireside*, the childhood magazine he wrote in January and February 1899 owes nothing at all to his schoolbooks. Possibly it was spurred by his school's plan to initiate the *Smith Academy Record* that spring; or by Tom's brother Henry's involvement with *Student Life* magazine at Washington University; or by the imminent publication of his mother's booklet *Easter Songs*.

Whatever its origins, with the *Fireside*, written in the dark days of winter, Tom became T. S. Eliot. Its front page announces it not only as 'Edited by T. S. Eliot' but also as a production of 'The T. S. Eliot Co., St Louis'. Like his father, working for 'The Hydraulic-Press Brick Co., St Louis', Tom, asking for subscriptions, was businessman as well as writer. The 'Printer' was also 'T. S. Eliot', and chapter one of the railroad adventure 'Bill's Escape' was announced as 'by T. S. Eliot'. Tom was signalling what he would become in adult life: author, editor and publisher, a poet with a business brain. The *Fireside* offers by far the most detailed window on the small boy's imaginative life and aspects of his St Louis milieu.

The first issue, a 'sample copy' of this new 'Weekly Magazine' featuring 'Fiction, Gossip, Theatre, Jokes' and other interesting material, is dated 'January 28, 1899'. It describes itself as both a magazine and 'A Little Papre' – Tom's spelling was not always assured. Borrowing from material in St Louis newspapers of the time, as well as imitating writers and genres that he liked, the *Fireside* is a lively melange. Its 'Gossip' section announces the engagement of 'Miss End and Mr Front'; a later issue mentions the elopement of 'Mr. Up and Miss Down'; the familiar advertisement 'EAT QUAKER OATS' becomes in Tom's version 'EAT QUAKER CATS', complete with a feline sketch.[22] Teleologically-minded readers can spot anticipations of the poet who, decades later, would pen *Old Possum's Book of Practical Cats*; who would link 'beginning' to 'end' in *Four Quartets*; and who would put at the head of 'Burnt Norton' a Greek epigraph from Heraclitus which means in English 'the way up and the way down are one'.[23] Certainly the little paper contains in its 'Poet's Corner' Tom's earliest surviving verses. Clearly imitative, the first of these mentions a family emblem, the elephant, cherished by Eliots since at least the seventeenth century; while it may have been a misleading 'family tradition' that '"Eliot" is merely a corruption of "Elephant"', Tom always liked the link, and in adult life chose for his bookplate an elephant emblem designed by David Jones.[24]

At ten he was haunted by verbal cadences. He could not get out of his head the Mad Gardener's song from Lewis Carroll's *Sylvie and Bruno*, published just nine years earlier. Carroll's poem begins:

> He thought he saw an Elephant,
>   That practised on a fife:
> He looked again, and found it was
>   A letter from his wife.
> 'At length I realise,' he said,
>   'The bitterness of Life!'[25]

Not yet ready for the bitterness of life, and perhaps feeling that writing poetry called for the invention of a slightly different self, Tom signed his poem 'Eliot S. Thomas':

> I thought I saw an elephant
> A-riding on a 'bus
> I looked again and found
> Alas! 'twas only us.[26]

From the very start, in such ludic childish efforts, he seems to have liked poetry's power to cross between mundanity and the wildly imaginative. Several times in the *Fireside* he imitates Carroll's poem, taking from it both 'a banker's clerk' and 'a hippopotamus', not to mention a 'kangaroo'. Judging from how often he followed its form, this was the ten-year-old's favourite poem, a completely mischievous one based on striking discrepancies between appearance and reality. Sometimes awkwardly, Tom made it his own, earthing it in the Mound City he knew:

> I thought I saw a kangaroo,
> A-jumping on the ground,

I looked again and lo!
It was an earthen mound![27]

Poetry and prose in the *Fireside* suggest, too, an early love of the writings of Edward Lear, a lifelong favourite who had died in the year of Tom's birth. When he presents *Fireside* recipes, Tom often ends with energetic advice on how to get rid of the food: 'Burn up as fast as possible' or (in the case of 'broiled fritters') 'Put out of the window as fast as possible.'[28] In imitative phrasing and inclination these follow Lear's nonsense cookery in 'To Make an Amblongus Pie', which ends, 'Serve up in a clean dish, and throw the whole out of the window as fast as possible.'[29]

Lear's genius for odd, memorable names – Quangle-Wangle, Yonghy-Bonghy-Bo, Scroobius Pip – is something Tom would develop. From 'The Story of the Four Little Children Who Went Round the World' he took the name 'Slingsby', used in one of his early mature poems, 'Aunt Helen'. Cat-loving Lear's self-portrait in 'How pleasant to know Mr Lear!' would beget, decades later, 'How unpleasant to meet Mr. Eliot!', where nonsense words 'porpentine' and 'wopsical' are fit to set beside such Learisms as 'crumpetty' or 'crumbobblious'.[30] In early 1899, under the guise of 'anon', he also attempted the literary genre most often associated with Edward Lear, but Tom's limerick about female suffering is below par in form:

There was a young lady name of Lu
Who felt so exceedingly blue
She was heard to state
That it was her fate –
And then she began to bu-hu.[31]

Clearly he was absorbing contemporary events, probably from reading newspapers that lay around the house. Tom's mention in *Fireside*, number 4 of a Brazilian balloonist in Paris picks up on the story of the rich young Brazilian Santos-Dumont whose 'sailing around Paris, driving his cigar-shaped balloon' was reported in the *St Louis Globe-Democrat* on 8 January 1899.[32] Again, Tom's use of comic plutocratic names including 'Mr and Mrs Bondholder Billion' in *Fireside*, number 3 and 'Miss Stockenbonds' in *Fireside*, number 11 involves close relatives of the creations of a *Globe-Democrat* cartoonist, Mr and Mrs Stockson Bond.[33]

Names such as Prufrock (which graced St Louis's Prufrock Furniture Co., a 'manufacturer of parlor furniture' one of whose branches in 1899 was 'between Locust Street & St Charles Sts') and Stetson (Mrs Stetson, a niece of Harriet Beecher Stowe, lectured to the Wednesday Club in

January 1899) stayed with Tom, absorbed apparently unconsciously, before emerging years later in his mature poetry.[34] Into the *Fireside* he also copied the picture of 'Dr Sweany' which regularly featured in the *Globe-Democrat*. This gentleman was one of several local pedlars of remedies for male ailments who advertised routinely throughout Tom's boyhood. Asking in anxiety-inducing capital letters, 'ARE YOU LACKING IN ENERGY, STRENGTH AND VIGOR . . . MEN WHO ARE WASTING AWAY?' and using such terms as 'Nervous Debility', Dr Sweany's advertisements addressed problems including nervousness and loss of manliness. Rhetoric of this sort flourished in an era when George M. Beard's *Practical Treatise on Nervous Exhaustion (Neurasthenia)* and its 1881 sequel *American Nervousness* were often reprinted, warning Americans that 'the relative quantity of nervousness and of nervous diseases that spring out of nervousness, are greater here than in any other nation in history'.[35] Shy, truss-wearing Tom, whose later verse would deal repeatedly with anxieties about manliness and who would develop poems featuring 'Apeneck Sweeney', copied from newspaper advertisements the doctor's substantial beard. In the printed ads, this hirsute appendage completely obscured Sweany's neckline. Tom also copied a version of the doctor's slogan – 'When Others Fail Come to *Me*' – and highlighted Sweany's ability to deal with insomnia.[36] Ironically, in Tom's 1920s melodrama 'Sweeney Agonistes', Sweeney's nightmares render him unable to sleep.

Other *Fireside* figures included 'Woodbury, The Facial Contortionist', based on John H. Woodbury who advertised 'painless operations for correcting featural irregularities'.[37] As a child Tom was acutely embarrassed by the perceived featural irregularity of his own protruberant ears. Sitting between two girls at a children's party he overheard one whispering to the other that she ought to look at this boy's ears. As a result, Tom bound a rope around his ears when he went to bed at night, but his mother removed it, telling him not to worry: in time the ears would fold themselves back.[38] In the childhood picture taken in the studio of 'Holborn's Dainties, 2320 Washington Avenue', those ears stick out like the handles on proverbial jugs.[39]

Conscious, too, of orthodontic problems, in the *Fireside* the boy drew an advert for 'Dr Chase, dentist' under which there is a picture of a protruberant-eared male with dog-like fangs.[40] From the age of ten, Tom was made to attend the dentist twice a week to have his teeth straightened. Over many visits, as he awaited this ordeal, he read all through an entire set of Edgar Allan Poe's *Collected Works* that were in the waiting room.

Nineteenth-century tooth-straightening could be gruesome, and Poe's narratives of horror may have seemed an appropriate preparation. The scholar Steven Matthews points out how 'The Assignation', one of Poe's *Tales of Mystery and Imagination*, especially impressed Tom when he read it before his regular dental appointment. This story of doomed love, attempted murder and the suicide of a beautiful young woman in Venice twice quotes lines from the seventeenth-century poet Henry King, memorialising his wife:

> Stay for me there! I shall not fail
> To meet thee in that hollow vale.

Tom went searching for that poem. Steven Matthews, calling attention to details in Poe's story, such as the hair 'in curls like those of the young hyacinth', makes a convincing case that not only did this reading resurface at moments in Tom's later poetry with its 'hyacinth girl', but it also prepared him for encounters with the often erotic and broodingly violent aspects of Elizabethan and Jacobean literature from which Poe liked to quote.[41] 'The Assignation', for instance, cites George Chapman's 'vigorous words' in the Jacobean tragedy *Bussy D'Ambois*. Later, Tom developed a marked taste for such plays, but his boyhood experience brought together his personal pain at the dentist's with darker aspects of literary imagination. Poe's work, so important to Baudelaire, underlay too the French Symbolist poetry Tom would come to love in his student years. Attracted to suffering women, Poe – recounter of mysterious crimes, morbidly erotic poet of 'For Annie' and provocative poetic theorist – went on mattering to him.

Whether it was his teeth, his ears or his hernia, his body was at times a source of anxiety, even before this shy boy reached puberty. The body in his mature work would be a recurrent focus for worry and pain. However casually, humiliatingly or light-heartedly, such a nexus of associations grew in Tom early, and was with him even as a ten-year-old. A good number of *Fireside*'s advertisements, usually copied from the newspapers, relate to ill health: Wine of Cardui was a tonic for female ailments; Munyon's Cures ministered to a plethora of ills, including common colds; Dr Franck's Grains of Health were good for 'C. C. and Headache'; Carter's Little Liver Pills, Dr Pearce's Pleasant Pellets for Pink People and Smith's Bile Beans spoke for themselves. Whatever else Tom Eliot was aware of, he certainly knew about illness.

'Avez vous *Fireside*?' ask that magazine's numbers 13 and 14; numbers 2 and 3 offer readers a story about 'duelests' (*sic*) set among 'the busy streets of Paris' complete with 'gamins'. Like Poe's tales, and like the *St Louis Globe-Democrat*, which often ran stories about life in Paris and London,

Fireside aimed to be Francophile and cosmopolitan. In December 1898 translations of Edmond Rostand's play *Cyrano de Bergerac* (which, as well as featuring French duellists, deals with men who find wooing an intellectual woman difficult) were selling out in Tom's home city.[42] This was because the actor Richard Mansfield and a large theatrical entourage were in town to perform at the Olympic Theatre 'the great play . . . for the first time in St. Louis'.[43] Rostand's drama juxtaposes poetic eloquence with chronic male shyness exacerbated by bodily oddity: Cyrano has a huge nose. A local fancy-goods store presented a prominent picture of Cyrano in its *Globe-Democrat* advertisement of 8 January and Mansfield's 'masterly production' got a rave review two days later. Here was 'a strong play, a great play, a beautiful play . . . perfection in a play' that featured 'a love song, the tenderest ever told'.[44] Though he would write his own, very different 'Love Song' eleven years later, this production also caught the attention of young Tom. He recorded in the *Fireside* of 28 January that it had caused 'a great sensation'. His chronicling that 'Mr Mansfield had a lame leg' suggests that either he or other family members may have seen it. *Fireside*'s 'funny artist' provided an illustration of Cyrano complete with sword, elaborate hat and convincingly voluminous nose.

The small boy editor was interested in other kinds of drama too. His piece on 'The Theatre' mentions as well as *Cyrano* the melodrama *Over the Sea*, then playing at the Music Hall, and the ragtime comic opera *By the Sad Sea Waves* with its lyrics by J. Sherrie Matthews and Harry Bulger. Matthews and Bulger played two wastrels taken on as instructors at a sanatorium where they wreak havoc. The show featured Gilbert and Sullivan parodies and minstrel songs which included the hit 'coon song and chorus' entitled 'You Told Me You Had Money in the Bank', published later that year.[45] This song began 'Mr Gideon Strong you've treated me wrong', and here too the ragtime mix of catchy tunes and lyrics that fused vernacular idiom with cheeky use of rhyme was perhaps all the more appealing for belonging to a world so different from that of Tom's parents.

As a student, Tom's brother had a taste for Tin Pan Alley songs. Writing his own advert for a 'great show' called *A Hot Time*, Tom also pencilled a lyric about 'Hasty Red, the Negro Hustler', and noted 'The coon dance': like the Eliots' odd-job man, Stephen, both African Americans and whites regularly used the words 'nigger' and 'coon' in the 1890s.[46] St Louis was clearly a city where African Americans, while no longer slaves, were regarded as an underclass; in newspapers such as the *Globe-Democrat* (whose politics were, like Tom's father's and like his uncle Ed's, Republican), they feature, if at all, largely in caricature drawings, in stories about crime or disease, or in entertainments such as the 'Coon Carnival'.[47] Tom grew up with a sense of a 'colour bar', but also with an awareness that there was valuable material in a wide spectrum of culture. His *Fireside* is evidence of that.

In his little magazine and in local newspaper cartoons, hoboes too were figures of fun. He showed them being given food by Mrs Rogers, apparently the Eliot family's cook, or begging in the street, sleeping rough or spending time in a lock-up. Spread across numbers 5, 6 and 7, the longest of the *Fireside*'s tiny short stories is about the adventures of a hobo called Mosly Wrags. Mosly has a taste for 'a saloon' where he can 'drown his sorrows'. The previous year in St Louis police raided 'cheap saloons where the hoboes hang out', and sixty-six hoboes had been rounded up; many found themselves jailed.[48] Released from his lock-up, Mosly Wrags returns to begging. His young creator, while clearly intrigued, turns away with mock fastidiousness: 'But *we* shall have no more to do with him.'[49] An interest both in the tones of decorum and in what contradicts or disrupts them would be characteristic of poems Tom wrote a decade later: readiness to mix high and low life, evident in the pages of this tiny journal, would remain part of his gift.

As a mature poet, he knew that he had learned not just from the opportunities to access elite culture that his childhood environment offered, but also from growing up in Locust Street with a sense of urban decay in

> A neighbourhood which had become shabby to a degree approaching slumminess, after all our friends and acquaintances had moved further west. And in my childhood, before the days of motor cars, people who lived in town stayed in town. So it was, that for nine months of the year my scenery was almost exclusively urban, and a good deal of it seedily, drably urban at that.

He came to realise that in his poetry 'My urban imagery was that of St. Louis, upon which that of Paris and London have been superimposed.'[50] He made verse that has its roots in a childhood sense of a tension between propriety and its enemies.

At ten, Tom copied out the first verse of Longfellow's early poem 'The Village Blacksmith': Longfellow was a poet taught at Smith Academy. Yet Tom knew, too, of other kinds of verse. In 1898 some St Louis men had established a local Indiana Society, and had invited Indiana 'genius' James Whitcomb Riley to read.[51] Riley had begun by imitating other poets, particularly Edgar Allan Poe, before becoming celebrated, as the *Globe-Democrat* explained, for his 'Annals of the Poor', his 'Character Sketches', and works such as 'Little Orphant Annie'. Hailed as someone who would 'one day stand at the head of American classics', Riley read this last poem to a packed theatre in St Louis in 1898, the local audience relishing Annie's account of the 'little boy' who refused to say his prayers and went 'to bed at night, away upstairs' only to be eaten alive:

An' the Gobble-uns'll git you
　Ef you
　　Don't
　　　Watch
　　　　Out![52]

In *Fireside*, number 14, Tom Eliot (who would use English and American dialect in his own, very different, mature poetry) wrote a little verse, 'The fate of the Naughty Boy', about 'A Boy who went to bed one night' only to be eaten by 'The Goblins', and in number 4 he included an advertisement for an invented work, '"The Bloomer Girl", A Poem, By J. W. Riley', accompanying it with a drawing of a female cyclist wearing bloomers, a piratical eye patch, and smoking a cigarette. No doubt she is one of those 'new women' noted by an 1896 *St Louis Globe-Democrat* parodist of Longfellow's 'Hiawatha' as 'Riding bikes and clad in bloomers'; Tom's sisters had been known to cycle, and several, perhaps all, shared his mother's commitment to extending opportunities for women.[53] Though belonging to none of the twenty 'Women's Clubs of St Louis' which, in 1898, discussed topics ranging from Michelangelo to the *Rubáiyát of Omar Khayyám*, Tom grew up well aware of debates around culture and gender.[54]

The little boy who not so long before had been smitten by a girl acting the part of a cherished, dying lass in a play at a seaside hotel continued to be interested in actresses. His story 'Pretty Belle, the Belle of the Actresses' mentions *The Belle of New York*, performed in St Louis in 1898.[55] This hit musical starred beautiful Edna May as a Salvation Army girl who ends up marrying a millionaire. Its Pretty Belle's most famous song was published later in the St Louis press:

I'm sure I look demure enough, as I go 'round the city;
And do my best to hide the fact that I am young and pretty;
And I therefore cannot see, when I go out to preach,
Why men must say to me that I'm a perfect peach!

With her teasing refrain that sings of young men and 'the light of faith', concluding that 'they never proceed to follow that light, but always follow me!', this Belle of New York was rather different from the ladies of 2635 Locust Street.[56] But, however flippantly, Tom was interested in such a theatrical milieu. Edna May was back in St Louis in early 1899, by which time he was also mentioning, in *Fireside*, number 13, another, more scandalously vivacious actress, Paris-born Anna Held.

Anna Held was in St Louis acting the part of Suzette in *The French Maid*, a Ziegfeld extravaganza. Suzette at a seaside resort romances the entire British fleet. '"Brazen", "sensual", "bawdy" and "wanton"', Held represented, as her modern biographer puts it, 'everything that was glamorous about Broadway, everything that was naughty about Paris'.[57] Already notorious for her 1897 'kissing marathon' and for being reported as bathing, like Cleopatra, in milk, she became one of the most photographed actresses in America, featuring in the St Louis press several times during Tom's boyhood and teens. When he mentioned her in 1899's *Fireside* (and mention her is all he did), she was being billed at St Louis's Century Theatre as 'the Peerless Parisian Beauty'. For the *Globe-Democrat*'s theatre reviewer she made 'a combined assault upon the sense of decency of every man and woman who went to that playhouse'; this was because of her tendency to '"skin down" closer in the matter of clothes than any other woman now before the public'.[58] Again, this seems a world away from the behaviour of Tom's mother and sisters, but the little boy, who was learning French and who noted a local performance of *Othello* starring Lawrence Hanley, paid just as much attention to the presence of Anna Held in *The French Maid*. She, too, was part of the allure of Paris, a city whose fashions, Moulin Rouge and risqué theatre life all featured in the St Louis papers. Paris was synonymous with style and sinfulness.

The 'editor' of the *Fireside*, whose vocabulary outpaced his spelling, liked to record 'flirtation' and 'elopments'. He also dedicated two issues of his magazine 'To My Wife', giving those two words triple underlining and an exclamation mark in number 6.[59] Who ten-year-old Tom's wife was we may never know. The boy's 'inamoratae' around this time or a little later included his freckled, athletic contemporary Margaret Lionberger, daughter of St Louis millionaire attorney, Isaac H. Lionberger, whose Henry Hobson Richardson-designed mansion at 3630 Grandel Square assuredly outclassed Tom's Locust Street home. Where the Eliots stayed put, the Lionbergers moved several times to more and more upscale neighbourhoods.[60]

Other local girls Tom had his eye on included Jane Jones (readily remembered decades later); Effie Bagnall 'whose family were considered distinctly *nouveaux riches*', probably because their money came from that newfangled thing an electricity company; and 'the reigning beauty of the dancing school: Edwine Thornburgh herself, who subsequently became Lady Peek of Peek Frean & Co Ltd.'[61] Tom met these fledgling eligibles from 'St Louis's smart set' at Professor Jacob Mahler's Dancing Academy, 3545 Olive Street, today the site of St Louis's Centene Center.[62] His parents consigned him to this Dancing Academy, often to his great discomfort: 'how I dreaded those afternoons, and my shyness'.[63]

Girls who danced with him in St Louis were struck by his shyness, and by his unreconfigured ears – that continuing source of embarrassment. Margaret Shapleigh, whose brother was a classmate of Tom's at Smith Academy, whose mother belonged to the Wednesday Club and whose doctor father lectured on 'diseases of the ear', called him 'Big-eared Tom'. So did her friends. Though not among his 'inamoratae', she recalled dancing with him at a fancy-dress party when his outfit was rather different from his usual attire:

> My clearest remembrance of him is when he was attending a 'Farmers' Party' because everyone was in farmers' costumes. I was a shy girl but on that occasion I saw (or thought I saw) my brother who from the rear looked exactly like every other boy (blue jeans, plaid shirt & huge straw hat). So being partnerless I tapped him on the shoulder and said 'Hi, kid, let's dance.' The form turned around. It wasn't my brother – just Tom turning redder than a turkey cock. I too was stunned – but we danced.[64]

Confronting and overcoming shyness, Tom danced in his boyhood and teens and grew to love it; twenty years later he would roll back the carpets of his London flat and foxtrot with his wife; he waltzed in old age. If dancing in St Louis brought him into contact with 'inamoratae', it also set a pattern. Just as he was interested in actresses, so he liked dancers. If he recalled his childhood in terms of shyness and being 'protected from . . . sexual precocity', he knew too that, for good and ill, his childhood had made him.[65] At Professor Mahler's and elsewhere, sometimes gauchely, it encouraged him to dance.

Tom remembered the Dancing Academy as deliberately 'Select', catering 'for the jeunesse dorée [gilded youth] of St. Louis'.[66] The Academy had its own printed 'catalogue' which could be mailed out to families wishing their children to attend.[67] Each season, from October until March, the theatrically imaginative Professor – who also organised small children's shows with 'fairy drills and cupid marches' – held a good number of dances at his house for local teenagers from the upper stratum of St Louis Society, as well as Saturday matinee events in his ballroom, typically including a 'Valentine matinee' and a 'farmers' party' like the one at which Tom danced with Margaret Shapleigh.[68] Jacob Mahler has been described as 'a terpsichorean titan, despite his light, lithe build and despite the fact that he always wore velvet ballet slippers'.[69] Well-off parents entrusted their children to this man's care, confident that 'the responsibility, the unseen but nevertheless unmistakable subtle refining influence, the ease of manner, and all the other essential things which go to make young people well bred are in the safest of hands when Mr. Mahler has the helm'.[70]

In his teaching Mahler was an enthusiast for the work of François Delsarte, the French theorist whose work influenced Isadora Duncan and who sought to relate mental to physical articulation, grounded in philosophy and theology.[71] Idealistic in its conviction that 'the artist needs an exactly-formulated definition of art', the Delsarte System was just the sort of dancing that was appropriate for high-minded Lottie Eliot's younger son.[72] Though Tom liked some of the girls at Mahler's, he disliked several of the boys. His 'most loathed enemy' was Atreus Hargadine von Schrader, Jr, who teased him mercilessly. When he was younger Atreus had lived nearby at 2648 Locust Street, but when Tom was nine the rich and ambitious von Schraders had moved away to more salubrious quarters.[73]

Soon so did another boy who aggravated him at Mahler's dancing classes. Lewis Dozier, Jr, sang in the Smith Academy Glee Club and was a rival admirer of Edwine Thornburgh. Though shorter than Tom, Lewis exuded self-assurance that only heightened Tom's shyness. In 1899 the Dozier family migrated to Westmoreland Place, arguably in Tom's boyhood the city's swankiest street.[74] Mixing with these very rich kids, and coming from a prosperous family himself, the boy who wrote up in the *Fireside* 'Miss Stockenbonds', 'Mrs Insessent Snob' and 'the Bondholder Fortunnes' was able to make fun of social pretension in a milieu where 'Miss Kamchatty de Havens gave a small tea of twenty covers.'[75] From a very young age he was able both to participate in polite elite culture and to mock it. That mixture of impulses would be crucial to the poems of his first collection; it never left him.

He read constantly. Photographed aged eight, he hunches, engrossed in a book while sitting at an odd angle, one leg curled under him, on a rocking chair on the porch of the house at Gloucester. In a portrait in oils, painted by his art-student sister Charlotte about five years later, Tom sits formally upright on a dining chair. He is wearing what looks like a dark jacket and white bow tie, reading one of the red leather-bound volumes of the Temple Shakespeare edition which his mother had given him and which remained in his library all his life. Tom remembered how his 'family advised or exhorted me to read' approved works, 'for they concerned themselves about my reading, and I remember my mother's anxiety because I devoted too much attention to the novels of Mayne Reid – she tried to interest me in Macaulay's History [of England] instead'.[76]

Unauthorised reading was exciting. Captain Mayne Reid, whose popular Victorian adventure stories included *The Boy Hunters* and *The Forest Exiles or the Perils of a Peruvian Family amid the Wilds of the Amazon*, was just the author to appeal to the St Louis lad whose *Fireside* contained such little tales as 'Up the Amazon', 'Rattlesnake Bob' and '"Pony Jim" by Dimey Novles'.[77] Tom may have seen pieces such as 'Up the Paraguay River' in the *Globe-Democrat*.[78] He had a taste for Mayne Reid-style adventures involving deserts and jungle locations, striking flora and fauna (the 'humming-bird' whose 'throat . . . glitters' in *The Boy Hunters* re-emerges as the 'glitter' of the 'hummingbird' in the 1930 poem, 'Marina'), and accounts of rites such as that of the '"rain-maker"' which are 'the *first dawning of religion on the soul of the savage*'.[79] These were tales Tom found for himself, some time after he had inherited from his older siblings the 'beloved Rollo books' authored around the time of his father's birth by New England clergyman and educationalist Jacob Abbott.[80] Abbott's educational stories about a polite little American boy, who learns about the world and eventually travels abroad (*Rollo in London*, *Rollo in Paris*), were the genteel, approved counterparts of the adventures among supposedly primitive peoples offered by Mayne Reid. Tom absorbed the lot.

There were books at school, too, of course. In his second year at Smith Academy in 1899–1900 these included not just Edward Eggleston's *History of the United States and Its People*, with its emphasis on 'correctness' and 'clearness', but also a more imaginatively alluring group of 'English Classics', including the Lambs' *Tales from Shakespeare*, Dickens's *A Christmas Carol* and a work entitled *Legends of King Arthur*.[81] Probably this was a book by Thomas Bulfinch, but there is a similarly titled volume by Sir James Knowles; either way, here was Tom's introduction to the legend of the quest for the Holy Grail which, reinterpreted by anthropological writer Jessie L. Weston, would play an important part in *The Waste Land*.

The boy worked assiduously. When his father signed to certify that he had 'examined' Tom's report card for the second term of session 1899–1900, Hal was pleased to see that whether for coursework or final examinations every grade – for Arithmetic, English Literature, English Grammar, English Composition, US History, Spelling, Drawing, Writing and Deportment – was an A.[82] Tom's performance in the first-year class of the main school was a marginal improvement on his report card for the comparable term in his previous year. Then he had dropped to a B for one element of Arithmetic coursework, and had scored consistent

Bs for Writing – probably meaning handwriting, not the separate subject of 'English Comp'. For composition, as in everything else, he had been awarded straight As for 'exceptional work'.[83]

Tom drew on his schoolwork for his writing at home, and sometimes anticipated it. He wrote in pencil the tiny booklet, *George Washington, A Life*, presenting the author on the title page as 'Thos. S. Eliot, S.A., Former Editor of the "Fireside"'. He then crossed out the word 'Former', so probably this briefest of works (which compresses Washington's life into just twelve lines of prose) was contemporary with the early 1899 *Fireside* productions. Tom's Washington 'wanted to go to sea but his mamma didn't want him to'.[84] Tom repeated this detail in a tiny piece on Washington in the *Fireside*.[85] Mammas were commanding figures.

In St Louis around 1900 there were local newspaper features on London life and on Charles Dickens – an author whose work Tom grew to love. One could attend a Literary Symposium lecture on St Paul's Cathedral and the area of London known as 'the City' centred round 'old London Bridge' near which had been the 'shrine' of 'Thomas à Becket'.[86] At schools like Smith Academy private education for boys was relatively Anglophile. Tom worked through a history of England during session 1900–1901, but read American literature too – not just *Hiawatha* but also Longfellow's 'The Courtship of Miles Standish', which, blending amorous pursuit with a rather plain name, anticipates 'The Love Song of J. Alfred Prufrock'. Another text the boy read in 1900 was Oliver Goldsmith's *The Vicar of Wakefield*; as he later acknowledged, words from a song contained there ('When lovely woman stoops to folly') entered *The Waste Land*.[87] When he was thirteen the third page of John Williams White's *First Greek Book* introduced him to the term *logos*.[88] The meanings of that word came to fascinate him.

His schooling sculpted his imagination, as, indeed, it was designed to do. Overseen by Washington University whose junior 'Academic Department' it had been from 1856, then financed by local philanthropists James and Persis Smith, Tom's all-male school was a private, non-residential establishment with about three hundred pupils and twenty teachers. Its substantial multi-storey brick building stood on land owned by Washington University at the corner of Washington Avenue and Nineteenth Street. Next door, but quite separate in gender and ethos, was the Women's Christian Home, a fifty-bedroom hostel for young women of good character but relatively low income: nurses, teachers and shop assistants.[89] A 'preparatory school for colleges, schools of engineering and business', Smith Academy attracted the sons of prosperous St Louis folk, just as the similarly constituted Mary Institute admitted their daughters.[90]

Entrance to Smith Academy was by examination. Pupils had to buy their own textbooks. Fees were about $70.00 for each of the year's two twenty-week terms. Facilities were good. There were chemistry and physics laboratories on the second floor equipped for practical experimental work as well as lectures, and a first-floor gymnasium 'handsomely furnished with the most serviceable pieces of apparatus of modern pattern'. Tom took part in daily gymnastic exercises to which each class was sent around the middle of the school day. The object was 'to give a systematic physical training, not only to those who enjoy athletic sports and would practice them of their own accord, but also to the large number who neglect bodily exercise, unless opportunity is furnished them'.[91]

Many Smith boys in their white shirts, neatly knotted ties and formal jackets went on to become students at Washington University, but the school also sent students regularly to Ivy League colleges including Harvard, Yale and Princeton. For all its ties to Missouri education, Smith in the 1890s boasted that 'The methods of instruction are such as prevail in the oldest and most popular preparatory schools of New England.'[92] Pupils intending to pursue a university arts degree followed a six-year 'Classical Course': Tom took this traditional option including Greek. Cautioning its students 'lest self-love should rule the mind', Smith Academy had a Ciceronian motto: '*Non nobis solum sed patriae et amicis*'; as one of the school's songs (written by Tom's favourite English teacher, Roger Conant Hatch) translated it, 'Not for ourselves alone but for / Our friends and native land'.[93] This ethic of subordinating self to community accorded both with Tom's grand-father's teaching, and with his own mature thought.

Smith's lean, experienced headmaster Charles P. Curd from Louisville, Kentucky, set the tone. Curd had arrived in 1879 at the age of twenty-eight and risen through the pedagogical ranks. Given at times to platitudes, he believed, as he put it when Tom was fifteen, that 'Energy, enthusiasm, honesty and an unbounded determination are among the chief requisites of success.'[94] His 'pupils' were 'expected to prepare at home a part of the lessons assigned for each day, and their hours of study should be regular and free from interruption'.[95] A Latinist, a Germanist and an English teacher who had studied arts at the University of Nashville, then law at Vanderbilt University, Principal Curd held forth at school-chapel morning assemblies. Enthusiastic about public speaking (the school had regular oratory contests), he was known in the press as 'an idolater of athletics'.[96] Neither of these passions Tom shared. However, Curd was keen to inspire his boys in other ways too. He invited the school's best-known former pupil, American author Winston Churchill (not to be confused with the British politician) to address the school on Citizenship when Tom was twelve.

Shortly before, an extract from Churchill's recently successful novel, *Carvel Hall*, had been read at the school's Christmas chapel exercise. Here, as one of the highlights of the school year, was work by a living writer.

Tom's was a markedly literary education. He went to a school where it was possible to encounter a practising author, and where writing of different kinds was celebrated. Curd's staff included outstanding English teachers such as young Percy H. Boynton, who taught at Smith from 1898 until 1902, lectured extramurally in St Louis on Tennyson, then went on to become a professor of English at the University of Chicago.[97] When Tom was thirteen Boynton, who ran the school's annual oratorical contest, launched a series of chapel exercises on the topic of 'Boys' Books'. There were sessions on Abbott's Rollo books and on Kipling's *Captains Courageous*.[98] After Boynton left, Harvard graduate Roger Conant Hatch arrived. A sporty, broad-shouldered young man of twenty-four, Hatch was completing his master's degree at Washington University and had written verse about striving to be 'An honest Christian man'.[99] When Tom was fifteen, Hatch took charge of 'higher English and elocution', but his passion was lyric poetry. He had a taste for Elizabethan verse and Robert Burns. Though his contributions to *Songs of Smith Academy* sang of the school's 'lofty halls' and 'feats of brawn', he could also pen erotic verse about a woman's 'warm soft arms'.[100] Hatch enjoyed teaching, later calling his Smith Academy pupils '"aygnorant young divils," God bless 'em'.[101] Tom liked him.

He did not, however, like every aspect of schooling. It no longer exists, but the earliest poem he remembered writing was about not wanting to go to school on a Monday morning. He regarded himself as having been well taught; yet, with the exception of 'Tom Kick' whom he knew before he went to Smith, he tended not to recall having close St Louis friends. Later he described F. Anstey's Victorian novel *Vice Versa* in which an older man is sent back to school as a 'nightmare'.[102] Back in St Louis as a sixty-five-year-old, he stated, with some qualification, that his 'memories of Smith Academy' were 'on the whole happy'; he wanted to 'pay tribute to' the institution as 'a good school', not least 'because of the boys who were there with me'. Yet he named no fellow pupils, and contemporaries from his schooldays recalled him as 'diffident and retiring' (as Tom Kick put it). To another, less well-disposed classmate he was 'dreary, bookish'.[103]

This last description suggests shy, hernia-afflicted Tom kept his mischievous side well hidden, maintaining a low profile in a school whose most celebrated pupils tended to be sports stars like August R. Krutzsch, fullback in the Smith football team.[104] In 1903, about a month after Tom's fifteenth birthday, Smith fielded burly, broad-shouldered Frederick Klipstein in centre position, though a week later he left the field when a fellow footballer, Otto H. Schwarz, was brought on as a substitute in a convincing Smith victory.[105] While playing no part at all in football, Tom knew these players' names well. He stored them up for decades only for them to re-emerge in unattractive contexts in his poetry. In the drafts of what became *The Waste Land* 'Gus Krutzsch' is one of several men out for a night on the town, while Eliot also used the name as a pseudonym when he published his 'Song to the Opherian' (later modified as part of 'The Hollow Men') in 1921.[106] Klipstein would appear in 'Sweeney Agonistes' as part of the American duo Klipstein and Krumpacker, who at one point sing a jazzy duet accompanied by 'Swarts' on tambourine.[107] J. Louis Swarts was at Smith along with Tom but when, years afterwards, Otto H. Schwarz (who had also captained the Smith Academy basketball team) was convinced that he recognised a version of his own name and that of Klipstein in Tom's writings, the poet confessed, adding that, in part at least, his character of Sweeney had been based on Klipstein.[108]

It is hard not to think that in giving such names to less than reputable characters in his work, Tom was taking a kind of revenge on some of the sporting boys from whose circles he was excluded at Smith Academy. In a footballing school where lads were routinely weighed, measured and examined, Tom's physique and shyness meant he did not conform to the gregarious norms of sporty masculinity.

When he did incorporate names from high school into his later work, several sound Jewish. As a little boy in his *Fireside*, he had advertised a book called 'History of the Jews by Fulish Writers', illustrating his advertisement with a drawing of a man with a bulbous nose.[109] Evidently the *Fireside* circulated among his immediate family, so presumably it was acceptable at Locust Street to link 'Jews' to 'Fulish Writers'. If so, this prejudice, very common indeed in his youth and early manhood, did not come from Tom's religion: his early minister, the Reverend Snyder, was aware of hostility towards Jews but sympathetic to them. Yet, with some embarrassment, Tom's mother commented much later, in 1920 when her younger son was dealing with a writer called Bodenheim:

> It is very bad in me, but I have an instinctive antipathy to Jews, just as I have to certain animals. Of course there are Jews and Jews, and I must be not so much narrow-minded, as narrow in my sympathies. There must be something in them which to me is antipathetic. Father never liked to have business dealings with them . . .[110]

The way his mother articulates this implies that anti-Semitism was a prejudice substantially unspoken in the Eliots' St Louis household, but indisputably present. Tom's attunement to it in the *Fireside* suggests that he took it on board early. His deployment of names like that of the sports star Klipstein hints that it may have stayed with him during his time at Smith Academy. It continued to dog him, part of an early conditioning which he sometimes went along with, sometimes questioned. Tom would benefit from Jewish critics and publishers, and during World War II would go out of his way to call attention to and denounce what was happening at Auschwitz. When directly confronted with the charge of anti-Semitism decades after his childhood, he denied it.

3

Schoolings

LIKE most people, Tom had not so much a schooling as schoolings. He learned from vacations as well as from classrooms. His home reading was as important as any set texts. Decades afterwards, when he thought back to his fellow Smith Academy pupils, he called them simply 'acquaintances'. Apparently he had lost track of them. Half jocularly he remembered disliking 'my only contemporary in St. Louis who has become famous: Gerard Lambert, whose family flourished by the manufacture of "Listerine". He was rich, he was good at mathematics (which I was not) and he was an athlete and won cups.'[1] When Tom was nearing sixteen, not just the World's Fair but also the Olympic Games came to St Louis. On 14 May 1904 Lambert won the pole vaulting competition, as well as coming second in 'running broad jump' and 'running high jump' during the Olympic Interscholastic Meet (State of Missouri) in which Smith Academy finished second overall.[2] Tom played no part in such success, though he did have a ticket for the World's Fair, one of whose principal displays covered 'Anthropology and Ethnology, including the Philippine Islanders'. As well as displaying live 'Aborigines' from America, Africa and Japan, there was a vast 'Philippine Encampment' featuring 'the most remarkable display of a people held at an exposition'. Here in lake encampments were 'Savage Moros' and 'Head Hunters' (described as 'all savage') and Viscayans ('civilized and devout Catholics') – who had come from 'Luzon and the surrounding archipelago'.[3] If all this seemed a world away from Smith Academy, Tom did publish the following year a story in his school magazine about a sea captain shipwrecked among Polynesian tribesmen – some 'beating bhghons (a sort of cross between a tin pan and gong) and chanting monotonously', but others converted by French missionaries and therefore 'quite civilized and uninteresting'.[4] His interest in juxtaposed cultures and

59

religions interpreted through anthropology is rooted in the world of his schooldays.

To an English friend he wrote in 1939, 'As for other of my childhood acquaintances, they were more mixed in origin than any of your playmates, I am sure. Butch Wagner, Pat Sullivan, Snowball Wolfert, Elephant-mouth Hellman, Gander Giesecke: what has become of them?'[5] Tom's schoolfellows were boys from 'good families' who did well and often went on to good universities; Milton 'Elephant-mouth Hellman' progressed to Yale.[6] Yet such 'acquaintances' were not trusted confidants. During his last years at Smith, Tom was part of a small group of five boys distinguishing themselves in the Classical Course. Standing in their midst for his formal class yearbook photograph, he looks hunched and a little uneasy. He seems not to have been very close to any of them: his fellow Classicist Lawrence Tyler Post, who had some talent for verse, penned the 'Class Song' for Tom's year, before going to Yale. As for the other boys on the Classical Course, Charles Hills Ryan proceeded to Longfellow's alma mater, Bowdoin College; wealthy banker's son Walker Moore Van Riper chose Yale, and later hymned the St Louis Mortgage Bond Co. in *What Every Investor Should Know* (1913); Frederick Clinton Lake, Jr, too headed for Yale, returning afterwards to the St Louis dry goods business.[7] These classmates were among the twenty-five chosen to participate in the school's preliminary speaking contest in February 1905. The organiser was Tom's admired English teacher, Mr Hatch; but Tom was not selected for the finals.[8] At times his best friends were his books.

Principal Curd's *New Method of English Analysis* was a set text. It offered tiny extracts from famous writers as examples of common English constructions. The chosen authors included Shakespeare, Pope, Poe and Byron – all important to Tom – but Curd also cited stylists including La Rochefoucauld and Seneca. Tom would mention La Rochefoucauld in his first book of poems, and would later write about Seneca, but more generally the bookish habit of deploying tiny quotations from other writers became second nature to him. Tom himself (then, much later, John Soldo and Jayme Stayer) identified his schoolbooks.[9] In its choice of such texts for study as *The Vicar of Wakefield*, *The Merchant of Venice*, *Silas Marner*, Carlyle's *Essay on Burns*, Tennyson's *Princess*, James Russell Lowell's *Vision of Sir Launfal* and Burke's *Speech on Conciliation with America*, Smith Academy's literature curriculum used works commonly set for admission to leading colleges.

Tom's curriculum was also tied to the contents of *Composition and Rhetoric for Schools* by Chicago educators Robert Herrick and Lindsay Todd Damon. Working through this text, he found mention of *The House of the Seven*

Gables (which became a favourite novel), *Captains Courageous*, and frequent references to Kipling and Stevenson. He imitated these last two authors in stories for the *Smith Academy Record*. Herrick and Damon also cited J. M. Barrie, that fashionable chronicler of hesitant masculinity whose *Sentimental Tommy* Tom later joked about. Tom encountered, too, the writerly advice of G. H. Palmer (afterwards one of his Harvard teachers) to look to 'speech' and 'conversation' in seeking 'the development of literary power'. Herrick and Damon argued that 'good writing does not differ essentially from good talking' and encouraged a productive relationship with modern spoken idiom. Their suggestion that a fine topic for writers was 'The Legend of the Holy Grail' was one Tom would take up later.[10]

Reading this book on composition, he was pointed towards Tennyson's *Idylls of the King* and Sir Thomas Malory's *Morte d'Arthur*. He recalled in 1934 that a children's edition of Malory (probably produced by Sidney Lanier, with illustrations of 'Eliot the Harper' and the castle of the Holy Grail) had been 'in my hands when I was a child of eleven or twelve. It was then, and perhaps has always been, my favourite book.'[11] Tom's inclinations were encouraged by his education. Throughout his boyhood Tennyson's *Idylls of the King* was still widely admired on both sides of the Atlantic. Edward Austin Abbey had recently painted *The Quest and Achievement of the Holy Grail* around the walls of Boston Public Library, its narrative written up by Henry James in 1895. Playing his part in such American Arthurianism, Tom was selected to read out his essay, '"A Vision of Sir Launfal", A Christmas Study', as part of Smith Academy's Christmas exercises in 1904. Though the essay has not survived, it was based on his reading of Lowell's Grail quest poem, *A Vision of Sir Launfal*, a staple of the Smith Academy curriculum and one of Tom's fifth-year texts that session. The standard school edition presented the poem as 'fraught with' a 'deeply religious element'.[12]

Lowell's 1848 *Vision* links its protagonists to nature and the seasons; it contrasts the 'leaves' and 'sap' of summer and youth 'lightsome as a locust-leaf' with the senescence of 'An old, bent man, worn out and frail', imaged as a wintry 'sapless and old' tree.[13] Beginning in the everyday, Lowell soon plunges into the visionary. Regarded as a classic in Tom's youth but now criticised for its 'disregard for form', Lowell's poem helped make the Grail legend seem 'democratic' to Americans.[14] Utterly different, Tom's poetry too would feature exhausted old men linked to seasonal cycles. Lowell uses the word 'tent' of green vegetation; the notes to the school edition call attention to an odd expression, '"the river's shroud"', perhaps picked up in that unusual phrase in *The Waste Land*, 'the river's tent'.[15]

Tom's appropriative poetic ear retained cadences, his imagination was sustained by images and stories. A striking number of the tales he read were about unfortunate love affairs. In German, Theodor Storm's *Immensee*, which he studied when he was fifteen, is an old man's narrative of lost love, memory and desire; Wilhelm Hauff's *Das kalte Herz* (*The Cold Heart*) has a protagonist who kills his wife; Paul Heyse's 'L'arrabbiata' ('The Fury') deals with a violent, difficult erotic relationship. In French George Sand's *La petite Fadette* features another problematic love affair, though *Mademoiselle de la Seiglière* by Sand's lover Jules Sandeau at least ends happily; Pierre Loti's sensuous novel *Ramuntcho*, presenting spring as sad for the aged, evokes lost love. Teaching such texts, Tom's French teacher at Smith Academy, Julia Juvet Kaufmann, born in Geneva to Swiss parents, was sophisticated and cosmopolitan. All his life Tom remembered her as 'the French Mistress who gave me my first taste for that language'.[16] When he was fifteen the local press reported that Mme Kaufmann 'goes abroad annually and has done so for many seasons'; in a socially conservative milieu this widow in her fifties was the only single woman listed among 'St. Louis Travelers who have made from Ten to Twenty Transatlantic Trips'.[17] For a time she had lived further along Locust Street at number 3200, a not-so-distant neighbour but one very different from Tom's parents who had never even set eyes on Europe.[18]

Classroom reading prepared the way for his subsequent work. Extended study of Xenophon's *Anabasis* in Greek when he was fourteen and fifteen set him up for his much later translation of St John Perse's *Anabase*. *Julius Caesar* and *The Merchant of Venice* yielded phrases used in his mature verse. As early as 1901 four purple stars and a gold star were placed on the board to indicate that he had given seventy 'excellent recitations in Latin'. Principal Curd as well as Tom's teacher, Miss Mabel Evans, a dedicated Washington University alumna, signed a 1901 report which told the boy's parents, 'We consider his work worthy of the highest praise.'[19] Soon he began reading Ovid's *Metamorphoses* (cited in *The Waste Land*'s notes), and Virgil's *Aeneid* which became a lifelong talisman.

In Palgrave's *Golden Treasury*, a set anthology when Tom was in his penultimate year at Smith Academy, poems LXV and LXVI were short extracts from Renaissance dramas: lyrics of the sort liked by Mr Hatch. The first, Shakespearian song (which Palgrave called 'A Sea Dirge') comes from *The Tempest*. It contains the line 'Those are pearls that were his eyes', which would become part of *The Waste Land*.[20] The second lyric, from John Webster's Jacobean tragedy *The White Devil*, was entitled by Palgrave 'A Land Dirge'. It concerns 'The friendless bodies of unburied men': its last couplet, 'But keep the wolf far thence, that's foe to men, / Or with his nails he'll dig them up again' would be recast in *The Waste Land*. A few pages further on in the first book of Palgrave's anthology is Edmund Spenser's 'Prothalamion' whose refrain 'Sweet Thames! Run softly, till I end my song' would haunt Tom.[21]

He was taught that 'committing a poem to memory . . . is most desirable'.[22] But the verse he memorised did not necessarily come from school. In the *Fireside* he mentions that 'There have been many parodys [*sic*] on "The White Man's Burden"', a well-known 1899 poem by Kipling addressed to Americans during a crisis in the Philippines, urging them to 'Take up the White Man's burden' of imperial responsibility over 'new-caught, sullen peoples, / Half devil and half child'.[23] In St Louis ten-year-old Tom, writing that 'The Philipines [*sic*] are dangerous' and that the word from '*England*' was that 'The Anglo-Saxon American is marching on', no doubt came into regular contact with racist rhetoric, but Kipling appealed to him for other reasons.[24] When Tom was ten or twelve, he fell in love with the sound of the Anglo-Indian poet's ballad about the hanging of a soldier, 'Danny Deever', and memorised it.[25] This ballad of 'drinkin' bitter beer' deploys Cockney speech; like Tom in later life, the Kipling of *Barrack Room Ballads* is a great poet of English pub-talk: his 'Tommy', a poem Tom afterwards picked out, begins, 'I went into a public-'ouse to get a pint o' beer'. But the lines of 'Danny Deever' that most fascinated the boy were in its last stanza, '"What's that that whimpers over'ead?" said Files-on-Parade. / "It's Danny's soul that's passin' now," the Colour-Sergeant said.' Remembering this poem all his life, Tom realised he loved the imperfect rhyme between 'Parade' and 'said'; 'the word *whimper*' was 'exactly right'. In adulthood, misquoting from memory, Tom turned Kipling's dying 'whimpers' into 'whimper', surely because by then it had been absorbed into his own most quoted line about dying, 'Not with a bang but a whimper'.[26]

Like most late-nineteenth-century children, he grew up familiar with death. His dead Grandfather's mores still dominated family life; his own birth had been preceded by the passing of his sister Theodora; he had been enamoured of the child actress who played the dying Carol in *The Birds' Christmas Carol*. At school during an outbreak of fever in early 1900, Dr Curd had to give a speech memorialising a pupil who had died; a week later an assembly of staff and pupils paid tribute to another dead boy.[27] In 1901 one of Tom's school contemporaries, Walter Crunden, whose brother had just died of meningitis, became 'nervous' and 'was stricken with brain fever' said to have been brought on by 'long-continued nerve strain in preparing for a school debate'.[28] Like Tom, Walter was a reciter of poetry, and had a marked taste for literature. Such events did nothing to lessen Lottie Eliot's fearfulness about her potentially vulnerable younger son. Long afterwards, when a commentator on Tom's upbringing remarked on the 'anxiety' and even 'distress' in his mother's face, he did not demur.[29] His mother worried he was lonely. As he moved through Smith Academy, she grew increasingly aware that, though her youngest child was 'most friendly', nonetheless 'We have lived twenty-five years on the old Eliot place, while all our friends have moved out, and Tom desires companionship of which he has been thus deprived.'[30] His lack of friends and his health concerned her.

Though Tom took part in 'gymnasium training' with the other boys, his mother was clear he 'could not participate in football and other such strenuous sports'. He was, she realised, 'almost the only fellow debarred from football'. She agonised about his 'physical limitations' and paid careful attention to what the family physician said when he examined Tom's 'congenital rupture'. By 1905 the doctor thought the condition '*superficially* healed, but as the abdominal muscles are weak, care must still be exercised'.[31] Personally as well as professionally, even if perhaps she 'saw herself as a failure as a teacher', Mrs Eliot cared passionately about bringing up children, and worried about their welfare.[32] Throughout Tom's early teens she was a leading, successful campaigner for the rights of youngsters in the St Louis penal system; by 1903 she had been 'for a number of years one of the managers of a temporary home for children'.[33] She knew how to influence her family too, encouraging them to continue her preoccupations: her eldest daughter Ada, already a student at Radcliffe during Tom's infancy, was secretary of Boston's Family Welfare Society when Tom started high school. Ada, who had once mouthed sounds to her baby brother, went on to specialise in child welfare issues, winning early in her distinguished social work career the nickname 'Angel of the Tombs'.[34] Yet, as Mrs Eliot grew increasingly deaf, and as Tom's siblings left home, the frustrated poet who was his mother grew all the closer to her shy, poetry-loving younger son. Sometimes she worried the nature of their closeness might be oppressive for Tom. 'I talk with him', this strong-willed woman wrote when he was sixteen, 'as I would with a man, which perhaps is not so good for him as if he had young people about him.'[35]

In the early 1930s, a few years after his mother died, and at a time when he had grown familiar with psychoanalysis, Tom remarked to a small audience of American students that the treatment of 'mother-love' in D. H. Lawrence's *Fantasia of the Unconscious* was 'better than all the psychoanalysts' had to say on the topic.[36] Lawrence (one of whose 'conspicuous weakneses', according to Tom, was that he 'gave his best to his mother') writes of how the middle-aged mother in particular can demand 'more love' from 'one who will "understand" her. And as often as not she turns to her son.' *Fantasia of the Unconscious* saw such an engulfing situation as 'a dynamic *spiritual* incest, more dangerous than sensual incest, because it is more intangible and less instinctively repugnant'. Such circumstances produced 'introversion' in sons when 'Child and parent' were 'intensely linked in adult love-sympathy and love-will', yet the child's developing sexuality, though roused by parental love, could not find adequate expression through the intense parent-child bond and so clashed against it. For Lawrence this state of affairs was bound up with the child's 'own shame and masturbation, its own cruel, secret sexual excitement and sex *curiosity* . . . There is an aversion from the normal coition act. But the craving to feel, to see, to taste, to *know*, mentally in the head, this is insatiable.' To suggest that every detail of Lawrence's argument should be read back into Tom's relationship with his mother would be unfair; but it is striking that he later called attention to this account of 'mother-love' as especially perceptive. Revealingly, where Lawrence (though he does write about love between a mother and a son) uses the non-gendered expression 'parent love', Tom substituted 'mother-love'.[37] The boy whose Mamma fretted over his health, and who shared with her a deep love of poetry, grew up to become the thirty-one-year-old poet who gratefully accepted her offer to make him a new pair of pyjamas: 'it would seem to keep us nearer together'.[38]

Little or nothing is known about sex education or possible instances of homosexuality at Tom's single-sex school, but traditionally Smith Academy did give its boys at the age of twelve or so some instruction in 'Physiology' through 'familiar talks'; at home Tom's father's strict views on sex and sex education grew severe as he aged.[39]

> I do not approve of public instruction in Sexual relations. When I teach my children to avoid the Devil I don't begin by giving them a letter of introduction to him and his crowd. I hope that a cure for Syphilis will never be discovered. It is God's punishment for nastiness. Take it away and there will be more nastiness, and it will be necessary to emasculate our children to keep them clean.[40]

Though these sentences date from 1914, they reflect the sexual code Tom's father passed to the boys in what Tom's older brother called 'such a fanatically conservative family as ours'.[41] Later Tom's brother became conscious of being attracted to girls who seemed exciting but unsuitable; he married late, happily, and had no children. For Tom, shy and sometimes fastidious, his father's attitude to sex was unlikely to relieve any anxiety he may have had about his body, not least when conscious of potential weakness caused by his congenital hernia. Yet photographs of him with his father suggest there was clear physical affection between them. As a couple, Lottie and Hal Eliot had produced seven children. Tom's parents were strict, but hardly sex averse.

On at least one occasion during his Smith Academy years Tom moved beyond parental control. In 1904, rather than staying for the summer at Eastern Point, he headed further north to Quebec. Though in another country (this was his only boyhood trip abroad), he was still in Eliot territory. The previous year his uncle, the Reverend Christopher Rhodes Eliot of Boston, had visited the St Louis Eliots and preached at the Church of the Messiah.⁴² Around that time Christopher also bought land on the shore of Canada's Lake Memphremagog. This became the site of a fifty-four-acre family camp, Camp Maple Hill, where everyone slept in tents. At Camp Maple Hill Christopher Eliot's Scottish wife Mary liked to read aloud Walter Scott's ballads, encouraging visitors to join in impromptu songs and amateur theatricals.⁴³ When Tom went in 1904, it was the camp's first season. His cousin Frederick was there, as were nine women and girls, including several other cousins.

There were trails to mark out on this plot of land, garden ground to plant, even a log cabin to build. This life by shores and forests was a world away from Locust Street, and much more basic than vacationing at Eastern Point. At least one of his cousins noted that it was liberating for Tom to be away from his parents.⁴⁴ He went swimming in the lake. He rowed on it. The weather was hot. He took part in an expedition to climb a 3,000-foot mountain from whose summit he could see as far as Mount Washington in the United States and Montreal in Canada.

Something of his excitement can be sensed in a verse letter he sent from this camp to his sister Charlotte. Married the year before to architect George Lawrence Smith, son of a Harvard Classics professor, she seems to have been unwell after the birth of her daughter, Tom's little niece Theodora. 'Hoping you are better, / At least enough to read my letter', fourteen-year-old Tom tells his sister about his expedition:

> We after breakfast took a start,
> Four of us, in a two horse cart
> Together with a little luncheon,
> Including things quite good to munch on . . .

Part gauche rhyming, part mischievous excitement, this letter exudes fun, though the writer does not seem entirely sure how his sister will receive it. 'I suppose now I should desist, / For I am needed to assist / In making a raft'.[45]

Raft-building was the sort of thing boys did in Captain Mayne Reid's stories. This summer delighted Tom, and at least one aspect of it entered the heart of his mature poetry. His time at Camp Maple Hill explains why the 'Drip drop drip drop drop drop drop' of *The Waste Land* is accompanied by a note that sounds surprisingly personal as it details, with its reference to Chapman's *Handbook of Birds of Eastern North America*, 'the hermit-thrush which I have heard in Quebec Province'.[46] Tom here brings together a memory of his time among the lakeside trees with the bird book his mother had given him. Under the surface of the mature poem are memories of relative freedom from his parents as well as a treasured maternal link. A sense both of escape from the constraints of home and of a powerful awareness of ties to his upbringing would condition all Tom's adult life. His first taste of this came in Quebec.

In 1905 he saw Ada married to Alfred D. Sheffield, an instructor at Harvard Preparatory School, Springfield, Massachusetts. The Unitarian marriage ceremony was a quiet one held at the family home in Locust Street. Christopher Eliot presided alongside the Reverend John William Day, who had replaced Reverend Snyder as minister of the Church of the Messiah. A significant figure during Tom's early teens, Day had established himself as a clergyman with marked philosophical concerns, at least some of which Tom would come to share. Day maintained that knowledge was in an important sense relational. He believed that 'every created thing is part of some larger life than its own. Learning about the world is a process of learning to what things belong. We do not know a thing by knowing that thing alone, we know it by knowing of what it forms a part.' Discussing the way 'the agnostic attitude . . . assumes that the part is the whole', this pastor argued for a 'logic of knowing' which made the 'valid inference, like the inferences of science' that the part can be related to 'the whole'. While he spoke up for 'The profound, indisputable significance of the resurrection of Jesus', Day saw this as affirming 'a science of the soul, a larger order than the order of birth and death'.[47] This for him was the meaning of Easter. Mixing philosophical rhetoric with invocations of Christ, Day continued his predecessor's custom of making the Unitarian Lent and Easter services a cultural as well as a religious festival. So, for instance, when Tom was eleven, Day preached in the Church of the Messiah at services where members of the St Louis Choral Symphony played, and singers and narrators performed parts of Gounod's 'Redemption' oratorio.[48] Like Lottie Eliot, this pastor emphasised the importance of those who had suffered for faith: in a sermon on 'The Cheer of Suffering', delivered when Tom was twelve, he stressed that, 'In all the bright armory of fame, nothing shines with quite the luster which is reflected from the deeds of those who have been tried as by fire and have not been found wanting.'[49]

In a 1901 Easter sermon on 'Death in Life and Life in Death', the intellectually ambitious Day examined the German philosopher and scientist Ernst Haeckel's thought. Day considered 'the result of mind and will being concentrated on one kind of reality, so that they lose all sense of every other kind'.[50] Tom's parents regularly took him to church. The boy who listened to this philosophically minded Unitarian preacher later developed into a student who would write on such matters as degrees of reality and who would question in his poetry what was real and 'Unreal'.[51]

While he could never match up to the Reverend William Greenleaf Eliot, the balding, bearded Reverend Day, who championed 'the survival of the faithful', shared several of Tom's parents' interests, secular as well as religious.[52] Not least, he argued that their Church should play a full part in the 1904 St Louis World's Fair, with aspects of whose planning Hal and Lottie, too, were involved.[53] Like those of the Eliots, Day's cultural loyalties lay with the legacy of New England transcendentalism, and in the spring of 1903 he held an ambitious evening at the Church of the Messiah to celebrate 'the centennial of the birth of Ralph Waldo Emerson'. At this event, speaking about philosophy, Professor A. O. Lovejoy argued that Emerson's teachings had 'done much to counteract "the modern disease of personality"'.[54] Tom Eliot would grow up to make fun of Emersonian optimism in his poetry, but he too would present a critique of 'personality'.

Tom's minister championed Unitarianism precisely because it was 'a denomination which publishes no authoritaritative declaration of faith' yet represented 'intellectual and spiritual strength'.[55] Day believed that 'human nature improves'. Though Tom would come to react strongly against such Unitarian beliefs, aspects of the faith shaped him. Preaching traditional adherence to the Ten Commandments, Day urged his congregation to 'Condemn our modern idolatries with the law which condemned ancient idol worship.' What he advocated was what Tom and his family generally practised: 'Reverence, sanctity, honor to parents, respect for life, chastity, honesty, truth and unselfishness'.[56] This was a lot to live up to, but the Eliots were schooled and churched to live up to it. In Tom's sixteenth year the Church of the Messiah celebrated Lent with a concert at which 'Several numbers were heard for the first time in St Louis, one of the most interesting being the Angels' Chorus from Elgar's "Dream of Gerontius"' with its libretto by the famous English Catholic convert

Cardinal Newman.[57] There had been discussion of Elgar's oratorio in St Louis beforehand and given that this performance was one of the highlights of his church's year, Tom was bound to have heard about it. 'Gerontius' gave him a name that, like other names garnered from St Louis, lingered in his mind. Retuned, it emerged fifteen years later in that geriatric poem-title, 'Gerontion'.

His brother Henry was surprised to hear Tom's later statement that it was reading Edward Fitzgerald's *Rubáiyát of Omar Khayyám* which had been his crucial early encounter with poetry. Instead, Henry remembered discovering Tom about the age of ten immersed in Milton's *Samson Agonistes*. When Henry, then a university student, reported this to the rest of the family, they were astonished.[58] Milton was regarded by many Unitarians as sharing their beliefs; he was a great religious poet, though a difficult one. Perhaps Tom was reading what he thought he *should* be reading; yet his being discovered poring over *Samson Agonistes* in private suggests that he genuinely wanted to come to terms with it. At the very least it is obvious that, albeit ironically, he did go on to make use of Milton's title in his own 'Sweeney Agonistes'.

Henry also recalled his brother reading Browning before he encountered Fitzgerald's *Rubáiyát*.[59] Browning too was a difficult poet. His interest in saints and in religious tensions, whether in 'St Simeon Stylites' or 'Fra Lippo Lippi', was both akin to and sceptically different from Tom's mother's pious literary commitment. Browning had perfected the dramatic monologue, the poetic form that 'The Love Song of J. Alfred Prufrock' would build on. At one point in later life, Tom would be dismissive of the Victorian poet in relation to his own work: 'Browning was more of a hindrance than a help, for he had gone some way, but not far enough, in discovering a contemporary idiom.'[60] However, it was precisely Browning's combination of conversational tone, intellectual rigour, passion and irony that would stand Tom in good stead, and on occasion he came to recognise that Browning among nineteenth-century writers was 'the only poet' to devise a way of speech which might be useful for others and that 'Browning's lesson' lay 'in [the] use of non-poetic material – in reasserting [the] relation of poetry to speech'.[61] Henry remained insistent that his brother was wrong about the age when he read certain books, maintaining that Tom read Milton before he devoured Fitzgerald, and that, by the time he was fifteen, Tom, reading voraciously in ways not suggested by his elders, had absorbed a good deal of Browning.[62] Tom's precocity struck some observers. Aged about fourteen and on holiday in Massachusetts, he was introduced to Harvard historian Professor Kuno Franke, a neighbour of his cousin Eleanor in

Cambridge. The professor asked Tom with a twinkle if he 'was a sub-sub-Freshman'.[63]

Certainly during this formative period Tom encountered Fitzgerald's *Rubáiyát*, the work which, from at least the 1930s to the 1960s (when Henry was no longer alive to contradict him), he consistently presented as having provided his first profound experience of enjoying poetry. Asked in 1959, 'Do you remember the circumstances under which you began to write poetry in St. Louis when you were a boy?' he replied, 'I began I think about the age of fourteen, under the influence of Fitzgerald's *Omar Khayyam*, to write a number of very gloomy and atheistical and despairing quatrains in the same style, which fortunately I suppressed completely – so completely that they don't exist. I never showed them to anybody.'[64] This poetic start is presented as totally private, and (though Tom does not explicitly say so) in complete opposition to his parents' values. When he wrote in the 1930s about being excited by poetry as an adolescent, his vocabulary was a sexual one of 'seduction' and 'infatuation':

Everyone, I believe, who is at all sensible to the seductions of poetry, can remember some moment in youth when he or she was completely carried away by the work of one poet. Very likely he was carried away by several poets, one after the other. The reason for this passing infatuation is not merely that our sensibility to poetry is keener in adolescence than in maturity. What happens is a kind of inundation, of invasion of the undeveloped personality by the stronger personality of the poet.[65]

This seems to be what happened to Tom when he 'happened to pick up a copy of Fitzgerald's *Omar* which was lying about', and found in the poem an 'almost overwhelming introduction to a new world of feeling' that was 'like a sudden conversion; the world appeared anew, painted with bright, delicious and painful colours'.[66] As Henry pointed out to him, there had been a vogue for Fitzgerald's poem when Tom was about ten or twelve.[67] In 1898 the St Louis Musical Club had performed English composer Liza Lehmann's settings of parts of the *Rubáiyát*; that same year the *Globe-Democrat* discussed poet Richard Le Gallienne, agreeing with 'those who laugh at his impudence in trying to improve upon Fitzgerald's version of Omar Khayyam'.[68]

The popularity of the *Rubáiyát* in America explains why Tom was able to find a copy of Fitzgerald's translation of the Persian poet 'lying about' a few years later. This poem about 'reviving old Desires' was unashamedly hedonistic as it invoked 'the fire of Spring' in a desert terrain of 'the Waste', a milieu of wine, longing, fear of 'the NOTHING', and admiration for the fleeting 'Nightingale that in the branches sang'. Here was a sensuous poetry which asserted heretically, "'I Myself am Heav'n and Hell'", and whose insistent message was *carpe diem* – something the shy adolescent Tom seemed unable to do at his dancing classes. One of Fitzgerald's images for desire involves an exhausting search for water in the desert:

> Would but the Desert of the Fountain yield
> One glimpse – if dimly, yet indeed, reveal'd,
> To which the fainting Traveller might spring,
> As springs the trampled herbage of the field![69]

Though Tom's quatrains sparked by his absorption in Fitzgerald are lost, it is clear his reading propelled him into an intense engagement with nineteenth-century Romantic poetry. 'Thereupon I took the usual adolescent course with Byron, Shelley, Keats, Rossetti, Swinburne.'[70] He was attracted not least to verse that mixed sexual longing with religious sentiment. A poem he mentioned along with Fitzgerald's *Rubáiyát* as part of the 'intellectual pubescence' of 'a boy of fourteen' was Dante Gabriel Rossetti's 'The Blessed Damozel'.[71] This work was classed among Rossetti's 'masterpieces' in one of Tom's textbooks, Henry S. Pancoast's *An Introduction to English Literature*.[72] Even more sensuous than Fitzgerald, Rossetti's poem portrays a woman longing for her lover as she leans out from 'the gold bar of Heaven', wearing 'Her robe, ungirt from clasp to hem'. Such poetry excited Tom. He read on: 'Her hair that lay along her back / Was yellow like ripe corn'.[73] Eventually he would ironise this material, not least by juxtaposing its phrasing with the repressed, polite milieu in which he came to move: 'The readers of the *Boston Evening Transcript* / Sway in the wind like a field of ripe corn'.[74] Probably such ironising began early, and indeed elements of it may be sensed in at least one piece Tom published in the *Smith Academy Record*.

This was 'A Fable for Feasters', a poem for Christmas published unseasonably in February 1905. Tom's tale about a ghost in a medieval monastery uses the stanza form favoured by Byron in *Don Juan*, another signal of the boy's liking for nineteenth-century poetry with an erotic tinge. Cheeky rhymes such as 'Mormon' and 'Norman' suggest Tom liked Byron's wit and acoustic nimbleness too.[75] Yet the immediate model, as readers from his brother Henry to modern critics have recognised, was the *Ingoldsby Legends, or Mirth and Marvels*, a once popular series of Victorian English comic verses about medieval life. The poems of the *Ingoldsby Legends* mix modern, sometimes slangy lingo ('You *will* have a kicking!') with mock-medievalisms ('Quoth his saintship, "How now!"'), and parody both actual medieval forms and nineteenth-century medievalising, such as that of Keats in 'The Eve of St Agnes'.[76] Where Tom's admired *Morte d'Arthur* and *Vision of Sir Lanfaul* were solemnly medieval, *Ingoldsby* capered; so does 'A Fable for Feasters'.

Tom's first printed poem describes the many-wived King Henry VIII as 'that royal Mormon' and presents monks as 'quacks'. Tom's brother relished the way, conducting an exorcism, the poem's Abbot douses a dining room with holy water, 'And watered everything except the wine'.[77] Into his poem Tom works expressions such as '"O jiminy!"' rhyming with 'the chimney'. As well as drawing on 'The Ghost' from *The Ingoldsby Legends*, he learned from the poem that follows it in the same collection, 'The Brothers of Birchington, A Lay of St Thomas À Becket'. When Tom wrote in his last stanza of how 'Each morn from four to five one took a knout / And flogged his mates 'till they grew good and friarly', his use of the unusual word 'knout' in this context probably owes something to the way in 'The Brothers of Birchington' we hear of 'such a knout! / For his self-flagellations! The Monks used to say / He would wear out two penn'orth of whipcord a day!'[78]

Reading and imitating this work, Tom began to put together allusions to older cultural forms with anachronistically modern colloquial language. He also found a way both to indulge and subvert the taste he shared with his mother for sometimes ascetic medieval religious life. Though later he would be fascinated by masochistic saints and as a mature poet would return more solemnly to Thomas à Becket, what he started to essay in this teenage poem was mixing modern and antique diction. In doing so he drew on some of his interests in older poetry and religion, yet developed an ironic edge. Tom did not succeed fully in 1905, but perhaps the untonsured man in 'The Brothers of Birchington' who worries about 'a little bald patch on the top of his crown' would return later as J. Alfred Prufrock with a 'bald spot in the middle of my hair'.[79]

In his penultimate year at school, though absent from the sports field, he did win respect for his academic performance. Like his brother before him, he was awarded the school's gold medal for Latin. Tom's medal made his parents proud. Pa gave him a reward of $25, but secretly Tom took ('stole' as he later put it) $2 of this to purchase a copy of Shelley's poems.[80] Reading the work of a poet who had written a notorious justification of atheism was in its way a rebellious act. It followed Tom's authoring of those 'atheistical' quatrains spurred by his reading of Fitzgerald. He perused Edward Dowden's edition of Shelley's poems excitedly. On the first page of his introduction Dowden presented Shelley's genius as 'primarily lyrical'. 'No poet ever sang more directly out of his own feelings – his joys, his sorrows, his desires, his regrets.' A little-known, fragmentary lyric poem towards the end of Dowden's edition, where it was entitled 'To the Moon', stayed with Tom all his life. He came to think it 'the most perfect short poem that Shelley wrote':

> Art thou pale for weariness
> Of climbing heaven and gazing on the earth,
>   Wandering companionless
> Among the stars that have a different birth,
> And ever changing, like a joyless eye
> That finds no object worth its constancy?[81]

Like 'The Blessed Damozel', this is a poem of longing and apartness that articulates a sense of the 'companionless' – just what Tom's mother worried about when she feared Tom had been 'deprived' of 'companion-ship'.[82] If his taste in poetry was something he kept (in part at least) hidden from his parents, his attraction towards the 'atheistical' may have led this boy perceived by outsiders as shy to feel cut off from some aspects of his family life too. This helps explain why at least once he said his Unitarian upbringing had formed him as an 'Atheist'.[83] In some rather despondent moods, looking back twenty years later, he could intuit that his growing commitment to poetry had isolated him, feeling he had been '*forced* into poetry by my weakness in other directions . . . I took this direction very young, and learned very early to find my life and my realisation in this curious way, and to be obtuse and indifferent to my reality in other ways.'[84]

Tom played no part in the editing of his school magazine, but he was published in it. His three short prose contributions in 1905 are undistin-guished, but hint how his reading continued to guide him. 'The Birds of Prey', about a vulture which comes to feast on a battlefield victim, has a title reminiscent of Kipling's '"Birds of Prey" March'. 'The Man Who Was King' (the narrative about a man shipwrecked in Polynesia) echoes Kipling's short story 'The Man Who Would Be King', but also inclines towards R. L. Stevenson. 'The Man Who Was King' is narrated by a retired captain, 'at present engaged in lobster-trawling and skippering summer visitors'. He sounds a bit like the skipper who taught Tom to sail at Gloucester. Terms such as 'mizzen top-gallant shrouds', 'flying jib-boom', 'fore staysail' and 'holystoning the deck' (all used in Tom's other story 'A Tale of a Whale') demonstrate that the young mariner had been well taught. Moments in these narratives, as when sailors on the back of a whale eat 'sponge-cake, made out of the sponges which grew on the bottom of the great animal', suggest Tom's more mischievous, Edward Lear-loving side.[85] So do occasional made-up words, including Tom's Polynesian 'bhghons'. Veering between the comical and the serious, these prose pieces also essay themes that became lifelong preoccupations. The captain, worried about being 'roasted for the consumption of his hosts', ends up being made king of an island where, later, colonists convert naked pagan 'natives', rendering them disappointingly 'civilised'.[86] All this came from an imagination which would grow fascinated soon by anthropology, by Conrad's *Heart of Darkness*, and would juxtapose the supposedly primitive with the civilised in *The Waste Land* and 'Sweeney Agonistes.'

Yet the production which most impressed Tom's family in 1905 was his lyric imitation of Ben Jonson, written on 24 January as an exercise for Mr Hatch.[87] In some ways it was a sensitive pastiche. Tom's *Golden Treasury* contained Shakespeare's 'Where the bee sups, there sup I' as well as several Jonson lyrics, including 'To Celia' whose stanzaic pattern Tom followed. His poem imitates Renaissance diction, lamenting flowers 'withered ere the wild bee flew / To suck the eglantine'; it urges lovers to 'pluck anew'. Tom's words impressed Mr Hatch. That teacher's own somewhat less delicate song, 'Smith Forever', promising to 'rear a kingdom wide of schools, / And set Smith on the throne', appeared in the *Smith Academy Record* in February along with 'A Fable for Feasters', just in time for the school's 'sing fest'.[88]

Reading Tom's lyric, Mr Hatch was admiring but sceptical; perhaps he knew Tom's mother wrote verse. Tom recalled that his teacher 'commended' the poem 'warmly' and 'conceived great hopes of a literary career for me', yet also asked 'suspiciously if I had had any help in writing it'.[89] Actually, though Tom remembered his lyric as 'the first poem he wrote to be shown to other eyes', it was some time before his family read it. He remembered the precise moment his mother mentioned it to him: 'she remarked (we were walking along Beaumont St. in St Louis) that she thought it better than anything in verse she had ever written. I knew what her verse meant to her. We did not discuss the matter further.'[90]

This conversation between mother and son on home ground marked the moment where both seem to have acknowledged that Tom's gift for poetry was not just something he shared with Mamma but also a talent that set him apart from her. Papa reacted with straightforward pride. Having made or got hold of a typed carbon copy of his son's lyric, 'If Time and Space, as sages say', he posted it to his brother Thomas in Portland, Oregon, scribbling at the top in pencil, 'Verses by Thomas Stearns Eliot for one of the classes in "Composition"', adding the comment '*good* for 16 yrs!'[91] He was right. The poem builds an argument uniting lyricism and the hint of a philosophical trajectory. John Donne, whose work also does this, was just a name to Tom at this stage – there was one Donne poem in his *Golden Treasury*, and a passing, slighting mention of him in Pancoast's *Introduction to English Literature*.

Now his contributions to the *Smith Academy Record* regularly appeared in or near pole position in the magazine. He won the respect of his family and Mr Hatch. Chosen to read his poem 'To the Class of 1905', he scanned the proud audience at the Smith Academy Fiftieth Annual Graduating Exercises on 13 June that year. His reading was preceded by the Smith Academy Glee Club, who accompanied the class heartily in singing 'Smith Forever' and 'Pull for Good Old Smith'. After Tom read, his classmate Frederick Lake led the Mandolin Club in another school song.[92] Tom's poem, dutifully declaimed from the stage on behalf of his fellow students ('We go . . . // We shall return . . . // We go . . . // So we are done'), was appropriately stagey. Occasional cadences suggested books he had been reading: '"Farewell", / A word that echoes like a funeral bell' calls to mind Keats's 'Forlorn! The very word is like a bell' from the 'Ode to a Nightingale'. Ending with a Latinate dramatic flourish, '*Exeunt omnes*, with a last "farewell"', Tom's poem marked his 'first appearance on a public platform before a large audience'. It should have worked. Destructively, however, one of his teachers remarked to him that while his 'poem itself was excellent, as such poems go', his 'delivery' had been 'very bad indeed'.[93] His classmate Lawrence Post, a more gifted public speaker, orated the 'Farewell Address'.

After that, Tom was off to Gloucester for the summer, then to the select Milton Academy in Massachusetts for a year's preparatory work before progressing to Harvard. He had already passed the examinations for Harvard by the spring of 1905. However, he was still just sixteen, and in March his mother was anxious again about his health – 'he has been growing rapidly, and for the sake of his physical well being we have felt that it might be better for him to wait a year before entering on his college career'.[94] Awkwardly, he had not done nearly as well in his last year at Smith Academy. As his mother confessed, 'My son's marks were "B" in History, and "C" in everything else except Physics, in which he was conditioned, receiving an "E".'[95] Taking all this into account, she looked at the course catalogue for Milton Academy with Tom in early April.

Housed in handsome buildings on a grassy campus, Milton, just eight miles outside Boston, was an established institution (founded in 1798) with a reputation as a gateway to Harvard. Tom's brother was already a Harvard student, and the family knew Harvard's procedures. Tom had been informed that he had done well in French and English when he sat the Harvard prelims; he was wondering if at Milton he might study some more science (his weakest area) and maybe some English and American history. He was rather uncertain, but, recognising he had been a 'faithful student' at Smith Academy, his parents were 'willing to have him wander a little from beaten paths this year and take a somewhat miscellaneous course', if that was what he wanted.[96]

Writing to Richard Cobb, the recently appointed headmaster at Milton, Lottie Eliot was, as so often, anxious about her younger son. She worried he might be 'lonely'. She assured Mr Cobb that 'although quiet and very dignified he is a most friendly boy, of sweet nature, and every inch a gentleman, withal very modest and unassuming, yet very self-reliant too'.[97] Dutifully, signing himself 'Thomas S. Eliot', her son transcribed a list of the recent courses he had taken and the books he had studied.[98] Some of these, such as *The Principles of Rhetoric* by Adam Sherman Hill, Boylston Professor of Rhetoric and Oratory at Harvard College, were also on the Milton curriculum. Emphasising 'clearness', 'force' and 'ease' in expression, Hill, though no 'Anglomaniac', was aware of charges of American 'provincialism'. His book is full of quotations from great writers, illustrating stylistic merits, and sometimes demerits. 'Browning at his best', for instance, is presented as 'a master of the suggestive style' and 'My Last Duchess' as a model of concision. Reading such books in the wake of Curd's *New Method of English Analysis*, Tom grew even more used to absorbing literature through illustrative snippets. Years later, the use of resonant quotations became part of his allusive compositional technique, but in the short term he was taught not just how to write but also that Harvard academics including 'Professor L. B. R. Briggs', 'Professor G. L. Kittredge', 'Dr Royce' and 'President Eliot' were themselves authorities on writing.[99] Schools like Milton Academy were designed to get boys accustomed to sharing Harvard assumptions. Soon Tom would encounter these professors for himself.

For a while it seemed touch and go whether he would proceed to Milton or head straight to Harvard. His parents had gone so far as to rent rooms for him 'in a private house on Mt Auburn Street' in Cambridge, a well-appointed location very handy for Harvard Yard, and favoured by some of the most prosperous students.[100] In August 1905, however, Lottie Eliot made arrangements to visit Milton with Tom, and it was fixed that he would be admitted as a boarding pupil in the Upper School. He was to reside in Forbes House, a substantial brick building whose supervising matron was Mrs Margaret Gardner Chase. Mrs Eliot was concerned that, even in such a small matter as the way Tom stowed his belongings in his room, he should perpetrate no 'infringement of rules to which Mrs Chase would object'. Anxious that he should not be expected to participate in 'strenuous sports' because of his 'physical limitations', his mother asked to be informed by telegraph 'Should Tom ever be ill'. Consulting her son-in-law Alfred Sheffield (familiar with modern Harvard), she felt on the whole that Tom should not repeat subjects at Milton at which he had excelled at St Louis. This is why, among other things, he applied himself to Physics during this final schooling. Tom's Physics notebook, signed by the Milton Physics teacher, Homer W. Lesourd, still survives at the school, but all his other records are lost, so we cannot be certain what else he studied. It is likely, however, that he was well taught. Lesourd had Harvard connections and would soon publish his *Principles and Formulas of Elementary Physics*. Milton Academy prided itself on its standards and attracted the children of ambitious, often rich parents eager for their sons to enter Harvard. Tom's brother was sure Milton friendships would benefit Tom.

Arguably, the social connections he made at Milton mattered more to Tom than the Physics or other subjects he learned there. A fellow Forbes House pupil was Scofield Thayer, scion of a wealthy Massachusetts family. This young New Englander had been schooled in his home town of Worcester, but entered Forbes House in 1905. Like Tom he was good at Latin and had literary interests. Though Thayer did not reach Harvard until later, their paths would cross afterwards in decisive ways. Another Forbes House boy was the overweight Howard Morris, whose nickname 'Fat' may date from his schooldays.[101] Both aiming for Harvard, Tom and Morris got on well enough to share accommodation there. As was the Harvard custom, so in Milton the graduating class had, Tom's brother recalled, a 'class president' – in Tom's case a boy called John Robinson, who came from Salem and was interested in sailing.[102] Tom and Robinson had at least that pastime in common, and would keep in touch at university. Others in Tom's circle at Milton included Harrison Bird Child, who became an Episcopal priest after studying at Harvard; and Roger Amory, who became the Treasurer for Tom's Harvard classmates.

At Milton he found himself part of a group of privileged boys with New England backgrounds, but since he had arrived only in 1905 he was regarded as among the 'immigrants' to his class.[103] Jayme Stayer points out that one fellow pupil (assistant business manager of the school magazine) was called Ronald A. MacAvity; his surname would become as notorious as that of Prufrock.[104] Learning to fit in, Tom wrote home to St Louis regularly from the time he 'first went to Milton', and his mother preserved his letters all her life.[105] He alarmed her in May 1906 by wanting to 'swim in a quarry pond near the Academy'.[106] Since Papa's sister had drowned in a pond, Tom's parents were none too keen on that.

When Tom came to graduate with twenty-one classmates from Milton Academy on 21 June 1906, Roger Amory wrote the 'Class History 1906' in one of the school publications, *The Milton Orange and Blue*, published on the fourth of July. Stayer has noted that Tom's was the very last name to be saluted by the class historian at the 1906 graduation. No mention of any misdemeanour by Tom appears in the school's surviving disciplinary minutes, but he was hailed at graduation as 'Big Slam Eliot, boisterous haranguer of Forbes House'.[107] Perhaps this indicates that at Milton he had reinvented himself. However, given the shyness that had characterised his boyhood, and which continued to be part of his demeanour at Harvard, the act of keeping his name to the very end of the list and then describing him as a 'boisterous haranguer' may have been designed to give his classmates one last laugh before leaving school.

4

A Full-Fledged Harvard Man

B Y today's standards, it is surprising that Thomas Stearns Eliot was admitted to Harvard. In a university run by the ageing, distinguished President Eliot, his surname and background probably did him no harm. Writing to Headmaster Cobb at Milton Academy in spring 1905, Lottie Eliot had glossed over Tom's precise grades, preferring to emphasise his Latin prize and extensive reading. Tom stated simply that he had 'passed' subjects at Harvard's 'Elementary' level, and was about to sit Greek, Latin, French and English at 'Advanced'. When Mr Cobb asked about the precise level of the passes, Tom's mother confessed they were mostly Cs.[1] John Soldo, who unearthed in the 1970s the full run of entrance examination grades, lists the Elementary passes as 'B+ in History; B in French; C in English, Greek, Latin and Algebra; D in Plane Geometry and E in Physics'. This last disaster, Mrs Eliot explained, was precipitated by a teacher who had succumbed to 'nervous prostration'.[2] In his four Advanced subjects Tom achieved a consistent row of Cs.[3] He was working, but not very hard.

That style, honed at Milton, shaped his time as a Harvard freshman in session 1906–7. Dominating small-town Cambridge, Massachusetts, just across the Charles River from Boston, 'Unitarian Harvard' (as Tom later styled it) was not just about education.[4] It was also, he knew, about privileged panache. His brother, who had edited the *Harvard Lampoon*, is credited as the author of 'The Freshman's Meditation', penned a few years before Tom arrived: 'Whoop! Hurrah! I've come to Harvard!' it begins, 'I'm a full-fledged Harvard man.' To his 'dandy room' (furnished by his mother), the freshman in this poem adds Harvard flags and crimson cushions matching the university colours, not to mention 'an ice-chest out of sight'. With 'So many things to do' on the sporting front, Henry's new arrival relishes his sense of freedom, convinced he 'Needn't trouble 'bout my studies'.⁵ No doubt alert to social cachet and guided by Henry who had graduated in 1902 before proceeding to Harvard Law School, Tom's parents had secured him accommodation at 52 Mount Auburn Street, right at the heart of Harvard's 'Gold Coast'. Just minutes from Harvard Yard in the direction of the Charles, this area of privately developed halls and upscale student boarding houses was home to the most cosseted under-graduates; the 'Silver Coast', classy but less exclusive, was down the road. Other boys from Tom's year at Milton, including Howard Morris, George 'Dago' Parker and Charles 'Chicken' Gilbert, were moving to the Gold Coast. It seemed right for Tom 'Big Slam' Eliot to be there too.

Earlier generations of freshmen had tended to live at the heart of the Harvard campus in the Yard's dormitories, most iconic of which was the early-eighteenth-century dark-red-brick Massachusetts Hall. However, 1906 freshmen from moneyed backgrounds enjoyed more opulent facilities if they lived outside the gated Yard with its expansive, well-kept lawns and lofty elms. Freshmen in Tom's cohort (the 'Class of 1910' – named after the year in which they would graduate) strolled to Massachusetts Hall to elect class officers – a president, a secretary, a social committee – and attended receptions as well as lectures and classes in the other build-ings of the Yard; then the most affluent ambled back to Mount Auburn Street.

On that thoroughfare and nearby some of the best endowed student societies had their clubhouses with private dining rooms. As the 1907 *Official Guide to Harvard University* puts it, this area 'between the Yard and the Charles River . . . has come to be the centre of those activities in which the social spirit, the college loyalty, and the literary, musical, and other interests of the student body express themselves . . . Along Massachusetts Avenue, facing the Yard, and in Harvard Square, southwest of the Yard, are the shops, restaurants, billiard rooms, etc., most frequented by the students.'⁶ Long afterwards, reminiscing to a Harvard pal with whom he had made undergraduate mischief, Tom mentioned billiard cues; it was easy on the Gold Coast to avoid one's studies.⁷ From 52 Mount Auburn a short stroll took him to a café such as the Dunster at Harvard Square which offered music every evening as well as food. One could buy stationery or have one's visiting card engraved at Aimee Brothers, fine purveyors of 'Student Supplies'; or, just off the Square at 5 Brattle Street, could eye fashionable clothing in the emporium of Alfred R. Brown & Co., Tailors and Outfitters, 'Sole Agents for Carlton & Co.'s English Hats'; next door, the Harvard Tailoring Co. prided itself as 'Importers of Woolen Novelties', offering a 'special Discount to Harvard Men'.⁸

Men they all were. Female students studied at nearby Radcliffe College, but none yet graduated from Harvard. Almost all Harvard men in Tom's day were white, many from the crème de la crème of exclusive New England private high schools. As well as Tom, three other freshmen are listed as lodging at 52 Mount Auburn for 1906–7: Robert Haydock, a well-behaved New Englander with a self-deprecating sense of humour, later pursued a Boston business career; C. C. Perkins, though listed as a freshman, was probably Charles C. Perkins, a sophomore of the Class of 1909 who went on to become a salesman; Constant Wendell, kinsman of Harvard literary professor Barrett Wendell, left the following year and eventually experienced a nervous breakdown.[9] Several further students lodged next door at number 54, none of them academic stars; whether or not one was as 'green' and inexperienced as the conventional 'verdant freshman', it was easy to be distracted on the Gold Coast.[10]

Hints of well-off student life in this vicinity come from some of the creative writing in the *Harvard Advocate*, confirming Gold Coasters' reputation for idleness. In a 1906 *Advocate* parody of an ancient Greek play the character 'Goldkoastides' determines 'to elect no courses but from ten o'clock to twelve'; any course whose class hour is 9 a.m. 'shan't exist for me'.[11] A story from the same year depicts a fashionable freshman trying to decide what pictures (presumably prints) to hang on his wall; he swithers between an image of a Cardinal or a 'nervy and spiritual' portrait of St John by Andrea del Sarto. Freshman bookshelves reveal what looks like 'the inevitable set of Stevenson', but turns out to be 'a French edition of du Maupassant in a false binding'. Two students return from a theatre visit, bringing 'a pail of raw oysters'. Meanwhile 'A warm spring breeze blew the window hanging to and fro, and up from Mt. Auburn Street came the familiar evening sounds, – the tramp of feet, the slamming of club-house doors, the calls for various heads to appear at upper windows and the shrill screams of muckers, fighting and playing.'[12]

Though starting university offered Tom an opportunity to reinvent himself as more outgoing, he seems not to have been particularly close to any of his immediate freshmen neighbours, and soon among classmates he acquired his customary reputation for shyness. Still, like other freshmen, he observed and sometimes participated in undergraduate pursuits. Harvard favourites ranged from consuming 'several Coca-Colas' or spending a morning 'drinking rum punches' to calling on a society hostess 'on Beacon Hill', the most genteel area of Boston.[13] Such visits were a way to meet women, perhaps including some from Radcliffe; if undergraduates were organised enough to invite girls to a polite tea, it was expected that they would arrange a chaperone. One student advised that while 'you might tastefully display a number of books by prominent authors in your sitting room to show that you are fond of good literature', nonetheless 'on general principles you had better remove all saucy pictures from the walls'; in Henry's day fashionable prints to display had included 'the more recherché ladies of Burne-Jones'.[14] Yet for most of his undergraduate years, apart from contact with members of his family including cousin Eleanor Hinkley and his sister Ada, Tom's shyness with girls appears to have remained inhibiting.

Educated almost exclusively among boys, and now at what was in many ways a single-sex university (Radcliffe had its own separate arrangements), Tom seems to have been assimilated into a predominantly masculine milieu where clubbableness might mask underlying insecurities. Before reaching Harvard, he would have heard from his brother about characters to look out for. While a student, Henry had written verses for an illustrated volume, *Harvard Celebrities*, and had sent a copy back to St Louis, inscribing it to his mother. One of the celebrities was among Tom's lecturers in English 28, a half-course he took as a freshman, and which outlined the history and development of English literature. Sketched by Edward Revere Little of the Class of 1904, Professor Barrett Wendell, a renowned historian of American literature who venerated Hawthorne and saw New England literary tradition as having declined, stands nattily dressed in fedora and checked suit. Smoking, he carries a stylish cane and gloves. Henry's accompanying verse suggested that Wendell's dress sense conjured up 'The atmosphere of London . . . instead of Harvard Square': Wendell was the 'guiding star' of Harvard, his mission 'To edify the vulgar, and abash the unrefined'.[15]

Another edifying local celebrity was Professor LeBaron Russell Briggs, Boylston Professor of Rhetoric and Oratory. Also dandyish, this lecturer impressed Freshman Tom in English 28. Almost a quarter of a century later he remembered how 'Professor Briggs used to read, with great persuasiveness and charm, verses of Donne to the Freshmen', though he confessed that 'I have now forgotten what Professor Briggs told us about the poet; but I know that whatever he said, his own words and his quotations were enough to attract to private reading at least one Freshman who had already absorbed some of the Elizabethan dramatists, but who had not yet approached the metaphysicals.'[16] Donne, a poet important to Harvard literary culture during this era, would matter greatly to Tom. Probably spurred by his mother and by quotations in Poe, as well as by his schooling in literary history, he had a good knowledge of Renaissance drama before he entered Harvard College. There, as he read Donne, Professor Briggs's enthusiasm set the tone, and in Tom's second year one of his classmates, Clarence Dewey

Britton, won a prize for writing on 'The Temperament of John Donne'.[17] Though Gold Coaster Tom was inspired to read Donne in 'private', he almost lost the opportunity to pursue his undergraduate course. Only months after his Harvard career began, it nearly came to an end.

For all his wide-ranging recreational reading (and perhaps in part because of it), he was not working hard enough. His poor performance was noted by the Assistant Dean E. H. Wells. Trepidatiously, Tom wrote to his father in St Louis, letting him know that, though he was doing well in English 28 (for which, eventually, he got an A), this half-course would not count when it came to overall consideration of his progress. He warned Papa what was coming. Shortly afterwards the Assistant Dean informed Tom's father that 'Thomas's November record is so unsatisfactory that the Administrative Board will place him on probation.' His work in English appeared 'satisfactory', but in several courses he had received 'unsatisfactory' D grades.[18] These included Greek B, a literature course that moved from Plato and Xenophon to Euripides' dramas *Medea* and *Iphigineia among the Taurians*. In some ways Tom was living the life of that caricature slacker Goldkoastides, who advised in 1906 that 'You mustn't miss taking Greek B, / You'll at least get a D or an E'.[19] Unfortunately, freshman Eliot was also awarded a D grade for Charles Homer Haskins's introduction to Medieval History; for the elementary course German A; and for Government 1, Constitutional Government, whose lecturers included Professor Abbott Lawrence Lowell, soon to succeed C. W. Eliot as Harvard's president.[20] Tom's performance was embarrassing: even in a subject like medieval history which had interested him from the days when he read Malory's Arthurian tales, wrote about Sir Lanfaul and created his 'Fable for Feasters', he was not pulling his weight. The Assistant Dean's letter stated that unless there was marked improvement 'Thomas' could be sent away from Harvard without further warning. 'Will you kindly co-operate', Henry Ware Eliot, Sr, was asked, 'in encouraging the boy to raise his record to a satisfactory standard?'[21] The father of 'the boy' replied speedily, emphasising that Tom was 'sufficiently concerned'. Pointing out that 'College advisors' had gone along with Tom's choice of courses that demanded much outside reading, his father, loyal to the son he loved, tried to excuse his offspring's waywardness. But the concluding paternal sentence was potentially more forbidding: 'When he comes home for the holidays I will discuss it with him.'[22] On the brink of failure just months into his Harvard career, Tom made the long rail journey back to St Louis in December 1906 preparing himself for awkward conversations.

Discussions ensued. It was time for new year resolutions. Tom returned to Mount Auburn Street in early 1907 resolved to avoid a repeat of his first-semester predicament. Released from the surveillance of his parents and Mrs Chase of Milton Academy, he had been enjoying the freedom to do as he pleased. 'Loafing' was Henry's word for such behaviour, and Tom later confessed that for his first two sessions at Harvard he 'loafed'.[23] Yet returning for his second semester he did make efforts to work a mite harder. He also took part in a disciplined university activity: rowing. Even if the weather was wintry, it was just a short walk from his lodgings to the boathouse on the Charles. The daily *Harvard Crimson* published an editorial in its 11 February 1907 issue, hoping 'that the call for Freshman crew candidates will meet with a prompt and hearty response'. Tom's response was prompt enough: his name appeared in a list of aspiring freshman crew members published the following day. After many summers' boating at Gloucester, this seemed a good idea, but Tom was not selected. He was five feet eleven inches tall, but rather skinny, and probably his physique was against him; all those years free of competitive team sports could not have helped. Later he did take up rowing in a wherry – traditionally a gentleman's rowing boat – and finally worked up to a single scull.[24] So, as he rowed, he remained alone, more disciplined and fitter, but not quite a team player.

Though still loafing, he did at least manage to come through his first year with an overall B in Greek, followed by overall Cs for Government, History and the German Elementary Course. Some lecturers, like Professor Briggs, were inspirational; others were not. Regarded as compulsory in an era when there was much discussion at Harvard of the German university system, Tom's course German A was, complained one of his three hundred or so classmates, a 'Horrible routine of fairy stories and trivial sentences – "Where are the old shoes of my grandfather," etc.' Like so many other Harvard literati, the instructor, Assistant Professor Heinrich Conrad Bierwirth (whose *Beginning German* Tom had read in 1905), had an interest in Dante, but when it came to German he failed to inspire; his assistants only made things worse. 'Instructor might as well have been a phonograph', wrote one unimpressed listener. Undergraduates complained their teacher 'deliberately antagonized' students in a course variously described by Tom's classmates as 'useless', 'an absolute waste of time' and 'a slaughter house'.[25] Tom put up with it. He chugged along at a level which at least kept him above that 'unsatisfactory' D grade, but he remained attracted to stylish loafing, and still stayed somewhat aloof.

Later he made friends with an immigrant Manhattanite classmate. William George Tinckom-Fernandez had been born in India, about which he wrote occasional poems. He was one of the very few in Tom's year not to have a permanent address listed when the *Crimson* published

its 'Directory of Freshmen' in October 1906; possibly this was because
the itinerant Tinckom-Fernandez was spending so much time in New
York. He seems to have been the person whom Tom recalled as a 'man
whose principle of choice of courses was that the lectures should all fall
on Tuesdays and Thursdays, with no lecture on Saturday: thus he was
free to spend four days a week in New York. I should add that he did
not follow even this course of study with sufficient application to qualify
him for a degree'.[26] Given that it took several hours to travel from Boston
to New York by rail, this was not quite loafing of the conventional sort;
but it did have style. Tinckom-Fernandez wrote considerable amounts
of verse, read contemporary poetry and was already publishing in the
Advocate while he and Tom were freshmen. Tom, whose avid interest in
poetry was not quashed by his academic mishaps, published far less.
His student friendship with 'Tinck' blossomed later, but literature
and a sometimes cavalier attitude to academic work was something they
both relished.

When they recalled Tom, 'shy' is the word fellow students regularly
associated with him. Some also thought him clever, despite the loafing,
and even perceived that, beyond his shyness lay a capacity for companion-
ship. An early college friend was Leon Magaw Little, who came from a
New England family brimming with Harvard connections; Tom's brother
had collaborated with Edward Little on *Harvard Celebrities*. As a freshman
Leon lived near Tom, sharing a suite of rooms with a fellow first-year at
133 Westmorly Court. A recently built Gold Coast private hall (now part
of Adams House), Westmorly charged some of the highest rents, but
boasted excellent plumbing, and even had its own ornate private swimming pool.[27] As an old man, Leon Little remembered the impression Tom
made from his first year onwards; he mentions a companionability and
academic accomplishments less evident to others.

> As a freshman T. S. Eliot was of the type that welcomes friendships
> but is too reserved to seek them. However, his scholastic brilliance
> and his charming personality quickly brought to him a circle of
> friends of two quite divergent types, the intellectuals on the one
> hand and, on the other, many of those who were not considered in
> that category. His requirements seemed to be a reasonable amount
> of brains but above all a happy, keen sense of humor. Within the
> circles of these friends he was a very gay companion.[28]

In late February 1907 Tom received another letter from Assistant Dean
Wells: the Administrative Board was taking him off probation. This

brought relief, not least to his parents. Tom had hardly become a 'grind' – a student devoted to his studies – but he had bought more time to come to terms with what Harvard had to offer.

He was enrolled at America's oldest university. In 1886, six years after the future United States President Theodore Roosevelt had graduated, Harvard had celebrated its 250th anniversary. That milestone encouraged intensive fundraising. New buildings went up across the campus. Still aligned to the older Calvinistic or Unitarian values of New England, Harvard was increasingly an academic centre of national and international renown. Its faculty were effortlessly cosmopolitan. So, for instance, Tom's Professor Wendell was not only a historian of American literature. He also authored *The France of Today* (1907), while Anglophilia was evident alike in his tailoring and in his knowledge of seventeenth-century English literature, on which he delivered the Clark Lectures at King's College, Cambridge, England. Years afterwards, so did Tom.

Leading American intellectuals such as philosopher and psychologist William James (Henry James's brother), fellow philosopher Josiah Royce and polymathic cultural critic Irving Babbitt – another Francophile – were distinguished figures around the campus. Under the ambitious leadership of President Eliot, arguably the most widely known academic in America, Harvard had attracted outstanding tenured and visiting faculty, and it went on doing so. Tom would benefit in a later year from the presence of Bertrand Russell as a visiting philosophy professor; and during his second semester the famous young classicist Gilbert Murray, formerly professor of Greek at the University of Glasgow and soon to move to Oxford, delivered in Harvard's capacious new Fogg Museum of art a series of lectures on ancient Greek poetry.

Editor and translator of Euripides (his *Medea* appeared in 1907) as well as an enthusiast for Aristophanes, Murray was associated with interdisciplinary thinking that linked literature to anthropology. Admired by several Harvard faculty members, an emergent intellectual movement connected poetry and plays to more ancient rites. Murray's *History of Greek Literature* had spoken up for 'the Greek of the anthropologist'.[29] Tom, fresh from studying *Medea* and hearing freshman lectures on Greek literary history, would study Aristophanes the following year. Not only were his teachers excited to host Murray, but Murray's lectures were reported regularly in the *Crimson*. His interest in linking literature to rituals was attuned to that student imagination which, spoofingly, had so recently brought together in the *Harvard Advocate* rituals of the freshman life of 'Goldkoastides' with the forms of ancient classical drama, 'Parodos', 'Choros' and all. Later Tom criticised Murray as a translator of Greek drama, but in his own

'Aristophanic Melodrama' 'Sweeney Agonistes' and elsewhere, he would fuse modern-day life with Classical scholarship that invoked anthropology. At Harvard Murray argued that the *Iliad*'s 'originality' lay precisely in the way it took materials 'ready-made from older books or traditions' and so registered 'an intensity of imagination, not merely of one great poet, but the accumulated emotion of generations'.[30] Such ideas were being discussed around Tom while he studied Greek.

'Abeunt Studia in Mores' read one of the inscriptions in Harvard's Memorial Hall: 'Our studies breed our habits'.[31] Tom's studies were magpie-like, and the Harvard of his day, with its 'elective system' which allowed students to assemble their degree in piecemeal fashion, encouraged that. Though in his second year he studied Aristophanes, Aeschylus and Sophocles, he did not major in Greek or in any other single subject. Between 1906 and 1910, when he graduated Master of Arts, he took twenty-five courses (some, to be exact, were designated 'half-courses') in ten subjects: English, Latin, Greek, French, German, Comparative Literature, Philosophy, History, Fine Arts and Government. In modern parlance, one might say that his undergraduate work was substantially in comparative literature. The elective system let students follow their instincts, with the result that, as one of Tom's lecturers put it in 1908, 'Boys drift.'[32] Generously bankrolling his son's student years, that was what Tom's father worried about.

As he loafed around Harvard Yard, Tom observed buildings familiar today, but his Harvard, smaller and less driven than now, was also subtly different. Including summer school participants, there were just over 5,000 students; across the whole institution the staff–student ratio was roughly one-to-twelve, and in Tom's part of the university, the Faculty of Arts and Sciences, there were a little over 2,200 students, most expecting to reside for three or four years.[33] Lecture audiences could number nearly four hundred in big courses like Government 1, and over three hundred for History, German and English; instructors and assistants led smaller group discussions and helped with grading.[34] Some undergraduates, including members of Tom's own Class of 1910, thought the university had grown excessively large, and that it was too easy for students to avoid notice. Yet, though the red-brick dormitory of Forbes House had prepared Tom for the look of Harvard Yard, after St Louis Cambridge was very small. One of his friends, who arrived in 1907, recalled it as 'a village', albeit an atmospheric one: 'Lilacs, white picket fences under elms, horse-drawn water-carts to lay the dust in the blindingly dusty streets of summer, board-walks put down on the pavements every winter and taken up every spring, sleighs and pungs [sleighs with box-shaped bodies] in the snow, and the dreadful college bell reverberant over all.'[35]

Though a few rich Harvard men brought with them those newfangled machines, motor cars, most, including Tom, did not. Cambridge was walkable. One could stroll to eat with over a thousand fellow students in the great dining hall attached to Sanders Theatre, its roofbeams over sixty feet above diners' heads, and stare at stained-glass windows depicting Chaucer, Dante and, less predictably perhaps, Sir Philip Sidney; or, as Tom sometimes did, one could scrutinise statuary and paintings in the Fogg Museum, or walk a few hundred yards towards the Weld Boat House if the weather was suitable for rowing. Everywhere, even in the newest buildings, there was a weight of tradition redolent of New England. Completed in the College Yard the year before Tom arrived, Emerson Hall, home to the Philosophy Department, had a large bronze statue of the seated Ralph Waldo Emerson in its concourse, positioned to confront all who entered the building; an inscription over the grandly pillared doorway quoted the biblical book of Psalms, 'WHAT IS MAN THAT THOU ART MINDFUL OF HIM?' Tom grew used to such imposing spaces. Later, he would craft a mock-grandeur of his own: 'The lengthened shadow of a man / Is history, said Emerson'.[36]

The present-day centrepiece of Harvard Yard, the great Widener Library, had not yet been built. In its place stood the several times extended Gore Hall. Cathedral-like outside and in, this library held about half a million books. Specialities including its Dante collection were not open for undergraduate browsing, but it had a large reading room accessible to all students, even if its librarians seemed stern. A member of the Class of 1907 noted a growing undergraduate wish to seem 'literary', a symptom of which was 'the falling off in attendance at Gore Hall, and the increase at the Union library'.[37] As he got used to Harvard, Tom came to prefer student-controlled reading spaces like that of the Harvard Union. Endowed by Henry Lee Higginson, founder of the Boston Symphony Orchestra, this extensive club had been built a few years earlier at the corner of Quincy and Harvard Streets, overlooking attractive gardens.

Costing just $10 to join, the Union gave 2,000 student members access to dining rooms, reading rooms and facilities including a billiard room and barber shop. Entering it brought Tom close to the centre of under-graduate literary life. A basement suite of rooms comprised the offices and composing room of the *Crimson*; the top floor housed the offices of student literary magazines, the *Harvard Advocate* and *Harvard Monthly*. Tom saun-tered through the entrance hall leading to a hundred-foot-long 'Living Room', its oak-panelled walls hung with grand portraits. In winter wood fires blazed in great open hearths at either end while students lounged around, reading ('Daily papers from the principal cities of the United States are kept on file'), or took coffee and refreshments at small tables. With its game room, writing room and periodical rooms adjoining the main Living Room, the Union was designed for privileged chaps: a separate, less impressive entrance provided access to a 'ladies' dining room'.[38]

Tom liked to wander upstairs to the Union Library, its windows overlooking the lawns, its shelves stocked with over 6,000 books in three connecting rooms. Here students could read unsupervised in 'agreeable privacy'. For an undergraduate like Tom who enjoyed pursuing his 'private reading' at least as much as his coursework, this was a refuge.[39] The Union Library was a great place for contemporary literature. New highlights added to its shelves – whether volumes of *Shelburne Essays* by St Louis-born critic Paul Elmer More or more risqué volumes such as Oscar Wilde's *Salomé* – were listed regularly in the *Crimson*.[40] Tom, who started reading *Shelburne Essays* at Harvard and whose 'Love Song of J. Alfred Prufrock' with its image of a 'head (grown slightly bald) / brought in upon a platter' would soon parody the Salome narrative, used the Union as an enlivening resource.[41]

Somewhat sobered after being placed on probation, he chose a more coherent assortment of courses for his second year. Ancient Greek became his centre of gravity and in 1907–8 he signed up for Fine Arts 3 (History of Ancient Art), taught by Classicist and art historian, Assistant Professor George Henry Chase. Chase was cataloguing the classical pottery collection of James Loeb, soon to be presented to Harvard's Fogg Museum. Chase's lectures were considered dry, but their subject matter complemented Tom's study of Greek Prose Composition in the half-course called Greek E, as well as another course he took that session, Greek Literature, where teaching was led by Assistant Professor Charles Pomeroy Parker. An Oxford graduate, Parker had an interest in Greek philosophy, but Greek 2, the literary course that he and Professor Earnest Cary taught, included very different material. The Eliot scholar Grover Smith points out that 'At Harvard there is a school copy of Aristophanes' *Acharnians* in W. W. Merry's edition, with marginal notes by Eliot.'[42] Merry, the Victorian editor, presented Aristophanes as 'burlesque'.[43] Schooled in choral Aristophanic comedies including *The Acharnians* and *The Birds*, both of which he read for Greek 2, Tom later fused their structure with modern burlesque in 'Sweeney Agonistes'. In his late sixties, he would still find the heartily obscene Aristophanes 'delightful'.[44]

As well as these Greek courses, in his second year he continued the study of German, an important language for Classical scholarship. He concentrated on grammar and written German, but also read some poetry and prose with a native speaker, the instructor Hermann Julius Weber, and his colleague William Arnold Colwell, whose interest in German literature in eighteenth-century England was a further example of Harvard's inclination towards comparative literature. Unfortunately Tom's German was not considered satisfactory. He slipped back into the danger zone with a 'D' grade. In French 2a (where his grade was 'C') his lead instructor, Assistant Professor Charles Henry Conrad Wright, was working on a compendious *History of French Literature*. Eventually published in 1912, it deals with the authors covered in Tom's course. These ranged from Corneille and Racine to the nineteenth-century writers de Musset, Sainte-Beuve and Rostand.

Wright was an assiduous scholar. His critical vocabulary included the terms 'dislocation' and 'impersonality', but his tastes show him to have been just the sort of critic that Tom, especially when discussing modern French literature, would come to attack. For Wright, de Musset, 'perhaps the most characteristically French poet of his century', was far more attractive than the Baudelaire who, influenced by Poe, had helped give a questionable 'vogue to Symbolism . . . and decadents who built their theory of poetry on the element of suggestion and the relations between things and the soul, precisely as they professed to see in the music of Wagner'. Sainte-Beuve was to be lauded as 'one of the greatest of critics', a man preoccupied with the literary examination of 'personality', even to the extent of becoming 'a Peeping Tom, especially of women'. Rostand, though he achieved a 'high level' in the 'long and rambling' *Cyrano de Bergerac*, had fallen away in his more recent, fashionable *Chantecler* with its 'evanescent modern Parisian wit, often sinking to the commonest slang'. Wright's French 2a stopped with Rostand. He disliked Symbolist poetry as 'obscure', 'unintelligible' and 'freakish' – just the sort of line that his most famous student would soon react against with creative vehemence.[45]

'C' was pretty much Tom's average grade throughout session 1907–8. Though he managed Bs in Fine Art and the more literary of the Greek courses, he got a C for Greek Prose Composition. Having chosen also two Philosophy courses, in one he got a 'C', in the other a B. Yet, set against his D in German, this run of marks made him an undistinguished student. His loafing contributed, but there was also a sense he was not yet finding quite what he needed. For an undergraduate so grounded in literature, the philosophy courses in Emerson Hall were a new departure. Taken together, Philosophy A (History of Ancient Philosophy) and the matching introductory course B (History of Modern Philosophy) were surveys providing a general overview to which students might add depth later. Tom was selecting courses that let him read around freely, indulging a taste for roaming across cultures: from ancient Greece and Rome through the Middle Ages to modern English, French and German. No one who has embarked on Goodwin's *Moods and Tenses of the Greek Verb* could argue that he chose only the easiest options; but he was hardly an academic star.

He had left Mount Auburn Street in his second year, but had moved no further than around the corner to a purpose-built Gold Coast residential hall. There he shared a suite of rooms with his former Milton school friends Howard Morris and John Robinson. While a freshman, nineteen-year-old Morris had lived nearby in sumptuously appointed Westmorly Court, sharing a suite with another friend from Milton days, twenty-year-old Californian Welshman Evan Cyfeilwig Evans, Jr, and his younger brother Harry Llewellyn Evans. Morris lost his two room-mates when their mother died and the Evans boys left Harvard after just a year, returning to San Rafael, California. Big, heavily built, Morris had comparatively little interest in literature, but was easy-going, enjoyed music and liked to eat and drink. Also, he was used to fraternising with people he had known from Milton. He spoke with Tom and John Robinson about sharing a suite of rooms in another of the Gold Coast's swanky privately-run residences, Russell Hall, very close to Westmorly.

Tom knew he could get on with Morris and Robinson so they signed up for accommodation during 1907–8 at 22 Russell Hall. This substantial five-storey building stood at the corner of Plympton Street and Bow Street. Now demolished, it was replaced in 1930 by another Russell Hall, today part of Adams House. A surviving photograph shows that the earlier building's design featured bow-windowed towers at its street-front corners. Each student in suite 22 had a separate bedroom, but they shared a large sitting room in one of these tower-like extensions, with three windows looking out over the street and a semicircular, cushioned window seat beneath them. In the fashion of the day, the windows were equipped both with blinds and lace curtains. Occasionally, in true student fashion, Tom and his flatmates drew their blinds half down in daytime. Hardwood-floored, their sitting room had dark woodwork, but its atmosphere was softened by an elaborately patterned carpet in the centre of the room. Furniture was à la mode: 'the general tendency is towards "mission" morris chairs', a 1907 *Harvard Advocate* article 'On the Decoration of College Rooms' had remarked, noting that as well as such recliner chairs with their wooden arms and cushioned leather seats, 'some steins' (ornamental beer mugs) and 'plaster casts' were desirable.[46] If you could afford the substantial rent, 22 Russell Hall was not a bad place to loaf.

A photograph of Tom and Howard Morris in their sitting room was perceptively if a little speculatively described in the 1970s by the journalist T. S. Matthews.

It was well lighted: in the middle of the ceiling hung a chandelier, fitted for both gas and electricity; two wall brackets, each with gas and electric fixtures; on a small table by the fireplace a 'student lamp,' with a green glass *art nouveau* shade. On the table, cluttered with tobacco tins and a small pile of books, was a copy of the *Saturday Evening Post* (that would be Morris's); on the other side of the fireplace a small bookcase, shaped like a truncated pyramid, filled with an encyclopedia and a set of 'the classics' (that would be Eliot's). A sizable oriental rug covered most of the floor. A chafing dish stood on top of the bookcase; a tea set was on another small table. The space under two of the three bay windows was filled by a divan, spread with pillows and rugs. There were two Morris chairs, with flat wooden arms and frame and leather-covered cushions; a third chair, uncompromisingly hard.

Over the fireplace and above the mantelpiece a large rectangular crimson banner, bearing the legend HARVARD 1910, was tacked to the wall; the 1910 was partly obscured by two photographs of football teams. Between the photographs stood a beer stein; on the second mantel shelf were four more, flanked by two silverplated trophy cups (Morris's). In the center of the shelf were a dozen books (common property). Just over the fireplace hung a pipe rack, a line of trolls' heads in plaster; at the side, a German peasant's pipe depended from a hook. The andirons in the fireplace were piled with short birch logs. The framed pictures that covered the walls were mostly photographs: family groups, classical buildings and statues, a framed diploma.[47]

When the photograph was taken both young men were in their characteristic dark suits. Tom, hair neatly combed, sat in one of the leather-seated chairs, legs crossed and hands folded in his lap. His dark leather shoes are typically gleaming. Beyond him, Howard Morris has adopted a characteristic student attitude of the day 'as he lounges on the proverbial window seat', one hand behind his head, smoking relaxedly.[48] Their body language is very different. Morris looks the more at ease.

Later Morris described himself as belonging 'to more clubs than I need'.[49] He and Tom shared jokes and got on fine, but Tom's intellectual life was separate. Rather than cooking much for themselves, it was customary for well-off students to belong to private Gold Coast dining clubs, but Morris and Tom tended to move in different circles. As an undergraduate Tom belonged to several societies. Probably the first he joined was the Southern Club whose other members drawn from his year included Texan Jack Harrold; at a time when, unlike Boston, Cambridge was a dry town, belonging to a private club brought access to alcohol. Tom remembered the Southern Club as a hell of drinking and poker-playing, perhaps indicating that he went there most during his 'unsatis-factory' period, or maybe that he did not frequent it much at all. Southern Club membership was appropriate, given his Missouri roots, but he seems to have avoided significant contact with other Smith Academy alumni at Harvard such as his fellow member of the Class of 1910, James Taus-sig, Jr. Tom's one-time childhood neighbour and foe, Atreus Hargadine von Schrader, Jr, was a year ahead, playing tennis – without notable success – in the Class of 1909.

A better tennis player was Tom's 'really closest friend' at Harvard, Harold Peters.[50] This New Englander had grown up on family land on South Street in the Forest Hills district of Boston, today part of Harvard's lush, green Arnold Arboretum with its Peters Hill.[51] In the spring of 1907 while von Schrader was being knocked out in the early rounds of the interclass tennis tournament, Peters was powering his way to the final of the Freshman Championship.[52] He continued to play, but not quite so well, in the following two years. As did Tom, Harold Peters came from a prosperous family that could trace their roots to seventeenth-century New England; if Tom's father had a house at Eastern Point, Harold's held property on Maine's North Haven Island.[53] Again, like Tom, Peters had a family background to live up to: his elder brother had enjoyed a successful Harvard undergraduate career before studying at the Law School. The age gap between these two brothers was even greater than that between Tom and Henry. By the time Harold Peters was winning at tennis, his sibling Andrew James Peters (Class of 1895) was a Democratic Congressman for eastern Massachusetts; later he became Mayor of Boston.

Like Howard Morris, Harold Peters was a good companion to Tom, but no intellectual star or civic leader. He was, however, passionate about sailing. He and Tom spent several energetic holidays cruising in small boats from Gloucester and other New England ports. While Tom was rooming with his ex-Milton pals Howard Morris and yachting enthusiast John Robinson, Peters at 106 Westmorly was sharing with his old school-friend Leon Little, who had grown up in Newburyport, Massachusetts, and was, like Tom's brother, another keen sailor. Little and Tom were members of the Digamma Club, founded about a decade earlier: a private Harvard society. Tom's sophomore room-mate Robinson knew Peters too, and was another member of the Digamma. So were other old school friends of Tom's such as Chicken Gilbert from Milton.[54]

With its substantial, white-doored clubhouse at 44 Boylston Street, the Digamma was an exclusive, all-male space where well-off young men could socialise, dine, drink and make merry in very fine surroundings.[55] Boasting three storeys and a substantial basement, the detached building was ornamented with imitation classical columns at its corners, though the Digamma was not among the very richest of Harvard's clubs.[56] Founded by six students in 1898, its name comes from the sixth letter of the archaic Greek alphabet; however, 'F', the archaic Greek letter digamma, just happens to look like the English initial associated with academic failure – and may hint at other F-words too. The Digamma's title made it sound like one of the elite intellectual 'Greek letter clubs' of the Ivy League colleges, best known of which in Tom's Harvard was the Phi Beta Kappa; but its coded moniker was partly parodic. Though it had numbered literary men, such as journalist Maxwell Perkins and poet Van Wyck Brooks, among its members (Brooks had been club librarian), bibulous sociability and even scandalous exclusivity, rather than remarkable brainpower, were its hallmarks; its signature 'F' led to its being renamed the Fox Club, its emblem a rampant fox slyly holding a letter 'F'.

Of the seventeen men in Tom's class who mentioned membership of the Digamma in their later class reports, five, like Harold Peters, had attended the Noble and Greenough School in Boston, and another three, including Tom, its traditional rival, Milton Academy. Peters's sporty old school friends, C. C. Little as well as Leon Magaw Little (in 1908 a member of the Digamma's House Committee), became friends of Tom's too. So did Dick Hall, who liked tennis and theatricals; Hall was yet another Digamma member schooled at the Noble and Greenough. Almost all Digamma men lived on the Gold Coast and had attended expensive private schools – Milton, Noble and Greenough, Boston's Volkmann School (soon amalgamated with Noble and Greenough) – which acted as feeders for Harvard.[57] Members were initiated into the Digamma in a secret ritual: Van Wyck Brooks's had involved 'harassing . . . with oarsmen and football players', but Brooks had been known to pass out after downing a straight whisky.[58] Bookish Tom Eliot, though less sporty than most other Digamma members, hoped he was made of sterner stuff.

Elected while a sophomore, Tom survived his initiation and, in the year when Leon Little was Digamma Secretary, went on to become the club's Treasurer for 1908–9; Leon thought the treasurer's job 'very distasteful' to Tom, though he reckoned that it stood his friend in good stead when, like so many Fox classmates, Tom later became a banker.[59] Attracting former members as well as current ones, Fox Club dinners were boozy affairs. Treasurer Tom was also the club's librarian and balladist. In its formal dining room on 15 May 1909, during his Junior Year, he recited his 'Ballade of The Fox Dinner':

Muse of the rye and ginger ale,
Muse of the Cocktail and the Bar,
Open a bottle ere you hail
The members met from near and far.

Tom's dinner ballad mentions no foodstuffs. However, as well as rye and ginger ale, it takes in top-of-the-range champagne ('When Cordon Rouge like water flows'), 'demon Rum', a 'cocktail chorus' and 'booze' generally. The song imagines futures for several fellow members: recently graduated Charles Wilkins Short, Jr, of the Class of 1908, who had been club president when Tom was elected, is glimpsed advertising liquor, while former Gold Coast room-mates at 44 Dunster Hall, Dudley Richards Leland (by that time living on Park Avenue, Manhattan) and Harold Franklin McNeil (graduated but residing nearby, in Brookline, Massachusetts), were also featured: the latter for his ongoing 'partnership with Venus' and the former for rowdiness; Tom imagines Leland crashing through a Fox Club window, summersaulting on his chair.[60] Laughing about sexual antics and uproar were clearly de rigueur. Tom's role as club bard was to encourage this. He did a good job.

Another Foxy friend, Winthrop Sprague Brooks, known to companions as 'Nick', also comes into Tom's poem. Clearly Nick, who came from Milton, had a reputation for running a 'gambling game'. Though there is no evidence that he experienced financial problems, between poker at the Southern Club and gambling at the Fox, Tom did not have to look far to be led astray. Much later, 'Nick' Brooks recalled 'Tom Eliot' as his 'old frat mate'. For Nick, a year ahead of Tom, the Fox meant having 'a stein of whiskey at my elbow'; he relished memories of how every club dinner grew 'pretty damned informal before its termination'.[61]

As well as remembering the Fox's liquor, Nick Brooks recalled his 'frat mate' not so much as 1909 balladist or future poet of *The Waste Land* (like Howard Morris, Nick looked on Tom's later published poetry as 'cryptic tripe'), but as the 'swell guy' with whom he spent 'many happy hours . . . going over the little known and, as far as I am aware, unpublished highlights of the career of the indefatigable Columbo'.[62] Tom's readiness to share this scandalous 'Columbo' material with his trusted circle helps explain why he got on so well with these much less literary frat pals. Within a close group that first of all included fellow diners Harold Peters, Leon Little and Nick Brooks, he delighted in coming up with bawdy 'Columbo' verses that might have made his mother pass out. Sexually explicit, overtly racist, outrageously carnivalesque and taboo-breaking, these, like the club initiation rites, functioned as part of a male-bonding routine. Though most people saw him as shy, carefully dressed and well mannered, there was a determinedly Aristophanic side of Tom that strove to rebel against the proprieties of an upbringing soused in genteel Unitarianism.

Digamma members had a taste for his most laddish imaginings, and he was not the only Foxite to purvey scurrility; many years afterwards Nick Brooks sent to London what Tom hailed as 'a very bawdy verse . . . quite a gem, up to his best style'.[63] Tom relished Nick's turns of phrase, such as 'I'll be horse-fucked.'[64] Designed to be as offensively subversive as possible, Tom's Columbo poems and their close cousins the King Bolo series are comically, anxiously and disturbingly over-assertive in their sexualised masculinity. They go all out to shock. All this went down well with whisky-drinking friends like Nick:

> One day the king & queen of Spain
> They gave a royal banquet
> Columbo having passed away
> Was brought in on a blanket
> The queen she took an oyster fork
> And pricked Columbo's navel
> Columbo hoisted up his ass
> And shat upon the table.

Knowing he was able to counterbalance his customary shyness and formality by unleashing among his mates a talent whose scatological, sometimes misogynistic, always beyond-the-pale brio would both delight and appal, Tom tried to make each performance more scandalous than the last.

> One Sunday morning out at sea
> The vessel passed Gibraltar
> Columbo sat up on the poop
> A-reading at the psalter.
> The bosuns wife came up on deck
> With a bucket full of cowshit
> Columbo grabbed her round the neck
> And raped her on the bowsprit.

Now when they were three weeks at sea
Columbo he grew rooty
He took his cock in both his hands
And swore it was a beauty.
The cabin boy appeared on deck
And scampered up the mast-o
Columbo grasped him by the balls
And buggered him in the ass-o.[65]

Relishing the outrageousness of such verses, Tom and his male cronies bonded. The Columbo stanzas, and their equally scandalous companion verses about 'King Bolo and his big black queen', could be chanted or sung (they suit the tune of 'Yankee Doodle Dandy'), though by around 1910 Tom was collecting several in a notebook. In a predominantly male milieu with marked strains of anti-Semitism, sexism and racial prejudice, rich white Harvard men, not least in a fraternity house like the Fox with its own private liquor store, might snigger and whoop at 'A great big whore' who 'bitched' Columbo 'with a pisspot'; or at 'the only doctor in his town / . . . a bastard jew named Benny', who 'With countenance so placid' went on to fill 'Columbo's prick / With Muriatic Acid'.[66]

To link Tom's most effortfully shocking poetry exclusively to the Fox Club would be misleading, though Nick Brooks, reminiscing years later, clearly associated the verses with its 'frat' nights. Nick, who shared with Tom not just a locker-room delight in bawdy rhyming but also an interest in bird-watching and sailing, graduated in 1909 and spent much of the next few years in Canada, Siberia and Alaska. So, while individual Columbo poems are impossible to date precisely, it is a fair assumption that when Nick, remembering Tom, writes of spending 'many happy hours with him' going over the Columbo poems, he is referring to the period before 1909, and specifically to the time when he knew Tom in the Fox (alias Digamma) Club.[67] Though in our own day ostracised by the Harvard authorities because of its refusal to admit women as members, the secretive Fox Club continues to exist in the building where Tom drank, recited and bonded with Nick Brooks, Leon Little, Harold Peters and their buddies. Flanked by elegant circular pillars and topped by a pale classical pediment, the clubhouse's front door at what is now 44 JFK Street is no longer white, but painted an imposing dark green and fronted by a foxy polished door-knocker. If you look at the society's website, it reveals only preening exclusivity: 'for members of the Fox Club only. Unauthorized access is strictly prohibited.'[68]

In some ways, at least, attitudes to gender, race and sexuality were strikingly different in early-twentieth-century America when compared with those of a century later. During the year when Tom became a freshman, the university's official *Harvard Illustrated Magazine* published solemn photographs of the naked buttocks and muscular bodies of student athletes demonstrating their 'organic vigor' in the university gymnasium while undertaking 'Dr Sargent's Physical Test for Strength, Speed and Endurance'.[69] The same magazine and other Harvard publications regularly printed pictures of male students posing cross-dressed as (usually young) women in college societies' plays; such cross-dressing, regarded as routine and ridiculous, brought its own dangers: the manly 1908 editor of the *Harvard Monthly* recalled later how he 'was dressed up as a chorus girl, laced with a very tight corset, and fainted in the midst of the evening'.[70]

Though Tom would not have used anachronistic twenty-first-century terminology, as it seems to have been at his high school, so at Harvard the social performance of masculinity was sometimes difficult for him. Handsome and hazel-eyed, he remained self-conscious about his shyness, but also determined to be articulate about it. One undergraduate friend familiar with his scandalous verses and who met him both in the context of an all-male student club and at mixed college dances (held in the elegant surroundings of Buckingham House in the female domain of the yard at Radcliffe College) remembered that Tom 'was early explicit, too, about the necessity, if one was shy, of disciplining oneself, lest one miss certain varieties of experience which one did not naturally "take" to. The dances, and the parties, were part of this discipline.'[71] In part, at least, the Columbo and Bolo poems let him fraternise with male friends who did not share his other literary interests and who were committed to uproar and sports. The boy who had grown up with a congenital hernia, and who had not been allowed to take part in team sports was 'chided about his frail physique' by at least one other Digamma Club member.[72] Stringing together his Columbo and Bolo poems let him present an absurd epic of masculinity that allowed this young man (who was, by his own later admission, still very much a virgin) to appear shockingly blasé about all aspects of sexuality from heterosexual 'fucking on the sofa' to 'syphilis' and homosexual buggery.[73]

That this was all an over-assertive performance is suggested not least by the way when Tom collected some of these poems in his notebook, he introduced them with an antique, somewhat risqué stage direction: 'Let a tucket be sounded on the hautboys. Enter the king and queen.'[74] The accompanying poems suggest a sequence built up over time (perhaps since his 'Big Slam' days at Milton Academy), and an imagination grown used to thinking up rhymes for words like 'masturbation'. Yet the staginess suggests the Columbo poems may even have been spurred by Tom's more literary reading. Performing and perusing Elizabethan plays by Ben Jonson, Thomas Heywood, George Chapman and other lesser-known Elizabethan and Jacobean dramatists was a Harvard habit of the era. It was encouraged particularly by Professor George Baker whose course on early English drama Tom would take in 1909–10; but he was reading plays by Donne's contemporaries considerably before then. An undated sheet of notes from his student days includes a very brief plot summary of James Shirley's 1641 play *The Cardinal*, an over-the-top drama of forced marriage and wedding-day slaughter set in Navarre and featuring 'Columbo', a character who is, Tom noted, 'a great captain'.[75] His own Columbo's vigorous feats were even more atrocious: an offensively crazy, overemphatic performance of maleness.

Perhaps, as at school and later, his shyness and physique made him feel awkward about his masculinity. After his close friend and fellow clubman Peters reproached him about his physical development, he began to exercise according to the published guidance of Eugen Sandow. Here was another hyperbolic performer of maleness. Famous as the world's first bodybuilder, Sandow, 'a Titan in muscle and thews', had studied heroic sculpture; he liked to display his physique in 'classical poses'. Tom used 'the Sandow system', and later remarked that he had hoped to expand his chest to forty-six inches.[76] Exhibited by Ziegfeld of the Ziegfeld Follies, Sandow, who emphasised (as the capital letters in *Sandow on Physical Training* put it) 'ATTENTION TO CHEST DEVELOPMENT', was very much approved of by Harvard men.

> Dr Dudley A. Sargent, Director of Applied Anatomy, Physical Training, and Personal Hygiene, at the Hemenway Gymnasium, Harvard University, has compiled an interesting Anthropometric chart of Sandow, recording accurate measurements of the different parts of the athlete's anatomy, and prepared a professional paper on him for the Press. In the latter he observes:
> 'SANDOW IS THE MOST WONDERFUL SPECIMEN OF MAN I HAVE EVER SEEN'
> He is strong, active, graceful, combining in his person the characteristics of Apollo, Hercules, and the ideal athlete.[77]

Tom may have exercised in a Harvard gym, but he could never compete with this. Several of his early poems, most notably 'The Love Song of J. Alfred Prufrock', exhibit in an ironic manner acute anxieties about

masculinity; Columbo and King Bolo are at the other end of the masculine spectrum: unintellectual, grotesque sexual Sandows posed forever in
flagrante delicto. Negotiating their way among misogyny, fear, over-
protestation, unconvincing knowingness, homoeroticism, heterosexuality,
wit, offensiveness and absurdity, such versions of manhood countered and
balanced one another. They also allowed Tom to entertain not only some
of his sporty frat buddies but also several of his literary chums; the former
knew he had begun to publish serious poems in the *Harvard Advocate*, while
at least one of the latter – his friend Conrad Aiken, an *Advocate* student
poet from the class one year below Tom's own – knew and enjoyed the
Bolo poems. In spite of his shyness, despite early teetering on the brink
of failure at Harvard, and for all he might be reproached for his 'frail
physique', polite, loafing, yet occasionally foul-mouthed Tom, formally
dressed and Gold-Coasty with his often inscrutable smile, was becoming
accepted by groups of his student peers.[78] In public and in private he was
learning how he could present himself; it took considerable effort to be
a full-fledged Harvard man.

5

A Rose

By the end of his freshman year, Tom was already publishing verse in the *Harvard Advocate*: a single, eight-line poem. The *Advocate* was perhaps less weighty than its rival, the *Harvard Monthly*, but this was a start. However much he Gold Coasted and may have produced obscene rhymes, nonetheless in his first two undergraduate years he continued to read poetry and fiction. Yet his published output was utterly minimal. No notebooks of verse survive from this period. Apparently, just as his academic work skirted the unsatisfactory, so, for the most part, his ability to write printable poetry had stalled.

Part of him was still at high school. With its 'flowers' and 'withered petals', Tom's 'Song' in the *Advocate* of 24 May 1907, like the poem Mr Hatch had praised in St Louis, was two stanzas long. Indeed, in a canny piece of recycling, Tom made minor adjustments to his Smith Academy lyric with its 'flowers . . . withered', and now submitted it to the *Advocate* where it appeared in the following issue (also as 'Song'). During the sophomore year when he shared rooms with Howard Morris and John Robinson, and was elected to the Digamma, he published nothing. In the first semester of his third year, his work resurfaced in the issue of 13 November 1908: another two-stanza lyric with 'Petal on petal' of 'withered flowers'. The near-repetition of phrasing across poems published several years apart indicates lack of development. Each of these pieces plays off the promise of what the revised 1905 poem calls 'flowers of life' (and the 1907 poem calls 'flowers' that 'bloomed' and the 1908 poem terms 'Fresh flowers') against an insistent awareness that 'time . . . runs away' (revised 1905), that 'roses' in a wreath have 'faded' (1907), and blooms soon turn to 'withered flowers' (1908). All conventional enough, but the flowers in the recent poems seem to wither as soon as they blossom, or at least budding and dying flowers are mixed up: 'Fresh flowers, withered flowers, flowers of dawn' as the plangent refrain of the 1908 poem, 'Before Morning', puts it.[1] Undistinguished, these poems signal fears of premature decline.

A withering parody of 'Before Morning' appeared in the *Harvard Lampoon*. Probably taking his cue from Aristophanes, whose *Frogs* shows the poet Euripides substituting for Aeschylus' grandest phrases the words 'little bottle of oil', the *Lampoon* spoofer swapped Tom's poetic flowers for bottles of milk. Apart from occasional other substitutions, the parodist completed his work by leaving most of the rest of Tom's poem, including its plangently monotonous rhyme words, devastatingly unaltered.

Before Morning
(With apologies to T. S. E. of the *Abdicate*)

While all the east was wearing red with gray,
The bottles on the backstep turned towards dawn,
Bottle on bottle waiting for the day,
Clean bottles, milk bottles, bottles of dawn.

This morning's bottles and bottles of yesterday,
Their contents drips across the steps of dawn,
Bottles of the fresh and bottles of decay,
Clean bottles, milk bottles, bottles of dawn.[2]

To be lampooned was distinction of a sort, and Tom was good natured. He had been spotted staggering from a drinks party or 'punch' held at the *Lampoon*'s office, probably in spring 1908. Conrad Aiken, an eagerly prolific poet who published frequently in the *Advocate*, clearly remembered one of their earliest encounters. Aiken was strolling along with a mutual friend when

a singularly attractive, tall, and rather dapper young man, with a somewhat Lamian smile, reeled out of the door of the Lampoon on a spring evening, and, catching sight of me, threw his arms about me – from the open windows above came the unmistakable uproar of a punch in progress. 'And that,' observed my astonished companion, 'if Tom remembers tomorrow, will cause him to suffer agonies of shyness.' And no doubt it did: for he *was* shy.[3]

Tom's shyness did not inhibit his developing friendship with Aiken. The two undergraduates relished Bolovian obscenities, and became good sparring partners, even as they developed into significantly different poets. Both had grown up in the South but came from New England families, yet Aiken's background was as shocking as Tom's was sedate. At the age of eleven Aiken in Georgia had discovered his parents' bodies after his father, a brain surgeon, had murdered his mother then shot himself. After a protected upbringing in his aunt's house in Massachusetts, the clever, traumatised boy had proceeded from Middlesex School in Concord to Harvard. At university, Aiken came to be fascinated by philosophy; the stylish philosopher George Santayana became his favourite professor. However, as his poetry developed, this young writer would gravitate towards an interest in psychology, desire and action rather than bookish cogitation. Tom cogitated more deeply, even though his early Harvard grades suggested otherwise.

Yet after two years of loafing, Tom had grown more ambitious as a poet. The next work he published, during the first semester of his third, junior year, has 'flowers' in it too, but is revealingly different. Greek scholar Tom contributed to the 25 November 1908 *Advocate* a poem with a Homeric title, 'Circe's Palace'. Its subject is the *Odyssey*'s famous seductress who turns men into beasts. Possibly owing something to Tennyson's 'Lotos-Eaters' and Swinburne's 'Hymn to Proserpine' and 'The Garden of Proserpine', its stanza form and brevity set it apart from theirs. Where Columbo and Bolo relish bestial sex, Tom's speaker of this significantly dissimilar poem fears it, and, in language that it is tempting to read as sexual, finds around Circe's 'fountain which flows / With the voice of men in pain' further 'flowers'. These, however, are blooms that 'no man knows' – a phrase used several times by Swinburne. 'Their petals are fanged and red / With hideous streak and stain'. Alarming, maybe menstrual, they are associated with a terrifying female enchantress who reduces her suitors to mindless animality. They become panthers, a 'sluggish python', 'peacocks' with the eyes of lost men.[4]

This poem's language shows originality. Though Swinburne had used the adjective 'fanged' of flowing water, Tom, in this lyric whose vegetation springs from the dead, seems to be the first poet to use it of flowers; towards the end of Act 3, Scene two of *Macbeth* 'Light thickens' just before mention of a 'wood': in Tom's poem it is a forest which 'thickens'. Sometimes, probably unconsciously, he takes over older wording but recontextualises it: Tom's phrase 'stately and slow' occurs in Lionel Johnson's 1890 poem, 'The Troopship'. Yet, though sometimes one can detect where phrases come from, there are wordings in 'Circe's Palace' that sound just right and are Tom's own: 'streak and stain' or 'sluggish python', for instance. Echoic and acquisitive but also accurate and original, his verbal imagination was developing.

As student poets jostled for position, not everyone recognised this. Before the *Lampoon* skewered him, Tom seems to have submitted work to the *Monthly* as well as to the *Advocate*, but the *Monthly*'s editors were not keen. Widely published John Hall Wheelock, then about to graduate, thought Tom's 'Song' beginning 'The moonflower opens to the moth' might be worth using if there was room in the *Monthly*; Tom's classmate John Silas Reed, later a famous journalist, agreed. Others, though, including Tom's pushy contemporary Edward Eyre Hunt (already well known in undergraduate magazines) advised against publication. Eventually, the *Monthly* men passed on the 'moonflower' poem as a gift to their neighbours on the top floor of the Union, the *Advocate* editorial committee. Tinckom-Fernandez thought their gift should be rejected. Tom's classmate Harford Powell agreed vehemently. Despite all this, the poem ended up being accepted, perhaps because another *Advocate* man, undergraduate poet Haniel Long, was really struck by it. For Long, Tom's was the stand-out *Advocate* lyric of the year. So impressed was he that after it appeared on 26 January 1909 he went round to the printer's to hunt for the original manuscript. He retrieved it, complete with *Monthly* and *Advocate* editorial comments scribbled on the back.[5]

Tom had fiddled with the first line of this lyric's second stanza. First he had written 'Whiter the flowers which you hold'; then he had changed 'which' to 'that'; then he took out the word 'that', and recast the line as 'Whiter the flowers, Love, you hold'.[6] As poets must, he cared about cadence: the word 'Love', a stressed syllable, sounded better than the unstressed 'which' or 'that'. Yet his capital 'L' shows this love is an idealisation, offering only the most pallid kind of experience. Despite regarding with horror the 'petals . . . red' of 'Circe's Palace', the poet has his speaker long for more exotic excitement. When this poem was written, the word 'scarlet' in an erotic context was associated with a 'scarlet woman' – a prostitute.

> Whiter the flowers, Love, you hold,
>   Than the white mist on the sea;
> Have you no brighter tropic flowers
>   With scarlet life, for me?[7]

Tom might write about 'scarlet life', but he was not experiencing much. If he overcame his shyness sufficiently to attend dances in polite Brattle

Hall and Radcliffe, that was as far as things went. For him neither his nearby cousin Eleanor Hinkley nor his sister Ada represented 'scarlet life'.

By the time he wrote those words Tom was living in 25 Holyoke House, just opposite the Yard. This five-storey hall of residence had been fully renovated over the summer, so fall 1908 was a good time to move in, even though rents had gone up.[8] It was easy to travel into Boston by electric tramcar, get away from Cambridge village life, go to the theatre and enjoy big-city restaurants. There were also exhibitions at Boston's Museum of Fine Arts, concerts and shows. Upscale theatres such as the Boston Opera House (opened in 1909) advertised regularly in Harvard's magazines. Tom, however, liked going with his friend Aiken to the much less reputable Grand Opera House, in the city's South End at Dover and Washington Streets.

Two rival melodrama theatres stood at this intersection. Painted white, festooned with electric signs that blazed at night, the New Grand Theatre offered cheap seats and 'low burlesque'. The larger Grand Opera House opposite charged more for its melodramas and vaudeville extravaganzas.[9] This was a poor part of town, with a substantial Irish, African American and Jewish population. Next to the Grand Opera and about two hundred feet from Dover Street Elevated Railway Station, the run-down Hotel Caprio had lain derelict for some time.[10] A decade earlier, it had been noted that 'prostitution . . . is much more deeply rooted in the South End than in any other part of the city'.[11] Though some zones had been cleaned up, this remained the case throughout Tom's student days in an area partly overshadowed by overhead train tracks. Along Washington Street near the Grand Opera House were cheap restaurants and saloons familiar to hookers and petty crooks.

After seeing a show at the Grand Opera House, Tom and Conrad Aiken would sometimes drink in a nearby bar Tom recalled as the Opera Exchange; the bartender was among the prototypes for the character of Sweeney in some of his mature poems.[12] This sort of slumming on the part of Harvard students was not unusual. Indeed, literature encouraged it. The Scottish poet John Davidson, recommended to Tom by 'Tinck', had written a whole collection called *In a Music Hall*, while Nineties poets like England's Arthur Symons (whose work Tom came to know 'pretty well') liked to write about working-class showgirls and savour the life of popular theatres.[13] Tom may have come to see 'scarlet life', but he enjoyed the shows too. In 1908 a fellow undergraduate wrote about popular comic operas in the *Advocate*, relishing the sort of show whose last act was set in 'a street in the Big City. On the right, palatial residence of Jacob Porous Plaster – on the left, a horrid slum.'[14] Some comic operas ridiculed higher learning and the genteel Bostonian milieu

Tom's cousins inhabited, or at least could be adapted to do so in ways Harvard students enjoyed:

> She learned, goodness gracious, that God is fallacious –
>   A theory that Boston reveres.
> But she grew pretty sour on old Schopenhauer
>   And Nietsche reduced her to tears.[15]

Tom didn't just like the clever-clever stuff, though. He remembered sitting 'entranced, in the front stalls', watching *No Mother to Guide Her*, an elaborate 1905 melodrama by Lillian Mortimer involving bigamy, beatings, an escaped convict and a soubrette from New York's Bowery called Bunco.[16] Probably it was at the Grand Opera House he saw George M. Cohan's *Fifty Miles from Boston*, a hit show that toured New England between 1907 and 1909. Featuring a Harvard student who fell in love with a postmistress, it centred round a bet on the Harvard baseball team. Onstage drama included a dastardly villain, a robbery and a raging post-office fire with firemen, tooting whistles and much raising and lowering of the curtain. Principally, the rickety plot was an excuse for musical numbers. One reviewer picked out a song called 'Harrigan' as having 'a catchy touch and go to it that was a bit exhilarating'.[17] Tom thought so too. Years later, working on what became *The Waste Land*, he drafted a long passage mentioning the Opera Exchange and quoting from 'Harrigan': '"I'm proud of all the Irish blood that's in me, / "There's not a man can say a word agin me"'.[18] Tom's lines also echo a song from Mae Anwerda Sloane's 'My Evaline' from the 1901 hit *The King's Carnival* ('Meet me in the shade of the old apple tree, / Ee-vah, I-vah, Oh-vah, E-va-line!'). He runs this together with 'Meet me pretty Lindy by the watermelon vine', a 1904 song by Thomas S. Allan.[19] Brought with him from St Louis, his taste for popular culture very different from the mores of Harvard classrooms took him repeatedly to the Grand Opera, a theatre never afraid to offer audiences pretty girls, choruses, staged knife-fighting, and even (when Tom was four years into Harvard) 'an electrical prairie fire, and an exhibition of lasso throwing'.[20]

Visits to his cousins were tamer affairs. Cousin Fred was now a Harvard undergraduate in the same year as Conrad Aiken, and had his own taste for theatricals, playing a minor part in a student production. Tom's sister Ada worked from 1909 for the Massachusetts State Board of Charities. Her scholarly husband, 'Shef' Sheffield, was interested in literature; long fascinated by oriental culture, he had written fiction for the *Advocate* as an 1890s undergraduate, and was someone with whom Tom could talk.[21]

Shef was also a sounding-board for Lottie Eliot, anxious about her son's university studies.[22] Tom seemed uncertain in what direction to go. He had published a few poems, and had withstood literary rejection and mockery. But other student poets were doing more. The year before Tom started at Harvard, Van Wyck Brooks and his friend John Wheelock had published a joint collection of poems while still freshmen; in Tom's own class Tinckom-Fernandez was a frequently praised *Advocate* contributor, already on the editorial board in his second year; Edward Eyre Hunt was well connected, and looked set to become a literary star; even Tom's poet friend Aiken, praised by an English professor for his 'most imaginative' freshman verse, had published far more than Tom.[23] Poetry is about quality, not quantity: Tom knew that. Fed up with Wheelock's Swinburne worship, Hunt's bluster and a milieu loud with echoes of Kipling, Andrew Lang and Yeatsian Nineties poets, he was trying to escape what he saw as a literary impasse.

Some friends helped. When he read 'Thirty Bob a Week', a poem by Tinckom-Fernandez's admired John Davidson, Tom savoured the way that as early as 1894 this Scot had caught a contemporary accent. Making use of internal rhymes as well as end rhymes, Davidson, nevertheless, sounded arrestingly 'unpoetic'. The Celtic Twilight Yeats, whose more conventionally poetic lyrics of lake isles and whispering reeds were so beguilingly plangent, seems to have meant almost nothing to Tom as he read recent poets' work, searching for notes of modernity. Attuned to London's streets and subway system, Davidson, however, offered an edgy presentation of a working-class urban clerk. With 'pipe all alight' this protagonist spends the day 'A-scheming how to count ten bob a pound', and finds something deeply unsettling in the state of his soul:

> I step into my heart and there I meet
>   A god-almighty devil singing small,
> Who would like to shout and whistle in the street,
>   And squelch the passers flat against the wall;
> If the whole world was a cake he had the power to take,
>   He would take it, ask for more, and eat them all.[24]

In 1908 Tom wasn't able to write like this. He was listening for something. He wasn't sure what. Then, at the end of that year, he found it.

He had gone to a favourite haunt, the Union Library. There, upstairs, warmly protected from the December weather outside, he was looking through recently received books. Alert University library staff helped stock the Union's shelves. Tom's eye was caught by the name of Arthur

Symons, and by his book's title, *The Symbolist Movement in Literature*. It was a small second edition published earlier that year and just imported from London. The volume's dedication to W. B. Yeats presented Symbolism as the pre-eminent literary movement in Europe from Ireland to Russia. 'Without symbolism there can be no literature', began the first chapter, but Symons's special Symbolism had a capital 'S' and was, he argued, something new: 'What distinguishes the Symbolism of our day from the Symbolism of the past is that it has now become conscious of itself.' This Symbolist poetry fused self-conscious rebellion against tired conventions with a sense of renewed religious mission. 'It is an attempt to spiritualize literature, to evade the old bondage of rhetoric.' Here was a 'revolt' against 'rhetoric' and 'materialistic tradition'; it had the power to speak 'as only religion had hitherto spoken to us, it becomes itself a kind of religion, with all the duties and responsibilities of the sacred ritual'.[25]

Symons's book invoked 'Mysticism', but in a very different way from Tom's mother.[26] It was full of modern French poets whose behaviour would have horrified Lottie Eliot, and who had certainly not been part of the curriculum of Professor Wright's French course. Probably Tom had been reading Baudelaire for some time. Years later, he recalled:

I think that from Baudelaire I learned first, a precedent for the poetical possibilities, never developed by any poet writing in my own language, of the more sordid aspects of the modern metropolis, of the possibility of fusion between the sordidly realistic and the phantasmagoric, the possibility of the juxtaposition of the matter-of-fact and the fantastic. From him, as from Laforgue, I learned that the sort of material that I had, the sort of experience that an adolescent had had, in an industrial city in America, could be the material for poetry . . . It may be that I am indebted to Baudelaire chiefly for half a dozen lines out of the whole of *Fleurs du Mal*; and that his significance for me is summed up in the lines:

> *Fourmillante Cité, cité pleine de rêves,*
> *Où le spectre en plein jour raccroche le passant . . .*
> [Swarming City, city full of dreams.
> Where the ghost in broad daylight accosts the passer-by . . .]

I knew what *that* meant, because I had lived it before I knew that I wanted to turn it into verse on my own account.[27]

Reading French poetry, he understood how his own childhood among the St Louis fogs could be an artistic asset. But Symons's book, with its account of Jules Laforgue and other poets, took him beyond Baudelaire. As he read about Gérard de Nerval (whose works he would buy – 'two copies' – and whom he would quote in *The Waste Land*), he discovered a poet haunted by his sense of isolation in the 'crowded and more sordid streets of great cities', a man who had found 'his ideal in the person of an actress' and craved 'the fatal transfiguration of the footlights' in a theatre where 'reality and the artificial change places with so fantastic a regularity' that men were drawn like 'moths into its flame'.[28] Such a process, Symons asserted, would continue 'as long as men persist in demanding illusion of what is real, and reality in what is illusion'. To its readers Symons's book offered heady, even bewildering stuff; but to Tom, divided between shy Harvard bookishness and slumming it in Boston's South End, it brought clarity too: it was a 'revelation'.[29] 'Every artist lives a double life', wrote Symons. Though poets were 'for the most part conscious of the illusions of the imagination', nevertheless there were peculiarly intense writers such as Villiers de L'Isle Adam, 'The Don Quixote of Idealism', for whom 'it was not only in philosophical terms that life . . . was the dream, and the spiritual world the reality'. Writing of 'hallucination' and of scandalous Paul Verlaine who had 'realised the great secret of the Christian mystics', or decadent Catholic novelist Huysmans or playwright Maurice 'Maeterlinck as a Mystic', Symons presented authors – principally poets – able to set forth vision with religious intensity, but not with vagueness: 'the artist who is also a mystic hates the vague with a more profound hatred than any other artist'.[30]

At times Symons wrote about his French poets with well nigh messianic zeal. It was 'on the lines of that spiritualising of the word, that perfecting of form in its capacity for allusion and suggestion, that confidence in the eternal correspondences between the visible and invisible universe, which [Stéphane] Mallarmé taught, and too intermittently preached, that literature must now move, if it is in any sense to move forward'. Yet, although Tom went on to read all Symons's Symbolists and would learn from them, one in particular obsessed him. Encountering Jules Laforgue, Tom, at the age of twenty, began reading a French poet who was also in his twenties; yet they could never meet, because Laforgue had died at the age of twenty-seven, about a year before Tom's birth. Markedly more than the Harvard student from Missouri, Laforgue was a displaced person: born in Montevideo, he had grown up in France. A poet of 'nerves', Laforgue had written, according to Symons, 'letters of an almost virginal *naïveté*', yet his literary art was peculiarly knowing, daring in content and, especially, in form:

[His] verse and prose are alike a kind of travesty, making subtle use of colloquialism, slang, neologism, technical terms, for their allusive, their factitious, their reflected meanings, with which one can play, very seriously. The verse is alert, troubled, swaying, deliberately uncertain, hating rhetoric so piously that it prefers, and finds its piquancy in, the ridiculously obvious. It is really *vers libre*, but at the same time correct verse, before *vers libre* had been invented. And it carries, as far as that theory has ever been carried, the theory that demands an instantaneous notation (Whistler, let us say) of the figure or landscape which one has been accustomed to define with such rigorous exactitude. Verse, always elegant, is broken up into a kind of mockery of prose.

> Encore un de mes pierrots mort;
> Mort d'un chronique orphelinisme;
> C'était un coeur plein de dandysme
> Lunaire, en un drôle de corps;
> [Another of my pierrots is dead;
> Dead from being chronically orphaned;
> He had a heart full of lunar
> Dandyism in a funny body;]

he will say to us, with a familiarity of manner, as of one talking languidly, in a low voice, the lips always teased into a slightly bitter smile . . .[31]

Tom, remembered for his own 'somewhat Lamian smile', clicked with all this. 'The Symons book', he stated later, 'is one of those which have affected the course of my life.'[32] At least two Symons phrases from the same page would find their way into his poetry. When Symons writes of Laforgue composing 'love-poems hat in hand', Tom in a 1909 poem has 'Romeo . . . hat in hand'. Symons's oddly phrased statement that 'In Laforgue, sentiment is squeezed out of the world before one begins to play at ball with it' surely ghosts Prufrock's thought of having 'squeezed the universe into a ball'.[33] In Symons's bibliography Tom noticed mention of Laforgue's three-volume *Oeuvres Complètes*, published in 1902–3. No Harvard library had these books. Tom ordered all three to be shipped from Paris. Probably he was the first person in the United States to do so. He knew exactly what he needed.

His interest in French literature may have been encouraged by his acquaintance with another young Harvard poet, Alan Seeger. Thirty-five years later, a fellow student, Gluyas Williams, who did not know Tom well, recalled how impressed he had been that Tom and Seeger shared rooms. Seeger had a reputation as an aesthete (he was rumoured to wear a golden fillet around his hair after he washed it), and Williams thought Tom 'an aesthete too'.[34] Haniel Long, in his 1908–9 diary, writes of Seeger as rather friendless, 'always in search of solitide' – so much so that he would sometimes lock himself into an unoccupied guest-room.[35] In his slightly self-mythologising prose, Seeger, who had a taste for Balzac and French literature, and would go on to become a celebrated American literary Francophile, recalled that 'at college' he had 'led the life of an anchorite . . . My books were my friends.'[36]

If Tom did indeed room with an 'anchorite' of whom he saw little, he shared some of Seeger's tastes, including an attraction towards Dante. Seeger's version of *Inferno* Canto XXVI, which ends, 'Over our heads we heard the surging billows close', seems to date from his Harvard student days and is interesting to set beside the drowning that concludes Prufrock's 'Love Song'.[37] Tom and Seeger were in the same year as undergraduates, but very different as people and poets; since 1908 Seeger had been working on his long Keatsian poem, 'The Deserted Garden', awash with fairyland imagery.[38] Yet his later poem, 'Paris', hymning that city of 'ragged minstrels', 'Uncorseted . . . adolescent loveliness' and 'Open café-windows', sums up a Francophilia that, increasingly, Tom shared.[39] After Seeger had been killed in World War I in France, Tom wrote a short, anonymous 1917 review that described Seeger's old-fashioned poems as 'high-flown': 'Alan Seeger, as one who knew him can attest, lived his whole life on this plane, with impeccable poetic dignity.' Tom singled out Seeger's 'Paris'.[40] He thought, though, that his old classmate seemed to live 'in a violet mist' so that 'The Paris of his verse', to its detriment, 'might be the Paris of a performance of "Louise" at the Boston Opera-House'.[41] When Tom followed Seeger in using the word 'Uncorseted' (in his 1917 'Whispers of Immortality'), he did so with ironic precision, deploying a very different tone. Tom and Seeger shared a deepening commitment to literature, especially in French; and sometimes they circulated in the same Harvard society: in 1909 Seeger was hoping to move to a Cambridge 'attic down on Ash St. No. 16', an address where Tom would reside a couple of years later.[42] However, Seeger, unlike Tom, wrote work that was 'well done, and so much out of date as to be almost a positive quantity'. Tom thought Seeger's poetry 'goes back to the early Keats'.[43] Seeger learned nothing from Jules Laforgue.

Some months before his three-volume Laforgue arrived, Tom wrote a sonnet, 'On a Portrait'. Published in January 1909's *Advocate*, it juxtaposes the narrator's sense of being outside in a busy street against a remote, dreamy female figure in a room; she seems cut off, like 'A pensive lamia' (that expression probably triggered Conrad Aiken's later description of Tom's own smile) or like Walter Pater's Mona Lisa, 'Beyond the circle of our thought'; if that sounds a little grandly eloquent, the poem's last rhyming couplet snipes ironically at its earlier rhetoric, and at the lady: 'The parrot on his bar, a silent spy, / Regards her with a patient curious eye'.[44] Though it has not yet got there, this poem heads towards the accurate, unsentimental perception and anti-rhetorical writing advocated by Symons and his Symbolists. '"Take eloquence, and wring its neck!" said Verlaine in his Art Poétique.'[45]

Symons's book excited Tom, and socially things were looking up too. Haniel Long, the student so impressed by Tom's *Advocate* 'Song' ('The moonflower opens to the moth'), spoke to him on Monday 8 March 1909 about his writing ability. Long thought Tom should be involved with both the *Advocate* editorial board and the Signet Society. One of the most writerly of Harvard's private clubs, the Signet was headquartered in a recently renovated large 1820s corner house at 46 Dunster Street where it joins Mount Auburn. A flamboyant heraldic crest over its door carried the words '*Mousikehn poiei kai ergazou*' (Greek for 'Make music and live it'), while another Signet motto, from Virgil's *Georgics*, was '*Sic vos non vobis Mellificatis apes*' (So, not for yourselves, you bees make honey). As Long was aware when he spoke to Tom, this most cultural of clubs, whose undergraduate members were called 'drones', needed to make money too. Over a thousand dollars in debt, the Signet wanted prosperous new members. There was a meeting on 19 March to discuss candidates for election. This went on for hours, with members trying to blackball various possibles, but Long waited and managed to get the name of 'Tommy Eliot' accepted.[46] On 21 March a handwritten letter on a small sheet of Signet notepaper went out to 'Mr. T. S. Eliot' from a member who also worked on the *Lampoon*:

Dear Sir,

It gives me great pleasure to inform you of your election to the fourth seven from the class of 1910. For your initiation, which takes place Friday evening, April second at seven thirty, you will prepare a part of not less than ten hundred words.

Very sincerely
Morton Peabody Prince[47]

This was an honour, even if Tom, in the 'fourth seven', was hardly among the first chosen. Held in its clubhouse, the Signet's secret initiations were less riotous than Digamma ones, but still formidable. Rumours circulated that there might be 'very drastic physical dangers'. We do not know the exact nature of Tom's initiation, but candidates were expected to prepare a 'part', or speech, for delivery to an intimidating jury of former members who then interrogated them, not necessarily on issues related to the 'part'. An account of another, less shy poet's 'quite overawing' interview with a Signet jury about three years earlier indicates the club's style. Candidates were kept waiting to make them nervous. Then they were led 'into this beautifully lighted room, and sitting before us were George Lyman Kittredge, the great scholar; William James, Professor of Psychology at Harvard; Josiah Royce, the philosopher; Hugo Münsterberg, the philosopher, I think was also there; and Charles Townsend Copeland, Boylston Professor of Rhetoric'. Questioning of candidates was carried out individually. Tom's jury would have been similarly constituted, and his questions may have been as unexpected as those of his fellow-poet candidate John Hall Wheelock, whose inter-rogation was opened by Kittredge:

'Spell "syzygy".' I couldn't spell it. He then said, 'That's spelled S-Y-Z-Y-G-Y.' He looked at the other inquisitors, and said, 'This candidate doesn't seem very promising to me.'

Then one of the other professors . . . said to me, 'Would you please let us know to which of Longfellow's sisters he addressed that beautiful line, 'Hail to thee, blithe spirit, bird thou never wert.' And I was confused, because I knew of course that this was from Shelley's 'Ode to a Skylark,' and it would seem rude to catch a professor in a mistake of that sort, so I had to claim that I wasn't familiar with that either. Then they looked very doubtful.

Then the third question was: 'could God make rocks bigger than He could lift?' I'd never heard this question before. I have heard since that it's sometimes been used by boys to stump a Sunday school teacher. But there didn't seem any answer to that. So I just said I couldn't answer it.

All unanimously agreed – James, Munsterburg, Royce, Kittredge, Copeland, and whoever else was there: 'This man is not fit for admission to the Signet. I'm sorry that we've subjected him to this ordeal' and so on. 'Next candidate, please.' And I retired in the most dreadful state of shame and annoyance. Then, when they'd all been listened to and been subjected, I suppose, to the same humiliation, punch bowls were brought in, and I was welcomed with the rest of them as a new member.[48]

Tom, having presented his 'part', was suitably initiated. After the news was broken to them that they had been admitted after all, new members were expected to drink from a bowl, a 'loving cup', and each received a red rose which he was expected to press and preserve before eventually returning it to the club after he had published his first book. Today the Signet Society at Harvard numbers among its proudest possessions Tom's rose.

In this club Tom fraternised with his fellow classman Robert Canby Hallowell (later to work for the *Century Magazine*) and with Thomas Powel, editor and secretary of the *Lampoon*; his friend Tinckom-Fernandez, who became President at the *Advocate*; and other student poets, including Eyre Hunt, soon to be editor of the *Monthly*, Haniel Long and Rogers MacVeagh (both *Advocate* men). Just as helpful was the fact that distinguished academics mixed with student members. The Signet was a place for inter-generational conversation as well as undergraduate discussion and sumptuous reunions where members and alumni would quaff Moët et Chandon, sing ('Champagne? Yes, yes. Rum punch? Yes, yes'), and smoke Romeo and Juliet cigars.[49] Tom's election to another club with a literary bent, the Stylus, brought him into contact with many of the same people – Hallowell, MacVeagh, Powel, Prince and Tinckom-Fernandez were all members there too – while again granting him access to an informal space where students sometimes mixed with faculty.

The Stylus attracted, for instance, flamboyant aphorist Pierre La Rose – also linked to the Signet. An enthusiast for heraldry, Catholicism, style and *bon ton,* 'le bon Pierre' had designed several of the Signet's splendid interiors as well as its vast, bee-crowded crest above the door. The Signet boasted a well-heated 18-by-40-foot library (with 'shelf-room for 6000 volumes', La Rose stated in 1903); a house speciality in Tom's day was Chateau La Rose claret.[50] Friendly with Harvard philosopher George Santayana, La Rose was associated by Tom's brother Henry with Mount Auburn Street and the *'elite'* welcomed by 'Mrs Jack' – Isabella Stewart Gardner – to gatherings at her magnificent Boston home.[51] Tom would go there too. Through these clubs he had the opportunity to meet socially men like the stocky, shrewd Josiah Royce, with whom he would later study, and other influential academics including the dapper English professors Copeland and Briggs. Some members, including Eyre Hunt, courted the faculty: in 1909 Hunt wrote the introduction to his modern translation of the medieval poem *Sir Orfeo*, prefacing it with a chunk from one of his English professor's books, ever so gratefully acknowledged.

Tom did not go in for such sycophancy, but his was a Harvard with friendly, club-level as well as formal, class-level contact between privileged circles of students and professors. If the former might caricature or adulate the latter, the faculty also reviewed the 'drones'. So, for instance, several professors involved with Tom's English courses were readers and reviewers of the *Advocate*. Others who took an interest included the great Sanskrit scholar Charles Lanman, with whom Tom would study as a graduate student, and the art historian, Professor Chase. Such contacts could work wonders. It was after reading Hunt's *Sir Orfeo* in the October 1909 *Monthly* that Professor Schofield suggested it should be 'published in separate form'; just months later, it was.[52] Nothing so promising happened to Tom, though he was 'cheered' to receive a letter from Thomas Head Thomas, an old student friend of his brother, praising his *Advocate* poems.[53] In print, less generous comments came from an anonymous November 1909 reviewer who merely mentioned that the new *Advocate*'s 'contributions of verse are from T. S. Eliot and C. P. Aiken'.[54] Yet Tom's membership of literary clubs and writing for the *Advocate*, to whose editorial board he was elected in his junior year, countered his often deserved reputation for shyness and brought him greater visibility. He obtained, too, first-hand experience of the business of literary publishing.

Among the professors Tom liked was George Herbert Palmer, whose survey History of Ancient Philosophy (Philosophy A) he had taken as a sophomore. In his sixties and recently widowed, Palmer had a 'splendid personality'; his 'high quality of lecturing' was particularly prized by students in Tom's year who gave Philosophy A 'more favourable "points" than any other course'. It was 'a good essential introduction' that 'no educated man can afford to neglect'.[55] A committed Christian as well as a scholar of Greek and Philosophy, Palmer was affable, polymathic and engaging. He made time to meet students in societies, to preach at chapel and to give public talks about George Herbert, the poet whose name he shared. Avidly, Palmer collected editions of Herbert, having edited the complete works in 1905. Encouraged by Palmer, a public 'exhibition of books by and relating to George Herbert' was held in the Treasure Room in Gore Hall during Tom's junior year – another indication of Harvard's interest in Metaphysical poetry.[56] Much later, Tom would write a small book about Herbert.

It was Palmer whose writerly advice had been quoted in *Composition and Rhetoric for Schools*, Tom's textbook at Smith Academy. The professor, who encouraged students to 'seek out the company of good speakers and writers', had translated Homer in his youth. He was revising his widely read *Self-Cultivation in English* when he first taught Tom. Interested in 'the transmission of the power to write', Palmer detected Tom's 'early promise'. Later, when he taught him as a graduate student, he decided Tom had 'a mind of extraordinary power and sensitiveness'.[57] Palmer liked to emphasise that writers should be 'obedient' to their matter, suppressing their own personality when they wrote:

> Great writers put themselves and their personal imaginings out of sight. Their writing becomes a kind of transparent window on which reality is reflected, and through which people see not them but that of which they write. How much we know of Shakespeare's characters! How little we know of Shakespeare![58]

In time, especially after engaging with Laforgue's poems, Tom adopted a similar aesthetic, at least when it came to dispelling a Romantic aura of 'personality'. Palmer's pleasurable classes introduced him to a subject beyond his high-school curriculum: philosophy. He started to learn about Heraclitus and Aristotle, Plato and Plotinus, to all of whose work he would return.

As well as Palmer's Ancient Philosophy survey, in that 1907–8 session Tom took Philosophy B, History of Modern Philosophy, taught by Pierre La Rose's friend and fellow Signet member, George Santayana. It seems to have been less this Spanish-born professor's philosophical stance that impressed Tom than his cosmopolitan sophistication. Like Palmer, Santayana enjoyed 'informal meetings with his students', and had a practitioner's interest in writerly style as well as in philosophy.[59] An agnostic powerfully shaped by several aspects of Catholicism, he used his philosophical training to think about poetry. Maintaining later that Santayana was 'more interested in poetical philosophy than in philosophical poetry', with a hint of misogyny or homophobia Tom stated that 'I have never liked Santayana myself, because I have always felt that his attitude was essentially feminine, and that his philosophy was a dressing up of himself rather than an interest in things.'[60]

When he taught Tom's class Santayana was at work on his *Three Philosophical Poets*, which devotes considerable attention to Dante. His earlier *Interpretations of Poetry and Religion* argued that

> The poet's art is to a great extent the art of intensifying emotions by assembling the scattered objects that naturally arouse them. He sees the affinities of things by seeing their common affinities with passion . . . By this union of disparate things having a common overtone of feeling, the feeling itself is evoked in all its strength . . .[61]

Tom would ponder similar ideas in his own philosophical way. Years afterwards, he theorised the 'objective correlative' and, when considering the Metaphysical poets, wrote of how 'a poet's mind . . . is constantly amalgamating disparate experience'.[62] His later ideas grew from a pervasive Harvard milieu in which Santayana, Palmer and others so readily linked philosophy to poetry, assuming it was a great thing to be a philosophical poet. Like most good students, Tom reacted against aspects of his teachers' teaching, but he came to share several of their enthusiasms, not least for Dante and Metaphysical poetry. In 1909–10 he took another course with Santayana, whom some considered a dilettante. Palmer's counsel to writers was to 'work day after day unwearyingly'.[63] Sophomore Tom hardly lived up to this ideal: he got a C on Palmer's Philosophy course, and a B for Philosophy B. Among his sophomore grades, B was his highest. Yet in his junior year he began to hit his stride academically – which meant at least that the Bs became more common – and, thanks to Symons and Laforgue, he worked more productively on his poetry.

Having already studied French, German, English and Greek in his first two years at Harvard, it seemed reasonable to Tom to proceed to take courses during 1908–9 in the small Comparative Literature department. This had been established in 1906 with the appointment of Professor William Henry Schofield to a chair in the subject. Conveniently for Tom, some of its classes were held right next to the Union in Warren House, a handsome 1833 building which had once been the residence of the Professor of Sanskrit. In the academic village of Cambridge, nothing was ever very far away. To register for his 1908 first-term classes Tom needed only to cross the road from Holyoke House to the Yard.

Relishing institutional history, Harvard asked students to present themselves for classes at the first meetings in the appropriate 'recitation rooms', a term dating from the days when undergraduates, instead of simply listening to lectures, were expected to recite and comment on their learning.[64] In the first week of October 1908, the recitation room for the first meeting of Comparative Literature 7, Tendencies of European Literature in the Renaissance, was in room 31, one of the smaller spaces in Henry Hansel Richardson's imposing red-brick Sever Hall in the Yard. In charge of the course, Assistant Professor Anthony Murray Potter had interests that ranged from Petrarch and Dante to Spanish literature. Deeply committed to the new department, Potter had just endowed Comparative Literature prizes (still awarded today) in memory of his mother. His doctoral thesis had been published in 1902 as part of a distinguished series of literary studies including volumes by his senior colleague, Professor Schofield, and by the anthropologically-minded English folklorist Jessie L. Weston, with whom Schofield would soon collaborate.

The new discipline of Comparative Literature encouraged people, as Gilbert Murray and others had sometimes done, to connect literary works through anthropology to supposedly primitive rituals. Professor Potter was given to citing anthropologists such as John Ferguson McLennan or Edward Westermarck, author of *The History of Human Marriage*. He liked to consider literature anthropologically: 'Miss Weston has conjectured that in the combat of Father and Son we have a romantic presentment of the struggle between the old and new divinities of vegetation, which finds ritual expression in so many spring and harvest festivals, and of which Mr. Frazer has claimed the Arician rite as an example.'[65] Tom was not yet used to thinking this way. However, over the next few years he too would read McLennan, Westermarck, Weston and Frazer. He internalised some intellectual habits familiar to his Harvard teachers. Schofield, his other Comparative Literature professor that year, thought this way too; at least on later occasions Schofield discussed the evolution of the figure of Tiresias who would come to feature in *The Waste Land*.[66] Tom acquired a copy of Schofield's *English Literature from the Norman Conquest to Chaucer* which he took back to St Louis; years afterwards, he was reminded of it when he was preparing to work on *The Waste Land*.[67] For Schofield the story of 'Tristram and Isolt' was 'the apotheosis of illicit love', and he was interested in the way that 'pagan' material underlay stories such as that of the Holy Grail.[68]

Tom would return to such thoughts when he read Jessie Weston's 1920 *From Ritual to Romance* and incorporated her thinking into *The Waste Land*, but in 1908, studying medieval Arthurian romance with Schofield, setting it in a wide comparative context, he was nowhere near that stage. Nevertheless, as John Morgenstern has argued, Schofield's interest in 'tradition', 'the individual' and the 'impersonal' may have influenced his most famous student.[69] In Comparative Literature 6a (The Literary History of England and its Relations to that of the Continent from the Beginning to Chaucer), Tom encountered again some of the Arthurian material with which he had grown up; in Schofield's Comparative Literature 6b (The Literary History of England and its Relations to that of the Continent from Chaucer to Elizabeth) he heard more about Dante. Around this time he began to absorb Dante for himself; Tom never formally studied Italian, and later admitted he 'read Dante only with a prose translation beside the text'; but, excitedly, he

began to puzzle out the Divine Comedy in this way; and when I thought I had grasped the meaning of a passage which especially delighted me, I committed it to memory; so that, for some years, I was able to recite a large part of one canto or another to myself, lying in bed or on a railway journey. Heaven knows what it would have sounded like, had I recited it aloud; but it was by this means that I steeped myself in Dante's poetry.[70]

In Dante he found great poetry wedded to a system of spiritual belief. Deploying with technical mastery his *terza rima* verse form, Dante begins his *Inferno* as a lost soul, and makes poetry out of uncertainty long before being guided towards certainty:

> E quale è quei, che disvuol ciò che volle,
>   e per novi pensier cangia proposta,
>   sì che dal cominciar tutto si tolle,
>
> tal mi fec'io in quella oscura costa:
>   perchè pensando consumai la 'mpresa,
>   che fu nel cominciar cotanto tosta.

Stumblingly pronouncing such lines to his inner ear, Tom grew fascinated by Dante's music – the alliteration, the hints of internal rhyme, the way one stanza picks up a rhyme from the last. Like his mother before him, he was drawn also to the spirituality of Italian culture, but, like Browning, he sensed its carnality. The pocket-sized Temple Classics version of Dante (Tom acquired a copy of the 1909 edition) made the Italian poet a portable travelling companion. In this version Dante's text came with a facing translation so that Tom could glance across at the English prose to reveal or confirm the sense of the sonorous Italian:

> And as one who unwills what he willed, and
>   with new thoughts changes his purpose, so that
>   he wholly quits the thing commenced,
>
> such I made myself on that dim coast: for with
>   thinking I wasted the enterprise, that had
>   been so quick in its commencement.[71]

Tom wasn't a quitter, but Harvard's elective system encouraged him to drift from course to course. Twenty years later he told his mother he was sorry about this: 'I was one of the victims of the "elective system". I have always regretted that as an undergraduate I did not stick to Latin and Greek, and some mathematics, and leave alone all the things I dabbled in year after year.' He felt he had been 'so interested in many things that I did nothing thoroughly, and was always thinking about new subjects that I wanted to study, instead of following out any one'.[72] Yet this was what he thought later. As an undergraduate he picked a melange of topics which mightily enriched his poetry. As well as reading that great Florentine, Dante, he went on to enrol in Edward Waldo Forbes's Fine Arts 20b course on Florentine Painting in his final undergraduate year. Often Tom's mature poems contemplate pictures or *objets d'art*. If his course choices seem capricious, his caprices were shrewd.

His third year at Harvard saw him taking two Latin courses. In Latin 2a (Latin Literature) he heard during fall 1908 an overview of poetry given by Assistant Professor Edward Kennard Rand, whom he came to know as 'Ken'. Herbert Howarth suggests Tom may have encountered Ken also in the rather more convivial surroundings of the Fox Club.[73] Well liked, Rand was yet another Dante scholar; he wrote, too, about St Augustine. Like Tom's mother, Rand had an interest in mysticism, especially that of St Ambrose. He admired Horace and Ovid, but also more obscure reaches of Latin literature. His lectures were 'too learned' to be 'popular', Tom decided, but that did not put him off. Rand's emphasis on 'the continuity of pagan and Christian culture' reinforced the line taken by his other anthropologically-minded teachers. Tom came to regard Rand as 'one of the finest classical scholars and humanists of our time', even if his lectures outshone his publications.[74] Most of the latter post-date Tom's student days, and one of them, on 'The Latin Literature of the West from the Antonines to Constantine', includes a consideration of the 'Pervigilium Veneris', a poem tied to the 'cult of Venus' that Rand links to the work of Apuleius; the poem, which Walter Pater had discussed, was something 'a poet, growing old and sad, might have written'.[75] It caught the attention of Tom, who would soon write his own 'Prufrock's Pervigilium', lines from which would form part of 'The Love Song of J. Alfred Prufrock'.

Latin 11, Tom's other Latin literature class in session 1908–9, dealt with the Roman novel, especially Petronius and Apuleius. Petronius' *Satyricon*, a mixture of prose and verse from Emperor Nero's Rome narrated by a man who has provoked the sex god Priapus, fired Tom's sometimes priapic imagination. Taught by Professor Clifford Herschel Moore (later founder of the Harvard Faculty Club), this Menippean satire included such Aristophanic elements as a whale-bone dildo, farting, much gluttony and all sorts of graphic sexual shenanigans – just the sort of thing to appeal to the student singer of 'Columbo' and to other male undergraduates of a Bolovian cast of mind. No Fox Club romp quite matched Petronius. Professor Moore, author of textbooks on Latin grammar and an editor of the *Harvard Studies in Classical Philology*, was a New England farmer's son who had studied in Munich and worked in Rome, so perhaps he was unshockable. Moore and his wife were renowned for hospitality at their Brattle Street home, and the professor was recalled as 'an accomplished figureskater'.[76] Like many Harvard students, Tom too would take skating lessons.

Having read Petronius' *Satyricon* for Moore's course, Tom kept a very old German edition in his library. A pencil note stuck inside suggests that this work, also, demonstrates how literature, customs and popular material might coalesce as anthropologists often suggested, mixing pagan and Christian material. The note records how a Roman story about 'The matron of Ephesus' (dealing with 'the faithlessness of women') was 'brought from the east by the crusaders' and can be found in works as diverse as medieval stories and George Chapman's early-seventeenth-century play *The Widow's Tears*.[77] A pencil gloss in Tom's copy of Petronius explains that the Latin 'tubere' could be translated 'mushroom'.[78] Years later, Tom would write his own poem of 'dried tubers' and would add to it a chilling, multilingual epigraph from Petronius.[79] Though the *Satyricon* (alluded to by F. Scott Fitzgerald in *The Great Gatsby* and by that libertine novelist Henry Miller) was more familiar to American undergraduates of Tom's generation than it is today, its priapic excesses were not what left their mark on *The Waste Land*. Instead, however fascinated Tom may have been by Petronius' millennia-old bawdy-meets-highbrow burlesque, he drew on it eventually for a passage about the Sibyl of Cumae who says in Greek, 'I want to die.'[80]

6

Secret Knowledge

I N 1909 Tom did not want to die. He wanted to read more Laforgue.
He was able to read some, along with poetry by Tristan Corbière,
Stéphane Mallarmé, Jean-Arthur Rimbaud, Paul Valéry, Paul Verlaine and
others in the Parisian '*Van Bever* anthology', *Poètes d'Aujourd'hui 1880–1900*,
edited by Adolphe van Bever and Paul Léautaud, but this was not enough.[1]
When Laforgue's three-volume *Oeuvres Complètes* arrived, it contained
more prose than poetry: sometimes, like a late-nineteenth-century
Petronius, Laforgue had intermingled the two. The first volume was all
poetry. Volume II was *Moralités Légendaires* in prose with a sprinkling of
verse, and volume III a *Mélange posthume* whose contents ranged from
reflections and aphorisms 'Sur La Femme' to art criticism, and selected
letters. This was the feast Tom had been waiting for. It took him some
time to digest. Steeped in Catholicism, Laforgue had lost his Christian
faith, acquiring interests in Buddhism and Indic religion. In diction, themes
and form, his verse had come to terms with urban modernity.

Laforgue was a twenty-something male obsessed with sex, disconcertingly and ironically direct about its mixture of fascination and repulsion.
He articulated anxieties involved in conversations – real, abandoned and
imagined – between men and women. Veering between styling himself a
'bon misogyne' (good misogynist) and attempting self-mocking declara-
tions of love, the hyper-intellectual protagonist of his poems sees women,
whom social conditioning seems to have groomed for reproduction, as
intensely desirable but deeply unsettling. Here was a poet of many
'Complaintes' who, taking the expression 'enfant-terrible' all too literally,
could write in the voice of a 'foetus' emerging from the 'mucus' of the
womb. For Laforgue, 'Vieille et chauve à vingt ans' (Old and bald at
twenty), spring was a 'cortège', or 'purges'. He rhymed 'Préaux des soirs'

(The evening quads) with 'Christs des dortoirs!' (Dorm Christ-Gods).[2] To Tom, this poet was, quite simply, astonishing. 'He gave me', he recalled in 1920, 'the same revelation which I imagine he has given to other people before and since: that is, he showed how much more use poetry could make of contemporary ideas and feelings, of the emotional quality of contemporary ideas, than one had supposed'. Tom admitted that Browning (whom he had read since boyhood) had done as much, but 'It is easier for a young poet to understand and to profit by the work of another young poet, when it is good, than from the work of a mature poet.'[3]

In an electrifying way, Laforgue was his contemporary. This young Frenchman who wrote poems with titles such as 'Complainte des pubertés difficiles' (Complaint of Difficult Puberties) and regarded the end of the world in terms of a puke-dish ('Vomitoire') was not necessarily a writer whose oeuvre Tom would show his mother, but that made him all the more exciting. Laforgue played subversively with religion. He flaunted his disconcerting sense of sex. He authored a poem about 'doublure' (underwear) with the title 'Maniaque' (Maniac). Tom, however, having written already of King Henry VIII as 'that royal Mormon', was delighted to discover a poet who could call the moon 'Pape / Des Mormons' (Pope of Mormons) in 'La Lune est stérile', or (in 'Esthétique') link up the Christian 'Galilee' to 'rites végétatifs de l'Inde' (Indian vegetation rites).[4] Laforgue made poetry out of the sort of anthropological speculations familiar to Tom's undergraduate lecturers. This Uruguayan Frenchman seemed absolutely at home, too, in writing about the modern city. His moon looks down not just on Paris but also on the Missouri, that river which shared its name with Tom's home state. Here was the only poet in the world who rhymed – the French pronunciation helped – 'Paris' and 'le Missouri' ('Complainte de la lune en province').[5] Metaphorically speaking, such a rhyme became Tom's goal too.

Sounding less than irreproachably French to the French (who still consider him a minor poet), this immigrant writer, Jules Laforgue, had a strange ear for words. Obsessively Anglophile – he married an Englishwoman – Laforgue was fascinated by Hamlet and Ophelia. Addicted to Shakespeare, he also loved oddly Byronic rhymes: 'défroques' (knee-socks) chimes with 'époque' (epoch) in his poem 'Esthétique'. The first significant Francophone poet to use a form of *vers libre*, Laforgue was, too, a master of rhyme and form. Indeed, possessing a compulsively insinuating music, his verse seemed to fuse the two together. Tom took some time to learn from all this, but learn he did. By the end of 1909 he was beginning to imitate Laforgue in his own 'Nocturne' (published in the *Advocate* that November) and 'Humouresque (after J. Laforgue)' (*Advocate*, January 1910). Laforgue released in him a new music, a fresh voice. This emergent ironic sound came at first a little falteringly, yet soon became not the acoustic of an undergraduate imitator, but the uncannily recognisable voice of T. S. Eliot.

Before late 1908, Tom had never heard of Laforgue. By late 1909 he was almost his reincarnation. The experience was like falling in love. A decade later, when his marriage was in trouble, Tom used strikingly erotic language to describe vital, transformational reading, implying, perhaps, that (though the object of attention was a dead man) it had been better than falling in love. 'When a young writer is seized with his first passion of this sort he may be changed, metamorphosed almost, within a few weeks, from a bundle of second-hand sentiments into a person.'[6]

Though he could not have expressed it so arrestingly in 1909, Tom's encounter with Laforgue had this remarkable power. At a deep level there is less a one-to-one mapping between Laforgue's poetry and Tom's than a weird sense of confirmatory consonance. The 'cosmiques chloroformes' of Laforgue's 'Jeux' (Games) is not the verbal equivalent of the verb 'etherised' at the start of 'The Love Song of J. Alfred Prufrock', but surely it nourishes that poem. From his childhood, Tom would have seen the famous Ether Monument – a tribute to pioneers of anaesthetic surgery – in the Boston Public Gardens.[7] The daring modernity of 'When the evening is spread out against the sky / Like a patient etherised upon a table', prefacing mention of 'half-deserted streets', has been spurred by a related daring in the Laforgue who could write in 'L'hiver qui vient' (The Coming Winter) of how 'La rouille ronge en leurs spleens kilométriques / Les fils télégraphiques des grandes routes où nul ne passe': lines which Peter Dale translated as 'Rust along deserted thoroughfares / Gnaws the kilometric spleens of telegraph wire'.[8] Laforgue's shocking modernity, born out of and clashing against his deeply felt Christian upbringing, is everywhere apparent; yet his quirkiness makes him a stunning nineteenth-century minor writer. Without his intoxicating example, however, Tom might have stalled forever.

In 1909 he read Laforgue with delight. Almost a decade later, he still had a vivid sense of 'sending to Paris for the texts', then poring over them after they arrived, acclimatising to the French poet's language.

> I puzzled it out as best I could, not finding half the words in my dictionary, and it was several years later before I came across anyone who had read him or could be persuaded to read him. I do feel more grateful to him than to anyone else, and I do not think that I have come across any other writer since who has meant so much to me as he did at that particular moment, or that particular year.[9]

Laforgue's most intent American reader was this shy, bright, sexually inexperienced twenty-one-year-old, anxiously desperate to sound utterly knowing in his Bolo poems and, though he had not yet managed it, in other poems too. Tom came to believe that Laforgue, 'if not quite the greatest French poet after Baudelaire, was certainly the most important technical innovator' in his development of a form of *vers libre* which 'contracts and distorts' traditional verse measures. Tom read Laforgue alongside 'the later Elizabethan drama' (which he heard in terms of a contracting and distorting of blank verse), and the French poet's ear for language astonished him.[10] In 'Complainte de cette bonne lune' (Complaint of This Good Moon), 'la Lune' (moon) rhymes with 'rancune' (rancour), a rhyme Tom's ear would retain for years and echo in his Laforguian 'Rhapsody on a Windy Night'.[11] Laforgue's devices, such as snapping off bits of the Lord's Prayer, or mixing Classical mythology with modern tawdriness and boredom, would become Eliotic hallmarks. Laforgue's sense of windy desolation, ennui and 'Néant' (Nothingness — a favourite word) haunts some of Tom's early poems. Moreover, in a number of poems Laforgue presents intimate judgements, overheard or imagined in a way that inhibits the speaker. In 1923, crediting this poet with inventing a 'particular type of fragmentary conversation', Tom confessed that he had 'been a sinner myself in the use of broken conversations punctuated by three dots'.[12] When a voice in one of the several Laforgue poems entitled 'Dimanches' (Sundays), begins 'J'aurai passé ma vie à faillir m'embarquer' (I will have spent my life in failing to embark), it offers, surely, an impossibility: a nineteenth-century J. Alfred Prufrock.[13]

'We must all develop our originality in the same way', Tom wrote in 1925, 'by steeping ourselves in the work of those previous poets whom we find most sympathetic.'[14] For him none was more sympathetic than this Frenchman. 'There was', he claimed in 1946, with perhaps a hint of exaggeration, 'no poet, in either country [Britain and the USA], who could have been of use to a beginner in 1908. The only recourse was to poetry of another age and to poetry of another language.'[15] Laforgue remade English speech for him. Several of the more unusual words of Tom's poetry — 'anfractuous', 'bocks', 'cauchemar', 'estaminet', 'hebetude', 'sempiternal' and 'velleities', for instance — also occur in Laforgue's French, while some Laforguian imagery, whether 'sous-marine' (submarine) strangeness or street-lamps or geraniums or bats or urban industrial smoke or horns or whirlpools or Philomel, becomes Tom's too. Laforgue's prose revealed interests in the 'cauchemar' (nightmare) quality of Egyptian art, in experimental metaphysics and mysticism, in the unconscious and a sense 'du moi et du non-moi' (of I and not-I).[16] In his *Moralités Légendaires* where he brought ancient myths and older works of literature disturbingly up to date, Laforgue has Salome encounter the Administrator of Death, conjuring up a labyrinth of corridors and deploying submarine imagery of molluscs and undersea 'silence'. Elsewhere he offers a rocky landscape of 'pittoresque anfractuosité' (picturesque anfractuosity).[17] In 'Pan et la Syrinx' the prose is perforated by weird Wagnerian 'clameurs de Walkyrie!'

Hoyotoho!
Heiah!
Hahei! Heiaho! Hoyohei![18]

Tom's most famous poem is famous not least for its own Wagnerian cries, those of 'Rhine-daughters' transposed from *Götterdämmerung* to the modern-day Thames. Their sounds disturb part III of *The Waste Land*:

Weialala leia
Wallala leialala . . .[19]

Quoting in English, Laforgue could take a familiar passage of Elizabethan drama and recontextualise it: '"*Good night, ladies; good night, sweet ladies! Good night good night!*" Ça chantait, et souvent des gravelures.' (It sings, often dirtily). In *The Waste Land* Tom would redeploy a version of the same line from *Hamlet*. When he wrote in 1928 that 'The form in which I began to write, in 1908 or 1909, was directly drawn from the study of Laforgue together with the later Elizabethan drama', this was true, and Laforgue had encouraged him even to make the connection.[20] Never in the history of English language poetry has the importation of three new French volumes had such spectacular results.

Compared with this, Tom's academic studies were comparatively unexciting. Yet, just as he was about to hit his poetic stride, so in his courses he found a new dedication. Laforgue boosted his confidence. He could be his own man. At times this carried over into his classroom tasks, though not always with stellar results. In the spring of 1909, he took the popular, preening Charles Townsend Copeland's course on English Composition, English 12. Tom submitted on 2 March a neatly handwritten essay about an author whose work he had known since childhood. He began with a title and an opening sentence that adopt a confident tone:

The Defects of Kipling

As the novelty of certain innovations dies away, as the school of literature of which Mr. Kipling is the most illustrious representative, the exotic school, passes with all its blemishes exaggerated more and more into the hands of less brilliant practitioners, so Kipling's fame is fading, and his unique charm is diminished.

Professor Copeland changed Tom's word 'brilliant' to 'able'. He described this as 'A mouth-filling sentence'. A seasoned public reader of verse, Copeland had a sense of the oratorical. He was strict with Tom, whose judgement he considered 'harsh', though 'with some elements of truth'. Tom thought some of Kipling's short stories such as 'the "End of the Passage"' (which later supplies an image in 'The Hollow Men') were 'masterpieces'; Copeland, grading Tom's essay B+, wanted to keep this student in his place. 'Youthful rashness', he wrote waspishly, 'is not likely to be one of your attributes, at least till you are middle-aged'.[21] Attempting to project mature confidence in his verdicts, Tom only succeeded in amusing his teacher. Still, B+ was a higher mark than any he had got for his previous year's courses. Overall on English 12, Copeland graded him B — also Tom's grade on Rand's two Latin half-courses, and on Comp. Lit. 7 with Murray Potter. Both of Professor Schofield's Comp. Lit. half-courses brought him As, however: his first such marks since his freshman-year English 28. Things were starting to look up.

During that spring of 1909 he absorbed not just Laforgue, but also a new book by a recent Harvard graduate who had served on the *Advocate* editorial board of 1908. Poet-critic Van Wyck Brooks, whom Tom later claimed to 'remember at Harvard as a dapper little man with a taste for Charles Lamb', had fallen in love with European culture.[22] Like Henry James he had crossed the Atlantic in pursuit of it. Precociously, Brooks had completed in October 1908 a critique of American mores, *The Wine of the Puritans: A Study of Present-Day America*. In his first published book review Tom wrote about this volume admiringly for the May 1909 *Advocate*. Brooks thought New England's Protestant and Unitarian values of thrift and industry (represented by Whittier and Emerson) 'unable to meet the needs of great prosperity, imperialism and cosmopolitanism'; Emerson's thought, 'the direct result of a provincial training', might have been 'rational as an explanation of the peculiar life of one corner of the world' but was 'inadequate to explain life in the wider sense'. Acutely aware of what he perceived as American provincialism and of a need to learn more about European culture, if only to establish a sophisticated 'tradition for those who come after', Brooks wanted an idiom to express 'full-grown, modern self-consciousness'. The American, he argued, was 'independent of tradition'; lacking an appropriate reservoir of myths and tradition suitable for 'modern, cosmopolitan life', he had 'to think it all out for himself'. That was what Tom, with Laforgue's help, sought to do. With apparent approval he quoted – or, not entirely uncharacteristically, misquoted – Brooks's wish for a future when 'the names of Denver and Sioux City will have a traditional antique dignity like Damascus and Perugia – and when it will not seem to us grotesque that they have'.[23]

Brooks's book, exposing, as Tom put it, 'the failure of American life (at present) – social, political, in education and in art', was 'if one take it rightly, a wholesome revelation'.[24] Yet, however increasingly Francophile, Tom felt strong New England filiations. 'Those of us who can claim any New England ancestors', he wrote in the *Advocate* three weeks later, 'may congratulate ourselves that we are their descendants', though he added that such descendants could 'rejoice that we are not' those ancestors' 'contemporaries'. Reacting against his American familial inheritance, he also loved and venerated it. This would become a lifelong pattern. Even as he read Jules Laforgue, he relished 'fine old ships' and locations such as Salem or nearby Baker's Island – which he probably knew through his own sailing exploits with his friends. He wanted to afford 'our New England forbears . . . the grace of recognition'.[25] Yet, commenting on Tom's article in a review, Harvard's Dean Briggs thought it revealed immaturity: '"Gentlemen and Seamen" treats of the old merchant sea-captains in New England and of Salem, the old seaport for trade with the East. The feeling in the article is good; but the imperfect workmanship and the tendency to moralize give the effect of a school composition.'[26] Harsh but fair, such criticism indicated Tom was not yet a fully fledged writer. That May, after reading *The Wine of the Puritans*, he contributed to the 'cocktail chorus' of the Fox. Having found a place in his life for Sandow exercises as well as for avant-garde French poetry, he argued there needed to be room at university both for the physical liveliness of the 'sport' and for the studious pursuits of the 'grind'.[27] Mixing immaturity and precocious brilliance, he bided his time.

Thanks to Tom's father's wealth, money for his studies was never a problem. By the time he had completed sufficient classes for his A.B. (Bachelor of Arts) degree in summer 1909, taking into account half-courses and whole ones, he had a total of 1.5 courses at grade A, 6.5 at grade B, 5 at C and 1 at D. It was hardly a stellar record, but his marks had improved in his third year (no Cs or Ds then), and he stayed on for a fourth, studying for a master's degree. As he matured, his interest in European culture increased. Henry James was the consummate novelist of New England society's engagement with Europe, and Tom read *The American, The Europeans* and *The Portrait of a Lady*. Friends including Conrad Aiken went off to Europe that summer, and considered living in London or Paris. Tom, though, as usual, summered in New England (sailing off the Maine coast), and could only read about those European capitals.[28]

Still, he was hardly leading a deprived existence. To his father's relief, he looked likely to graduate as a credit to the family. Generously bank-rolled, the young man made arrangements to live during his master's year in one of the largest rooms in Apley Court, the swankiest private dormitory in Cambridge. Built in ornamented red brick, this lavish, five-storey block on Holyoke Street towered over the small wooden house next door. Its fine lobby led to a marble staircase; its large rooms boasted magnificent woodwork and handsome fireplaces. Apley Court was associated with wealth, aestheticism and such figures as Pierre La Rose, termed by Tom's brother 'The nifty Prince of Apley Court'.[29] Moving into this regal splendour, now Tom applied himself more intensively to his studies as well as to extra-curricular reading and writing. In the first term of 1909–10 Tinckom-Fernandez 'made a desperate effort to get editorials from him' for the *Advocate* and was forced 'to run him to earth in his room' at Apley Court where Tom, 'working harder than ever', had become 'a recluse'.[30]

He took three courses in 1909–10 with Professor William Allan Neilson. One was English 1 (on Chaucer), which Neilson co-taught with Fred Robinson; the others were Neilson's own courses: Comparative Literature 18 (Studies in the History of Allegory) and English 24 (Studies in the Poets of the Romantic Period). The terms Classicism and Romanticism were important to Neilson. He used them not so much to designate literary periods as to highlight 'persistent tendencies'. Just as he saw the Middle Ages and the Renaissance as interlinked, so Neilson was wary of splitting apart a Classical from a Romantic era. In 1911 he gave a lecture series, published the following year, drawing on his teaching 'of students in Harvard University':

> Romanticism is the tendency characterized by the predominance of imagination over reason and the sense of fact. Classicism is the tendency characterized by the predominance of reason over imagination and the sense of fact. Realism is the tendency characterized by the predominance of the sense of fact over imagination and reason.

Deprecating Rousseau, Neilson was suspicious of a vagueness associated with 'Romanticism'. Enumerating prose writers from Balzac, Flaubert and

Tolstoy to 'Howells and James in America', he thought that the temper of the modern age was 'truth to fact'. A scientific age was interested not least in the 'psychological', though 'in poetry . . . we are still in the romantic age'. For Neilson 'We have suffered, and we continue to suffer, from a defect of the classical qualities, both in creation and in appreciation: we have much to gain from a greater reverence for tradition, a finer sense of the beauty of retained and regulated form, a more rigorous intellectual discipline.'[31] These became Tom's beliefs too.

Neilson's views had a good deal in common with those of another of Tom's teachers that session, Professor Irving Babbitt, whom Neilson signed up to write on 'literary criticism' for his series of volumes, The Types of English Literature.[32] When Tom took his half-course French 17hf, Literary Criticism in France with Special Reference to the Nineteenth Century, Babbitt was an Assistant Professor best known for his recent volume, *Literature and the American College: Essays in Defense of the Humanities.* Unlike most of Tom's other teachers, but like Matthew Arnold, whose work Babbitt admired, this professor wrote for a wide audience; much of his recent book had appeared in the *Atlantic Monthly* and the *Nation.* As a young man, Babbitt had studied at Harvard and in Paris, and, though he taught modern literature, his background was in Classics, Sanskrit and Pali. He had an interest in Buddhist as well as in Christian thought, but was not a Christian. Like Neilson, Babbitt disparaged Rousseau's Romantic 'horror of every form of discipline', arguing that 'Liberty, to be humanized, must be tempered by true restraint'. Babbitt supported democracy, but, attuned to the writings of France's Charles Maurras, advocated 'an aristocratic and selective democracy'. In a culture dominated by capitalism and commerce, Babbitt spoke up for 'Academic Leisure', saw the value of 'monasteries' and argued that to benefit society colleges must 'insist on the idea of quality'. He was suspicious of Harvard's cafeteria-style elective system, and even of the 'sudden prosperity' of 'Comparative literature' if it took students away from '"the constant mind of man"'. Defending an ideal he termed 'humanism', he wanted 'Genuine originality', which was 'a hardy growth, and usually gains more than it loses by striking deep root into the literature of the past'.[33]

Influenced by Babbitt, Tom came to share many of these ideals. The half-course he took drew on material soon developed in Babbitt's *The Masters of Modern French Criticism* which sought 'to criticise critics' and to portray the 'ideal critic'.[34] Tom, future author of *To Criticize the Critic* and 'The Perfect Critic', would recommend Babbitt's book in 1916. It saw the fashionable French thinker Henri Bergson as 'perhaps the chief spokesman' of a 'new tendency' in French thought which foregrounded anti-intellectualism.[35]

Though later he came to disagree with some of Babbitt's non-Christian emphases, over the next few years Tom inclined towards Paris, towards the study of Sanskrit and Pali, towards Buddhist thought and towards a politically conservative ideology engaged with adventurous aesthetics and expounded through prose that might reach beyond academic classrooms. At the end of his life Tom wrote that Babbitt was the 'one teacher at Harvard' who 'had the greatest influence on me'.[36]

In 1909–10 he also studied with George Pierce Baker, taking his course English 14 on The Drama in England from the Miracle Plays to the Closing of the Theatres. This professor introduced students not only to medieval English religious dramas but also to Ben Jonson's stagecraft and work by lesser known Elizabethan and Jacobean playwrights including Dekker and Heywood.[37] Baker's interest in theatre was practical. Plays were scripts for performance, and he liked to mingle with students. Tom's cousin Eleanor Hinkley was developing an interest in drama, as was his cousin and fellow Harvard student, Fred Eliot. The taste for drama that Tom shared with Baker ran alongside his rather different enthusiasm for vaudeville and melodrama – all part of what his father complained about when he complained in 1910 that Tom was 'too dramatic busy' at Harvard.[38]

Poetry, though, was his first love, and several fellow students knew it. For session 1909–10 'Thomas S. Eliot' was elected secretary on the *Advocate*'s Board of Editors.[39] His friend Tinckom-Fernandez began that session as president, though he left before its end, heading back to New York. Other companions and acquaintances such as Haniel Long and Conrad Aiken were on the Board too, along with 1910 classmen including poet Rogers MacVeagh. Tom's position as 'Secretary' suggests that, even while immersed in the poems of Laforgue, he was regarded as a safe pair of hands. On 13 December 1909, he was nominated Odist of the Class of 1910 in a ballot held in the Lodge of Harvard's Class of '77 Gate, one of the entrances to the Yard. Alan Seeger stood for Class Poet, a separate position, so he and Tom were not in direct competition. When the votes were counted that Monday evening at the *Crimson* office, Seeger lost to Edward Eyre Hunt, but Tom beat his rival, MacVeagh, comfortably.[40] In the summer he would have to stand in front of a vast audience at his class graduation and read his poem aloud. Even more than at Smith Academy, this was bound to make his parents proud.

In due course Tom wrote to inform his mother. 'You must be sure', she replied, 'and secure tickets when the time comes for Father and me to hear your Ode'.[41] He mentioned, too, that he was about to give a lecture (probably to a student society) and to visit New Haven. He had been in the habit of sending home copies of the *Advocate* when he had work

Young Eliot

published there. Lottie, conscious of her own relative failures as poet and teacher, was very keen that her 'dear Boy . . . receive early the recognition I strove for and failed'. She wished he would send letters more frequently. What were his most recent marks? Would he please send them now? She was, she assured Tom, 'interested in every detail of your life'.[42]

Apparently, he had not been going into full details about his latest reading and writing. Some knowledge was best kept secret. He had been drafting several poems influenced by Laforgue and other French poets. He did, though, signal to his parents that his work, encouraged by courses such as Babbitt's, was taking him in the direction of French culture and that he would like to go to Paris. His mother made it clear in April 1910 that she had 'rather hoped you would not specialize later on in French literature', and wondered if he might change his mind. 'I cannot bear to think of your being alone in Paris, the very words give me a chill. English speaking countries seem so different from foreign. I do not admire the French nation, and have less confidence in individuals of that race than in English.'[43] In Lottie Eliot's St Louis, fashionable Paris was still the City of Sin. To Tom it meant Baudelaire, Laforgue and others whose work fascinated him; it was that heady philosopher Bergson's headquarters, the capital of sophistication, a compass point for Americans, from Henry James to Van Wyck Brooks, eager to engage with European culture. He made clear his resolute Francophilia. Probably his mother didn't know the half of it.

That session Tom took cosmopolitan Santayana's course Philosophy 10 (Philosophy of History) which examined ideals of society, religion, art and science in their historical development – further reminders that there was a world out there much greater than St Louis or New England. Santayana's teaching seems to have drawn on his recent five-volume *The Life of Reason, or the Phases of Human Progress*, a vast comparative survey of intellectual life which, like Babbitt's writings, considered aristocratic and democratic ideals while showing a marked, if agnostic, interest in religion. As would Tom, Santayana speculated about knowledge and experience, from the mores of 'savages' to the world around him: 'Progress, far from consisting in change, depends on retentiveness. When change is absolute there remains no being to improve and no direction is set for possible improvement: and when experience is not retained, as among savages, infancy is perpetual. Those who cannot remember the past are condemned to repeat it.'[44]

Born in Spain, though schooled at Harvard, Santayana was fascinated by the aesthetics of Catholicism. He left Harvard not long after teaching Tom's class, and his later novel, *The Last Puritan*, satirises New England

132

life as repressedly small-minded. Tom remembered 'when an undergraduate' thinking Santayana 'rather a poseur, who chose to look down upon New Englanders as provincial Protestants'.[45] Determined to come to terms with any threat of provincialism, early that session Tom had been reading the work of yet another American Francophile. In October 1909 he contended that 'Now that Arthur Symons is no longer active in English letters, Mr. James Huneker alone represents modernity in criticism.' He had found Huneker's biography of Chopin interesting and, cheekily, he made clear just what he loved about this critic's writing: 'he is far too alert to be an American; in his style and in his temper he is French'.[46]

'I suppose I am not enough of a scholar to know what is termed the "particular genius" of any people', Tom's mother wrote, rather woundedly, to her son, cautioning him against undue Francophilia.[47] Over half of Huneker's *Egoists: A Book of Supermen* was given over to French culture, and some of the rest to Nietzsche. Allusively, Huneker ranges from the 'colossal and muscular humanity' of Michelangelo to 'Rochefoucauld', Dostoevsky's *Crime and Punishment* and 'Jules Laforgue'. He links Laforgue's Hamlet to Stendhal's 'timidity with women'. Huneker is interested in Stendhal's dislike of America for being too 'democratic' and 'utilitarian' to produce art. Quoting Stendahl's remark, 'My head is a magic lantern', Huneker regards Stendahl as a 'man of action paralysed little by little because of his incomparable analysis'. Some of this inveigled its way into Prufrock who has his own nervously cerebral 'magic-lantern'. Writing of 'muffled delirium' (an arresting phrase which anticipates, perhaps, Tom's later 'chilled delirium' in 'Gerontion'), Huneker linked John Donne to Baudelaire. He admired Baudelaire's 'power of blasphemy', seeing him as a 'strayed' Manichaean Christian, 'the patron saint of *ennui*' whose 'disharmony of brain and body' and 'spiritual bilocation, are only too easy to diagnose; but the remedy? *Hypocrite lecteur – mon semblable – mon frère!*' Tom, who had been reading Baudelaire as well as the other French poets in *Poètes d'Aujourd'hui*, would remember that line too. It ends the first section of *The Waste Land*, while his later Baudelaire essay too owes debts to Huneker.[48]

Tom's extra-curricular student reading was remarkably resilient in shaping his subsequent work. Huneker's 'The Pessimist's Progress' praised French novelist Joris-Karl Huysmans (whose work Tom read), not least for depicting 'the nervous distaste of a hypochondriac for meeting people'. Huysmans was a 'singer of neurasthenia' whose characters 'suffer from paralysis of the will, from hyperaesthesia'. Yet Huneker also pointed to Huysmans's preoccupation with 'the perverse odour of perfumes', and the figure of Salome, 'symbolic deity of indestructible Lust, the goddess of immortal Hysteria'. A Catholic convert with a penchant for writing about Paris, Huysmans delighted in reading 'the mystics' including 'St. John of the Cross'. Huneker admitted that Huysmans's 'union of Roman Catholicism and blasphemy has proved to many a stumbling block'.[49] Yet Tom was fascinated by 'the genius of faith' he read about in Huneker as well as by other kinds of 'perverse and lunary genius'.[50]

Chatting with Tom in early 1909, Haniel Long was struck by his discriminating knowledge of modern fiction. They discussed novels by Thomas Hardy and George Meredith.[51] Tom was particularly interested in Henry James. Revealingly, 'in the matter of English style', he found what Huneker (in *Overtones*) had to say about James especially 'illuminating'.[52] Huneker's James was 'in rebellion against conventional art forms'. *What Maisie Knew* and *The Ambassadors* revealed a 'fastidious artist' who was nonetheless (like fastidious Laforgue) 'among the revolutionists'. This writer, 'a Puritan tempered by culture', had learned from Hawthorne. James showed how a New England inheritance might be fused with the sometimes scandalous stylishness of France. Thanks to 'French influences', Henry James, fascinated by how 'Americans abroad suffer a rich sea change', and preoccupied, like his brother William, by the workings of psychology, had developed a style which was 'a jungle of inversions, suspensions, elisions, repetitions, echoes, transpositions, neologisms'. This 'elliptical method' free of 'descriptive padding' drew on Flaubert's 'oblique psychology', producing more than one 'exquisite portrait'. Thanks to French influences, and in an era when so many Americans flocked to Paris that they had been accused of turning the French capital into 'a "sinister Chicago"', James had issued 'a declaration of independence' and created 'companion work to the modern movement in music, sculpture, painting'.[53] Tom, though he had not yet discovered how to do so, sought to do likewise. Paris was the place for it.

Could one be Parisian without leaving America? Tom remembered seeing Van Wyck Brooks in a 'French restaurant', Petitpas, at 317 West Twenty-ninth Street in Manhattan – a venue redolent of 'little corners of Montmartre' – where 'Van Wyck Brooks, Alan Seeger', the rich lawyer turned art patron John Quinn and the artist Jack B. Yeats, nicknamed 'the seer of Petitpas' (and famous as brother of the poet), often foregathered.[54] Yet being Parisian in Gloucester, Massachusetts, was harder. Nevertheless, Tom was keen to sound as Parisian as he could. Probably in the summer of 1909, in Procter Brothers Co., based at Gloucester's Old Corner Bookstore, he bought a lined seventy-two-page notebook. At some point he wrote in black ink on its front flyleaf 'Inventions of the March Hare', and by November he was beginning to invent poems in it, such as 'Short

Romance' (published in 1916 as the more French-sounding 'Conversation Galante') in which a nervously wordy (presumably male) speaker and a female interlocutor discuss such topics as the moon and piano-playing. The interchange is brittle, nervy, Laforguian; underlying it are fears of inanity. The poem's discussion of the music of an 'exquisite nocturne', and the repeated word 'eternal' (used of 'madam'), may owe something to Huneker's *Overtones*, whose essay 'The Eternal Feminine' asks whether women can play Chopin as well as men. Like this poem and the later, Jamesian-titled, Chopin-related 'Portrait of a Lady' and Prufrock's self-conscious 'Love Song', Huneker's work presents women as 'other' and as intimidating in their retorts: 'These long-haired, soft-eyed animals, as Guy de Maupassant describes them, are our true critics weighing us ever in scales that are mortifyingly candid.'[55] Huneker thought Chopin 'the favourite composer of women'; The 'Lady' in Tom's 'Portrait' thinks 'Chopin' is 'So intimate' that 'his soul / Should be resurrected only among friends'.[56] In another poem which Tom wrote into his notebook about a month later, 'a lady' is overheard exclaiming, '"Where shall I ever find the man! / One who appreciates my soul". . .'[57]

Tom juxtaposed such soulfulness with very different material. Setting out to write about the lower-class area of North Cambridge, but taking motifs and rhymes from Laforgue, Verlaine and others, in his notebook he would deploy seedy urban images with conviction for the first time: 'yellow evening . . . dirty windows . . . broken glass . . . tattered sparrows . . . the gutter'; his 'First Caprice in North Cambridge' – rhyming a little dissonantly the word 'patience' with a rather mannered last line, 'Oh, these minor considerations! . . .' has all the calculated awkwardness and dismissive shift of tone that characterise Laforgue's poetry.[58] Exclaiming over 'The charm of vacant lots!', eyeing 'debris of a city' and juxtaposing such observations with ironic invocations of 'aesthetic laws', Tom was writing French American poetry.[59] Practising for Paris, he was finding his style. Almost casually, later in 1910 when he went to the French capital, he would delete the words 'North Cambridge' from the title of his 'Fourth Caprice in North Cambridge' and pencil in instead 'Montparnasse'.[60]

For now, his Harvard teachers, fellow students and the books he read were his guides to European culture. In March 1909, Haniel Long had written, Boston was 'crazy over Wagner'.[61] *Tristan und Isolde* was performed that month at the Metropolitan Opera in New York; Tom mentions 'New York' in his 'Humouresque (after J. Laforgue)', published in January 1910, shortly after Boston's new Opera House had opened in November. The Met performance led a reviewer to enthuse over 'all the emotions that sweep through the soul of Wagner's heroine'.[62] For Huneker in *Overtones*, *Tristan und Isolde* represented 'the subjugation of man by woman'; its 'epic sweep' made it comparable with the *Divine Comedy* and *Hamlet*. 'One of the most complex scores in existence', it was, nonetheless, 'built upon but one musical motive'. Within it lay 'the seeds of the morbid, the hysterical, and the sublimely erotic – hallmarks of most great modern works of art'.[63] Tom, when he first responded to Wagner in 'Opera' in November 1909, wrote in terms of 'love torturing itself'. With Laforguian defensiveness his poem reacts with 'a feeble smile'. Its speaker concludes, 'I feel like the ghost of youth / At the undertakers' ball'.[64] This tone, in part young and in part beyond all youth, was one he would perfect in other poems. He sought an armature of sophistication that would allow him, like Laforgue, to voice powerful emotion and vulnerability, yet avoid the sentimental. Watching Romeo woo Juliet under 'a bored but courteous moon', his 'Nocturne', published in the November 1909 *Advocate*, takes a similar tack. Its mixture of blood, tears and 'climax' is mocked through the speaker's 'best mode oblique'.[65]

His last six months at Harvard saw Tom perfecting his Anglophone French voice. 'Spleen' sounds like a title from Baudelaire, but belongs to a poem Tom published in the *Advocate* in late January. Its first word, 'Sunday' (repeated in the second line), was produced, surely, by Laforgue's several poems entitled 'Dimanches' (Sundays), and the 'fastidious' figure of 'Life' who stands, 'a little bald and gray', is Jamesian but also Laforguian, in his 'tie and suit', waiting 'On the doorstep of the Absolute'.[66] Tom, too, was waiting, waiting to go. He and Tinckom-Fernandez had encountered 'in college' some of the early work of that transplanted American poet, Ezra Pound, who had crossed the Atlantic some years earlier.[67] Tom didn't like it much (it sounded old-fashioned), but did ponder the idea of moving to Europe to write. By the summer he had completed all his coursework, including his final art history course, Florentine Painting, taught by Emerson's grandson Edward Waldo Forbes, a Europhile Boston Brahmin recently appointed Director of Harvard's Fogg Museum.

At Forbes's lectures Tom took copious notes, not least on the work of Filippo Lippi. Forbes, who had studied English at Oxford and possessed a lifelong interest in poetry, was a shrewd observer of paintings. To sharpen their powers of observation he sent students to look at works in the Fogg and in books. From late February until mid-April 1910 Tom made regular careful pencil sketches of religious images from Italian art. He reproduced two studies of the head of Christ, and of three female saints. He drew the head of a man, after the fifteenth-century Florentine painter Masaccio; and the head of an angel, after Giotto's *La Speranza*, as well as the kneeling figure of a neophyte – again after Masaccio. Waldo Forbes kept Tom's sketches, and later donated them to Harvard. Tom's written answer to a question asking him to describe a work by the Florentine painter Antonio Pollaiuolo has been preserved: he examines a painting of St Sebastian 'on a warm light ground'.[68] This is the picture (now attributed to Piero del Pollaiuolo) in London's National Gallery, and later ticked in Tom's London Baedeker (bought in October 1910).[69] It shows a near naked Sebastian tied to a stake and raised aloft, surrounded by archers firing arrows at him. Different from his mother's pen-portraits of martyrs, yet linked perhaps to that interest in mysticism and strange visions of saints enjoyed by Huysmans and other scandalous French writers, this visual image of the tortured saint would stay with Tom and would soon be supplemented by others. These were images of tormented masculinity.

Making tiny, nuanced verbal revisions to further comments on Renaissance art (e.g., by scoring out 'charm' and substituting 'interest'), Tom took extensive notes, for instance, on the 'spiritual sensualism' of Leonora Buti as seen by Florentine monk-cum-artist Filippo Lippi, '*The painter of Women*' : 'Leonora was in somewhat the same condition that F had been. Shut up. This was the 1st opportunity she had to gratify her instincts, and she took it. She is supersubtle & delicate, sensual, nervous, languid, the instinct of sex stronger than the instinct of maternity.' Tom made extended notes as Forbes, mentioning Robert Browning's poem 'Fra Lippo Lippi', lectured about how poetry, repression and sexuality could come together in art.

> I do not think that Browning's characterization of Filippo gives quite all of the personality which is found in the man's work. Browning's Lippo is a sort of jolly Rabelaisian peasant, hating the task of painting saints and saints, longing for freedom and licence. This is true so far as it goes, but the temper of Lippo does not seem to me that of the healthy sensual man of the lower class. True, he was a different man from what he would have been if he had had a normal youth, if he had not been shut up in a monastery at the age of 8, but far from checking and crushing his personality, his misfortune gave him the subtlety and refinement which take him out of the rank of a mere genre painter, and gave his sensuality its peculiar interest. It is not the splendid sensuality of the Venetians, nor the stolid bestiality of Rubens, but the morbid and *maladif* craving of the enforced monk. Filippo is very emotional, & interested in his own emotions: that gives us the feeling of a personal, self conscious confession. His emotions have the refinement of Angelico's, but lacking Angelico's idealism, they are turned in on themselves.[70]

Fascinated by the intense self-consciousness of Laforgue, Tom wrote all this down carefully. Obsessed with women who talk of Renaissance art, yet turned in on himself, J. Alfred Prufrock would soon articulate his own 'morbid and *maladif* [sickly] craving'.

Suddenly Tom himself was ill. His father wrote anxiously to his uncle, Thomas Lamb Eliot, on 12 May: Tom had been hospitalised in Cambridge. He had suspected scarlet fever, said to have reached epidemic proportions in Boston. In distant St Louis his parents were desperate for information: 'Lottie goes to Boston tonight.'[71] Tom lay in Harvard's Stillman Infirmary, which had its own quarantine facility. Scarlet fever was potentially fatal. His brother Henry had been left partially deaf after contracting this disease in childhood. Yet apart from the awful matter of having to confront the possibility of dying, the worst that happened to Tom, who weathered the storm, was that he missed his concluding examinations in English 14, Fine Arts 20b and French 17. Special arrangements were made for him to receive final grades.[72] About a month after he was released from hospital in Cambridge, he wrote a poem about a fearful 'Silence' linked to 'the ultimate hour'. It was not ostensibly autobiographical, but its account of being 'terrified' at having to face up to an absolute 'peace' registers emotional disturbance.[73]

From dramatic hospitalisation in May, he progressed to June graduation. He was designated to do duty as one of two students charged with supervising the 'second spring collection of clothing, magazines and text-books' from Apley Hall when the end-of-term recycling 'wagon' called on Friday 20 May – another indication that he was considered a safe administrative pair of hands.[74] Though not on course to graduate with great distinction, he had recovered. His graduation 'Ode' was ready for publication in the June *Advocate*. He received grades of B+ for his Chaucer course and B for Professor Baker's Drama course, but got A- for English 24, and straight A's in Babbitt's French class and Santayana's Philosophy 10.[75] Even his relieved father recognised that he had been 'working so hard'.[76]

Then, on Friday 24 June, graduation day arrived. The *Boston Evening Transcript* recorded how 'A pleasant east wind tempered the heat, yet left the air warm enough to tempt the girls to wear their filmiest of Class Day gowns.' Harvard's lawns were verdant after the previous week's rain. In the Yard, where the old elms looked sadly 'moth-eaten', most of the Seniors assembled in front of Holworthy Hall and 'marched' to Appleton Chapel where Tom's Philosophy professor, G. H. Palmer, offered prayers. Then at 10.30 a.m. there was a procession to Sanders Theatre. During the ceremonies there Edward Eyre Hunt read an interminable poem of his own composition; William Richard Ohler, emphasising 'service', orated on the topic of 'Harvard and the Community'. Tom's proud parents heard the Class Ode 'recited by Thomas Stearns Eliot and then sung by the class to the tune "Fair Harvard," the singing being led by the class chorister, Twining Lynes'. Tom's ode's two eight-line stanzas concluded elegantly, formally, and in a style as far removed from that of Jules Laforgue as can be imagined. Piously he wished for a Harvard-centred vision:

> And only the years that efface and destroy
> > Give us also the vision to see
> What we owe for the future, the present, and past,
> > Fair Harvard, to thine and to thee.[77]

Twenty-first-century readers may hear in that penultimate line an antici-pation of the opening of the first of *Four Quartets*, but for the Eliot family on 24 June 1910 there was the much more pressing matter of 'a monster garden party'. Bands were 'playing in all parts of the grounds'.[78] For twenty-one-year-old Tom, who had managed to get his own way, there was summer, and the promise of Paris.

7
Voyages

BEFORE going to Paris, Tom went to Gloucester. That was his custom every summer, though often, with student friends, he voyaged beyond. So scanty are the records of these voyages, it is impossible to date most of them accurately, but they were important parts of his youth. Boyhood sailing lessons had given him both the assurance and dexterity necessary to handle a boat. With his 'sensitive nature', he may have kept a good deal of his imaginative life to himself, but on the water he felt relaxed.[1] He and his brother loved to put the sailboat *Elsa* through her paces, tacking alertly on the waters off Eastern Point.

His confidence at Gloucester surprised Harvard classmates. Tinckom-Fernandez, who knew him well, recalled that 'in his sophomore year he decided to complete his course in three years and take a master's degree'. Occasionally at 'initiations and punch nights', Tom came 'to expand, in the midst of our hilarity, into his quiet, subtle humor'. Though friends like Howard Morris, relishing the Bolo poems, knew Tom's humour could be anything but subtle, Tinckom-Fernandez recalled him in thoughtful mood: 'He was always ready to lay his book aside and fill his pipe. With his analytical mind his curiosity was insatiable as to the meanings and motives in the literary and social currents of our day. He was always the commentator, never the gusty talker, and seemed to cultivate even then a scholarly detachment.' Yet in vacation time, visiting Tom at the Downs 'in a quiet, charming family circle of parents and sisters', Tinckom-Fernandez was impressed by how his friend 'used to take me sailing in his catboat, and he could handle a sheet with the best in Gloucester'.[2]

He and Tom kept in touch, even after 'Tinck' set off for Europe in 1913, the year he married. Tom saw him off from the Boston docks. They corresponded for a time, but their letters are lost. So is all Tom's correspondence with his closest sailing partner, Harold Peters. Their maritime exploits are recorded in written fragments and photographs. Tom's sense of the sea pervades his poetry. Some of his coastal cruising, especially while he was younger, was along the granite shore of Cape Ann, or past the Dry Salvages, familiar, he later explained, as 'a group of three rocks off the eastern corner of Cape Ann, Massachusetts, with a beacon: convenient for laying a course to the eastward, Maine, or Nova Scotia'.[3] This was the direction he liked to sail in, though sometimes, too, he seems to have headed south towards John Robinson's Salem, or Marblehead. According to Leon Little, Harold 'Pete' Peters introduced Tom

to small-boat cruising and they made many cruises together between Marblehead and the Canadian border. The most spectacular episode of any in these cruises was when, in a 19-foot knockabout, before the days of power, they rounded Mt. Desert Rock in a dungeon of fog, a rough sea and a two-reef breeze. The log book, the next day, shows a sketch of Tom in the tender in a heavy wind unmooring from an enormous pile mooring at Duck Island. The title of the sketch is 'Heroic work by the swab.' They had spent an uncomfortable night at that mooring and had decided in spite of the continuing fog, wind and heavy sea, to leave there for Mt. Desert and a protected harbour. So, now with three reefs, they headed inshore and finally anchored at the little land-locked harbour of Somesville. The last entry in the log for that day was 'Ashore for supper at Somes House, $1, excellent.'[4]

This voyage to what is now part of Acadia National Park was probably Tom's most dangerous. Mount Desert Rock is a remote, treeless island with a nineteenth-century lighthouse and keeper's accommodation. Peters had cruised that part of Maine since at least 1908, when his name and that of Chuck Cobb, another of Tom's Harvard acquaintances, appear in the register of the old inn in the village of North Haven.[5] In 1909 Tom post-carded his mother to say he was having a 'pleasant and lazy' time in 'very warm weather' not far from 'North Haven'.[6] Leon Little, an experienced sailor, thought the trip Tom and Peters made 'around Mt. Desert Rock in the Lynx' was 'crazy'; the *Lynx* was probably the smallest sailboat ever to accomplish such a voyage without power.[7] Little was amazed Tom and Harold Peters had survived.

That they did so is a tribute to their seamanship and luck. An experienced sailor, Peters was naturally sporty in a way that Tom was not. Unsettled, he never married, and would go on to spend much of his life at sea. On a boat, both he and Tom fitted in. Tom liked the camaraderie of such voyages. They introduced him to characters very different from his Harvard professors, though the on-board food was no Signet dinner. When Peters and Leon Little made a trip on the *Lynx* together, Leon boasted they lived entirely on 'bacon, beans, bread and bananas'.[8] A surviving photograph shows Tom in casual hat and short-sleeved shirt, at the wheel of a boat, steering while his companion ('probably Harold Peters') smokes; there was ample liquid refreshment.[9] Though he remembered sleeping at Peters's mother's house, usually Tom and Peters slept on board the *Lynx* or, later, the *Arethusa*.[10] It is clear from Little's correspondence at Harvard that he expected Tom and Peters would have shared Bolovian compositions as part of their close association. Another of Tom's Harvard sailing pals, Clarence Little (also nicknamed 'Pete'), treasured memories of Columbo and Bolo verses.

At least among some of the young men of Tom's circle, these scurrilous poems were useful currency, but he was impressed when, in small-town Maine ports, he met old sailors whose vocabulary might be even more shocking. 'About COARSENESS', he wrote, years later, to Ezra Pound, 'I don't want to boast, so I wont tell you what Capn Eben Lake of Jonesport said to Capn Joe Tibbetts of East Machias about me.' Gleefully he mentioned 'old Ike Carver of Mosquito Cove . . . who fucked the whole of Marshall's Island in one night, at the age of 70'.[11] For the rest of his life he remembered meeting locals when he sailed to places such as Jonesport, Roque Island and Cutler, Maine. '(I shall never forget', he wrote in a parenthesis to Leon Little almost half a century later, 'Pete leading the Grand March at the Jonesport Summer Ball with Mrs. Willie Carver, you never saw anything more respectable) and Lakeman's (we never got to the Wolves, there were said to be some tough lads there)'.[12] Mrs Willie Carver, then in her forties, was Martha Guptill, married to Jonesport lobsterman William Carver and part of a local lobster-fishing family.[13] In the 1950s, remembering this incident, Tom tried to recall a 'nautical ballad' that 'starts so magnificently: It was the schooner Lapwing / From Jonesport bore away . . .'[14] This was the ballad 'Cruise of the Lapwing', composed in 1870 by John Radley, a Jonesport commercial fisherman; it was still being sung by celebrated local balladeer and storyteller Joshua Alley in 1936 when he was ninety-three. It may well have been Alley's singing that Tom remembered from the early twentieth century:

> The good schooner Lapwing, from Jonesport bears away
> She being all spars and canvas, from her bows she heaves the spray
> And as she passes through the Reach and down Kelley stand
> We are going winter fishing to the Isle of Grand Manan.

The air is very cold and vapour o'er the ocean spread
With her lofty spars and canvas, she nobly leaps ahead
And by the wind and on her course, looks up for Cutler head.
Now in Cutler Harbor and safe at anchor rides
With plenty scope ahead of her, to stem the winter tides.

From there this ballad takes the *Lapwing* northwards, away from 'girls on shore' who are 'most jovial company, to pass away the time'. The boat enters stormy waters where 'The wind is fast a-canting, and blowing a half a gale'. Finding few fish, the voyagers reach an ice-scape: 'the ocean is one white sheet; the air is filled with snow and hail'. Here 'amid the ice and snow' the crew hear of a race between schooners 'down by the Duck Islands'.[15] Though he seems never to have sailed in winter up into the ice, Tom loved to recall his adventures in the maritime world of such ballads, the milieu he had read about, too, in *Captains Courageous*. Grand Manan, an island between Maine and New Brunswick (familiar territory to Gloucester fishermen), was at the northern extremity of Tom's voyaging. Years later, recalling 'those places along the coast where Harold Peters and I used to cruise so regularly', he relished again 'the famous occasion on which Peters and I spent the night moored to a spar buoy on the lee shore of Duck Island during such a fog, combined with half a gale of wind'.[16] Eventually they had gone ashore and called at a dwelling.

Such voyaging could be dangerous. This strain of Tom's experience, mixed with and submerged beneath his reading, would permeate his mature poetry, whether in the 'Gull against the wind, in the windy straits / Of Belle Isle' in 'Gerontion' (the Strait of Belle Isle is between Quebec and Newfoundland), or in that long voyage 'From the Dry Salvages to the eastern banks' on which 'everything' goes 'wrong' in the drafts of *The Waste Land*. Tom cut most of that passage, which involved sailing away from 'girls and gin' onshore at 'Marm Brown's joint' and voyaging beyond 'the farthest northern islands' to 'a long white line', a white-out landscape of 'bears' and 'cracked ice'. In the end, he excised everything except the final, eerie drowning of 'Death by Water'. Re-imagined and modified, details there come from experiences he and his student friends had shared: 'The canned baked beans were only a putrid stench'. As in 'The Dry Salvages' itself, the vocabulary is that of a man familiar with sailing: 'the main gaffaws / Jammed . . . A spar split . . . then the garboard-strake began to leak'.[17] That leaking 'garboard strake' would recur in 'Marina', a poem whose pencil manuscript draft locates its foggy setting 'Off Roque Island' in Maine, and which still in its published version communicates wonderfully a sense of lying offshore in fog: 'What seas what shores what grey rocks and what islands / What water lapping the bow'.[18]

By the end of Tom's Harvard days Harold Peters was getting ready to set off on much more distant voyages. Capable yet boyish, he liked Tom, and may even have had a crush on him, but there is no evidence it was reciprocated. Later in life Tom realised that these voyages up the New England coast had become indelibly fixed in his memory. They were a valuable part of him that few of his subsequent friends knew about. His poetry alone shows how deeply such experiences affected him. His days at sea, watching the coast and the fog, or coming ashore to communities of lobstermen and yarners were in their way just as formative as his time spent in the classrooms of Irving Babbitt or hunched over the poems of Laforgue.

Tom's rounding of Mount Desert Rock might have resulted in his failing to come home. So, in a different sense, might his 1910 transatlantic voyaging. Long afterwards he made it clear that during the academic session 1910–11 he thought very seriously about 'giving up English and trying to settle down and scrape along in Paris and gradually write French', as had two earlier minor, Symbolist-affiliated American poets, 'Stuart Merrill and Vielé-Griffin'.[19] Such behaviour would have horrified his parents. He embarked on his first ever transatlantic journey in October 1910, in an era when the crossing took about a week. These voyages were phenomena in themselves. Alan Dale's *The Great Wet Way*, illustrated with comic sketches, gives a fine flavour of what passengers might expect. On board ship there was the chance to '"loaf" a bit'. Dale eavesdrops on typical on-board conversations. '"If I loved Parrus, I should think myself a very poor sort of American", says one woman. "I tell you that Syracuse could give lessons to Parrus any day in the week. Parrus belongs to the past; *we* belong to the future."'[20]

This was not Tom's attitude. Instead, recalling 1910–11, he told a French audience, 'Tantôt Paris était le passé; tantôt tout l'avenir: et ces deux aspects se combinaient en un présent parfait' (Paris, on the one hand, was wholly the past; on the other, it was wholly the future; and these two aspects combined to make a perfect present).[21] If this magnificent European capital was vibrant, then even the journey there was exciting. According to Alan Dale, crossing the Atlantic in this era involved Americans in constant 'flirtations' on board ship. Though some 'nervous passengers' were 'distracted' by the 'Wagnerian *leit-motif*' of the fog horn, transatlantic sailing also furnished an abundance of the sort of popular music Tom enjoyed: 'The banjo-soloist flourishes in mid-Atlantic . . . They have a repertoire of awe-inspiring rag-time.' Passengers contributed their own songs, even when ill with *mal de mer*. Dale recalled a choir of twenty in deckchairs who 'gave us the classic numbers of Vesta Victoria, Alice Lloyd, Vesta Tilley, Harry Lauder, and all the rest of the "vaudeville" nightingales of both sexes'.[22] A young poet with a keen satirical eye, Tom disembarked in Europe with no shortage of material. Paris, though, for all that he had read about it, was stimulatingly new.

He stopped off in England for a short time en route: his London Baedeker carries on its title page the solemnly dated black-ink inscription 'Thomas S. Eliot, October the 14th, 1910'.[23] But Paris was his destination. Bankrolled from St Louis, he had set up an arrangement with the stunningly palatial headquarters of Crédit Lyonnais at 19 boulevard des Italiens, in the second arrondissement not far from the Opéra, which allowed him to receive mail there. Tom, however, lived some distance away, on the other side of the Seine, in the Latin quarter. There he had secured a 'petite chambre' in a house looked after by an old French couple, the Casaubons. Madame Casaubon refreshed lodgers with tea from her gleaming silver teapot, and white-bearded Monsieur Casaubon was strikingly elegant. This French husband and wife were used to taking in Anglophone as well as Francophone boarders.[24] There was 'a prim but nice English lady' whom Tom got to know a little; 'she does not understand the American dialect'.[25] Several other residents were Harvard men: liking to sport a 'gold *pince-nez*' the resonantly named, socialist-inclined Henry Wadsworth Longfellow Dana, grandson of the author of *Two Years Before the Mast*, shared Tom's taste for Dante. Dana had come from Harvard two years earlier to lecture on English at the Sorbonne.[26]

Arrested decades later in New York for allegedly propositioning a teenage boy, Dana, like another of the Pension Casaubon's residents, Matthew Prichard, was probably homosexual.[27] Tom's brother had introduced him to Prichard, an Englishman who had worked for Boston's Museum of Fine Arts and had known Isabella Stewart Gardner. Tom later mentioned Prichard's 'very remarkable sensibility'; in Paris, like Tom, Prichard discussed Bergson's philosophy. He was also friendly with English art critic Roger Fry and enthusiastic about Byzantine art at Ravenna and San Marco.[28] Prichard had got to know Henri Matisse in 1909, introducing him to Byzantine visual culture. In 1910 he took Tom to meet Matisse.[29] Going beyond Gauguin, Matisse was then experimenting with non-naturalistic colour, and had recently painted the 'primitive' frolicking female nudes of *La Danse*. Yet, later at least, Tom was wary of Prichard: 'I should prefer not to see him again.'[30]

When Tom arrived, Dana was already used to Paris. Certainly he could advise Monsieur Eliot who was to enrol as a foreign student at the Sorbonne and attend Bergson's lectures at the Collège de France. Prichard was able to tell Tom about Bergson, and emerging artistic developments such as Cubism and Futurism: Cubist art became a Paris sensation at an April 1911 exhibition; Futurism had featured in *Le Figaro* since at least 1909.[31] 'My opinions on art, as well as other subjects, have modified radically', Tom wrote in 1911. In Paris, he recalled, 'discussion of Bergson was apt to be involved with discussion of Matisse and Picasso'.[32]

Yet at the Pension Casaubon Tom grew close not so much to fellow Americans as to a French lodger who remarked with a certain sarcasm how 'Monsieur Dana en tressaillerait derrière ses lorgnons d'or' (Monsieur Dana would shudder behind his gold pince-nez). This French medical student, Jean Jules Verdenal, found Prichard boring, prone to being taken in by charlatans. Verdenal joked with Tom about these visiting, apparently gay aesthetes, but it would be wrong to assume Verdenal was either homophobic or anti-American; likewise, it would be naïve to decide that Verdenal, who could use expressions in letters to Tom such as 'Cher ami, je vous serre la main' (Dear friend, I shake your hand), was homosexual.[33] He was a young Frenchman of 1910, who spoke, behaved and wrote as one; in his letters to Tom he used the more formal 'vous' (you), rather than the more intimate 'tu'. Tom, eager to become as much of a young Frenchman of 1910 as he could, found Jean Verdenal the best of companions. He was delighted by how much they shared – from a taste for Laforgue's poetry to philosophical interests, and from tentative habits of mind to astutely ironic observations. Verdenal had friends in Parisian literary circles, and knew such young writers as Jacques Rivière, brother-in-law of the aspiring novelist Alain-Fournier. Remarkably, right here in his lodgings, Tom had found a soulmate.

Even if, in response to his former professor's request, he sent back to Harvard's Edward Waldo Forbes a catalogue from the Trocadéro and offered him brochures from the Luxembourg Museum, Tom had come to Paris to loosen his ties with New England. Situated a short stroll from the Sorbonne and the Collège de France, the Pension Casaubon welcomed Americans, but was most attractive when most Parisian. At 151 bis rue Saint-Jacques it stood between a poultry shop and a café-restaurant. The restaurateur liked to set out chairs and tables on the pavement. Above the Pension's doorway was a balcony with an ornamental wrought-iron railing. A street lamp stood right beside the front door, and at night, when in this part of Paris (as a fellow lodger put it) one could hear at ten o'clock 'all the bells in the area . . . ringing and, almost at the same time . . . a tinkling of fairly distant chimes, soon blotted out by the measured pealing of a deeper bell', the Pension Casaubon's street lamp lit up rows of plucked fowls hanging in the adjoining poulterer's window.[34]

To come from the 'village' of Cambridge to Paris, a capital city of 3,000,000 people still substantially bounded by its ancient city walls, was wonderful. Aged twenty-two, Tom was just a year older than the Eiffel Tower. Four years earlier, not far from his lodgings, Rodin's famous statue, *The Thinker*, had been set up outside the Panthéon. The area around the Pension Casaubon was steeped in several nations' history. Just off the rue Saint-Jacques (an ancient pilgrim route) was the church of St Séverin, its stained glass depicting the murder of England's St Thomas à Becket; near Tom's pension, in the direction of the River Seine, was the medieval rue de Bièvre where Dante (said to have attended lectures nearby) was reputed to have written some of his *Divine Comedy*. Walking by the Seine, Tom could catch a glimpse of 'Anatole France'; then in his mid-sixties, this writer had produced his earliest work while Baudelaire was still alive.[35] The American student liked to saunter in the 'Luxembourg Gardens' near the place Edmond-Rostand, a few hundred yards downhill from his lodgings. There, as young 'Uncle Tom' (aka 'L'Oncle Tom') explained to his six-year-old niece Theodora, children sailed boats in a pond, spun tops and rolled hoops in 'a sort of park like the Boston Public Gardens'.[36] Sketching French infants surrounding him as he bowed, he sent his scribbles to Theodora, who preserved them. She liked Uncle Tom.

The Pension Casaubon was close to both the Collège de France with its imposing statue of Dante, and the Sorbonne, one of the world's oldest universities. Intellectually, Tom found himself at an intersection between ideas emanating from both insitutions. 'At the Sorbonne', where he was now a student, 'the sociologists, Durkheim, Lévy-Bruhl', he observed, 'held new doctrines'.[37] The great Jewish thinker Émile Durkheim, a Sorbonne star, established sociology as a fully-fledged academic discipline. He stressed that individuals were bound to a greater cultural whole, a tradition, though in Europe this bond had been weakened by Christianity's decay. Durkheim had studied at Marburg in Germany; his work's philosophical underpinnings drew on epistemological as well as anthropological thought. From 1906 onwards in his Sorbonne lectures Durkheim outlined the matter of his last great book, *The Elementary Forms of the Religious Life* (1912), which Tom would read in French. Reviewing its 1918 English translation shortly before writing 'Tradition and the Individual Talent', he described it as 'intensely interesting', not least for its ideas about '"group-consciousness"'.[38]

Durkheim's Sorbonne colleague, philosophy professor Lucien Lévy-Bruhl, was also concerned with epistemology, anthropology and religion; in 1910 he published *Les fonctions mentales dans les sociétés inférieures*, arguing that there was a separation between the mentality of 'savages' and that of modern civilised people. Soon Tom took issue with this: Lévy-Bruhl 'appears to me to draw the distinction between primitive and civilized mental process altogether too clearly'.[39] Following those intellectual currents, familiar at Harvard, which linked anthropological thinking to literature, Tom's greatest poetry would juxtapose modern-day life with the rituals of societies supposedly '*inférieures*'. Though the Sorbonne's records of his studies do not survive, he encountered the work of its leading thinkers. He mentioned once working on 'un travail de quelque envergure que je désirais présenter à l'Université' (a project of some magnitude that I wanted to submit to the university).[40]

At that time, he thought, '[Pierre] Janet was the great psychologist.'[41] A correspondent of William James, Janet had lectured at Harvard Medical School on hysteria in 1906, and coined the terms 'subconscious' and 'dissociation' (indicating a psychological detachment from reality). Tom, soon to write a poem called 'Hysteria', would adopt and adapt the word 'dissociation' when, a decade later, he argued that English poetry suffered from a 'dissociation of sensibility'.[42] These Sorbonne thinkers were an important stimulus for his reading about the intersection between religious mysticism, asceticism and hysteria in 'primitive' and modern life. Among his student notes a substantial reading list of works in French and English contains nothing published later than Edward Scribner Ames's *The Psychology of Religious Experience* (1910); almost all the books Tom listed are in the Sorbonne's library. His notes from Janet's 1898 *Névroses et Idées Fixes* include (from Volume II) a summary of 'Observation 95. Woman who showed hereditary traces of hysteria', and cover such topics as hearing voices in different languages and links between sexual pathology and religious rapture. Tom, whose first collection of poems would be made up of 'Observations', noted down, too, details of articles by Maxime Bernier de Montmorand in the *Revue philosophique de la France et de l'étranger* between 1903 and 1905 with titles such as 'L'érotomanie des mystiques chrétiens'. These studies investigated the relationship between asceticism, mysticism and sexual ecstasy. At least one of them argued with the work of 'M. le Dr Pierre Janet' on 'les hystériques' and on those described as '*abouliques*'. Tom jotted down the relevance of this 'to Janet' and 'aboulie theories'.[43] This material and terminology would haunt him.

While these might seem weirdly arcane interests, connections between erotomania and Christian mysticism were also part of the most exciting avant-garde culture Paris had to offer. They not only featured in Janet's lectures but, as Nancy Hargrove points out, were seen also on stage in May 1911 when the Théâtre du Châtelet premiered a shocking five-hour extravaganza, *Le Martyre de Saint Sébastien*, which became 'the talk of Paris'.

With a script by Gabriele d'Annunzio, specially composed music by Debussy, choreography by Mikhail Fokine and costumes by Leon Bakst, its star was Jewish Russian ballerina Ida Rubenstein. She had played Cleopatra in a Ballets Russes production the previous year. Now, cross-dressing, she was Saint Sebastian, dancing ecstatically over burning coals, her ultimate fate to be bound to a tree and martyred by being shot full of arrows. This Sebastian was, one reviewer wrote, 'a woman with a supple and voluptuous body of pale and gleaming flesh who portrays, in languid and sensual dances, the Stations of the Cross' in 'a savage, insane, but very impressive work of art, which produces piercing sensations, divine or diabolical, in our minds'. Jean Cocteau put it more succinctly, '*She is delicious.*'[44]

The Pope had just proscribed d'Annunzio's works. In Sebastian the erotically excited and anthropologically-informed Italian playwright sought to fuse, as he put it, 'Christian myth' with 'the beautiful wounded god' Adonis. 'Let me know your love / again, in the arrows', Sebastian begs the archers. The archbishop of Paris denounced the play, threatening Catholics with excommunication if they went to see it. The row became a public scandal. *Le Figaro* published a cartoon on 25 May depicting a fashionably dressed young woman confessing to a priest that she has seen the drama. 'Combien de fois?' he asks her – 'How many times?'[45] Tom enjoyed Parisian theatre, seeing, for instance, a performance of *Les Frères Karamazov* at the Théâtre des Arts that spring. Whether or not he attended *Le Martyre de Saint Sébastien*, he surely knew about it, and had previously described Pollaiuolo's St Sebastian. Three years later, writing to Conrad Aiken (who had also been in Paris in 1911), enclosing his poem of erotic violence 'The Love Song of St Sebastian', Tom asked, 'no one ever painted a female Sebastian, did they?'[46]

Though no match for d'Annunzio's wild eroticism, the Collège de France nonetheless attracted large audiences – including Parisians who were not students – thanks to the sheer excitement of its lectures. Alfred Loisy, its professor of religion, had been excommunicated recently by the Pope for implying the Catholic Church had betrayed Jesus Christ. 'Loisy', Tom recalled, 'enjoyed his somewhat scandalous distinction'.[47] Even more popular were the Collège de France lectures of Durkheim's old classmate, Bergson, whom Tom remembered as a 'spider-like figure' dangling above Parisian intellectual life.[48] Crowds flocked to Bergson's lectures, so to secure a seat Tom needed to arrive early. He took out his squared-paper exercise book (map of France on the back, illustration of the Paris Odéon on the front), and inked on its cover in block capitals, '**BERGSON** = VENDREDI'. Every Friday in January and February (and perhaps later too, though only these jottings survive), he took notes in French as Bergson discussed 'la psychologie' and 'la personnalité'. Fundamental to these lectures was David Hume's sense of the self not as singular and fixed, but made up of fleeting impressions. Bergson quoted Hume in English, and Tom wrote down the words, 'I always stumble on some particular perception. I never can catch myself.' Though Bergson went on to contend that 'La question de l'unité ou la multiplicité de la vie de la personnalité n'est pas une question vitale' (The question of the unity or multiplicity of the life of the personality is not a vital question), and passed on to Kantian ideas of personality, that notion of the self as fragmentary and in flux would pervade Tom's poetry.[49]

He was far from the only clever Harvard man excited by Bergson's rhetoric. In a piece in the 1909 *Hibbert Journal* (a magazine Tom sometimes read), William James had enthused about the 'lucidity' of Bergson's style: 'It seduces you and bribes you to become his disciple. It is a miracle, and he a real magician.' Harvard enthusiasm for Bergson was part (though only part) of what made Tom so keen to reach Paris in 1910. Iconoclastically, this French philosopher challenged the supremacy of the intellect, and the belief 'that fixity is a nobler and worthier thing than change'. Emphasising the vital 'flux of life', Bergson, explained James, argued that 'Thought deals . . . solely with surfaces. It can name the thickness of reality, but it cannot fathom it.' You must 'Dive back into the flux itself, then, Bergson tells us, if you want to *know* reality.' With regard to past, present and future as well as other supposedly different categories, Bergson's philosophy in *Matter and Memory* and *Creative Evolution* (both of which Tom read eagerly in French) 'presents, *as if they were dissolved in each other*, a lot of differents which retrospective conception breaks life's flow by keeping apart'. Like Tom for a time at least, James was captivated. 'Open Bergson, and new horizons open on every page you read. It is like the breath of the morning and the song of birds. It tells of reality itself, instead of reiterating what dusty-minded professors have written about what other previous professors have thought.'[50] Sitting in Bergson's presence, Tom felt the full force of this almost messianic figure. He experienced a 'conversion'. It would only be 'temporary'.[51]

By the time he listened to Bergson, his French had improved. He was greatly assisted by a private tutor, recently married Henri Alain-Fournier, the brilliant young writer who lived with his wife at 2 rue Cassini in Montparnasse. To reach their house Tom headed southwards about half a mile along the rue Saint-Jacques. Just two years his senior, Alain-Fournier was at the heart of Parisian literary life. So was his twenty-four-year-old friend and brother-in-law, Jacques Rivière, whom Tom also visited 'chez lui' (at his home), who had recently begun to write for *La Nouvelle Revue*

Française, and who knew Tom's fellow-lodger Verdenal.⁵² 'Gauche' Tom had published nothing outside school and student magazines.⁵³ Yet these young men, virtually his own age, were already writing for leading publications in Paris, a city whose international 'predominance' in literature was then, he was sure, 'incontestable'.⁵⁴ Observing and listening to them, he learned not just how to improve his French but also how to raise his game.

He eyed not only the internationally-minded *Nouvelle Revue Française*, to which he soon subscribed, but also other journals including the philosophically and socially engaged *Les Cahiers de la Quinzaine* with its stark 'cover of austere grey paper'.⁵⁵ This was a world away from the *Harvard Advocate*. Yet Alain-Fourier, whom he recalled as a 'quiet-spoken, witty, elegant young man, who spoke with real conviction of his ambition to write a great novel in the tradition of the established French masters', had a combination of ambition, sense of tradition (he made Tom 'recite passages from the classics' of French literature) and apparent reticence that came close to aspects of Tom's own personality.⁵⁶ Tom was given suggestions about what to read: not older French classics, but recent work which, like Laforgue's poetry, helped show this young American writer how he might draw on aspects of what he knew already. 'When I came first to Paris', he recalled, 'I first read *Bubu de Montparnasse*.' This relatively little-known novel of slum life by Charles-Louis Philippe became for him 'a symbol of the Paris of that time' and was admired by Alain-Fournier and Rivière.⁵⁷ Around December 1910 when Tom's 'Fourth Caprice in North Cambridge' became 'Fourth Caprice in Montparnasse', he had begun (he recalled) to work together some earlier fragments into a poem involving the name 'Prufrock'. Featuring a walk through run-down urban streets of the sort familiar to him from America, 'Prufrock's Pervigilium' may feature American-sounding 'drugstores', but its sense of 'narrow streets', 'evil houses' and 'Women, spilling out of corsets' who 'stood in entries / Where the draughty gas-jet flickered/ And the oil cloth curled up stairs' owes debts also to Bubu's Paris.⁵⁸ Tom's French 'romantic year' (as he later termed it) was not 'romantic' in the usual sense.⁵⁹ It left us no poetic descriptions of the Eiffel Tower or kisses in the Champs Élysées. Instead, it helped him incorporate into poetry vignettes of a kind of life he had seen in the alleys of America as well as on the lanes of Montparnasse. It helped him, too, to draw less on the 'romantic' itself than on intense anxieties about it.

Ultimately, Tom became a great poet through learning how to access and articulate unforgettably the wide spectrum of his inner life, his experience and his voracious reading. He learned to face up to and make poetry out of his own hurts, but gave his material a wider resonance through blending it with what he read. Apparently completed in Paris in 1910, the third of his 'Preludes' carries an epigraph from *Bubu*, and steals Philippe's 'sordid images', including 'the yellow soles of feet'. *Bubu*, along with Philippe's *Marie Donadieu*, which Tom read in 1911, also haunts 'Rhapsody on a Windy Night'.[60] That poem features a 'street-lamp' that 'sputtered' and 'muttered', calling attention to an inviting yet intimidating woman of the night, 'the corner of her eye' twisting 'like a crooked pin'.[61] Tom missed female company acutely in Paris; though he conversed with women there, he knew none well, and certainly, as he made clear three years later to Aiken, he did not sleep with any of them. Instead, feeling intensely self-conscious, in 'Paris' he suffered from 'nervous sexual attacks'.[62] He attempted to ward these off at times with over-compensatory imaginative bravado. Some fragments, later excised from his notebook but apparently penned in late 1910 begin:

> There was a jolly tinker came across the sea
> With his four and twenty inches hanging to his knee
> *Chorus* With his long-pronged hongpronged
>   Underhanded babyfetcher
>   Hanging to his knee.

Tom might delight in such an imagined sexual epic, but in his less rowdy poems he investigated more anxious aspects of sexuality, psychology and modern life.[63] Completed in March 1911, his 'Rhapsody', in which 'the floors of the memory' are made to 'Dissolve', fuses Bergsonian flux with precise, sometimes sexualised images of nocturnal streets. Its crazy synaesthesia, perhaps drawing on Janet's psychology, ranges far beyond the street lamp that stood outside the Pension Casaubon:

> Every street lamp that I pass
> Beats like a fatalistic drum
> And through the spaces of the dark
> The midnight shakes my memory
> As a madman shakes a dead geranium.[64]

No one had written like that in English before. The geranium was Laforgue's. A sworl of exciting ideas and images surrounded Tom, and he was able to synthesise many of them in startling combinations. Undergirded by all his American reading and experiences, this was the making of him, the making of his style.

Alain-Fournier urged him to read recent French poetry by the Catholic poet Paul Claudel. Also verse by Charles Péguy, as well as prose by André Gide and Dostoevsky. 'Under his [Alain-Fournier's] instigation', he read *Crime and Punishment*, *The Idiot* and *The Brothers Karamazov* 'in the French translation during the course of that winter'. They 'profoundly impressed' him, and he 'had read them all before *Prufrock* was completed'.[65] Sometimes it can seem that all he did in Paris was read. Yet the city showed him how literature and cultural values were intermixed. Such fusion impressed him: 'in 1910 I remember the camelots cheering the cuirassiers who were sent to disperse them, because they represented the Army, all the time that they were trying to stampede their horses'.[66] This is a reference to a near riot at the Théâtre de l'Odéon, not far from Tom's lodgings, on 3 November 1910 when the young dramatist René Fauchois criticised Racine in a public lecture, and there were street demonstrations by the Camelots du Roi who championed the tradition-alist nationalist beliefs of the faction known as L'Action Française. Tom, receiving some informal 'leçons de philosophie' from Alain-Fournier, read a good deal of the writings of Charles Maurras, anti-Semitic intel-lectual leader of L'Action Française. Maurras's *L'Avenir de l'Intelligence* was on Tom's 1911 bookshelf.[67]

This pessimistic, anti-Romantic work saw literary intellectuals as increasingly enslaved by a sterile capitalist society. To Tom, in flight from America's version of such a society, it spoke compellingly. Its influence ('l'importante influence') has been traced on *The Waste Land* and else-where.[68] During 1913 Maurras would be defined in the *Nouvelle Revue Française* (which had published criticism of his views) as 'classique, catholique, monarchique'; fifteen years later, Tom used those terms of himself.[69] His interest in Maurras was one of many traits he shared with Jean Verdenal who, a fellow medical student recalled, 'took a small interest, literary and political in Charles Maurras and his Action Française. He may have been inclined to be monarchist theor[et]ically, but not to take part in this extremist movement.'[70] Verdenal's interest in Maurras was at once thoroughly French, yet also in some ways consonant with Tom's familial conservatism.

Maurras's vision of a great tradition of European culture impressed this young American. He paid tribute to Maurras for much of his life, addressing him later (as his supporters did) as 'Cher Maître'.[71] He knew Maurras had precious little liking for foreigners (of whom Tom was one) and virulently detested Jews.[72] Deeply attached to what he told Tom were 'les qualités les plus françaises de subtilité, de grâce et d'héroisme', yet also with a background as an 'internationaliste', Alain-Fournier borrowed

Tom's English-language books. He spoke with him about the novel he was writing, *Le Grand Meaulnes*, a lyrical account of lost youth, a paradisal French milieu and an unattainable woman. Tom, 'tres jeune et gauche' (very young and gauche), and a person for whom all women were as yet sexually unattainable, was profoundly impressed. He was also conscious that Alain-Fournier had in him an increasing resentment towards Germany.[73] Aided by Alain-Fournier's tuition, Tom's French was improving rapidly. He could read almost non-stop.

By the end of his year in Paris he was being addressed by Alain-Fournier in customary French style as 'Mon cher ami'.[74] Jean Verdenal used the identical form of address and became an even closer friend. Twenty-year-old Verdenal was a doctor's son from the small, historic medieval city of Pau in the Pyrenees, about thirty miles from the Spanish border. Birthplace of France's King Henry IV, whose fourteenth-century chateau dominated the town, Pau throughout Jean Verdenal's boyhood had been a favourite resort for British, American and other tourists. Thanks to the late-twentieth-century detective work of George Watson and Claudio Perinot, we know Verdenal excelled at school there. Sporty, clever, he had been considered delicate and introverted as a boy. Well read in English and German, he had read Dante in French, learning passages by heart. He loved poetry and, like Tom, had 'a remarkable knowledge of things cultural'. Surviving books from his library include volumes by Laforgue, Mallarmé, Gide and Claudel, as well as Charles-Louis Philippe's *La mère et l'enfant*, a work Tom read too after Verdenal recommended it. When Verdenal, who had travelled little, came to the French capital as a provincial in his late teens to study medicine at the Sorbonne, he lodged with old family friends, the Casaubons. Gradually he began to love Paris. He attended art exhibitions, plays and concerts; Wagner was an especial favourite. He liked discussing philosophy with fellow lodgers and, like Tom, went to Bergson's lectures. Brought up to be patriotic, he was interested in Maurras, but 'didn't think of him as a model leader'. Psychology, philosophy and poetry fascinated him; he read William James. Long afterwards, his nephew recalled him as 'a kind of mystic, not the Saint Catherine type of course, but he did have a strong inner life, a personal spiritual life. He was a profound believer and rather shunned the exterior rites of religion.'[75]

This was the man who became Tom's closest friend. Each was haunted by passages in Laforgue, by Bergson, by Wagner, by Maurras. Each combined a serious intellectualism and formality with a wryly amused take on life. Inked in his clear, never florid hand, this young Frenchman's surviving letters to Tom are always signed 'Jean Verdenal'. Occasionally they contain tiny changes (such as replacing 'habitude' (custom) with 'études' (studies)) which suggest a fine sense of verbal nuance; only once, on a scribbled postcard, does he sign himself simply 'Jean'.[76] If Laforgue, amalgamating improbable materials, was 'fascinated' (as Tom later remarked) not just by the alluring English governess he married but also 'by the Kantian pseudo-Buddhism of Schopenhauer', then the student Verdenal could tell Tom about whores' supple busts and a glimpse of shapely leg through the slit of a fashionable split skirt; yet he might also shoot the breeze in a letter mixing almost mystical rhetoric with amusing trivia:

l'histoire conte que le terrible Schopenhauer en était fort amateur. Il jouait aussi de la clarinette, mais c'était peut-être pour embêter ses voisins. Voilà bien assez de choses pour nous rattacher à la vie. La volonté de vivre est mauvaise, cause de désirs et de peines mais la bière est appréciable – et l'on continue. O! Raison.

history tells us that the formidable Schopenhauer was a great beer-lover. He also played the clarinet, but perhaps that was just to annoy his neighbours. Such things are quite enough to make us cling to life. The will to live is evil, a source of desires and sufferings, but beer is not to be despised – and so we carry on. O Reason![77]

Unlike other lodgers, such as the sometimes boring Prichard, Verdenal combined brilliance with fun. None of Tom's Harvard companions had been on his wavelength in quite the same way: Harold Peters was great company on a boat, but hardly the man for Laforgue. Verdenal came from another country. He spoke another language. Yet those things made him all the more valuable as a friend. He'd wander downstairs to Tom's room in his slippers, collarless, in an old jacket, ready to chat about anything: anything, usually, except his medical studies. Often those seemed to interest him less than literature and philosophical speculations.

Later, it would be suggested by some commentators that Tom and Verdenal had been lovers. They were close, kindred spirits. Tom, at least, was so clever and complicated that he almost never found a kindred spirit, which made this friendship, so unexpected and strong, matter all the more. They went walking together, sometimes with Prichard and with Harrison Bird Child, that old acquaintance of Tom's from Milton and Harvard, who was studying during 1910–11 in England. They strolled among the trees at the large parklands of Saint Cloud a few miles along the Seine.[78] They talked culture and philosophy. But there is no evidence that Tom and Jean Verdenal slept together or even that their mutual attraction was essentially homoerotic. Certainly they liked each other enough to be daft with one another. Spotting Verdenal outside in the garden, Tom 'threw a lump of sugar at him'.[79] The two students went on corresponding after Tom left Paris, and some of the daftness lingered. The Frenchman sometimes felt trapped in a Pension Casaubon time-warp: 'everything is just the same (this evening, for the 2474th time, I shall see Madame Casaubon hold her napkin between her chin and her chest as her wrinkled hands mix the salad)'.[80]

These student friends shared hopes and dreams. At times, despite their different native languages, they even seem to share turns of phrase: Verdenal's 'Ce n'est pas facile de se faire comprendre' sounds almost like a recollection of Tom's 'It is impossible to say just what I mean' from his Prufrock poem.[81] There is no evidence that Tom showed Verdenal his verse, but he kept his French friend's letters and occasionally a usage or a phrase in them seems to anticipate his own later work: Verdenal's 'C'est un homme charmant' (used of Harvard philosopher B. A. G. Fuller), for instance, becomes Tom's '"He is a charming man"' in 'Mr. Apollinax', a poem based on incidents at Fuller's Massachusetts home.[82] Tom's friendship with Verdenal may have been the closest friendship he ever enjoyed with another man. It stayed with him particularly intensely for a terrible reason. In 1934, recalling that year in Paris, Tom confessed 'that my own retrospect is touched by a sentimental sunset, the memory of a friend coming across the Luxembourg Gardens in the late afternoon, waving a branch of lilac, a friend who was later (so far as I could find out) to be mixed with the mud of Gallipoli'.[83]

The last letter Tom kept from this friend, who died in the Great War at almost the same age as Jules Laforgue, was sent at the end of 1912. The young Frenchman signed off characteristically: 'Au revoir, mon cher ami, et bien à vous . . . J. Verdenal.'[84] Five years later, when Tom published his first collection of poems, he added the simple dedication, 'For Jean Verdenal, 1889–1915'. Some years again after that, he appended to the dedication the words 'mort aux Dardanelles', and some lines from Dante's *Purgatorio* in which two poets meet in the afterlife. Virgil speaks first to his 'brother' ('Frate'), Statius; then Statius replies:

> 'Or puoi la quantitate
> comprender dell' amor ch'a te mi scalda,
> quando dismento nostra vanitate,
> trattando l'ombre come cosa saldi.'

which Tom translated into prose in 1929 as

'Now you can understand the quantity of the love that warms me towards you, so that I forget our vanity, and treat the shadows like the solid thing.'[85]

These Dantescan words are not just a declaration of fraternal love. They state, too, an enduring literary bond.

Tom's voyage to Paris for that academic year 1910–11 brought him a sense of deep, unexpected personal kinship, but also an excitingly immediate sense of European culture. Like many Americans on a year's study abroad, he planned several side-trips. During the Christmas vacation he travelled for two weeks, including visits to 'Poitiers, Angoulême, Toulouse, Albi, Moissac, and other places in the south west'.[86] All these towns were on railway lines. Conceivably Tom visited them with his good friend and fellow lodger if Verdenal went home to Pau, about sixty miles from Toulouse. In mid-May 1911 Tom visited Rouen, planning visits to further 'towns about Paris'.[87] By then he had also crossed the English Channel to spend a good deal of the Easter vacation in the city that he had read about in childhood and which would one day become his home. It was the place where Jules Laforgue had married, the metropolis of Dickens and Sherlock Holmes.

'At London one pretended it was spring', he wrote to his cousin Eleanor on 26 April. He had returned to Paris the night before, finding a note from her among 'a pile of letters'. In Paris it was 'full spring', but London's spring had been a mere pretence and 'one continued to hibernate among the bricks'.[88] That last phrase also formed part of his poem, 'Interlude in London', written the same month. Christopher Ricks has pointed out this poem shares phrasing with 'The Love Song of J. Alfred Prufrock', 'Preludes' and even, perhaps, *The Waste Land*, while drawing at times on French poetry.[89] Apart from the word 'London' in its title, the urban details could come from almost any city. In London, though, Tom went to a number of specifically English churches. Mainly in the financial district – the City – they were mentioned in his Baedeker, and included the Church of St Bartholomew the Great. The Baedeker entry for this carries Tom's pencilled note 'St. B. Inscription "John Eliot" gave £30 for the poor.'[90] Even here, he was among Eliots.

His letter to Eleanor Hinkley contains a list of places visited that roughly corresponds to a pencilled tally on one of the back pages of his Baedeker. These sites include the 'National Gallery', the 'Brit[ish] Mus[eum]', 'S. Kensington' (i.e. the Victoria and Albert Museum) and the 'Wallace Collection'.[91] Ticks in Tom's Baedeker suggest his particular interests included the 'Egyptian Antiquities' and 'Religious Collections' dealing with 'Early Christianity' in the British Museum; also rooms XVIII and XIX in the Wallace Collection, which contained respectively 'a charming series of fêtes champêtres, conversations galantes, pastoral and romantic scenes, etc., by *Watteau*', and Fragonard's painting *The Swing* in which a man looks up a lady's skirt as she swings.[92] Tom wrote to Eleanor that he had 'made notes!!' at the Wallace Collection, but did not say what they were about.[93] About five years later, he would write about 'Priapus . . . Gaping at the lady in the swing' in 'Mr. Apollinax', and would publish another poem 'Conversation Galante'.[94] Visual images and fragments of text lingered long in his mind. So did snatches of song and music. He always associated this youthful visit to London with Herman Finck's tune 'In the Shadows' which was made popular by a 1911 show featuring the glamorous Palace Girls at the Palace Theatre.[95]

In London, despite cool weather, he spent much time outdoors. He perused the banking hub, 'The City – Thoroughly', and mentioned to Eleanor 'Whitechapel (note: Jews)'. Perhaps the anti-Semitism of Maurras's Paris made him all the more alert to Whitechapel's Jewish presence, though visitors often noted it. At London Zoo he 'gave the apterix a bun'; fond of the word 'apterix' (kiwi bird), years later he signed a review 'T. S. Apteryx'.[96] London offered music-hall treats: while Tom was there, George Robey was performing at the Empire Theatre, and Marie Lloyd at the Pavilion.[97] As well as visiting the zoo, he went to Cricklewood – in those days a semi-rural village on the Edgware Road, though already on its way to becoming a suburb. Maybe, as with 'apterix', he simply liked the sound of the name; or perhaps he went because, though easily accessible, Cricklewood was *not* a place mentioned by Baedeker.

> I made a pilgrimage to Cricklewood. 'Where *is* Cricklewood?' said an austere Englishman at the hotel. I produced a map and pointed to the silent evidence that Cricklewood exists. He pondered. 'But why go to Cricklewood?' he flashed out at length. Here I was triumphant. 'There is no reason!' I said. He had no more to say. But he *was* relieved (I am sure) when he found that I was American. He felt no longer responsible. But Cricklewood is mine. I discovered it. No one will go there again.[98]

Cheered by this exotic English adventure, and safely back in Paris, he planned further foreign trips: 'After the middle of June I shall go to Munich for some time, to study German. I hope to spend a few weeks, at least, in Italy.'[99]

When he reached Munich in July, he found another great city of European culture. Its Maximilianstrasse, a broad, tree-lined royal avenue whose monumental buildings led the eye towards the heroically imposing Maximilianeum across the River Isar, was one of the Continent's grandest streets. In London Tom had stayed in a hotel. Here in this Bavarian capital of 600,000 people he had arranged lodgings in a boarding house, the Pension Bürger, which occupied two storeys at 50 Luisenstrasse. On the half mile or so journey from the main railway station to this address visitors passed the 765-foot long Glaspalast; opened in 1854, it was modelled on London's Crystal Palace. Munich was full of palatial architecture. Beyond the Glaspalast was the imposing Basilika St Bonifaz (built in imitation of an early Christian basilica). Tom's lodgings were close to a great Corinthian-style art gallery opposite the magnificent marble halls of the Ionic Glyptothek (sculpture-hall), built for King Ludwig I of Bavaria to house classical statuary. 'A walk through Munich', the 1911 *Encyclopedia Britannica* article about that city proclaimed, 'affords a picture of the architecture and art of two thousand years'. From the Luisenstrasse one could walk along Briennerstrasse, passing through a great stone gateway in the Propyläen (built to imitate a temple on the Athenian acropolis) to the massive Residenz (Palace) complex of the Bavarian monarchs. The Arcades to the west and north of the Hofgarten with its several open-air cafes contained one-hundred-twenty-five pier-arches and had been adorned with frescoes, including Joseph Rottmann's Italian landscape pictures depicting classical ruins – a veritable 'Ruinenpanorama', to use a word that circulated in the Munich of July 1911 – though when Tom visited they were in poor condition.[100]

So was he. 'In Munich', he recalled during a later bout of low blood pressure, 'in 1911' he had experienced 'cerebral anaemia'.[101] At its worst, this disease is fatal. Usually accompanied by intense diarrhoea, dizziness, faintness and pallor as well as some mental confusion and general sensation of physical weakness, the illness in its milder forms (which seems to have been what Tom suffered) can be treated with drugs backed up by healthy eating, fresh air and exercise. 'Most unpleasant', he later summed up his ordeal.[102] Following not so long after scarlet fever, this was the second time in just over a year that he had contracted a potentially life-threatening disease. Being ill alone in a foreign city is never easy. Yet for Tom it coincided with a poetic breakthrough. Later in life he came to suspect that sickness and poetic creativity could be linked. During his stay in Munich he completed his first great poem.

It deals with weakness. Some of its fragmentary drafts mention 'nausea' and even 'Madness'. However, 'The Love Song of J. Alfred Prufrock' is not directly autobiographical; nor is it set in Munich.[103] Tom appears to have brought with him the notebook he had bought in Gloucester, and copied into it extended sections – at one time, perhaps, intended as separate poems – that drew on earlier fragments. This way of hoarding bits of older material, then piecing them together, would become a compositional strategy. Schooled but not confined by Laforgue's style, his new poem with its generalised yet tellingly memorable cityscape of 'restless nights in one-night cheap hotels / And sawdust restaurants with oyster shells' tosses and turns restlessly. It presents a masculinity hampered by incisive self-consciousness and inhibition.

Three titles were in play: 'The Love Song of J. Alfred Prufrock', 'Prufrock among the Women' and 'Prufrock's Pervigilium'. Eventually Tom spliced together what may have started life as at least two different related works. In draft his first line began with '. . .' Those dots sent a signal at the very start of hesitancy and, perhaps, of something ending before it had even begun. The final version, not published until 1915, four years after he completed it at the age of twenty-two, begins more confidently.

> Let us go then, you and I,
> When the evening is spread out against the sky
> Like a patient etherised upon a table . . .[104]

That 'Let us go', which so soon lapses into an unforgettable image of illness and paralysis, may owe nothing specifically to Tom's illnesses in Harvard's Stillman Infirmary or in Munich with its 'Lazarett' (hospital). Boston's Ether Monument is surely present in the background. But this poem of a man who fantasises about saying, '"I am Lazarus, come from the dead / Come back to tell you all"', yet who cannot bring himself to behave with any assurance in his obsessive, nervously imagined interactions with women, may draw more deeply on Tom's own lack of achieved love life. Several years later, he was still worrying in a letter to Conrad Aiken (one of the earliest readers of the unpublished Prufrock poem) about sexual anxiety and about not having lost his virginity. 'The thing is to be able to look at one's life as if it were somebody's else', he wrote around that time to Aiken.[105] The 'Love Song of J. Alfred Prufrock' constructs a voice and state of mind which, however much the poem draws nutrients from other poets' voices, bravely confronts, mines and metamorphoses anxieties that lay deep within Tom and may lie within some of his audience. With its speaker who is at once intimate with the reader yet afflicted by seeming cut off from life, Prufrock's 'Love Song' is one of the bravest poems about gender ever authored.

The male speaker, worried he will be perceived (especially by women) in terms of his thinning hair, thin arms and thin legs, is afflicted by a sense of how 'I grow old . . . I grow old . . .' Yet many readers sense it as a young man's poem, a staged yet secret utterance by a speaker disconcertingly articulate about his tongue-tiedness. Echoing with overheard and imagined comments from women much more assured and sophisticated, it ends with an over-protested attempt to look fashionably attractive – 'I shall wear white flannel trousers, and walk upon the beach'. There is a vision of alluring, unattainable and dangerous mermaids, then death by water. The poem's last word is 'drown'.[106] Furnished with lines from Dante's *Inferno* which, ironically or otherwise, add to its cultural resonance, this 'Love Song' requires no biographical knowledge of its author. Yet, like most hypnotically alluring poems, it is powered by real emotion. Anyone with an interest in its young poet may be tempted to recall several photographs in which he looks thin; in at least one he appears to be wearing white flannel trousers.

Responding to enquiries decades afterwards, Tom made clear that 'The poem of Prufrock was conceived some time in 1910', though it may have drawn on some 'earlier fragments' written before he went to Paris; it was 'not completed until the summer of 1911'; he finished it 'in Munich'.[107] In the cosmopolitan Bavarian capital, as in Paris, he was in a city where sex was on display as it was not in Cambridge or Boston. The conventional artists in a huge exhibition shown all that summer at the Glaspalast offered many titillating female nudes; avant-garde painters, some of whom were about to exhibit in the famous Blue Rider show later that year, went much further. Franz Marc, photographed drawing the reclining naked Marie Schnür outdoors on a grassy slope, was only one of Munich's artistic figures famous for their sexual explicitness. 1910's 'Bachusfest in Old Rome', held in a local brewery, had resulted in photographs of happily naked revellers: a sometimes orgiastic, sometimes lyrical eroticism was part of the temper of this city where the reputedly mad King Ludwig II (before drowning in the nearby Starnbergersee) had been Wagner's greatest patron.[108] 'Try, if possible, to hear something by Wagner in Munich', urged Jean Verdenal, who had just enjoyed *Götterdämmerung* in Paris. Verdenal's view of *Tristan und Isolde*, he explained to Tom later, was that it 'is terribly moving at the first hearing, and leaves you prostrate with ecstasy and thirsting to get back to it again'.[109]

Suffering from cerebral anaemia, Tom may or may not have been in the mood for *Tristan*. However, the Pension Bürger was just round the corner from Richard-Wagner-Strasse, and it was impossible to walk around 1911 Munich without being aware of the city's erotically-supercharged artistic atmosphere. Tom pencilled the date 'July 1911' on his 'Ballade pour la grosse

Lulu'. That poem juxtaposes actual or supposed reports about Harvard's President Eliot and others from the worthy American Christian periodical *The Outlook* with much more shocking shenanigans associated with 'Lulu' – a name made scandalous throughout Munich and the rest of the German-speaking world by Frank Wedekind's *fin de siècle* plays about a sexually provocative dancer: 'But, My Lulu, "Put on your Rough Red Drawers / And come to the Whore House Ball"', reads Tom's markedly un-Prufrockian refrain.[110] Though he never succeeded in publishing this piece, at some point (maybe later) he came up with an arresting rhyme for a German city's main railway station – 'Hauptbahnhof'. Turning that word into a 'frightful cry' of sexual excitement, he rhymed it, a little clumsily but in a style of which avant-garde Munich might have been proud, with 'pulled her stockings off'.[111] Ironically, the highly sexed Munich milieu may have heightened and crystalised J. Alfred Prufrock's memorable sexual anxieties.

Fresh air, good food and exercise were recommended to anaemics, and one of the 'most popular excursions from Munich' at the time was to the thirteen-mile long Starnbergersee, Germany's greatest lake. In those days it was accessible by rail from Munich's Hauptbahnhof in well under an hour. Especially beautiful in summer, it lay calm in front of the mountains beyond.[112] Perhaps in July 1911, though we do not know when or how, Tom met Marie Larisch, one of whose titles was Countess of Munich.[113] A remembered conversation with this middle-aged aristocrat, unhappy in her marriage and associated with sexual scandal, would be recalled, mixed with other memories and desires, in the first section of *The Waste Land*.

> Summer surprised us, coming over the Starnbergersee
> With a shower of rain; we stopped in the colonnade,
> And went on in sunlight, into the Hofgarten,
> And drank coffee, and talked for an hour.
> Bin gar keine Russin, stamm' aus Litauen, echt deutsch.
> And when we were children, staying at the arch-duke's,
> My cousin's, he took me out on a sled,
> And I was frightened. He said, Marie,
> Marie, hold on tight. And down we went.
> In the mountains, there you feel free.
> I read, much of the night, and go south in the winter.[114]

Readers sometimes ignore the punctuation of these lines: it is not the people but the summer that (as in 1911) is 'coming over the Starnbergersee / With a shower of rain'. The people, making the most of sunshine, coffee and conversation, are where Tom was – in Munich.

Recovered, he headed south about a hundred and fifty miles from Bavaria to northern Italy. Guided by his own earlier studies and probably by advice from the Byzantinist Prichard, he travelled for about two weeks on a carefully choreographed trip that took in Verona, Vicenza, Venice, Padua, Ferrara, Bologna, Modena, Parma, Milan and Bergamo, cities linked by a good rail network. Everywhere he went in Italy he carried with him a small black leather-covered pocket notebook. Its pages were ruled with the squared paper he often chose to write on. This was not a notebook for poems, but for observations on art and antiquities. His use of technical language – detailing the 'ceiling' of San Zeno Maggiore in Verona with its 'shallow coffers, or rather a grating' – indicates how attentive a student he was, pausing to make a pencil sketch and draw a floorplan. Such architectural exactness would benefit his poetry: the 'coffered ceiling' of 'A Game of Chess' in *The Waste Land* is followed by a 'carvèd dolphin' and an 'antique mantel'.[115] A trained art historian from his undergraduate days, Tom noticed, and noted. On a sunny summer Sunday in Vicenza, a place he found 'altogether charming', he walked among a crowd of locals up the steep road to the Basilica S. Maria di Monte Berico where the Virgin Mary (represented by a striking statue) was said to have appeared twice in the fifteenth century. He gazed out over the city below. Enjoying life, he wrote in his notebook on the spot or shortly afterwards: 'View from near church is superb, over the flat plains on one side and toward Alps on other. Blue haze and talking bells. Road leads to narrow lane, very fine, between high brick walls (lizards and rosebushes) to Villa Valmarana. Villa and garden charming, but Tiepolo rather a disappointment.' Perhaps from one of those rosebushes he plucked the flower which he pressed in his notebook, and which still survives, dry and fragile, in Harvard's Houghton Library. Then he went to sketch a floor plan of the Rotonda.[116]

By the time he got to Venice he was determined to be cowed neither by Baedeker nor by conventional assumptions. He wanted to look, and take notes, for himself. About San Marco he wrote somewhat grudgingly, 'The piazza is not so attractive as the P. Erbe (or P. Vitt. Eman.) in Verona. It is large and magnificent (I suppose) but has an oddly businesslike, mercantile appearance. Its effect, at least, like that of the Grand Canal, is all in the first moment.'[117] Readers of Tom's American-in-Venice poem 'Burbank with a Baedeker: Bleistein with a Cigar', published in 1919 and opening with an epigraph that conjures up 'charming' Venice, are often struck by the ensuing poem's sense of modern tawdriness. They register, too, its apparent distaste (shared with Shakespeare's *Merchant of Venice*) for 'The Jew'.[118] In the summer of 1911 Tom was prepared to be unimpressed: 'unattractive gold' he wrote of the Pala d'Oro, the Byzantine masterpiece in the Basilica di San Marco; '*Libreria Vecchia* is an impressive bldg. which does not impress me.'[119]

Yet, almost despite himself, he could be bowled over, as he was by the elongated, grey-clad Byzantine-style mosaic figure of the Mater Theou – the Mother of God – on the golden apse inside the cathedral of Santi Maria e Donato on the Venetian island of Murano. 'The Interceding Virgin is the finest mosaic I have seen; the finest Virgin, and one of the finest religious expressions I have anywhere seen. *Note* effect of curve in apse, which bends the Virgin forward over you, enhancing the evocation of divinity. Color first-rate.'[120] For all his interest in Janet, Bergson and the sceptical interrogation of religious belief, and despite his apparent determination not to be wowed by Venice, he could still be profoundly affected by religion made manifest in art.

Tom progressed round the galleries, churches and other attractions of northern Italy. His notebook shows he disliked the over-elaborate. The Certosa di Pavia monastery complex he saw as 'One of the most repellent buildings in Renaissance art. The production of a rotten art.'[121] When he returned to Paris it was as a seasoned, opinionated European traveller. He had cheated death – again. He had completed his first masterpiece – not that he seems to have shown it to anyone in the Pension Casaubon. He was beginning to think, albeit with some reluctance, about returning to Harvard. Sceptically full of the heady ideas of Bergson, he would probably become a philosopher.

8

A Philosopher and Actor
Falls in Love

Rᴇᴛᴜʀɴᴇᴅ to Massachusetts to pursue doctoral work in philosophy, Tom was keen to remain Parisian. For some time he wore what Conrad Aiken considered 'exotic Left Bank clothing'.[1] Like composer Maurice Ravel and others in 1911 Paris, Tom at Harvard sported a Malacca cane. He also parted his hair behind, and took out a subscription to the *Nouvelle Revue Française*. He had come back from the Left Bank having written 'Entretien dans un parc' (a poem dated February 1911 about romantic 'uncertainties' around holding hands with a woman 'under the April trees')[2] as well as the more scandalous 'Ballade pour la grosse Lulu'. Before Aiken married in 1912 and left for Europe, he and Tom conversed regularly during the academic session 1911–12. Knowing Tom and Paris, Aiken was well placed not only to become one of the first readers of the unpublished 'Love Song of J. Alfred Prufrock', but also to observe his friend's post-Parisian reinvention.[3] Tom hung on his wall a reproduction of Gauguin's disconcerting crucifixion painting, *Yellow Christ*, and from time to time letters arrived with stamps bearing the words 'République Française'.

'Ne croyez pas que je vous oublie' (Don't think I have forgotten you), Jean Verdenal wrote in a short, mid-October note after hasty farewells. He added that they would talk again in the future.[4] Tom had already written to Verdenal. He may have missed Paris, but he was busy. He had taken lodgings at 16 Ash Street, that address his Francophile classmate Seeger had mentioned a few years earlier. Unlike his previous Cambridge abodes, this one was a wooden three-storey private house in a quiet, leafy residential street. Here he would live for the next three years: clearly he and his landlady, Miss Caroline J. Carroll, were mutually agreeable. His lease for 1913–14 survives, neatly signed in ink, 'T. S. Eliot', and recording that from September until June he rented 'the suite of 2 rooms on the third floor'.[5] During the same session 'a nice fellow', Elmer Keith, had rooms on the same floor; Keith had just been studying at Oxford and was able to tell Tom about that experience.[6] The two men got on well, though Keith seemed 'very English – thoroughly so', which Tom found 'baffling'.[7] Tom's parents could scarcely have disapproved of this genteel street where Harvard students conversed about Oxford and older residents might advertise they were 'at home' on Mondays or Thursdays.[8] Overlooking trees and gardens, Tom's upper-storey rooms were a haven of birdsong and concentration. At 16 Ash Street he demanded of himself far more philosophical brainwork than he had displayed as an undergraduate.

Leafiness suited him. Harvard Yard was a ten-minute walk away; he was closer to Radcliffe, and not far from where his cousin Eleanor lived in a similar, suburban-style house. 'For rent of rooms' in 1912–13 Miss Carroll charged him $40 per quarter plus a few dollars more for coal and wood – New England winters were chilly after Paris.[9] There were two other 'principal residents', Miss Mary Stimpson and Miss Ella M. Palmer.[10] Verdenal could share a joke with Tom about the 'label "elderly American spinster"'.[11] Now back in Cambridge, Tom shared a house with several unmarried ladies in the markedly feminine Radcliffe part of town. That November he returned to a poem he had worked on in Paris, 'Portrait of a Lady'. Like Prufrock's 'Love Song', this work about strained nuances of etiquette between a young man and an older woman conscious of her 'buried life, and Paris in the spring' seems to have developed alongside raunchier writings, each perhaps spurring the other. In manuscript the first part of 'Portrait of a Lady' has, Christopher Ricks notes, 'Bolo verses on the other side'.[12] Apparently drawing on Tom's undergraduate interaction with the considerably older Miss Adeleine Moffatt who 'lived behind the State House in Boston and invited selected Harvard undergraduates to tea', the poem's third section involves an awkward conversation about 'going abroad'. The male speaker, nervous about his 'self-possession', envisages smiling after the lady's death, but questions whether he has 'the right' to do so.[13] His mind wanders from talk of Chopin to popular culture – Tom and Aiken were fans of comic-strip characters Mutt and Jeff. Tom anatomises male (and sometimes female) anxieties, several of which seem hard to separate from his own shyness, however offset by a dash of Parisian swank.

Some French passions he shared with his family. His mother, always eager to understand her younger son, read Bergson's newly translated

Creative Evolution, and even attended 'lectures thereon, largely influenced by Tom's enthusiasm', though she noticed less Bergsonian ardour now her son was back from France.[14] Further ongoing interests – Boloesque and otherwise – he kept more private. He and Verdenal went on corresponding, still sharing the same wavelength, but the Frenchman's letters show no awareness of Bolo or Columbo. In the Pension Casaubon the Parisian medical student had moved to Tom's old room:

> the pattern of the wallpaper (do you remember it?) often gets on my nerves. Damn. It occurred to me a moment ago to send you a little bit of wallpaper – then I immediately realised that the idea was not mine but that I had got it from a letter by J. Laforgue, so I will abstain. I am not quite sure of ever having had an idea that really belonged to me.

Though committed to pursuing his studies, Verdenal had regrets about having chosen a scientific career. He worried he read too much, and had 'little gift for action'. He invoked Bergson with an ironic tone, and his rather Prufrockian concerns about his own self-consciousness make it clear why he and Tom felt close: 'if I act (O action, O Bergson), I am bright enough to take a sincere look at the joy of action and destroy it by analysis.'[15] Tom's poems show he, too, pondered how self-analysis could inhibit action. Like Verdenal, he went on with his reading in French. April 1912 saw him buying from Boston's Schoenhof Book Company works by Corneille and Racine as well as Charles-Louis Philippe's *Lettres de jeunesse*, newly published by the *Nouvelle Revue Française*.[16] Yet his Paris life was fading. For all their friendship, he and Verdenal were rather dilatory correspondents. If Verdenal's final surviving note to him dates from December 1912, then as early as April, in his last extended letter, the young Frenchman realised that, continents apart, they were each getting on with their considerably different lives.

> Mon cher ami, nous ne sommes pas très loin, vous et moi, de la limite au dela de laquelle les êtres perdent, l'un l'autre, je ne sais quelle influence, quelle puissance d'émotion naissant à nouveau quand ils sont rapprochés. Ce n'est pas seulement le temps qui peut faire l'oubli – la *distance* (l'espace) y a une part qui est grande. Elle déjà pèse entre nous, sans doute (avouons le franchement) puisque des occupations stupides, et beaucoup de paresse ont tellement raréfié ma correspondance.

(My dear friend, we are not very far, you and I, from the point beyond which people lose that indefinable influence and emotive power over each other, which is reborn when they come together again. It is not only time which causes forgetfulness – distance (space) is an important factor. It is already, no doubt, making itself felt between us (let us admit this frankly), since my stupid occupations and considerable laziness have made my letters few and far between.[17]

Tom's academic interests were removing him, too, from his under-graduate friends, most of whom had left Cambridge. His doctoral work in philosophy would involve about five years' further study. Now he was safely home from Paris, his parents were happy to fund this.

Partly perhaps under Babbitt's lingering influence, and aware of his brother-in-law Shef's interest in Eastern thought, Tom began studying Sanskrit. Among other things, this involved leaving Western alphabets far behind. His professor was Charles Rockwell Lanman, whom he may have known through family connections: Lanman's wife was a Hinkley. Then in his sixties, Professor Lanman had developed Harvard's outstanding collections of Sanskrit books and manuscripts. His Sanskrit *Reader*, one of Tom's set texts, introduced such topics as ancient Indic customs and the transmigration of souls. Lanman liked to point out that 'The belief that a man must be born and live and die, only to be born and die again and again through a weary round of existences, was widespread in India long before Buddha's day', and that 'the "Jataka", the most charming of all Buddhist story books', contained 'a narrative of not less than 547 former existences' preceding the 'birth' of Buddha. Benign but exacting, Lanman drew parallels between Buddhist and Christian traditions. He emphasised Buddha's analysis of 'the cause of human suffering' which

he finds in the craving for existence (no matter how noble that exist-ence) and for pleasure. If you can only master these cravings, you are on the road to salvation, to *Nirvana*. This, so far as the present life is concerned, means the going out of the fires of lust and ill will and delusion, and further a getting rid thereby of the round of rebirth.[18]

Such thinking would condition *The Waste Land*, and during these graduate student years Tom wrote in black ink on square-lined paper lines that underpin parts of that poem. In their original form they begin, 'So through the evening, through the violet air'. They describe wandering among 'sunbaked houses' and encountering 'strange images'. Among these is an image of a woman drawing 'her long black hair out tight'. Conrad Aiken recalled reading this passage years before it was revised as part of *The Waste Land*. Imagery of 'bats' leads to mention of 'A man' with 'abnormal powers' who is seen to 'creep head downward down a wall'.[19] This derives from a passage in Bram Stoker's *Dracula*, that vampire narrative in which cycles of reincarnation involve the tormenting sexuality of the undead: a very different cycle of rebirth and destruction from the Buddha's, but one which would also be pertinent to Tom's famous poem.

During session 1911–12 he took Lanman's courses Indic Phililogy 1a and 1b (Elementary Sanskrit). He embarked on the *Panchatantra* and *Bhagavad Gita*. Meeting thrice weekly, on Monday, Wednesday and Friday afternoons, these were intimate classes. In 1a the students were a freshman, V. N. Banavalikar (who seems to have dropped out), Thomas Brown Kite, Jr (a Quaker graduate student of German), John Van Horne (a graduate student linguist), Levi Arnold Post (another graduate student, who went on to become a distinguished Greek scholar) and Tom. Course 1b was even smaller; Tom, Post and Van Horne got straight As.[20] Around this time, pondering world religions, Tom authored a fragment that draws on the *Bhagavad Gita* and ends, glancing towards sacred sacrificial 'ghee' butter, 'I am the fire, and the butter also'.[21] This tries to juxtapose Christ's words from the Gospel of John 11:25, 'I am the resurrection, and the life', with allusions to the *Gita*; but the lines risk bathos: 'butter' to many readers sounds a bit comical. Nonetheless, Tom hung on to this fragment, which clearly signals his continuing interest in religious rites, and forms part of the drafts from which *The Waste Land* would emerge.

Fired up by Paris, he now excelled in demanding areas of graduate scholarship. The following session he took two further Lanman courses on Pali, the language of the earliest Buddhist scriptures. 'These courses in the language of the sacred books of Buddhism', Harvard's *Official Register* explained in 1913, were intended 'for students interested in the history of religions and folk-lore', of whom Tom was certainly one.[22] He obtained a catalogue of books, published by the Vedanta Society in New York, on topics including 'Reincarnation' and the 'Theory of Transmigration'.[23] In Indic Philology 4 and 5, there was one other student. Shripad Krishna Belvalkar, a Hindu, had come to Harvard intending to edit Pali texts after he had met another of Tom's professors, James Haughton Woods, in India. Together Tom and Belvalkar read selections from the sacred books of Buddhism, the *Jataka* and Buddhagosa's commentary on the *Anguttara Nikaya* – lives of the Buddhist saints – as well as a selection of dialogues of the Buddha himself. The two graduate students shared an interest in chess. Conversing with this Indian fellow student and, later, reading about contemporary India made Tom wary of generalisations about 'the Indian mind', and sympathetic towards Indian 'aspirants after autonomy' at a time when India was still subject to 'British rule' that often involved a 'lack of sympathetic imagination'.[24]

For Indic Philology 4, Tom and Shripad Belvalkar read through the first eighty-one pages in Part I of Copenhagen librarian Dines Andersen's *Pali Reader*. It contains 'The Fire Sermon' in which the Buddha maintains all things are afflicted with burning (in the Pali text the word 'addita' is repeated hypnotically); the noble disciple, disgusted with all these things, becomes divested of passion: the Pali word 'nibbinah' (disgusted with) recurs again and again.[25] Encouraged by Lanman and Woods, Belvalkar (graded 'A') would become a distinguished editor, publishing in Lanman's *Harvard Oriental Series*. Tom, too, was a favoured, straight-A student. Within a decade his use of 'The Fire Sermon' with its sense of disgust and repeated 'Burning burning burning burning' would make this piece of preaching the best-known Pali text in Western literature.[26]

Lanman liked Tom. During the academic session before they read 'The Fire Sermon' in class, the great scholar presented his student with a 1906 Bombay edition of the *Upanishads*, inscribing its flyleaf, 'Thomas Eliot, Esq., with C. R. Lanman's kindest regards and best wishes. Harvard College, May 6, 1912'.[27] Inside Tom kept a sheet of headed notepaper from 9 Farrar Street, Cambridge, Lanman's family home. Dated 'May 22 1912', it is a handwritten list of passages from the *Upanishads*, including one (which has been ticked) from the Brihadaranyaka Upanishad, an ancient mystical and philosophical text about unknowability and the Absolute. In one passage thunder and lightning are envisaged as consciousness interrupting the darkness of sin. Lanman has listed a section where, as he notes, 'Da-da-da = damyata *datta dayadhvam*'.[28] Thanks to *The Waste Land,* along with the concluding utterance 'Shantih' ('a formal ending to an Upanishad'), these words would become known to readers of poetry around the world.[29]

'*Life is pain*' was simply 'a matter of fact, not necessarily pessimistic', Tom jotted in his notes on Eastern philosophy on 3 October 1913.[30] Next day he went to the Harvard Cooperative Society to buy an Indic text.[31] That September, bookish as ever, he had been browsing in the Coop's Sanskrit section, and had bought for $4.50 Paul Jakob Deussen's *Die Sutras des Vedanta,* along with Deussen's *Sechzig Upanishads des Veda* ($4.95). Though he didn't know it, his $9.45 was a shrewd investment in the future of poetry; he would refer readers to Deussen's book in his notes to *The Waste Land*.[32]

For the previous session, 1912–13, he had enrolled in philosopher James Haughton Woods's Indic Philology 9 (Philosophical Sanskrit). Years later, in the midst of mental and emotional pain, his Harvard studies in Sanskrit and Pali – or moments from them at least – returned to him offering an articulation of burning, torment and disgust. Yet during his graduate student years these studies formed part of his preoccupation with the nature of reality. He read as a philosopher. In 1911–12 he had taken his old teacher George Herbert Palmer's ethics course, Philosophy 4, considering the theory of morals; also Woods's Philosophy 12, Greek Philosophy with Especial Reference to Plato. There were connections between these two courses. Woods, who began by outlining the 'Origins of the Ethical Point of View of the Greeks', was well placed to compare and contrast Greek with Indic philosophy: 'Read the Vedas and then Homer and you will feel that the Greeks have discovered a new kind of freedom', Tom noted. Woods took it for granted that poetry and philosophy could be bonded; he praised the way in Greek 'Each thing is described with scrupulous honesty.'[33] Tom had sought such honesty in creating Prufrock, and continued to do so. Woods spoke not only of Greek 'self-restraint' and the effort to be 'disinterested', but also of Greek ideas of the 'Independence of soul from body-ecstasy', of 'a round of rebirth' and 'transmigration' different from that of 'India' and the 'Buddhist'.[34]

Tom took copious notes on the Presocratic philosophers, especially Heraclitus whose work had survived in fragments, Woods explained in October 1911, because it was 'quotable'. Deploying alliteration, repetition and even rhyme, it was 'Poetic'. Reading G. T. W. Patrick's *Heraclitus of Ephesus*, Tom noted Patrick's view that it was 'Impossible to understand Hct. unless we consider the ethical and religious character of his mind.'[35] Speaking of Heraclitus' belief in a 'primary substance – *pur*', Woods explained that this substance was not quite 'fire as we should say', but was 'accepted because he can find no better word'. Heraclitus presented a vision of flux that involved the elements. Tom took dictation:

anathumiasis: a difficult word. Means the movement from earth towards *pur*. A kind of substitute for *air*. While the fire is solidifying into water and earth you have the contrary action going on in the same substance. And the world is merely the result of these contrary strains.

The essence of the substance is the flux.[36]

This was oddly fascinating. Tom wrote of 'fire' and 'flow' in a poetic fragment of his own.[37] Woods pointed out there were three worthwhile modern editions of Heraclitus; the best arrangement of the fragments was that of Hermann Alexander Diels. Heraclitus, Woods explained, 'complains of the inability of the ordinary man to pierce the appearance of stability and see the finer play of the world movement'. He was the 'originator of the idea of opposites . . . He shows that the opposites do not neutralize each other, but may sometimes be the same thing.' More than two decades after noting all this down, Tom returned to the Heraclitus section of Diels's *Die Fragmente der Vorsokratiker* and took from it two fragments as epigraphs for 'Burnt Norton', first of his *Four Quartets*. The initial epigraph means, 'Though the law of things is universal in scope, ordinary people live as if they had their own insight'; the second means, 'the way up and the way down are the same'.[38] Each of the *Four Quartets* seems to correspond to one of the elements: air, earth, water, fire. All this is just one of many indications of how even the most recondite details of his graduate learning bore fruit in later poetry.

Yet larger-scale philosophical thought processes also shaped his poetic procedures. Discussing Heraclitus' habit of seeing 'the same object in different relations', Woods encouraged ideas of juxtaposition and shifting interpretations.[39] In poetry Tom was always open to recontextualising older materials so that, without altering the original words, he let them be read in new ways. In retrospect, we can see that he shared this technique with other well-read modernist writers from Ezra Pound to James Joyce and Hugh MacDiarmid; it was encouraged, too, by his philosophical studies. Grounded in Western thought from the ancient Greeks through Descartes, Spinoza and Leibniz to Kant and recent speculation about the nature of reality, he grew increasingly interested in fundamental questions of knowledge and interpretation; his awareness of these was enhanced by his schooling in Indic and Oriental philosophy. Reading Spinoza's *Ethics*, he jotted comments in the margin: 'Intellect an abstraction. There is only the stream of ideas.'[40] Ideas, reality and flux obsessed him. He was not infallible but was – and remains – hard to keep up with. Reading Bergson in French, then in English, he also read Patanjali in the original Pali, the *Upanishads* in Sanskrit, Heraclitus in Greek, Kant in German, Dante in Italian – and, as for Spinoza, he read that great Jewish philosopher in elegant seventeenth-century Latin. No other major twentieth-century poet was so thoroughly and strenuously educated.

Though focused on the philosophy classroom, his studies involved, too, aspects of modern scientific culture. Psychology was a field in which William James's work and the establishment of a psychological laboratory upstairs at Emerson Hall had made Harvard a centre for advanced investigation. In 1912–13 Tom studied in Philosophy 20b the relations between mind and body with leading psychologist Hugo Münsterberg, a German Jewish intellectual hired by James and trained in Berlin by Wilhelm Wundt.

Practically-minded, the prolific Münsterberg had recently published *Psychotherapy*; he had little time for mysticism, though he did admit, in his idiosyncratic idiom, that it could have value for those with personal problems. 'The own personality is submerging into a larger all-embracing hold and thus inhibits the small cares and troubles of merely personal origin. The consciousness sinks into God, a mental process which reaches its maximum in mysticism. The haphazard pains of the personality disappear and are suppressed by the joy and glory of the whole.'[41] Tom was much more fascinated by this sort of thing than was Münsterberg, but eventually Tom's doctoral thesis would contain a chapter entitled 'The Psychologist's Treatment of Knowledge'. During the previous session, having come into contact with the Parisian explorations of Janet, he had also embarked on an elementary laboratory course in Experimental Psychology, Philosophy 21, taught by Münsterberg's colleague, Dr Herbert Sidney Langfeld. Dutifully, Tom took notes on how the skin reacted to touch, pain, heat and cold. These jottings, which appear burned at the edge, make it look as if at some point his practical experiments went too far, but perhaps he was just careless with one of the pungent Gauloise cigarettes he favoured for much of his life: a Parisian vice that may not always have endeared him to the other residents of 16 Ash Street.[42]

Langfeld's scholarly concerns included synaesthesia and the effects of fasting. Tom had shown interest in synaesthesia in poems he had worked on in Paris; this phenomenon fascinated several Symbolist poets as well as writers on mysticism. Still thinking of his friend as working in this vein, Conrad Aiken, probably his closest poetic associate during these years, wrote to him from Rome where he had gone to enjoy life with his wife Jessie, asking if Tom had a 'superfluous copy of the Love Song of J. Alfred Prufrock', which Aiken could not get out of his head. He mentioned he had written 'a caricature of T. S. Eliot Esq., – O, a most seductively horrible pome – entitled "Decadence." – It is a caricature worthy of Beerbohm. It has you, and your poems (the earlier Lamia kind as well as the later Prufrock variety) and your hoisted Jesus, and all; a complete composite photograph. Tom posed as a decadent!'[43] Though this poem does not survive, and Aiken did not mail it, clearly Tom's print of Gauguin's yellow Christ – which could be linked to synaesthesia, martyrdom and Paris – appeared part of his 'Decadence'. 'What have you been writing – futurist poems?' Aiken asked, mentioning that he had written 'some dozen or less of long narrative poems' himself. He also asked about Tom's 'latest meditations'.[44] With no wife, no long narrative poems and no grand travel plans, Tom in Ash Street was finding that philosophical 'meditations' took up a demanding amount of his time.

After the excitements of Europe and the poems he had made there, his decision to return to the States and to pursue graduate work in philosophy may have curbed his writing of verse. His courses were intellectually strenuous. Pursuing them involved unremitting interrogation of the grounds of knowledge and belief.

Eastern and Western philosophical and religious systems overlapped, but also conflicted. Though Tom grappled with them in ways that most people could not manage, they posed apparently impossible choices. Studying Greek philosophy alongside Sanskrit and Pali was almost mind-boggling. However much, sitting in class beside Belvalkar, or chatting with professors Lanman and Woods, he was attracted to and deeply impressed by Indic thought, he found it unsettlingly problematic. In Woods he saw a professional able to teach both Greek Philosophy and Philosophical Pali. Yet for Tom the two came to clash in ways he could not reconcile.

Two years spent in the study of Sanskrit under Charles Lanman, and a year in the mazes of Patanjali's metaphysics under the guidance of James Woods, left me in a state of enlightened mystification. A good half of the effort of understanding what the Indian philosophers were after – and their subtleties make most of the great European philosophers look like schoolboys – lay in trying to erase from my mind all the categories and kinds of distinction common to European philosophy from the time of the Greeks. My previous and concomitant study of European philosophy was hardly better than an obstacle. And I came to the conclusion – seeing also that the 'influence' of Brahmin and Buddhist thought upon Europe, as in Schopenhauer, Hartmann, and Deussen, had largely been through romantic misunderstanding – that my only hope of really penetrating to the heart of that mystery would lie in forgetting how to think and feel as an American or a European: which, for practical as well as sentimental reasons, I did not wish to do.[45]

This later (1930s) account may telescope chronology somewhat – Tom's interest in Buddhism continued for several years – but it shows how, even as he made excellent academic progress, he was studying systems of belief which, potentially, might overwhelm everything he had been brought up to be. As with his momentary conversion to Bergsonism, this had its attractions, bringing real intellectual excitement, and a sense of wide horizons. In the long term it would be of most use to him as a poet in providing, through its very clash of styles of thought, a way of helping to articulate torment, unknowability and breakdown.

Yet it offered valuable philosophical guidance. If psychologists including Janet questioned the nature of the self, then in Buddhism Tom found a profound scepticism about the desirability of such a thing as personality. Indic Philology 9 involved, among other things, a study of the Yoga system and Patanjali's *Sutras*. These *Sutras* contained an examination of what Woods, working on his Harvard Oriental Series translation of *The Yoga-System of Patanjali: Or the Ancient Hindu Doctrine of Concentration of Mind* while he taught Tom, termed 'sense-of-personality'. But the ultimate aim was to move beyond and even extinguish this in achieving a transcendental 'higher passionlessness' or enlightened 'Isolation' beyond what the Indic text termed the 'Rain-cloud of knowable things'.[46] Tom's intellect was moulded by such ideas. They would return, sometimes as metaphors, in his poetry, encouraging praise of 'impersonality' in his prose. More generally, they shaped his character.

So interested was he in Eastern thought that in 1913–14 he attended an additional Harvard lecture course given by Masaharu Anesaki, a visiting professor from the Imperial University of Tokyo. Anesaki pioneered religious studies as an academic subject in Japan, and had published on 'How Christianity Appeals to a Japanese Buddhist' in the *Hibbert Journal*. He maintained that 'No religion, not even the most catholic or cosmopolitan in its character, can claim an absolute unity and homogeneity.'[47] Invited by his 'old friend' J. H. Woods, Anesaki held Harvard's newly endowed Professorship of Japanese Literature and Life. His course Philosophy 24a, Schools of Religious and Philosophical Thought in Japan, ranged from 'Buddhist Transcendentalism' through 'Mystic Pantheism' to 'Confucianism' and aspects of Western thought in Japan.[48] Auditing Anesaki's lectures in the winter of 1913–14, Tom noted in black ink on his favoured square-lined paper not only the statement that life was pain but also the notion of the cyclic 'turning of the wheel' in Buddhist thought, and that 'Everything is interrelated.'[49] In the disturbingly interrelated, painful cycles of *The Waste Land* such ideas would return with a vengeance. The thought that Anesaki expounded was mind-bending: 'does reality exist or not? . . . The views that the world exists, or not; both are false; the truth lies in the middle, transcending both views.'

Increasingly preoccupied with considerations of the nature of reality, Tom took notes attentively. He was fascinated, too, by Anesaki's imagistic details. Used to reading about lotus flowers in Sanskrit and Pali, he noted how 'the lotus alone is perfect, because it has many flowers and many fruits *at once*. The flowers & fruit are simultaneous. The real entity represented in the fruit, its manifestation in the flower. Mutual relation of final reality and manifestation.'[50] Tom transcribed, too, Anesaki's explanation of a Pali text's conception of 'past present and future', as well as absorbing Anesaki's class handouts about 'the parable of plants nourished by rain' and ideas about 'Apperception of reality', the 'Hallucinatory' and 'Neither being nor non-being'.⁵¹ Studying the thirteenth-century Buddhist thinker Nichiren, Tom was asked to consider 'the connection between individual salvation and universal salvation'.⁵² So, in a Japanese context, he thought again about the relationship between individual, society and belief which, in a very different environment, had been an issue central to the work of Maurras in Paris. Over twenty years later, considering past, present and future in 'Burnt Norton', Tom returned to the image of the lotus, to ideas of ultimate reality and to hallucination. No other Western poet of his era was more professionally schooled in traditional Indic and Japanese thought.

A good sense of his wrestling with complex theories of knowledge is afforded by essays that he wrote for Philosophy 15 (The Kantian Philosophy). This was one of two courses he took in 1912–13 with Charles Montague Bakewell, a visiting Yale professor who had studied at Harvard with Woods, William James and Josiah Royce, before establishing himself as an authority on ancient Greek philosophers including Heraclitus. Bakewell had served recently as President of the American Philosophical Society. He thought well of Tom, grading his essays A and A-. Supplying 'an irreverent burlesque of Kant's thought', Tom, that fan of music halls, wrote a 'Report on the Kantian Categories', trying to set out Kant's thinking on how different systems of thought and interpretation might interact:

> We are here in face of an infinite regress, dealing with interpenetrating systems; so we handle the world, just like any object, through categories, and can arrive at a metaphysical construction which will be part of another system, bearing just the necessary and systematic relation to that which we have been handling as the world system, as the perception does to the object. Hence we can know neither an object, nor our own ideas, nor the world, except as phenomena: and our knowledge is itself a phenomenon – as known.⁵³

This, like Tom's work for Bakewell's 1912–13 metaphysics course, Philosophy 20c (dealing with the nature of reality), is the stuff of grad-school seminars, hard going for non-philosophers. Yet a sense of potentially infinite regress involving interpenetrating systems is just what *The Waste Land*, questioning what is real and unreal, would offer readers – not because it is a drily Kantian speculation but because its poet, striving to express his mental agony, had been nourished by such complex ways of thinking.

Studying Kant with Bakewell, Tom grew interested in agnostic, critical and especially 'sceptical' attitudes which called 'any dogmatic point of view' into question. Sceptics he had in mind included '[David] Hume [F. H.] Bradley [Harold] Joachim' and '[Arthur] Balfour'. The Oxford philosopher Bradley (and to a lesser extent his colleague Joachim) began to preoccupy him. Tom's philosophical essays could be quite metaphorical: as spring came to Ash Street in 1913, that April, he discussed philosophical ideas almost as if they were forms of vegetation:

> . . . the germ of scepticism is quickened always by the soil of system (rich in contradictions). As the system decomposes, the doubts push through; and the decay is so general and fructifying that we are no longer sure enough of anything to draw the line between knowledge and ignorance. For Bradley the only recourse is an Absolute which maintains some of the visual features of German Idealism, but none of the *Gemüth*; which represents in fact only the pathetic primitive human *Credo* in ultimate explanation and ultimate reality which haunts us like the prayers of childhood. This Absolute is mystical, because desparate. Ultimate truth remains inaccessible; and it only remains for Mr. Joachim to shatter what little Bradley has left standing, by urging upon us that we have no right to affirm (though he still affirms it!) that there is truth at all.

Tom was fascinated by such intense scepticism, even as he studied the 'mystical' and explored the idea that 'in order to know we must begin with *faith*'.[54] What was going on in his philosophical investigations highlighted a continuing clash. On the one side stood the values of religious commitment so prevalent in his mother's writings and (however scornful he now was of Unitarianism) part of his own upbringing. Opposite were ranged intellectual forces of corrosive scepticism, questioning the very bases of thought and belief. Out of that clash came not just philosophising but also, in succeeding years, poems simultaneously fascinated by questions of knowledge and provocatively sceptical or hostile towards established systems of faith.

Keeping up his interest in Bergson, he read the French thinker's article on consciousness in the October 1911 *Hibbert Journal*. Yet despite Bergson being the subject of a popular 1912 series of Harvard lectures by E. C. Wilm, Tom's scepticism eroded his earlier Bergsonian fervour. Some time after reading the *Hibbert* piece, he attempted to 'raise objections' to and highlight 'inconsistencies' in *Matter and Memory* and *Creative Evolution*. He subjected the original French texts to close scrutiny, bringing to bear some of his reading in Greek philosophy. 'Bergson's critics', he summarised, 'call him a mystic. With this appellation I am not disposed to quarrel; though, as at present elaborated in Bergson's work, it is rather a weakling mysticism.'[55]

Conrad Aiken was glad that by March 1913 Tom had 'shunted Bergson down the hill'.[56] Yet Tom remained fascinated by mysticism – and not just from Asia. 'I'm eager to have wisdom from you *in re* these your Buddhistic and Indic mysteries', Aiken wrote; but Tom read about other mysticisms too.[57] Sometimes drawing on ways of thinking that he had encountered in Paris, he took copious notes from books on mysticism, asceticism and primitive religion. In November 1912 he purchased his own copy of William James's *The Varieties of Religious Experience*. Making notes from this book, he concentrated on considerations of Eastern and Western mystical thought, interested in 'signs' associated with mysticism, including 'Ineffability' and 'Passivity'.[58] James's was only one of many works in this area that he perused. Others included such slightly older writings as W. R. Inge's *Christian Mysticism* (1899) and Ernest Murisier's *Les Maladies du sentiment religieux* (1903), from which he took notes on such topics as 'L'extase' and 'lévitation'. He read recent publications including Henri Delacroix's *Études d'histoire et de psychologie du mysticisme: les grands mystiques chrétiens* (1908), which interested him with its detailing of St Theresa's sexualised ecstasy, and the 1912 edition of Evelyn Underhill's six hundred-page *Mysticism*, which he summarised on notecards.

From Underhill he copied out the words, 'If we would cease, once for all, to regard visions & voices as objective, and be content to see in them forms of symbolic expression, ways in which the subconscious activity of the spiritual self reaches the surface mind, many of the disharmonies noticeable would fade away. Visionary experience . . . is a picture which the mind constructs . . . from raw materials already at its disposal.' Though Underhill did not say so, this argument brought mystical experiences close to Symbolist poetry and the kind of verse that interested Tom. As he read about St Theresa and St John of the Cross, he pondered experiences of 'The Mystic Way' as outlined by Underhill, noting that its stages were

1. Revelation of Divine Reality
2. Purgation
3. Illumination
4. Dark Night of the Soul
5. Union

Tom stored away images and ways of thinking that would fuel his poetry for decades. Yet he read as a fascinated sceptic, taking on board not just Underhill's sympathetic commentaries but also the more distanced treatment in Josiah Moses's 1906 *Pathological Aspects of Religion*. Its accounts of phallicism led Tom to note the 'Sexual element' was 'very dominant'.[59] His note-taking in this and related areas, and the subtle changes in the handwriting of his notes suggest that his interest, though tied at times to particular papers he was writing, went on for an extended period.

It was spurred in part by his encounters with Parisian intellectual life. There were also links to the work of Harvard philosophers including Josiah Royce. Tom jotted down that the chapters dealing with 'Realism and Mysticism in the History of Thought' and 'The Unity of Being, and the Mystical Interpretation' in Royce's *The World and the Individual* (1900) constituted 'An excellent exposition of philosophical mysticism'.[60] There was intellectual grit in all this, but also voyeuristic fascination in some of the stranger psychosexual aspects of religious extremism. All added fuel to Tom's poetic as well as his philosophical, often religiously inflected imagination. Sitting by the fire in his Ash Street lodgings, or more sumptuously provided for in Harvard's libraries, he read books, papers in specialist journals, essays, memoirs and scriptures.

His unusual intellectualism may have made him intimidating, but he knew how to counterbalance it. Besides, it also made him friends among some of the ablest graduate students. The most remarkable of these was the American Jewish thinker Norbert Wiener, a prodigy from infancy and later the pioneer of cybernetics. Like Tom, Wiener had been born in Missouri; his family had moved to Boston when he was very young. His father, who taught Slavic languages at Harvard, had home-schooled his nervous, introspective son; by fifteen this prodigy was a Harvard graduate student with a background in zoology and philosophy, though he also suffered from depression. Interested in the border zone where philosophy and mathematics overlapped, he had wanted to study with Royce, but Royce was ill. So the teenager worked instead on mathematical logic first with E. V. Huntington of the Mathematics Department, then with a visiting professor from Tufts, Karl Schmidt, who supervised Wiener's PhD. This compared aspects of the algebraic thinking of Ernst Schroeder, A. N. Whitehead and Bertrand Russell.

Intellectually hungry, Tom, too, was studying with Schmidt. In 1912–13 he took his course in advanced logic, Philosophy 8. It included an introduction to the algebra of logic. This helps explain why, a little later, Tom made reference to 'my friend Dr Wiener'.[61] Wiener, who obtained his Harvard doctorate in 1912 at the age of eighteen, was someone with whom he could discuss his most abstruse philosophical interests. A problem for advanced graduate students in the humanities can be intellectual isolation. As Tom progressed through graduate courses, probably no other Harvard student covered quite the same range. However, though his explorations in the algebra of logic and the nature of reality may have cut him off in some senses from many people around him, his philosophical agility gave him a position of clear utility within the Harvard system. Having impressed his professors, on 10 June 1912 he was appointed 'Assistant in Philosophy for one year from September 1st 1912'.[62]

Renewed the following session, this teaching post demonstrated that at least some of his studies could be useful to other people. It paid him, too, for the first time in his life, a small monthly salary. His job was to teach 'sections' (seminar groups with about two dozen students in each) from the big undergraduate class Philosophy A. Drawing sometimes on Professor Bakewell's *Source Book in Ancient Philosophy*, this course covered Greek Philosophy, concentrating on the Pre-Socratics, Plato and Aristotle; then, moving through Plotinus and Seneca, it explored Christian thought of the medieval Patristic and Scholastic periods as well as their legacy. Philosophy A's reading list involved work by several authors who mattered to Tom, including Dante and St Augustine. In *The Waste Land* and elsewhere he would draw several times on Augustine's *Confessions* where he encountered an intense sense of self-consciousness to match his own.

He was quite able to teach this material, but it kept him on his toes: Plotinus and Seneca one week, Augustine the next. He had to set exercises and prepare students to answer such exam questions as 'Compare very briefly the doctrines of Heraclitus with those of the Eleatics'.[63] Administratively, he occasionally stumbled. On Friday mornings in the fall and winter of 1913, he had to teach two Philosophy A sections in Emerson Hall – at 10 a.m., then at noon – and was expected to take a roll-call, sending details of this to the university authorities. When no list was received for Friday 7 November's 10 a.m. meeting of section G, an official named Cram sent Tom a solemn pro-forma: 'It is important for me to know whether there was an exercise held that day, and if possible to have the names of the absentees. Awaiting your reply . . .'[64]

If Tom was annoyed to receive this message, he could console himself that it was addressed, flatteringly but inaccurately, to 'Dr T. S. Eliot'. Still doing his coursework, he had not even started writing his doctoral thesis, but was recognised nonetheless as a distinguished student. Active in Harvard's Philosophy Club, he participated in its twice-monthly meetings in Emerson Hall room C during session 1912–13, and was elected its 1913–14 president.

His interest in Indian philosophical studies, as well as in poetry, led him to go to hear Rabindranath Tagore, who gave a series of lectures (later published as *Sadhana*) in the Philosophy Department in the early part of 1913. Tagore's topics included 'The Problem of Evil' and 'Man's Relation to the Universe'. He was also invited to speak to the Harvard Philosophy Club on 18 February 1913 about 'Brahma' – the creator, self-born in the lotus flower, a fundamental topic that Tom had pondered. Admired by Professor Woods, Tagore was asked back for further lectures in April when Robert Rattray, a Unitarian student who knew Tom through the Philosophy Club, was particularly enthusiastic about the 'famous philosopher-poet of India', and wrote to the *Crimson* on 8 April to 'call attention' to Tagore's significance:

In the Times Literary Supplement for March 20, 1913, leading article, is the following:

'A new star, perhaps of the first magnitude, has lately appeared in the Indian poet, Rabindranath Tagore, whose exquisite art and keen vision of the eternal through the temporal stamp him as a religious genius of rare power. It may be hoped that the appreciation of his poetry in Miss Underhill's new book (The Mystic Way, by Evelyn Underhill) will procure many readers for the cheaper edition of "Gitanjali.". . .'[65]

Tagore's prose translations of Bengali 'song offerings' in *Gitanjali* (1912) had been published with an introduction by W. B. Yeats. They were likened to biblical texts. Yet their conventional poetic diction was far removed from what Tom was attempting. He listened to Tagore, but any comment he made does not survive. Writing poetry involves resisting some influences, integrating others. It would be several years before elements important to Tagore – Indic traditions, mysticism, philosophy and poetry – would be configured very differently by Tom.

Just before Tagore gave his last two Harvard lectures, on Friday 4 April 1913, Tom, Robert Rattray, Norbert Wiener and other members of the Philosophy Club including Dr Harry Todd Costello (a young teaching assistant recently returned from attending Bergson's lectures in Paris) met in Emerson C to participate in 'A Review and Discussion of "The New Realism"'.[66] This was a debate about *A Preface to Politics* by Walter Lippmann, one of Tom's undergraduate classmates. Tom worked carefully on the paper he read that evening. It reveals much about his habits of mind. A clear satirical impulse surfaces in his vignettes of current philosophical tendencies, whether 'Mr B. Russell directing with passionate enthusiasm' what Tom calls a 'ballet of bloodless alphabets' (Wiener, interested in Russell, might have liked that), or 'Professor Bosanquet' as 'a prophet who has put off his shoes and talks with the Absolute in a burning bush'. Drafting this talk, Tom dithered over what to say about Royce. Initially, and somewhat flatteringly, he was going to say that Royce (who that year published *The Problem of Christianity*) 'as a relativist is a wholly sympathetic figure'; eventually he settled for something more arrestingly sharp: 'to Professor Royce we owe the realisation of Christianity by the method of last aid to the dead'. With sideswipes at 'Bergsonians in various degrees of recovery from intellect', Tom was trying hard to impress fellow grad students.[67]

His opening vignettes come closest to the social satire of his early poems; his mockery of radical chic reveals a sympathy with conservatism inherited from his Republican father and quickened by his time in Paris. After much scoring out, rephrasing and the inserting of bons mots about Boston's Beacon Street (whose well-to-do mansions were then being turned into apartments), he continued:

> The present furthermore is a time of lively agitation of political theory. Radicalism is become conventional. Socialism has settled down on Beacon St.; but no radical is so radical as to be a conservative. Where are all the conservatives? They have all gone into hiding. All the old ladies with cozy shares of telephone stock, all the clergymen of subsidised goodness – now socialists waiting not for the millennium, but for the minimum wage which shall abolish prostitution; all our millionaires are socialistic theorists who will dispose of their incomes – later – according to their own theories.[68]

With a fine ear for dramatic effect, Tom inserted that word '– later –' as he redrafted. His remarks lean in one direction towards the mockery of the progressivist clergyman Lyman Abbott in 'Ballade pour la grosse Lulu', and in a slightly different direction towards the skewering of modern New England life in such poems as 'Cousin Nancy', 'Aunt Helen' and 'Mr. Apollinax', written not so long afterwards.

Attacking Rousseau, Tom's paper on Lippmann's book mocked 'the fallacy of progress'. It shows him still wrestling rather sarcastically with his religious upbringing: 'I belong to a church of which one of the tenets refers to the Progress of mankind onward and upward forever.' Referring to Lippmann's admiration for Frenchman Georges Sorel's 'doctrine of the "Social Myth"', Tom protests, 'I do not understand how M. Sorel avoids seeing that his theory of myths is itself a myth; that the aspirations and impulses which his myth bodies forth will inevitably be reinterpreted by history.' Underlying fashionable enthusiasms, including those of Bergson and Nietzsche, Tom finds 'fundamental pessimism and despair'. He worries that 'if *all* human meaning is human meaning, then there is no meaning. If you assume only human standards, what standards have you? History, if it is to be interpreted at all, must be interpreted from a point of view itself outside the process.'[69]

Tom's critique of notions of progress involved a perception that one myth comes to be interpreted by another, then by another again in a potentially infinite regress. This can be aligned with the direction of thought in some of the comparative literature classes he had taken as an undergraduate; those saw older pagan myths and practices being overlaid with Christian symbolism. Such a way of thinking would be reinforced by his reading in anthropology and primitive religion. Eventually all this would feed into the consciousness that produced *The Waste Land*, where it seems impossible to find a point of view outside the process of history from which history can be interpreted.

In his 1913 paper, Tom perhaps surprised his philosophical audience as they listened to his thoughts on Lippmann's book. Having written first of all the words 'we do not need to wait for Bergson to tell us that', he later changed this to 'for we know already that'; then he quoted Dante's *Purgatorio*:

Lo naturale è sempre sanza errore,
    ma l'altro puote errar per malo obietto,
    o per troppo o per poco di vigore.[70]

A few years later, once more considering poetry beside philosophy, Tom would quote these lines again in 'Dante', the essay which concludes his 1920 book *The Sacred Wood,* seeing them as 'pure exposition of philosophy', but maintaining that 'We are not here studying the philosophy, we *see* it, as part of the ordered world.'[71] Dante's lines are about the love of what is good. In Purgatory Dante's guide Virgil tells him that 'Neither Creator nor creature was ever without love, either natural or of the mind'. He continues, in the lines Tom quoted in Italian:

The natural is always without error,
    but the mind's love may go wrong through a wrong object
    or else through excess or defect of vigour.[72]

By the time he copied out these lines in 1913, Tom was falling in love, though he seems not to have been able to give voice to what he felt. Yet the lines are not about sexual but about intellectual passion. Speaking them in a philosophical discussion with his friends on an April evening, Tom quoted them in an apposite context; but he also hinted that, despite all his intellectual commitment and rigour, the most important form of expression for him would not lie in politics or even in philosophy but in Dante's medium, poetry.

Still, he was on course to become a philosopher, and he took that seriously. Conrad Aiken, who had missed Tom's company and who returned to Cambridge with his wife in 1913, was keen to emphasise the importance of living – and, indeed, having sex – rather than just sitting thinking. Though Aiken had his own philosophical interests, he asked Tom, 'Why indeed *study* philosophy?'[73] Aiken was gearing up to publish his first collection of poems, *Earth Triumphant,* which appeared in September 1914. Tom, who had probably seen much of it earlier, read it in proof. It scorns 'Clutching philosophy's vapid wraith', and mocks poets who deploy 'fantastic' symbols yet lack 'warm blood' in their 'veins'. Aiken's poems are sexually knowing, but often banal: 'Like blossom-fires of spring her body went, / He closed his eyes and knew now what life meant'. Trying hard to be modern but sounding notes from the 1890s, *Earth Triumphant* includes glimpses of the sort of vaudeville shows Aiken and Tom had relished in Boston, hymning

> The latest musical comedy, –
> To sink back in a front-row seat
> And watch the intricate flash of feet
> Of well-trained chorus-girls, who came
> To give him ecstasy and shame –
> With legs of lustrous saffron silk,
> White frills, and skin as white as milk,
> With sexual laughter, nods and becks,
> Mechanical display of sex, –[74]

If Aiken somewhat show-offishly urged more life and sex, and less philosophy, then Tom remarked on his friend's naively excited poem 'Youth' that 'the hero was perhaps not as innocent and romantic as he was made out to be, and maybe carried rubber goods in his hip pocket'.[75]

Aiken could not help stealing rhythms and phrases from Tom, who had to put up with this in Aiken's volumes for years even before his own first collection was published. However, the perceptive Aiken recognised Tom's poetic genius before almost anyone else, and, perhaps despite himself, was impressed by Tom's studies. Later, in the 1920s, linking

Tom's poetry and personality, Aiken would write about his friend that 'From the outset his poetry was the poetry of a sceptic, an ironist, an intellectual; it was detached and convictionless; but it was also the poetry of a highly sensitive and shrinking individual with exceptionally acute insight, and imagination and a very fine sense of the values of rhythm.'[76] Conrad remembered being with Tom and the young philosopher George Boas (who spoke to the Philosophical Club on 13 March 1914 about 'The Fine Arts and Expression') in a Greek restaurant near the waterfront on Boston's Kneeland Street while Tom held forth about 'using words of which I don't know the meaning'.[77] Tom was obsessed with issues of meaning and interpretation, but, despite his 'shrinking' tendencies, he also worked hard at getting on. Now president of the Harvard Philosophical Club, he wrote from 16 Ash Street to a Yale professor ('My dear Professor Hocking'), inviting him to come and speak; then, after William Ernest Hocking had spoken on 5 December 1913 about 'Bergson's Philosophy of Art', Tom thanked him fulsomely.[78] Another visitor (whose Seminary in Metaphysics on the nature of reality he took in the earlier part of session 1913–14) was Professor R. F. A. Hoernlé from the University of Durham. Later Hoernlé would be asked to comment on Tom's PhD.

Tom addressed the Club of which he was president on 24 October 1913, taking as his title 'Philosophy and Politics'. This talk built on the earlier 'New Realism' discussion in which he had played a prominent part. He knew how to get himself known. During the second part of 1913–14 he studied ethics in Philosophy 20d with William James's former student, Professor Ralph Barton Perry; and for the whole year he participated in Philosophy 20c, a seminar in logic overseen by Josiah Royce who had chosen as the topic for that session a comparative study of various types of scientific method. Royce had appointed as recording secretary for the seminar Harry Todd Costello, whose PhD Royce and Perry had examined and whom Tom knew from the Philosophical Club. Costello was a recent holder of Harvard's Frederick Sheldon Fellowship which provided money for educational travel to Europe; on 31 March 1914 the president and fellows of Harvard appointed Tom as a Sheldon Fellow in Philosophy.

All this confirms he was not just talented but could make the most of the Harvard system. He was keen, too, to demonstrate to his parents, and not least to his father whose financial support had made his Harvard life possible, that he was not simply an indulged incumbrance. He wrote to tell his folks his good news, and expressed something of his gratitude and his anxiety. His father replied generously,

My dear Tom:

I am much pleased that you have rec[eive]d the Scholarship, on ac[coun]t of the honor, as you couldn't get it unless you deserved it. You have never been a 'burden' to me, my dear fellow. A parent is always in debt to a son who has been as dutiful and affectionate as you have been.

Yrs.

P.[79]

This note meant a lot. Later, after his parents died, Tom made sure almost all his correspondence with them was destroyed. But these words survived.

He remained close to his parents emotionally, even if the relationship was at times problematic. In class, he was in a different world. Encouraged by Hoernlé's seminar on the nature of reality, he postulated that 'There are I believe degrees of *reality*.' He wrote a paper in which he began, 'I do not intend to draw any absolute distinction between perception, image and judgment, between real and unreal.' Discussing the epistemology of hallucination, appearance and judgement, he tried out materials that, in revised form, would find their way into his doctoral thesis. Undermining distinctions between real and unreal, he worked on fascinating but vertiginous ideas. His sense of humour helped him preserve both mental agility and psychological balance. 'Metaphysical opinions', he pronounced, 'ascend like a rocket and come down like a stick. The struggle of life is to eat your cake and have it too: to go up on your Jacob's ladder of reality and stay on the ground at the same time.' Addicted to image and metaphor even as he discussed philosophical abstractions, he added, 'If we have good long legs, the attempt to keep one foot on sea and one on shore does not become embarrassing until the boat is well under way.'[80] So Tom, the experienced sailor, tried to navigate precariously through metaphysics.

Of the many philosophical papers he wrote during these years one in particular stands out for readers of his later poetry. It was written for discussion in Royce's seminar on scientific method, and dealt with the interpretation of primitive ritual. In a seminar that included researchers from several backgrounds, discussing everything from 'protoplasm' to Einstein's 'relativity' and its 'new analysis of physical space and time and their relation' with regard to 'simultaneity', Tom on 9 December 1913 read a paper which asked the question, 'On what terms is a science of religion possible?'[81] Beyond that, he wondered, 'Can it be treated wholly according to the methods of sociology?' Drawing on Durkheim and Lévy-Bruhl, he brought to bear also his reading in psychology and anthropology. Works such as E. B. Tylor's Victorian classic *Primitive Culture* and other anthropological tomes are alluded to, but Tom critiques these, arguing that 'What seemed to one generation fact is from the point of view of the next, a rejected interpretation.'[82]

He sees the roots of religion as ultimately inscrutable. It may be possible to reconstruct an 'external order in ritual and creed and in artistic and literary expression', but only approximately, and examination of the elements of that order moves us immediately from unstable 'fact' into interpretation. 'The actual *ritual*' is part of 'a complex which includes previous stages' interpretations of the ritual of the preceding stage, and so on back indefinitely'. Though Tom's interest here was in the way '"*fact*" melts into interpretation, and interpretation into metaphysics', later this sense of ritual, artistic expression and religious forms being layered one on top of another in a possible order that went 'back indefinitely' would be part of the underpinning of *The Waste Land*, and of other poems.[83]

By 1913 he had been reading parts of anthropologist J. G. Frazer's vast 'comparative work', *The Golden Bough*. He was in awe of it, but critical of how it imposed interpretations on its data:

> I have not the smallest competence to criticise Dr Frazer's erudition, and his ability to manipulate this erudition I can only admire. But I cannot subscribe — for instance to the *interpretation* with which he ends his volume on the Dying God. He is accounting for the magical rites of spring festivals: —
> P.266[84]

At this point he seems to have read to the seminar group some of Frazer's words from the opening of his section 'The Magic Spring'. After supplying accounts of various vegetation ceremonies, including Indian ones involving Siva and Parvati and European ones featuring 'the May Bride, Bridegroom of the May, and so forth', Frazer (on page 266) opines:

> The general explanation which we have been led to adopt of these and many similar ceremonies is that they are, or were in their origin, magical rites intended to ensure the revival of nature in spring. The means by which they were supposed to effect this end were imitation and sympathy. Led astray by his ignorance of the true causes of things, primitive man believed that in order to produce the great phenomena of nature on which his life depended he had only to imitate them . . .[85]

Convinced such speculations are unjustified in terms of philosophical method, Tom exclaimed pointedly to his 1913 seminar group that 'This volume appeared as recently as 1911!' Yet he argues, too, that other thinkers such as Durkheim, more methodologically up to date, also blur lines between fact and interpretation, and between individual and group consciousness, in ways that are untenable. A science of religion is impossible, however much craved. 'I do not think that any definition of religious behavior can be satisfactory, and yet you must assume if you are to make a start at all that all these phenomena have a common meaning; you must postulate your own attitude and interpret your so-called facts into it, and how can this be science?'[86]

Tom the impressive graduate student cut through other thinkers' assumptions with commendable incisiveness. Yet he also tied himself in knots. Tom the poet retained several ideas and images his reading supplied. This can be seen only in retrospect. In Cambridge, as he walked between Emerson Hall and Ash Street for the umpteenth time, he had other thoughts on his mind. He was very struck by the arrival of the English philosopher Bertrand Russell, lionised as a visiting professor at Harvard where he was delivering a lecture series on 'Our Knowledge of the External World'. Russell (who found Harvard 'soul-destroying') invited students to visit him in his office, and on 27 March 1914 Tom went there along with a friend of his, fellow philosophy graduate student Raphael Demos whom he knew through the Philosophical Club. After talking to the two students, Russell observed that

> one, named Eliot, is very well-dressed and polished, with manners of the finest Etonian type; the other is an unshaven Greek, appropriately named Demos, who earns money for his fees by being a waiter in a restaurant. The two were obviously friends, and had on neither side the slightest consciousness of social difference.[87]

Tom described himself later that year as 'a thorough snob', but that was not how Russell saw him.[88] Tom audited some of Russell's logic classes at Harvard and they spoke about Heraclitus (whom Russell was about to discuss in a lecture on 'Mysticism and Logic'). 'Yes, he always reminds me of Villon', said Tom – presumably linking the medieval French poet François Villon's lament for the vanished snows of yesteryear with Heraclitus' perception of transience expressed through the idea that one cannot step into the same river twice. Russell thought Tom's remark 'so good that I always wished he would make another'. But Tom, in whom shyness and incisive eloquence often contended, was 'extraordinarily silent'.[89]

They met again on Sunday 10 May 1914 at a garden party held at the house of Santayana's and Jean Verdenal's Francophile friend Benjamin Apthorpe Fuller, high-minded author of *The Problem of Evil in Plotinus*, which saw 'Evil' as linked to 'the body'.[90] Fuller lived in the country with his wife and his mother, and Russell thought him 'an Oxfordized Harvardian, cultivated, full of the classics, talking as like an Englishman as he can, full of good nature, but feeble – quite without the ferocity that is needed to redeem culture'. Noticing Tom, too, at this party, Russell decided he was 'a very similar type, proficient in Plato, intimate with French literature from Villon to Vildrach [Vildrac], very capable of a certain exquisiteness of appreciation, but lacking in the crude insistent passion that one must have in order to achieve anything'.[91] As Russell observed the shy graduate student, so Tom watched Russell. His observation of this visitor at the Fullers' home prompted his later poem 'Mr. Apollinax', in which the physicality, behaviour and 'dry and passionate talk' of a visitor to the United States discomfit his academic hosts, whose logic is less than perfect: '"His pointed ears . . . He must be unbalanced."'[92] Apollinax comes over as clever, disruptive, ready to violate the proprieties. Unsettling this genteel milieu, he makes the poem's speaker think of the Classical sex god Priapus juxtaposed with the 'shy figure' of the delicate-sounding 'Fragilion': this (though the poem was authored considerably later) was perceptive, for Russell liked to give free rein to his sexual appetite. Tom, customarily far more repressed in his conduct, remained part of the polite New England milieu, but knew well that it needed disrupting. As a forceful personality and as a philosopher, Russell was fascinating. However, for some time, though philosophical argument was certainly important to Tom, he had known it was not his sole concern.

Since at least the previous summer he had had lines to learn, and had been enjoying mixing with people who were not philosophers. He had been playing the leading man, Lord Bantock, in *Fanny and the Servant Problem*, performed in summer 1913 by the Cambridge Social Dramatic Club in Brattle Hall, not far from Harvard Yard. The female lead, Lady Bantock, was a dark-eyed, sophisticated young woman called Amy de Gozzaldi. Schooled at Cambridge's Berkeley Street School along with Tom's cousin Eleanor (who lived along the road at 1 Berkeley Place), Amy had grown up at 96 Brattle Street. Both girls loved acting; their school had a tradition of performing plays. Amy would act in the Social Dramatic Club for much of her life. For a few years she and Eleanor had been schoolfellows with another girl with a passion for drama, Emily Hale from Boston. Emily's mother had had a mental breakdown, so the girl had been brought up by her uncle and aunt, the Reverend and Mrs Joyce Carroll

Perkins. After Berkeley Street School Emily had attended Miss Porter's School in Connecticut where the headmaster was married to a Hale. Tom's parents knew the Perkinses, and were familiar with the circles in which Emily and her friends moved. Amy's mother was active in the recently founded Cambridge Historical Society; Eleanor, who wrote plays as well as acting in them, had played with the Eliot children at East Gloucester and Cambridge since infancy. Emily's uncle was a music critic for the *Boston Globe*; her father Edward was, like several of Tom's uncles, a Unitarian minister. He had taught at Harvard Divinity School and became first assistant to the Reverend Edward Everett Hale in Boston. At one point, in 1900, it had been expected that the Reverend Edward Everett Hale would be succeeded in his ecclesiastical 'pastorate' by one of Tom's relations, the Reverend Samuel A. Eliot.[93] Each of them born in 1891, Amy, Eleanor and Emily belonged, like Tom, to the cultured upper echelon of New England society.

Lord Bantock was a major part. Since it was customary for the players to work up from minor roles to larger ones, probably Tom had done so too; later in life Eleanor Hinkley stated that his 'first dramatic appearance' was in February 1913, but his interest in drama predates that.[94] Certainly he enjoyed the work of the Social Dramatic Club. Though much of its archive was destroyed in a flood, a list of productions survives, and Tom's enthusiasm would fit with his father's concerns about his son spending too much time on drama. During Tom's junior undergraduate year the Social Dramatic Club, an amateur group mounting three or four shows annually, had as its 75th performance *She Stoops to Conquer*, a work alluded to in *The Waste Land*. While he was away in Paris they had performed J. M. Barrie's *The Admirable Crichton*; as one of Tom's friends put it, this was long remembered since 'one of our better actresses walked on stage clad in a rather short leopard skin with no shoes or stockings – quite a sensation in those days and a fine conversation piece for the rest of the season'.[95]

His friend's delight in the frisson that a glimpse of leopard-skinned flesh could cause in Cambridge would be matched by Tom's own mischievous coining of the name 'Professor Channing-Cheetah' in his priapic poem 'Mr. Apollinax'.[96] The 1911–12 season had seen the Club performing Robert Marshall's comedy *The Second in Command*, in which a young woman reads aloud to a young man from a romantic novel and enacts what she reads: '"She stood gazing into his eyes, the sunlight turning her soft hair to golden lustre. Scarce knowing what she did her arms crept round his neck (*places her arms round* HILDEBRAND'S *neck*) And in a moment as a wild and sudden blush leapt to her cheek, she kissed him passionately." (*kisses* HILDEBRAND).'[97] Tom's poems liked to mock such stagey, self-conscious romantic effusions. Sometimes, however, as in the sense of 'a gesture and a pose' in his poem 'La Figlia Che Piange', his verse shows an acute awareness of theatricality:

Weave, weave the sunlight in your hair –
Clasp your flowers to you with a pained surprise –
Fling them to the ground and turn
With a fugitive resentment in your eyes:
But weave, weave the sunlight in your hair.[98]

Henry Arthur Jones's *The Manoeuvres of Jane* in which an English lord wonders how 'self-possessed' he really is and Anthony Hope's *The Adventures of the Lady Ursula* completed the Dramatic Club's 1911–12 season.[99] 1912–13 brought John Hartley Manners's *The House Next Door*, which staged English anti-Semitism ('Jews, Jews, Jews everywhere one turns')[100] and Israel Zangwill's *Merely Mary Ann,* the production that preceded *Fanny and the Servant Problem.* During Tom's last year as a Harvard graduate student, the Club mounted productions of Somerset Maugham's *Jack Straw,* with its disconcerting waiter, and Hubert Henry Davis's 1914 comedy *A Single Man* in which a middle-aged writer is attracted to and eventually marries his secretary.

In such English plays well-bred men fall in love with actresses; upper-crust characters sport names like Agatha; situations unfold in country houses; upper-class mores and cockney dialect mix; scenarios are clever and traditionally plotted. Tom's poems might mock these kinds of romantic comedy, but they would supply narratives and images for his future life and work. Sometimes, much later, his own plays would mix their style with plots taken from ancient Greek drama, attempting to render 'degrees of reality' and to appeal to popular audiences. The most striking theatrical moment in Davis's *A Single Man* is when, at the end of the second act, a confused group of lovers dance round and round to the nursery rhyme 'Here we go round the mulberry bush'.[101] Having read much about interpretations of dances and rituals, about a decade later when his own love-life had become a disaster, Tom would move from thoughts of 'Lips that would kiss' to a parody of that same nursery rhyme:

Here we go round the prickly pear
Prickly pear prickly pear
Here we go round the prickly pear
At five o'clock in the morning.[102]

Acting provides a way for people to overcome their shyness. Tom, whose shyness was often perceived as arrogance, had worked hard to transform himself from the schoolboy whose public speaking was poor into the graduate student suitable for a starring role. Just as his St Louis dancing classes had been a way to meet girls, so, the Social Dramatic Club offered similar opportunities. It had been set up as a merger between two older societies in 1891 to meet 'in Brattle Hall on Saturday evenings' with 'some dramatic performance or other entertainment given in the early part of the evening, followed by simple refreshments and – from eleven to twelve o'clock – dancing'.[103] The 'Brattle Hall dances', where Conrad Aiken remembered seeing Tom, were probably descendants of these functions. Very different from his all-male philosophy seminars, and from the all-female schools attended by Amy de Gozzaldi, Eleanor Hinkley, Emily Hale and their friends, the 'Social Dramatic' encouraged respectable Cambridge young folk to mingle. Harvard's drama clubs were male-dominated, though some Radcliffe students participated; the Social Dramatic drew on a wider gene pool. Under its auspices young women and men danced, flirted, and even indulged in onstage kissing.

The kissing was famous. Dick Hall, whom Tom later described as one of the 'old theatrical friends of mine from the days of the Cambridge Dramatic Society', told heroic tales about it.[104] It was also remembered by a local Unitarian minister's son called Edward who had grown up in Irving Street, just along the road from Josiah Royce. At the age of eighteen Edward played the part of Ernest Bennet, Lady Bantock's second footman, in the summer 1913 production of *Fanny and the Servant Problem*. During the play the second footman has to kiss Lady Bantock, but in real life the young actor was intimidated by the well-travelled, sophisticated twenty-two-year-old Amy so his kissing was too tentative. 'At rehearsals the director continually encouraged him to be more bold. At length, on the night of the performance, he outdid himself in a kiss that he remembered for months.'[105] In fact, he remembered it for decades: 'billions cheered:I shall never forget'.[106] The second footman's name was Edward Estlin Cummings, later better known as E. E. Cummings.

Tom got to kiss and be kissed by Amy de Gozzaldi several times in the play. Amy played Fanny, an actress who has married Vernon, Lord Bantock, and turns out to be the niece of his butler. That butler seeks to order Fanny about, despite the machinations of her agent, Newte: hence the 'servant problem' in English humorist Jerome K. Jerome's play. Tom's onstage interactions with Amy were rather different from his exchanges with the members of the Harvard Philosophical Club:

FANNY (*she laughs — takes his hand in hers*). I wish you hadn't asked Newte any questions about me. It would have been so nice to feel that you had married me — just because you couldn't help it — (*laughs*) — just because I was I; and nothing else mattered.

VERNON. Let's forget I ever did. (*He kneels down beside her.*) I didn't do it for my own sake, as you know. A man in my position *has* to think of other people. His wife has to take her place in society. People insist upon knowing something about her. It's not enough for the stupid 'County' that she's the cleverest, most bewilderingly beautiful, bewitching lady in the land.

FANNY (*she laughs*). And how long will you think all that?

VERNON. For ever, and ever, and ever.

FANNY. Oh, you dear boy. (*She kisses him.*) You don't know how a woman loves the man she loves to love her (*Laughs.*) Isn't that complicated?

VERNON. Not at all. We're just the same. We love to love the woman we love.

FANNY (*laughs*). Provided the 'County' will let us. And the County has said: A man may not marry his butler's niece.

VERNON (*laughing*). You've got butlers on the brain. If I ever do run away with my own cook or under-housemaid, it will be your doing.

FANNY. You haven't the pluck! The 'County' would laugh at you. You men are so frightened of being laughed at.[107]

Gently exploring issues of gender, social class and English mores, such plays were just the sort of thing that the markedly Anglophile Social Dramatic Club relished. E. E. Cummings seems to have felt some jealousy of Tom's role and the relationship with Amy de Gozzaldi that it afforded him; Tom, who later imagined Amy dancing to the music of *Carmen* with 'huge eyes', did not complain.[108] The woman he had fallen in love with, though, was not Amy (who went on to marry Tom's fellow actor and Harvard classmate Dick Hall) but her friend Emily Hale. Given that Emily had known Amy and Tom's cousin Eleanor so long, it seems inconceivable that she was not watching Lord and Lady Bantock's performance closely.

Later, Emily Hale acted in several Dramatic Society productions, and taught acting at various colleges, but in her youth her family forbade her to go on the professional stage — it was not considered respectable. Having returned from Miss Porter's School to the Boston area, she was a regular visitor to Eleanor's house. Planned from early in the year, the June 1912 fiftieth anniversary of the Berkeley Street School and the setting up that February of a Berkeley Street School Association (in which Amy's mother was to the fore) brought together a number of former pupils.[109] It was in 1912 that Tom met Emily through Eleanor.

Shrewd, observant, musical, slim and elegant, Emily, like Tom's mother, was intelligent but had not gone to university. She had the polite manners of an upbringing in Chestnut Hill, just outside Boston, and of her several single-sex schools. Her ability to act helped conceal a history of familial damage: in early childhood she had had to cope with the death of her infant brother, then with separation from her increasingly mentally ill mother. Those close to Emily (including Tom) detected a vulnerability about her, as well as a gift for friendship. She could be very fine company; with those whom she really trusted she was a prolific, entertaining correspondent. People who knew her less intimately sometimes thought her snobbish, aloof and repressed. Tom, too, could be perceived this way. His intellectual brilliance, and the persistent shyness he had fought hard to overcome through various pursuits from acting to taking some boxing lessons in Boston, could set him apart. Many years later, Cummings, when it was pointed out to him that his fellow actor had been T. S. Eliot, remembered 'a snob, cold, older than me, aloof, never sat with the rest of the cast at rehearsals, immaculately dressed; you know, a type "the frozen jeunesse dorée"'.[110] In choosing this 'gilded youth' for the part of an English lord, the play's director may have detected something similar too, yet could not have thought Tom too 'frozen' to kiss Amy convincingly.

At twenty-four, Tom knew St Louis, Boston, Cape Ann and parts of Maine. He had been to London, Paris, Munich and Italy; he was sophisticated, nattily dressed. He had written unpublished poems such as 'Preludes', 'The Love Song of J. Alfred Prufrock', and 'Portrait of a Lady'. For all his effortfully bawdy poems (shared only with his male buddies), he could dissect subtly and minutely social awkwardnesses between men and women. Yet his insight came not least from introspection. He was as vulnerable as anyone to such social awkwardnesses, but knew how to prepare a face to meet the faces that he met. He possessed, too, the skill and courage to interrogate his own vulnerability as well as to observe the awkwardness and assurance of other people.

On 16 December 1912 the Tom who had rhymed about Lulu and the whorehouse ball purchased from the Schoenhof Book Company a copy of Pierre Loti's *Le roman d'un d'enfant* with its account of young dreams of 'l'amour' and 'tendresse infinie', and its sense of 'une commotion intérieure'.[111] Three days later he went back to the same Boston shop to buy popular English novelist Leonard Merrick's 1908 short-story collection, *The Man Who Understood Women*. Its opening words could be taken as speaking, at least indirectly, to his own situation in an accent that owed something to J. M. Barrie and Jerome K. Jerome:

> Nothing had delighted Wendover so much when his first book appeared as some reviewer's reference to 'the author's knowledge of women.' He was then six or seven-and-twenty, and the compliment uplifted him the more because he had long regretted violently that he knew even less about women than do most young men.[112]

At eight o'clock on the wintry Massachusetts evening of Monday 17 February 1913, Emily Hale sang several songs at the very beginning of the 'Stunt Show' held in Eleanor Hinkley's home to raise money for the Cambridge Visiting Housekeeper scheme which Eleanor's mother helped organise. It trained unskilled young women to be domestic servants, and the evening's entertainment, with its own printed programme, was well fitted to genteel taste. Despite her family's reservations, Emily was allowed to act and sing in this private performance for relatives, neighbours and friends. Her opening the show suggests that she had, and was seen to have, presence and a good voice. Eleanor, though, was the moving spirit. She had recruited old school companions, neighbours, brothers of her friends and some cousins to take part. She had written two original sketches, and had 'arranged' several 'scenes' from literary works such as Dickens's *Bleak House*, for small group performance.

Certainly Tom could mock mannered domestic theatricality ('You have the scene arrange itself – as it will seem to do –'), but he also had a taste for it, and Eleanor Hinkley had his measure.[113] She played a strict mamma in 'Rosamond and her Mother', dramatised from Maria Edgeworth's *Rosamond* – one of whose stories, 'The Purple Jar', was a favourite in America. Eleanor also acted Emma in 'An Afternoon with Mr. Woodhouse' from her beloved Jane Austen. In this scene Tom (whom Eleanor had known from his delicate childhood) was cast as the prematurely aged hypochondriac Mr Woodhouse. To fine-mannered Emily Hale in the same *Emma* 'stunt' went the part of the vain but vulgar Mrs Elton. In another sketch of Eleanor's own, entitled 'Arnold Bennett chooses a Heroine', Tom's sister Marion (who had studied at Miss Folsom's school for social service in Boston) was cast as 'The Sunday School Teacher'.[114]

The evening was carefully choreographed and full of teasing. 'Mr. Thomas Eliot', that would-be Parisian, found himself cast as 'Monsieur Marcel' in a sketch Eleanor had written specially, 'Monsieur Marcel and his latest Marvel'. Here Tom played opposite Amy de Gozzaldi, who acted the part of his 'Marvel'.[115] Casting Tom alongside two of her friends, Emily and Amy, Eleanor knew what she was doing, but Emily rather than Amy was positioned as star of the show: she sang at its start as well as after the interval, and she was central to the evening's conclusion.

Number 1 Berkeley Square is not a vast house. Conditions for performers and audience were intimate. Eleanor recalled that 'The scenes were laid by the parlor fireplace, in a space no bigger than seven square feet, so that the actors could be seen by the audience in the next room, through a door-way that was four feet eight.'[116] At home in this house that he had known from childhood, and among trusted relatives and friends, Tom listened to Emily singing 'andantino con molto espressione' a song called 'Ecstasy', which opened the evening:

Only to dream among the fading flowers,
Only to glide along the tranquil sea;
Ah dearest, dearest, have we not together
One long, bright day of love, so glad and free?

Only to rest through life, in storm and sunshine,
Safe in thy breast, where sorrow dare not fly;
Ah dearest, dearest, thus in sweetest rapture
With thee to live, with thee at last to die![117]

Written by pioneering Boston composer Mrs H. H. A. Beach, this was passion New England-style, but passion it assuredly was: as she sang the words 'dearest, dearest' the soprano's voice soared into the lyric ecstasy of the title. Here was the woman with whom Tom was ineradicably smitten.

Emily sang five other love songs that evening: James Hotchkiss Rogers's 'Julia's Garden' (Tom came to associate her with flowers and gardens), Francesco Paolo Tosti's 'La Serenata' (another song of longing and the sea), an 'Old Air', Luigi Denza's 'A May Morning' ('For you are the Queen of the May, my sweet, / And all the world to me'),[118] and Boston composer Margaret Ruthven Lang's 'Mavourneen'. This last song had been sung as an encore at the Boston Symphony Orchestra the previous autumn, and was particularly popular; Emily's uncle Philip, a devotee of the Boston Symphony and one of America's leading music critics, was among the composer's admirers.[119] Formally entitled 'An Irish Love Song', though often called 'Mavourneen', its anonymous lyrics liltingly articulated both love and separation. The distinctive, constantly repeated Irish woman's name was drawn out for emotional effect across rising chords:

O the time is long, Mavourneen,
Till I come again, O Mavourneen;
An' the months are slow to pass, Mavourneen,
Till I hold thee in my arms, O Mavourneen!

Shall I see thine eyes, Mavourneen,
Like the hazel buds, O Mavourneen;
Shall I touch thy dusky hair, Mavourneen,
With its shim'rin glint o' gold, Mavourneen?

O my love for thee, Mavourneen,
Is a bitter pain, O Mavourneen;
Keep thy heart aye true to me, Mavourneen,
I should die but for thy love, O Mavourneen.[120]

Emily Hale was not Irish, but Tom, who later went to some length to send her a bunch of Killarney roses, may have associated her with this Irish love lilt, and it is possible she accompanied him to the Boston Opera House's *Tristan und Isolde* when he went to hear Edoardo Ferrari-Fontana as Tristan and Margarete Matzenauer as Isolde in the production of 1 December 1913.[121] Tom, like his friend Jean Verdenal, found *Tristan und Isolde* profoundly moving; later, in the context of intense erotic desire, he quoted in *The Waste Land* those lines where Tristan, in the first act of Wagner's opera, longs for his Irish girl:

Frisch weht der Wind
Der Heimat zu
Mein Irisch Kind
Wo weilest du?[122]

[The wind blows fresh
To the homeland
My Irish child
Where are you lingering?]

In the poem Tom follows these lines with a passage of his own about giving a 'girl' flowers (hyacinths) and being unable to speak or to move for intense emotion. Then he returns to *Tristan und Isolde* for a sense of the sea that separates the lovers as 'wide and empty': '*Oed' und leer das Meer*'.[123]

Tom enjoyed an intense bout of concert and opera-going during the 1913–14 season. He had relished classical performances before, experiencing, for instance, Debussy's *Pelléas et Mélisande* when he was an undergraduate, but now he kept the printed programmes.[124] Several are for Boston Symphony Orchestra concerts in Sanders Theatre at Harvard and for concerts and recitals at the orchestra's base, Boston's Symphony Hall. Emily was clearly musical and her uncle Philip wrote all the programme notes for performances given by the Boston Symphony.[125] At Harvard in October and November 1913, Tom heard that orchestra playing Beethoven's Seventh Symphony, Sibelius's Fourth Symphony and Brahms's Second Piano Concerto. Then, heading into Boston, he went to *Tristan und Isolde*, then on Tuesday 2 December to a Chopin piano recital by Josef Hofmann at Symphony Hall. Next, on Sunday 7 December, while gearing up to read his paper on interpreting primitive ritual to Royce's seminar group that Tuesday, he attended an afternoon violin recital by Fritz Kreisler (Symphony Hall again). He saw *Tosca* at the Boston Opera House on the evening of Monday 22 December; its sets depicted the splendid architecture of Rome.[126]

Apparently insatiable, he was back at the Boston Opera House on the evening of 2 January 1914 for *Madama Butterfly*, then attended a Mischa Elman violin recital on the afternoon of Saturday 10 January (more Beethoven) and a recital the next week by the 'celebrated Belgian Violinist' Eugène Ysaÿe on the afternoon of Sunday 18 January. Throughout this period he was arguing in Royce's seminar about the difference between description and explanation, between reality and illusion. On 30 January at the Boston Opera House the graduate student of philosophy, who had not so long before walked the streets of Montmartre, listened to the ravishing aria of young love 'Depuis le jour' sung as part of a staging of Gustave Charpentier's Montmartre opera *Louise* whose present-day Parisian characters included, the programme noted, 'Premier Philosophe' and 'Deuxième Philosophe'. On 5 February in Sanders Theatre, Tom heard the Boston Symphony play at their evening concert Schubert's Unfinished Symphony and Beethoven's powerfully emotional 'Emperor' piano concerto.[127]

Beethoven would be a lifelong love for Tom. He had an especial fondness for that Seventh Symphony he had heard performed at the outset of this period of intense musical gratification. In it, Emily's uncle wrote in his programme note, 'as Beethoven achieved in the *scherzo* the highest and fullest expression of exuberant joy – "unbuttoned joy," as the composer himself would have said – so in the finale the joy becomes orgiastic'.[128] If not quite orgiastic, Tom's attendance at these deeply moving concerts and operas was certainly as committed as his philosophising. These performances were very different from the shows he and Aiken went to. Perhaps he just wanted a break from endless seminars; but combined with the fact that (supplementing the knowledge he had gained at Mahler's Academy of Dance in St Louis) he paid teacher Emma Wright Gibbs $7 for three hours of 'dancing lessons' on 15 December 1913, following up with a lesson at the Cambridge Skating Club on 4 April – and since this was the period when his relationship with the music-loving singer Emily was deepening – it seems likely that he was going on a full-blown series of dates.[129]

Yet by the start of 1914 he had clear plans to leave for Europe that summer. 'Mr T. S. Eliot of Harvard College' had been 'admitted as a Commoner' of Merton College, Oxford, 'for the Academical Year 1914–1915' on 21 January, some months before being awarded the Sheldon Travelling Fellowship.[130] Though his absence was unlikely to last more than a year, this planned departure was a deadline to concentrate the heart as well as the mind. Never a man to reveal his emotions readily, about two years after meeting her, Tom managed to tell Emily that he was in love with her. Having made a 'declaration' of what he felt, he found her response crushingly disappointing. According to an account that he set down in old age in a private memorandum, and which is the most authoritative record of his intimate reactions, Tom 'had no reason to believe, from the way in which his declaration was received, that his feelings were returned "in any degree whatever"'.[131]

Probably in his excitement and nervousness he misread elements of the situation. In his twenties he was, as he later put it, 'very immature for my age, very timid, very inexperienced'.[132] Aged twenty-two in the summer of 1914, Emily, who later made it clear to friends that she did love Tom, seems also to have been inexperienced in matters of the heart, however eloquently she could sing about them. Her brilliant, sometimes intimidating but witty and sensitive twenty-five-year-old philosopher who knew all about Paris and was teaching, as Emily's father had done, at Harvard, was heading soon for Europe once again. Though his travelling fellowship might involve no more than twelve months' absence, the future was far from certain. Possibly Emily knew that, whatever he said to his parents, he wanted to be a poet at least as much as he aspired to become a professional philosopher. Neither he nor she had any permanent employment. All this made an engagement seem unwise.

Intelligent, vulnerable, strictly brought up and defensively 'proper' in a bygone ladylike way that may be hard for us now to understand, Emily was schooled in Bostonian restraint. An observant woman who met her later, when she was middle-aged, thought her 'like a sergeant major'; in her youth she was softer, but still correct.[133] Perhaps inexperienced in relationships with suitors, she did not give Tom a signal that he could interpret as encouragement. They went on being friends and she remained unmarried. Though all their early letters are destroyed, they corresponded for some time after he sailed for Europe. As months and then, unexpectedly, years kept them apart, each thought of the other with longing and new understanding. Tom came to regret profoundly the loss of this woman he loved and who shared so much of his own background; Emily felt troublingly wounded by their separation. These feelings were modified over the rest of their lives, but remained central to their pained relationship. It was something they could never put right.

In Princeton University Library are twelve boxes containing 'approximately 1,131 letters and related enclosures' sent by Tom to Emily Hale. No correspondence survives from their youth: the Princeton collection begins only around 1930; 'by agreement with the donor, Emily Hale', it 'is sealed until January 1, 2020', so it will be discussed in the second volume of the present biography.[134] The archive's principal significance lies in what it says about the later years of the relationship. Though Tom sent Emily only seven letters in 1930, the next year he sent her ninety-two letters and in 1932 he sent a hundred. Throughout the 1930s they met face to face on both sides of the Atlantic. On average he mailed Emily at least one letter a week, usually more. While tapering off, their correspondence continued throughout the 1940s and 1950s. It ended abruptly when Tom married his secretary, Valerie Fletcher, in 1957. His connection with Emily lasted forty-five years. Late in life, recalling his sense of how in 1914 she gave him no reason to believe his feelings were reciprocated 'in any degree whatever', he still articulated a pang of hurt.[135]

9

The Oxford Year

Sure he had failed in love, he turned to poetry. One of his early poems, which he never published, addresses a 'beloved' linked to 'song'; but that poem's speaker, associated with broken glass, sees his fate as 'To be swept away'.[1] Convinced he had been rejected by Emily, during summer 1914 Tom read in proof Conrad Aiken's debut collection of poems. Dedicated 'To My Wife', it was thronged with images of young love, happy and otherwise.

> And so he lay awake long hours,
> Traced on the wall the patterned flowers,
> And while the clock ticked, cold and slow,
> Carefully backward would he go
> In hushed mind over memories of her
> To ask if she were friend or lover . . .[2]

The first poem in Conrad's forthcoming book lasted sixty-eight pages, the second sixty-three. Neither was first rate. Yet the volume would be published by a good publisher; it attracted decent reviews, appearing alongside titles by Tom's former classmate Edward Sheldon and collections by noted American poets including Vachel Lindsay, Harriet Monroe and Amy Lowell. Tom could only be patient, and bide his time. Annoyingly, Aiken's poems contained moments reminiscent of Tom's own unpublished verse. Sometimes he despaired. 'I have done nothing good since J. A[lfred] P[rufrock] and writhe in impotence', he complained late that summer. It was now three years since he had completed Prufrock's 'Love Song' in Munich. With his relationship with Emily confined to epistolary friendship and his poetry apparently stalled he had to face up to 'having made a failure of one's life'.[3]

He went to Germany. On the transatlantic liner bound for England he was mistaken for an Englishman, and was asked if he had enjoyed his visit to America. Undeterred, he danced to the captain's phonograph; sat 'astride a pole, a pillow in each hand', competing in a pillow fight; partnered 'Miss Mildred Levi of Newton, the belle of the boat' in a 'Thread the Needle contest'.[4] On board ship during the 4th of July celebrations, he joined in singing 'Rally, rally round the Flag, Boys!' with piano accompaniment.[5]

From his 'snug little cabin' he wrote to his cousin Eleanor about the voyage. Probably she had some inkling of his situation with Emily, and recognised he was putting a brave face on things. Witty, kind, attentive to details, his letter shows how charming he could be with women he trusted. He had always liked Eleanor. Alert to theatre dialogue, she shared his alert ear for phrasing; for her he transcribed transatlantic snippets: 'Well I never should have said you came from St Louis.'[6] Ironically, at least one of Tom's early ocean crossings was made on a ship called the USMS *St Louis*. On its notepaper he wrote a prose poem (perhaps imitating the 1912 French prose poetry of Charles Vildrac) called 'The Engine'. The steamship's engine hammers and hums, oblivious to its American passengers. The engine stops and the speaker imagines what would happen if the ship sank.[7]

After a London stopover where he seems to have acquired a copy of avant-garde 'Vorticist' magazine *Blast*, Tom headed through Bruges ('charming if you like that sort of thing'), Ghent, Antwerp and Brussels, visiting art galleries en route. Improving his knowledge of paintings of St Sebastian, he noted as among the best Hans Memling's in the Brussels Musée des Beaux-Arts. By 19 July he had reached Marburg, the small, ancient German university town where he was to attend a philosophy summer school. Delightfully, Marburg was built on a steep hill terraced with rose gardens; his window looked across these and the River Lahn beyond. Tom lodged with a pastor, Herr Happich, and his kindly family. Embarrassed to arrive with 'only one (torn) pair of pajamas', he could not find the German for pyjamas in his dictionary, but noticed it did contain the German for 'pudibund' – a word he offered to Conrad Aiken, but squirreled away for his own poetic use.[8] From the cultured Lutheran rectory he sent Conrad a new Bolovian opus rhyming 'Fried Hyenas' with 'bit of penis'. He drew a bald, bewhiskered 'Herr Professor'. The solemn, goggle-spectacled academic sports a knee-length double-breasted coat.[9]

Tom liked the Happichs, and ate heartily: 'five meals a day'. He swam, and hiked beautiful paths in the woods – 'but not far, because I must always be back in time for the next meal'. In a university town noted for its philosophers he bought Edmund Husserl's *Logische Untersuchungen* – (Logical Investigations), and noted approvingly that you could purchase Abdulla cigarettes, an upmarket English brand.[10] Modern German philosophy interested him; he seems to have attended at least some of the 1912 Harvard lectures by Rudolf Christoph Eucken, whose *Can We Still be Christians?* was translated in early 1914. Marburg's professors were strong in neo-Kantian epistemology and links between theology and philosophy. It made sense for the Harvard graduate student who had studied Kantian metaphysics and who remained interested in religious thought to come here. Yet, as on his previous visit to Europe, Tom was impelled towards poetry.

He was trying to write an ambitious long sequence provisionally entitled 'Descent from the Cross'. One part was uttered by a philosopher: 'Appearances appearances he said / I have searched the world through dialectic ways'. This speaker's concerns related to Tom's more abstract speculations about degrees of reality: 'Appearances appearances he said / Are nowise real; unreal, and yet true; / Untrue, but real – of what are you afraid?' Juxtaposed with such abstract material were to be a tormented love song, 'an Insane Section, and another love song (of a happier sort)'; then a piece about a 'married girl' who 'Wraps her soul in orange-coloured robes of Chopinese', a 'mystical section', and a 'Fool-House section' beginning by parodying a religious scene:

'Let us go to the masquerade and dance!
I am going as St John among the Rocks
Attired in my underwear and socks . . .'[11]

In Tom's mind, around the time he sketched all this in a letter to Aiken, were different notions of sex and love: from the taboo-breaking, sex-mad Bolo sort and Swinburne's poem in praise of Venus, 'Laus Veneris' (which imprisons its German hero with a tormenting erotic goddess who kills all her lovers except the speaker) to Goethe's Faust, another German protagonist famously fascinated with '*Das ewig weibliche*' – the Eternal Feminine.[12] The sequence of poems he was working on draws on his preoccupations with philosophy, mysticism, psychology, martyrdom and religion.

Most striking, though, is its troubled eroticism – an exploration of violent, sometimes self-loathing behaviour that may emanate from sexual frustration. The poet of J. Alfred Prufrock was now authoring further love songs; but whereas in 1911 Tom had mixed worries about declaring love with finely judged ironic wit, in 1914 he presents a far more extreme scenario. In 'The Love Song of St Sebastian' the speaker flogs himself until he stands in a pool of blood. Scourged, he approaches the bed of his white-gowned beloved:

> Then you would take me in
> Because I was hideous in your sight
> You would take me in to your bed without shame
> Because I should be dead . . .

This poem's first stanza presents a saint who mortifies himself to death; its second shows him strangling the object of his affections with obsessive erotic attentiveness: 'Your ears curl back in a certain way / Like no ones else in all the world'.[13] Mentioning how 'the world shall melt in the sun', the phrasing echoes Robert Burns's famous promise to stay faithful to his sweetheart until 'the rocks melt wi' the sun'.[14] However, designed to lead readers towards a planned 'Insane Section', Tom's lines present the lover as a possessive psychotic killer:

> You would love me because I should have strangled you
> And because of my infamy.
> And I should love you the more because I had mangled you
> And because you were no longer beautiful
> To anyone but me.[15]

Surely conscious that St Sebastian had become associated with homosexual imagery, Tom, unable to have Emily Hale, ponders the psychology of sex, possession and martyrdom. His covering letter to Aiken (who had his own fascinations with disturbed psychology) maintains, a little anxiously, 'there's nothing homosexual about this'.[16]

Having been in Paris when d'Annunzio's scandalously female *Martyrdom of St Sebastian* was performed (it had been staged, too, at the 1912 Boston Opera House), Tom was aware that this saint's 'Love Song' could speak of heterosexual as well as homosexual experience. His 1914 poem should not be interpreted as direct autobiographical revelation. Yet, counterbalancing Aiken's predictable celebration of young love, it plumbs the psychology of religious and sexual obsession. Tom's experience with Emily Hale had done nothing to calm his sense of sex as a source of unease. His poetry saw the sexual and the religious coming together not just in ancient primitive rites, but also in the present-day realm of 'underwear and socks'. 'The thing is', he wrote to Aiken that September, 'to be able to look at one's life as if it was somebody's else – (I much prefer to say somebody else's)'.[17]

That grammatical construction (already old-fashioned in 1914) calls to mind his writing of 'ones else' in his St Sebastian poem. This new 'Love Song', he feared, wasn't working: 'Does it all seem very laboured and conscious?' he asked Aiken.[18] In it and other verses that Tom tried to fit together in Marburg, he drew indirectly on aspects of his recent experiences, fusing them with his philosophical and religious reading, then distorting both with disturbing aesthetic impact. Yet as in his attempt to woo Emily Hale, so, trying to assemble this ambitious poetic structure, he felt failure.

Despite intellectual sophistication, he could be naïve. 'We rejoice that the war danger is over', he wrote on 25 July from Marburg.[19] Discussing 'the Balkan Question' with his hosts, he enjoyed listening to the Happichs' daughter Hannah (later described to Eleanor as 'my old flame') playing Beethoven on the piano or singing. Tom spent part of Sunday 26 July doodling pictures of dachshunds on a witty illustrated letter.[20]

On Saturday 1 August he found himself in a changed country. Germany had declared war on Tsarist Russia. Having only just commenced, his summer school was over. On Sunday its director warned the students not to speak foreign languages in Marburg's streets, and explained no one could leave for two weeks. On Monday 3 August, the Germans declared war on France. At 4.21 that afternoon, conscious his parents would realise that their son was stranded in a European conflict, Tom spent 10 of the 20 marks he had on him and managed to get a cablegram through to his father at East Gloucester. Slightly garbled, the German operator's message arrived the same day: 'Ver staate nordamerika Keine angst haben [*sic*]' (Have no fear about the United States).[21] Immediately there were further developments. On Tuesday the Kaiser's army invaded Belgium; Britain declared war on Germany.

Tom never forgot the Happichs' kindness to their anxious lodger. Realising his letters of credit were not being accepted in Marburg, they did not charge him for board (he repaid them years later). Down to about 40 marks, he worried if he stayed longer he might not have enough cash to reach the frontier. Russian and French summer-school students were detained indefinitely. Foreign nationals faced the poorhouse if their money ran out. Tom sent a postcard in German to his parents requesting cash, but could not be sure it would reach them. For two weeks he and other English-speaking students met each evening at a local hotel, trying to work out what was happening. Eventually, on Sunday 16 August with several companions, he set out on the ninety-minute rail journey to Frankfurt. It took five hours. Many passengers were soldiers and reservists: jumpy, on the lookout for bombs and bidding anxious farewells to sweethearts. Having said goodbye to his own loved ones just over a month earlier, Tom registered these scenes acutely: 'I shall never forget one woman's face as she tried to wave goodbye. I could not see his face; he was in the next compartment. I am sure she had no hope of seeing him again.'[22]

From Frankfurt he headed to Cologne. Changing trains, he ran short of food, and had a long wait. Eventually, he departed Cologne at 3 a.m. after a meal and a kip in the station waiting-room. Twelve hours and several trains later he and other Americans reached the German-Dutch border. 'We were very nervous, expecting to be searched, but they did not even open our bags; looked at our passes – *"Amerikaner – ach, schoen!"* ["American – oh fine!"] let us by.'[23] By Thursday 20 August he was in England. A week later he wrote flippantly to his brother about his German difficulties: 'an intolerable bore'.[24]

He had found London accommodation at 28 Bedford Place in Bloomsbury – a central location identified on a sheet glued into his London Baedeker as '*Aiken's Lodgings*'.[25] Other tenants were Continental refugees. Here in the huge capital city of the largest empire on earth Tom was safe for the moment, and chatted in French about the war. Nearby he could hear 'English, American, French, Flemish, Russian, Spanish, Japanese' being spoken. He listened rather scornfully as an old woman in the street sang a sentimental American song about 'memories that bless – and burn'; people threw her coins from their windows. Afterwards he watched as 'the housemaid resumes her conversation at the area gate'.[26] He found he could work among the din, and liked cosmopolitan, noisy London better than before. In his poem 'Morning at the Window' a speaker upstairs in a foggy urban street hears 'rattling breakfast plates in basement kitchens' and is 'aware of the damp souls of housemaids / Hanging despondently at area gates'.[27]

Eager for female company, he had met a 'very interesting' French woman and enjoyed her shrewd remarks; he told Eleanor he had encountered, also, Ann Van Ness, a mutual friend who was, like Emily Hale, an American Unitarian minister's daughter. Ann was living not far away. Tom had tea with her in early September – 'very pleasant company'. They walked to Regent's Park Zoo, but, though before she left London she 'said that she "would be glad to hear from me"', Ann did not hold the same attraction for him as Emily.[28] Being abroad was exciting, but lonely too. Despite seeming Angicised to some Americans, on his own in London – a metropolitan area of 7,000,000 people – Tom felt foreign: 'I don't understand the English very well.' His sympathies lay with Britain in the war, but he had been impressed by Germany, and mocked gung-ho patriotic efforts in some Boloesque verses entitled 'Up Boys and at 'Em' which he mailed to Aiken. Even as he began to find his bearings and enjoyed dining in London with Martin Armstrong, an English literary friend of the Aikens, there seemed 'a brick wall' between him and most Englishmen; English women were at least as hard to fathom.[29] Still, he admired the way 'an Englishman is content simply to live'. He appreciated 'the ease and lack of effort with which they take so much of life . . . I should like to be able to acquire something of that spirit.'[30]

More by accident than design, along with the ensuing summer, the academic session 1914–15 that Tom would spend in Oxford would be a turning point. He was pleased one day to encounter Bertrand Russell in the street near Bedford Square. Russell invited him back to his flat for tea, chatting about pacifism, Germany and 'the European situation'.[31] 'I naturally asked him', the pacifist Russell recalled, 'what he thought of the War. "I don't know," he replied, "I only know that I am not a pacifist."'[32] Tom kept in intermittent touch with Russell. Yet the rest of his most important early contacts in England were Americans. Aiken, attempting to help his friend, had tried to interest London editors in Tom's poems, only to be rebuffed: Harold Monro of the Poetry Bookshop thought them insane. 'Go to Pound,' urged Aiken. 'Show him your poems.'[33]

Recently married to Englishwoman Dorothy Shakespear, the expatriate American Ezra Pound was lodging in London. With his shock of wild hair, bohemian friends and enthusiasms for everything from Japanese drama to the paintings of Whistler, Pound was a passionately committed artistic intellectual. Just three years older than Tom, this prolific and ambitious Idaho-born poet had published his collection *Ripostes* in 1912, and was employed as W. B. Yeats's secretary. Having left behind an academic career when he sailed from America in 1908, Pound worked, too, as a talent scout both for Harriet Monroe's Chicago journal *Poetry* and for London's *Egoist* magazine, which in 1914 started publishing James Joyce's *A Portrait of the Artist as a Young Man*. Pound knew everyone, though not everyone liked him. His abrasive manners could be disconcerting. As Tom was aware, Pound's own poetry had featured in the Vorticist artist Wyndham Lewis's magazine *Blast*, where a few of his lines about sex had been blacked out to placate the censor. Quoting himself – 'An Image is that which presents an intellectual and emotional complex in an instant of time' – this unsettlingly energetic young American had stated that summer in 'Vortex. Pound.' that 'The primary pigment of poetry is the IMAGE.' 1914 saw the Poetry Bookshop publish his anthology *Des Imagistes*. Tom was warily familiar with Pound's writings before they met that September. When Tom showed him 'The Love Song of J. Alfred Prufrock', the Imagist poet loved it, insisting it should appear in *Poetry*, and giving the author a few days to get it ready for the press.[34] Here, Pound wrote to Harriet Monroe, was 'the best poem I have yet had or seen from an American. PRAY GOD IT BE NOT A SINGLE AND UNIQUE SUCCESS.'[35]

By the end of the month Pound was trying to set up a dinner at which he and Dorothy could introduce Tom to Yeats. What so impressed Pound was the way that as a poet Tom had modernised himself on his own. At Harvard Tom had had little time for what he saw as Pound's old-fashioned early poetry. Now he was excited to be welcomed by this fellow countryman who was at the heart of London's avant-garde: 'Pound has been *on n'est pas plus aimable'* – couldn't have been kinder – he told Aiken, adding that he 'wants me to bring out a Vol. after the War'.[36] Awkwardly, such encouragement brought a crisis of confidence. Showing Pound a range of his work, Tom reflected that he had accomplished nothing really good since 'Prufrock'. His ambitious plan for 'The Descent from the Cross' had failed. Neither love nor work seemed to be prospering. 'But', he reflected phlegmatically, 'it may be all right in the long run'.[37]

About to go to Merton College, Oxford, and resume his philosophical studies, Tom was unsure about his future. Alluding to J. M. Barrie's *Sentimental Tommy*, whose hero, somewhat confused about women, finds it hard to mature, he wrote to Aiken: 'I should find it very stimulating to have several women fall in love with me – several, because that makes the practical side less evident. Do you think it possible, if I brought out the "Inventions of the March Hare", and gave a few lectures, at 5 p.m. with wax candles, that I could become a sentimental Tommy.'[38] Then, on the 6th of October, he headed for his next university.

War was denuding Oxford of its students. Predominantly upper-class English public schoolboys, they were regarded as ideal British military officers. That October Merton had just under fifty students, including six Americans, four Indians and two Canadians. About three-quarters of the undergraduates drilled every afternoon in the Officer Training Corps; among the Britons who started at Merton alongside Tom, over half would be killed in the war. 'I should have liked to go into the officer training corps myself', Tom wrote to Eleanor Hinkley, 'but they won't take a foreigner'.[39]

Like Marburg, Oxford was a medieval university city, though one experiencing peripheral industrial growth, giving rise to what Max Beerbohm called in 1911 'those slums which connect Oxford with the world'. After London, it was small, its population around 50,000. Tom was well placed to savour central Oxford's 'last enchantments of the Middle Age'.[40] On arrival, he turned in off the busy High Street, heading along quieter, narrower medieval Merton Street, lined with honey-coloured sandstone academic buildings. Entering Merton College through its fifteenth-century gatehouse surmounted by relief sculptures of Bishop Walter de Merton, St John the Baptist and other religious figures was like stepping into a monastery. Its hefty wooden gate led through a stone archway past a porter's lodge where a college servant kept a suspicious watch on all incomers. Having introduced himself to the porter, Tom was directed to his room. Turning left, he walked across the uneven flagstones, looking for staircase 2:1 in the St Alban's Quadrangle.

Though the oldest of Merton College's four stone quadrangles dates from the thirteenth century, the later St Alban's buildings had been reconstructed in 1910, so their plumbing, while not up to American standards, was in advance of the rest of the college. Merton hygiene could be an ordeal. A fellow American student recalled how 'Stored away under the bed was a tin tub, refilled daily, which you were supposed to pull out each morning, leap into, throw water over your quivering torso, and then rub down with a towel so moist that you could almost wring it out before using.'[41] Unfazed by Merton's Spartan regime, Tom boasted to Eleanor Hinkley, 'I think I am the only man in the college who takes *cold* baths.' A college servant asked him, '"Do you keep it hup all winter, Sir?"'[42] To Tom English working-class accents were exotic. Cold baths or not, Oxford was 'exceedingly comfortable and delightful – and', he added, 'very "foreign"'.[43] Just yards away stood Merton's imposing medieval chapel, its ornamental screen designed by Sir Christopher Wren.

He had to climb several stairs to reach his room. It had an odd atmosphere due to the differing levels of Merton Street to the north and the college quadrangle to the south. Tom looked out of a small raised window at street level on to Merton Street, but when he turned round and looked out the larger window on the other side, into the quadrangle which had no buildings on its southern border, he had a fine, elevated view across a lawn to the broad green expanse of Christ Church Meadow. 'You can leave the curtain up, sir', a college servant told him. 'It ud take a seven footer to look in your window.'[44]

On Tom's staircase were several students from England. Clergyman's son John Legge Bulmer, a second-year undergraduate from Yorkshire, had studied at Marlborough fee-paying boys' school and come to Merton on a scholarship. He and Tom attended the college's debating society. Finding the undergraduates agreeable, Tom was struck by the way (though Merton was an all-male college) 'girls attend the lectures here – come right into the college buildings, and attend the same lectures as the men', he wrote to Eleanor (having just expressed his hope that 'Emily' was thriving). 'P.S.

No one looks at them.' Emily Hale had been writing to him from her home at 5 Circus Road, Chestnut Hill, in Brookline (a handsome, tree-lined street rather like Ash Street) to let him know that she was likely 'to start in acting very soon'.[45]

Tom had grown up with St Louis family servants. He hoped Miss Hale in Brookline would 'have a good servant'. At Oxford, disliking 'having to look out for myself', he acclimatised himself to 'being taken care of'.[46] As his fellow American graduate student Percy ('Brand') Blanshard, then in his second year at Merton, put it later: 'the class system was still strong: a man old enough perhaps to be your grandfather waited on you like a footman, built a fire daily in your grate, served in your rooms (and I mean rooms) a hearty English breakfast and a lunch of bread and cheese'.[47] Used to being waited on, sometimes Tom wrote letters before breakfast; he had his own typewriter. He came to enjoy getting up at 7.15 a.m. since students were required to sign a 'roll call' sheet at ten minutes to eight each morning. This meant rushing 'across two quadrangles', often in the rain ('dreadful climate'), then waiting more than half an hour for breakfast.[48]

Dinners were served in the sombre college hall, rebuilt in Victorian times in imitation of medieval traditions. As they still do, students sat side by side on dark wooden benches, dining at long, hefty refectory tables; dons ate separately at High Table beyond. In such conditions, and given the small number of students, Tom soon got to know people. He tried to blend in, dressing, Blanshard recalled,

> like most of us, in a brown tweed coat, a sweater, and gray flannel trousers; but the trousers would be punctiliously pressed in spite of the incessant autumn rain. He wore the same jacket-length gown that we commoners did, for unless one held an Oxonian scholarship or degree, one could not wear a scholar's gown . . . My first impression, an impression never removed, was that though he was friendly and ready with his smile, he was shy, reticent, and reserved.[49]

Tom knew some other Americans in Oxford. Eleanor Hinkley's Anglophile acquaintance Francis Wendell Butler-Thwing had published several mediocre poems in the *Harvard Advocate*, assembling them with other juvenilia in his 1914 *First-Fruits* with its epigraph from Dante's *Inferno*. Butler-Thwing had just arrived at New College. He impressed Tom by telling him he was going to be 'naturalised as an Englishman' so he could join up.[50] Along the road at Magdalen College, Scofield Thayer, familiar from Milton and Harvard, had come, like Tom, to study philosophy; Tom renewed his acquaintance. Soon he lent Thayer Aiken's new poetry collection. Taking long walks, that autumn Tom hiked to Cumnor, a nearby village of quaint thatched cottages. He liked the countryside, eyeing it as a fascinated foreigner.

His closest English friend at Merton was also something of an outsider. Bright, independent-minded, Karl Culpin was a bespectacled twenty-year-old, literature-loving Yorkshireman. A third-year undergraduate reading history, he had an English father and a German mother: a difficult background in World War I England. In October 1914, as they had done a year earlier, the college authorities granted Culpin a scholarship 'on the ground of poverty'.[51] He was considered outspoken. On 9 February the college debating society had voted on whether he should be ejected for 'a seditious speech'; two weeks later, after he defended the motion 'that the time has come when civilised nations should settle their disputes by arbitration rather than by force of arms', the motion was carried but Culpin found himself chucked out of the meeting.[52]

Culpin was still a controversial figure when, probably encouraged by Blanshard (elected secretary of Merton's Debating Society for 1914–15), Tom got to know him. In early November 1914 the club's President ruled against a proposal that voting procedures should 'conform entirely to American models'. Culpin tried to censure this decision. Later, when Tom's neighbour, John Bulmer, moved 'that in view of the state of international relations revealed by the war, it is desirable to introduce conscription into the British Empire', Culpin opposed this, bolstering his case with convincing statistics. The vote was lost by 13 to 6. Tom liked Culpin whom he regarded as 'the most intelligent of the Englishmen at Merton', and he got on with Blanshard well enough: 'an excellent butt for discourse', exhibiting 'all the great American fallacies', including vagueness and diffuseness.[53] On 23 November the motion was debated 'that this Society abhors the threatened Americanization of Oxford'. Bulmer spoke against it. So did Tom, who, the minutes record, 'preserved the appearance of gravity, which was more than the house did'. Sure he had not been so grave, Tom was pleased to have worked in references to a brand-new ragtime dance-craze: the fox trot. 'I pointed out to them frankly how much they owed to Amurrican culcher in the drayma (including the movies) in music, in the cocktail, and in the dance', he informed Eleanor Hinkley.[54] The meeting's twenty-two voters included several Americans, Indians and a Frenchman as well as students from England. Debate was lively: a visiting speaker from Magdalen College 'showed the House how dreadful the American accent was by mimicking it'. Another, unEnglish speaker attempted to assume the most Oxonian English voice. The motion was lost, narrowly, by 12 votes to 10.[55] Tom was on the winning side.

As in Paris, so in Oxford, he made a small number of close friends. He spent part of the Christmas vacation in London, surrounded by more Americans, in lodgings at 1 Gordon Street off Gordon Square, Bloomsbury. Nearby, at a table under the great dome of the circular reading room in the British Museum, he perused another commentary on Aristotle. On one occasion, probably through Pound, he found himself invited to a 'cubist tea', meeting 'two cubist painters, a futurist novelist, a vorticist poet and his wife, a cubist lady black-and-white artist, another cubist lady, and a retired army officer who has been living in the east end and studying Japanese'.[56] A long time afterwards, Tom remembered attending an artists' soirée during this period. He recalled 'Bomberg, Etchells, Roberts, Wadsworth, Miss Sanders and Miss Dismorr as being present'.[57] In London he chatted, too, with Charles Abraham Ellwood, a University of Missouri professor, staying at 1 Gordon Square surrounded by his family. Interested in eugenics and social psychology, Ellwood was spending session 1914–15 in Oxford, consulting works on sociology and anthropology in the Bodleian Library. He told Tom that Lottie Eliot was one of his 'three dearest friends in St Louis'.[58] Far from his own family, Tom found the Christmas period very quiet. A card came from Adeleine Moffatt in Boston, whom he had portrayed in 'Portrait of a Lady'; she sent him 'ringing greetings of friend to friend at this season of high festival'.[59] Norbert Wiener, then spending time at the University of Cambridge, working with Bertrand Russell, recalled meeting Tom for 'a not too hilarious Christmas dinner together in one of the larger Lyons restaurants'.[60] As gifts and loans Wiener brought a handful of his own recent philosophical publications on such topics as relativism and logic. Christmas turkey was inappropriate. Jewish Wiener, Tom noted, was 'vegetarian, and the lightest eater I have ever seen'.[61]

Usually in London Tom felt a certain big-city excitement, confessing (or perhaps boasting) to Aiken, 'Oxford is very pretty, but I don't like to be dead.'[62] Like many people, he altered his tone to take account of his correspondent: as far as his Harvard professors were concerned, Oxford was splendid. To Aiken he explained that London made him feel very alive, but also lonely, not least on New Year's Eve. He wandered the city streets, and had 'tea when there is anyone to have it with'.[63] Though in correspondence with his cousin Eleanor he did his best to sound buoyant and busy, to Aiken he confided that his sense of isolation had a sexual dimension. Joking that he longed for 'concubinage and conversation', he wrote from London with perceptive introspection about problems in his sex life.

How much more self-conscious one is in a big city. Have you noticed it? Just at present this is an inconvenience, for I have been going through one of those nervous sexual attacks which I suffer from when alone in a city. Why I had almost none last fall I don't know – this is the worst since Paris. I never have them in the country . . . I am very dependent upon women (I mean female society); and feel the deprivation at Oxford – one reason why I should not care to remain longer – but there, with the exercise and routine, the deprivation takes the form of numbness only; while in the city it is more lively and acute. One walks about the street with one's desires, and one's refinement rises up like a wall whenever opportunity approaches. I should be better off, I sometimes think, if I had disposed of my virginity and shyness several years ago: and indeed I still think sometimes that it would be well to do so before marriage.[64]

Marriage, though, did not seem on the cards. Aiken was privy to at least some secrets of Tom's love life, or lack of it. From Oxford Tom had written asking if in early December Aiken would buy 'some red or pink roses, Killarney I suppose', and send them with a card to Emily Hale at Brattle Hall.[65] She was going to be acting there in the Cambridge Dramatic Club's production of a three-act comedy about social climbing, *Mrs Bumstead-Leigh*. Tom was eager that Aiken in America make sure the roses reached Emily, if not at the play then later at Christmas, but there is something tentative and sad in his specifying not that they should be red but that they should be 'red or pink'. As well as Emily, Amy de Gozzaldi came into his mind over the vacation. Both were out of reach.

With Culpin and Blanshard he had been on a mid-December holiday to Swanage in Dorset. This south-coast seaside town was the sort he liked – an English version of Gloucester, Massachusetts. Staying over a fortnight with a local landlady, each student had his own bedroom, reading there mornings and evenings. They ate together in the dining room, and enjoyed long afternoon walks by the sea or over the soft-turfed, treeless downs. Visiting tourist sites including Corfe Castle and the Tilly Whim caves, they had enjoyed themselves. Culpin and Blanshard sensed Tom's reserve, but were conscious he liked them. They were appropriately impressed when he propped Bertrand Russell and A. N. Whitehead's *Principia Mathematica* open in front of him at the breakfast table, eyeing its symbols with *savoir faire*. 'He said that manipulating them gave him a curious sense of power.' Blanshard thought he was friendly, 'but preferred to wear that Mona Lisa smile and listen with laconic remarks rather than to initiate or develop subjects himself'.[66]

In this small seaside town, the holidaying students had checked out the local female talent. 'We had met a pretty, apple-cheeked English girl from Bournemouth whom we all liked, and we thought it would make for merriment to shivaree her. We divided the forms of celebration between us, and one of them was to indite a poem in her honour.'[67] Blanshard made the poem. Tom had not even revealed that he wrote verse. To his friends he was simply available company, a young and dauntingly clever visiting American.

Back in Oxford the philosopher who interested him most at Merton was one of the college fellows, the idealist thinker F. H. Bradley, author of *Appearance and Reality* (1893). Eventually Tom came to think Bradley's 'the finest philosophic style in our language'; it possessed a 'reserved power'.[68] Then approaching seventy, and having long enjoyed a fellowship without teaching duties, the long-faced, bearded Bradley was notoriously reclusive, his manner reminiscent of Merton's 'mediaeval schoolmen'.[69] Still active, in 1914 he had just published *Essays on Truth and Reality*, critiquing the work of William James and Bertrand Russell while developing his own thinking on epistemology, God and the Absolute. Bradley's colleagues, including Tom's college tutor Harold Joachim, protected the elderly don from students. Tom's shyness meant that, though the enterprising Blanshard dared submit a note with questions for the Great Man, who subsequently invited him for conversation, to Tom's disappointment he and Bradley never once met. Instead Tom went, sometimes accompanying Blanshard, for regular Oxford-style tutorials with the Hungarian immigrant's son Harold Joachim. Joachim's formidable 1908 study, *The Nature of Truth* (a copy of which Tom had brought from Harvard), censures Bertrand Russell, presenting an idealist theory of truth accompanied by detailed readings of Aristotle, Descartes, Spinoza and the elusive Bradley. At these meetings Tom or his fellow tutee would read a paper aloud, after which the erudite, pipe-smoking Joachim, then in his mid-forties, would do his best, intellectually speaking, to shred it.

This shredding could be gruelling, but Tom learned from it. He had been used to producing Harvard student papers prinked with literary allusions or metaphorical flourishes. Joachim disliked these. 'He taught me', Tom recalled, 'in the course of criticizing weekly essays with a sarcasm the more authoritative because of its gentle impersonality.' The Oxford philosopher wanted clarity, not quasi-literary distractions. Between October 1914 and July 1915 Tom worked hard for these tutorials. As well as meeting Joachim to read Aristotle, once a week he presented 'a short paper dealing with some one of the questions considered in the thesis which I hope to present for the degree of Ph.D. at Harvard.'[70] Discussing these papers with Joachim 'in detail', he wrote on such subjects as 'real, unreal, ideal, and imaginary objects'. Thinking strenuously, he found himself taking a stance on what is 'wholly real', only to realise that he must also argue against it: 'But there is another point of view, obtained by standing this one upon its head, which I find equally necessary to insist upon. From this point of view it may be suggested that the absolute is the one thing in the world which is real. Reality is the one thing which doesn't exist.'[71]

Working intensively, even risking the occasional disturbingly vivid phrase as he contemplated 'the suicide of knowledge', Tom in these tutorials came to realise that Joachim 'was concerned with clearing up confusion rather than with scoring off his victim'. The Merton philosophy don wanted to instil the ideal 'that one should know what one meant before venturing to put word to paper'.[72] Reading Aristotle in Greek with Joachim, whose lectures on the *Nicomachean Ethics* he attended thrice weekly from 13 October 1914 throughout the session, was demanding. Tom had written to J. H. Woods at Harvard on 5 October to say he had been reading Aristotle's *Metaphysics* in the original Greek, and was expecting to go through the *Posterior Analytics* in Joachim's tutorials.[73] From the college library he borrowed Giacomo Zabarella's weighty Renaissance Latin commentary on the *Posterior Analytics* in October and kept renewing it until the following June: he considered Zabarella 'probably the greatest of all Aristotelian commentators'. Later, in January 1915, he consulted Pacius's sixteenth-century Latin commentary on Aristotle's *Organon*.[74] Supplementing Joachim's lectures, he attended R. G. Collingwood's on Aristotle's *De Anima*, consulting Pacius's commentary on that too: almost forty years later he still recalled how Joachim 'made me read' Pacius.[75] Tom's third lecture course during his first term was on Logic with Professor J. A. Smith, who was then in the first decade of his more than thirty-year-long editing of Aristotle. Conscious that as part of his doctoral ordeals at Harvard he could face an examination on Ancient Philosophy, Tom annotated thoroughly his Greek copy of the *Metaphysica*. Aristotle entered his bloodstream.

In Collingwood's lectures, he took detailed notes, sometimes drawing on his Harvard reading to annotate them. So, for instance, on 29 October as he recorded one of Collingwood's points about the *De Anima* — that 'If the soul moves in space, it might move out of the body and back again' — Tom scribbled the words 'Golden Bough', remembering the anthropologist Frazer's accounts of souls being said to leave bodies.[76] Soon he acquired 'the highest respect for English methods of teaching'.[77] 'For anyone who is going to teach the Oxford discipline is admirable', he wrote to Professor Woods at Harvard, taking care to impress him by offering to type up and send his lecture notes.[78] Tom gave Woods the clear impression in November 1914 that university teaching was his goal. Yet working with Joachim also sharpened his literary education in ways that matter to poets: 'To his *explication de texte* of the Posterior Analytics I owe an appreciation of the importance of punctuation.' Tom remained proud of his sometimes rhetorical sense of punctuation, especially in verse; paying tribute to Joachim (a highly gifted musician) he maintained that 'Any virtues my prose writing may exhibit are due to his correction.' He thought Joachim 'perhaps the best lecturer' at Oxford, 'really almost a genius, with respect to Aristotle'.[79] Tom credited no other academic in England or America with such a detailed influence on the style and structure of his writing.[80]

Just three years after teaching him, Joachim wrote of Tom as 'a man of very exceptional ability', stating, 'it was a great pleasure to work with him'. He praised Tom's 'thorough knowledge of ancient Greek' as 'scholarly & profound'; his American 'pupil' was 'excellent in every respect'.[81] During his strenuous philosophical training Tom argued for 'a more minute examination of the question of truth'.[82] Joachim expounded a 'coherence theory of truth'. Truth was made up of 'significant wholes'.

> A 'significant whole' is such that all its constituent elements reciprocally involve one another or reciprocally determine one another's being as contributing features in a single concrete meaning. The elements thus cohering constitute a whole which may be said to control the reciprocal adjustment of its elements, as an end controls its constituent means. And in this sense a Centaur is inconceivable . . .[83]

The philosophically-minded poet and theorist Tom, fresh from Royce's theories of how communities construct interpretations, would recast ideas like Joachim's in his thinking about tradition and the individual talent. As a poet he would draw on them too, sometimes subversively. Whereas the Merton tutor declared centaurs 'inconceivable', his 'pupil' wrote in verse around this time about the wonderfully disruptive presence of that foreigner Bertrand Russell at Fuller's Harvard tea-party: 'I heard the beat of centaur's hoofs over the hard turf.'[84] Tom's training in precision made him change 'soft turf' to 'hard turf' – at once consistent with those beating 'hoofs' and more surprising.[85] Even as he imbibed philosophy and was warned off metaphor, he reconceived his learning, sometimes mischievously, to lasting poetic benefit.

Rigorous study of Aristotle and regular 'Informals' – intimate tutorials – with Joachim and J. A. Smith required antidotes. The River Thames flows through Oxford and, as he had done at Harvard, so here Tom took up rowing. He was, he confessed to Aiken, increasingly fed up with 'professors and their wives'. Tom sounded off: 'As you know, I hate university towns and university people.'[86] Typically, in an often pleasantly and honestly contradictory way, he sought to counterbalance one side of his experience with another. However much he was excited by London and complained of lack of 'intellectual stimulus' in Oxford, at Merton he excelled in argument; and when he went rowing with fellow students, American and English, he enjoyed that too. If he could be ratty about dons and donnishness, he could also describe himself in Oxford to Aiken as 'contented and slothful, eating heartily, smoking, and rowing violently upon the river in a four oar'.[87] He rowed in the position of stroke, and was pleased to boast in later life that he and his crew had beaten wartime Oxford's only other passable four-oar. He was awarded a pewter mug.

Offering a 'Social Column of Births, Funerals, and Broken Hearts', Eleanor Hinkley's letters kept him abreast of life in Cambridge, Massachusetts.[88] As he had done from boyhood onwards, Tom offset high-brow material with popular entertainment. So, when not reading Aristotle, he amused himself and Eleanor by 'working' (he used the word loosely) on outlining his 'great ten-reel cinema drama, EFFIE THE WAIF'. Jokingly, he suggested which of their mutual friends, including Ann Van Ness, might act in this full-scale piece of 'Amurrican culcher', a mock-movie 'drayma' featuring, like his speech at the college debating society, Anglo-American contrasts. He assured Eleanor that this cinematic spoof whose characters included 'SEEDY SAM, the blackmailer' would be set partly in Medicine Hat among 'the mountains of Wyoming', partly in England at 'the stately manor' of 'Gwendoline, Lady Chomleyumley' and partly in imperial Kashmeer.[89] Involving abduction, a man-eating tiger, a fakir and a German spy, Tom's ten-reel extravaganza shows his taste for vaudeville now extended to silent cinema. Well informed, he developed this parody over several months in transatlantic letters. For Amy de Gozzaldi he created the part of Mexican dancer Paprika, 'one of our best eye-rollers'.[90]

Early in Oxford's Lent term, Tom's friend Culpin had fun in a 25 January debate. The motion deplored American attitudes towards British naval policy: 'Mr Culpin attacked the American attitude with the greatest gusto, inspired to an unwarranted height by various specimens of the objectionable genus which he saw before him.' John Bulmer joined in, 'audacious enough to think America was not all hopeless; many of the people were reported to have reached real respectability; only their govern-ment was a tragedy'. Culpin was handed a bouquet for his efforts; the motion was carried convincingly.[91] If light-heartedness energised the college, there was also grim uncertainty. Tom stared across soggy Christ Church Meadow, hearing news of commissions and casualties. Winter brought endless rain. Several Merton students were being called up to fight. London was experiencing Zeppelin raids. Self-evidently, Tom was a resident alien, a young non-combatant foreigner.

No mere intellectual game, his hard thinking at Oxford revealed aspects of his deepest beliefs. He perceived a division between carefully articulated philosophical accounts of behaviour, and the necessarily more instinctive conduct of day-to-day existence. 'In a sense, of course', he told Norbert Wiener in January 1915, 'all philosophising is a perversion of reality; for, in a sense, no philosophic theory makes any difference to practice.' Tom saw how philosophical theories claiming 'completeness' teetered into preposterousness. They made 'the world appear as strange as Bottom in his ass's head'. Tellingly, just days after writing to Aiken about sexual frustrations, he used this image of one of Shakespeare's most grotesque frustrated lovers. Admitting that 'one cannot avoid metaphysics altogether', he looked to a great poet to put philosophy in its place.[92]

During this period, no philosopher came closer to his thinking than Norbert Wiener. Like Tom, Wiener had engaged profoundly and sceptically with Harvard intellectuals including Royce and James; also with Bergson, with Bradley and with Russell's mathematical logic. A fellow Sheldon Fellow in philosophy and occasional poet, Wiener had come from Harvard to Cambridge via Göttingen, at the same time as Tom had reached Oxford via Marburg. There was intellectual respect between them, but also awkwardness. Sharp-tongued, Wiener was socially clumsy. For all his usually impeccable manners, Tom, too, could be viperish; perhaps his view of Wiener was conditioned by familial anti-Semitism. Yet when, days after they shared Christmas dinner, Tom described Wiener to Aiken as 'like a great wonderful fat toad bloated with wisdom', those mocking words 'fat toad' were more than countered by 'wonderful' and 'wisdom'.[93]

Wiener's recent paper on 'Relativism' struck a chord. Tom wrote to its author with unusual enthusiasm. Clearly the two were used to exchanging philosophical ideas face to face:

The Relativism I cordially agree with, but nearly all of the subject matter I think we had already touched upon, at one time or another, in conversation. I hope that you will have reprints taken of it, in order that the doctrine may be promulgated. Such a doctrine can however, as it seems to me, be worked out, under different hands, with an infinite variety of detail. One can, I should think, be a relative idealist or a relative realist. What it seems to me to lend itself to most naturally, is a relative materialism – or at least this is the way in which my sympathies incline.[94]

Wiener's 'doctrine' was that the human self was a 'system of experiences internally relevant to one another'; 'we must experience in relation from the very beginning everything we ever know in relation'. According to this theory of 'Relativism', 'Our mind is continually stretching out tentacles to the past and the future: here we search for a memory forgotten, there for the verification of a prediction.' Truth was relative and relational, no knowledge either 'self-sufficient' or 'absolutely certain'. Acknowledging the 'infinitely complex' nature of the universe, 'relativism insists that the supposed absolute rigidity of the definitions used in metaphysics is but a fiction, that no concept can mean what it does entirely independently of everything else'.[95]

Restated in aesthetic-historical terms, such thinking would be crucial to Tom's idea (expressed several years later) of a tradition in which 'No poet, no artist of any kind, has his complete meaning alone. His significance, his appreciation is the appreciation of his relation to the dead poets and artists. You cannot value him alone.'[96] Wiener had argued that 'The relativist believes that everything, in so far as it is understood adequately, is understood in relation to other things.'[97] Tom would maintain that every creative artist, to be understood and evaluated, must be set 'for contrast and comparison, among the dead'. He went beyond Wiener in contending not just that present experience was conditioned by a network of relations with previous experience, but that in art the present can re-arrange the network of the past:

> The existing monuments form an ideal order among themselves, which is modified by the introduction of the new (the really new) work of art among them. The existing order is complete before the new work arrives; for order to persist after the supervention of novelty, the *whole* existing order must be, if ever so slightly, altered; and so the relations, proportions, values of each work of art toward the whole are readjusted; and this is conformity between the old and the new.[98]

This way of thinking about 'relations' between artworks or poems was not simply derived from Wiener's 'Relativism', but his was arguably the single most important philosophical paper Tom ever read. It helped him develop ideas about the fruitfulness of constantly changing systems of relations – ways of thinking that conditioned some of his sharpest critical insights, and also helped him find in poetry ways to maintain complex networks of mutually interpenetrating meanings. These he brought into place through allusion, echo and suggestion as well as more directly. Tom was incubating such insights before Christmas 1914, but Wiener's thinking spurred him on.

'New knowledge we acquire must be internally *relevant* to our previous knowledge', argued Wiener: 'the steam-hammer of to-day is the lineal product of the first stone hammer used by primitive man'.[99] Tom sought a similarly panoramic perspective, coming to think about art as the product of 'a mind which changes', but 'which abandons nothing *en route*, which does not superannuate either Shakespeare, or Homer, or the rock drawing of the [stone-age] Magdalenian draughtsmen'.[100] Wiener had a sense of scientific progress; for art, though he used the word 'development', Tom did not envisage straightforward 'improvement'. Both men's insights developed through relational thinking. Though they flowered by moving apart, their philosophical interests were strikingly contiguous. The young Wiener published on aesthetics and was fascinated by theories of reality and knowledge. His mention in his 'Relativism' of 'mysticism, and all philosophical views which claim to be supported by some brand of knowledge essentially different from the sort of knowledge we recognize ourselves to possess' signals that Wiener, like Tom, was interested in mystical experience. Wiener's slightly later sceptical but thoroughly engaged and anthropologically informed article on 'Ecstasy' reveals a familiarity with authors that Tom too had been reading, including William James on religious experience, Janet on hysteria, E. D. Starbuck on the psychology of religion and Underhill on mysticism.[101]

In dialogue with Wiener, Tom explained he had written a thesis about 'Bradley's theory of judgment', but, unhappy with it, he planned to recast it. This would become his Harvard doctoral submission. Joachim's input was crucial, even if Tom (as he soon told J. H. Woods) found that his own 'fatal disposition towards scepticism' led him constantly towards 'criticism' rather than 'construction'. Tom wrestled with this tendency. However, he also made clear to Wiener that 'I am quite ready to admit that the lesson of relativism is: to avoid philosophy and devote oneself to *real* art or *real* science.' Conscious that Wiener like himself had studied with Santayana, he added that 'For *me*, as for Santayana, philosophy is chiefly literary criticism and conversation about life.'[102] These comments hint that Tom realised Wiener's future lay in science and his own future lay in literary art. For all that he continued his philosophical studies, this was true.

Still interested in Buddhism (he attended a Buddhist Society meeting in February), Tom maintained a Unitarian aversion to creeds, intensified

by his philosophical studies. 'I have had for several years', he told Eleanor
Hinkley, 'a distrust of strong convictions in any theory or creed which
can be formulated'. Then he added, 'One must have theories, but one
need not believe in them!'[103] Back in Oxford after Christmas, he worked
hard, auditing lectures by Professor J. A. Stewart on Plotinus, whom
Wiener later characterised as 'a mystic' and 'the last of the ancient thinkers
to have added anything to the theory of aesthetics'.[104] Tom made it clear to
Eric Dodds, the only other student willing to keep listening to the
sixty-eight-year-old Stewart's unexcitingly delivered lectures, that he was
'seriously interested in mystical experience'. In this tiny class Tom opened
up to his sole classmate. Like Tom, the independent-minded young Irish
Classicist Dodds had been in Germany the previous summer; he had also
been to Serbia, working in an army hospital. Tom and Dodds enjoyed
chatting. 'What astonished me as I came to know him better', Dodds
recalled, 'was the wide knowledge of contemporary European literature,
poetry in particular, which he gradually revealed. Then one day he
confessed shyly that he had written some poems himself.'[105]

Dodds told Tom he too wrote verse. He belonged to a small undergraduate poetry-reading group, the Coterie, headquartered nearby in
Beaumont Street. A few members, including E. H. W. Meyerstein, had
already published books or pamphlets; others were about to do so. Though
their poems' diction was often old-fashioned, nonetheless some of these
people were enthusiasts for French Symbolist verse. Among them was a
gangly, rather cynical, short-sighted twenty-one-year-old undergraduate
from Balliol College, Aldous Huxley. Dodds invited Tom to come along.
Becoming a regular member of the Coterie, characteristically he 'said little,
but that little was always pungent and to the point'. To these fellow students
Tom read aloud 'The Love Song of J. Alfred Prufrock'. 'We were startled',
Dodds recalled, 'and, yes, a little puzzled, but less puzzled than excited'.[106]

Tom's circle of acquaintances was expanding in quite different directions. Ezra Pound had put him in touch with musician Arnold Dolmetsch
and his wife Mabel, with whose family Tom 'passed one of the most
delightful afternoons I have ever spent'. Being in a family pleased him.
Aged between three and eight, the four children danced for their visitor.
Always good with youngsters, he was 'wild to see them again'.[107] Also
through Pound, he was in contact with Wyndham Lewis. Six years Lewis's
junior, Tom met this sometimes pugnacious painter and novelist in a tiny
'triangular sitting-room' – 'the only room in the Pound flat where there
was any daylight'. Decades later, and after he had painted Tom's portrait,
Lewis recalled their first encounter:

As I entered the room I discovered an agreeable stranger parked up one of the sides of the triangle. He softly growled at me, and we shook hands. American. A graceful neck I noted, with what elsewhere I have described as 'a Giaconda smile.' Though not feminine – besides being physically large his personality visibly moved within the male pale – there *were* dimples in the warm dark skin; undoubtedly he used his eyes a little like a Leonardo. He was a very attractive fellow then; a sort of looks unusual this side of the Atlantic. I liked him, though I may say not at all connecting him with texts Ezra had shown me about some fictional character dreadfully troubled with old age, in which the lines (for it had been verse) 'I am growing old, I am growing old, I shall wear the bottoms of my trousers rolled' – a feature, apparently, of the humiliations reserved for the super-annuated – I was unable to make head or tail of.[108]

Not long afterwards, and making a rather different impression, Tom sent Lewis his poem 'The Triumph of Bullshit'.[109] Ostensibly addressed to 'Ladies, who find my attentions ridiculous', Tom's bullshitting included the refrain 'For Christ's sake stick it up your ass'. The disconcerted Lewis also received what he called 'Ballad for Big Louise' – presumably a version of the 1911 'Ballade pour la grosse Lulu'.[110] Eager to be a twenty-six-year-old *enfant terrible*, Tom thought these suitably scandalous for *Blast*; the Vorticist editor, Lewis, however, turned them down, maintaining (he told Pound) that while they were 'excellent bits of scholarly ribaldry', he would 'stick to my naïf determination to have no "Words ending in -Uck, -Unt and -Ugger"'. Pound tried to cajole him – 'I dare say Eliot will consent to leaving blanks for the offending words' – but Lewis would not be cajoled.[111] He did, though, take 'Preludes' and 'Rhapsody on a Windy Night' for *Blast* number 2. Bolovian Tom told Pound he found Lewis's response disappointingly 'puritanical'.[112]

By around springtime in his Merton College tutorials Tom was attempting to outline what he called 'an idealism *à rebours*' – his phrasing suggests a coupling of the reclusively donnish Bradley with the scandalous French Symbolist Catholic J. K. Huysmans, author of *À Rebours*.[113] During mid-March the Oxford student spent several days in Cambridge, where his friends Wiener and Russell were of use to him. He brandished Wiener's term 'relativism' when he gave a paper on 'The Relativity of the Moral Judgment' to the Moral Science Club in Russell's impressive Trinity College rooms. Visiting just a few days after Russell had hosted D. H. Lawrence, on 12 March Tom 'attempted to compromise between an absolute idealist position and a relativist view'.[114] He was invited also to the Heretics, 'the leading literary society' whose 'most *brilliant*' members – whom perhaps he associated with Wiener – put him in mind of the intense but scattered 'clever Jew undergraduate mind at Harvard'. Snooty about 'serious, industrious, narrow and plebeian' Cambridge students, Tom sat up till 1 a.m. with 'Bertie' Russell, and visited George Santayana 'who was in Cambridge too'.[115] Tom claimed to argue 'As a relativist (to use my friend Dr Wiener's word)'; but in the typescript of this paper designed for oral delivery, he scored out the words 'my friend', making the youthful Dr Wiener sound more impersonally authoritative.[116]

For a piece of abstract argument, his Cambridge talk was rich in biblical language, jokiness ('the more tough-minded philosopher sometimes presents the aspect of an elderly German mathematician learning to dance') and phrases such as 'the hysterically minded' which reflect his reading in Janet and other psychologists.[117] Such literary flourish, well judged to impress and amuse at Trinity, was just the sort of thing Joachim disparaged. Tom's use of it hints at how his poetic and philosophical selves, though often aligned, might also war with one another. Writing about ethics, he discussed 'the origin and development of the moral ideas'.[118] On Saturday 27 February, preparing for this paper, he had borrowed from Merton's library *The Origin and Development of the Moral Ideas* by Edward Westermarck.[119] Tom's Cambridge discussion drew on Westermarck. Its treatment of '"desires" or "satisfactions"', 'compulsions' and 'needs' may relate to topics covered in Joachim's lectures, which dealt around 27 February with '*normal* human bodily appetites' and even 'diseased or abnormal bodily appetites' in the context of the topic of pleasure in Book VII of Aristotle's *Ethics*.[120]

But Tom had, too, a sense of appetites outside the classroom. However mocking he had been in an untitled Jane-Austen-cum-Dickensian playlet which he had written and sent to Eleanor Hinkley on 27 January, its sense of what one speaker calls 'the impetuosity of my blood' was a reaction to the news that Tom's earnest, churchy younger cousin Fred had become engaged. Still virginal, and acutely conscious of his own desire, Tom wrote around April 1915 an untitled poem, 'The Death of a Saint Narcissus', later retitled 'The Death of Saint Narcissus'. Its speaker walks 'between the sea and the high cliffs', then 'over the meadows', then 'in city streets', always intensely aware of his sexuality. The poem features masturbatory imagery:

Then he knew that he had been a fish
With slippery white belly held tight in *his* own fingers,
Writhing in his own clutch, his ancient beauty
Caught fast in the pink tips of his new beauty.

Seeming to partake of both male and female experience, this man is entranced yet horrified by his ecstatic eroticism. He becomes 'a dancer to God', his flesh, Sebastian-like, 'in love with the burning arrows'.[121]

Not long before, Tom had walked by the high cliffs near Swanage, as well as over Oxford's meadows; he had experienced a recurrence of his 'nervous sexual attacks' in London. However, while perhaps spurred by his own anxieties, his poem is not confessional. Its cliffs and meadows could be anywhere; its city is named 'Carthage', the place where that keen student of Plotinus, St Augustine, had spent his licentious youth in sexual 'burning'. This poem about a man 'stifled and soothed by his own rhythm' who seems in the city 'to tread on faces, convulsive thighs and knees' powerfully mixes desire and 'horror'.[122] Its narcissistic anxiety appears in part homoerotic, in part heterosexual. It dramatises intense, confused eroticism. On 2 February Tom sent another poem to Pound. In 'Suppressed Complex' a woman is seen lying still in bed; the speaker dances 'joyously in the firelight' and, eventually, as the woman clutches the blanket, passes 'out through the window'.[123] Sexual experience is implied rather than stated in this other poem of clutching fingers. Conscious at once of powerful desire and suppression (our word might be 'repression'), these works articulate a sense of compulsion and control which, during that term, featured, far more tamely, in Tom's philosophy classes.

As winter turned to spring, he made sure to tell Eleanor Hinkley he had met several young women. At Oxford he had dined with the polite daughters of Sir John Rhys, principal of Jesus College. In London, where he spent the Easter vacation and took a keen interest in work by Jacob Epstein, Henri Gaudier-Brzeska, Wyndham Lewis and especially Edward Wadsworth in the Vorticist-dominated Second London Group Exhibition at the Goupil Gallery, Tom had encountered 'delightful' red-haired Sheila Cook from New Zealand; also 'very pretty Miss Cobb' with her oppressively genteel Bostonian mama, and three young sisters whose surname was Petersen, the youngest (sixteen) 'very beautiful indeed . . . I shall have to take her punting next term.' Miss Petersen confirmed his frustrated sense that 'English girls' were 'completely managed by their mothers – but perhaps it is merely that the ones I have met have been rather young'.[124]

Compared to Conrad Aiken, whose second son died at birth on 11 February, Tom, at twenty-six, was himself in some ways 'rather young'. He felt frustrated and under the weather, but, as often for him, such sensations were conducive to poetry. Coping with 'indigestion, constipation, and colds constantly', he was gathering together some verse.[125] By early April, Pound, eager to foment an American-led 'Renaissance' of which Tom approved, was planning to feature his work as part of a 'small anthology in the autumn'.[126] Eventually published in London in November, it would be called *Catholic Anthology*, would sell badly, and would mark the first appearance of Tom's poetry in a book. As spring turned towards summer, Pound 'was enthusiastic about my poems, and gave me such praise and encouragement as I had long since ceased to hope for'.[127]

Happily married to a young Englishwoman of literary tastes, Pound urged Tom to stay in England too. Assembling poems including 'Aunt Helen' and 'Mr. Apollinax' that April, Tom denounced what he saw as characteristically stifling American phenomena.[128] These included 'the Maiden Aunt and the Social Worker': his mother and at least one sister fit this last description.[129] In works written against Bostonian repression, including 'The Boston Evening Transcript', he chafed against the confinements of a way of life he had aspired to escape:

When evening quickens faintly in the street,
Wakening the appetites of life in some
And to others bringing the *Boston Evening Transcript*[130]

'Something might be said', he added to Pound in April, 'about the Evil Influence of Virginity on American Civilization'.[131]

Tom knew about Vorticist art and avant-garde poetry, but didn't know what to do. He imagined marrying (not that he had anyone to marry yet), having a family (he seems to have taken it for granted that he would become a father) and living in America, buttoning his lip and forfeiting his 'independence for the sake of my children's future'. Alternatively, he considered saving hard, then retiring to France at the age of fifty, watching the world go by as he sipped his 'aperitif at 5 p. m.' Neither possibility compelled him, but a crisis was coming: he had to decide whether or not to accept a renewal of his Sheldon Fellowship. 'The great need is to know one's mind, and I don't know that.' He wrote respectfully to J. H. Woods, postponing his decision. More vividly and a touch melodramatically he presented to Aiken, 'The idea of a submarine world of clear green light – one would be attached to a rock and swayed in two directions – would one be happiest or most wretched at the turn of the tide?'[132]

Tom seems never to have gone punting in Oxford with sixteen-year-old Miss Petersen. Instead he punted and danced there with vivacious twenty-six-year-old Vivien Haigh-Wood. Born in 1888, she was a young woman exactly the same age as himself. They met in March at a lunch party in Scofield Thayer's Magdalen College rooms. Punts were moored at the adjacent Magdalen Bridge: one thing led to another. Slim, dark-haired Miss Haigh-Wood was a talented artist; one of her most lovingly detailed sketches, made around this time, is of an empty punt by the grassy bank of Oxford's River Cherwell, which flows under Magdalen Bridge.¹³³ Tom took pride in how 'from one virginal punt' he and Thayer could glide along 'charming the eyes and ears of Char-flappers' (coquettish young women on the Cherwell), even though he remembered himself as excelling in his 'voracity for bread and butter' rather than in flirtatious eloquence; it was Thayer who spouted 'Sidneian showers of discourse upon Art, Life, Sex and Philosophy'.¹³⁴ Anyhow, this exciting day finished with dancing. Vivien was pretty, and an eager, excellent dancer.

Born in the northern town of Bury, Lancashire – which she loathed as provincial – this young Englishwoman had grown up in sophisticated London. She had known Thayer's unstable, lively cousin Lucy since 1908: they had met on holiday in the Alps. Clever, artistic, Francophile, Vivien Haigh-Wood, like Tom, savoured poetry, sailing and acting. Having topped up his St Louis terpsichorean skills with those extra Harvard dancing lessons, Tom was attracted to this lively, petite companion. Soon on Saturday nights he was spending time in London where one could go to dance parties in big hotels.

Vivien, Tom recalled, had 'a genius for dancing'.¹³⁵ At first neither he nor she enjoyed each other's exclusive attention. To his delight he found his American style of dancing gave him an almost dangerous appeal: 'I terrified one poor girl (she is Spanish at that) by starting to dip in my one-step', he informed Eleanor Hinkley, mentioning also two other women – 'very good dancers' who, with his help, 'caught the American style very quickly'. By no means the reserved young ladies of Boston Unitarianism, such women excited him all the more for that.

> As they are emancipated Londoners I have been out to tea or dinner with them several times, and find them quite different from anything I have known at home or here. (I fear my previous generalisations were misleading – they do not seem to apply to London girls over twenty-five.) They are charmingly sophisticated (even 'disillusioned') without being hardened; and I confess to taking great pleasure in seeing women smoke, though for that matter I do not know any English girls who do not. These English girls have such amusing names – I have met two named 'Phyllis' – and one named 'Vivien'.¹³⁶

To Tom 'Vivien' was an exotic English name. Vivien was the famous, gossipy seductress who enthralled Merlin in Tennyson's *Idylls of the King*. Lithe Miss Haigh-Wood, who shopped at London's Poetry Bookshop and had worked as a Cambridge governess in the winter of 1914–15, was not *that* Vivien, but she did enjoy attracting clever men; pleased he could impress her, Tom relished her vivacity. She was Scofield Thayer's friend when he met her at Magdalen, and Thayer knew more than Tom about her background. Thayer had been in touch with her in February about his and Tom's American poet friend Butler-Thwing whom Vivien's brother was going to contact; she had invited Thayer to a dance. When he did not go, Vivien made sure to tell him what a wonderful experience he had missed. Impressed he was a philosopher, she teased him about his studies and urged him to visit her at her parents' substantial home, 3 Compayne Gardens in Hampstead: 'I need cheering up badly – *awfully* – just now. You'd better come & do it!'[137]

In childhood Vivien (or 'Vivienne' as she sometimes styled herself) had had a 'terror of loneliness'.[138] Her artist father was distinguished enough to be elected to the Royal Academy. Vivien was his favourite model. He had painted her with her younger brother Maurice in a picture originally entitled *Small Girl Sulking*, 'an early indication', her biographer Carole Seymour-Jones points out, 'of the moods from which Vivienne suffered increasingly from the age of twelve'.[139] Vivien had painful (possibly menstrual) problems for which, from her sixteenth year, she took various drugs. As Scofield and Lucy Thayer knew, she had become engaged to a London schoolteacher Charles Buckle. Her best friend married in 1914, and Vivien hoped to emulate her. However, familiar with Vivien's disturbing mood swings and apparent hysteria, and sure she suffered from 'moral insanity', her mother 'warned CB off', as Maurice put it.[140] The engagement – a sexual relationship Maurice termed 'a *real* affair' – was broken.[141] Vivien went on seeing at least one specialist doctor.

Summoned to cheer her up, Scofield Thayer went. Through Lucy he had first met Vivien in spring 1914 while she was going out with Buckle. Vivien had felt attracted to the young American philosophy student Thayer. Now, visiting her at her parents' house on Thursday 25 February 1915, and telling her she looked radiant, he compared her with Mona Lisa. They chatted. She showed him Buckle's photograph. No sooner had Thayer left than Buckle phoned up. Home from the army on leave, he called for Vivien at 10 p.m. and, though she had a high temperature, took her dancing to the Savoy. Mrs Haigh-Wood was annoyed. Immediately, Vivien fell ill with influenza. 'Please excuse pencil, I am in bed', she wrote to Thayer in a letter sent on 3 March in which she complained of 'a good deal of mental, as well as physical distress & depression'. She felt boxed in. Thinking of his likening her to Leonardo's *Mona Lisa* (which thieves had carried off in Paris in 1911), she told Thayer she wished someone would cut her out of her frame. She asked if he liked some of the poems she had been reading in Ezra Pound's *Ripostes*, especially 'A Girl', and other erotic pieces including 'An Immorality' and 'Virginal', as well as T. E. Hulme's poem of sexual indiscretion, 'Conversion'. She made it clear she wanted Thayer to move to an opulent London bachelor's flat – much closer than Oxford. Would he be willing to teach her Italian in the Easter vacation?[142] She tried, too hard, to attract him.

Tom got to know Vivien better in April, May and June. In Oxford he was attending demanding, inspiring lectures on Aristotle. Harold Joachim was discussing pleasure and control of the passions – largely among men. In late April Tom heard a long discussion of 'attraction'; by 13 May the topic was 'reciprocal affection'; on 27 May Joachim outlined Aristotle's idea that 'pleasure is an *energeia*' – an energetic force – both 'timeless' and sudden. 'Whatever we may say about the conditions of pl[easure] it is not gradually produced – it has no history.' Aristotle encouraged a 'comparison of pleasure to the bloom of youth'. It was, Joachim explained on 1 June, 'in many cases due to novelty'. He spoke of the headiness of hedonism. He said other things too, but these points were to the fore in what Tom, who was seeing more and more of Vivien by then, chose to write down in his notebook. At the end of the course, though Joachim spoke about knowledge, his summation on 8 June was that 'Knowledge in all its forms is the activity of a mind grasping a real. This relation presupposes a fundamental identity. What we really have is not two actualities in relation, but a single *energeia*.' Now Tom, closer to 'the bloom of youth' than his professor, was about to 'grasp a real', and to exchange his sense of 'two actualities in relation' for that of 'a single *energeia*'.[143]

Maurice Haigh-Wood and Ezra Pound perceived that Vivien and Thayer were 'going out' together.[144] They visited each other, they danced; he bought her a lavish dinner at the Savoy. Yet their relationship was problematic: she was keener than he to take things further. A couple of weeks before he was due to return to America (the Oxford term stopped in June), Vivien grew annoyed. She felt she had been stood up on what sounds like a double date involving herself and Thayer as well as Tom and Thayer's cousin Lucy. Staying at her family's holiday house, Thyme Cottage at Upper Bourne End near Marlow in Buckinghamshire (about halfway between Oxford and London), Vivien complained to Thayer, 'Re our visit to Oxford, Lucy & I were both given to understand by Eliot & you, severally and definitely, that we were to keep both Saturday & Sunday free, & that if Sat. was wet, we should be expected to come on Sunday.' Vivien had turned down an attractive dance invitation to keep herself available. Thayer had then cancelled at short notice – on that very day, 'Thursday'. Vivien suggested to him with an element of moral blackmail that his behaviour could adversely affect her mental health: 'Remember the specialist's words, Scofield, & do not be the instrument of pushing me more quickly than is necessary into an untimely melancholia, or else, as he also prophesied, an early grave.' What she wanted was for Thayer to 'come to me in London'. He would enjoy having, as she put it, 'little Vivien to jog along beside you & gaze longingly upon you with her golden eyes'. She told him he was a fool for returning to the 'savage land' of America. Once he left,

> from that day I do *solemnly promise* you I will never have speech, or correspondence with you, nor will I *ever* look upon your promising-much and fulfilling-little countenance again. Never. I have made up my mind, really. And you will never meet such another as I. & one day, I assure you, you will grind your teeth at the raw, childish *folly* which prevented you distinguishing between a yellow diamond – a white flame – & an ordinary toy of coloured glass. A fool there was, & *she* made her prayer – to a rag & a bone & a hank of hair. Why indeed cast pearls before swine – yellow diamonds & white flames before hide-bound, unawakened limited savages of Wall Street calibre? O God – *WHY*?

Wishing Thayer could write her a letter of matching passion, she told him he 'should snatch *every hour* in these last days & *try*, try to burn just one of your fingers in the white flame – just for the experience you know'.[145] What Tom admired as Thayer's 'passionate detachment' annoyed Vivien precisely because Thayer was not attaching himself to 'little Vivien'.[146]

Unable to spur Thayer to take the plunge with her, Vivien in this letter adopts the position of the foolish lover in Kipling's poem 'The Vampire' who is cast aside after an affair. In Kipling's verse it is a female vampire who jilts a man: 'A fool there was and he made his prayer/ . . . / To a rag and a bone and a hank of hair'.[147] Vivien, however, has reversed the gender roles. She makes the scorned lover pointedly a '*she*', implying that Thayer has abandoned her. Probably her reference is not simply to Kipling's poem but to its recent, scandalous use to underpin the internationally-popular silent movie *A Fool There Was*, launched in January 1915 and based indirectly on the poem, whose words feature in its captions. Starring femme fatale Theda Bara as the cinema's first 'vamp', it dealt with the seduction and ruin of a Wall Street lawyer who has sailed from America to England

and becomes enthralled by the seductive 'Vampire'. Playing with references to the vamp, the Wall Street figure and urges to 'burn' in a 'white flame', Vivien teases the plutocratic American Thayer after their relationship has failed to reach a passionate consummation. The letter makes clear that Thayer would sail in about two weeks, so she must have sent it on Thursday 3 June.[148]

Tom, too, was due to leave for the States that summer. On 23 June the President and Fellows of Harvard had appointed him once more an Assistant in Philosophy for the coming session.[149] Yet, to their surprise, his plans took a very different turn. He sent in his resignation. About ten days after Thayer sailed from England, and without either Vivien or Tom telling their respective parents, on Saturday 26 June they met Lucy Thayer and Vivien's aunt Lillia Symes at Hampstead Register Office. There, not far from Vivien's home and a few miles from where Tom, quit of Oxford now the term had ended, was living at 35 Greek Street in Soho, Vivien and Tom (listed as 'of no occupation') were married.[150] Almost secret, it was, in its way, a sudden elopement. They got a 'special licence', which meant that, after they swore to the registrar that there was no legal impediment to the wedding, and once a fee had been paid, advance announcement need not be made. Such marriages were a feature of World War I England where soldiers often wed in haste before setting off for the battle front.

Quick-witted and determined, Vivien was on the rebound. So, in a subtler way, was Tom. He had by no means forgotten Emily Hale. Just as each of them had felt rebuffed, so both he and Vivien were eager for erotic experience. Flirtatious, vivacious Vivien could offer such experience in a way that Emily did not; indeed, part of Vivien's allure was that she might become what Thayer later described to Tom as 'a wife who is not wifely'.[151] Poetry-loving Vivien, deprived by her mother of her lover Buckle the year before, and now failing to secure her handsome American literary-cum-philosophical beau Thayer, was genuinely attracted by Thayer's striking, even cleverer American friend Tom Eliot. She shared several of Tom's interests, and – encouraged by her own poetic sense and Pound's confidence – believed in what she knew about his gifts as a poet. Marrying Tom, whom she had known for three months, was impulsive, but hardly ridiculous. Becoming his wife, she would rescue him for poetry, for England and, most importantly, for herself: she secured a brilliant, sensitive husband, a fine dancer, an indisputable catch that her mother could not now rob her of.

Anxiously eager to lose his virginity and his 'suppression', Tom had long been uncertain whether he could put his commitment to poetry before his predicted career as a philosopher; he had wondered about staying in England rather than returning to be immured in American academia. In marrying Vivien, he cut through all his problems at a single stroke – or so it seemed. Later he wrote,

> I think that all I wanted of Vivienne was a flirtation or a mild affair: I was too shy and unpractised to achieve either with anybody. I believe that I came to persuade myself that I was in love with her simply because I wanted to burn my boats and commit myself to staying in England. And she persuaded herself (also under the influence of Pound) that she would save the poet by keeping him in England.

When he wrote these words almost half a century afterwards, he knew it had all been a disastrous mistake – not only for himself. 'To her the marriage brought no happiness', he recorded in one of the bleakest accounts of any union. From one perspective, Pound had been right to encourage Vivien and Tom to throw in their lot together; from another, he had been wildly wrong. 'To me', Tom wrote in this same account of their relationship, 'it brought the state of mind out of which came *The Waste Land*'.[152]

10

V. S. Eliot

No sooner were they married than Vivien was ill. Keeping plans secret from her parents could not have been easy; her brother had to set off for the battle front on the wedding day itself; a combination of Tom's sexual inexperience and Vivien's worries probably made their nights together at least as problematic as delightful. About three years later Tom published a poem (soon suppressed) called 'Ode on Independence Day, July 4th 1918'. Dealing with a wedding night, it contains three one-word-long verse paragraphs – 'Tired', 'Tortured' and 'Tortuous'. The bride appears a disembowelled female sexual demon; the bridegroom smooths his hair; there is blood on the bed. An epigraph to the published version conjures up Shakespeare's *Coriolanus*. That lonely, proud Roman, accused of betraying his country, and suffering from having his career manipulated by his mother, came to fascinate Tom.[1] As usual with his poems, this one deflects autobiographical readings: he was not a bridegroom on 4 July 1918. Yet often his verse was conditioned by his ability to draw on his own sensations and emotions, cladding these in allusion, refraction and ironic distancing to produce devastating observations and to face the worst. His 'Ode' presents the most disastrous wedding-night consummation in literature.

'Eliot has suddenly married a very charming young woman', wrote Ezra Pound to his parents on 30 June 1915, four days after the event.[2] Friends liked both Tom and Vivien. Excitedly, the newlyweds did their best to put a brave face on things. On 30 June a conventional announcement appeared under 'MARRIAGES' in the London *Times*. It reads as a demonstration of unity. Just as her surname was the double-barrelled, rather upper-class English-sounding 'Haigh-Wood', so his became the double-barrelled 'Stearns-Eliot'. Perhaps confused by complex instructions, the typesetter gave the bride, 'Vivienne', an additional middle name:

STEARNS-ELIOT: HAIGH-WOOD. On the 26th June, by special
licence, THOMAS STEARNS-ELIOT, youngest son of Mr. and
Mrs. Henry Ware Eliot, of St Louis, Missouri, U.S.A., to VIVIENNE
HAIGH HAIGH-WOOD, only daughter of Mr. and Mrs. C. H.
Haigh-Wood, of 3, Compayne Gardens, Hampstead.[3]

Mentioning 'unusual preoccupations', Tom signed himself 'T. Stearns-
Eliot' when he thanked Harriet Monroe ten days later for payment for
the publication of 'The Love Song of J. Alfred Prufrock'. It had appeared,
appropriately or otherwise, in the issue of *Poetry* that coincided with its
author's wedding. Though he soon dropped the hyphen, he went on
calling himself 'Stearns Eliot' in formal letters for the next eighteen months
or more. When signing more than just her first name, Vivien styled herself
variously to Tom's family and to Scofield 'Vivien S. Eliot', 'Vivien S-E.'
and 'V. S. E.' The young couple wanted to rhyme.

None of this 'Stearns-Eliot' stuff cut much ice in America. There, on
the front page of the *St Louis Globe-Democrat*, above a story headed 'SLAYS
GIRL AND KILLS HIMSELF', appeared an item, 'THOMAS ELIOT
OF ST. LOUIS WEDS ABROAD'.[4] His family were summering as usual
at Gloucester, and probably hoping that their younger son, like his friend
Scofield Thayer, would soon be home. Tom did his best to manage how
they received the news. Though his own announcement to his parents
does not survive, they took it badly. Conscious they would think he was
throwing everything away, Tom had lined up Pound (whose own father
was closely involved in his son's literary life) to send a long, reasoned
epistle to Henry Ware Eliot, Sr, setting out what one might call the 'business case' for Tom's remaining in London to pursue a literary career.

Sent on 28 June, Pound's arguments were in many ways shrewd, if as
much about himself as about Tom. However, they were unlikely to go
down well with the bridegroom's father. For one thing, they revealed that
Tom had discussed his personal plans – financial and otherwise – in considerable detail with this obscure, eccentric young poet in London whom
Lottie and Hal had never met, while not even breathing a word to his
own parents about his impending marriage. Disquisitioning on everyone
and everything from Theocritus and Rihaku to Imagism and the *Mercure
de France*, Pound focused on literary and commercial arguments. His line
of pleading was not always geared to encourage a sympathetic reception:

As to his coming to London, anything else is a waste of time and
energy. No one in London cares a hang what is written in America.
After getting an American audience a man has to begin all over again

here if he plans for an international hearing. He even begins at a disadvantage. London likes discovering her own gods. Again in a literary career mediocrity is worse than useless. Either a man goes in to go the whole hog or he had better take to selling soap and gents furnishings. The situation has been very well summed up in the sentence: 'Henry James stayed in Paris and read Turgenev and Flaubert, Mr Howells returned to America and read Henry James.'[5]

Henry Ware Eliot, Sr, did not sell gents' furnishings; his company sold bricks. He had never been to Paris. He knew how little his wife had wanted Tom to go there in the first place. His father loved Tom, but had little love for what he saw as the insanity of *Blast* and London's avant-garde. The fact that Tom's peculiar poem 'The Love Song of J. Alfred Prufrock' had appeared in *Poetry* (tucked away towards the back because the editor did not greatly care for it) was unlikely to mollify him. Did Tom think his father would welcome this Mr Pound's letter which concluded with advice hinting at how much money he, Henry Ware Eliot, Sr, should give his own son?

It was almost three weeks before the marriage of 'Oxford student' Tom to his English bride was announced in his home city. This suggests that the family, in shock, bottled things up as they tried to work out how best to manage the situation. It was not Tom's parents but his brother who stated awkwardly to the inquisitive St Louis press on 15 July:

> that he had been notified of his brother's marriage, through his mother. He said that Thomas Eliot had been in London taking a year's course in philosophy at the Oxford University. He said he knew little of Miss Haigh-Wood, but understood that she was a daughter of a member of the Royal Academy of Arts.[6]

Tom had been trying to stress Vivien's respectability. Yet St Louis readers who read between the lines might conclude that there was something suspect about this hasty marriage. That was what Tom's parents thought too. His niece, Theodora, eleven that summer, remembered the family 'row'. The consensus was that Tom had been 'caught' by Vivien.[7] Having contacted his father and mother, on 2 July (using Vivien's parents' address), Tom wrote to his brother, telling him: 'I feel more alive than I ever have before.' His letter suggests that with Henry he had discussed in the past a general wish to marry, to commit himself to literature and to escape the milieu of the *Boston Evening Transcript*. Loyal, hard-working Henry, a single man who liked writing and had some similar aspirations, was sympathetic. Tom hoped that, to a degree, the family might be 'prepared for my decision'. Mentioning that his bride, just days after the wedding, 'is not very well at present', he told Henry how much he and Vivien appreciated his kindness.

> Dear Henry,
>   You will have heard by this time of the surprising changes in my plans. You know, however, what I always wanted, and I am sure that it will seem natural enough to you. The only really surprising thing is that I should have had the force to attempt it, and when you know Vivien, I am sure that you will not be surprised at that either. I know that you will agree that the responsibility and independent action has been and will be just what I needed. Now my only concern is how I can make her perfectly happy, and I think I can do that by being myself more fully than I ever have been. I am much less suppressed, and much more confident, than I ever have been.[8]

Then, advised by Pound, Tom requested several favours. His brother might help him secure him good contacts with American editors. Henry, supportive and generous towards both Tom and his parents, sent a photograph taken on a visit to Chicago in June. It showed Henry with writer Dorothy Dudley. From a leading Chicago literary family, she too had work in the June issue of *Poetry*. Keen to aid Tom, Henry pointed out that Dorothy's sister Helen, painted that year by Vanessa Bell, was 'now in London'.[9] She was also, though probably Henry did not know this, one of Bertrand Russell's lovers.

Tom hoped to persuade his parents to come to England to greet his bride, and strove to develop his growing network of London friends and acquaintances. Though they had not yet met, he heard through Pound about Richard Aldington, who had married the American poet H. D. (Hilda Doolittle) in 1913. An Englishman in his early twenties, Aldington was one of the original Imagists and assistant editor of the *Egoist* magazine. Publication in *Blast* had brought Tom a certain notoriety. He socialised with that journal's dynamic editor Wyndham Lewis whose Vorticist circle included the young artist Edward Wadsworth and a more senior figure, forty-three-year-old novelist Ford Hermann Hueffer (Ford Madox Ford), who had edited the *English Review*. Through Pound, Tom met 'Imagists and others', including poets 'John Gould Fletcher and F. S. Flint'.[10] If any American writer was well placed to undertake what he called two years later the literary 'siege of London', it was Tom.[11] Maybe, if they visited, his parents would come to understand his situation better.

The newly-weds had been living in a small studio flat. His in-laws, Vivien's brother recalled, 'very quickly recognised Tom's sincerity & high character', taking him 'to their hearts as a son-in-law'.[12] Trying hard to get a job as a schoolteacher – in London if possible – he had withdrawn his application for a Harvard assistantship, while asserting that his commitment to London 'literary work' would not derail his thesis submission. His marriage, he explained awkwardly to Professor Woods, 'was hastened by events connected with the war'.[13]

Unsurprisingly, Tom was somewhat dizzied: he was adjusting to life with Vivien; seeking employment; negotiating a new, more 'independent' relationship with his family – and with the Harvard philosophy department; courting editors on both sides of the Atlantic. Some days he started to write letters, failed to finish them before he had a train to catch, then took them out again to continue in a station or in the open street. 'It is hard to make a foothold', he told the wealthy Isabella Stewart Gardner in Boston, whom he hoped might help him with American editors, 'but I felt that the work at Harvard was deadening me.'[14] If marriage brought new vitality, less 'suppression', it was also testing. Telling Mrs Gardner of his 'happiness' with Vivien, he wrote too about the demands of the relationship:

> You said once that marriage is the greatest test in the world. I know now that you were right, but now I welcome the test instead of dreading it. It is much more than a test of sweetness of temper, as people sometimes think; it is a test of the whole character and affects every action. This is what I have discovered.[15]

Sixteen years older than his former student, Betrand Russell, who dined with the newly-weds on 9 July, just days after Tom wrote those words, thought the young husband was failing the test. Russell knew there had been 'trouble between' Tom and Vivien. Himself upset and writing to his married lover Lady Ottoline Morrell (a woman his own age with whom he had an intense, difficult and non-exclusive relationship), Russell is no objective witness. Yet his account is devastating:

> Friday evening I dined with my Harvard pupil Eliot and his bride. I expected her to be terrible, from his mysteriousness; but she was not so bad. She is light, a little vulgar, adventurous, full of life – an artist I think he said, but I should have thought her an actress. He is exquisite and listless; she says she married him to stimulate him, but finds she can't do it. Obviously he married in order to be

stimulated. I think she will soon be tired of him. She refuses to go to America to see his people, for fear of submarines. He is ashamed of his marriage, and very grateful if one is kind to her. He is the Miss Sands type of American.[16]

Ethel Sands was a wealthy, exquisitely cultured and apparently lesbian American painter, long resident in England. Comparing Tom to her, Russell implies Tom lacks masculine vigour. Clearly, however, the philandering philosopher was struck by how 'adventurous' and 'full of life' Vivien was, and thought the marriage would fail. Three weeks later, finding herself alone, Vivien, while enjoying what she called her 'very nice' status as 'Mrs Stearns-Eliot (notice the hyphen)', wrote to Scofield Thayer, telling him she had had 'blessings called down on my head' as 'the Poet's Bride' in the latest *Blast*. She also let Thayer know how 'He is all over me, is Bertie, & I simply love him.'[17] Russell had just invited her to dinner.

An older man highly experienced in seduction, Russell made these moves as soon as Tom was off the scene. The poet's parents were refusing to visit London: the transatlantic liner *Lusitania* had been torpedoed by the Germans in May, causing the loss of 1,200 lives, 128 of them American. The Eliots had summoned their son home. 'Too frightened of the voyage & the submarines', Vivien would not undertake the crossing. Tom went alone, attempting to balance his new, 'independent' husbandly self against his deeply ingrained sense of family duty. He reached America on 1 August, having told Vivien he would return in a month. They looked forward to 'a second honeymoon', and some security: thanks in part to a strong reference from the Dean of Merton, Tom had secured a job as a teacher at a school in High Wycombe in Buckinghamshire, not far from Vivien's parents' holiday house at Upper Bourne End.[18] In Oxford, the Dean wrote, Tom with 'a genuine interest in fine literature' had 'made many friends and proved his ability and taste'. He was 'likely to be a sympathetic and stimulating teacher and to exercise a good influence moral and intellectual over his pupils'.[19]

Nevertheless, the newly-weds were anxious. Before departing England on 24 July, Tom left with Vivien a sealed letter to be opened in the event of his death. Beginning with the words 'My dear Father' and signed, 'Your loving son Tom', it made clear to his wary parents that Vivien had 'not seen this'. The letter requested, in the event of Tom's not surviving the Atlantic crossing, that Henry Ware Eliot, Sr, give Vivien the proceeds of a $5,000 insurance policy which he had taken out for Tom. The young husband explained, 'I am *convinced* that she has been the one person for me. She has everything to give that I want, and she gives it. I owe her everything. I have married her on nothing, and she knew it and was willing, for my sake. She had nothing to gain by marrying me. I have imposed upon you very much, but upon her more, and I know you will help to make her life less difficult.'²⁰ Reaching Gloucester, Massachusetts safely, Tom had to advance these arguments face to face.

His parents listened. However much they felt he had been 'caught', that 'he ought to have known better & certainly ought not to have married', they could not unmarry him.²¹ They argued over his 'blunders'.²² The senior Eliots thought Tom naïve and foolish. Later, his mother made it clear she believed that 'up to the time of his marriage and residence in England' he had 'dwelt in an ideal world'.²³ Years afterwards, having met both Vivien and her parents, Lottie Eliot wrote to Tom's brother that Vivien's mother was 'not congenial . . . not a person of high principle . . . The standards in the female branch of that family are not as high as they should be.' Tom's mother continued to regard her younger son's marriage as 'a great misfortune'.²⁴ 'He married an English lady', she explained curtly to the outside world.²⁵ In August 1915 his parents tried to talk him out of his determination to stay in England. If Tom remained there, his father stated he would pay the rent but Tom must 'support his wife'.²⁶ It would be folly to throw away Harvard. Though he had declined it, Tom had already been offered an academic position at Wellesley College where his brother-in-law Shef had once taught. There was further work on offer at Harvard itself. Why couldn't Tom be sensible? His parents wanted him to behave like an Eliot.

After a few days he began to weaken. By 5 August he was writing to Conrad Aiken, telling him that, despite having secured the school-mastering job in England, he might stay the winter in America to complete his doctorate in accordance with 'my family's wish'. 'What I want is MONEY!$£!!' he added, conscious of his father's stance. 'We are hard up!'²⁷ The 'We' shows he had no intention of abandoning his wife, but by 16 August he was writing to Professor Woods to say he would be returning to Harvard in September. Vivien, with absolutely no wish to come to America, mounted a transatlantic campaign to bring him back. Her telling Scofield Thayer, whom she expected to meet Tom, all about Bertrand Russell's attentions was part of this tussle, though Russell's attentions were no invention. Calling herself 'a grass widow', Vivien told Thayer she had been dancing at the Savoy 'with two male friends' who were 'consoling' her. 'Tom has gone to America without me . . . Rather unwise perhaps to leave so attractive a wife alone and to her own devices!'²⁸

1. Henry Ware Eliot, Jr, with his baby brother Tom
in St Louis around 1890.

LEFT: 2. Tom's father, Henry Ware
Eliot, sitting on the porch of the
family's summer home at Eastern
Point, Gloucester, Massachusetts.
ABOVE: 3. Tom's mother, Charlotte
Champe Eliot.

4. Tom, sitting on the front gate of 2635 Locust Street, St Louis, with his mother
and, from left, his cousin Henrietta, his sister Marian (obscured, with her hand to
her head), and his sister Margaret on the morning after the 1896 cyclone.

5. 2635 Locust Street was screened by dense foliage in a city often loud with the sound of cicadas.

6. The hallway of 2635 Locust Street, with the grandfather clock (at left) that Tom's father brought from Massachusetts as a present for his wife.

7. Tom, aged about four, posing for a formal photograph.

8. Tom, aged about six, with his nursemaid, Annie Dunne, in St Louis.

9. Tom, aged about seven, in St Louis.

10. Tom, aged about ten, standing in the yard of Smith Academy, St Louis.

11. The Downs, the Eliots' extensive summer house at Eastern Point, Gloucester, Massachusetts, when recently built in the 1890s.

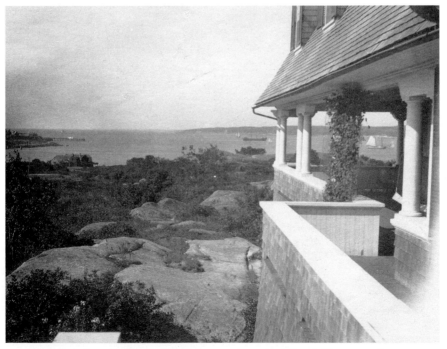

12. The view to the sea from the porch at the Eliots' Gloucester house.

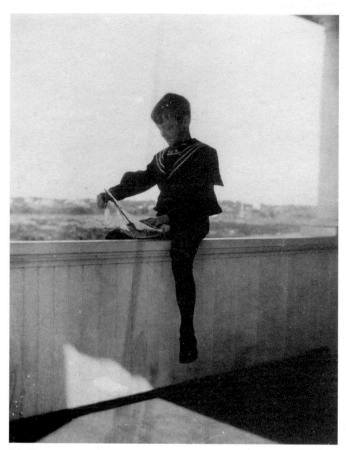

13. Tom in a sailor suit, sitting astride the balustrade of the porch at the Gloucester house, contemplating a model boat.

14. Tom as a boy at Gloucester, learning to sail.

15. A damaged
photograph of Tom,
aged about eight,
with his cousins
Eleanor and Barbara
Hinkley on rocks
at Eastern Point,
Gloucester.

16. Tom, aged about
twelve.

17. Harvard Yard at the beginning of the twentieth century.

18. Tom as a thin Harvard under-graduate in 1907, wearing what look like white flannel trousers on the porch at Eastern Point, Gloucester.

19. Tom as a student, sailing in the catboat *Elsa*.

20. A modern photograph of the house at 16 Ash Street, Cambridge, Massachusetts, where Tom lodged as a graduate student.

21. Emily Hale, aged twenty-three, in 1914
(her favourite picture of herself).

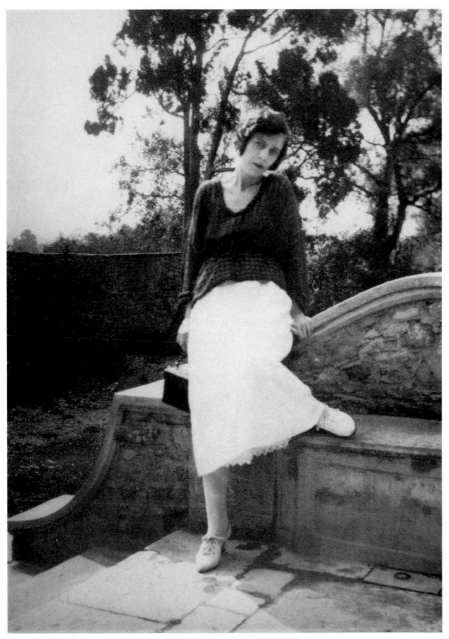

22. Vivien Eliot as a young woman.

23. Vivien and Tom as a young married couple in 1916 in their flat at 18 Crawford Mansions, Marylebone, London.

ABOVE: 24. Vivien's photograph of Tom with Violet and Sydney Schiff in the living room of the house the Eliots leased with Bertrand Russell at Marlow, Buckinghamshire.

LEFT: 25. Bertrand Russell in 1916.

26. Vivien at home in the Eliots' London flat.

27. Tom, Osbert Sitwell, young Jeremy Hutchinson, and Mary Hutchinson at West Wittering, Sussex, in July 1919.

28. A modern photograph of London's Clarence Gate Gardens. The Eliots' flat was in the far block on the left, just before the church.

29. An early twentieth-century postcard showing the Hôtel-Pension Ste-Luce, Lausanne, where 'What the Thunder Said' was written.

LAUSANNE. — Hôtel-Pension Ste-Luce.

30. Vivien's summer 1920 photograph of (right to left) Violet Schiff, Tom, Sydney Schiff, Lady Tosti (widow of the composer F. P. Tosti), Wyndham Lewis, and two Italian visitors, Signora and Signor Emanueli, in the Schiffs' garden at Eastbourne.

31. Tom's photograph of Vivien with the same group on the same occasion.

THE WASTE LAND

BY

T. S. ELIOT

" NAM Sibyllam quidem Cumis ego ipse oculis meis
vidi in ampulla pendere, et cum illi pueri dicerent:
Σίβυλλα τί θέλεις; respondebat illa: ἀποθανεῖν θέλω.˝

NEW YORK
BONI AND LIVERIGHT
1922

32. The title page of *The Waste Land* when first published as a book.

Thayer, who had earlier cabled his congratulations on the nuptials, made it clear he was unhappy with Tom's behaviour, and sought to meet in Massachusetts. Tom avoided encountering him, pleading that he had promised the time to his 'relatives'.[29] The aggrieved coldness of Tom's reply shows that Thayer (who kept several of Vivien's letters for the rest of his life) had expressed annoyance at Tom for having apparently poached Vivien from him. 'I must confess', Tom wrote on 9 August,

> that at the time I was surprised at the extent to which you were 'nettled'. You had never given me the impression that your interest in the lady was exclusive – or indeed in the slightest degree a pursuit: and as you did not give *her* this impression, I presumed that I had wounded your vanity rather than thwarted your passion. If I was in error, at least Time (let us say) is the anodyne of disappointment rather than the separation of friends.
>
> Sincerely yours
Thomas Stearns Eliot[30]

Though transatlantic communications between Tom and Vivien do not survive, it is clear that, sensing she was losing the battle for her husband's attention, she now played her trump card. She sent a message to Eastern Point that she was 'very ill', convincing Tom that he must sail 'at once' for England. Without even having time to deliver all the presents he had brought, Tom booked a passage back, setting sail on 21 August, though still telling Professor Woods that he did 'not anticipate that her illness will prevent my return before the opening of college'.[31] Tom's sister Margaret was struck by the family's 'anxiety' over Tom's leaving for London; but they could not stop him.[32] As she had tried to do earlier with Thayer, so now Vivien invoked her illness as a way of exerting control over her husband. 'I fought like mad to keep Tom here', she wrote later, 'and stopped his going back to America. I thought I could not marry him unless I was able to keep him here, in England.'[33]

She and Bertrand Russell had been making plans. Vivien and Tom would move into the spare bedroom in Russell's London flat at 34 Russell Chambers, Bury Street. By early September, when the young couple had what Russell snidely termed 'their sort of pseudo-honeymoon' at Eastbourne, that was settled.[34] Back with Vivien, Tom wrote to Thayer apologising for his earlier letter. He hoped Thayer would visit London soon. Having succeeded in using her illness to retain Tom, Vivien established a pattern that would be repeated over the ensuing years; Tom would learn to respond with illnesses of his own, and by steeling himself. Both he and Vivien could be manipulative. She seemed confident of her power over the middle-aged Russell also, and Russell was all too ready to offer help to his former student and his petite young wife. His motives, as Ottoline Morrell recognised, were scarcely disinterested. 'I don't think it would *help her* and help towards making the Eliot life happier to let her fall in love with you', she warned him.[35] It was too late.

Vivien had already sent Russell what he interpreted as a 'desperate' letter from Eastbourne. The 'pseudo-honeymoon' was 'a ghastly failure'. She seemed 'in the lowest depths of despair & not far removed from suicide'. Russell, who had exchanged several letters with Vivien, saw himself as just the man to step in: 'she seems to have come to rely on me more or less'. He went on, 'I think she will fall more or less in love with me, but that can't be helped.' Perhaps attempting to reassure his lover Ottoline, he drafted a rather devious letter, explaining that Vivien had 'a great deal of mental passion & *no* physical passion, a universal vanity, that makes her desire every man's devotion, & a fastidiousness that makes any expression of their devotion disgusting to her'. Clearly Vivien had been telling Russell in considerable detail about her relationships: 'She has suffered humiliation in two successive love-affairs, & that has made her vanity morbid.' He thought her ambition 'far beyond her powers': she needed discipline, religious or otherwise. Treating her rather as a psychological case or a character from J. M. Synge's *Playboy of the Western World*, Russell saw her as capable of destroying Tom, and (though Ottoline perceived otherwise) presented his own motives as wholly benevolent: 'At present she is punishing my poor friend for having tricked her imagination – like the heroine of the "Playboy". I want to give her some outlet rather than destroying him. I shan't fall in love with her, nor give her any more show of affection than seems necessary to rehabilitate her.'[36] So it was that the wily Russell encouraged Tom to contact a member of the editorial committee of the *International Journal of Ethics*, who gave him some philosophy books to review, while, with characteristically unethical behaviour, Russell set about seducing Tom's young wife.

Thanking 'Mr Russell' for 'kindnesses' which had 'quite overwhelmed him', Tom at Eastbourne progressed like a lamb to the slaughter, or, perhaps, like a man at his wits' end. Still conducting transatlantic negotiations by letter, he felt 'quite exhausted each day'. Vivien was 'still so unwell'; they were calling a doctor. Russell asked if Tom would mind if he – Russell – slept in the London flat sometimes when Tom was teaching at High Wycombe and Vivien was alone. Increasingly dependent on Russell, Tom replied,

As to your coming to stay the night at the flat when I am not there, it would never have occurred to me to accept it under any other conditions. Such a concession to conventions never entered my head; it seems to me not only totally unnecessary, but also would destroy for me all the pleasure we take in the informality of the arrangement.[37]

Committed now to remaining in England, Tom wanted his mother to send on his clothes 'as soon as she can'. The position at High Wycombe was 'still open'. Assuring his 'dear father' that he remained 'Always your affectionate son', he explained that, though they were struggling financially, 'Vivien's resourcefulness and forethought are inexhaustible.'[38] After the honeymoon debacle at Eastbourne, he set off for his lodgings at High Wycombe to teach at the Royal Grammar School.

Term began on 21 September. Set in fourteen-acre grounds on Amersham Hill, this fee-paying boys' school, which catered for about two hundred locals and boarders, looked not unlike Milton Academy. Yet it was both older and more modern. Founded in 1562, it had moved in mid-1915 to substantial neo-Georgian buildings. Excellent facilities included science labs and (appropriately in wartime) an 'Armoury'.[39] That summer Cumbrian George Wright Arnison, the ambitious, Cambridge-educated headmaster, recorded with pride that 88% of his school's eligible former pupils were serving in the military. Tom's new colleagues included 'gay, debonair and popular' Lieutenant Matthews, who commanded the school's Officer Training Corps.[40] Arnison was a stickler for order. Soon Tom became conscious that 'where work really shows (in the eyes of a headmaster) is in working the boys hard, keeping discipline, and making the red tape run smoothly'.[41] His headmaster kept a graph of every individual pupil's progress, insisting each have 'fortnightly progress reports for parents to see'.[42] A demanding Classicist, Arnison was sympathetic to Tom's erudition. He encouraged him to continue his doctorate.

The young master lodged with a landlady, Mrs Toone, in Sydney Cottage, Conegra Road, near the railway station. Nestling in the scenic Chiltern Hills, and situated on a historic route between Oxford and London, High Wycombe had been mentioned in the Domesday Book. In 1915 it was a prosperous market town coming to terms with intensive army recruiting, tales from the front, casualty lists, 'Charliechaplinitis' at the Grand Cinema and fears of zeppelin attacks.[43] The Grammar School, whose classes began at 9.30 each morning, was about a mile and a half's uphill walk away. Tom taught French, mathematics, history, drawing and swimming to boys of various ages on a salary of £140 a year plus school evening meals – when possible he popped back to Mrs Toone's for lunch. Tuesday and Thursday afternoons were free, but there were always lessons to plan.

This regime required quick thinking: sometimes, directed by Mr Arnison, Tom had to superintend games or take 'a scripture class at five minutes notice'.[44] Toing and froing between High Wycombe and London, he had to cope, too, with Vivien's doctors' bills and with his anxious father who had been cabling the Haigh-Woods and Ezra Pound. Not keen for Pound to receive such cables, Tom tried to reassure his father while also asking for extra cash. Salvation of a sort came when Bertrand Russell, who felt that his own views about pacifism obliged him to rid himself of investments in a munitions manufacturer, made over his £3,000 holdings to Tom. Though much later (in 1927) Tom returned the debentures, in the short term they did provide a financial safety net; and intensified a sense of indebtedness to Russell.

On Sunday 3 October, the day after the Wycombe Royal Grammar School Officer Training Corps commanded by Lieutenant Matthews had joined a torchlit parade as part of a big local recruiting rally and had heard a 'stirring speech' maintaining that the war could certainly be won without 'the Americans',[45] Russell wrote to St Louis at Tom's request, reassuring his mother about her son's prospects in England. Praising Tom, the Cambridge don assured Lottie Eliot he had also 'taken some pains to get to know' Vivien 'who seems to me thoroughly nice, really anxious for his welfare, and is very desirous of not hampering his liberty or interfering with whatever he feels to be best'. This, surely, was what Tom thought his mother should hear. Russell praised Tom's literary talent, while mentioning that Vivien had ensured he was 'no longer attracted by the people who call themselves "vorticists"'.[46] Though not quite true, this too was designed to go down well; when Tom's father had perused *Blast* his opinion had been that 'he did not know there were enough lunatics in the world to support such a magazine'.[47] Tom was keen to reassure his parents, and also anxious to move back to London. Already thinking about another job, he told his mother about his reviewing for the *International Journal of Ethics*, and mentioned he was joining London's leading philosophical association, the Aristotelian Society.

If only the St Louis Eliots had known, they would have realised that, still fraternising with the scandalous Vorticists, their son was interested, too, in another unconventional artistic coterie. Along with her husband, Liberal MP Philip Morrell, Russell's mistress, Lady Ottoline, hosted gatherings of the avant-garde elite in the rural hamlet of Garsington, a few miles from Oxford. There, next to the Norman St Mary's Church whose vicar Edward Hastings Horne, a graduate of Russell's Cambridge college, was at work on his biblical commentary *The Meaning of the Apocalypse*, stood the picturesque, brick-chimneyed, three-storey seventeenth-century manor house which Ottoline and Philip Morrell had bought with a three-hundred-and sixty-acre estate in 1913. Enjoying views over open countryside to distinctively shaped hills, the Wittenham Clumps, the Morrells' house was approached between stunningly high yew hedges, and some of the goings-on in its grounds were rumoured to be positively apocalyptic. Bertrand Russell had stayed in a Garsington cottage for part of summer 1915 when he, D. H. Lawrence, artist Mark Gertler and author Gilbert Cannan (recently married to Mrs J. M. Barrie after her notorious divorce) had painted one drawing room in the manor house hot Venetian red with gold highlights, and the other a contrasting sea green. Upper-class freethinkers, the Morrells had recently moved in with their young daughter Julian. They made the place a refuge for controversial pacifists like Russell, and for artists, academics, homosexuals, heterosexuals, bisexuals, lovers and mistresses.

By that autumn, when copies of Lawrence's new novel *The Rainbow* had been confiscated by police as obscene, Tom too was 'planning' to rendezvous with Russell at Garsington.[48] However, it appears this meeting did not take place, so he did not encounter Lady Ottoline until the following spring.[49] Over the next few years, sometimes accompanied by Vivien, he would visit Garsington regularly, enjoying sitting outdoors in sunny weather, chatting and smoking with other well-dressed guests among birdsong in the sloping grounds where charismatic Ottoline developed a large rectangular pond (painted as emptily Edenic by Gertler in 1916) and an 'Italian garden' with copies of naked and semi-naked Classical statues of Vulcan and other deities.[50] Just as Garsington juxtaposed echoes of Classical grandeur with present-day avant-garde decadence, so would several of Tom's new poems. Flamboyantly dressed, Lady Ottoline liked unusual costumes with green, violet, yellow and turquoise silks.[51] She assembled guests including Russell, Lawrence, Gertler, Lytton Strachey, Bloomsbury art critic Clive Bell, aristocratic artist Dorothy Brett (who had a crush on Lady Ottoline), Julian and Juliette Huxley, and the young Aldous Huxley. Tom knew Aldous from Oxford's Coterie reading group; Huxley's *Crome Yellow* (1921) with its phoney fortune-teller Sesostris (her name so close to that of *The Waste Land*'s 'Madame Sosostris, famous clairvoyante'[52]) sent up Garsington in a novel of apocalyptic prophecies, frustrated love, philosophers, artists and poets. Even better known is D. H. Lawrence's metamorphosis of Lady Ottoline into the character of Hermione Roddice in *Women in Love*, which led Ottoline to try to sue him.

When Tom began gravitating towards this often unconventional, intellectually starry and sometimes fractious company, he was received less as an obscure, struggling schoolteacher than as Bertrand Russell's smart young friend, the unusually promising American poet. Russell's contacts would help secure Tom's welcome also into the Bloomsbury set that included novelists Leonard and Virginia Woolf, though Tom was reluctant to be co-opted by any one artistic grouping. The celebrated Cambridge philosopher's poet-protégé was welcomed into top-drawer English society. Between them, those very different mentors, Russell and Ezra Pound, gave Tom access to several English artistic elites.

Meanwhile Russell, who had had an affair with his previous typist, hired Vivien to type up his thoughts on pacifism. 'I would not for the world have any scandal', he had written to Lady Ottoline when she worried about the consequences of Vivien's falling in love with him, 'and as for the Eliots it is the purest philanthropy'.[53] Spending time with Vivien while Tom was in High Wycombe, Russell grew 'very fond' of her, though he assured Lady Ottoline 'she does not attract me much physically'.[54] That adverb, 'much', sounds weaselly. Ray Monk's biography of Russell traces his developing relationship with Vivien in astute detail. On 10 November the childless Russell wrote to Ottoline Morrell that he had 'come to love' Tom 'as if he were my son':

He is becoming much more of a man. He has a profound and quite unselfish devotion to his wife, and she is really very fond of him, but has impulses of cruelty to him from time to time. It is a Dostojewsky type of cruelty, not a straightforward every-day kind. I am every day getting things more right between them, but I can't let them alone at present, and of course I myself get very much interested. She is a person who lives on a knife-edge, and will end as a criminal or a saint – I don't know which yet. She has a perfect capacity for both.[55]

By this time Vivien, corresponding with Scofield Thayer, was showing Thayer's letters to Russell. She was proud to be 'the wife of a poet whose fame is rapidly increasing through the length & breadth of more than one land'. However, 'in order not to become merely "T. S. Eliot's wife"', Vivien was embarking on a career in ballet. She went to practise in an underground Soho room where she wore a short black skirt and 'Bertie or Tom' came to watch her.[56] Joking, she compared herself to the theatrical dancer Jenny Pearl in Compton Mackenzie's 1912 novel *Carnival*; pursued by several lovers, Jenny finds 'The ennui of life' sometimes 'overwhelming' and is eventually murdered by her husband.[57] Again, jokily, she told Thayer, 'We have more or less of a triple ménage. Bertie Russell has taken us to his bosom. I cheer him up, he says – & the flat rings with his raucous mirth.' She then mentioned that she and Tom would be going to America in the spring, perhaps for an extended stay. He would sit his doctoral exams, and she would bring some of Russell's 'seditious writings' to distribute in New York. 'Will you help me Scofield *deeear*?'[58]

In sickness and in health Vivien enjoyed exercising flirtatious power. Russell, like others, felt it. Awkwardly combining paternalism with sexual attraction, he promised he would go on holiday with her in January 1916, and chose the Torbay Hotel, Torquay, in Devon. Though Vivien had been corresponding pleasantly with the Eliots in America, her planned transatlantic trip with Tom in the spring was off. Now back in London, Tom had found another teaching job at Highgate Junior School while intensively rewriting his thesis. He worried about the war, which was ruining so many lives. The shocking news had reached him that Jean Verdenal had been killed in action: that death of such a close friend would haunt him. Immediately, though, war brought other problems. Due to conscription, he might be about to lose his 'putative publisher' to the army. Moreover, Vivien had been 'very ill', triggering further anxieties – not least about medical bills.[59] With all these stresses, it was a relief when Russell took her on holiday.

Self-protectively reverting to a former self, Tom wrote to Aiken, summoning up the old Bolo spirit and rhyming 'klassic' with 'ass sick'. He congratulated Aiken on his new collection of poems. Probably as a result of appearing in *Poetry*, Tom had entertained hopes of getting a volume of verse published by Sherman French and Company of Beacon Street, Boston. 'They wrote asking me to send them a book, and when I wrote back asking for terms they said they hadn't known I was an Englishman and they could only boom books by native talent.' Disgusted, he told Aiken he had 'written their name on bumwash'. He also said he was 'having a wonderful life', emphasising that he had '*lived* through material for a score of long poems, in the last six months'.[60] None of these, however, had he written.

After five days, Russell left Vivien in Torquay and Tom, at Russell's expense, joined her there. Tom wrote to Russell expressing great gratitude: he was sure the older man had 'handled' Vivien 'in the very best way – better than I'. He felt they owed Russell a huge amount, perhaps even Vivien's life. She was still, however, sick with exhaustion, headache, faintness and stomach problems. Such ills would become central to their married life – frightening for both of them, and hardly conducive to conjugal bliss. Tom knew sex could be exciting, but could also pall; its urges might be controlled or deflected. Observing schoolboys in the classroom, he summarised, with approval and a certain chilled, schoolmasterly clarity, the arguments of A. Clutton Brock's *The Ultimate Belief*:

For the boy whose childhood has been empty of beauty, the boy who has never learned the *detached* curiosity for beauty, the sexual instinct when it is aroused may mean the only possible escape from a prosaic world. Hence a danger which may be followed by a still greater disaster, the passage from a period of violent excitement into a maturity of commonplace. We must learn to love always, to exercise those disinterested passions of the spirit which are inexhaustible and permanently satisfying.[61]

This was 'T. Stearns Eliot', reviewer in the *International Journal of Ethics,* perfecting his magisterial tone; but around the same time in later 1916, writing to Henry about how he felt, he described his year as 'the most awful nightmare of anxiety that the mind of man could conceive'.[62]

As he struggled to write up a revised version of his PhD, his worries were financial, literary and academic, but at the heart of them lay Vivien and her health. When they married he had not known her medical history in detail.[63] Now he saw all her difficulties. Early in the year she exhausted herself agonising over an impending visit to the dentist. Toothache and that dentist's mention of 'a possibility of an abscess' reduced her to a state of 'shock'. Tom, who thought the dentist lacking in tact, turned to Russell; Vivien was now 'very ill', suffering 'very great pain, both neuralgia and stomach'.[64] Russell told Woods at Harvard in early March that Tom, when not schoolteaching at Highgate, spent his spare time looking after his wife 'with the most amazing devotion and unselfishness'.[65]

Having moved out of Bertie's London quarters, the Eliots were now in a rented flat at 3 Culworth House in St John's Wood, a neo-Georgian, mansion-style block about a mile from Vivien's parents. Almost at once they sought alternative accommodation. Vivien was 'very ill all the winter', Tom told Aiken. No sooner did he suggest she was 'gradually getting better' in the summer of 1916 than there was another bout of 'neuralgia' and sinus trouble.[66] In September a doctor told her she was not eating properly. As she put it,

He said I was chiefly starved! The headaches are called hemicranial migraine, and they are really 'nerve storms' affecting one whole side of me – they make me sick and feverish and they always last 15–24 hours – and I rise up weak and white as if I had been through some long and dreadful illness. He explained that they are caused in me by starvation – I do not eat enough to nourish my nervous system – and brain.[67]

On new medication, she hoped to improve, but slowly. It is tempting to speculate that this sounds like an eating disorder, but in early-twentieth-century parlance Vivien's troubles were variously assumed to involve nerves, hysteria, colitis, neuralgia, stomach cramps, migraines and other ailments. Troubled, and never long in remission, she always felt exhausted by her illnesses. So did Tom.

Constantly worried about her, he now spent his weekdays teaching small boys at the fee-paying Highgate Junior School. Described by him in 1921 as 'near London', it was a sixteenth-century foundation.[68] The poet Samuel Taylor Coleridge, who had ended his days in Highgate, was buried in the school chapel; another poet Gerard Manley Hopkins had been a pupil in the 1850s. Based in Cholmeley House, the Junior School catered for boys around the age of ten. Tom's immediate boss was E. H. Kelly, a competent teacher with a talent for woodturning. In these war years he impressed Tom by turning 'crutches beautifully' on a small lathe.[69] More forbidding, in mortar board and billowing silk gown, red-faced Dr J. A. H. Johnston, Highgate's scientifically-minded headmaster, was an irate Scottish mathematician. Passing regularly through the school 'like a tornado', and said to be the victim of a gastric ulcer, Dr Johnston annoyed boarders (who breakfasted on 'bread and scrape' and lunched on 'lentil pie') by ostentatiously 'necking into roast chicken'.[70] A junior teacher under Mr Kelly, Tom could seem quiet and remote, but at least one boy – ten-year-old fledgling poet John Betjeman – remembered 'The American master, Mr Eliot' as 'That dear good man'.[71] Tom taught 'French, Latin, lower mathematics, drawing, swimming, geography, history, and base-ball'.[72] Vivien and his mother thought he was wasted in the job. However, as with all his adult employments, he gave it his best, and taught at Highgate until the end of 1916. He thought hard about education that year, sympathetic to the idea that 'Boys should be taught to respect the values of truth, beauty and goodness for their own sake . . . They should learn *why* knowledge is valuable, apart from purely practical success, the pursuit of which may fail to excite the more independent.'[73]

In March the young schoolteacher and his wife dined in Soho with Bertrand Russell, and Ottoline and Philip Morrell. Russell had shown Lady Ottoline the October 1915 *Poetry* containing 'The Boston Evening Transcript', 'Aunt Helen' and 'Cousin Nancy'. Thinking these 'very remarkable', Lady Ottoline welcomed the Eliots into her London circle, which included painters Dorothy Brett and Dora Carrington as well as the novelist Molly MacCarthy. Ottoline was struck by Vivien's refusal to accompany Tom to America 'as she was afraid of submarines'. In Soho, however, she recalled,

The dinner was not a great success. T. S. Eliot was very formal and polite, and his wife seemed to me of the 'spoilt kitten'-type, very second-rate and ultra feminine, playful and naïve, anxious to show she 'possessed' Bertie, when we walked away from the restaurant she headed him off and kept him to herself, walking with him arm-in-arm. I felt rather *froissée* at her bad manners.

Next day I gave a tea-party at Bedford Square. One of the drawing-rooms had been turned into my bedroom. The bed was a large, very high four-poster, with Cardinal-coloured silk curtains, trimmed with silver; it was very lovely looking into that room from the Great Drawing Room. Molly MacCarthy and Dora Sanger, Brett and Carrington and Gertler and Mr. and Mrs. Eliot and Bertie came. It seemed a happy gay tea-party, at least thus I always remember it.[74]

Conscious Vivien would be too ill to accompany him to America, and did not want to go, Tom aimed to submit his PhD as soon as possible. He worked hard on the new version, 'The Nature of Objects, with reference to the philosophy of F. H. Bradley'. Drawing heavily on his Oxford work, its first chapter dealt with knowledge of immediate experience.

A toothache, or a violent passion, is not necessarily diminished by our knowledge of its causes, its character, its importance or insignificance. To say that one part of the mind suffers and another part reflects upon the suffering is perhaps to talk in fictions. But we know that those highly-organized beings who are able to objectify their passions, and as passive spectators to contemplate their joys and torments, are also those who suffer and enjoy the most keenly.[75]

If Vivien and her toothache were in his mind as he wrote, so was Thackeray's manipulative lover Becky Sharp, as well as ideas that would nourish his own aesthetic theory. Discussing imagination and memory, he argued that 'It is not true that the ideas of a great poet are in any sense arbitrary'; rather, 'the apparent irrelevance is due to the fact that terms are used with more or other than their normal meaning'.[76] Drawing on his earlier work, Tom stressed the importance of 'relation' and of 'degrees of reality'; he confronted, too, issues of solipsism. The only poet mentioned is the French Symbolist Mallarmé (defended against being read solely in terms of 'morbid psychological activity'), and only one poem features − revealingly misquoted. Substituting the word 'shadows' for 'visions', Tom altered the first line of Elizabeth Barrett Browning's sonnet 26 from *Sonnets from the Portuguese*, that begins 'I lived with visions for my company'; the poet thanks her beloved for coming to 'be' what earlier dreams only 'seemed'.[77] Though she supported his writing of the thesis, Vivien believed Tom's real bent lay in poetic vision, not philosophical shadow-play. In this, as in other ways, she was the inspiring opposite of his mother. Lottie Eliot explained in a May 1916 letter to Russell that she had 'absolute faith' in Tom's 'Philosophy but not in the *vers libres*'.[78] Vivien was in some regards just what her young poet husband needed: 'Tom is *wonderful*', she assured Henry.[79] 'Of course', she added later that year, 'he has me to shove him – I supply the motive power, and I *do* shove.'[80]

Like his mother, Vivien saw Tom's potential; but each woman regarded that potential differently. Vivien shoved, but held Tom back too. As the time drew near for him to sail to the States on 1 April 1916 to sit his doctoral examinations, Tom was urged by Pound to take an extra trunk filled with Vorticist paintings for a planned New York exhibition. Wyndham Lewis did not want all his pictures sunk 'in these torpedoing times': sending half with Tom and the rest in a different vessel should reduce the risk.[81] Vivien, more anxious about her new husband than about any paintings, grew increasingly worried Tom's ship would be vulnerable. Foul weather hardly helped. Aware on 29 March that her nerves were 'all to pieces', Russell contacted Tom's father, strongly advising him to cable Tom not to make the trip unless his doctorate was worth risking his life.[82] Next day Tom cabled to say he was not coming. He and Vivien had just moved flats; the strain was telling on them both.

To give him a change of scene, in early April Russell took him on his first visit to Garsington. 'Rather lonely, and very lovable', Tom (Russell assured Ottoline Morrell) had 'an *intense* desire to see you again'.[83] Tom did not shine. A disappointed Lady Ottoline, conscious of the attraction between Russell and his former student's wife, nicknamed the young poet 'The Undertaker' and described his tense, guarded demeanour in her journal, adding further reflections later.

> I never feel my best with Bertie. I cannot tell why. He always quenches my light-headedness and gaiety and puts a blight on me. T. S. Eliot, his American poet friend came with him. I was very excited that T. S. Eliot was coming with him, but I found him dull, dull, dull. He never moves his lips but speaks in an even and monotonous voice, and I felt him monotonous without and within. Where does his queer neurasthenic poetry come from, I wonder? From his New England, Puritan inheritance and upbringing? I think he has lost all spontaneity and can only break through his conventionality by stimulants or violent emotions. He is obviously very ignorant of England and

imagines that it is essential to be highly polite and conventional and decorous, and meticulous. I tried to get him to talk more freely by talking French to him, as I thought he might feel freer doing so, but I don't think it was a great success, although better than English. He speaks French very perfectly, slowly and correctly. As I remember this I feel how odd it was, but it shows how very foreign Eliot seemed to me then; but I generally found that Americans are as foreign to us as Germans are.[84]

Socially, maritally and professionally, Tom was struggling, even if Russell thought Vivien 'all right again'.[85] 'In a state of mental confusion', Tom told Woods at Harvard that his ship's departure had been postponed for five days at the last minute, but assured his former professor he would come '*at the first opportunity*'.[86]

The new London flat, 'nearly a top one' and overlooking a courtyard, was at 18 Crawford Mansions, a newly built, five-storey red-brick neo-Georgian building on the corner of Crawford Street and Homer Lane, Marylebone.[87] Five pale stone steps led to a handsome communal front door whose panels included art nouveau ironwork. Vivien liked it. Though there were pubs, 'slums and low streets and poor shops close around us', tantalisingly near were expensive, fashionable squares.[88] Noise came from neighbours' gramophones, but the plumbing was good – constant hot water and 'every modern convenience' – even if by Vivien's standards the apartment was small. There was a hall, dining room (which doubled as Tom's dressing room and study), drawing room, substantial bedroom, kitchen and a good bathroom. Vivien chose fashionable decor: orange wallpaper in the dining room, black-and-white stripes in the hall. For all her illnesses, she still liked to excite. Signing herself 'the most fervent Vivien S-E', she wrote to Scofield Thayer, who had announced he too was getting married. She urged him to 'Try black silk sheets and pillow covers – they are extraordinarily effective – so long as you are willing to sacrifice *yourself*.'[89] But not long afterwards she was 'very ill in the night', Tom told Russell anxiously. 'She seems very overdone.'[90]

At Harvard Tom's doctoral thesis was extremely well received, even though its author was absent. Royce considered it 'the work of an expert', Hoernlé 'a most valuable piece of work'. Asking Tom to confirm that his interest in philosophy was as strong as ever, Professor Woods hinted at the possibility of a Harvard appointment.[91] This was just what Tom's mother hoped for, and what Vivien sought to avoid. Tom strove to keep options open. Continuing to be solicitous, Russell had put him in touch with Philip Jourdain, a mathematician assembling a special feature on

Leibniz for the October issue of Chicago's prestigious philosophy journal the *Monist*. Jourdain was the magazine's editor in England. As a result, two academic articles by Tom appeared in the issue, though one, drawing very substantially on his Oxford work, was more about Aristotle than Leibniz. Tom told Aiken that autumn 'I am still a relativist.'[92] Presenting Aristotle's account of matter as 'relativistic', he continued to explore, as he had done for years, the relationship between soul and body.[93]

'Our interest in art cannot be isolated from the other interests in life, among them interests in philosophy and religion', he had written in late 1915, deprecating both 'a distorted puritanism' (which he hoped he had escaped) and 'an orgiastic mysticism', which he had read much about.[94] Yet in 1916, though Pound helped him 'select the poems for his first volume' in April and urged London publisher Elkin Matthews (who had published some of Pound's own early collections) to bring it out, Tom's poetic output was in decline.[95] Instead, in the hope he could give up schoolteaching, he was taking on reviewing. Sydney Waterlow, an editor of the *International Journal of Ethics*, had put him on to literary editors at the *New Statesman*, *Manchester Guardian* and *Westminster Gazette*. For these general-interest publications the books he reviewed were often related to America, India or France: he was, after all, a Francophile American who had studied Sanskrit. Cloaked in the confidence of anonymous reviewing – which ensured none of his Harvard teachers would identify him – he relished what he saw as an accurate picture of 'the essential faults of American education' and 'some of the reasons for the insolvency of American literature'. The Canadian humourist Stephen Leacock highlighted 'the sterility of American literature' when compared with British work.[96] Tom enjoyed reading Leacock on the life of a schoolmaster, and even more on the slog of writing a PhD. 'Mr Leacock', he wrote,

> draws a truthful picture of the American graduate student, the prospective Doctor of Philosophy: his specialisation in knowledge, his expansion in ignorance, his laborious dullness, his years of labour and his crowning achievement – the Thesis.
> Now it is not to be thought that this post-graduate work upon the preparation of a thesis, this so-called original scholarship, is difficult. It is pretentious, plausible, esoteric, cryptographic, occult if you will, but difficult it is not.
> This labour is fatal to the development of intellectual powers. It crushes originality, it kills style. Few, very few, of these 'original contributions' are well written or even readable.[97]

These words hardly suggest someone eager for an academic career.

Initially naïve about reviewing, he was convinced he could earn significant money by doing vast amounts: 'I crave a new book every few days.'[98] He received volumes ranging from philosophical and critical works on topics with which he was familiar (Durkheim, Bergson, theories of religion) to new poetry by Edgar Lee Masters and adventure fiction by Henry de Vere Stacpoole about hunting for gold among the New Guinea Dyaks. To his mother he explained that 'the editress' of the *Saturday Westminster Gazette* 'told me that she could read and review *six* novels in an evening!' and advised him to do the same: short appraisals of eight novels would earn £1; then the books could be sold to a second-hand shop for 2 shillings each. 'Vivien can do some of them for me', he added, taking care to show his mother how carefully he was calculating their household finances, and that his wife was readily supportive.[99] Perhaps, even if Tom wrote it, the *Westminster*'s verdict that in *The Reef of Stars* Stacpoole's account of a mad New Guinea gold-hunter 'leaves us in a state of complete exhaustion' owes something to Vivien's predicament.[100] Or maybe it was just Tom's own sense of being 'worried and nervous'.[101]

As he discovered the longstanding nature of Vivien's illnesses, she told him that, 'afflicted with tuberculosis of the bones', she had endured 'so many operations before she was seven, that she was able to recall nothing until she reached that age'.[102] Later, doctors came to describe her to him as 'extraordinarily undeveloped' as if she were in a state of 'extreme youth and almost childishness'.[103] Sometimes she dreamed of having children; more often she expressed a horror at passing on 'something of yourself'.[104] Not so long before, Tom had envisaged becoming a father. Vivien's dancing, her intellectual and physical brightness, her prettiness and rushes of energy had drawn him to her. Other men, she knew, sensed these too. Yet more than thirty years after they met, reflecting that no one was ever wholly a success or a failure, he described marriage as a continuous learning: 'married people must always regard each other as a mysterious person whom they are gradually getting to know, in a process which must go on to the end of the life of one or the other'.[105] This use of 'must' makes the process sound somewhat gruelling. Sometimes Vivien's quirks were simply a nuisance: back in London from the countryside for a day to work in the library of the British Museum, Tom could not access his own books in a locked bookcase in their flat because she had hung on to the key. But her constant ill-health was an ongoing ordeal for them both.

In summer 1916, during the school holidays, he had a new photograph taken for his wartime Identity Book. This document meant he and Vivien could move freely beyond London. They spent several weeks 'vegetating and gaining health' in the attractive historic village of Bosham. Pronounced 'Bozzum' by locals, it lies on the south coast of England near Portsmouth, conveniently accessible from London by train. Bosham's lowest street was (and still is) submerged at high tide. Its cottages, ancient church and sailors' pub looked out on the sunlit sea. Like Gloucester, Massachusetts, Bosham offered 'bathing, boating and bicycling'.[106] Accommodated and well fed by their 'bouncing kindly landlady' Kate Smith, and conscious of other vacationers such as Gilbert Cannan, art critic Roger Fry and Bloomsbury-affiliated writer Mary Hutchinson, the Eliots went on learning about each other, relishing the seaside.[107] Relaxing in shirt and flannel trousers, Tom walked with Vivien to a farmhouse where they bought mushrooms. They cherished small pleasures, but things went wrong. Their lodgings were damp: Vivien experienced prolonged neuralgia as well as rheumatism in her feet ('nearer to gout'); Tom got mild rheumatism in his left leg.[108] The two twenty-eight-year-olds tried to cheer up, yet sometimes, in pain and under the weather, they felt acutely miserable.

At Bosham they had a familiar visitor, also unhappy. Convicted for impeding British military recruitment, Bertrand Russell had been sacked from Trinity College in June. Vigorously he supported the No-Conscription Fellowship. Though the philosopher was ordered to pay a £100 fine, Tom 'rejoiced' to hear accounts of his spirited courtroom defence; Russell had dined with Vivien soon after his trial, and they had 'discussed money'.[109] The sacked don had been assisting the Eliots financially with their household expenditure, as well as funding Vivien's dancing lessons. He realised, as he put it to Lady Ottoline, that 'it would save my pocket if her husband got better-paid work'.[110]

Impressed with what he knew of Tom's reviewing, Russell suggested to Ottoline that Tom might send her samples of his writing, so she might ask the influential critic Desmond McCarthy (a frequent Garsington guest) to help him out – maybe with regular work for the *New Statesman* or *Guardian*, for both of which, occasionally, Tom had written. Economising, Russell had rented out his London flat. He flitted now among several bolt-holes, writing public lectures for the No-Conscription Fellowship to be delivered that autumn. Among his places of refuge were Garsington, and Bosham – where Vivien more than Tom seems to have been the attraction. Lady Ottoline was fed up with her lover's apparent infatuation with Vivien:

I had a long talk with Bertie about Mrs. Eliot. I don't really under-stand her influence over him. It seems odd that such a frivolous, silly, little woman should affect him so much, but I think he likes to feel that she depends on him, and she looks up to him as a rich god, for he lavishes presents on her of silk underclothes and all sorts of silly things, and pays for her dancing lessons. It takes all his money and now he expects us to raise a fund to pay the £100 fine.[III]

None of this stopped Russell arriving in Bosham on more than one occasion that August. Following his 'long talk' with Lady Ottoline, he promised to disengage from Vivien, but feared 'the result will be a violent quarrel'.[112] He felt he could not immediately axe his financial support. 'It will be difficult to do anything sudden', Russell prevaricated, '& *really*', he told her ladyship on 4 August, 'the whole thing is not as bad as you think'.[113]

By 20 August, away from Bosham, Russell was writing to Ottoline about how Vivien cared for him. He felt 'affection' for her; he worried her 'faults' sprang from 'a root of despair'.[114] He could not break with her immediately and felt awkward. Writing to Aiken on 21 August, Tom listed various Bosham visitors, but not Russell; nor, though she knew him, did he mention the philosopher to Eleanor Hinkley on 5 September when he wrote from London, giving her an account of Bosham and 'friends' they had seen there.[115] On 31 August Russell and Tom had discussed Vivien, who was then ill and whom Russell did not see. No detailed account of their conversation survives, but Russell conveyed the gist to Lady Ottoline:

It was rather gloomy, but I got quite clear as to what must be done, so I shan't worry any more. It is fixed that I go to Bosham Monday to Friday; then I don't expect to see her during the winter. Seeing her is worrying, and takes up my time and money and her health. I shall go on doing what I have done in the way of money during the winter, but beyond that I have said I can't foresee what will be possible. I can't now decide anything beyond this winter.

Conscious that his behaviour could be regarded as shabby, Russell told Lady Ottoline he would like to come to Garsington after his week at Bosham with Vivien while Tom was in London. 'Matters with Mrs. E. will be decided then. I never contemplated risking my reputation with her, & I never risked it as far as I can judge.'[116] On 4 September Russell was served with a banning order by the authorities, prohibiting him from visiting any coastal areas or other militarily sensitive sites. Vivien remained in Bosham alone; Tom stayed in London.

'Tell me how Emily is', he wrote the next day to Eleanor.[117] This short sentence occurs as part of a much longer letter, composed with a determined lightness, in which he describes life in Bosham. The words about Emily Hale conceal much more than they reveal. In June Tom and Vivien had had their first wedding anniversary. Yet, recalling his 1915 marriage, he wrote as an old man, 'I was still, as I came to believe a year later, in love with Miss Hale.'[118]

As far as he could, he suppressed that thought. He did not write to Emily. He knew he had burned his boats. Yet his time in Bosham with Vivien made him think of Massachusetts. 'The villagers', he told his mother, 'are very much like New England fishing people, but rather more complete in their way'.[119] Even as New England came into his mind, he sounded a note of admiration for old England: a reminder he was staying put. His father seems never to have accepted his decision, but Tom went on playing chess with him by post. Transatlantic family relations were generally improved, and he strove to keep them so, thanking his mother profusely for offers of help and his father for ongoing financial support. From time to time Henry too sent money. English friends including Russell and Ottoline Morrell, not to mention Pound and his many contacts, were encouraging the publication and reception of his work in England and America. Sent to *Poetry* by Pound in May, four poems ('Conversation Galante', 'La Figlia Che Piange', 'Mr. Apollinax', and 'Morning at the Window' – none of them new) appeared in the September issue of that Chicago journal under the collective title, 'Observations'. This term, cool and distancing, would linger in Tom's mind.

While determined to stay in England, he remained an American. To his brother he confessed his fear 'that "J.A.P." is a swan song'. Nonetheless he had hopes to publish his first collection that autumn in New York: 'a small volume', but a personal milestone.[120] Instead, when this aspiration came to nothing, he had to content himself with reading Conrad Aiken's second collection, *Turns and Movies*. Published in Boston and New York, it was filled with vignettes of dancers and theatre performers such as those he and Aiken had watched as students. Tom found a certain power in the work. Continuing to review books on primitive religions, he could still joke with his friend in verbally inventive, quasi-Bolovian fashion about 'the sacred ritual of the rpat'; but as he read Aiken's poems he felt a 'nausea with life'.[121]

Editors hardly rushed to publish his verse, but at least it was appearing. In August 1916, composing on the typewriter, he wrote a review (published that October in the *New Statesman*) of a volume memorialising French poet Charles Péguy. Tom had read Péguy's work during his student year in Paris. Now he saw Péguy as 'a witness to the eternal fertility of the French soil'. That phrasing is unusually fulsome; the book moved him:

'It is like the account of the death of a friend.'¹²² Less than a year had passed since he had heard of the death of his own friend Verdenal, and from Vivien's young brother Maurice (invalided home from the front suffering from insomnia, and spending his nineteenth birthday sailing with them at Bosham) came accounts of battlefield horrors. 'WORN OUT' and prematurely aged, Maurice spoke about seeing scattered body parts and spending sleepless nights shooting trench rats with a revolver.¹²³ Increasingly, the war spoiled life in London, and threatened artistic endeavours. From editing *Blast* Wyndham Lewis had gone to be a gunner in the army; Lewis's friend and fellow Vorticist Edward Wadsworth was now in the Royal Navy; England's philosopher-poet T. E. Hulme, whose championing of Classicism and whose poetry mattered to Pound and to Tom, had been sent home wounded in 1915, but had returned to combat and would soon be killed. Conscious that he was far from such battlefield ordeals, the little known American philosopher-poet 'T. R. Eliot' (as *Poetry* termed him that September) felt 'comparatively immature'.¹²⁴

To bring in more cash he took on lecturing for the Oxford University Extension Delegacy, a form of academic outreach. Apparently he applied to this body while teaching at High Wycombe. He offered six different courses on French literature – from 'French Literary Criticism' to 'Contemporary French Poets and Novelists' – but the bureaucracy moved slowly; only one course was requested. It was to run on Tuesday afternoons from 3 October until 12 December in Ilkley, a town on the West Yorkshire moors, about two hundred miles north of London. Tom must have had to negotiate time off school – even today the rail journey takes three hours. Covering topics from the egotistical spontaneity of Rousseauistic Romanticism to modern French literary nationalism, royalism, socialism and Catholicism, the lectures culminated with an account of Bergson. The young, less than happily married 'T. Stearns Eliot, M.A. (Harvard)' stressed that 'The beginning of the twentieth century has witnessed a return to the ideals of classicism' whose 'point of view has been defined as essentially a belief in Original Sin – the necessity for austere discipline'. Belonging to no church, he was particularly scathing about those who made religion sound easy. With his familial 'Unitarianism' in mind, he published a review that October containing a sentence etched with irony: 'Certain saints found the following of Christ very hard, but modern methods have facilitated everything.'¹²⁵

Deep down, religion continued to trouble him. His reading of Durkheim helped convince him that 'the struggle of "liberal" against "orthodox" faith is out of date. The present conflict is far more momentous than that.'[126] His relativism and scepticism continued; yet he inclined in a direction encouraged by his time in Paris. Once, while at Harvard, he had written of a wish to overturn 'romantic irritations' by 'classical convictions'.[127] Now his Ilkley lectures on modern French literature stressed the need for form and restraint. 'A classicist in art and literature will therefore be likely to adhere to a monarchical form of government, and to the Catholic Church.'[128] If this sounds a surprising attitude for an American to propagate, it had been encouraged not only by Tom's study with Babbitt but also by his reading of *The Drift of Romanticism* (1913) and *Aristocracy and Justice* (1916). In these books the conservative Paul Elmer More argued, as Tom put it during that World War I summer, that 'At the bottom of man's heart there is always the beast', and that 'man requires an askesis'.[129]

Tom's Yorkshire lectures were probably ill-suited to their audience. To buy all the set texts alone cost almost £5. Attendees used a wartime local library as best they could. Almost sixty turned up – mainly women – but only a quarter of them stayed on for the ensuing discussion classes. The subject matter was so unfamiliar that he had to admit there was no 'discussion of an argumentative nature' at all.[130] The students thought 'he seemed a nice young man but he would fiddle with his watchchain'.[131] Nervously, he over-prepared. Scripting his first hour-long lecture in full, he had attempted to memorise it, but he realised his oration was in danger of lasting two hours. Undaunted, he had also applied to the University of London Extension Board to deliver another course, this time on better-known material. The former Oxford Classics don Alfred Zimmern had mentioned Tom's name to an official of the Workers' Educational Association; in October London University's Joint Committee for the Promotion of Higher Education for Working People agreed this young American could be a tutor in Southall, London, 'provided that there is satisfactory evidence that he will be remaining in England for a reasonable period'.[132]

Tom started not long afterwards giving a twenty-four-week course of lectures on 'Modern English Literature'. It began with Tennyson, the Brownings, Carlyle, Newman and Dickens, then continued through Thackeray, George Eliot, Arnold and the Brontës, before concluding with George Borrow, Ruskin, Edward Fitzgerald and George Meredith. Given that for Tennyson alone students were recommended to read *Maud, In Memoriam, The Idylls of the King* and a range of shorter poems, this was again very demanding. Lectures were on Monday evenings. The Ilkley series was not yet over. So in some weeks Tom had to speak for an hour in Southall, then give a follow-up tutorial in the ensuing hour, then be in Yorkshire for the Tuesday afternoon's lecture and discussion class, before heading back to complete his curtailed week's teaching at Highgate School. He was also working on reviews and articles. Vivien, complaining of her own 'nerve storms' in October, noted that Tom felt '*dried up*' as a poet.[133] By around the end of October 1916 he had decided to give up his work at Highgate completely.

He got better at the lecturing, and enjoyed it. This seemed a more promising way to make money. Bertrand Russell, a seasoned orator, was giving a series of public lectures on such topics as 'Political Ideals' in Manchester from 16 October.[114] Perhaps coincidentally, Vivien decided she was well enough to go to Lancashire to stay outside Manchester with an old girlfriend for ten days or so from 11 October. Ten days later Russell, with Vivien on his mind, was writing to one of his current lovers, the aristocratic actress 'Colette O'Niel' (Lady Constance Malleson, whose husband Miles, active in the No-Conscription Fellowship, was one of Russell's admirers) about how he had become 'enmeshed'. Protesting his 'very great affection' for both Tom and Vivien, he confessed that 'my relation to her especially is very intimate'; he thought Lady Constance would 'think her a common little thing, quite insignificant', but made it clear how much he cared about her.[135] Aware that Vivien had been hurt emotionally in two earlier relationships, Russell presented his own emotional involvement with her as altruistically benign, though he admitted they had had 'a long disagreement':

> The root of the matter is that she had become filled with fear through having been hurt, and out of defiance had become harsh to everyone including her husband, who is my friend, whom I love, and who is dependent on her for his happiness. If I fail her, she will punish him, and be morally ruined. During the disagreement, I thought this had happened, but it turns out that it hasn't. I am really vitally needed there, and one can't ignore that.[136]

Not mentioning Russell or their disagreement, and hardly short of snobberies of her own (in which she encouraged Tom), Vivien complained, part jokingly, in a letter to Tom's brother that her friends in Lancashire and North Wales were 'most dreadful people' who were 'so provincial that my American friends tell me they are very much like Americans!' Lecturing in Ilkley, Tom had been struck 'how much more like Americans' the people in Yorkshire were 'than the South of England people', but he didn't seem to mind.[137] His forthright friend Karl Culpin had come from Yorkshire, and Tom, unlike Vivien, developed a lasting fondness for such northerners.

No sooner had he developed his journalistic contacts than Vivien (who saw how successful Russell's lectures could be) was encouraging her husband to change direction: 'I feel *very* strongly that Journalism is bad for Tom. It is. If he was not a poet it would be excellent for him. He loves it. But I am sure and certain that it will be the *ruin* of his poetry – if it goes on. For him – he ought never *to have to write*.' She wanted him to take on more lecturing: the Southall lectures paid £60 plus a £3 expenses allowance, and 'directly Tom gets sufficient lectures to keep us, he will do no more *journalism*'. Vivien's tone in this letter to Tom's brother Henry is confidently directorial, but, unlike his parents (and perhaps quickened by their scepticism), she had an insightful, brave and absolute faith in his verse: 'I *do* think he is made to be a great writer – *a* poet. His prose is very good – but I think it will never be *so* good as his poetry.'[138]

This was Vivien at her most inspiring. Incited by her, Tom sought further lecturing opportunities; but, frightened not least by her erratic health, he felt unable to abandon journalism. His hope in November 1916 was to become self-supporting, relying on lecturing, literary contacts and several kinds of writing. Henry sent money; his parents were also supportive. Tom felt 'proud of my family' as they rallied round.[139] Along with Vivien he urged his brother to take the plunge and come to London too in order to pursue literary work. Partly reflecting on his own circumstances, he set forth to Henry an ideal of risk and commitment: 'I do think that if one makes up one's mind what one wants, then sooner or later an occasion will come when it is possible to seize it, for I think everybody gets the kind of life he wants, and that if he doesn't know, or doesn't want strongly enough, he will never get anything satisfactory.'[140] The sole recklessness, he added, lay in taking a risk without sufficient willpower to carry it through. However awkward their circumstances, that was where Vivien helped.

Yet still he worried. He was coming to have a sense of what he called 'the deeper reality behind ordinary superstition'. Conscious of war, financial anxieties and dangers of overwork, he wondered what would happen to Vivien if he died. 'I want her to seem quite real to you', he wrote to his brother, 'literally one of my own family, and I should not trust her care to anyone but one of my own family.' He repeated the point in a postscript, asking Henry explicitly if he would be responsible for Vivien in the event of his death: '*Will you do that?*' There was no time for a longer letter. Tom very rarely underlined words in his correspondence, but towards the end of this handwritten missive he underscored six separate words and phrases – a habit characteristic of Vivien's notes. He added yet another postscript: 'I want *all* of my family to take the sort of interest in her which would persist after my death; but I depend *especially* on you.'[141]

II

Observations

WHEN Vivien first slept with Bertrand Russell is uncertain. It may have been as early as mid-1915 when she boasted that he was 'all over me'.[1] However, it seems unlikely that after only weeks of marriage she would announce her infidelity. Charismatic rather than handsome, poetry-loving Russell was an older man who could seem to exude confidence. A powerful orator, an intellectual star, a Fellow of the Royal Society and the son of an English viscount, he lived among England's social elites. Witty, self-obsessed, orphaned at an early age and haunted by dark family secrets, Russell had a powerful, problematic allure that attracted many women. Seen by some as a feminist, by others as a libertine, in 1916 he advocated 'advanced' views on sex, marriage and adultery: 'A rather small section of the public genuinely believes that sexual relations outside marriage are wicked . . . and a very rapidly increasing number of women . . . do not believe the conventional code.'[2] The poem 'Mr. Apollinax' (which Russell liked) certainly recognises its subject's associations with bold sexuality.[3] Tom's poetic intuition was eerily perceptive.

Russell's use of the word 'intimate' usually denoted sexual relations. Decades later, he assured one of Tom's acquaintances that 'I never had intimate sexual relations with Vivienne.'[4] This conflicts with Russell's having told Constance Malleson that his 'relation to' Tom's wife was 'very intimate'.[5] Russell's biographer, Ray Monk, demonstrates that his denial was a lie: by 28 September 1917, Lady Malleson was describing Russell as a 'lover' of Vivien. Asked about 'the idea that Vivien and Russell had sexual relations', she recalled, '"I always took it for granted that they had; & when I wrote so to BR he never contradicted me . . . He once appeared in my bedroom wearing black pyjamas, saying that VSE likes them."'[6] Nicholas Griffin, the twenty-first-century editor of Russell's letters, thinks it was 'At some point in 1916' that Russell and Vivien, who had become increasingly close, 'began an affair'.[7] Certainly by 30 October 1917, Russell, writing to Malleson to emphasise that he still loved *her*, made it quite clear what had been going on:

> I intended to be (except perhaps on very rare occasions) on merely friendly terms with Mrs Eliot. But she was very glad that I had come back, and very kind and wanting much more than friendship. I thought I could manage it – I led her to expect more if we got a cottage – at last I spent a night with her. *It was utter hell.* There was a quality of loathsomeness about it which I can't describe. I concealed from her all I was feeling – had a very happy letter from her afterwards. I tried to conceal it from myself – but it has come out since in horrible nightmares which wake me up in the middle of the night and leave me stripped bare of self-deception. So far I have said not a word to her – when I do, she will be very unhappy. I should like the cottage if we were merely friends, but not on any closer footing – indeed I cannot bring myself now to face anything closer.
>
> I want you to understand that the one and only thing that made the night loathsome was that it was not with you. There was absolutely nothing else to make me hate it.[8]

By the time Russell wrote that letter, Tom had published *Prufrock and Other Observations*. Just forty pages long, his first collection of poems was not dedicated to Vivien, whose belief in his poetry had helped sustain him. Instead, it was dedicated to Jean Verdenal, now utterly lost. The poems register a fascinated fear of women and sex, often ironically treated in a Laforguian manner. Most if not all, including 'The Love Song of J. Alfred Prufrock' and 'Portrait of a Lady', had been written before Tom and Vivien met. The new book belonged to a time and a self now irrecoverable. Over the next few years his poems treated sex much less from the angle of fascinated, wary fear than from the standpoint of disgust. Sexual impropriety in *Prufrock*, whether in 'Aunt Helen' or 'Mr. Apollinax', has a liberating potential, hinting perhaps that there is no such thing as erotic propriety. Yet the poems Tom wrote after those in his first collection feature seedy seductions, shabby affairs, couplings between the monstrous and the lovely, between the sexually voracious and the pale or horrified. The word 'adultery' does not feature, but terms such as the French 'Adultère' and the English 'adulterated' come close.[9] Darker, savage even, these poems have at times what one of them, 'Gerontion', terms a 'chilled delirium'.[10] However much, or however little, he knew of the details of Vivien's adultery with Russell, Tom's poetic perceptiveness remained stingingly acute.

He had his own infidelity to cope with. Having realised that he was still in love with Emily Hale, he was, in terms of the code in which he had been educated, unfaithful to Vivien. Though many might dismiss this idea as ridiculous, to someone as deeply grounded in Christian scripture as Tom, Christ's words in Matthew's gospel carried a disturbing charge: 'whosoever looketh on a woman to lust after her hath committed adultery with her already in his heart'.[11] When, years afterwards, he wrote of remembering having experienced 'minor pleasures of drunkenness and adultery', this odd phrasing may refer specifically to minor rather than major indulgences of being unfaithful: flirtations, for instance, in which he several times engaged, and close, emotionally dependent friendships with women.[12] But, in the absence of any clear evidence that Tom matched Vivien's carnal betrayal, it may refer just as much to a guilty sense of inescapable 'adultery . . . in his heart'.

Both the Eliots had tribulations and secrets. He appears to have attempted to numb himself in order to cope with the combined pressures of work, illnesses (his own and his wife's) and erotic distress. A decade after his wedding, he told Bertrand Russell that Russell's early, pessimistic verdict on the marriage had been accurate: 'You are a great psychologist.'[13] Tom wrote, too, in 1925 a shocking letter in which he stated that 'In the last ten years – gradually, but deliberately – I have made myself into a *machine*. I have done it deliberately – in order to endure, in order not to feel – *but it has killed* V.' He stated that he had 'deliberately killed my senses' and had even 'deliberately died' in 1915 – the year of his marriage – simply to 'go on with the outward form of living'. Tom here reproached himself, rather than Vivien, and worried he had damaged her irreparably. Painfully aware of all that was wrong in their relationship, he recounted how he had '*tried* to kill myself' in order to keep going. He wrote of struggling, and apparently failing, to 'exorcise this desire for what I cannot have, for someone I cannot see'.[14] This person appears to have been Emily Hale, whom by 1925 he had not even glimpsed for almost eleven years, and with whom, for nearly as long, he had had little or no communication.

If Lawrence Rainey and Lyndall Gordon are correct in dating the unwatermarked paper, then some time after September 1916 (it may have been as late as 1919) Tom typed up his poem 'The Death of the Duchess'. It begins with a vision of 'The inhabitants of Hampstead', the London district Vivien came from. Trapped in constricting routines, they resemble readers of the *Boston Evening Transcript*. Considerably different are the poem's couple 'in leafy Marylebone' (the area where Tom and Vivien lived from 1916 until 1920), but they too have their problems. The speaker is in a relationship, but unsure whether to say "'I love you'" or "'I do not love you'"; he fears having to make conversation with the chambermaid and being left alone with his partner, playing chess while, bleakly, 'The ivory men make company between us'.[15] For all that a later partial inventory of the Eliots' household effects includes a chessboard, this poem is deliberately distanced from contemporary life by its title, which refers to John Webster's Jacobean tragedy, *The Duchess of Malfi*. Other allusions are to a scene where Webster's Duchess, who has made a clandestine marriage, thinks she is talking privately to her husband and maid as she brushes her hair, but actually betrays her secret with terrible consequences. The 'intensity' of this scene haunted Tom, who saw the play performed in late 1919 but brooded on Webster some time earlier.[16] Tom never published 'The Death of the Duchess', but elements of it found their way into *The Waste Land*, whose 'Game of Chess' alludes to another Jacobean drama.

Though we cannot be sure exactly when 'The Death of the Duchess' was written, factors that conditioned it – however fiercely repressed – were present from early in Tom's marriage. Eager for Russell's affections even as she supported her husband, Vivien maintained the appearance of a lively, respectable married woman. Both she and Tom had been enmeshed by their benefactor; just how far was hard – and perhaps too painful – to calculate. The young husband made the best of things; so did Vivien. Occasionally the pain, the exhaustion, the steely need to withstand it all, emerged, refracted and meticulously crafted, into his poems, or sparked unexpectedly, almost undetectably, in his prose. However distanced, his art is made out of damage and woundedness. A short story entitled 'Eeldrop and Appleplex', one of his strangest pieces, appeared in the *Little Review* in mid-1917. Encompassing some of Tom's own intellectual interests, it touches too on 'adultery', 'marriage' and the murder of a mistress. As regards the man who has killed his mistress, 'for the brief space he has to live, he is already dead. He has crossed the frontier. The important fact is that something is done which can not be undone – a possibility which none of us realize until we face it ourselves.'[17]

If emotional turmoil underlay the surface, there were also unignorable practicalities of finance. During February 1916, just after America broke off diplomatic relations with Germany, Tom asked his father to advance money for a year's rent. He was worried lest transatlantic communication grew more difficult. Tom's mother, who seems to have sent her younger son letters about once a week (his father wrote regularly too), became increasingly anxious and craved reassurance. Sometimes with Vivien's help,

Tom tried to reply to all her communications. Correspondence was his emotional lifeline to his family and to those aspects of America he loved; yet it was exhausting to keep up with. However emphatically and effusively he signed himself 'Always your devoted son' or 'With very fond love' or with 'infinite love', his residence in England remained a cause of strain.[18] 'I have never been so glad to get letters; the interval seemed as if it would never end', he wrote to his father at the start of March: wartime conditions meant that no mail from the States had reached him for a month. He concealed many difficulties, but did reveal some of Vivien's health problems. 'Worries over our affairs have pulled her down', he wrote on 1 March, then changed his phrasing to 'have held her back a great deal'. In this letter he gave a little more detail: 'When she worries she bleeds internally, in a metaphorical sense, as well as other internal pains, like migraine and stomach trouble, in a literal sense.'[19]

Vivien alternated between attempts at wifely frugality – repeatedly darning Tom's underwear or pyjamas – and pained protestations of anxiety. Never having met her, Lottie Eliot offered guidance: surely Vivien's temperament must resemble her own, so Vivien must be sure to get lots of sleep. 'I worry a great deal', Vivien replied. 'Often when I lie down to sleep I feel that a wheel is going round in my head, and although my body is dead tired my brain gets more and more excited.' She wrote of relapsing into further sickness. She complained about Tom's having had influenza and being 'most gloomy and depressed and very irritable and I knew he felt that life was simply not worth going on with'. Each day, facing illness and wartime conditions, Vivien wrote excitedly, 'the screw turned a little tighter'.[20] No wonder the Eliot parents fretted.

Yet in the midst of this, and steeling himself against it in order to cope, Tom articulated a poetic credo. His work gave him a focus that let him go on when his private life was difficult; though the two could not be separated completely, he valued all the more the sense of shape, the mixture of intuition and form that dedication to verse might offer. Turning to the technique of poem-making, he discussed French poetry and *vers libre* with Pound, to whom Tom grew closer and whose Francophilia reinforced his own. Tom had been perusing a pamphlet published during his year in Paris, Georges Duhamel and Charles Vildrac's *Notes sur la technique poétique*. It pondered through aphorisms and brief reflections the relationship between *vers libre* and the central metre of French classical poetry, the alexandrine. Partly reacting to this, and making clear he was talking about tradition and verse form rather than 'imagism', Tom maintained in a March 1917 *New Statesman* essay that '*Vers libre* does not exist.' There was, he concluded, 'only good verse, bad verse, and chaos'. Citing examples from

Webster's drama to new poetry by Hulme and Pound, his 'Reflections on *Vers Libre*' argued that while 'Scansion tells us very little' and 'It is probable that there is not much to be gained by an elaborate system of prosody', nonetheless, 'the most interesting verse which has yet been written in our language has been done either by taking a very simple form, like the iambic pentameter, and constantly withdrawing from it, or taking no form at all, and constantly approximating to a very simple one. It is this contrast between fixity and flux, this unperceived evasion of monotony, which is the very life of verse.'[21] He did not oppose rhyme, he explained, though 'it is possible that excessive devotion to rhyme has thickened the modern ear'. If rhyme was removed, then 'the poet is at once held up to the standards of prose'. While this may seem odd for a poet to advocate, it was a way of banishing the too predictably 'poetic' and replacing it with subtler sound patternings, as well as content whose truth was all the more apparent for being as robust and immediate as prose. Tom wanted the poetry not of a 'moralist' but of an 'observer'.[22]

That last word picks up on the title 'Observations' which had headed the group of his poems in *Poetry* six months earlier. *Observations* is what he would call all the work in his first collection. In early 1917, he was optimistic that it would be published soon – in England, if not in America; by April the slim volume was 'in press'; eventually it appeared in June.[23] Some people found it odd that Tom 'call[ed] his "observations" poems'; they detected a 'notion of poetry' that was 'uninspired', lacking 'any genuine rush of feeling'.[24] The title *Prufrock and Other Observations* does not sound conventionally 'poetic'. Yet the poems possess the minute and telling precision of 'observations'. Readers encountering Tom's book title were and are struck by the name 'Prufrock'; new to poetry, this was, though none of his English readers would have recognised it, an import from St Louis. Yet the neutral-sounding term 'observations' is at least as important since it sets out the poems' approach.

Frequently used in titles of scientific, legal and other prose writings, 'Observations' had never before featured as part of the title of a book of English-language verse. Its deployment fits with the way often the poems are voiced with humorous detachment, even when the speaker – frequently gendered as male, never as female – is an observer observing himself and hyper-conscious of how others, not least women, may see him. Tom's poems utilise and even flaunt the conventions of poetry – no rhyme could be truer than that between 'I' and 'sky' at the start of 'The Love Song of J. Alfred Prufrock'. However, his writing also departs from such conventions: the lack of a rhyme with 'table' (easy to supply in English) in that poem's famous third line, 'Like a patient etherised upon a table', adds to its memorable weirdness. This line would not sound strange in prose; but (like the ensuing, plainer phrase, 'cheap hotels'), when taken from prose into poetry, it marks something unsettlingly new.

The form of this landmark in the history of poetry is not really *vers libre*. Iambic pentameter is heard in the opening verse paragraph – in 'Of restless nights in one-night cheap hotels', for instance.[25] Nevertheless, the departures from pentameter, like the resistance to poetic diction, are more striking. Simultaneously such departures and resistance both ironise and heighten those moments when (as in the famous title's use of the term 'Love Song') the poetry invokes the traditionally 'poetic'. Authoring his manifesto 'Reflections on *Vers Libre*' (proudly sent to his parents) and contemplating his first collection in the early part of 1917, Tom formulated in his prose and in that book's title an aesthetic which he had originated years earlier in America and during his first visit to Europe.

As he did so, his sense of creativity returned. He contemplated producing an article on 'Introspective Consciousness'.[26] His interest in that topic, like his wary conviction that 'individual psychology' could be understood in new ways through 'psycho-analysis', matched his imaginative use of self-observation as well as observations of people around him.[27] Such perceptions were recast, shaped through artistry, to take them far from autobiography, but the results are all the more impressive for drawing, however indirectly, on Tom's own consciousness and reading. Some topics remained off limits: nothing parental is explored in his early verse, for instance; but there is a continuing, increasingly cutting observation of ways in which the sexes interact.

Having long discussed French poetry with Pound and others, in summer 1916 he had tried to translate more Laforgue. Along with his perusal of Vildrac and Duhamel, this led to an odd experiment that complemented Ottoline Morrell's belief that Tom might release in French what he could not say in English. Attempting to trick his consciousness into allowing him to create poetry again, he chimed French rhymes off each other: 'Le directeur / Conservateur / Du Spectateur'.[28] The ploy worked, and one of the resulting poems was uncharacteristically autobiographical.

Its title was 'Mélange Adultère de Tout', and it presented a peripatetic speaker with a variety of professional identities: 'En Amérique, professeur; / En Angleterre, journaliste' were the first two; others included being a lecturer 'En Yorkshire' and, in Germany, a philosopher.[29] Drawing on personal experience, Tom, who had kept up his reading in anthropology, also moved disconcertingly beyond it, incorporating a range of attributes and naming several international locations that he had never seen – from Damascus and Omaha to Mozambique. Pulled in many directions, the speaker tells of being a London banker, and of celebrating his feast day at an African oasis, dressed in a giraffe skin. Autobiographical and weirdly imagined elements meld. The poem suggests not only a protean, over-stretched existence, but also a disconcerting sense of not feeling at home anywhere. Tom's experience of being a foreigner in England could pay dividends, both in affording him easy access to other foreigners, and in quickening his ability to articulate a sense of displacement profoundly important in modern literature. 'Mélange Adultère de Tout', written in a foreign language, is one of the first poems in which he explores an imaginative seam whose continued investigation would help make him, in due time, the greatest immigrant poet in Anglophone verse. Meanwhile, declaring itself 'A Magazine of the Arts, Making No Compromise with the Public Taste', Chicago's *Little Review* had just taken on that other displaced person Ezra Pound as its 'foreign editor', which is why, in 1917, Tom's new Francophone poems appeared there. Not all this literature of immigrants and emigrants won plaudits. 'Your magazine is rubbish', complained a New York correspondent in the same issue; nonetheless, the self-exiled Irishman 'James Joyce, Zurich, Switzerland', had recently praised its 'many good writers' and hoped to send 'something very soon'.[30]

However English he sounded to Americans, occasionally Tom played up his 'outsider' status. 'I am very dependent on such aids', he wrote to Mary Hutchinson at the start of 1917, after she sent him a map of part of London. He had met Mary, a writer, and her lover Clive Bell the previous year. She recalled that the first time she saw Tom was 'in August, 1916' when he 'was sitting alone on a sea-wall in the estuary of Chichester Harbour'; he was wearing 'white flannels and was looking out to sea'. Around this time 'he used to carry in his pockets a very small Virgil and a very small Dante' which, she believed, he read 'by the water's edge'. Tom, too, remembered their encounter precisely: Mary was carrying 'an unusual flower'.[31] Slightly younger than Tom, this Indian-born upper-class woman was married to a radical lawyer, St John (known as Jack) Hutchinson, who was, like Tom, a fan of music-hall stars including George Robey. Mother of two young children, Mary wore bright frocks designed by the avant-garde Omega Workshops; local working-class kids nicknamed her 'The Queen of Sheba'.[32] She was also a half-cousin of the provocatively camp biographer Lytton Strachey; her lover, the art critic Bell, was married to artist Vanessa Bell, Virginia Woolf's sister. After painting Mary Hutchinson's portrait in Matisse-like tones in 1915, making her look sly and big-lipped, Vanessa Bell pronounced the picture 'perfectly hideous . . . and yet quite recognisable'.[33] Partying with Mary and friends, Tom was received now into the heart of the sometimes spiteful, aesthetically daring Bloomsbury group. He mixed in 'fast', witty artistic circles whose sexual mores were completely different from those of the St Louis and New England Eliots. In January 1917 he and Mrs Hutchinson had parts in a play written for private performance by Strachey, whose risqué farces sometimes involved cross-dressing. Their acting seems to have involved Tom – as he had once done with Amy de Gozzaldi – giving Mary 'a prolonged kiss'.[34] Clive Bell exclaimed to her that she was 'flirting with Eliot!'[35]

In such company, with his intellectual acuteness masking the hurts of his private life and his fashionable garb concealing his darned underwear, Tom could shine. Intelligent, handsome, observant, and with a dash of foreign exoticism, he had the ability to quote poetry in several languages and had a taste for words like 'pococurantism'.[36] His poetry was regarded, even in the Hutchinsons' circle, as provocatively racy. By April 1917 the jealous Clive Bell was complaining half seriously to Mary Hutchinson that she was probably kissing Tom 'or at least squeezing his hand'. He suggested she ask the American poet to show her how (as Tom put it in 'Aunt Helen'), 'the footman sat upon the dining-table / Holding the second housemaid on his knees'.[37]

Long afterwards, Vivien's brother claimed Mary Hutchinson had 'made a pass' at Tom; there does seem to have been a close chemistry between them.[38] Tom would 'come over on the ferry' frequently from Bosham to the Hutchinsons' country cottage, Eleanor House at West Wittering, a few miles from Itchenor. From Bosham to the ferry was about twenty minutes' walk and people had to call across to the ferryman to sail over; when Tom came Mary 'would walk to meet him', and they might stroll the four or so miles together from the ferry to Eleanor House; he read her his poetry, and discussed *The Waste Land* with her before it was published, but her children considered his formal manner 'very tight in'.[39] Yet they liked this American visitor who was happy to stay at Eleanor where there was no electricity and only an earth closet for sanitation. Soon, as a little boy, Mary's son Jeremy grew to find Tom '*friendly*, and smiling'. Over the next few years Jeremy and his sister Barbara observed Tom closely. He was both likeable and 'prim'; in particular he 'had a prim way of speaking'. Barbara, who would be eleven when *The Waste Land* was published, liked to imitate 'the Bloomsbury Voice': '*What* have you been doing *today? Well . . . saw* the most *extrAOrdinary* thing!' But when she came to imitate Tom 'it was "*prim*, rather *prim*"', with a certain over-emphasis on the plosive 'p' sound and the concluding 'm' at the end of that word.[40]

Prim he may have seemed, but he grew very close to Mary Hutchinson, though there is no conclusive evidence that they became lovers. Indeed,

Mary's handwritten recollection of their relationship suggests that, though intimate and tinged with erotic feeling, it remained an unconsummated 'perhaps'. She writes of how she met Tom

> on the sea-wall at Bosham, and after this we walked by the Estuary, arranged to meet for pic-nics (à quatre) and wrote letters to each other. He came to stay with us at Wittering and later took a house nearby. In London he would meet me to dance at the *Hammersmith Palais de Danse* with dinner afterwards at some little restaurant (often in Baker Street) . . . I imagined that, as I grew to know him, a subtle, poetic, sophisticated character would emerge in tune with his writing.
>
> He seemed 'difficult'; a slow and painstaking dancer, often a silent tongue-tied companion. This filled me with dread for I felt I was failing in understanding and communication. I did not know then that people are often 'not of a piece'; that there can be strange opposites in their natures. Later I realised that in personal relationships [he] was far from being subtle and sophisticated; he was simple, inexperienced and even unimaginative. Had I seen clearly I could have been bolder perhaps, stimulated his imagination perhaps, given him experience perhaps![41]

Mary at that time was 'overwhelmed' by reading Proust, and 'stirred by Rousseau's account in the *Confessions* of his gentle seduction by Madame de Warens, by the life and letters of Byron and Benjamin Constant, by the novels of Turgueniev [sic], Tolstoy, Mérimée and Flaubert, by *Les Liaisons Dangereuses*'.[42] Unseen by Eliot's earlier biographers, her handwritten account of her relationship with Tom includes several quotations from these writers, all of which signal sexual desire. She encouraged him to read Flaubert as well as Keats's letters, while he 'wanted me to read the poems of Ezra Pound and Hulme, and the stories of Henry James, particularly *The Finer Grain* and *The Ambassadors*. We read each other's suggestions and quarrelled over them. He was the first to tell me about Joyce.'[43] In her manuscript memoir, after citing several quotations (mostly in French and copied from her private notebook) that deal with intimate sexual liaisons and the wish for them, Mary wrote 'These were my apéritifs for living and loving – far away surely from the tastes of Boston and Harvard?'[44] Yet Tom's tastes, too, were Francophile and open to literature that was frank about sex; in his writing he was a connoisseur of unconsummated intimacies, as *The Waste Land*'s 'hyacinth girl' episode, or those words 'your heart would have responded' suggest.[45]

For a time, he and Mary were intensely close, reading each other's work in draft and taking part in what she called 'a moving enquiry into one another's nature, frustrated by ignorance and hesitation'.[46] It was so intimate that it was probably what he had in mind when, later, he confessed to having known at least some of those 'minor pleasures' of 'adultery'.[47] After a while, Mary recalled, their relationship 'drifted towards a calm loyal friendship that lasted for nearly fifty years'; but she thought wistfully about its 'perhaps', and seems to have regarded herself as a subtler confidante than Vivien, whom she remembered as 'very lively, pretty, and direct, and it almost seemed that she could "bring him out", but she was too roughly impetuous, in a sense "common" and insensitive ever to have seduced him away from his natural path. Instead she exasperated and shocked him into rage and despair.'[48] If Vivien sensed Tom's temper and his desperation, sometimes finding them as hard to cope with as he found her behaviour difficult to bear, she, too, confided in Mary on occasion, and enjoyed those picnics 'à quatre' when she and Tom and Mary and Jack Hutchinson lunched together in the West Sussex countryside. Sometimes, if not always, Vivien accompanied Tom to Mary's and other avant-garde parties; but, however much she could attract Bertrand Russell, in general at such events it was her husband who exercised more fascination. Vivien, more than once, felt insecure.

Russell had published recently *Principles of Social Reconstruction*, his manifesto for post-war intellectual life. Advocating 'mental adventure' as well as greater sexual freedom, rather windily he presented 'thought' as 'anarchic and lawless'.[49] Predictably, Tom disagreed. Attempting an article in response, he showed it to Russell, but neither man liked it. Tom wanted to write about 'Authority and Reverence', expressing his conviction that 'there is something beneath Authority in its historical forms which needs to be asserted clearly without reasserting impossible forms of political and religious organisation which have become impossible'. Yet, as even his awkward repetition of 'impossible' here hints, Tom could not complete this piece satisfactorily. Complaining to Russell about lack of peace of mind, he craved 'better nerves and more conviction in regard to my future'.[50] Tom may have thought Russell's book 'very weak', but where the older man had the confidence to set forth his vision and to seduce Vivien, Tom, even as he began writing poetry again and setting out his writerly credo, did not feel able to compete.[51]

He had, though, found a new job. 'Mélange Adultère de Tout' presents its speaker as 'A Londres, un peu banquier' because Tom, now 'combining the activities of journalist, lecturer, and financier', had started work on

19 March 1917 in the Colonial and Foreign Department of the London headquarters of Lloyds Bank, one of Britain's biggest lending institutions.[52] Previous talk of a job at the *Manchester Guardian* had come to nothing, so a commercial career was an opportunity. Paying £120 a year, the bank position was less remunerative than schoolteaching, but provided better prospects, security of income and a regular routine, even if Tom worried about leaving Vivien (who had been complaining of laryngitis) on her own at home all day. Often on Sundays they dined with her parents in Hampstead, and Tom explained to his mother that it was a friend of Mr and Mrs Haigh-Wood, E. L. Thomas, Chief General Manager of the National Provincial Bank, who 'gave me an introduction to Lloyds'.[53] He was eager to show his parents that in business as in literature, his decisions and commitments might pay off.

In the financial district, the City, not far from London Bridge, he shared a small office. His colleague, Mr McKnight, who liked to regale Tom with stories about his son, carefully polished his silk hat before stepping outside. Tom sat at a gleaming mahogany desk scrutinising balance sheets of foreign banks, reporting on them, then filing them. A little like his character Appleplex, he transcribed details on to large cards under headings such as 'Cash in hand' or 'Correspondents'.[54] Painstakingly investigative, these tasks appealed to the side of him that always enjoyed Sherlock Holmes. To Vivien's surprise he found the work 'fascinating'; in this, as in his sense of order, authority and (occasionally) rebellion, he was his father's son.[55]

The business was notably polylingual. Checking and cross-checking banks' reports, evaluating their activities and solvency in wartime, Tom absorbed texts in French, Spanish, German, Portuguese, Danish, Swedish and Norwegian. The way *The Waste Land* would flit among an array of different languages is indebted, surely, to his Harvard education, but also to his London bank work. During the day Mr McKnight (on whom, decades later, Tom based the character of Eggerson in *The Confidential Clerk*) told his new colleague about suburban gardening; at night Tom lectured to his students on nineteenth-century literature and received from two of them ('Both are mad') advice about spiritualism, head colds and astrology.[56] From a metamorphosed version of horticulture ('"That corpse you planted last year in your garden, / "Has it begun to sprout?"') to a 'famous clairvoyante' with 'a bad cold' and a 'horoscope', details of Tom's Lloyds Bank days and his literary night-school teaching found their way later into *The Waste Land*. Its City workers crowd across London Bridge where the church bell of St Mary Woolnoth 'kept the hours / With a dead sound on the final stroke of nine' – 'A phenomenon', Tom wrote, 'which I have often noticed'.⁵⁷ Starting at 9.15 each morning, his office day ran until 5 p.m., though he enjoyed a very English cup of tea at precisely 4 o'clock.

Most lunchtimes, sometimes with Dante's *Inferno* in his pocket, he snatched 'half an hour in Cheapside' not far from the most famous of all Wren churches, St Paul's Cathedral; or else he wandered closer to the river – 'la malheureuse Tamise' (the unlucky Thames) as he called it in one of his French poems. Here several pubs were located on or near Lower Thames Street beside the site of the old Billingsgate fish market.⁵⁸ Close by, overlooking the Thames and affording panoramic views of the city, stands Wren's Monument to the 1666 Great Fire of London, and another Wren Church, St Magnus Martyr, where each year the Fish Harvest Festival was celebrated. A section Tom marked in his London Baedeker explained that Miles Coverdale, first English translator of the Bible, was buried in St Magnus Martyr; Chaucer 'the "father of English poetry"' had lived just yards away.⁵⁹ On the once adjacent Old London Bridge (eventually demolished in the mid-nineteenth century and replaced by a more modern structure) an ancient chapel had been dedicated to St Thomas à Becket; this chapel had been a staging post for pilgrims, including those in Chaucer's *Canterbury Tales*, heading to Canterbury Cathedral where Thomas was murdered.⁶⁰ Tom, a 'solitary visitor at noon' escaping 'the dust and tumult of Lombard Street' in an area crisscrossed by narrow alleys, had an eye for such details. He visited many of the churches in this part of London, ticking them off in his Baedeker. In 1921, when there were controversial plans to demolish City churches, he protested vehemently, praising their 'beauty';⁶¹ in the 1930s he would write his play about Becket, *Murder in the Cathedral*. Since it was almost as popular in nineteenth-century America as in England, probably he had known from childhood the rhyme and dance beginning 'London Bridge is falling down'. That, too, became part of *The Waste Land*, a poem peculiarly nourished by his time in the City.

As Tom discovered, St Magnus Martyr in Lower Thames Street had been devastated during the Great Fire. Wren rebuilt it. Inside the church's white, columned interior can still be seen the centuries old Benefactors' Board, recording among other things that in 1640 a 'Mrs Susanna Chambers' had left 'Twenty-two Shillings and Sixpence', so that a special 'Sermon' be preached there every 12 February to celebrate 'God's merciful preservation of the said Church of Saint Magnus from Ruin' after an earlier 'Terrible Fire on London Bridge'.⁶² The church, another memorial records, had been threatened by a further 'dreadful Fire' in 1760, and when

Tom started work in the bank, London was again threatened with conflagration – this time started by German bombing.[63] Among the details of
the section of *The Waste Land* called 'The Fire Sermon' is an account of
calmer details familiar to Tom:

> Beside a public bar in Lower Thames Street,
> The pleasant whining of a mandoline
> And a clatter and a chatter from within
> Where fishmen lounge at noon: where the walls
> Of Magnus Martyr hold
> Inexplicable splendour of Ionian white and gold.[64]

For a poet who had read the Buddha's Fire Sermon in Sanskrit, and who
recalled fishmen working at the fishsheds of Gorton and Pew and other
businesses in Gloucester, Massachusetts, these London sites had oddly
unEnglish resonances. Yet Tom was impressed, too, by their historic associations, even if the modern Thames, with its 'Oil and tar' was hardly
unpolluted.[65] Those sounds in the 'public bar' and that glimpse of
'Inexplicable splendour' in St Magnus Martyr are perhaps the most positive moments in *The Waste Land* – remarkable products of Tom's snatched
half-hour lunches, and of Mrs Chambers's bequest.

Away from the bank, Tom continued to humour Harvard's Professor
Woods, promising him further notes on Aristotle. Occasionally on
Thursday nights he attended meetings of the Omega Club, an offshoot
of Roger Fry's Omega Workshops design studio at 33 Fitzroy Square.
There he sat on a mat '(as is the custom in such circles)' exchanging a few
words with W. B. Yeats or listening to the novelist Arnold Bennett. Yeats,
in whose poetry he continued to show little interest, struck him at this
time as willing to talk only about 'psychical research' and 'Dublin gossip'
– neither of which Tom cared for much. The poet of 'The Love Song of
J. Alfred Prufrock' and the poet who was then writing 'The Wild Swans
at Coole' seem to have avoided conversing about poetry. Tom thought
Bennett like 'a successful wholesale grocer' whose accent, very different
from the tones of Anglophile Boston and the upper-class 'Bloomsberries',
struck him as unpleasantly 'Cockney'.[66]

Most Saturday afternoons and a good part of Sundays were spent
preparing for the coming week's evening lecture. More practised now, he
did not script his lectures in full, delivering them instead from notes.
Keeping ahead of the class was challenging, but he came to relish his
contact with the working-class students, one of whom, a thoughtful
grocer, was an astute enthusiast for Ruskin. If some of his listeners amused

him, Tom liked to entertain them too. In April he made his predominantly female English audience laugh by reading aloud a passage from Ruskin's *Time and Tide*:

> My American friends, of whom one, Charles Eliot Norton, of Cambridge, is the dearest I have in the world, tell me I know nothing about America. It may be so, and they must do me the justice to observe that I, therefore, usually *say* nothing about America. But this much I have said, because the Americans, as a nation, set their trust in liberty and in equality, of which I detest the one, and deny the possibility of the other; and because, also, as a nation they are wholly undesirous of Rest, and incapable of it: irreverent of themselves, both in the present and in the future; discontented with what they are, yet having no ideal of anything which they desire to become.[67]

Tom suspected Harvard's Charles Eliot Norton was just as 'crusty' as Ruskin.[68] His evening-class students made him think more about differences between America and England. While 'not so petrified in snobbism and prejudice as the middle classes', working-class English people had, he decided, a 'fundamental conservatism'; their American equivalents were often 'aggressive and insolent'.[69] Politically he regarded himself at this time as 'Labourite in England, though a conservative at home'.[70] Even taking into account that he made this remark to a fellow American, his use of 'at home' is revealing. He saw it as sheer 'snobism' [*sic*] that drove England's middle classes to buy their children private education at what are called in Britain 'public schools', and felt they lacked respect for true learning. 'Some day I shall write a book on the English; it is my impression that no one in America knows anything about them. They are in fact very different from ourselves.'[71] In the spring of 1917 reviewing books on American politics quickened his consideration of such differences.

Hoping the war would end, eager to keep in touch with America and finding the world sometimes 'a complete nightmare', Tom felt he was living through an 'unreal' era.[72] Though the bombing of London was far less destructive than that of the 1940s Blitz, aerial bombardment was a new, terrifying phenomenon. Geopolitics brought minor as well as major reverberations. No sooner had it been confirmed in March 1917 that Tom's first book would be published in London than the political landscape changed. On 2 April in Washington DC, President Woodrow Wilson addressed Congress, proposing to resist Germany. America declared war four days later. As the horrors of conflict increasingly consumed public attention, it became more and more likely that *Prufrock and Other Observations* might not appear; yet, thanks to Pound's help, Tom had found one of the twentieth century's most remarkable publishers.

Her name was Harriet Shaw Weaver – 'the Weaver', Tom called her. Determined and distinguished, she was then at the start of her forties. Having grown up, like Vivien, in Hampstead, she came, as Tom did, from a wealthy family with a streak of religiously inflected tenacity. After subscribing to the *Freewoman*, a feminist journal edited by Dora Marsden, Weaver had stepped in as financial backer when newsagents refused to stock it. By 1913, at the suggestion of Pound, who acted as talent scout, the magazine had been retitled the *Egoist*; James Joyce's *A Portrait of the Artist as a Young Man* soon appeared there. When no other publisher would take the risk in 1917 Weaver not only bankrolled Joyce but also set up the Egoist Press at Oakley House in Bloomsbury Street specially to publish his novel. Now, encouraged by Pound and hoping it would not cost more than £15 to produce, she took on *Prufrock and Other Observations*. Shortly afterwards, once the magazine's handsome young assistant editor the poet Richard Aldington had gone off to war, Weaver and Marsden (whom Tom, with the arrogance of a young man, regarded as 'old maids') hired Prufrock's author to replace Aldington's wife Hilda Doolittle as assistant editor from June.[73] Tom continued full-time at the bank.

Miss Weaver (to whom in 1932 a grateful Tom would dedicate his *Selected Essays*) was supportive, but it was Pound who encouraged her to take on his friend's book and Tom himself. Pound was sick of attempting to place *Prufrock* with the more traditional Elkin Matthews, based near London's Piccadilly Circus. Matthews fussed about the wartime cost of paper, and the risk; wanted a subvention; prevaricated. Fed up, as Pound explained in a letter to John Quinn in New York, he told Matthews that if his firm would not publish Tom's volume 'without fuss, someone else would. *The Egoist* is doing it. That is *officially* The Egoist. As a matter of fact I have borrowed the cost of the printing bill (very little) and am being The Egoist. But Eliot don't know it, nor does anyone else save my wife, and Miss Weaver of the Egoist & it is not for public knowledge.'[74] Helped by the Haigh-Woods, then by his outstandingly generous fellow American poet (who had borrowed the money from his wife, Dorothy, and from Harriet Weaver), in the space of a few months Tom had an additional new job, a publisher for his debut collection, and his first editorial position. Vivien, tired and feeling their life was 'a long scramble', felt he was less irritable and prone to 'black silent moods' than he had been; but she feared lest now, as an American, he would have to fight. 'I think he would almost like to', she wrote to his mother, worrying that his 'highly strung' temper-ament would take it badly.[75]

Tom thought of Harold Peters and Leon Little, who had been in the United States naval reserve. He knew one of his cousins, George Parker, was in the military. The young poet had some contact with the American Embassy in London. Still, conscious of Vivien's situation, he thought he would not fight unless called up. Coughing, *'full* of catarrh', she worried he was overworking. Yet she was proud of his success as lecturer and banker; if Tom were promoted at Lloyds, she explained to his mother on 30 April, 'there is no reason why he should not obtain through it his greatest ambition: viz: a congenial and *separate* money-making occupation *– of a sort* that will leave his mind and brain fresh enough to produce good literature, and *not to have to depend on writing for money at all'*. She thought him more youthful – more like the 'boyish' person she had married.[76] With money from St Louis, he ordered a new grey suit.

Published in early June, his book attracted some attention, but not a lot. It sold very slowly. In London's *English Review* Edgar Jepson saw it as 'new in form' and 'musical with a new music'. Jepson was right. Here was work by a 'real' and very American poet: 'United States of the United States'.[77] Across the Atlantic, however, William Carlos Williams was lukewarm. Grudgingly, he admitted *Prufrock* had elements of attenuated New England merit. The *Literary World* saw Tom as 'one of those clever young men' – too clever by half; snootily, *The Times Literary Supplement* thought Mr Eliot's 'observations' were 'of the very smallest importance to anyone – even to himself'. More helpfully and crustily abusive was Arthur Waugh in the *Quarterly Review*; he likened Tom to a 'drunken slave' exhibited as a warning in 'the family hall'. Pound picked up on this with gusto. Alert to the value of publicity, and characteristically spoiling for a fight, he published a substantial piece in the *Egoist* entitled 'Drunken Helots and Mr. Eliot': 'And since when have helots taken to reading Dante and Marlowe? Since when have helots made a new music, a new refinement, a new method of turning old phrases into new by their aptness?' Insightfully, Pound associated Tom with Joyce. May Sinclair, a novelist with interests in idealist philosophy whose work Tom had been encouraging, praised the collection, contending that '"The Love Song of Prufrock" is a song that Balzac might have sung if he had been as great a poet as he was a novelist.'[78] Tom was pleased that at least his book was out, but knew it had found few appreciative readers. Four years later, despite the print run of just 500 copies priced at 1 shilling, pristine examples were still for sale.

All around, the war was obscenely unignorable. At Lloyds Bank, Tom was being trained in new duties. During a break, his mentor read aloud a letter from a brother, fighting in France. Then the man was called away from the room. Five minutes later he returned: 'My brother's been killed.'[79] At home, Vivien, about to have her twenty-ninth birthday, received word that a friend's fiancé was a casualty. Next day, as chill spring turned to hot summer, Tom heard Karl Culpin had been critically wounded. Culpin's weak eyesight had delayed his being sent to the front, but he died, Tom recalled almost half a century later, 'I think, on his first day in the trenches.'[80] Vivien's brother Maurice, battle-hardened since the age of eighteen, tried to explain to them what it was like. Sometimes sickened by political rhetoric in England and America, Tom recognised powerful writing when he saw it. Concealing the author's identity, he sent one of his brother-in-law's letters to the *Nation*, a publication critical of war policy. It described

> a leprous earth, scattered with the swollen and blackening corpses of hundreds of young men. The appalling stench of rotting carrion mingled with the sickening smell of exploded lyddite and ammonal. Mud like porridge, trenches like shallow and sloping cracks in the porridge – porridge that stinks in the sun. Swarms of flics and blue-bottles clustering on the pits of offal. Wounded men lying in the shell holes among the decaying corpses: helpless under the scorching sun and bitter nights, under repeated shelling. Men with bowels dropping out, lungs shot away, with blinded, smashed faces, or limbs blown into space. Men screaming and gibbering. Wounded men hanging in agony on the barbed wire, until a friendly spout of liquid fire shrivels them up like a fly in a candle.[81]

Tom's sending that letter for publication was a moral act. For several years he had been reading war poems. In Pound's 1915 *Catholic Anthology* his work had appeared alongside pieces including T. E. Hulme's 'Trenches: St Eloi' with its 'lines' and 'corridors' and carnage. Tom considered Hulme 'a really great poet', and perhaps, as George Simmers has suggested, an undated manuscript of Tom's, once possessed by Maurice Haigh-Wood and ending with the smell 'Of the alleys of death / Of the corridors of death', contains an image of trench warfare; but in 1917 Tom's most powerful reaction to the conflict was what he did with Maurice Haigh-Wood's letter.[82]

Nothing could have seemed further from the 'unreal' War enthusiasms and horrors than *Prufrock and Other Observations*. Tom had a copy mailed to his parents as soon as it appeared. 'I am lucky to get it printed at all without cost to myself', the young banker told his businessman father, explaining that the cover (whose plain black type on buff-coloured paper might have let the book pass for a bank report) was not quite what he might have chosen: he accepted what he could get.[83] Clive Bell took copies to a Garsington party and handed one to Mary Hutchinson, who told Tom how much she liked it, and invited the Eliots to dinner; others went to the Morrells, to Aldous Huxley and to two further Garsington visitors, John Middleton Murry (an English novelist, editor and poet who had recently published a book on Dostoevsky) and the New Zealand short-story writer Katherine Mansfield with whom Murry had a long, often strained marital relationship. At Garsington Mansfield read 'The Love Song of J. Alfred Prufrock' aloud – probably the first time it was read in public by a female voice. She came to believe 'Prufrock' was 'by far and away the most interesting and the best modern poem'.[84] Intrigued by Tom Eliot, she wrote to Ottoline Morrell in late June about meeting him at a party and walking home with him while 'a great number of amorous black cats looped across the road'.[85]

Later that same Wednesday evening, Tom wrote to his mother. He told her how tired he was and how he had been going to bed 'very early lately' – though also that the following Saturday he was going to play tennis: doubles with himself and Maurice Haigh-Wood (home from the battlefield) against Pound and a friend.[86] Tom expressed longing for summers at Gloucester, remembering how sometimes he had reached there from Harvard before his parents, then seen them arrive, strolling across the grass and clambering over a break in the stone garden wall at Eastern Point. He recalled with regret his old catboat, the *Elsa*. Vivien, who was continuing with her dancing lessons, wrote to Lottie Eliot next day, emphasising she was doing her best to be frugal with money. Tom seemed 'always tormented' by overwork.[87]

They were living for a spell in Vivien's parents' house, while Mr and Mrs Haigh-Wood were away on holiday, but were discontented. The day after the tennis match Vivien lay indoors (probably in her old bedroom) on 'my divan' staring at a portrait of Scofield Thayer which stood on 'my cabinet' and smoking a Gold Flake cigarette.[88] Making him aware of her posture and her 'half open lips', she wrote teasingly but ruefully to Thayer, whose own recent marriage was in trouble. Not so long ago, he had compared her smile to Mona Lisa's; now, quoting Walter Pater, she compared him in a cleverly allusive but mannered letter to Leonardo's masterpiece. Invoking times they had spent together, she quoted Horace on the loss of a dear friend, and Swinburne on a lost love.[89]

Aldous Huxley, who had visited the Eliots about ten days earlier, sensed something of the troubled intensity of relations between Vivien and Tom

– though not their full complexity. Annoyed at Russell's interest in Vivien, Ottoline Morrell read a letter from Huxley dated 21 June: 'I met Mrs. E. for the first time and perceive that it is almost entirely a sexual nexus between Eliot and her: one sees it in the way he looks at her – she's an incarnate provocation – like a character in Anatole France.'[90] Tom, whose piece on *vers libre* that spring had mentioned in passing a novel about a love triangle, had been reading not Anatole France but Paul Bourget's *Lazarine*, about a husband who kills his 'odiously fascinating' wife, a 'syren' who has taken a lover. For him this French novel dealt with 'the struggle between the desire for happiness and the fact of marriage which is something more than merely a Christian dogma'. He picked out as 'very sound' on 'the subject of marriage' one character's remarks: 'de vraies fiancailles . . . ce n'est pas une ivresse de coeur . . . c'est le don mutual de toute une vie, de toute cette effrayante longeur de la vie' (real marriage . . . is not a wildness of heart . . . it is the mutual gift of a whole life, of all that frightening length of life).[91] The words Tom selected are hardly redolent of married bliss.

That spring he had written in French the first of his two poems about terrible honeymoons. In 'Lune de Miel' (Honeymoon) an American couple in Ravenna, Italy, lie awake on a hot night, scratching their bedbug bites in an atmosphere of summer sweat and 'une forte odeur de chienne' (a strong smell of bitch); the man's concerns about budgeting and modern European travels are set against a sense of Ravenna's early Christian basilica of St Apollinaire which, 'raide et ascétique' (perpendicular [or stiff] and ascetic), still holds in its crumbling stones the precise form of Byzantium.[92] This is not a poem about Tom and Vivien's honeymoon; it is determinedly detached. At times Tom sought detachment as if his sanity – and the life of his verse – depended on it. That year, reviewing the French poems of Jean de Bosschère, he located in them 'an intense frigidity which I find altogether admirable', though he could also admire in John Davidson's poetry 'an occasional passionate flash of exact vision'.[93] In his own work he mixed both, each reinforcing the other. Yet, however distanced, as an American who had travelled in northern Italy looking at churches, who had money worries and who (encouraged by the sense of 'l'odeur de femme' in the work of Tristan Corbière) had a pronounced awareness of 'female smells' long before he met Vivien, he incorporated into this unsettling piece at least some aspects of his experience.[94]

Other poems from 1917 and the ensuing years repeatedly present troubled couples and couplings. Scarcely new to his verse, this theme intensified. Sometimes, as bombs fell and he laboured in the bank while continuing to review books on religion, it was juxtaposed with stinging irony beside religious and financial imagery as well as against impending mortality. In 'la saison de rut' (the rutting season), aware during Lent of 'une odeur fémelle', the protagonist of 'Petit Epître' (Short Epistle) – a poem Tom never published – speaks to a priest and dreams of a paradise where good things are shared; but this is attacked as 'promiscuité' and the speaker is condemned by outraged judgmental voices.[95] 'At mating time' the rutting sounds of a hoarse hippopotamus are set against the singing of the well-off 'True Church', rejoicing smugly with God at weekly worship; in 'The Hippopotamus' the hippo, not the Church, reaches Paradise.[96] Heaven is imagined as a place of money and scandalous sex in 'A Cooking Egg', where the speaker will 'lie together' with wealthy Jewish financier Sir Alfred Mond and wed exotic, highly sexed Lucretia Borgia, rather than remaining with the markedly less experienced 'Pipit' – associated with a 'penny world' of polite Englishness.[97] In 'Whispers of Immortality', a poem of death, 'lusts and luxuries' that Tom revised repeatedly, Pipit was set initially against the more overtly sexual Russian 'Grishkin' whose 'friendly bust' when 'Uncorseted' affords 'promise of pneumatic bliss'.[98]

Despite that ironically fantasised pleasure, sex in these poems by a young married man who that summer enjoyed dancing with his wife remains deeply problematic: there are no happy couples. Writing in French or else, encouraged by Pound, imitating Francophone poets including Théophile Gautier, Tom interlaced the transgressive with the formal. 'I have been living in one of Dostoyevsky's novels, you see, not in one of Jane Austen's', he wrote to Eleanor Hinkley in July. Though, ostensibly, when he typed these words he had the war in mind ('I have signed a cheque for £200,000 while bombs fell about me'), they signal a wider, profound disturbance.[99] Odd, and under-appreciated, the poems he was writing at this time are brave in the forthrightly anti-romantic way they confront sexuality: in them the most disturbing male sexual imaginings are anatomised.

'Dans le Restaurant' features a waiter in a stained waistcoat, whom the narrator regards as a 'vieux lubrique' (a dirty old man), recalling how as a boy of seven he gave a little girl flowers ('primevères'), then tickled her, experiencing a moment of power and delirium, before being stopped from going further by the pawing of a big dog. 'De quel droit payes-tu des expériences comme moi?' asks the disgusted narrator – by what right do you have experiences like me?[100] Underlying part of 'A Cooking Egg' is a passage about middle-aged John Ruskin's fixation on a little girl; 'Pédéraste' is one of the charges levelled against the speaker of 'Petit Epître'.[101] Troubled in his own sex life, Tom was no pederast, but, through refraction and the artifice of art he faced up to the sometimes vertiginous nature of sexuality, and knew that this was unsettling. Just as he presented astonished comments provoked by 'Mr. Apollinax', so in 'Petit Epître' he supplied a litany of affronted, sometimes conflicting reactions. Some, but not all, might have been occasioned by his own life and work.

> —'Certes, c'est un homme de moeurs impures.'
> 'Ne nie pas l'existence de Dieu?'
> —'Comme il est superstitueux!'
> 'Est-ce qu'il n'a pas d'enfants?'
> —'Il est eunuque, ça s'entend.'
> 'Pour les dames
> Ne réclame
> pas la vote? Pédéraste, sans doute'

> [—'Certainly, he's a man of impure morals.'
> 'Doesn't he deny the existence of God?'
> —'How superstitious he is!'
> 'Are there no children?'
> —'He is a eunuch, I've heard.'
> 'Doesn't he claim
> The vote
> For women? A pederast, no doubt.'][102]

In poetry Tom liked to provoke. In life he suffered, but also joked: a not unusual human combination. He could play tennis, yet his teeth were 'falling to pieces'.[103] Recently he had to use reading glasses, and had endured rheumatism, but soon he was receiving fan mail (though hardly a lot) for *Prufrock*, and going sailing at Bosham – his new Gloucester. A few highs countered the lows, but his relationship with Vivien was recurrently exhausting.

Still, his thinking about poetry assumed a more confident shape. Pound had edited a selection of letters by Irish painter Jack Butler Yeats, and Tom enjoyed reading them. Overworked himself, he prized the way Yeats had 'the kingdom of leisure within him' so that he wrote 'well even when not writing for publication'. Convinced that 'England seems drifting toward Americanization', Tom relished the painter's sense of Americans as unable to feel 'the inward and innermost essence of poetry, because it is not among the American opportunities to live the solitary life . . . Poetry is the voice of the solitary.' Quoting these words with approval, Tom, with only some qualification, made the point in his first article for the *Egoist* that 'It is only in England, Mr. Yeats thinks, that in the modern world poetry is possible.'[104]

As well as editing these Yeats letters, Pound, one of literature's consummate plotters, had managed to install himself as Foreign Editor of the *Little Review* while also remaining Foreign Correspondent for *Poetry*. Nominated by him, Tom had agreed to write a booklet championing Pound's work for New York publisher Alfred A. Knopf. 'Few poets have undertaken the siege of London with so little backing', Tom wrote of the fellow American who had supported him staunchly in the same enterprise. In *Ezra Pound: His Metric and Poetry*, masked by anonymity, Tom stood up for his own ideals. While separating Pound from the 'deadness' of 'scholarship in American universities', he defended this English-based American as 'one of the most learned of poets', his knowledge drawn not least from 'Gautier, Laforgue and Tristan Corbière' (Tom wrote a poem called 'Tristan Corbière' around this time.) But he stressed also Pound's variety. Among the poems quoted entire in the booklet was 'A Girl', the piece which had so impressed Vivien just before she met her future husband. 'Any poet, if he is to survive as a writer beyond his twenty-fifth year, must alter', wrote Tom, interested that Pound had now embarked on a much longer work.[105] Though he did not say so, he knew much of his own verse in *Prufrock* had been written by a poet under twenty-five.

Stray references in the Pound booklet – to myth, Malory and Arthurian legend, for instance – show that topics which had long fascinated Tom and would resurface in *The Waste Land* were abiding reference points. His authoring of this pamphlet was an act of generosity, showing how close he and Pound had become. In the August *Egoist*, Tom wrote about Pound's work on Japanese Noh theatre. At times the two Americans worked hand in glove. Tom's review of Pound's selection of Yeats letters was followed closely in the July 1917 *Egoist* by Pound's piece on 'vers libre', which, Pound argued, 'has become a pest'.[106] Pound must have supplied Tom with many of the reviews quoted in *Ezra Pound: His Metric and Poetry*. Moreover, it was Pound who suggested French exemplars which Tom imitated, and who (along with Toulouse-born, London-based book illustrator Edmund Dulac) scribbled on poems Tom produced in French and English in 1917.

Though not formally an 'Imagist', Tom approved of many Poundian and Imagist doctrines: 'Only in something harder', he wrote that summer, 'can great passion be expressed; the vague is a more dangerous path for poetry than the arid'.[107] American males allied in a foreign land, Tom and Pound shared enthusiasms, literary techniques, banter and attitudes. Whether rejoicing in transatlantic slang, obscenity, tones of masculinist superiority towards 'the feminisation of modern society' or subtle shrewdness, they went on corresponding and working in tandem.[108] 'You let *me* throw the bricks through the front window', Pound reportedly quipped. 'You go in at the back door and take the swag.'[109]

If Tom was generous as well as insightful in praising his friend, then Pound did more than ensure the London debut of *Prufrock*; in June 1917 he also attempted, unsuccessfully, to get it published by Knopf in New York. In this Pound was seconded by John Quinn. Quinn sent Knopf a copy of the English printing in August, remarking that he relished everything about the book except its title. 'I do not know whether it is great poetry or not', Knopf replied, but it was 'great fun and I like it.' However, the publisher maintained the collection was too small to issue 'except to give it away as advertisement'.[110] The booklet on Pound was even shorter, but would supplement Knopf's publication of Pound's poems. Tom would have to wait several more years before a collection of his own poetry appeared in his native land.

Until then, though he published a few poems, he hoarded more. Editing his oeuvre fiercely, he was also thrifty. From his 1917 work published in magazines he would recast and recycle material in later books. By far the best known part of 'Dans le Restaurant' is not the reminiscence of childhood sexual fumbling but the conclusion where, apparently in a more ancient time, 'Phlébas, le Phénicien', a trader concerned with profit and loss, drowns at sea under 'les cris des mouettes et la houle de Cornouaille' (the cries of gulls and the sea-swell of Cornwall). Tom had been to sites in Dorset sometimes associated with Phoenician tin traders, also said to have visited Cornwall; he probably associated Cornwall, too, with Tristan and Isolde. More recently, he and Vivien had had to confront their fears of death at sea in the dangerous wartime Atlantic. Typically, in 'Dans le Restaurant' as elsewhere, he has drawn on aspects of his own life, but has 'othered' them. Conceivably his imagination was guided by a novel he may have encountered in childhood, *The Wonderful Adventures of Phra the Phoenician* by Edwin Lester Arnold, son of Sir Edwin Arnold whose *Light of Asia* Tom relished as a boy. In this fantasy tale, a time-travelling Phoenician sailor falls in love with a beautiful Englishwoman and accompanies her to Britain after he has witnessed from his ship the crew of another vessel drowning, 'swirled about' and 'drawn by the current' as overhead 'gulls were screeching'.[111]

Drawing on his fears, emotions and experience, yet transforming and distancing those by meshing them with other writings and allusions became Tom's modus operandi. Though he had worked this way previously, now he did so in a more deliberately allusive style. Vivien quoted from at least three literary works in the sometimes self-dramatising letter she sent Scofield Thayer that July. Some of her habits of mind surely nourished

Tom's – sometimes for good, sometimes not. He seems, for instance, to have been fond enough of Joseph, his precociously money-wise Jewish office boy at Lloyds Bank; yet Vivien's dislike of 'Horrible Jews in plush coats by the million' from 'the East End of London' reinforced a familiar prejudice that Tom did not always subvert in his poems where 'red-eyed scavengers are creeping' from London's traditionally Jewish areas of 'Kentish Town and Golder's Green'.[112]

Though her husband flitted between Bosham and London for part of August and September 1917, Vivien stayed in Bosham much of the time. When not at the bank, Tom spent his spare hours preparing two further sets of evening lectures to be given at opposite ends of London: twenty-five Friday lectures on Victorian literature for delivery at the County Secondary School in Sydenham from 28 September; and for Southall, Middlesex, on Mondays until the following Easter, a series entitled 'Modern English Literature'. These extended from Emerson to Hardy. Limbering up for such demanding commitments, he immersed himself in nineteenth-century authors, some of whom ('Brontë, George Eliot, Emerson') he knew 'very little' about.[113]

Since Mary Hutchinson and her husband often holidayed near Bosham, Vivien and Mary enjoyed being in touch. Vivien wanted Tom to read a short story Mary had shown her; it appears to draw on Mary's own affair with Clive Bell, and its sophisticated, Mary-like protagonist, Jane, comes to doubt the 'reality' of relations with her lover. Jane's Francophile friend Sabine, described as a 'panther' as she eats, advises her to seek out 'Some poet . . . who can appreciate you'.[114] Eventually Tom published Mary's story in the *Egoist* after discussing with its author the handling of emotion in literature: 'I like to feel that a writer is perfectly cool and detached, regarding other people's feelings or his own, like a God who has got beyond them; or a person who has dived very deep and comes up holding firmly some hitherto unseen submarine creature.'[115] In his letters he still called her 'Mrs Hutchinson', and signed himself formally 'T. S. Eliot'.

Though Vivien had been seeing Russell earlier that summer, now he was off vacationing in Shropshire with his lover, Lady Constance Malleson. After they returned, he suggested to Constance they have a child together, but she demurred, and her husband Miles was growing tired of feeling sidelined. The Eliots had some sense of what was going on. Tom and Russell had been talking, as had Tom and Miles Malleson. Aldous Huxley came to visit and, passing on gossip, Vivien told Mary Hutchinson on 9 October that 'he quoted a saying of Gertler's that rather amused us – viz. that the Mallesons might be said to keep "*open bed*". It's true, from all I hear!'[116] While Tom, facing the possibility of military service and an attendant medical examination, was corresponding with his worried mother about his apparently healed 'Rupture' – his hernia – Russell was turning his attentions to Vivien again and thought he was finding encouragement.[117] Having caught influenza on returning from Bosham after spending hours shivering in the cellars of Crawford Mansions during air raids, Vivien feared further bombing. With Tom's agreement she was searching for a place to rent outside London. On 3 October Tom told his mother the plan was that he would commute into London 'every day', but Vivien struggled to find anywhere suitable.[118]

'Bertie', Vivien wrote to Mary Hutchinson that day, 'now says he wants to go shares in a country cottage. That will probably mean being out of the frying pan but *in* the fire!'[119] As during the early days of the Eliots' marriage, so once again, while his relations with Lady Constance and Lady Ottoline were fraught, Russell now used his clout and connections to share accommodation with Vivien and his former student, Tom. He saw a manipulative opportunity. Writing on 16 October to Lady Constance, who had been growing close to a man called Maurice Elvey, Russell mentioned that

> I found accidentally that the Eliots don't want to go on being always together, and that she was looking out for a place where she could live alone in the country and he would come for week-ends. So I suggested that, as I too wanted to live in the country, we might be less dreary if we lived in the same house. She was pleased with the idea, and no doubt it will happen. I want, for everyday, reliable companionship without any deep striving of emotion; if I don't get it, I shan't do any more good work. I feel this plan may hurt you, and if it does I am sorry; but if I let myself grow dependent on you, we shall have all the recent trouble over again next time, and I can't face that, and I don't suppose you can.[120]

Very soon Vivien was installed at Senhurst Farm, surrounded by pine woods in a high hollow among the hills two miles from Abinger Common in rural Surrey. Previously, as Tom put it to his mother on 24 October, the farmer and his wife had been 'gardeners to Lord Russell'; however 'fairytale', the old farmhouse was six miles from the nearest rail station. With his commitments to Lloyds Bank, lecturing and the *Egoist*, Tom could 'only be there at weekends'. This, Vivien told Tom's mother on 22 October, was 'a great disappointment'.[121] Vivien stayed at the farm for three weeks, during which time, on at least one weeknight, she slept with Russell, and, afterwards, sent him her 'very happy letter'.[122]

'I distrust the Feminine in literature', Tom wrote to his father from London on 31 October. He was explaining how things were at the *Egoist*, though he also sniped at 'the women' in his bank. Mentioning how 'beautiful' and 'delightful' the farm and its food were, he explained, 'As you know, Vivien has been in Surrey, which suits her very well, and I have been with her over weekends. This will be the last.'[123] However little or much she told him about her affair with Russell, Tom knew Vivien, knew Russell and was no fool. Russell (who seems to have destroyed most of Vivien's letters to him) told Lady Malleson he felt an 'odour of corruption' and a 'nausea' after what had happened. Protesting himself 'tortured and miserable', he felt he would 'have to break Mrs. Eliot's heart and I don't know how to face it. It mustn't be done all of a sudden.'[124] Nonetheless, following an ecstatic making-up with Constance Malleson, he met Vivien on 6 November after her return to London, presumably while Tom was at work. Next day Russell pronounced the encounter 'very satisfactory'. He had 'got out of the troublesome part of the entanglement by her initiative – she behaved very generously – it is a *great* relief'.[125] Vivien went on writing to him, and they met again a week later. Russell dreaded encountering Vivien once more, he explained to Lady Constance, with whom he was about to share a flat. However, they were due to rendezvous on 13 November. He felt that 'the relief of having done something irrevocable persists, though I feel this is shameful.'[126] On 13 November, he was delighted: 'Mrs E. behaved like a saint from heaven', he wrote next day. 'She put away her own pain & set to work to make me less unhappy – & she succeeded.'[127]

Probably Vivien succeeded too well. Giving Tom's mother on 22 November a detailed 'account of the money you sent for T.'s underclothing', and mentioning how she and her own mother had gone 'carefully thro' all Tom's winter underwear', checking what needed replacing, she enclosed receipts to prove she had spent the cash appropriately. She noted, too, that she had bought her husband a quilted satin chest protector to wear under his shirt against the cold. Having shared these impressively wifely details and exclaimed that Tom was 'very rough with his pyjamas and shirts – tears them unmercifully!', Vivien then proceeded to explain that Bertrand Russell had 'promised to go shares' in renting a country cottage if they could find one. Though Tom had to be based in London, it would be a 'refuge' for them.[128]

That same evening, working late at the bank, Tom was writing to his father. He was concerned that Vivien, nervous, had had a chill. She had seemed unwell since returning from the farm. Feeling she was healthier in the country, Tom too expressed the hope that they might find a cottage, and asked his father for money. Vivien had been trying to get work in a wartime government office – a plan Tom disapproved of, since he thought her health would not stand it; she had been rejected, apparently because she was married to a foreign national. Matters were difficult, but the solution they adopted brought further complications. In early December Russell took on a five-year lease with the Eliots to share a property at 31 West Street in Marlow, a small Buckinghamshire town on the Thames. Vivien liked the idea, hoping Mary Hutchinson would come and visit her and Tom so 'we can be just three by ourselves'. They could have a lively party: punting on the river, then dancing. Her letter suggests that, sleeping badly and suffering headaches, she dreamed of recreating something of the circumstances when she and Tom had first met.[129] Russell, however, thought that *he* was going to be the one enjoying Vivien's company. He wrote about his ideas for Mrs Eliot on New Year's Day 1918 to Constance Malleson:

I am not in love with her, & I do not care whether I have a physical relation with her or not. But I am happy in talking to her and going about with her. She has a very unselfish affection for me, and but for her I don't know how I should have lived through the unhappiness of these last months. I am intensely grateful to her, and I expect that she will be an essential part of my life for some time to come.[130]

As for Tom, whatever Vivien did or did not tell, and however much he tried to make himself 'a machine' in order to cope with the insistent routines of banking, lecturing, editing and writing, as well as marital difficulties, his poetry and his body signalled that things were wrong. While 1917 drew to a close, he became ill, struggling to cope. He was invited by well-connected Lalla Vandervelde, wife of a Belgian politician, to join Osbert and Edith Sitwell, Robert Graves and others in giving a poetry reading for charity at the grand house of Lady Sibyl Colefax in London's Onslow Square on 12 December. Since it was a weekday evening, Tom hurried there straight from the bank. For his late arrival he was 'rebuked publicly' in front of the audience of about one hundred and fifty people by the influential man of letters Sir Edmund Gosse. Hiding his tiredness, he then caused a stir by reading 'light satirical stuff', including 'The Hippopotamus'. Some 'didn't know what to make of it', but Arnold Bennett thought it the best poem read all evening.[131]

At mating time the hippo's voice
Betrays inflexions hoarse and odd,
But every week we hear rejoice
The Church, at being one with God.[132]

Soon Tom was unwell. There had been minor signs of trouble over the last few months: he had forgotten to write to his mother on her seventy-fourth birthday on 22 October, and apologised afterwards. In one frame of mind, he confessed to his brother, he might never want 'to see America again'.[133] Yet, conflictedly, he missed his American family intensely: 'I have parents whom I can be so convincedly proud of, who represent to me absolutely the best that America can produce', he told his mother in November.[134] Vivien, who *had* written to Lottie Eliot on 22 October (though, with other things on her mind, she had forgotten it was her mother-in-law's birthday), also apologised in November; later, when Tom's parents, anxious about their son's marriage, seemed concerned that she had spent a long time away from her husband, she explained it had only been a fortnight, 'and Tom came for both weekends'.[135] She said she would send Lottie for Christmas a small piece of crochet lace she had made '– I am afraid it is rather useless – '.[136] With 'infinite love' Tom, who did his best to make Vivien sound appropriately wifely to his parents, sent his mother as a Christmas gift a book on American history that he had reviewed.[137] He was feeling very, very weary.

As he often did when times were hard, Tom flexed his sense of humour. The December *Egoist* filled a spare half page with his spoof letters from a variety of English places real and imaginary – Hampstead, Thridlingston Grammar School, The Carlton Club – deftly parodying a variety of ever-so-English tones ('my old Oxford tutor'; 'our brave boys in the trenches'), and rejoicing in his genius for invented names: Helen B. Trundlett, Charles Augustus Conybeare.[138] Yet in a revealing letter to his father, reflecting on life and the war, he wrote that 'everyone's individual lives are so swallowed up in one great tragedy, that one almost ceases to have personal experiences or emotions, and such as one has seem so unimportant!'[139] If this made it sound as if he was hiding from his own emotions, he sensed, though he gave no details, that something might emerge sooner or later in his literary work: 'I have a lot of things to write about if the time ever comes when people will attend to them.'[140]

Meanwhile, Vivien had been hoping to accompany him to a party with Mary Hutchinson, and was excited about what she called 'my new house' at Marlow, but she worried Tom might not be well enough to dance.[141] He had a two-day holiday from the bank on 25 and 26 December, and no lectures for three weeks. A sense of 'nervous strain' oppressed him; he felt it would be 'a sad Christmas'.[142] Vivien told Mary he was 'overworked and tired of living'.[143] On Christmas Day when they opened their presents, he found his brother had sent him a portfolio of family photographs and familiar American scenes. Tom pored over them intently, as he confessed to Henry, with 'a lot of pleasure, some of it of a pathetic (but pleasant) sort'.[144] Christmas lunch was spent with Vivien's parents at their Hampstead home; Vivien would have preferred dinner in the evening, but a full moon made air raids more likely: after lunch she and Tom headed for the country before work at the bank resumed. As they both coughed, nursing colds in the December English weather, they felt miserable. Her sympathy tinged with a dash of spite, Vivien expressed a wish that Tom 'could break his leg, it is the only way out of this that I can think of'.[145]

12

American

As the war continued, Tom's thoughts focused more intently on American relations with Europe. Justifying his commitment to a literary career in England, he began to articulate views that would become among his best known. Soon, trying to enrol for military service, he had to confront in new contexts the consequences of being an American. As it had done when he lived there, his native land frustrated and even infuriated him; but it also defined him. His Americanness both excited and annoyed Vivien.

He was preparing a special issue of the *Egoist* memorialising an exemplary novelist from the United States. Henry James had died in early 1916. The previous year, partly in protest against America's refusal to declare war against the Kaiser, James had become a British subject, but to Tom he mattered most as a literary artist. Though Pound and others contributed to this special issue, published in January 1918, it was Tom's idea, emerging from his 'great admiration' for James's combination of the creative and the critical.[1] He agreed with most of James's criticism of New England life; whether considering James or Turgenev (another émigré writer he admired), he argued for 'the benefits of transplantation'. Tom sought examples of 'how to maintain the role of foreigner with integrity'; yet at the same time, in language that now seems problematic, he asserted 'a writer's art must be racial – which means, in plain words, that it must be based on the accumulated sensations of the first twenty-one years'.[2] Apart from his boyhood visit to Quebec, his own first twenty-one years had been spent wholly in the United States.

Proclaiming itself 'the most notable magazine of its kind in the world', London's *Poetry Review* had paid no attention to *Prufrock*. Instead, in 1917 it had featured 'Alan Seeger: America's Soldier Poet', killed in France on

4 July 1916.³ Tom, to whom Seeger's work was so manifestly 'out of date', thought his former classmate's poems 'not unworthy of the attraction they have attracted'; but the future was Jamesian.⁴ Seeing James's friend Edith Wharton as 'the satirist's satirist', Tom praised her New England novel of sexual betrayal and unhappy marriage, *Summer*, in the January 1918 *Egoist*, interested both in its attack on sentimental localism and in its 'suppressing all evidence of European culture'.⁵ James himself was even better: he had taken on Europe and triumphed. 'I do not suppose that any one who is not an American can *properly* appreciate James', Tom wrote. 'It is the final perfection, the consummation of an American to become, not an Englishman, but a European – something which no born European, no person of any European nationality, can become.'⁶

As Europe's warring nationalities tore the Continent apart, this insolent argument made a kind of sense. It may have goaded both English and American readers, but it let Tom follow in James's wake by turning his perceived New England provincialism into an asset. Bringing with him American perspectives to which he had added French, some German and English ones, he argued that the literature of England was too provincial. England's Georgian poets seemed weakened by lack of engagement with French verse. James, the transplanted American, had relatively few readers who understood him; but for Tom, who had even fewer, he was an inspiration:

> The fact of being everywhere a foreigner was probably an assistance to his native wit. Since Byron and Landor, no Englishman appears to have profited much from living abroad. We have had Birmingham seen from Chelsea, but not Chelsea seen (really *seen*) from Baden or Rome. There are advantages, indeed, in coming from a large flat country which no one wants to visit: advantages which both Turgenev and James enjoyed.⁷

Tom loved the way James refused to present Americans as 'commercial buccaneers'; instead, rejecting stereotypes that even Americans relished, James exemplified nuance. Tom had read with interest Frank Norris's 1903 novel, *The Pit*, which (as would *The Waste Land*) juxtaposed snatches of opera with urban commercial life; its artistic St Louisan, Corthell, falls in love with Laura but, despite her 'married life' being 'intolerable', and despite her 'affair' conducted with Corthell in richly ornate, plutocratic rooms, she remains with her businessman husband.⁸ Norris's narrative came into Tom's mind in early 1918, convincing him James's work was much subtler in its psychology and sense of Americans. James's 'superior intelligence' could make both America and England so uncomfortable that this writer's death, if properly understood, might have 'cemented the Anglo-American Entente'.[9]

Resistant to the 'all-American propaganda' of Amy Lowell, Tom brooded on what it meant to be an American author, while contending that 'Literature must be judged by language, not by place.' 'Provinciality of material may be a virtue', but 'provinciality of point of view' was 'a vice'.[10] He had been thinking more widely, too, about tradition and theology. To innovate, he argued, required consciousness of tradition, even if only to avoid repeating what had been accomplished already. Yet 'Tradition' with a capital T could be a mere repository of unexamined practices. Strikingly, when reflecting on contemporary poetry in late 1917, he had suggested that 'for an authoritative condemnation of theories attaching extreme importance to tradition as a criterion of truth' readers should consult a nineteenth-century papal encyclical.[11] Few perusers of the *Egoist* are likely to have done so, but Tom's commitment to avant-garde work by Joyce and Wyndham Lewis accompanied his reading of Catholic theologically-minded philosophers including Father John Rickaby, Cardinal Joseph Mercier (whose *Manual of Modern Scholastic Philosophy* was published in English in 1917) and Father Peter Coffey on interpretation of the tradition of 'modern Catholic thought'. Tom belonged to no church. Yet, visiting Anglo-Catholic City churches in his lunch hours, he was conscious of Catholicism as 'the only Church which can even pretend to maintain a philosophy of its own, a philosophy, as we are increasingly aware, which is succeeding in establishing a claim to be taken quite seriously'.[12] Despite mocking the 'True Church' in 'The Hippopotamus', as he continued reading philosophy and anthropology, he went on pondering literature side by side with religion.

Some details that caught his attention seem revealing. In late 1917 he was writing about *Eugenics Review* articles which dealt with sexual problems and arguments for birth control – 'as in cases when a woman lacks the physical strength for child-birth'.[13] Probably Vivien viewed herself in such a light, and Tom may have been aware that his mother (as she put it later) did not consider his 'an eugenic marriage'.[14] Writing with approval about marital conditions in Burmese culture where 'marriages are civil and can easily be dissolved on reasonable grounds, even on the ground of incompatability', he suggests that 'the primitive Shan tribes are undoubtedly more civilized than ourselves'.[15] Even as he remained locked into many of his society's conventions, his habit of aligning the supposedly 'primitive' with the present day, familiar from his Harvard studies, guided his poetry and criticism. He warmed to 'the anthropological aspect' of

Durkheim's thinking about the relationship between 'group-consciousness' and 'individual consciousness'. In late 1917 he wrote about Durkheim's *Elementary Forms of the Religious Life* with its 'reinterpretations of the principal social phenomena of primitive peoples'.[16] Such concerns recalled his earlier graduate-student paper on interpreting primitive ritual. Along with recent reflections on literary and Catholic tradition, they fed, too, into one of his most important essays, 'Tradition and the Individual Talent'. That work was not published until 1919, but there are anticipations of it in his articles throughout the previous year.

The 'primitive mind' compelled his interest. He thought 'The psycho-analysis of myths, pursued by some of Freud's disciples', could cast light on it.[17] Conrad Aiken was devoted to deploying Freud's ideas, but Tom, whose path diverged more and more from Aiken's, was wary of doing so crudely.[18] Nevertheless he knew work by Freud's exponent Ernest Jones, and had read Edwin B. Holt's *The Freudian Wish and its Place in Ethics* which he thought 'possibly' one of the most 'notable productions' among recent philosophical works.[19] Strikingly, Holt's book had linked a fixation with a woman's 'teeth' to 'hysteria'. The terms 'suppressed', 'complex' and 'dissociation' were borrowed by Holt from Freud and Janet; in turn, they were adopted by Tom, not just in his poems 'Suppressed Complex', sent to Aiken in 1915, and 'Hysteria' (in which a woman's 'teeth' are 'accidental stars'), but also in subsequent essays where the 'dissociation of sensibility' (a partial echo of Bostonian Morton Prince's 1906 *Dissociation of a Personality*) would become famous.[20]

If Tom's awareness of Freud made him concerned about his own sex life, more evident was his annoyance at America's prudery in depriving 'the small public that cares for literature' of Wyndham Lewis's sexually explicit story 'Cantleman's Spring Mate'. Under a US law that declared '"non-mailable"' by the postal service any material with a '"tendency to excite lust"', distribution of the *Little Review* had been halted in early 1918, despite legal efforts by John Quinn in New York.[21] Tom in the *Egoist* expressed outrage. He wanted a literature ready to face up to the seismic complexities of sex.

Long used to erotic vagaries, Bertrand Russell was looking forward now to an ongoing relationship with Vivien, while hoping to continue sleeping from time to time with Lady Constance Malleson; he was annoyed that Lady Malleson had become pregnant by another of her lovers. Spending several weeks in the New Year at Ottoline Morrell's Garsington, Russell wrote to Malleson on 6 January, 'My work-a-day life will be at Marlow, with Mrs. E. I shall come up to London one or two nights a week, according to how busy I am. If you are prepared to give me those nights & a day, we shall keep in touch . . .'[22] Unsurprisingly, his relationship with Malleson continued to be stormy, but other squalls, too, were brewing. Before he could establish a life 'at Marlow, with Mrs. E.', Russell was charged in early February with publishing statements 'likely to prejudice His Majesty's relations with the United States of America'.[23] He was found guilty in a London court, having suggested that, if war continued, an 'American Garrison' in England would be used for 'intimidating strikers, an occupation to which the American Army is accustomed when at home'.[24] While appealing against his conviction, Russell went on delivering public lectures on 'The Philosophy of Logical Atomism'. Still in London with Vivien and having suffered a bout of flu, Tom calmly and supportively reviewed Russell's *Mysticism and Logic* in the *Nation*: 'Mr Russell reaches the level of the very best philosophical prose in the language. The only contemporary writer who can even approach him is Mr Bradley.'[25]

Among those who rallied to Russell's support were the editor of the liberal free-trade paper *Common Sense*, of which Tom approved, and Raphael Demos, Tom's philosopher friend from Harvard, who visited him at the bank while in London. Tom had a detailed conversation with Russell about philosophy and the biological sciences in March, not long before Russell was once more reconciled with Constance Malleson. Later, in early May, the former don was gaoled for six months, his loneliness in Brixton prison alleviated by a flow of visitors, including Tom. Vivien was not on Russell's prison-visitors list, but Tom's readiness to support his devious mentor is striking: a triumph, perhaps, of generosity and intellectual loyalty over common sense. Certainly Russell's imprisonment meant the Eliots' marriage was less imperilled, though the strain caused by Vivien's adultery contributed to other stresses. In the midst of chilblains, neuralgia and exhaustion, she and Tom looked forward to small pleasures: letters, American newspapers, dancing, Orange Pekoe tea from St Louis.

As was becoming his habit, Tom managed to numb himself with work. Some weekends he spent all Sunday labouring on the *Egoist*, or preparing lectures. Weekdays, there was the bank; Saturday had long been the only time when he was free to meet his literary friends for extended conversation over lunch. A sense of personal pressures, intensified by the constant background menace of the war, disturbed both the Eliots, though they tried to cope in different ways. 'Everything looks more black and dismal than ever, I think', Tom wrote to his mother on 4 March. 'The whole world simply lives from day to day; I haven't any idea of what I shall be doing in a year, and one can make no plans. The only thing is to try to fill one's mind with the things in which one is interested.'[26]

One thing that interested him was editing. Harriet Weaver and he hoped to publish 'Mr. James Joyce's new novel, *Ulysses*'. It was to begin appearing in March in serial form in the *Egoist* simultaneously with publication in the *Little Review*, but very soon there were 'difficulties in regard to the printing'.[27] Wartime England's paper shortages continued. More challengingly, Joyce's work could be considered obscene, rendering its printers liable to prosecution. The Egoist Press brought out its second edition of *A Portrait of the Artist as a Young Man* in March. Tom, Weaver's assistant editor, was right behind her in trying to get *Ulysses* published in Britain, commenting in June that Joyce was 'The best living prose writer' and his new novel 'superb'.[28] His frustration at American refusals to countenance publication of Lewis's short story in March should be seen in the context of the *Egoist*'s struggles that same month to publish *Ulysses*.[29] Campaigning for and regularly conversing with other writers, Tom was at the very centre of literary life in London. His knowledge of tradition, theory and practice came to him through face-to-face discussion as well as via his remarkable formal education and a lengthening list of correspondents.

His work with Weaver introduced him to the travails of book publishing – both as author and editor. It confirmed, too, that he had an outstanding editorial eye – evident not just in material he published in the magazine, but also in his reviewing. He could take an eleven-line poem and see that it would be far better if 'the first four lines' were 'printed alone'. He could point out to a poet – his new friend Osbert Sitwell – that the word '"gigantic" should not be followed by "immense" in the next line'; and, having done so, he could remain friends.[30] The courtesy that may have been problematic in Tom's relations with Russell came into its own when he was making stringent but accurate editorial interventions. He took pride in knowing how to review work by his allies without betraying his principles. Interested in Pound's move towards longer poems – the first *Cantos* – he also went over some of his friend's verse before it was submitted for magazine publication. In due course, honed and strengthened, such skills would make Tom the twentieth-century's most celebrated literary editor. Pound, whose work in 1918 he valued 'far higher than that of any other living poet', certainly repaid the favour.[31]

Tom learned the hard way too: in early 1918 a rumour reached him from New York that recently established New York publishers, Boni & Liveright ('young Jews' as the sometimes virulently anti-Semitic Quinn termed them) aimed to produce a pirated American edition of *Prufrock*.[32] Actually, this firm was interested in publishing Tom's book in a perfectly legal way, but Quinn advised him to delay until he had enough material for a more substantial American debut with a publisher such as Knopf.

Grateful for Quinn's staunch support, Tom was prepared to wait, but concern that his work might be pirated increased his vexations: he had 'only written half a dozen small poems in the last year' and was usually 'too tired to do any original work'.[33] Often he would write letters or lectures until very late at night. One weekend Vivien worried he had spent a whole day without moving from his seat, except to eat. She found the days before his lectures 'terrible', and told Lottie Eliot how white and thin he looked. In describing her husband, Vivien expressed something of her own anxiety. 'It is more than one can endure to see a young man so worn and old-looking . . . It wears me out to see him.' Such statements exerted pressure on the Eliot parents, whose support continued – in cash as well as in kind. Tom got two new suits, 'a very jolly-looking over-coat' and a new hat to supplement the sweater, muffler and pyjamas sent across the Atlantic by his ever anxious septuagenarian mother.[34]

Frustrated in her earlier search for employment, Vivien was trying her hand at 'cinema acting', but with little or no success.[35] When they both felt well enough, she played the part of hostess at home, too, assisted by Ellen Kellond, the household servant on whose labour they relied. That March the Eliots hosted their most ambitious lunch to date, packing their small dining-room-cum-library with five guests who joined them in tucking into fish and spaghetti. Determinedly, they kept the 'obsessing nightmare' of war at bay; Tom, eager to 'preserve values', tried to do this in almost all his writing.[36] Yet occasional moments of civilised poise and personal success were swept aside: Vivien failed to sustain her career as an actress; Tom missed small things like the boneless cod boxed by Gorton and Pew in Gloucester or the Sunday evenings with baked beans, toast, cocoa and chat about friends at Eleanor Hinkley's Berkeley Place house. He felt pangs of nostalgia for America and his family, even as he resolved to stay in England.

Still thinking about Henry James – 'his always alert intelligence is a perpetual delight' – he reread some of that author's work, discovering further material while preparing another article, this time for the *Little Review*. Connections between James and Hawthorne made Tom interrogate more profoundly his own American filiations. Jamesian subtlety was invaluable, but insufficient. Thinking of his brother-in-law Alfred Sheffield, a thoroughgoing New England academic, he remarked that 'He has not preserved any wildness, any liberty!'[37] However demanding his work at the London bank might be, and however conventional his bankerly demeanour, Tom hoped that at some deeper level they let him preserve qualities Harvard might well have snuffed out.

His 'wildness' had never been much in evidence. Among friends and acquaintances he was often reserved. His speech, when it came, was carefully measured, exact. Yet he prized a vein in his poetry which, like some of the supposed 'obscenity' in Joyce's work, could offend readers because it was ready to say things that remained unsaid in tamer, lamer, sentimentalised writing. The crude, 'bad boy' aspect of his Bolo verse was related to this; elsewhere, when he wrote about a rutting hippopotamus or about sex and epilepsy, there is a compelling mixture of taboo-breaking and disciplined formality, as if wildness, disgust and composure were at one. Such an amalgam features in some of the poems in quatrain form that he wrote during the spring and summer of 1918. Several exhibit that man called Sweeney who seems like Bolo's avant-garde cousin. These poems do not seek psychological interiority. Instead, focusing on externals, they present a two-dimensional puppet show which comments on human folly. Cunningly intellectual, they are also cartoonish. Serious, outré and incisive, indebted to the music hall as much as the library, they can offer what Ronald Schuchard terms a 'brothel burlesque'.[38]

'Sweeney' was a name associated with manliness in Dr F. L. Sweany's St Louis and boosted by Tom's knowledge of the Irish-accented Boston where as a Harvard student he had gone for boxing lessons. His Sweeney represents a wild maleness overlapping with the bestial. In 'Sweeney Among the Nightingales' the protagonist is described as 'Apeneck', and associated with 'zebra' and 'giraffe'; a woman he is involved with – probably in a brothel – tries to sit on his knees but falls off and, 'Reorganised upon the floor', starts to yawn, then 'draws a stocking up'. Rather reminiscent of Mary Hutchinson's panther-like female, the women here can seem almost as bestial; and, just as Quinn, Vivien, Pound, Tom and his mother and father could share a scorn for Jews, so in this poem it is hard not to detect a designed aversion as 'Rachel *née* Rabinovitch / Tears at the grapes with murderous paws'. Sex comes across as seedy, animalistic, horrible; it involves a rapacious violence heightened when the poem concludes with complexly compacted imagery that juxtaposes Catholic religious orthodoxy – 'The Convent of the Sacred Heart' – with ancient rituals of violence and a strangely elegant image of bird shit as 'liquid siftings'. Some of the final, carefully chosen words, such as 'stiff' and 'bloody', are freighted with further hints of sex and death.[39]

Other poems from the same time or a little later, including 'Sweeney Erect', have related resonances. Analysing the paper on which it is typed, Lawrence Rainey dates 'Mr. Eliot's Sunday Morning Service' to between March and August 1918.[40] Its title invites us to relate it to its author. Drawing on Tom's reading in Plotinus and in theology, as well as on other preoccupations including art history and Renaissance drama, it juxtaposes money with churchiness, sexuality with philosophy in a style both elaborately knotted and unsettling. Probably the most shocking of the year's poems, the honeymoon 'Ode' bearing the date 'Independence Day, July 4th 1918' once more shows sex as anguished.[41] As well as registering erotic disturbance, in deploying the poet's surname and the date 'July 4th', these poems show, however ironically, a tenacious engagement with the writer's sense not just of what it meant to be an Eliot but of what it meant to be American.

Writing to fill a small gap on a page in the March *Egoist*, Tom employed the spoof address 'Little Tichester' to make clear 'in response to numerous inquiries' that Captain Arthur Eliot, who had co-scripted a London music-hall hit featuring a soldier suspected of betrayal, was 'not, roughly speaking, a member of my family'.[42] This was the light-hearted flip side of such concerns about identity. It also hinted that his earlier fondness for music-hall entertainers had been transferred from American theatres to the London of popular stars like Little Tich. If Little Tich was 'an orgy of parody of the human race,' then so was Sweeney.[43] With wildness, formality and precision, Tom too ridiculed humanity in poems written between 1917 and 1919; but, usually with great indirectness, he also probed his deepest worries.

His worries surfaced, too, in his lectures and reviews. Reading George Eliot (almost all of whose work he disliked) for his evening lectures, he picked out what he saw as her 'one great story': 'Amos Barton' deals with a broken man; its plot includes a marriage viewed by a family as unacceptable, and a suspected adultery. When Tom came to Thackeray, more than once in early 1918 he singled out as excellent 'the Steyne part' of *Vanity Fair* where the artist's daughter, manipulative seductress Becky Sharp, apparently betrays her estranged husband with the older philanderer Lord Steyne. That aristocrat has provided introductions into high society, has helped finance Becky's household and has plied her with presents.[44] She protests her innocence and Lord Steyne backs off, but her husband is left with torturing questions: 'What *had* happened? Was she guilty or not?'[45]

Vivien, now that Russell was in jail, hoped to devote herself to the not insubstantial garden at the back of the red-brick three-storey house in Marlow. These days she was spending more time there with Tom. Though in the April *Egoist* he had shown interest in novelist Gilbert Cannan's understanding of 'domestic warfare', his life with Vivien was by no means all dreadful.[46] An attractive place, Marlow boasted medieval and fine, red-brick, Harvard-style Georgian buildings: 'a charming old little town', Tom called it.[47] Percy Bysshe and Mary Shelley had resided not far along West Street, and had boated on the Thames; in 1918 the philosophically-minded,

India-obsessed English novelist L. H. Myers lived with his American wife just a short walk away, commuting to work in London; about a quarter of a century before Tom and Vivien moved to Marlow Jerome K. Jerome (who dwelt nearby while the Eliots were resident) had presented the place in *Three Men in a Boat* as a 'bustling and lively' location for sailing, 'one of the pleasantest river towns I know of'.[48] Today the riverside Compleat Angler Hotel still boasts that T. S. Eliot was among its several literary diners, and Jerome's description of Marlow, site of regattas and the occasional summer 'river concert' even during World War I, remains true: 'There is lovely country round about it, too, if, after boating, you are fond of a walk, while the river itself is at its best here.'[49] Tom liked the area, especially in summer when, he told his mother, 'the gardens of Marlow' were 'brilliant with hollyhocks, which start after the foxgloves and lupins and larkspur'.[50]

Then as now, 31 West Street was situated beside a quaint narrow alley. That summer in its secluded garden roses were in full bloom. Two grocers and a baker's shop stood a few doors away, so shopping was easy. When Tom's literary friends Sydney and Violet Schiff came to visit, there was a fresh, uncut loaf on the table in the small, plain dining room, along with manuscripts and pale china teacups.[51] Outside, though West Street was relatively busy, the garden was peaceful. By May Tom was travelling frequently between Marlow and London, thirty miles away. The Buckinghamshire town, its population around 6,000, was 'the terminus of a branch line of the Great Western Railway' and had 'an excellent train service'.[52] Finding the journey 'restful', he bought a season ticket so he could commute daily.[53] Though it was frustrating to have 'our chances of seeing anyone' in London limited, he kept in touch with Pound and newer friends such as May Sinclair and American actress Elizabeth Robbins, then in her fifties, who had corresponded with Henry James.[54]

In Marlow, sometimes at least, the Eliots felt healthier. June was hot. Temperatures in Buckinghamshire reached the 70s Fahrenheit (low 20s Centigrade) and London's sultriness reminded Tom of St Louis – but he felt he thrived on heat, and relished it after the winter. Both he and Vivien had been consulting doctors. Tom's had suggested country air would benefit him. Sitting out in the walled back garden all day on a blazing Sunday in early June, he thought the roses 'wonderful', and wrote of how in Henry James 'the soil of his origin contributed a flavour discriminable after transplantation in his latest fruit'.[55]

In this Marlow garden, thinking of the shade of 'the Harvard elms', Tom felt a strong sense of something both he and his native culture seemed too often to lack: leisure. 'There seems', he wrote, 'no easy reason why Emerson or Thoreau or Hawthorne should have been men of leisure; it seems odd that the New England conscience should have allowed them leisure; yet they *would* have it, sooner or later'. Admiring that, he set it against present-day American drives to 'at any price avoid leisure'. Those earlier American writers had been denied 'leisure in a metropolis', but had taken it under the best conditions they could achieve. While he sniped at Boston ('quite uncivilized but refined beyond the point of civilization'), he admired that dignified, rather aristocratic leisure which some nineteenth-century American authors had found, and which (though he did not say so explicitly) he could not. However, his principal interest in Henry James was that he had learned from French culture and from a sense of 'deeper psychology' in Hawthorne. Leaving relatively young, James had managed to escape the New England oppressiveness which defined Hawthorne. Unusually, Tom wrote that 'gentleness' was needed when criticising Hawthorne; for 'the soil which produced him with its essential flavour is the soil which produced, just as inevitably, the environment which stunted him'. Brooding on these Americans' 'sense of the past' was again a way of thinking about tradition and identity with a particularly New England inflection. As in sunny Marlow he read James on Hawthorne's sense of 'the shadow of the elms' on a Massachusetts summer's day, and on 'the "shrinkage and extinction of a family"', he thought about America, and about his own kin there.[56] He wanted his parents to know he was writing this American-accented piece, and hoped his mother might look up Marlow 'on the map' of England.[57] He was close, but very far away.

Marlow was a 'relief' after London.[58] Aldous Huxley, teaching at nearby Eton, visited the Eliots there on Saturday 22 June. Loftily, he found Vivien 'vulgar' but without snobbery since she made 'no attempt to conceal her vulgarity'. He thought 'Eliot in excellent form and his wife too'.[59] Yet the short-sighted Huxley missed some worrying signs. Both the Eliots remained vulnerable. Tom was thin: his weight had fallen by over a stone since he had left Oxford. Vivien, ever fearful of dentists, had been suffering from dizziness and migraine after 'very painful' dental work; she was also having eye problems. 'We feel sometimes as if we were going to pieces and just being patched up from time to time', Tom wrote to his mother the day after Huxley visited.[60] Tom knew his parents were struggling too. The Brick Company was in financial difficulties and his father's health poor. Lottie and Hal Eliot had decided to stay in St Louis that summer, rather than making their customary trip to Gloucester. Tom worried about them, but worry was all he could do. He knew, too, that they were anxious about him.

Yet in literature at least he was resolute. 'Every writer', he wrote in the *Egoist*, 'who does not help to develop the language is to the extent to which he is read a positive agent of deterioration'. Poets had to know their duty. 'England', wrote this banker, 'puts her great Writers away securely in a Safe Deposit Vault'. This led to them going 'rotten'. As a result, the great Romantic poets returned, like the undead, to 'punish us from their graves with the annual scourge of the Georgian Anthology'. Standing against such 'forces of death' were Pound, Joyce, Lewis and (in French) Jean de Bosschère, as well as 'probably' someone Tom had never met but who had published alongside him in Alfred Kreymborg's New York anthology *Others*: 'Miss Marianne Moore'. He saw her poetry as sharing qualities with that of Laforgue. 'Being an American has perhaps aided her to avoid the diet of nineteenth century English poetry. (Mr. Henry James and Mr. Conrad were also foreigners.)'[61] Such vitally disruptive foreigners could let the English language live in new ways. Tom aspired to be among their number.

Taken together, several prose pieces he published in summer 1918 constitute a manifesto. With a dash of that New England Puritanism which, despite his admiration for leisure, he could never throw off, he emphasised that poets had to work hard and be professional about their labours. Like scientists, they were 'contributing toward the organic development of culture'. To attack writers such as Joyce and Lewis for '"cleverness"' was a typically English mistake: the English loved the idea of the 'Inspired Bard', but poets needed intelligence and critical acumen as well as inspiration. Academically trained and now honing his skills as an editor, Tom sought to develop such a combination in himself, and demanded it of others. He was enthusiastic, too, about learning from prose: reading the serialised *Ulysses*, he found it stimulatingly 'volatile and heady'; it was 'immeasurably an advance upon the *Portrait*'. Pleasingly, 'Sweeney Among the Nightingales' and some of Tom's other recent poems appeared alongside 'Episode VI' of *Ulysses* in September's *Little Review*, helping to make that periodical one of the greatest of America's literary magazines.

Among his contemporaries James Joyce was certainly the prose writer from whom he learned most in ways that benefited his poetry. Joyce's use of literary allusion parallelled what Tom was perfecting in poems including 'Burbank with a Baedeker: Bleistein with a Cigar'. Published the following year, its epigraph is a tessellation of quotations from other works, relying on allusion and resonance to establish milieu. In Lewis's 'thick and suety', sometimes Dostoevskian novel *Tarr*, which Tom described in terms that sound close to his animalistic Sweeney poems, he found that deep wildness he liked, fused with intelligence: '*Tarr* is a commentary on a part of modern civilization: now it is like our civilization criticized, our acrobatics animadverted upon adversely, by an orang-outang of genius, Tarzan of the Apes.'[62] *Tarr*, especially in its treatment of 'Humiliation . . . one of the most important elements in human life', was a book that helped clarify his thinking about art: 'The artist, I believe, is more *primitive*, as well as more civilized, than his contemporaries, his experience is deeper than civilization, and he only uses the phenomena of civilization in expressing it.'[63] Tom's sense of underlying primitive wildness was, if anything, strengthened by his dedicated formality. He may have been a dapper, dark-suited banker, but was also the poet of 'Apeneck Sweeney'.

He admired purposeful clarity. Stylised forms, whether in theatre, music hall or painting attracted him. In the visual arts he preferred the strong, distinctive imagination of Vorticist Edward Wadsworth to the crowded artwork of proto-Surrealist Alan Odle. 'A distinguished aridity' impressed Tom – 'a single trail of fire', not 'a shower of sparks'.[64] Truthfulness to complexity demanded single-minded design. As he read poems by contemporaries, he grew convinced that 'the profession of poetry is fatiguing'; it required 'toil'.[65] Exerting himself, he had a kleptomaniac ability to adopt or adapt lines and phrases from older writers to nourish his work. These phrases were not always 'allusions'; often they simply added a sense of resonance, allowing his own verse to tap into deep cultural roots. Struggling to find something good to say about Lancelot Hogben's booklet, *Exiles of the Snow*, he picked out for its effective simplicity the line, 'When I am old and quite worn out'.[66] He published in the *Egoist* a poem by his recent acquaintance Sacheverell Sitwell (brother of poets Osbert and Edith Sitwell) about a parrot associated with the 'dry' and 'immemorably old'.[67] The summer weather Tom found 'very dry' and conducive to an outbreak of 'Spanish flu' which was decimating his colleagues at the bank.[68] Exhaustion, dryness and ageing would be at the heart of his poem 'Gerontion', on which he worked later in 1919; but by then his own sense of ageing had been further intensified by encounters with American military bureaucracy.

On the 4th of July 1918 Tom was underwhelmed by the way the day was (he employed ironic inverted commas) '"celebrated"' in London 'as a very serious act of international courtesy' in wartime. He longed for 'the hilarious 4th of boyhood', not least 'the strawberry icecream and the yacht race' he recalled at Gloucester.[69] Whatever else it does, with its mention of 'Children singing in the orchard', that 'Ode' dated 'Independence Day' marks the chasm between him and his lost past.[70] Among his American friends he was still in touch with Harold Peters and Scofield Thayer –

people of very different temperaments. Wealthy, bookish Thayer was going to fund and edit the American literary monthly the *Dial*. He wanted both Conrad Aiken and Tom to contribute; Tom wondered about sending 'Reflections on American Literature, by one NOT on the spot', and Vivien asked him to pass on the (perhaps coded) message to Thayer that she was 'homesick for America'.[71]

Still in love with the sea, Peters had sailed to New Zealand and to South America since he and Tom had last seen one another. After working 'intermittently' in real estate, he had been called up for active service in March 1917, being 'in the Massachusetts Naval Militia with the rank of Ensign' on a coastal torpedo boat. Since February 1918 as watch officer and navigator aboard the USS *Lakewood* Peters had played his part in 'carrying coal to Cuba and mines and mine anchors to Scotland'.[72] He hoped he and Tom might meet up. They had aimed to rendezvous in April, but Peters had got no further than Glasgow; in July, though, the timing was better; Peters managed to get a day off and visit Tom. 'He seemed not much changed, except matured by responsibility and authority', Tom wrote to his mother, who would have remembered Harold from Gloucester. This American visitor 'was just as nice as ever, and he and Vivien liked each other very much indeed'.[73]

As the English summer's 'long drought' turned to 'constant rain for a month' during July, the US Navy and the sea were much in Tom's mind.[74] At Bosham there was a British naval officers' club close to the house where he and Vivien had stayed. Sailors frequented the Anchor pub. Tom had felt again the allure of sailing. Now, with America fighting alongside Britain and her allies in the war, it seemed to him he might be of service to the US Navy. This need not mean voyaging abroad – Vivien was anxious not to be left alone again – but could involve work in England. Polylingual, Tom was, several of his referees pointed out, unusually talented in French. One of his Oxford friends, Willie King, worked for Military Intelligence in London; Tom had 'seen him occasionally' during a period when he was also in touch with the US Navy there, aiming to join its Intelligence Corps; another friend from Harvard days was attached to the American Embassy.[75]

Gathering testimonials, Tom was aided by Osbert Sitwell who approached Lady Nancy Cunard, the wealthy, American-born London hostess, for her backing. Colonel Jacob Schick, commanding the US Navy's London Division of Intelligence and Criminal Investigation, met and encouraged Tom. Undergoing a military medical examination, he hoped to pass but be graded 'low', so that he would not be sent into combat but could be enlisted nevertheless.[76] Eventually, though his doctor emphasised the examinee's poor health, he was graded by the official medical examiners more highly than he had expected. Taking his 'hernia and tachycardia' into account, they passed him as 'fit for *limited* service'.[77] In mid-August, all Americans in England were called up. Tom filled out an official US military Registration Card. Describing himself as a brown-haired, hazel-eyed 'Clerk' of medium build, he applied for 'exemption from draft', since he had a 'dependent wife'. Approved by the London Consul, his form was sent to his 'Local Board' in St Louis, where it was countersigned on 14 September.[78] Vivien grew terrified of the outcome. She pleaded with Mary and Jack Hutchinson to help rescue her husband: 'If he goes to America he will not be able to come back while the war lasts. That means years. If he stays here he will be killed, or as good as. If we don't save him he'll never write again.'[79] When it came to dealings with the military, Vivien maintained Tom could never be trusted to be 'worldly wise' and say the right thing at the right time. Writing out for him points she thought he should make in interviews, she was exasperated when he was thrown 'off balance' and did not stick to her script. She became 'Iller and iller all summer', intensifying both their anxieties.[80] A specialist gave her detailed advice, to which she paid little heed.

Trying to secure war work, Tom worried that if he were given the rank of private then he would struggle on a much reduced income. He described Vivien to his brother that August as 'an invalid dependent wife'.[81] Henry continued sending money. Complaining of 'incessant strain', Tom obtained references from the great and good including Arnold Bennett, soon Director of Propaganda at Britain's Ministry of Information.[82] Tom's plans involved moving back to the London flat, which he and Vivien had sublet while in the country. She proposed to stay in Marlow.

September saw him in contact with an American colonel, J. B. Mitchell, to whom Russell's lover Constance Malleson had introduced him. Nothing came of this, but Tom spoke also to a London-based St Louisan, Major Turner of US Intelligence. Initially, the US Navy had explained that he could only qualify for Intelligence work by enlisting as a seaman, then taking a laborious examination in several subjects. Changing tack, and armed with sixteen testimonials from everyone from the Dean of Merton to Jack Hutchinson, he had been encouraged to join the Quartermaster Corps, but was approached instead by an American lieutenant aiming to start up a new political intelligence section; eventually, its establishment was vetoed from Washington.

Next, Major Turner thought he could help get Tom a commission in US Army Intelligence, so long as he had three strong references from America to add to his English testimonials. His father helped him secure referees including Emeritus President Charles W. Eliot from Harvard: Tom had been 'an excellent student in all respects'.[83] Cables and letters criss-crossed the Atlantic. In a surprising development, he was summoned by US Navy Intelligence. Their London Commander told him he was just the man for them. If he enrolled as a chief yeoman locally, then they would try to get him a commission soon. On the strength of this, he was released from Lloyds Bank, which generously offered to rehire him when the war was over.

This naval appointment required Washington approval. Delays ensued. Eventually he received a Navy cable: 'Appointment received as requested – no further difficulty.'[84] However, the Navy's London office had assumed wrongly that he was not already registered for service. Tom pointed out that legally he had been required to register as an American in England, otherwise he would have been liable for British Army call-up. The US Navy consulted the US Army. No clarification came. There would have to be further exchanges of cables; the matter must be referred upwards to the provost marshal general in Washington. Angry, Tom, backed by Lady Cunard, tried to lay his case before the American admiral in London. He secured a meeting with the chief of staff, who was called away just as Tom was due to speak with him. The head of personnel stepped in at this point, explaining he could do nothing without explicit instructions from Washington. Meanwhile, official paperwork arrived from St Louis, requiring Tom to explain his situation at once with regard to military call-up.

He lost his temper. 'You *sent* for me, asked me to come as soon as possible', he told the Navy in London.[85] He had given up his job. Vivien's health seemed even worse. He had put his elderly father to the trouble of soliciting references from people who hardly knew him. He had spent a small fortune on cables. He might end up bankrupt. 'I feel years older than I did in July!' he exclaimed in a November letter to his 'dearest father', who, not in good health, was probably feeling that way too.[86] 'Very sore', in the second month of his thirtieth year, Tom confided to his brother that 'Three months of trying for a job, and for a month or so expecting to get it any day, has told on my nerves; and I feel very old at present, and mentally quite exhausted.'[87]

Had he been more stolidly thick-skinned, or more phlegmatically accustomed to military bureaucracy, he might have fared better; he was lucky that the bank renewed his employment, but his nerves got to him: 'this ends my patriotic endeavours', he declared to Jack Hutchinson in November.[88] Accustomed to thinking in terms of 'us (Americans)', he did not cease to care about his homeland, but it did annoy him.[89] 'As an

American of some years' residence in this country', he wrote a long public letter published in the *Nation* that November. It offered a critique of the politics of Republican Henry Cabot Lodge, a man with 'the best connexions in Boston society'. Backing the ideals of Democratic President Woodrow Wilson who advocated American participation in the League of Nations, Tom argued, 'It would mean universal disaster if the participation of America in the war does not lead to closer friendships and understanding, to freer intercourse of ideas, between America and England.'[90] If in public his convictions showed him still engaged with American ideals, in private his battling with American bureaucracy had taken its toll. 'This has been the most terribly exhausting year I have ever known, and one unfortunate event has crowded another.'[91] He craved 'Peace and peace of mind and freedom'.[92]

In the midst of all this, he had written to John Quinn explaining that he had a book typescript: containing prose criticism, verse from his first collection and more recent poems, it was ready to send to Knopf in New York. Despite Quinn's help, Knopf held off. But in London Tom received an important letter. It came from an English novelist in his thirties with a talent for satire, Leonard Woolf. With his wife Virginia, he had established the previous year a small press based at their three-storey red-brick home, Hogarth House, in Richmond, south-west London. Thin-faced and intellectually intense, the Woolfs were leaders of the Bloomsbury group of writers and artists. Leonard, a socialist of Jewish descent and a former colonial administrator, was eight years older than Tom. An alumnus of Trinity College, Cambridge, he knew Bertrand Russell. The Woolfs' friend Roger Fry had mentioned to them that Tom was seeking a publisher for some poems. Leonard and Virginia had brought out some of their own writings as well as a pamphlet by Katherine Mansfield. They had 'very much liked' *Prufrock*.[93] Would Tom allow them to look at his new poems with a view to having them published by the Hogarth Press?

Like writer and publisher John Rodker, some of whose work Tom welcomed to the *Egoist*, the Woolfs were part of that literary London in which he was learning to manoeuvre with a suavity that contrasted sharply with his inability to navigate the choppy waters of America's military bureaucracy. Leonard Woolf was compulsively hard-working. Affectionate, but childless, the Woolfs' marriage of six years was troubled by sexual difficulties. Nursed by her husband through more than one breakdown, Virginia Woolf had published a novel, *The Voyage Out*, in 1915. Tom had not met her, and knew little of her work. Interestingly, they shared several tastes, including a childhood fondness for Hawthorne and an admiration for Henry James. Independent-minded and brilliantly perceptive, Virginia, like Tom, came from a high-caste, markedly bookish family; socially, she seemed to have married beneath her; for a time she too had taught working-class students in evening classes. She had about as few readers as the author of *Prufrock*.

Though Leonard Woolf wrote to Tom, it was Virginia who had made sure to discover his address; she had contacted Clive Bell in September, asking him to get Mary Hutchinson to send it on since she had lost it. Tom took about a week before replying to Leonard's letter. Virginia Woolf noted on 28 October 1918 that he was 'asking to come & see us'.[94] She encouraged him. On Monday 11 November, a cloudy, still day in London, Tom, hard at work (Lloyds Bank had taken him back, promising a pay rise), heard guns firing, announcing peace. Sirens hooted on the grey, oily Thames. The Great War had ended. Armistice Day bells rang in churches, bands paraded, crowds cheered. Working late that night, he could not celebrate with Vivien because she was in the country, but she returned to be with him two days later. Then, on Friday evening, he first met Virginia Woolf.

She was scribbling in her diary when he arrived after work, at the imposing front door of Hogarth House. Henry James was on Woolf's mind, but she broke off to go and join her dinner guest along with her husband. Six years Tom's senior, Mrs Woolf found this foreign visitor 'a strange young man'. His enthusiasm for James Joyce she could just about agree with, but not his championing of the 'humbug' of Pound.[95] Returning to her diary soon afterwards, she set down a penetrating impression:

Mr Eliot is well expressed by his name – a polished, cultivated, elaborate young American, talking so slow, that each word seems to have special finish allotted it. But beneath the surface, it is fairly evident that he is very intellectual, intolerant, with strong views of his own, & a poetic creed. I'm sorry to say that this sets up Ezra Pound & Wyndham Lewis as great poets, or in the current phrase 'very interesting' writers. He admires Mr Joyce immensely. He produced 3 or 4 poems for us to look at – the fruit of two years, since he works all day in a Bank, & in his reasonable way thinks regular work good for people of nervous constitutions. I became more or less conscious of a very intricate & highly organised frame-work of poetic belief; owing to his caution, & his excessive care in the use of language we did not discover much about it. I think he believes in 'living phrases' & their difference from dead ones; in writing with extreme care, in observing all syntax and grammar; & so making this new poetry flower on the stem of the oldest.[96]

As writers – especially male ones – often do, the 'young American', who had just published an article on 'dead language' versus expression that was 'alive', and whose ideas derived from French Symbolist Rémy de Gourmont's 1900 *Le Problème du style*, fell back in conversation on what he had just been writing about.[97] He intrigued Mrs Woolf. She found herself talking about him next day to Desmond McCarthy, an Old Etonian friend as upper-class and English as she was. McCarthy, too, knew Tom. He told Virginia he had asked the poet about one of his clearly American productions, 'The Boston Evening Transcript'. With an exclamation mark that denoted her bemusement, Woolf recorded how, when asked about that poem's juxtaposition of La Rochefoucauld and a long street, 'Eliot replied that they were a recollection of Dante's Purgatorio!'[98] This American poet was hard to read as a person. His poems could be equally complicated; but they impressed. Woolf thought they made readers fetch up thoughts 'from the depths of silence'.[99] Within four months she would handset some of his lines of verse for her printing press, then print and bind by hand his small pamphlet, entitled simply *Poems*.

Presenting himself to the Woolfs, Tom confirmed his editorial astuteness. He had written more than four poems in the preceding two years, but, as he had done when assembling *Prufrock*, he suppressed all but the best. From early on he knew he would make his mark most effectively by releasing tiny amounts of utterly first-rate work to a discerning audience. The poems he gave the Woolfs were 'Sweeney Among the Nightingales', 'The Hippopotamus', 'Mr Eliot's Sunday Morning Service' and 'Whispers of Immortality'; to these he added three others in French: 'Le Spectateur' (later retitled 'Le Directeur'), 'Mélange Adultère de Tout' and 'Lune de Miel'. If his poems' quality and editing were high, the proofreading of them was patchy. Two mistakes in French were corrected during the Woolfs' small, early 1919 print run – about 250 copies; other errors slipped through. In the year of publication, Tom's sixteen-page pamphlet gleaned very, very few reviews: the anonymous critics seem to have known the author. *The Times Literary Supplement* warned him he was 'fatally handicapping himself with his own inhibitions', and risked 'becoming silly'.[100]

An unnamed reviewer in the *Athenaeum*, on the other hand, maintained that 'The poetry of the dead is in his bones and at the tips of his fingers: he has the rare gift of being able to weave, delicately and delightfully, an echo or even a line of the past into the pattern of his own poem.'[101] This was spot on, and might almost have been dictated by Tom; he had published a piece on Pound the previous September emphasising the need for the poet to cultivate 'the historical sense, of perception of our position relative to the past, and in particular of the poet's relation to poets of the past'. Effortfully relativist, here was a demanding manifesto: 'this perception of relation involves an organized view of the whole of European poetry from Homer'. Tom would develop such ideas and phrasing during 1919 in 'Tradition and the Individual Talent'. In his 1918 piece on Pound he praised the way 'James Joyce, another very learned literary artist, uses allusions suddenly and with great speed, part of the effect being the extent of the vista opened to the imagination by the very lightest touch.'[102] These techniques, on which Tom would continue to build, characterised his quatrain poems and other verse published by the Woolfs. Tom the Harvard-trained critic had praised 'laboratory work' and the way science was 'internationalized'; he wanted 'persons of equivalent capacity' in literature.[103] Yet the *Athenaeum* reviewer of his poems warned him against the mere *jeu d'esprit*; seen as a would-be 'scientist' of verse, he would have to work hard, this shrewd commentator warned, to remove the suspicion 'that he is a product of a Silver Age'.[104]

America was seldom far from his thoughts. He was contemplating going back there, at least to visit. With plans to apply for unpaid leave from the bank, probably that summer or autumn, he might try to visit his parents every future summer. This was part of a recurrent pattern: he longed for aspects of the United States, especially his family; yet he kept his distance. In late November he wrote to Woods, asking for news of Professor Lanman. Tom had not forgotten his years studying Sanskrit and Pali. Reviewing books on Indian ideas had brought back memories of that facet of his American education. As he pondered crossing the Atlantic, Vivien was less sure. She told Tom's brother she felt she '*really must . . . ought to*, go to America', but feared she never would.[105] Her health was dire: more dental work – 'I scream the whole time!' Writing up their major and minor health worries, she blamed Tom for passing on colds and influenza. He had to have his ears syringed to clear them of wax; the doctor was recommending he had one side of his nose cauterised because he seemed so prone to colds. Tom had shared her anxieties over the war and cash: 'We were off our heads all the summer.'[106]

Yet immediately the pressure seemed off as regards military service and finance, his health slumped. His bank salary was now £360 per annum – three times what it had been when he started the previous year – so, he told his mother, 'I ought to be practically self-supporting.' Unfortunately, he was getting splitting headaches, and had had to postpone some evening lecturing (one of his courses appears to have ended); he had been told by his physician to rest, ease up on moonlighting for the *Egoist* and read rather than write.[107] Vivien couldn't sleep. He fretted about her.

She reciprocated: he must take cod liver oil and a daily walk. They argued. He had an attack of sciatica; she suffered from migraines – a deepening problem – whenever she felt mental or physical strain. 'I do not understand it, and it worries me', Tom told his mother.[108]

Eventually, anxious about her husband's mental and physical health, Vivien got Tom to sign a written agreement not to do 'writing of any kind, except what is necessary for the one lecture a week which he has to give, and no reading, except poetry and novels and such reading as is necessary for the lectures, for three months'.[109] Tom had been reading voraciously for his lectures. An overdose of verbose literary criticism had made him ratty. J. A. Symonds's six-hundred-page *Shakspere's Predecessors in the English Drama* was 'absurdly long'; Felix E. Schelling's seven-hundred-page *Elizabethan Drama* was 'painful'.[110] What he liked was criticism by practitioners – 'the workmen's notes on the work' – though he added testily, 'Very few creative writers have anything interesting to say about writing.' Still, 'they ought to have the sense of what is actually important in older works'.[111] He had been using his compendious reading for his own ends as well as to benefit his students. He trained himself continually; but it was too much. Vivien realised that, and Tom paid heed. For about four months he published nothing. At last, emerging from this self-imposed embargo, he produced some of his most brilliant criticism.

For Christmas 1918 more money came from his parents, but also sad news. Tom's Aunt Marian Stearns in Cambridge, Massachusetts, had died. He remembered being visited by her during his student days in Paris. Slowly his American family was changing. His English in-laws came to Christmas dinner, but the next day – '"Boxing Day", the day after Christmas (a holiday here)', as he explained to his distant parents – Tom went with Vivien to see his president. They stood for more than two hours among cheering crowds in central London's streets, waiting to catch a glimpse of Woodrow Wilson. He had reached England on a European tour, celebrating the end of the war, and promoting his ideal of 'a just and lasting peace.'[112]

No serving United States President had ever visited Britain. It was only about a century since British troops had burned down Washington DC. Now London's streets were festooned with American flags. Church bells rang out. Artillery fired ceremonial salutes. Decorously, the British capital went wild. When President Wilson's train arrived from Dover at Charing Cross Station on a bright winter's day, it was met by King George V, Queen Mary, Prime Minister Lloyd George and assembled dignatories from Britain and America. Escorted by the Household Cavalry in ceremonial uniform, president and king rode together along the Strand in the first of a procession of horse-drawn royal carriages. Passing Trafalgar Square, they headed on by Pall Mall and Piccadilly to Buckingham Palace. 'It was', wrote Tom, who felt 'very pessimistic' about the 'chaos' of contemporary British politics, 'an extraordinary and inspiring occasion'.[113] With about thirty rows of people in front of them, Vivien, considerably shorter than her husband, could make out nothing as the procession approached. Then, just as the first carriage passed near them, Tom lifted her up. She glimpsed President Wilson: 'It was a most moving and wonderful sight to see him sitting next the King, and having such a glorious welcome.'[114]

Vivien cherished her most American moment, but it soon passed. Later, Tom decided the Paris Peace Conference and the ensuing Versailles treaty, which drew up several new European national boundaries, marked 'a bad peace'. Wilson had 'made a grave mistake in coming to Europe'.[115] Vivien's immediate worries were more familial. She had been too ill to get Christmas presents sent to St Louis in time, but wrote to Tom's parents on 30 December wishing them a happy New Year. A few days before her letter was received, Tom's father, now aged seventy-five, had been writing about money matters to his brother in Oregon. Hal complained about deafness, but expressed some pride in his sometimes exasperating younger son: 'My Tom is getting along now and has been advanced at the bank so that he is independent of me.' Independence, that most American of virtues, was something Henry Ware Eliot, Sr, prized in finance. He added, honestly but stingingly, 'Wish I liked his wife, but I don't.'[116]

13

Old Man

ON Tuesday 7 January 1919, Tom's father died. Vivien received a cable around noon on Wednesday. Wisely, she kept the news to herself until Tom got home from the bank. When she told him, he felt poleaxed. '*Most terrible*', her diary records; 'a fearful day and evening'. He stayed at home the following day, and she consulted her doctor. Afterwards she thought Tom 'very wonderful'; on Friday Aldous Huxley came to dinner: a 'nice evening'; but for several 'awful' days Tom was unable 'to feel as if anything was real'. He seemed to himself a restless sleeper in a nightmare, anxious lest he 'wake up and find the pain intolerable'.[1]

That Thursday in St Louis the funeral was held at the Church of the Messiah. The old man was laid to rest in Bellefontaine Cemetery. Tom's brother was there to support his mother: 'Men of every station crowded to do honour' to a well-known figure regarded as consistently conservative and loved as a pillar of the community. 'Not only his peers, but men of toil in every walk of life grieved to lose a true friend.' At the Eliots' church the Sunday sermon included a tribute to Henry Ware Eliot, Sr's 'modest character, and to the distinction he gave to citizenship'.[2] Tom had not seen him for over three years. The last time they had met, his father had reproached him. Tom's mind flooded with images of his boyhood, his cultured, strong-willed parents, St Louis and Gloucester: 'I have been all over my childhood.'[3] Tom believed his generous father thought of him as having 'made a mess' of his life.[4]

A cable arrived on Saturday from his brother: 'Do not come now plans uncertain mother well.' The next day Tom wrote his mother a short letter. It was all he could manage. Honest, characteristically slightly formal, it was also heartbroken. 'I do long for you, I wanted you more for my sake than yours – to sing the Little Tailor to me.'[5] Vivien wrote, explaining how for a long time Tom had felt acutely 'the fearful inadequacy of correspondence'.[6] There was too much to say; now it could hardly be said. He remembered beloved details: the funny little sketches his father sometimes put in letters: a trait Tom had inherited. He longed to frame one; he wanted some of his father's books. He felt guilt at not being in Missouri. His mother, seeking practical things to do, understood: 'this has been very hard on you – you were so far away'.[7] Bereavement made him feel all the more sharply a wish to prove himself: not just by doing well at the bank (a kind of success his father had valued), but also by publishing a book in his homeland. The Hogarth Press pamphlet was due in the spring, but in New York Knopf eventually turned down his typescript. Even before his father's death, Tom had written to Quinn to explain why 'for family reasons' he wanted 'to get something in the way of a book published in America'. Now his desire to do so intensified: 'my mother is still alive'.[8]

Work was a refuge. The bank needed him to stay focused. He composed his weekly lectures – now on Elizabethan lyric poetry. He visited the Woolfs to finalise details of his pamphlet. At Crawford Mansions the Eliots' servant caught pneumonia in February. Collapsing in the flat, she had to be nursed on the sofa for five days before being transported to hospital by ambulance. Taking over housework and disinfecting the premises, Vivien too became ill. She had been consulting her family's doctor, Lewis Albert Smith, at 25 Queen Anne Street. He had treated her since childhood, sometimes prescribing bromide – a sedative then given to women thought nervous or hysterical; but she was 'losing confidence'. Her meeting with Smith was 'Not satisfactory'.[9] Tom arranged to see Bertrand Russell, who had been in touch with Vivien again about whether they should go on sharing the rent of the Marlow house, and was complaining she 'won't reply'.[10] According to Vivien's biographer, Carole Seymour-Jones, she had written to Russell that she 'disliked fading intimacies, and must therefore break off all friendship'.[11] Sharply, Tom told Russell that Vivien was too unwell to deal with the strain of rental arrangements; they might get rid of the property altogether. Yet Vivien told Tom how much she loved the house in West Street and its garden. Even while the place was sublet, she had gone to check on it. Tom had to backtrack. Next, Russell started requesting the return of his Marlow possessions – a tea table, a coffee grinder – as soon as possible, and asked Tom to give his 'Love to Vivien. How are your troubles?'[12]

However troubled, life went on. Wanting Tom back at Harvard, James Woods wrote at least twice in February, trying to lure him to a new Philosophy post. Attempting to persuade his colleagues, Woods championed Tom's cause: 'He has shown extraordinary subtlety in writing.'

Unfortunately, Professor Hoernlé, now Department Chairman, was being lobbied by his predecessor in favour of someone more 'solid', more engaged with contemporary issues, less 'bookish and literary'. Tom's old teacher, G. H. Palmer, argued that, for all his 'extraordinary' intellectual 'power and sensitiveness', this unusual alumnus had 'allowed himself to be turned into weak aestheticism by the influence of certain literary cliques in London'. To counter such arguments, Woods needed Tom to help him. The retired chairman, Ralph Barton Perry, worrying that, judged by 'his recent poetry', Tom might be 'a sort of attenuated Santayana', gave the thumbs down.[13] The last thing Tom wanted was to be sucked into Harvard academic politics. He did not answer Woods's letters for almost two months, pleading exhaustion and bereavement. They were genuine excuses, but determinedly he burned his bridges.

'I have simply had a sort of collapse', he explained to his brother on 27 February. 'I slept almost continuously for two days, and now I am up, I feel very weak and easily exhausted.'[14] As had happened before, illness helped him release poetry on which he had been brooding. Substantial and different from his quatrain poems, this new work would draw on worries about a wasted life, which his father's death intensifed; it was fed, too, by failure to fight in war; by a sense of utter exhaustion; by trepidation about how the peace might turn out; by ongoing anxieties about sex, religion and death. It involved everything from hot, dry weather (like that of the previous summer) to Tom's absorption in Elizabethan, Victorian and American literature: even texts for his evening classes and his reviewing activities were raided with heightened magpie alertness to fuel this poem which he completed during summer 1919.

Initially it was called 'Gerousia'. Used by Aristotle, this noun denoted an ancient Council of Elders. Soon the title became 'Gerontion', a term used by Aristophanes and Xenophon, meaning 'little old man'. In English the title conjures up words such as 'geriatric' and 'Gerontius' – a name from Tom's childhood when Elgar's 'Dream of Gerontius' had had its St Louis premiere. Typed out not so long after his Greek-loving father's interment, 'Gerontion' carried two epigraphs – one from a speech about death in Shakespeare's *Measure for Measure*, and the other (which Tom abandoned) from Dante's *Inferno* where a spirit replies to an interlocutor surprised to see him dead, 'How my body stands in the world above, I have no knowledge'.[15] 'Gerontion' announces its sense of witheredness right from the start:

> Here I am, an old man in a dry month,
> Being read to by a boy, waiting for rain.

That rain never seems to come. The poem ends with 'a dry brain in a dry season'. It is an anatomy of exhaustion. Its speaker is oppressed by a consciousness of not having 'fought', of coughing, sneezing, feeling 'old' and 'dull' in a 'rented house' associated with 'lost . . . passion' and the 'adulterated'. Waste, wastedness and wasting predominate:

> I have lost my sight, smell, hearing, taste and touch:
> How should I use them for your closer contact?

Later Tom considered 'Gerontion' with its uneasy references to 'the Jew', to displaced people, to 'fractured atoms', extinction and drought, as a possible prelude to *The Waste Land*.[16] As it developed, he showed his draft typescript to several people, including his Jewish friends Violet and Sydney Schiff. They sent him a critique after 'analysing' it 'carefully', but apparently expressed no horror at anti-Semitism.[17] Twenty years older than Tom, Sydney Schiff was a wealthy Englishman who had worked in America and who wrote fiction. He and his intelligent, musically gifted wife Violet, then in her forties, liked to encourage writers and artists, including John Middleton Murry, Katherine Mansfield and Wyndham Lewis who painted Violet's portrait in the 1920s. In such company Tom could relax, chatting about life and art; he was sustained by the Schiffs' undemanding, shrewd affability.

In due course, circulating his work among his closest literary friends, Tom also passed his new poem to Pound, and sought to give it its final form. He was uncertain, for instance, whether or not to mention 'the windy straits / Of Belle Isle' – a nod towards those waters off the north-eastern United States where he had once sailed. This detail was in lines Tom added, and Pound emended. His poem's sense of exhaustion extends spectacularly from the deflected, masked and displaced personal origins of its immigrant author to the whole course of 'History', but its awareness of 'reconsidered passion' is not directly autobiographical.[18] 'Gerontion' incorporates reworkings of Renaissance divine Lancelot Andrewes's '*Christ is no wild-cat*' – a phrase Tom quoted in an April 1919 review – and material from the autobiography of 'a cousin', Boston Unitarian sceptic Henry Adams; Tom reviewed Adams's *Autobiography* that spring, recommending it to his mother as 'very interesting'.[19] Yet 'Gerontion' also focused his personal troubles, distancing them and letting them resonate widely through manifold echoes, dislocations and shifts of tone, transmuting them into unflinchingly crafted art.

Tom remembered the long-ago sound of his father's flute-playing. He stared with pleasure at two of Hal's drawings of cats. His mother was thinking of moving to Cambridge – nearer her daughters in Massachusetts. Tom supported that idea, though it meant a further sundering from the St Louis he remembered. Not all the family library could be 'saved', but he hoped his mother might take with her volumes epitomising 'New England civilisation', including Andrew Eliot's sermons, and works by or related to Emerson. He told her he had 'an idea that such of these things as you could save would be of use to me eventually'.[20] Consciousness of unavoidable breakage made him determined to maintain some semblance of old links. Gladly he accepted a selection of his father's Greek and Latin texts. Intuiting how Tom felt, his mother sent him a packet of letters saved from twenty years back. Her husband had written them lovingly to his younger son. Tom urged his mother to settle in Cambridge and look ahead. 'I shall come to visit you and bring you back with me.'[21] However, Vivien, used to her mother-in-law being kept at a distance, was keener for Tom to holiday in Europe.

The London Eliots needed cheering up. On Sunday 2 March, having gone to a dance with some acquaintances, Vivien was pleased to be 'Picked up by 3 Canadian flying men, all exquisite dancers', and felt she had 'danced as I never have since before the war'.[22] Next day she was exhausted, and feared Tom was 'not fit'.[23] When she told him she was lunching with Mary Hutchinson in early March, he invited Mary to an early evening dance the same day: he wanted to learn new dance steps, and to see Mary. There was also the possibility of a new job in literary journalism. His intelligent but hasty friend Middleton Murry had been appointed editor of the revamped *Athenaeum*. While Woods sought to bring Tom back to Harvard, Murry tried to hire him as assistant editor for a salary of £500. Eventually, Tom turned this down.

Restless and ambitious, at the start of the decade the stern-faced, chain-smoking Murry had made his name as editor of *Rhythm*, an avant-garde magazine whose contributors ranged from D. H. Lawrence to Picasso. Now, at the start of his thirties, he was among London's most sophisticated men of letters. His showily emotional poetry was very different from Tom's. Sometimes the two disagreed vehemently, but, if they could be rivals, they were bonded, too, by shared concerns. Each enjoyed editing; they had friends in common; their wives (Mansfield had tuberculosis) knew the burden of long-term illness. Still, Murry's *Athenaeum* was not for Tom. He had fresh, confidential duties at Lloyds, heading a research department working with an official from the British Foreign Office: with this came more lucrative, secure prospects. He liked the bank work because he could compartmentalise it; a full-time literary day-job with Murry as his boss was more likely to drain off his creative energy, and might be chancy. 'If one has to earn a living', he explained to Woods, 'the safest occupation is that most remote from the arts'.[24] Confidently advancing at the bank, he splashed out on a landscape picture by Edward Wadsworth.

Additionally, as bereaved people sometimes do, he got a dog. This 'very small Yorkshire terrier' was acquired by accident.[25] Apparently abandoned, though well trained, she followed Tom home in the street one day. Vivien welcomed her company. They named her Dinah Brooks, and Dinah soon regarded their three-room flat as her territory. When April brought fears of a rabies outbreak, Tom had to buy the dog a muzzle. It was the wrong size. Painstakingly, he managed to adapt it, using a specially purchased file and pincers. The dog's needs were a distraction, which was good for him.

In the wake of his father's death he took stock of his position, analysing it with his ambitious intelligence. This strengthened his resolve to prove to his mother that he was prospering. 'There is a small and select public', he wrote to her in late March, 'which regards me as the best living critic, as well as the best living poet, in England'. If true, such an achievement was individual, but also important in terms of his background: 'I really think that I have far more *influence* on English letters than any other American ever has had, unless it be Henry James. I know a great many people, but there are many more who would like to know me, and I can remain isolated and detached.'[26]

Increasingly, as emotional exhaustion took its toll, Tom idealised detached isolation. Hawthorne, he contended that April in a piece entitled 'American Literature', had 'the true coldness, the hard coldness of the genuine artist', something 'no one else in Boston had'. This was an accomplishment. Hawthorne had 'sucked every germ of nourishment out of his granite soil', but England's cultural loam was more fructifying.[27] Here, as in his use of Henry Adams in 'Gerontion', Tom continued to skewer Boston even as he encouraged his mother to move to Massachusetts. For himself, he implied that to pursue an artistic vocation was almost like following Christ: 'The Arts insist that a man shall dispose of all that he has, even of his family tree, and follow art alone. For they require that a man be not a member of a family or of a caste or of a party or of a coterie, but simply and solely himself.' In England Tom's goal now was to be an 'Individual'.[28] He sought to achieve uniqueness and to find a tradition that would help.

Building confidence in himself enhanced his critical boldness. He decided Swinburne and Kipling were immature when compared with the 'unmistakable' uniqueness of Joseph Conrad. To write for a large audience was misguided, though better than deliberately to tailor one's work to a small one. Best was 'to address the one hypothetical Intelligent Man who does not exist and who is the audience of the Artist'.[29] Encouraged by Murry, Tom produced several *Athenaeum* reviews, having fulfilled his 'contract' with Vivien to take a break from writing prose. He could not choose his topics so freely as at the *Egoist*, but the *Athenaeum* enjoyed a much wider readership. As editor, Murry published Tom alongside Mansfield, Santayana, the Woolfs, English poet Walter de da Mare and many others. Writing for it brought contacts and 'a critical notoriety' that Tom relished.[30] The *Athenaeum* featured and was devoured by the 'Bloomsberries' too; Lytton Strachey, one of its more vigilant readers, pointed out to Tom that he had mixed up two translations of the Bible, the King James and 'a modern edition'.[31] Tom admitted he had, and apologised. He liked to write more and more *ex cathedra*, but it was good for him – and he knew it – to be told he was not infallible.

On paper as in life he could provoke rebuke, and be intense in his dislikes. Vivien wrote to Mary, 'Tom would never speak to me again . . . would *hate* me' if she fell out with the Woolfs.[32] He could get 'angry and stubborn'.[33] Brigit Patmore, a strikingly beautiful thirty-seven-year-old literary friend with whom the Eliots went sometimes to the theatre, was angered by a 'judgment' he had made of her; he told her around this time she was 'mentally lazy'. Tom responded to Patmore's annoyance with an effort at flirtation, but sounded too like a drily academic philosopher: 'I can only observe, and correct by further observation.'[34] As his poetry suggests, he did observe keenly – whether paying attention to the seraglio at a Mozart opera, or listening to so-called 'actresses' in the flat below at Crawford Mansions who played loud gramophone music, and yelled to their 'gentlemen friends' in the street outside. 'The *immediate* neighbour-hood and some of our neighbours', the poet of 'Sweeney Among the Nightingales' wrote to his brother, 'are not what we should like'.[35] Still, the flat close to the pub was affordable, and they hoped to have it redec-orated soon. Henry had cabled more money.

The Marlow house needed attention too: Bertrand Russell persistently requested his belongings back but did not seem prepared to fetch them himself. Vivien was to go to West Street and superintend their return. Despite her earlier letter breaking things off, she sent a short note, begin-ning 'My dear Bertie'. She would get the job done as soon as her health allowed. Signing herself 'Yours ever', she encouraged him to 'come and see us when you have a free evening'.[36] But Russell's dreams of spending time with Vivien in his Marlow bolt-hole were over and grew more distant. Whatever she might have wanted at one time from her older lover, Vivien realised all along that her home was with Tom.

Now approaching her thirty-first birthday, when she felt well she dressed stylishly, combed her long dark hair and radiated vivacity. On other occasions, her self-esteem vanished and she seemed completely different. According to Virginia Woolf who met her for the first time on 6 April 1919, she was 'a washed out, elderly & worn looking little woman'. After Tom's first visit, Woolf had decided to count him as a friend. When she and Leonard had started typesetting his poems on 22 January, she had expected to 'probably see more of' him; but by the spring she had decided (wrongly, apparently) that Tom had turned against her. Having the Eliots to Sunday lunch with other visitors on 6 April, she noted how the atmosphere became easier when one of the guests took up Vivien's attention with stories about the king. Warily, Woolf decided Tom had become 'sharp, narrow, & much of a stick, since he took to disliking me'. Sometimes she felt awkward with him, which increased his own awkwardness, not least when his wife was present. Soon Woolf was aggrieved at Murry for saying 'the orthodox masculine thing about Eliot' and 'belittling my solicitude to know what he said of me'.[37]

After Tom, at the Woolfs' request, supplied a list of contacts to whom flyers about his poetry pamphlet could be mailed, none was sent out. Tom fretted. Vivien worried the pamphlet might never appear, after Tom had told people it would. Through Vanessa Bell's husband Clive, gossip circulated that Tom had spoken ill of Virginia Woolf. Mary Hutchinson, Clive's lover, rang Woolf on 3 April 'in great agitation': Tom had 'only abused Bloomsbury in general', not Woolf in particular.[38] Vivien maintained that Tom 'hates and loathes all sordid quarrelling and gossiping and intrigue and jealousy, *so much*, that I have seen him go white and *be ill* at any manifestation of it'.[39]

In the febrile, often incestuous world of literary London, such spats were frequent. From a safe distance they sound petty and comical. Shortly afterwards Woolf heard Tom had been 'praising me to the skies' in conversation with Mansfield and Murry.[40] As tensions flowed and ebbed, his pamphlet, *Poems*, with a cover designed by Roger Fry, appeared on 12 May. Publication coincided with that of two other Hogarth Press productions, one of them Woolf's *Kew Gardens*. Behind Tom's back, she explained to a friend, 'Mr Eliot is an American of the highest culture, so that his writing is almost unintelligible.'[41] Face to face, relations between poet and publisher were better, but a mutual wariness remained.

In 'Gerontion' Tom wrote about a disturbed state of mind. He may have drawn on his own, but certainly he contemplated that topic in literature. Dostoevsky's best work involved 'the continuation of the quotidian experience of the brain into seldom explored extremities of torture'. Tom was impressed, too, by the presentation (in Stendhal's *Scarlet and Black*) of Julien Sorel and Mathilde de la Mole, lovers who were passionate yet unsure of one another's love, doubting yet still desiring. To Tom some of Stendhal's scenes and phrases 'read like cutting one's own throat; they are a terrible humiliation to read, in the understanding of human feelings and the human illusions of feeling that they force upon the reader'. Such 'exposure' and 'dissociation of human feeling' fascinated him, and are essential to the pain of 'Gerontion'. There, as in his account of several of the greatest novelists, a sense of waste is bound up with 'the awful separation between potential passion and any actualization possible in life'. He felt acutely 'the indestructible barriers between one human being and another'.[42] This may have made him hard to understand as a person, even for Mary Hutchinson and Virginia Woolf. It accompanied, too, the strain of his marriage to Vivien and worries in the wake of his father's death.

Still, he did not want to write like a tired man. Essayist Robert Lynd, he observed, knew how to compose for the periodical press – a knack Tom had just about mastered – but seemed 'a tired man like other tired men who have to make a living by literature and also have consciences; tired men who want to make a book and cannot allow themselves that luxury; and the tired men do make books – they cannot wholly deny themselves – but the books are mutilated and unfinished'.[43] This was insightfully hard-hitting. The great thing about the bank was that it saved Tom from having to become an over-productive author of feeble books. Journalism could be a threat: 'In writing for a paper one is writing for a public, and the best work, the only work that in the end counts, is written for oneself.'[44] In 'Gerontion' and elsewhere he defeated tiredness by anatomising it; he knew only too well what it meant in life.

Self-knowledge brought pain, but also a hardening of determination. As he wrote to J. H. Woods in late April about poetry:

There are only two ways in which a writer can become important – to write a great deal, and have his writings appear everywhere, or to write very little. It is a question of temperament. I write very little, and I should not become more powerful by increasing my output. My reputation in London is built upon one small volume of verse, and is kept up by printing two or three more poems in a year. The only thing that matters is that these should be perfect in their kind, so that each should be an event.

As to America: I am a much more important person here than I should be at home. I am getting to know and be known by all the

intelligent or important people in letters, and I am convinced that
I am more useful in the long run by being here. Finally, one changes.
I have acquired the habit of a society so different that it is difficult
to find common terms to define the difference.[45]

This was not what Woods wanted to hear. Still, however hard-headedly
arrogant, it is a strikingly self-aware presentation of Tom's authorial
strategy. Any poet who reads his views on writing will gain a confirmatory, compelling education; but Professor Woods felt lingering regret.

Woods was not alone in trying to persuade Tom to return to America.
His mother, proposing to sell the St Louis and Gloucester houses, hoped
he would visit. He maintained that, though he longed to see her, he could
not yet ask for sufficient leave from the bank; perhaps he might arrive
with Vivien the following spring. From Lottie came his father's chessmen,
and an offer, graciously accepted, of Papa's bathrobe. The Eliots had to
decline Ottoline Morrell's invitation to Garsington in April, because Vivien
was unwell. Soon afterwards, when they needed to vacate their flat while
it was being decorated, she felt 'on the verge of collapse'. Temporarily
she moved to an address in Bayswater; Tom, who explained to Brigit
Patmore that he 'could not get in there', stayed at a hotel a few streets
away.[46] Why they did not cohabit at the hotel is unclear, but time apart
gave each some space.

In early May they went to Garsington, relishing the visit. Lanky, bearded
Lytton Strachey watched them through his small, round spectacle lenses,
and dined with Tom very soon afterwards, thinking him 'rather ill and
rather American: altogether not gay enough for my taste. But by no
means to be sniffed at.'[47] Surviving letters suggest the brilliant, squeaky-
voiced Strachey was flirtatious towards Tom, who attempted on occasion
to match Strachey's tone, but kept his distance.[48] Vivien enjoyed Garsington,
not least because she could talk frankly about Bertrand Russell to Lady
Ottoline. Tom's wife liked to believe Russell had been more generous to
her than anyone else; yet 'I have really suffered awfully in the complete
collapse of our relationship, for I *was* fond of Bertie (I think I still am).
But it is of course *hopeless*, I shall never try to see him again.'[49] It seems
unlikely that Vivien communicated all this to Ottoline (who could be
cutting about Vivien's 'affair') without Tom having any inkling of what
was going on.[50] Distanced, numbed and hurt, his poetry of 'reconsidered
passion' contained this kind of awareness: 'After such knowledge, what
forgiveness?'[51] Though 'Gerontion', whose speaker exudes despairing self-
rebuke, does not ask that question of the poet's household, it was a question that belonged in 18 Crawford Mansions.

Bertrand Russell came back to live in a cottage in Garsington Manor's grounds, and Lady Ottoline discussed Vivien with him around the end of July. It was then she confided to her journal that Vivien was 'a frivolous, silly, little woman', and Russell had been foolish to fall for her, plying her with all those presents such as 'silk underclothes'.[52] Vivien's confiding in Lady Ottoline was naïve, but she was both unnerved and entranced by Garsington society. Tom, too, however much he might recline smoking his cigarette in a Garsington summer deckchair, could be socially awkward. Going to see Diaghilev's Ballets Russes perform Stravinsky's *Firebird* at London's Alhambra Theatre on 13 May, he waited with Brigit Patmore until the Hutchinsons arrived, telling her nervously how cultured they were. Afterwards, he worried he had abandoned Patmore and wrote her overwrought notes. These suggest his nerves were on edge, and that, with clumsy flirtatiousness, he was trying to atone.

It was around then he wrote about 'humiliation' in Stendhal between illicit lovers. He knew he could be an awkward man to be with. Yet he enjoyed the company of women other than Vivien. Protesting her love for Mary Hutchinson, Vivien wrote to her saying how pleased she was Mary would be having Tom to stay at Wittering. Tom joked to Mary about how he could be 'seduced'.[53] More wistfully, he thought about a woman who was much further distant. In June he let his cousin Eleanor know he had sent a letter to Emily Hale, anxious about how it might be received. He could not forget her. 'I should, I think, like her to know what a keen interest I take in everything that happens to her.'[54] But there is no evidence Emily was writing to him.

Though Vivien's affair with Russell was over, and she was back from Marlow, she and Tom continued to spend periods apart, even after returning to their redecorated flat. One reason was Tom's work: towards the end of May the bank sent him on a tour of 'unknown provinces', including Manchester, Birmingham and Cardiff.[55] Vivien was unsure whether to accompany him; eventually she did not. Instead, 'ill in a sort of way', she went into what she described to Lady Ottoline as 'a sort of retirement which is so necessary to me at times that I should die without it'; she also invited Russell to tea in London while Tom was away, but that plan went badly. Russell seemed to flinch when he saw Vivien. Still, she asked Ottoline Morrell, 'Isn't it hard to put him *quite* out of one's mind?'[56] While Tom thought of Emily Hale, Vivien, spending a good deal of the summer at Bosham – sometimes with her husband and sometimes not – continued to dwell on her former lover. Marriage was difficult. During his travels, Tom sent letters, on occasion playfully, to Brigit Patmore and to Mary Hutchinson – who, when it suited her, used for correspondence the address of her lover, Clive Bell. Tom was toughening the shell that allowed him to cope. 'One must develop a hard exterior', he explained to Patmore, 'in order to be spontaneous – one cannot be that unless nothing can touch what is inside'.[57]

He had another publication planned: a small edition (250 copies) that poet John Rodker's new Ovid Press would print with artwork by Edward Wadsworth. Initially, the idea was to include Tom's earlier published verse from *Prufrock*, along with the contents of the Hogarth Press pamphlet and several new poems, among them 'Burbank with a Baedeker: Bleistein with a Cigar', 'Sweeney Erect' and 'Ode'. Tom aimed for the Egoist Press to bring out a cheap edition later, in the spring of 1920. Slyly, he did not consult the Woolfs about the Rodker scheme. They might not have welcomed it, given that his new book would appear long before they had sold out their pamphlet. Disappointed by Knopf and still attempting to find a good American publisher, Tom sought to prove he was flourishing in London. This fresh, expanded collection would help him do so. It would be a further slim volume of verse, but now other publishers' approaches were coming: Sir Algernon Methuen (interested in a collection of essays) and Martin Secker who had been impressed by Tom's thoughts on Stendhal and wondered if he might author a book about that novelist. Eventually the Methuen enquiry resulted in his essay collection, *The Sacred Wood*; the Stendhal proposal came to nothing. Secker was offering just £25.

Tom's evening-class teaching ended on 5 May. Grateful students gifted him *The Oxford Book of English Verse*, but he wrote to his mother, 'I hope I have done with education; the pay is not bad, but it seems such a waste!'[58] He made sure, however, to let her know he was about to lecture on 'the younger poets' on 31 May at London University.[59] To his family and himself he wanted to demonstrate success. Yet, touring the provinces, he felt both 'disdain' for London, and that he was 'sojourning among the termites'.[60] The fit between his American loyalties and his life in England was repeatedly uneasy. Once again, in mid-June, he had to cancel a Garsington visit at short notice when his former classmate Harold Peters arrived unexpectedly: 'the oldest and loyalest American friend I have', though Harold shared none of Tom's intellectual interests.[61]

Demobilised from mine-sweeping in the Orkney Islands, 'Pete' was about to sail to the States and had come from Liverpool for a long weekend just to see his Harvard pal. Tom tried his best to behave as if little had altered. Vivien returned from Bosham on Saturday 21 June to find the flat in an 'awful condition', with Tom entertaining Peters. The three of them went out to dinner, but the Eliots felt worn out, Tom 'looking very ill'.[62]

Nevertheless, on Sunday Tom and Peters went to Greenwich, walking for miles along the Thames by the docks, and through London's East End. Other trips took them to the theatre and the zoo. While Tom was at work in the bank, Peters simply sat nearby, waiting for his trusty companion to emerge. Vivien, who found Peters's attachment to her husband rather comical, complained their visitor had 'the development of an average boy of ten. *Boring!*'[63] Yet Tom told his mother (who knew Pete) that his former classmate was 'the most lovable fellow in the world, and I think really devoted to me, and time cannot alter that'.[64]

Immediately after Peters sailed home for America, Tom had to settle down to a week of banking and review writing before weekending at Bosham where Vivien, delighted to be back there and free of 'very boring' Peters, was spending a good deal of time.[65] Tom enjoyed picnicking with her and the Hutchinsons in nearby woods at Itchenor; other Bosham visitors that summer included the Schiffs, who came by car. On a fine summer's day, with Sacheverell Sitwell and Mary Hutchinson the Eliots hired a boat and sailed down Chichester Harbour for lunch at Wittering. This voyage was less adeptly accomplished than Tom's earlier excursions with Peters: the vessel grounded on a sandbank. Vivien, 'splendid in a boat', took off her stockings, jumped into the water and tried, unsuccessfully, to push.[66] Attempting to sort things, Tom broke a boathook. Eventually he anchored and they all waded ashore on planks across tidal mud. Peters's visit and this nautical fiasco meant sailing was very much in Tom's mind around the time he finished 'Gerontion', with its mention of seagulls and hazardous Belle Isle.

Again he pondered being American in England. On the whole he loved having escaped his homeland's 'gregariousness'. In London he could be 'an individual', finding more easily the contemplative solitariness he needed as a writer, yet, when he wanted it, enjoying ready access to like-minded literary friends. If Vivien thought Peters too boyish, Tom found himself reflecting now that not just his 'American friends' but 'any American I meet' manifested '*immaturity of feeling*, childishness'. He discerned a maturity in English society, yet never quite felt part of it. As he wrote to Henry, 'Don't think that I find it easy to live over here. It is damned hard work to live with a foreign nation and cope with them – one is always coming up against differences of feeling that make one feel humiliated and lonely. One remains always a foreigner – only the lower classes can assimilate. It is like being always on dress parade – one can never relax. It is a great strain.'[67] Yet he liked being valued for his particular talents in a literary metropolis. Being a foreigner in England was 'never dull'.[68] 'America outstrips the world in the development of the text-book', he wrote that summer, well aware that it was imaginative writing, not text-books, that compelled him.[69]

Hints in his poetry and prose register deeper disturbance. 'We may not be great lovers; but if we had a genuine affair', Tom wrote in the *Egoist*, 'with a real poet of any degree we have acquired a monitor to avert us when we are not in love'. He was writing about poetry here, not about his personal life, yet his imagery and preoccupation with the 'close analogy between the sort of experience which develops a man and the sort of experience which develops a writer' are striking, given what was happening in his marriage. Published during July, the piece considers how literary development can become advanced in 'a soul left immature in living' and on how 'difficult' it is for a writer 'to mature in America'; it must have been written around the time of the visit of the supposedly childish Peters.[70] Perhaps the way Tom describes Peters to his mother as 'the most lovable fellow in the world', as 'really devoted to me' and 'devoted to his mother', reveals a shared, tacit acknowledgement that Peters may have been gay.[71]

Like most people, Tom was alert to a spectrum of sexual experience. This alertness powers some of his shrewdest work. In summer 1919 he wrote, for instance, of the 'passion' involved in being 'intimate' with another writer, and of how perhaps 'not one man in each generation is great enough to be intimate with Shakespeare'. The language of love here describes relations between male writers, and there is a shifting between procreative sexuality and the implied homoerotic. 'Experience in living may leave the literary embryo still dormant', Tom contends, whereas there is an important relationship that one can have with another author which is undeniably quickening. Probably uppermost in his mind was his own transformational relationship with Laforgue, or, perhaps, with John Donne, about whose 'experience' and ability to 'penetrate' he had written in his poem 'Whispers of Immortality'. Pondering such relationships, he continued:

This relation is a feeling of profound kinship, or rather of a peculiar personal intimacy, with another, probably a dead author. It may overcome us suddenly, on first or after long acquaintance; it is certainly a crisis; and when a young writer is seized with his first passion of this sort he may be changed, metamorphosed almost, within a few weeks even, from a bundle of second-hand sentiments into a person. The imperative intimacy arouses for the first time a real, an unshakeable confidence. That you possess this secret knowl-edge, this intimacy, with the dead man, that after few or many years or centuries you should have appeared, with this indubitable claim to distinction; who can penetrate at once the thick and dusty circumlocutions about his reputation, can call yourself alone his friend: it is something more than *encouragement* to you. It is a cause of development, like personal relations in life. Like personal intimacies in life, it may and probably will pass, but it will be ineffaceable.[72]

Daringly but perceptively, Tom applies erotic language to the experience of a writer's empowering reading of another author. Since most of the poets he read were male, and since, at the start of this piece, he presents the writer as 'a man', the homoerotic element in the imagery is inevitable; but his use of it seems at least partly conscious. When he goes on to talk of 'lovers' and 'friendship', he is overt and alert. To a degree he is being provocative, but he is also drawing on gay mores familiar to him in Bloomsbury, at Garsington and elsewhere. Not just Lytton Strachey and Virginia Woolf (who idealised androgyny in literature) enjoyed same-sex relationships and flirtations; Vivien felt a teasing attraction to the apparently bisexual Mary Hutchinson whom she called 'little cat' later in 1919, signing off a letter, 'Goodnight my dear. When may I come and spend the night? I embrace you. V.'[73]

While both Tom and Vivien could be teasing on occasion with members of their own sex, that teasing seems to have gone no further than play. Vivien thought 'the sex business' made 'a vast difference' between her and Mary Hutchinson, even if 'we are very much alike'.[74] If what Tom writes about 'intimacy' between writers is conditioned by what he had sensed in Peters, or (some might argue) in Jean Verdenal, to suggest this is not to assert either that he slept with those men or even that he wanted to. The 'affair' he was closest to was that of his wife; when he wrote in July's *Egoist*, 'We may not be great lovers', those words might relate to his own marital predicament. Yet what this piece (whose use of quotations drawn on in 'Gerontion' indicates its closeness to his poetic imaginings) does indicate is that, as with the figure of Tiresias in *The Waste Land*, so here Tom's literary imagination passes readily and fearlessly across a wide sexual spectrum. This strengthened him as a writer. He composed his contribution to the *Egoist* when he was considering embarking on another long poem to set beside 'Gerontion', and when, having just read new work by Conrad Aiken, he was pondering links between writing, 'psycho-analysis' and the 'borderline of the subliminal'.[75] In his poetry, as in his prose, he investigated such territory with daring, but also with a subtlety that some critics belie when, lacking clear evidence, they attempt to read back too crudely from his writings into his conduct in life or to conscript, for whatever cause, his sexuality. His imagination was polymorphous; his mind did not run on one track.

One thing that obsessed him, however, was tradition. He was coming to see the poet as a tradition bearer; in this context, not least, his imaging of poets as passionately overwhelmed by their reading should be understood. 'We do not imitate, we are changed; and our work is the work of the changed man; we have not borrowed, we have been quickened, and we become bearers of a tradition.'[76] Using rather different imagery, he would restate this perception a few months later in 'Tradition and the Individual Talent'.

From Aiken's 'Senlin: A Biography', which Tom discussed briefly in print in June 1919, he filched (or stole back) some elements. Aiken had written of how 'The city dissolves about us'; conscious of Tom's earlier work, he had sought to fuse individual and urban consciousness in a metropolis 'Dumbly observing the burial of its dead'. In 'The Burial of the Dead' and elsewhere in *The Waste Land* Tom would mix familiar urban with other, more dreamlike images, from a violin and horns to bells and lilacs – all present in 'Senlin'.[77] He thought Aiken in that poem 'oversensitive and worried'.[78] Tom, who had his own worries, sought not to imitate his friend, but to outdo him now in the long poem he was planning. Its gestation would be painfully slow.

Vivien shared some of her husband's preoccupations. They were both 'carried away' by *Ulysses*, though Tom realised that few other people in London were; sadly, by the publication of the thigh-smacking, panting and sweating Blazes Boylan episode in the *Little Review*, Vivien began to find Joyce 'abominable'.[79] Threats of prosecution had halted serialisation of *Ulysses* in both the *Egoist* and the *Little Review*. Harriet Weaver and Dora Marsden decided to suspend publication of the *Egoist*, but before they did so Tom prepared to publish his most significant essay there. He was conceptualising 'Tradition and the Individual Talent' in early July when he wrote to Mary Hutchinson (whom more and more he had enjoyed visiting, and to whom he had recently sent Pound's *Personae*) about the need for 'civilisation which is impersonal, traditional' and 'which forms people unconsciously'. A transposed American, he explained that by 'tradition' he did not mean simply 'stopping in the same place'; deliberately, one had to develop a '*historical sense*'.[80]

Tom's essay would appear in two parts, printed in the *Egoist*'s final two issues. In part one he wrote, also, of contemporary literature's relationship with the dead, but did not deploy the imagery of lovers. When he first set out his ideas to Mary Hutchinson, however, there were hints of flirtatiousness: writing of 'you', Tom seems to mean Mary herself (whom

Vivien admired as 'such a "*civilised*" rebel'), though she may have represented, too, an English culture which remained sometimes hard for him
to read.

> I don't know whether I think you more complicated than you are
> – but I have fewer *delusions* about you than you think – but no doubt
> a great deal of *ignorance*. I certainly don't recognise the portrait you
> hold up as painted by me. But remember that I am a *metic* – a
> foreigner, and that I *want* to understand you, and all the background
> and tradition of you. I shall try to be frank – because the attempt is
> so very much worthwhile with you – it is very difficult with me –
> both by inheritance and because of my very suspicious and cowardly
> disposition. But I may simply prove to be a savage.[81]

Inevitably, Tom the *metic* thought of his father when packages arrived
from St Louis in early July containing childhood treasures and the paternal
bathrobe. When he saw the great 'care' with which his mother had packed
them, he almost wept.[82] He went to Garsington for the weekend of 12–13
July, but Vivien was 'in bed with cold' both days.[83] The following weekend
she and her husband travelled to Eastbourne to stay with the Schiffs. Vivien
found this 'unsatisfactory': the Schiffs were 'very fatigueing [*sic*] & irri-
tating to me', though 'Tom got on allright.'[84] It could be hard when her
husband was lionised; she took pride in his talent, yet did not welcome
being treated as his appendage. Still jobless, she took up an afternoon
dressmaking class. 'Where would I be without my dirty piece of crochet
which I have been doing for five years, or my failures of dresses and
underclothes?' She went, too, to the Russian Ballet with friends, but, tired
much of the time, worried she 'looked horrible'.[85]

His writing, however, attracted further admirers. Recently returned from
active service, twenty-seven-year-old Richard Aldington, his predecessor
Sometimes she felt too ill to go out at all. She took to her bed with a
terrible migraine after Lady Ottoline came to tea on 23 July, leaving Tom
to head off to the ballet with the Hutchinsons. Yet Tom, too, was ailing.
Before visiting the Schiffs, Vivien found him '*IM*possible – full of nerves,
really not well, very bad cough, very morbid and grumpy'; she complained
to Mary Hutchinson, 'He gets angry and stubborn.'[86] As soon as they
returned from Eastbourne Tom went to his doctor, John Robert Whait,
whose practise was at 124 Finchley Road in Hampstead and whose interests included neurology.[87] More than once Whait advised Tom to rest.
Conscious he needed dental work also, he was in bed 'several times' in
July and August, 'very much run down'.[88]

as assistant editor at the *Egoist*, wrote to express 'admiration' and 'envy' of his gifts as a critic; Aldington, the dashing young officer-poet of *War and Love*, had been struck particularly by Tom's incisiveness in the July *Egoist* article, though he felt obliged to add that he disliked Tom's verse greatly: 'it is over-intellectual and afraid of those essential emotions which make poetry'.[89] Later, he came to realise Tom's avoidance of sentimentality enhanced poetic power. Yet if some English men of letters praised aspects of Tom's talent, he continued to provoke American objections for transplanting himself. Just after his father's death he had received a letter from President Eliot, formerly of Harvard, asking him about his situation. During the summer, they corresponded further. Justifying residence in England in terms of its practical and intellectual benefits, Tom cited the example of Henry James; perhaps aware that some at Harvard were still hoping to recruit him, President Eliot found it 'quite unintelligible' that 'you or any other young American scholar can forego the privilege of living in the genuine American atmosphere – a bright atmosphere of freedom and hope'. It was just such facile optimism that Tom had fled. Where he sought a cosmopolitan, international literature, President Eliot countered that 'Literature seems to me highly climatic and national as yet; and will it not be long before it becomes independent of these local influences, and addresses itself to an international mind?'[90] This senior Eliot wanted a much more junior Eliot back in his Unitarian home.

Tom was adamant. That summer he considered several ideas of national culture, not just American. Irish literature involved 'crudity and egoism', though these qualities in some of Yeats's work and in *Ulysses* were exploited 'to the point of greatness'.[91] Thinking about 'the Romantic Generation in England', Tom detected 'decadence' (albeit 'decadence of genius') in Wordsworth and 'immaturity of genius' in Keats and Shelley; at least the German Romanticism of Goethe showed a 'completely awakened intelligence'.[92] 'Scotch literature' had something akin to the book culture of the New England he had left behind: flickering in its achievement, it had become 'provincial'. 'Edinburgh in 1800 . . . is analogous to Boston in America fifty years later'; inevitably, 'the important men turn to the metropolis' of London. 'The basis for one literature is one language.' This view saw America, Scotland and Ireland as peripheries nourishing the central tradition of a language rooted in England. The expatriate American cautioned against the 'intemperate and fanatical spirit' of France's Charles Maurras, who denounced undigested 'foreign forces' threatening French literature.[93] Tom thought Britain faced no such imminent danger.

These arguments are debatable: the assumption that 'The basis for one literature is one language' can seem self-evident; but it is equally apparent that the literature of England has been produced in several languages, including Latin, Old French and English, while the literature of Scotland – ranging from Gaelic and Scots to Old Norse – is even more polyglot.[94] Perversely, in 'Was There a Scottish Literature?' Tom never mentions Robert Burns, Walter Scott or Robert Louis Stevenson. However, he was formulating confidently the thinking on which his own work depended, and England was central to his internationalised view. In his mind, too, at this time were techniques such as Tristan Tzara's Dadaist mixing of French and alien, even on occasion Indic-sounding elements; Tom quotes 'Bonjour sans cigarette tzantzanza / ganga'. He cites uses of rhetoric in Elizabethan drama, from 'the furibund fluency of old Hieronymo' to Shakespeare's Cleopatra seen in a consciously dramatic light; he takes words from the famous speech beginning, 'The barge she sat in . . .' Unexpected patterns were generated by his panoptic examination of traditions: links, for instance, between 'Dickens' and Elizabethan drama.[95] All these perceptions, and even particular passages that caught Tom's ear, would be reconfigured in *The Waste Land*.

Though he may have revised it after his return, he seems to have been composing at least the first part of 'Tradition and the Individual Talent' before, on 9 August 1919, he set off for a French holiday. Following his July letter to Mary Hutchinson discussing 'tradition' and the 'impersonal', a 6 August letter to her (requesting the return of a draft of 'Gerontion') considers relations between 'individuals' and 'groups'.[96] Published in the September *Egoist*, his essay continued to contemplate national literatures: 'Every nation, every race, has not only its own creative, but its own critical turn of mind.' He also cautioned against looking for those aspects of a poet's oeuvre which least resemble the productions of other poets; instead, 'the most individual parts of his work may be those in which the dead poets, his ancestors, assert their immortality most vigorously'. This is what it means to be part of a tradition. Yet the essay glides away from ideas of national traditions to a wider concept of what tradition might signify. Indeed, probably spurred by his reaction against his own national tradition – though not mentioning America – he asserts counterintuitively that tradition 'cannot be inherited, and if you want it you must obtain it by great labour'. To do so involves acquiring 'the historical sense' (he repeats the phrase he had used to Mary Hutchinson), which brings with it awareness 'not only of the pastness of the past, but of its presence'. This sense compels the poet to write with a deep awareness of his own time; he needs, too, a feeling that the 'whole of the literature of Europe from Homer and within it the whole of the literature of his own country has a simultaneous existence and composes a simultaneous order'.⁹⁷ The historical sense makes a writer simultaneously traditional and contemporary.

Eurocentric, taking in England and its literature, but also internationally-minded, this essay was Tom's greatest manifesto, his 'programme for the *métier* of poetry'. No poet or artist could be appreciated alone; each must be set alongside the dead poets of many earlier generations. Only then could significance be assessed. There are some parallels between such a way of thinking and J. G. Frazer's comparative method in anthropology – invoked, perhaps, in Tom's later book title, *The Sacred Wood*. Yet if this project seemed to place a poet in conformity with the dead, it entailed, too, disruption.

The necessity that he shall conform, that he shall cohere, is not one-sided; what happens when a new work of art is created is something that happens simultaneously to all the works of art which preceded it. The existing monuments form an ideal order among themselves, which is modified by the introduction of the new (the really new) work of art among them. The existing order is complete before the new work arrives; for order to persist after the supervention of novelty, the *whole* existing order must be, if ever so slightly, altered; and so the relations, proportions, values of each work of art toward the whole are readjusted; and this is conformity between the old and the new. Whoever has approved this idea of order, of the form of European, of English literature, will not find it preposterous that the past should be altered by the present as much as the present is directed by the past. And the poet who is aware of this will be aware of great difficulties and responsibilities.

Writing this, Tom set out to achieve what he believed his fellow American Henry James had accomplished: to become fully European. In the twenty-first century that may sound odd, presumptuous, too Eurocentric. Yet for Tom it was a move beyond the limitations of national sensibilities that was enabled by being a '*metic*', by discovering that there was a 'mind of Europe' and accepting this as 'the mind of his own country' – 'more important than his own private mind'. Such an overarching 'mind' to which the poet had his crucial relationship might change and develop, but did not improve. Neither Homer nor the prehistoric rock art of 'the Magdalenian draughtsmen' nor Shakespeare went out of date. Requiring 'learning', and depending on 'relations', Tom's aesthetic may owe something to his philosophical training – and not least to his interest in 'relativism' and anthropology – as well as to his upbringing and poetic gift.⁹⁸

This way of thinking about literature across great swathes of cultures was something encouraged by Rémy de Gourmont's 1902 *Le Problème du style*. De Gourmont ranged from Homer and the Vedas to modern fiction and poetry; he admired and wrote about Laforgue and the Symbolists. Like Pound, Tom thought him a 'great critic'.[99] The 'knowledge' that mattered to poets, Tom argued, was not simply that of 'examinations'. It was something better: a sense of tradition to which the poet must continually 'surrender'. As a result, 'The progress of an artist is a continual self-sacrifice, a continual extinction of personality.'[100]

Such 'self-sacrifice' sounds tinged with the religion and family values of his childhood. He presents poetry as a demanding calling, and tradition as a form of communion linking the living to the dead. Yet his talk of 'extinction' also hints that poetry can offer a way out of dilemmas in personal life. The artistic process purges away irrelevant quirks of 'personality' in an art that may 'approach the condition of science' in its 'depersonalisation'. As Tom explained things a month or two later, 'In the man of scientific or artistic temper the personality is distilled into the work, it loses its accidents.' It becomes 'a permanent point of view, a phase in the history of mind'.[101]

Tom left his readers – and one wonders how many were able to do so – contemplating what happens when 'a bit of finely filiated platinum is introduced into a chamber containing oxygen and sulphur dioxide'.[102] Like so many of his most striking pieces of writing, this one was produced when he was feeling unwell. Once again, it was as if illness let him release material that had been building up, but which he could not otherwise let out. Making sure the piece was ready to appear in the September *Egoist*, he then set off without Vivien but with the draft of 'Gerontion', for his French holiday. 'Perhaps', he exclaimed to Mary Hutchinson in a letter, 'I won't ever come back!'[103]

On 9 August, a very hot Saturday, Vivien saw Tom off at 5 p.m. at London's Waterloo station. She was going to Eastbourne for a fortnight with the Schiffs, taking her dressmaking with her; he was catching an overnight boat train which would reach Le Havre at 8 a.m. on Sunday morning. Having crossed the Channel for the first time since the war had ended, he soon got into conversation with a French couple. He sailed with them for an hour on a small steamer from Le Havre across the mouth of the Seine to Trouville, a pretty resort town frequently depicted in its airy brightness by the painter Eugène Boudin. Tom delighted in the 'blazing bright August day, the boat crowded with people going to the races, and men with violins and singers passing their hats'. Out of England, he became elated: 'It was all so French and so sudden that I was dazed by it.'[104] Then he boarded a train from Trouville to Paris. A taxi via the place de la Concorde let him catch another train south. Slightly embarrassed because he had forgotten how to recognise some of the French coins, he had counted out his money slowly for the taxi driver, whose honesty was impressive. "'That's enough'", the man said, 'indicating a small tip'. Happy, Tom insisted on giving him more: "'That's because I have not been in Paris for eight years.'"[105] The driver roared with laughter, waving as he sped off. Tom travelled overnight south to Limoges, then changed trains, heading into the Dordogne at the start of his three-week vacation.

With a rucksack on his back, stepping off the train at Périgueux at 7.30 a.m. and looking for breakfast, he remembered being there before as a student in January 1911. Ahead of him now lay a walking tour through the Dordogne and Corrèze regions, a part of France Ezra Pound had written about a few years earlier in his poem 'Near Perigord' – all medieval castles, pine trees, poplars and rivers 'filled with water-lilies'.[106] Tom found it 'beautiful', and there to meet him on his arrival was Pound himself.[107] Tom's delight was no less for the wave of tiredness that hit him: as soon as they reached the hotel, he went to bed and slept till lunchtime. Then, 'I stuffed myself with good French food.'[108]

They spent several days together in Excideuil, the village where Pound and his wife Dorothy were holidaying from Toulouse. With its narrow streets, pale stone dwellings, castle associated with troubadour poetry and ruined tenth-century monastery, Excideuil was a fine place in which to recharge. Sunburnt, Tom savoured the taste of fresh melons, mushrooms called ceps, free-range country eggs, truffles, and, as he put it, 'good wine and good cheese and cheerful people'.[109] Lloyds Bank this was not; he loved it. He feasted too on 'Roman ruins, and tall white houses, and gorgeous southern shrubs, and warm smells of garlic – donkeys – ox carts'.[110] Leaving Dorothy sketching, he and Pound hiked together through the small, picturesque medieval towns of Thivier (proud of its foie gras and set between the Rivers Cole and Touroulet) and Brantôme on the Cole with its beautiful abbey and historic bell tower, said to be among the oldest in France. Occasionally, Tom postcarded Vivien. Pound informed Dorothy, 'T. has 7 blisters.'[111] When Tom showed him 'Gerontion', his friend scribbled suggestions on it; if Pound's poetry is a trustworthy record, Tom also revealed something of his ongoing wrestling with religion: 'I am afraid of the life after death.' Then he paused and added with satisfaction that at last he had managed to shock his companion.[112] Even in the French sunshine a dark substratum of religious anxiety continued to perturb him, filling him at times with a sense of dispossession, of emptiness, though usually he hid this from his friends.

After Pound headed back to rejoin his wife, Tom walked on alone to see the Magdalenian prehistoric art of the grottoes at Font de Gaume and Les Eyzies, south of Périgueux. His mention of 'Magdalenian draughtsmen' in 'Tradition and the Individual Talent' suggests that he had those places in mind when he wrote the essay, but, given that it had to be typeset for publication in the September *Egoist*, and that Tom got back from France on 31 August, he may have been anticipating his trip when he wrote it. On Tom's return, his wife was surprised to see he had 'begun to grow a beard'; Pound was bearded, but for Tom this was an unusual look.[113] Though she had not told him when she wrote to him in France, Vivien had felt ill during his absence, as had the dog Dinah. Tom's return was 'Very nice at first', but in her diary Vivien added the words 'depressed in evening'.[114] Later that week, Dinah grew worse: Tom accompanied Vivien in a taxi to take the dog to the vet, who 'put her to death at once'.[115]

The next day Vivien felt dreadful, but spent the morning packing. She and Tom were off to the coast, to Bosham. The weather was good, and there was a pleasant picnic with the Hutchinsons. Vivien stayed in Bosham for several weeks; Tom came down from the bank at weekends. Sometimes she felt 'very very nervous'.[116] She had a pain in her side and, though she enjoyed sea bathing, sketching and long talks with Mary, her exhaustion returned; she complained of neuralgia. Meanwhile, in London, Tom's new Lloyds Bank Information Department had been set up, giving him a 'fine impressive room' one floor above the entry level at 75 Lombard Street. Here, at the heart of British imperial finance, he could work at a table beside a large south-facing window looking out 'over the square toward the Mansion House'.[117] Bearded, he was a rarity in the City, and might well make a bad impression. The clean-shaven young ex-army officer Aldington feared as much when he arranged for the hirsute banker to meet the considerably older editor of *The Times Literary Supplement*, Bruce Richmond, on 29 September. Richmond wanted to know if Tom would write for the paper. In 'derby hat and an Uncle Sam Beard', Tom, thought Aldington, 'looked perfectly awful, like one of those comic-strip caricatures of Southern hicks'.[118] Richmond, whose reviewers had damned Tom's earlier work, was not deterred, but wary. He published just two pieces by this young American during the next twelve months.

France had refreshed Tom, and he knew it. Hoping to go to Italy the following year, he was wondering if, instead of his travelling to America, his mother might visit him. He tried to convince his brother that this plan would give their mother 'the chance to rest that she badly needs' after her bereavement and her proposed removal to Massachusetts.[119] For the moment, because Murry had gone to the Riviera with Katherine Mansfield whose tuberculosis was worsening, Tom had extra commissions for the *Athenaeum*. He was writing several reviews, including what became his celebrated piece on *Hamlet* – 'the "Mona Lisa" of literature', but a 'failure'.[120] Convinced that 'the notes upon poets by a poet' were worth reading, he was willing to risk unusual and provocative judgements: George Chapman (whose work he used in 'Gerontion') was a 'great poet', fit to set beside Donne.[121] The 'failure' of *Hamlet*, this play about 'the "guilt of a mother"', came from the fact that, 'like the sonnets', it was 'full of some stuff that the writer could not drag to light, contemplate, or manipulate into art'.[122]

As he considered embarking on a new, long poem of his own which would deal with, among other things, problems of sexual relations and religion, Tom attributed to Shakespeare difficulties that he was having to face himself. He was fascinated by *Hamlet* as 'a stratification': it 'represents the efforts of a series of men, each making what he could out of the work of his predecessors'. This makes Shakespeare's play sound a little like a repeated ritual of the sort Tom had considered at Harvard; it conjures up, too, his own poems where, through quotation and allusion, he builds on, alters and recontextualises the work of earlier poets. Consideration of *Hamlet* led him to confront another challenge essential to his poetry: how to express emotion. He did not emote as, say, Murry did. Several critics censured Tom's verse as unfeeling. Instead, he argued,

> The only way of expressing emotion in the form of art is by finding an 'objective correlative'; in other words, a set of objects, a situation, a chain of events which shall be the formula of that *particular* emotion; such that when the external facts, which must terminate in sensory experience, are given, the emotion is immediately evoked.[123]

This assumption that great art finds an 'exact equivalence' for emotion, so that the precise emotion can be recreated in the reader, seems too neat. It rather assumes all readers can be controlled in an identical manner. Yet finding a way to eschew sentimentality while profoundly moving the reader's feelings was of fundamental importance.

Hamlet, Tom argues, experiences a 'disgust' provoked by his mother's conduct, a disgust that is excessive and goes far beyond that behaviour: 'It is thus a feeling which he cannot understand; he cannot objectify it, and it therefore remains to poison life and obstruct action.' Tom's writing about this resonates more generally in ways that include not just his literary audience but also himself.

The intense feeling, ecstatic or terrible, without an object or exceeding its object, is something which every person of sensibility has known; it is doubtless a study to pathologists. It often occurs in adolescence: the ordinary person puts these feelings to sleep, or trims down his feeling to fit the business world; the artist keeps it alive by his ability to intensify the world to his emotions.[124]

In another piece written around this time, Tom saw contemporary poets as divided between struggles to convey 'pure feeling for which there is no equivalent in the visible world' and perhaps less ambitious attempts to write according to the doctrine of 'the Image'.[125] He sought in his own poetry to negotiate between these, yet was preoccupied, too, by something deeply bottled up.

The most profound disturbances in his own adolescence would seem to have been around sex and his insistent shyness, and around the religion linked to his mother and father. Marriage to Vivien, sexual difficulties and living with adultery had only heightened his discomfort; philosophical investigations had quickened both his scepticism and a confused religious hunger. Later in 1919, considering the sermon as 'perhaps the most difficult form of art', his poet's imagination would do what no one had done before: connect the Church of England sermons of Donne and Lancelot Andrewes with 'the Fire-Sermon preached by the Buddha'.[126] Tom's complex knot of feelings and thoughts about loss, sex and religion had not yet found full expression, even if 'Gerontion' was a crafted groan of despair. Reviewing recent work by Aiken (which, yet again, contained inferior echoes of his own) he saw a failed but 'consistent direction' which was 'to express the inexpressible by expressing the impossibility of expression'.[127]

As so often in his life, success and hurtful failure intersected awkwardly. He felt physically healthy again. His career at the bank was taking off; he looked prosperous: for the winter, with Vivien's encouragement, he bought a 10-guinea coat of 'the best cloth, and lined with wool'.[128] With luck, in early 1920 London would see two volumes of his essays – one on the art of poetry, expected from the Egoist Press after the demise of the *Egoist* magazine, and the other on Renaissance drama due from the elegant publisher Richard Cobden-Sanderson, son of Bertrand Russell's godfather. Thanks to Quinn's outstanding drive and efficiency, Knopf would be publishing his poetry in New York in the spring. Yet Tom's marriage was freighted with pain, and his sense of religion, occasioning his use of a ferocious tiger image in 'Gerontion', involved distress but little consolation.

On his thirty-first birthday, a Friday, he was in London; Vivien remained at Bosham. She wished she had gone back to be with him, but she had her period and a migraine. Aching, her face grew slightly swollen, but she packed her things to travel to London on the chilly Saturday, only to find a railway strike meant she could not go. Wretched, eventually she paid 30 shillings for a seat in a car leaving Chichester on Monday. She rose at 6 a.m. and wired Tom to say she was coming, but there was a mix-up. In London Vivien waited, exhausted, at Putney Bridge with a hamper and blackberries she had picked to make jam, expecting her husband to arrive; but Tom had gone to London Bridge instead. After two hours and no lunch she abandoned her luggage and managed to get home. Where was Tom? He came back at 7 p.m., having hung on for nearly four hours at London Bridge. They 'wept'.[129]

For society as a whole, these were testing times. As in the United States, so in post-war Britain social unrest led in 1919 to several large-scale strikes. Tom now defined himself as 'Liberal' in politics, but was not in sympathy with the coalition government led by Liberal Prime Minister Lloyd George.[130] Thanks to stoppages, for several days that September he had to walk the four miles to work. However, fresh from hiking greater distances in France, he coped. He was above such things, and, while he might feel distressed in private, could appear loftily elitist. For his new book of poems, the small one (opening with 'Gerontion') to be published in London by Rodker, he chose the title 'Ara Vus Prec', a quotation from Dante meaning 'Now I pray you'. It seemed to him 'non-committal' and 'unintelligible to most people'.[131] He approved of 'the individual against the mob', but this *de haut en bas* tone got him his comeuppance.[132] It turned out that, not knowing Provençal and following a faulty edition of Dante, he had got the quotation wrong. That is why, embarrassingly, the book appeared in December with *Ara Vus Prec* on the title page, but *Ara Vos Prec* on labels pasted outside.

Tom made sure to tell his mother he had been invited to write for *The Times Literary Supplement,* and might be producing 'the Leading Article from time to time. This is the highest honour possible in the critical world of literature.'[133] He also told her he expected to have 'three and possibly four books out next year': new editions of his poems in London and New York, as well as the two planned books of essays. When, in October at the Conference Hall, Westminster, he addressed the Arts League of Service on modern poetry, he reported the size of the audience (three hundred): 'My lecture was said to be a great success.'[134] His need to impress his family remained strong; he was in correspondence, too, with his siblings.

Yet, at a deeper level, his imaginative work was developing. Where his relatively short quatrain poems had stacked allusions to earlier texts and myths in variegated strata, now he was fascinated by ways of doing so, as *Ulysses* did, on a larger scale – one hinted at when 'Tradition and the Individual Talent' ranged from the prehistoric to the contemporary. Reviewing an anthology of Native American chants for the *Athenaeum*, he had no time for these as drawing-room exotica. They did, though, rekindle his sense of the importance of anthropology, that subject whose influence seemed inescapable.

> Within the time of a brief generation it has become evident that some smattering of anthropology is as essential to culture as Rollin's Universal History. Just as it is necessary to know something about Freud and something about [the entomologist] Fabre, so it is necessary to know something about the medicine-man and his works. Not necessary, perhaps not even desirable, to know all the theories about him, to peruse all the works of Miss Harrison, Cooke, Rendel Harris, Lévy-Bruhl or Durkheim. But one ought, surely, to have read at least one book such as those of Spencer and Gillen on the Australians, or Codrington on the Melanesians. And as it is certain that some study of primitive man furthers our understanding of civilized man, so it is certain that primitive art and poetry help our understanding of civilized art and poetry. Primitive art and poetry can even, through the studies and experiments of the artist or poet, revivify the contemporary activities. The maxim, Return to the sources, is a good one. More intelligibly put, it is that the poet should know everything that has been accomplished in poetry (accomplished, not merely produced) since its beginnings – in order to know what he is doing himself. He should be aware of all the metamorphoses of poetry that illustrate the stratifications of history that cover savagery. For the artist is, in an impersonal sense, the most conscious of men; he is therefore the most and the least civilized and civilizable; he is the most competent to understand both civilized and primitive.

More than once in this piece Tom links 'the poet and the anthropologist', but he also connects poet and 'savage'.[135]

He sought to develop what he admired in Pound's new collection *Quia Pauper Amavi* (published by the Egoist Press that October): 'a constant aim with a deliberate and conscious method'. Yet pursuing such a course in poetry would involve him in tapping into his own hidden convulsions and compulsions. His verse in *The Waste Land* would carry a lancing sense of pain that surpassed Pound's sometimes lacquered bookishness. However,

Tom saw that Pound, drawing on aspects of Browning's oeuvre, had found a new way to write poetry.

> As the present is no more than the present existence, the present significance, of the entire past, Mr Pound proceeds by acquiring the entire past; and when the entire past is acquired, the constituents fall into place and the present is revealed. Such a method involves immense capacities of learning and of dominating one's learning, and the peculiarity of expressing oneself through historical masks.[136]

Though he associated his friend with translations and versions of older poems, including several from the Provençal, Tom was fascinated by Pound's recreation of a two-thousand-year-old erotic voice in 'Homage to Sextus Propertius'. In this sequence Latin poetry, rendered into English, had been spliced, concentrated, quoted in snippets and rearranged so that ancient and modern were inextricable. Here was 'a final concentration of the entire past upon the present'.[137] Tom was struck, too, by Pound's new 'Cantos'. Ranging from an account of a Classical rape to details of present-day sounds and sights, they brought together a 'rag-bag' of quotations, allusions and historical parallels in an ambitious attempt to convey universalism.[138] Pound could make this function in a way 'no other poet living' could do.[139] Preoccupied with something similar in Joyce's recent prose, Tom would strive to better these achievements.

A year that had begun with one family death drew to its close with others. Vivien's Aunt Emily died in October. Accompanying her brother to the funeral, Vivien found the experience 'terrible'.[140] In November her beloved aunt Lillia Symes, the only family member present at the Eliots' wedding, passed away suddenly in her flat in Eastbourne. Again, Vivien was deeply distressed. Reminding Tom of his father's demise, further packages of books arrived from St Louis. With the works of Thomas Jefferson lined up in his bookcase, just as once they had been arranged at 2635 Locust Street, he worked on several essays, including his first leading article for *The Times Literary Supplement*.

Determinedly, he stayed up until 3 a.m. one morning to finish it. If it was hard to find time to write such pieces, it was difficult, also, to research them. The British Museum reading room, a wonderful resource, was 'useless', Tom complained, to most people with day jobs since it did not open in the evenings or on Sundays. Instead, he subscribed to the London Library, 'its terms . . . generous and its manners gracious'.[141] Registering there first as a 'journalist', he would be a lifelong supporter of this institution.[142] Today it boasts a wing named after him.

In late November he read the proofs of his books that Rodker and Knopf were soon to publish. He was now a poet with a small but substantial body of work exhibiting both consistency and variety; he had, too, a clear poetic stance. The second part of 'Tradition and the Individual Talent', published in December in the final *Egoist,* confirmed that. 'Honest criticism and sensitive appreciation' were to be 'directed not upon the poet but upon the poetry'. This 'impersonal theory of poetry' made clear it was not what the poet had in him to say that mattered; it was how he said it. There was a crucial difference between personal experience and poetic craftsmanship. Tom was fascinated, he made evident elsewhere at this time, by something in Donne's work: 'the sense of the artist as an Eye curiously, patiently watching himself as a man'.[143]

For the reader, and the poetry, however, it was the crafting that mattered. 'The more perfect the artist, the more completely separate in him will be the man who suffers and the mind which creates; the more perfectly will the mind digest and transmute the passions which are its material.' Yet revealingly, even in writing those words, Tom selected the verb 'suffers', rather than, say, 'loves', 'exults' or 'experiences'; and he chose to equate poetry with a corrosive, damaging material – sulphurous acid. The verse he was authoring now was a poetry of suffering ('Gerontion' is a poem of human corrosion); the last thing he wanted was for this to result in painful invasions of his rigorously guarded privacy. The more, as a poetic 'Eye', he watched his own hurts, the more he stressed impersonality. Instead of presenting poetry as soul-baring, he set it forth as a scientific operation, likening it to the making of sulphurous acid out of two gases, oxygen and sulphur dioxide; only when platinum was present would the gases combine, yet the platinum stayed seemingly 'unaffected'; it remained 'inert, passive, and unchanged'.[144]

Metallic, the poet's mind was that piece of platinum. This arresting analogy fits with Tom's later description of his having had to harden himself 'into a *machine*' so as 'to endure'.[145] Registering and combining materials in striking new ways, the poet's intelligence seems of necessity detached. It is not, this essay explains, 'the intensity, of the emotions' that matters in the making of a poem, but 'the intensity of the artistic process, the pressure, so to speak, under which the fusion takes place'. No good poet expresses what journalists call a '"personality"'. Poets present a medium: poetry. There is deep, clarifying insight in this separation of 'personal emotions, the emotions provoked by particular events in his [the poet's] life' from the 'emotion in his poetry', and in this emphasis on 'the emotion of art' as 'impersonal'. Yet, revealingly, the passages of verse Tom cites as examples often feature reactions to recent death or adultery, whether they come from Dante, *Othello* or Aeschylus. 'Only those who have personality and emotions know what it means to want to escape from these things.'[146]

Tom's thinking may have been sharpened by the discussion of 'person-nalité' in Rémy de Gourmont's essay on style. However, that French writer's presentation of the Flaubert who 'transvasait goutte à goutte' (decanted drop by drop) his sensibility into his work – an idea that fasci-nated Tom – is not quite the same as this theory of impersonality.[147] Transmuting personal sufferings into art might be a way of transcending them while fashioning something worthwhile out of the damage. 'The ways in which the passions and desires of the creator may be satisfied in the work of art are complex and devious.'[148] In one of the finest of all essays about poetry, Tom both concealed and revealed. He gave a superb account of how 'The poet's mind is in fact a receptacle for seizing and storing up numberless feelings, phrases, images, which remain there until all the particles which can unite to form a new compound are present together.'[149] That is how *The Waste Land* would come into being. It is how most poems are made. His 1919 account in 'Tradition and the Individ-ual Talent' is hard to better, even if, with a necessary instinct for self-protection, it hides underlying pain.

For all his consciousness and self-consciousness, Tom's poetry came together by accident as well as strategy. On 19 November 1919, Vivien enjoyed a London concert by African American musicians of the Southern 'Syncopated Orchestra', whose players included Sidney Bechet; such synco-pations reconnected Tom with sounds from his St Louis childhood.[150] His reviewing and evening lectures brought back to him material encountered at Harvard and elsewhere – from the Buddha's Fire Sermon to 'Petronius' – adding to it and keeping it fresh.[151] Inevitably, over the years some phrases, images and sensations had stuck. Now, mixed up with experiences from his recent life, they were almost ready to combust.

Here he was in another country, still receiving packages of his dead father's belongings. Tormented in his marriage, he remained close to Vivien and valued her – as she did him; yet their divergent experiences and behaviours kept them apart. Problematically insistent, too, was his intense link to his ageing mother. At the start of December he wrote, 'I should love to have pyjamas made by you.'[152] He was responding to her offer – sensing it as a gesture of nearness.

He missed the dead: not only his father (to whom he would dedicate his first book of essays), and Jean Verdenal (to whom he dedicated the Knopf edition of his *Poems*), but also others, including Karl Culpin and dead poets to whom he felt at times a preternatural closeness. '*Tu sei ombra ed ombra vedi'* (thou art a shade and a shade thou seest) was a fragment of a ghostly meeting from Dante's *Purgatorio* that appeared unexpectedly in his first *Times Literary Supplement* leader – on Ben Jonson – published that November.[153] Haunted by the literary and unliterary dead, when he wrote about Jonson he argued that we must put 'ourselves into seventeenth-century London' and find a way of 'setting Jonson in our London' to appreciate him not just as a respected dead poet but also as 'a contemporary'. Tom quoted 'the learned, but also the creative' Jonson's soliloquy of a 'ghost' on Rome, with its imagined earthquake-shaken 'towers', its 'ruin', its river and its famous topography. Eventually *The Waste Land* would populate London with the dead as well as the living. It would move present-day urban scenes into the past, into Dante and elsewhere, fusing them in a haunted, often hallucinatory panorama. Tom's technical skill, hoard of learning and profound sense of loss would unite to animate his poem. 'Every creator is also a critic', he argued. As he articulated his thinking in commanding criticism he created a grounding for poetry to come.[154]

His sense of being loss-haunted was hardly unique. Having lived in England throughout World War I, he had a profound experience of deso-lation unfamiliar to most American contemporaries. Almost a million British men had been killed in action; German and other losses were even higher. Richard Aldington and all former soldiers shared this oppressive sense of wasted lives, but non-combatants like Pound had it too. Pound and his wife came to dinner at Crawford Mansions on 17 November 1919, then the Eliots dined with them six days later before going to see *The Duchess of Malfi*. In 'Hugh Selwyn Mauberley' (written in early 1920), Pound articulated how 'There died a myriad' among 'wastage as never before'.[155] Tom, used to seeing Pound's poems in draft, knew the battlefield horrors of the front only at second hand but had heard distressing accounts from his brother-in-law and others. Impressed by the pessimism of his brilliant acquaintance John Maynard Keynes's 1919 *Economic Consequences of the Peace*, he was struck during the aftermath of the war by the 'destitu-tion' and 'starvation in Vienna' amid 'the "Balkanisation" of Europe'.[156]

All too aware of a Europe-wide post-war malaise, in his personal life Tom had experienced bereavement and intimate suffering. He may have been thirty-one in late 1919, but he felt like an old man. Bedridden for a time in mid-December, he was told by his physician 'not to think of going out' for several days more.[157] Dr Whait, whom Vivien summoned, gave him a special spray for his nose, warning him again he might have 'to have the membrane cauterized'. Telling his seventy-six-year-old mother that he always slept on his left side 'because I breathe more easily', he suggested that his ailment was similar to one she had suffered from. In this prematurely aged condition, he was also, he informed her, harbouring a 'New Year's Resolution'. It was '"to write a long poem I have had on my mind for a long time and to prepare a small prose book from my lecture on poetry"'.[158] That poem would become *The Waste Land*.

'Xmas is awful, *awful*', wrote Vivien, but they had a small tree and, as usual, in a consolingly childlike way, they hung up their stockings.[159] Cheques – and 'beautifully made' pyjamas – arrived from Tom's mother whom Vivien hoped might come and visit them in '*April*' which she regarded as 'just in time for the most beautiful time of the year in England'.[160] After Christmas lunch at home, she and Tom went on to Christmas dinner with her parents. Perhaps enthused by the rhythms of the Southern Syncopated Orchestra, she took along a gramophone, but felt the evening was 'not a very nice' one.[161] All Boxing Day, it poured with rain. Vivien ventured to the Schiffs for tea; but she and Tom would spend the next few days apart: he had accepted, but she had turned down, an invitation to visit his friend Sydney Waterlow, to whom he felt obligated and who was now 'a very important official in the Foreign Office'. Tom realised Vivien was sleeping 'very badly'.[162] She felt 'most wretched, & fearfully tired'.[163] They had the chance to rent out the Marlow house, but she was determined they should hang on to it, associating it with a dream of happiness that seemed lost, for the moment at least. On 30 December, now that Tom was back from Waterlow's, they went together to a 'very drunken & rowdy' dinner party at the Hutchinsons. The sexually voracious Nancy Cunard, the beautiful young poet and model Iris Tree, Osbert Sitwell, painter Duncan Grant and others were there, but Vivien, worried she looked unwell, did not enjoy it. Her father was ill; she feared he might die: another ailing old man. 'Glad this awful year is over', reads her diary entry for 31 December. 'Next probably worse'.[164]

14

Professional

In 1920 Tom's annual salary was £500 – a good income for a professional in his early thirties. On 6 January, when he informed his mother he had just been given a pay rise, *The Times* advertised a vacancy for a fully qualified 'clinical pathologist' of comparable age, which paid £600.[1] Including reviewing and other activities, Tom probably earned around that sum. Nevertheless, writing a cheque that day for a £14 dentist's bill, he felt, as so often, that he was not making quite enough to be able to look after Vivien, to maintain his position in society and to buy himself time sufficient for the work – not least the poetry – that he most wanted to create.

Generally he wrote 'in the evenings and Sundays'.[2] On weekdays in his Information Department, he collated economic data from several areas of the English-speaking world and Europe. He was expected to understand economics and as many European languages as necessary. Facts and figures impressed him: 'England and Germany use the most sulphuric acid.'[3] His limited knowledge of industrial chemistry was not great, but did make its mark on 'Tradition and the Individual Talent'. As he won the respect of his bosses at Lloyds, in the wake of the Treaty of Versailles they put him 'in charge of settling all the pre-War Debts between the Bank and the Germans'. This, he informed his mother, was 'an important appointment'.[4] 'Occupied', as he recalled, 'in a humble capacity, with the application of some of the minor financial clauses' of the Treaty of Versailles, he read Keynes's *Economic Consequences of the Peace*, which dealt with social psychology as well as economics.[5] Quoting poetry as well as statistics, Keynes (whom Tom met at Garsington) set forth his view of 'ruin', of 'the fearful convulsions of a dying civilization', of 'nightmare' and the 'morbid'. War debts were 'a menace to financial stability everywhere'.

The peace was flawed; the book's conclusion quotes Shelley's *Prometheus Unbound*: 'In each human heart terror survives / The ruin it has gorged'.[6] For Tom, as for the polymathic Keynes (a generous supporter of artists and writers), poetry and banking were instructively and darkly aligned.

Lacking formal commercial or legal qualifications, though aided by assistants, Tom had to weigh up complex economic issues. He produced financial reviews; he made digests; generating substantial correspondence, he got used to having a secretary. Office personnel changed repeatedly. One of his early clerical assistants, a military officer's wife called Mrs Lord, 'had no knowledge of shorthand and had some difficulty in reading her own handwriting' with the result that she 'occasionally pied the correspondence'. Another secretary, Miss Holt, was the sister of twin boys whom Tom had taught at Highgate School: 'She came to me to weep', he recalled of this typist. Before long, in *The Waste Land*, he would present a figure who has become the most famous typist in English literature. He liked to observe his professional colleagues – whether Mr Saunders, who enjoyed a 'matitudinal visit to Short's Wine Rooms in Pope's Head Alley', or Mr Crewdon, 'a real swell who had been to Uppingham and King's College Cambridge' – but the customers interested him too.[7] Meeting former millhand Sir James Roberts, whose clothing business at Saltaire outside Bradford in Yorkshire had been damaged by the financial consequences of the Russian Revolution, Tom was impressed. Sir James, who had known the Brontës in Haworth, was then in his seventies and so hardly the model for the young 'carbuncular' clerk who forces himself on *The Waste Land*'s typist, but he did provide the impetus for those unsettling lines: 'One of the low on whom assurance sits / As a silk hat on a Bradford millionaire'.[8] Every inch the businessman's son, in white shirt, dark tie and three-piece suit, Tom acted the banker with aplomb, and was respected for it. Yet, eyeing some of his richer friends who enjoyed freer lifestyles, he confided to Lady Ottoline that 'So very few of one's acquaintance realise what it means to have sold the whole of all of one's days, – except at most a month a year – and old age – to a huge impersonal thing like a Bank.'[9]

Bankerly professionalism carried over into his literary dealings too, and sometimes into domestic life. He contained elements of calculating ruthlessness that young poets – not least male ones – often possess. His work for the *Athenaeum* and his *Egoist* editorial activities overlay his earlier experience at the *Harvard Advocate*. Thoroughly familiar with how journals operated, he knew about reviewing from the reviewer's side as well as from the perspectives of author and publisher. He could boost his income by critiquing the same book for two paying periodicals. Professionally he became one of the best networked younger figures in London literary publishing. J. C. Squire had tried to court him to write for the new *London Mercury*. Politely Tom declined; he thought its editorial standards too low. Squire might be 'the cleverest journalist in London', but 'he knows nothing about poetry'.[10] As far as possible, Tom wanted to associate only with people whose professional judgement he trusted. He was more favourably disposed when during January 1920 publisher John Rodker sounded him out about becoming a 'Director' for a 'scheme' he was hatching; at around the same time he was visited by Lincoln McVeagh, a former Harvard student now working with Scofield Thayer at the New York *Dial*, to see if Tom would help secure work from English writers.

Though he introduced McVeagh to Murry, Tom was wary; he didn't want to solicit work from friends, only to find they were not treated with professional courtesy by the *Dial*. So, mixing helpfulness with a certain bossiness and signing himself 'Yours ever, Tom', he wrote direct to Thayer, advising him to come and hire 'a person of discrimination and intimate knowledge of London letters' to commission material 'on the spot'. Thayer might have thought Tom just such a person. However, matters were finessed by John Quinn and others so that Ezra Pound was made 'agent' at a salary of $750 (then worth about £200) per annum. Slyly, Thayer, who had met Pound and knew his name might disconcert people, kept it off the *Dial*'s notepaper.[11]

In March, Tom, who had already used his 'influence to get [Wyndham] Lewis into the *Athenaeum*', seems to have wangled Pound's appointment by Murry as that journal's theatre critic; fed up with England, Pound was spending much of his time in France, so this arrangement was short-lived and not entirely friction-free.[12] Conscious that 'Pound's lack of tact has done him great harm', Tom made sure to deploy manners, tenacity and skill to avoid antagonising influential people, whatever he thought of them. Socialising with minor poets including Osbert Sitwell, four years his junior, he was well aware Sitwell produced 'rather clever imitations of myself'.[13] Observing English society with a foreigner's amusement, he explained to his mother that on 24 February he had dined at the Woolfs' home with Sydney Waterlow, 'Lord Robert Cecil's right hand man' – 'very pompous and smokes cigars'. On Saturday he responded to Sir Algernon Methuen's invitation to have a volume considered for publication.[14] Though the Egoist Press had already announced that they would be publishing Tom's essays, this was a better offer, and he accepted it.[15]

Essay-writing consumed a good deal of his time. Occasionally he contributed to Sydney Schiff's favoured *Art and Letters*; he sent a much revised 'Brief Treatise on the Criticism of Poetry' to Monro's *Chapbook*; he went on writing, provocatively, for the *Athenaeum*, suggesting William

Blake with his 'peculiarly terrifying' honesty was no mere 'wild pet for the supercultivated', and examining why, in the age of 'Mr. James Joyce or Mr. Joseph Conrad', Swinburne's verse was 'no longer' enjoyed. Provocatively, he mocked the 'Civilized Class' for their failure to support performances of plays by Dryden, Webster and other classic English dramatists revived by London's Phoenix Society – a group whose work he championed.[16] All this writing was insightful, and often commandingly professional. For the critic, Tom stated later that year, 'there is no method except to be very intelligent'.[17] Such crisp judgements indicate an authoritative confidence accompanying his sense of being grounded in the art he professed: 'all the best criticism of poetry is the criticism of poets'.[18] His earnest professionalism, his literary socialising and his telling his mother how very busy he was established a pattern which became second nature: using professional obligations to cover up deeper troubles.

There were hints of sadness in verses he quoted. He recalled for their 'beauty' in January 1920 lines of Shelley he had known since boyhood, and that came to haunt him with their melancholy:

Rose leaves, when the rose is dead,
Are heaped for the beloved's bed;
And so thy thoughts, when thou art gone,
Love itself shall slumber on.[19]

It was now over five years since he had asked Aiken to buy roses for Emily Hale, but considerably later when Tom was well into his forties and had visited an English garden with her, those lines came back to him; they help explain why it is not roses but 'rose-leaves' which lie under dust as he ruminates in 'Burnt Norton' on lost possibilities.[20] In early 1920 as an example of Blake's 'naked vision', he quoted a stanza about an unhappy love match:

Love seeketh only self to please,
To bind another to its delight,
Joys in another's loss of ease,
And builds a Hell in Heaven's despite.[21]

Yet there were also moments of affection and respite. Early in the year, one Sunday morning he joined Vivien and one of her women friends for a 'dancing practice'.[22] Both Eliots still enjoyed dancing. He knew they appeared an odd couple, if not to casual observers then certainly to the folks of Bloomsbury and Garsington whose sex lives made their own seem tame. 'I live', Tom explained to Henry in March, 'among a set of people some of whom would probably shock your friends (all of them) terribly by varieties of "immorality" with no pretense; but these people are capable of being shocked in the way that I am. (They may consider myself and Vivien exceptionally moral, but they do not think any the worse of us for that — it merely seems to them interesting).'[23]

Seeking to bring his American family and his London life into balance, Tom used his professional judgement to advise his mother about finances, and pressured her relentlessly to travel to England. Writing to her, his brother Henry found this almost obsessive: 'Tom seems to be worrying himself sick over the prospect of your not going; it seems to be on his mind all the time.'[24] Tom urged her to 'seize the opportunity' and arrive 'next spring'. Otherwise, he would cross the ocean to America, 'because I should regret it every hour of my life if I did not'.[25] Well into her seventies, bereaved, suffering from 'renal troubles' and still having to face moving house to Massachusetts, Lottie Eliot prevaricated.[26] Ostensibly, Tom's reluctance to travel to the States was because even if the bank granted him extra leave, his visit would be painfully short; he wanted his mother to see London and their life there, and maintained he could not afford to pay transatlantic fares for himself and Vivien. Yet, with Woods still trying to recruit him to Harvard that spring, and with Vivien remaining fearful about voyaging to the land of the Eliots or about being ill if Tom went there, other psychological factors were involved. Tom's mother was a clever, sometimes domineering woman. His arguing with her was a battle of love as well as a trial of wills that he needed to win.

For months he had been saving up. He took Vivien to Paris for Easter, securing the necessary leave of absence from the bank. They went to glut themselves on the French capital in springtime: 'Paris est si *gai*' (Paris is so *jolly*), he wrote in a postcard to Mary Hutchinson. Both Eliots were 'very happy' in a post-war city of flourishing patisseries, galleries and dance halls. It was a place where one could enjoy everything from chic new hats to Dadaist magazines; from quaint horse-drawn carts to books and prints sold from lock-up boxes perched on the parapet wall beside the Seine near Notre Dame. Their time was short, but 'nous avons à voir tout' (we want to see the lot), he wrote.[27] Yet, after all their anticipation, Tom caught flu in Paris. They returned exhausted, and almost immediately Vivien went off with friends to rest. Tom soldiered on determinedly, conscious he had a book to deliver to a publisher in June.

Professional literary life brought strain as well as pleasure. As always among poets, there were excitements, jealousies and sniping. Tom happily mocked reviewing: 'From the point of view of any man of the slightest intellect or taste, there is not enough good verse to occupy a reviewer one week out of the year.' However, he was enjoying new verse in manuscript by his close friend and compatriot Pound, whose 'Hugh Selwyn Mauberley' he acclaimed in March. 'There is,' he declared,

no more useful criticism and no more precious praise for a poet than that of another poet:

'Fu miglior fabbro del parlar materno . . .
e lascia dir gli stolti . . .'[28]

These words from Dante's tribute to the supremely musical Provençal poet of heterosexual love Arnaut Daniel (whom Pound had translated) acknowledge him as 'a better craftsman of the mother tongue . . . and let the fools mutter . . .' In Purgatory Arnaut sings as he goes, grieving over his past erotic follies while aspiring towards possible salvation. This passage preoccupied Tom, who had his own secret follies and hopes. Arnaut's speech had already supplied his title *Ara Vos Prec*, and the concluding line in which Arnaut vanishes – 'Poi s'ascose nel foco che gli affina' (Then he hid himself in the fire that refines them) – would feature in *The Waste Land*, a work eventually dedicated to Pound, whom Tom liked to think of as sometimes operating 'behind the mask of Arnaut', as *'il miglior fabbro'*.[29]

There was a competitive aspect to Tom's friendship with Pound. The two Americans read one another's work regularly, occasionally with envy; Pound had a book of essays forthcoming from Boni and Liveright in New York early that summer; Tom still had not finished his. Cultural incest was part of avant-garde life, but could be enlivening. Mischievously, Tom in the *Athenaeum* had already described his own verse as 'curious'; gladly he had written the booklet *Ezra Pound: His Metric and Poetry*. However, the niceties of professional conduct were harder to negotiate when Murry wanted Tom to review for the *Athenaeum* a new verse play by none other than Murry himself. Featuring locations including 'Nectarine' and 'Aspidestra', and with characters 'to whom he gives names like Cinnamon, Angelica, Caraway, and Vanilla Bean', Murry's play was dreadful. Tom managed to write fifteen hundred words around it without ever saying just how bad it was, while maintaining a teasing tone that Murry may have smiled at wincingly: 'It is . . . a real pleasure, an exceptional pleasure, to have a patient like Mr. Murry extended on the operating table; we need our sharpest instruments, and steadiest nerves, if we are to do him justice.'[30] Tom's review appeared on 14 May; the Eliots dined with Murry and Mansfield that evening. After Tom and Vivien left,

Mansfield wrote in her diary that the room was still '*quivering*'. If there was jokey unease between the two men, between the women there was intense dislike. 'She really repels me', Mansfield confided to her diary. 'I am so fond of Elliot . . . But this teashop creature . . .' Tom sided with his wife, 'leaning towards her, admiring, listening, making the most of her', and later told Pound that Mansfield was 'a dangerous WOMAN' (the capitals carry a sexist spite), and that she and her husband were 'sentimentalists'. [31]

Yet Murry and Tom could be allies of a sort. In the hothouse, gossipy world of Bloomsbury and environs, Virginia Woolf, publisher of Tom's 1919 *Poems*, revealed later in 1920 that Murry had asked her to review that very publication for the *Athenaeum*. Eventually Leonard Woolf had written the piece, and, at Murry's request, Virginia had reviewed in the *Athenaeum* Murry's own essay, *The Critic in Judgment*, despite having published it herself at the Hogarth Press. Now, if Tom wished, Leonard 'would very much like' to write about Tom's book of essays – again for the *Athenaeum*. [32] Murry then went on to review Tom's book elsewhere, while Leonard Woolf produced a further appraisal of Tom's work, quoting with approval a poem which the Woolfs had published.

If such shenanigans seem less than professional, they are hardly unknown in the literary world, and neither Tom nor his reviewers wrote sycophantically. He continued to depend on personal contacts. In America one of the most important of these would be his wife's old admirer, Scofield Thayer. He cabled Tom in March to check about the suitability of E. E. Cummings as a benign reviewer for the Knopf edition of Tom's poems. In London, Tom's publisher Rodker brought out Pound's *Hugh Selwyn Mauberley* in June; Tom suggested to Rodker that it be sent to the *Athenaeum* for review. His position at the heart of London's poetry and reviewing scene made T. S. Eliot a figure that younger writers, including the twenty-seven-year-old Yorkshire-born poet and critic Herbert Read, looked up to. Often, as Tom made clear to his mother that summer, all this made him feel older than he was.

> I do not know why it is, but men five years younger than I seem to me much younger, and if they become my friends I feel a sort of paternal responsibility, yet men five years older seem to me about the same age. Murry is my age, Pound is four years older, Lewis is five years older, and Strachey is nearly forty; so is Sydney Waterlow. But Osbert Sitwell and his brother, Aldington, Huxley, Herbert Read, and several Americans whom I only know by correspondence, all seem children almost. [33]

Ill health, his own and Vivien's, added to their sense of being older than their years. 'Tired and depressed', Tom was off to Marlow for three or four weeks, he told Murry in April, 'to rest and to work'.[34]

He was polishing his book of essays, *The Sacred Wood*, and overworking. Murry seems to have suggested he might apply for a lectureship at 'a provincial university'; having avoided Harvard, Tom chose not to. If he ever left the bank, he favoured the relative freedom of journalism, rather than the 'fatiguing and worrying' business of endless lectures.[35] Throughout spring and summer 1920 he and Vivien engaged in bouts of flat-hunting. In the wake of several arrests near Crawford Mansions, they decided there was too much 'noise and sordidness'; Tom was aware of 'prostitution' in the area.[36] Annoyingly, the flats they viewed were unsuitable or unaffordable. They contemplated living without a servant; but, so long as finances allowed, aimed to keep on their current domestic, Ellen. She would work for them only if they did not move too far off.

Exhausted or not, Tom kept abreast of literary developments. Probably it was on 27 May in *The Times Literary Supplement* that he first came across a detailed account of Jessie L. Weston's new book *From Ritual to Romance*. In a substantial piece the reviewer showed how, gladly accepting Frazer's *Golden Bough* and anthropologists' accounts of vegetation rites, Miss Weston claimed 'to have connected the secret ritual of a Fertility Cult dating from far-away antiquity, and its survivals in the present, with the Grail romance of the Middle Ages'. Fascinated by Arthurian tales since boyhood, and long familiar with links between anthropological and literary materials, Tom was interested in Weston's argument that more recent narratives were patterned on ancient ones. As the sympathetic reviewer explained,

> in what relates to the Fisher King and the Waste Land, there is evidently postulated a close connexion between the vitality of the one and the prosperity of the other; and the hero's task consists in renewing the vigour of the ruler so that the land may cease to be desolate. The case is excellent, and excellently well pleaded. Behind the elements Christian or semi-Christian, and the Celtic elements of the high legend, there is reference to the hoary mystery cults of Fertility of Life that is victorious over evil and darkness and death. The Holy Grail and the Golden Bough henceforth are like to be associated in memory.[37]

Exactly when Tom got hold of Weston's book is not clear, but the Houghton Library at Harvard possesses a first edition with his inscription:

'This is the copy I had before writing The Waste Land.' It is virtually unannotated. Pages 137–40 and 141–4 remained uncut.[38] Nonetheless, this book gave him a mythic structure in which the sexually wounded mythical Fisher King seeks to be healed in order that the waste land may thrive. Weston linked that structure to the Arthurian Grail quest and Wagner's *Parsifal*. Bringing in everything from Tarot cards to Sanskrit scriptures, she ranged across history and cultures providing antecedents and parallels in a search for fertility and healing. Much more jaggedly and emotionally, as its parts came together over the next eighteen months, Tom's long poem would follow a related trajectory.

All this took time to happen. More pressingly, Conrad Aiken was in London ('stupider than I remember him . . . in fact, stupid', Tom added spitefully), with a younger American writer, Max Bodenheim. Bodenheim, whom Tom had published in the *Egoist*, arrived with his heavily pregnant wife, hoping Tom could help him establish himself in English literary life. 'Being Semites I suppose they will survive somehow', Tom remarked to Pound, unattractively; he did try to help this young fellow countryman, but explained that

> I told him my history here, and left him to consider whether an American Jew, of only a common school education and no university degree, with no money, no connections, and no social polish or experience, could make a living in London. Of course I did not say all this; but I made him see that getting recognised in English letters is like breaking open a safe – for an American, and that only about three had ever done it.[39]

With a photograph of him propped on her typing table, it was in response to this letter that Tom's mother confessed to her 'Dearest Son' her 'instinctive antipathy to Jews'.[40] Readers may detect readily where Tom's prejudice originated, even if his thinking about how hard it was for Americans, Jewish or otherwise, to crack the safe of literary London may have been correct. Impressively and imperiously, Lottie Eliot set out her plans for the visit that, at last, she was proposing to make to London in the spring of 1921.

Though hardly the man to be troubled by Tom's attitude to Jews, Pound, who was in Paris, worried about his friend's ongoing incarceration in London banking – not Pound's preferred haven for poets. In strict confidence Tom explained that if he were ever to give up the bank, he would want an income of £800 per annum 'and must provide for old age'.[41] The idea of spending an extended spell abroad, as Pound was doing, held some appeal, but Tom wanted to maintain a London flat. He thought if he escaped the bank he might produce an article a week. On average throughout 1920 he published something every three weeks, though sometimes his productions were simply letters to the literary press. Principally Pound hoped to spring his friend from the City for the sake of poetry.

In Marlow for most of July, behindhand with *The Sacred Wood*, apparently Tom tried to persuade Murry to publish some of Pound's poems in the *Athenaeum*.[42] Poets, as ever, had to look out for one another. Still, each had to find his own way of working. Once his essay collection was delivered, Tom was considering a further foray to rural France, maybe visiting Pound and going on a walking tour before rendezvousing with Vivien in Paris. He hoped things would turn out better than at Easter time; possibly he could contact 'anybody worth seeing' in the French capital – and particularly, because they had not yet met, James Joyce.[43]

Even as he struggled to shape *The Sacred Wood*, discovering that assembling a prose book was a dauntingly 'colossal task' compared to writing individual essays, Tom's professionalism brought him further offers of work, though not necessarily remunerative ones.[44] He had been 'invited to collaborate' in *La Revue de Genève*, an international journal seeking to draw together post-war European culture.[45] In 1920 it was publishing writers from Joseph Conrad to Sigmund Freud and from Ernst Robert Curtius to Georges Duhamel. Tom did not have time to take on this task, but the idea of such a magazine appealed to him. More locally, Wyndham Lewis sought his help in launching a new 'art and literature review' to occupy the ground vacated by the now defunct *Art and Letters*.

Tom was due to holiday in France with Aiken during August, but Aiken pulled out at short notice; so, having finished *The Sacred Wood* in late July while 'supposed to be ill', he took a few days off from the bank, still with thoughts of crossing the Channel.[46] He and Lewis had been planning the new magazine: since Lewis was to run it, Tom suggested its core comprise writing about art, with literature playing a subsidiary role. He liked, though, 'the idea of a large number of (anonymous) topical paragraphs', and wanted to consult Pound.[47] The magazine, *Tyro*, would not emerge until the following spring, with Tom contributing prose and the first new poem he had published in a journal for almost two years.

Summer brought professionally useful socialising. At the very end of July the Eliots travelled to Garsington; Ottoline Morrell photographed Vivien, inviting her to return for a solo stay. Aldous and Maria Huxley were there, and Mark Gertler; Vivien, having felt ill, grew worse: Tom decided he 'ought to have prevented' the visit.[48] Back in London, she took to her bed, but got up to accompany her husband and his visiting American cousin Abigail ('very young for her age') to the theatre; the following weekend, Vivien insisted on going with Tom to the Schiffs at Eastbourne.[49] Wyndham Lewis and some Italian visitors were fellow guests, and it was around this time that Tom and Lewis decided to excurse to France together. At Eastbourne, chattering in English and Italian, the Schiffs' visitors enjoyed hot, sunny weather. Taking chairs out into the garden, they sat among flowering shrubs by the greenhouse, then motored along the coast road to Burling Gap where they strolled beside the cliffs and took photographs. In pale three-piece suit and bow tie, Tom appeared happy and relaxed. He smiled affectionately at his wife as she photographed him with their friends. Vivien found the trip rekindled their sex life. Possibly her sense that he would soon leave for the Continent intensified her feelings. She wrote to Mary Hutchinson, implying this was the first time for a while that things had felt right in the bedroom: 'I had rather an affair with him . . . It began when we were staying with the Schiffs for the Peace weekend. Don't you yourself find that staying in people's houses together is very conducive to reviving passion?'[50]

Lewis and Tom went to France on Saturday 14 August. Vivien was returning to Eastbourne to stay with the Schiffs.[51] Tom had dashed off a hasty letter to Joyce on the Wednesday, saying he would be staying on Sunday night at the hôtel de l'Elysée on the Left Bank at 3 rue de Beaune, where Joyce himself, Pound and other avant-garde figures had resided. Entrusted with a brown-paper package from Pound – a gift for the Irish novelist – Tom wondered if they could meet for dinner that evening about 6.30. There was no time for Joyce to reply, but he turned up with his son Giorgio and Tom handed him the parcel. When Joyce unwrapped it, he found inside a second-hand pair of brown shoes. '"Oh!"' he exclaimed, 'very faintly'.[52] Rather like Joyce's subsequent meeting with Marcel Proust, his encounter with Tom, important in retrospect, was low-key, and slightly comical. Lewis, Joyce, Tom and the art critic of the *Petit Parisien*, poet Fritz Vanderpyl, all dined together at a nearby restaurant. Carrying a straw boater, Joyce was their generous host, tipping the waiter munificently but saying nothing specifically memorable. Still, the food was acceptably French, and Fritz's knowledge of cuisine encyclopedic; he knew the finest Parisian restaurants, and was, in Tom's view, 'an archimage in the arts of eating and drinking'.[53]

Wanting to record something of this dinner, Tom sketched the scene in a letter: the four men in hats, Joyce with goatee beard and spectacles. The author of *Ulysses*, like Lewis, was six years older than Tom, but all three had a strong sense of being artistic contemporaries. As they sized each other up, though Tom and Lewis worried that the Irish could appear

'Provincials', the observant, reserved novelist of Dublin deeply impressed the shrewd, shy poet from St Louis.[54] Mr Joyce, Tom wrote a few days later to Schiff, was 'a quiet but rather dogmatic man, and has (as I am convinced most superior persons have) a sense of his own importance. He has a sort of gravity which seems more Protestant than Catholic. He is obviously the man who wrote his books – that is, he impresses you as an important enough personage for that.'[55] While detecting an arrogance underlying Irish politeness, Tom liked conversing with Joyce, with whom he dined again on his return journey. Over the next couple of weeks, as they travelled together, Lewis and Tom chatted more extensively. 'I do not know anyone more profitable to talk to', Tom decided; 'highly strung, nervous', Lewis was also 'witty and amusing'.[56] The two men had more in common than art and writing: both had recently lost their fathers, and Lewis, for all his combative reputation, had suffered recent bouts of illness. Together these two North American-born Francophiles holidaying from England excursed via Nantes to Vannes, on the north coast of the Bay of Biscay. Vannes turned out to be unseasonably cold, so they headed inland to Tours and Saumur in the Loire: a new part of France for Tom.

If he had felt exhausted when he left London, then, as so often, France revived him. He relished, not least, its 'good wine', even if each evening Lewis saw him tot up 'most scrupulously in a small note-book the day's expenses', then reach the decision that 'There was not much more he could spend before he got into bed.'[57] When, after hiring bicycles at Saumur, Lewis crashed and injured his knee, Tom used his fluent French to persuade a local landlady to ply his companion with brandy. Taking charge, Tom headed to Saumur, 'chartered an open barouche', and, with the driver's help, brought Lewis and his faulty bicycle back to the bicycle shop where they argued vehemently with the owner.[58] Vehemence was one of Lewis's hallmarks.

While Tom was rescuing his friend with *savoir faire*, Vivien in England was growing increasingly jittery. The day after he left, she had 'a most incredibly horrible migraine'. She wrote to tell him so, anxious he keep her constantly posted about his address, '*so that I can get at you. I must write. I am not very well, but will be allright if I can keep in touch with you, and not have uncertainty and upsets.*' In her next sentence she assured Tom she was not ill. Receiving these unsettling, contradictory signals, he sent her at least two wires and a postcard during his first five days in France. Clearly she missed him intensely, and was in a state of anxiety – for him as well as for herself . She wanted him to know how much she loved him. Her first letter to him on this trip is signed 'Yr. most adoring. V.' [59]

The two letters Vivien sent her husband on this French trip are the only correspondence between them that survives from their early married years. Both notes are markedly anxious. The second, mailed from Eastbourne on 20 August, addresses him fondly as 'my darling', and again shows her missing him acutely: 'Yesterday I felt so ill and despairing that I went to my room and cried and called yr. name. Today I am so much better.' Repeatedly this letter sends mixed signals: Vivien is having a fine time; Vivien is ill. Photographs taken at Eastbourne show her looking strikingly pretty and enjoying the company of Sydney Schiff's 'nephew in law'; with Tom away, her 'actress' side came to the fore, and she and this man had fun, capering and striking poses in the garden.[60] Her correspondence emphasises that while getting 'the last ounce of health' out of his holiday, Tom must keep in touch yet should 'not think about me at all'. Other concerns surface too. Fearful lest Sydney Schiff 'fall into K[atherine] M[ansfield]'s hands', Vivien presses Tom to write to him.[61] Yet the most striking thing about this rather self-involved second letter to Tom is that it begins, 'My dearest Wonkypenky'.[62]

The way this odd term of endearment is used suggests 'Wonkypenky' was Vivien's intimate nickname for Tom. 'Wonky' is English slang for 'faulty', and, though the word is not in the *Oxford English Dictionary* (which lists only the verb to 'penk', meaning to throb), it seems clear 'penky' is slang for penis. So the letter, anxious and affectionate, also hints that Vivien was used to Tom having physical problems: 'wonkypenky' surely implies a difficulty in sexual performance. Though he had mentioned his hernia in a letter to his mother when he was undergoing his military medical examination, it does not seem to have troubled him unduly for some time. However, in the early 1920s there are indications that its condition deteriorated: by 1923, when he was 'examined by the doctor for Life Insurance', he was told, 'my hernia was worse (on the other side) and I should wear a truss and perhaps have an operation.'[63] Intimate physical trouble may have intensified a wider sense of woundedness within the Eliots' marriage, and may even have quickened Tom's imaginative interest in Jessie Weston's wounded Fisher King and his Waste Land. Still, Vivien uses the nickname 'Wonkypenky' endearingly – not reproachfully – and her letter reveals as much about its writer as about its addressee. This characteristically anxious short note, in which she has underlined a dozen separate words and phrases, confirms their sex life as problematic, with clear difficulties on his side.

Vivien signs her letter, 'Your loving Wee'.[64] Though 'Wee' can refer to urine in modern English slang, this seems a fairly recent usage; more probably, she is engaging in baby talk that refers either to a childish pronunciation of her first initial, or to her height: she was wee, slim and elegant; when she walked beside Tom the top of her head was level with his shoulder. At times biographers have sought to speculate in detail about the couple's sex life and medical conditions. Peter Ackroyd, who had access to her brother and to people who had known the Eliots in early married life, thinks Vivien's periods were unduly heavy and hard to manage; he claims that she regularly stained sheets, so much so that she insisted on removing bedlinen from hotels, then sent it back after it had been laundered.[65] Yet the evidence of Vivien's 1919 diary suggests her periods were regular, and there are dangers – when considering Vivien *or* Tom – in advancing theories for which evidence is so slender and which risk sounding too reductive or even misogynistic. What the tiny amount of surviving correspondence between wife and husband suggests is that their relationship was anxious, loving and, while containing elements of passion, sexually awkward. Vulnerabilities on both sides, Vivien's adultery, Tom's longing for Emily Hale and possible physical difficulties as well as flirtations in which both husband and wife engaged could not have helped. Later, at the end of the 1930s, Tom wrote of how his 'desire for progeny' had been 'very acute once', but he came to accept being childless. In his most despairing recollection (in 1939) he wrote that 'I never lay with a woman I liked, loved or even felt any strong physical attraction to', yet, early in their relationship at least (as Aldous Huxley among others had detected), there had been a strong element of sexual attraction between himself and Vivien.[66]

At his City bank Tom was the professional Mr Eliot; in literary company he was the sometimes inscrutable poet; in his most intimate moments with 'Wee' he was 'dearest Wonkypenky'. Unlike most folk he was remarkably intelligent and had a genius for verse, but like the majority of people he had public and private selves which could seem hard to reconcile. His triumph in his greatest poetry was to be able to draw on all of these, fusing them together and transmuting them through language that acquired almost infinite reach. He reshaped public and private issues into forms at once designedly impersonal, yet shot through with searing personal pain.

Getting to know him better in 1920, Virginia Woolf suspected he had 'a good deal of concealed vanity & even anxiety' about his own writing. She perceived 'A personal upheaval of some kind' had happened to him 'after Prufrock', and had 'turned him aside from his inclination – to develop in the manner of Henry James'. Woolf found him fascinating, but hard to read as a man: 'There is much to be said about Eliot from different aspects – for instance, the difficulty of getting in touch with clever people – & so forth

– anaemia, self-consciousness; but also, his mind is not yet blunted or blurred. He wishes to write precise English; but catches himself out in slips . . .' Yet while she registered Tom's punctiliousness, and associated him at times with 'anaemia', as Woolf watched him she was aware of a deeper life underlying his solemnity, and a sometimes stinging self-reproach.

> The odd thing about Eliot is that his eyes are lively & youthful when the cast of his face & the shape of his sentences is formal & even heavy. Rather like a s[c]ulpted face – no upper lip; formidable, powerful; pale. Then those hazel eyes seeming to escape from the rest of him. We talked – America, Ottoline, aristocracy, printing, Squire, Murry, criticism. 'And I behaved like a priggish pompous little ass' was one of his comments on his own manner at Garsington. He is decidedly of the generation beneath us – I daresay superior – younger, though.[67]

If Woolf, six years his senior, might be struck by something youthful in thirty-two-year-old Tom, few people saw it. In June 1920 Richard Aldington thought Tom 'a really polished American' whose 'conversation' was 'really witty, his point of view always finished and sometimes profound'; yet Katherine Mansfield complained in September 1920 that his writing had an 'opaque frigidity'; she thought he never 'risks himself'.[68] As Vivien, worried lest Mansfield turn the Schiffs against them, urged him to do, Tom wrote to Sydney Schiff from France, making clear he regarded him as a true friend, and sending him the sketch of dinner with Joyce. The Eliots' friendship with the Schiffs was genuine, even if, awkwardly, he described them to his mother (perhaps to counter her prejudice) as 'very nice Jews'.[69]

Returned to London from Eastbourne, Vivien took to bed with influenza symptoms. She hoped to go to Bosham soon and to see Mary Hutchinson, with whom she enjoyed discussing Tom. Such talks were 'an exciting joy that I couldn't be without.'[70] She also wanted to sort out any possible offence Tom had caused Mary in a letter. Vivien's time without her husband had taught her she should try, if possible, to feel less reliant on him. Just as when he was applying to join the American military forces she had attempted to school him in what to say, so she still harboured such an impulse, but strove to resist it. 'In future', she told Mary, 'I am going to simply wash my hands of Tom and refuse politely to explain him or interpret him or influence or direct him. I mean to have some sort of individual existence, and Tom must manage his own muddles.'[71] Being Mrs T. S. Eliot was difficult.

For some time Tom had been hoping to turn again to poetry. To Edgar Jepson, who had praised his work along with that of Pound, he mentioned before going to France that 'perhaps I shall try some verse now'.[72] Returned, he told Schiff he aimed soon 'to show you what I hope to have written'.[73] Yet the material did not come as desired. Complaining of 'the spiritual decadence of England', he was grumpy.[74] 'As the world becomes worse to live in, every month', he wrote despondently to his brother in mid-September, 'so the minutiae of existence seem to consume more time and energy'. He and Vivien were once more seeking a new apartment, while still aspiring to maintain a place 'in the country'.[75] At the same time 'younger men' were constantly after him for literary advice. Blighted by war, they seemed an 'unfortunate generation'.[76] Tom felt afflicted by a keen sense of 'the horrible waste of time, energy, life, of the struggle with post-war machinery of life'.[77]

In September 1920, just as they thought they had secured a new flat, and while Tom, with a view to moving in mid-October, was negotiating about alterations, the proofs of *The Sacred Wood* arrived. Methuen wanted to publish in October. Ezra and Dorothy Pound helped Tom proofread, correcting mistakes not least in quotations. His prose sorted, verse pressed in on him. 'I feel maddened now', he wrote on 26 September, 'because I want to get settled quietly and write some poetry; there seems no likelihood of it for some weeks at best'.[78] Henry wrote about selling St Louis Hydraulic-Press Brick Company stock left to Tom by his father. Turning his professional banker's brain to the matter, Tom calculated that interest from the sale of the stock could give him additional income of at least £100 a year. While not a huge fortune, added to his salary it was a marked help. Money from the United States continued to boost his London household finances, but never seemed quite enough. The new flat would cost more, and it looked as if moving would eat up time in October when Tom had hoped to 'take Vivien away'.[79] It might be November before he could settle to verse.

He couldn't find time. 'I want a period of tranquility to do a poem that I have in mind', he told his mother on 20 September, just as she was completing her own move to a new house in Cambridge, Massachusetts.[80] 'Am I writing much? Only signing my name to leases and agreements', he complained to Mary Hutchinson, adding that he was 'about to have an operation'.[81] This, he later explained to Leonard Woolf, was 'on my Nose'.[82] Probably he was having it cauterised: hardly a cheering prospect. Barbara and Jeremy, Mary Hutchinson's children, nicknamed him 'The Eagle' because of the size of his nose.[83] Aggravations multiplied. By mid-October he complained to Lewis he was 'in almost hourly consultation with somebody or other about the flat which I am trying to take from an insane she-hyena.'[84] This woman insisted Tom pay all her 'solicitors' fees' as well as his own.[85] His temper was not improved by having read Aiken's derivative new book of poems, *The House of Dust*, which, once again, seemed unduly indebted to 'myself'.[86] Struggling with his commitments, he asked Lewis to help with the removal.

His imagination flooded with ideas and images, including some from his past and from his reading as a student. Earlier in 1920 he had gone to see a performance of Euripides' *Medea* starring Sybil Thorndyke at London's Holborn Empire theatre. The verse translation of this play about a fearsomely strong mother was by Gilbert Murray. Though Tom thought Murray's poetry poor, he recognised him as a major Hellenist. Thinking about Murray's work led him to go over in his mind the way literature, anthropology and psychology had converged over the last few decades: something which his Harvard education and some of his recent reviewing had brought home to him. Having written a few years before about the interpretation of primitive ritual, Tom could treat this scholarship with a certain mockery in *Art and Letters*. Nonetheless he sensed in it a new intellectual dawn.

This day began, in a sense, with Tylor and a few German anthropologists; since then we have acquired sociology and social psychology, we have watched the clinics of Ribot and Janet, we have read books from Vienna and heard a discourse of Bergson; a philosophy arose at Cambridge; social emancipation crawled abroad; our historical knowledge has of course increased; and we have a curious Freudian-social-mystical-rationalistic-higher-critical interpretation of the Classics and what used to be called the Scriptures. I do not deny the very great value of all works by scientists in their own departments, the great interest also of this work in detail and in its consequences. Few books are more fascinating than those of Miss [Jane] Harrison, or Mr. [F. M.] Cornford, or Mr. Cooke, when they burrow in the origins of Greek myths and rites; M. Durkheim, with his social consciousness, and M. Lévy-Bruhl, with his Bororo Indians who convince themselves that they are parroquets, are delightful writers. A number of sciences have sprung up in an almost tropical exuberance which undoubtedly excites our imagination, and the garden, not unnaturally, has come to resemble a jungle. Such men as Tylor, and Robertson Smith, and Wilhelm Wundt, who early fertilised the soil, would hardly recognize the resulting vegetation; and indeed poor *Wundt's Völkerpsychologie* was a musty relic before it was translated.[87]

Reviewing all this, and writing about scholarship on primitive fertility rituals as if it was itself a form of fertile 'vegetation', Tom concluded what was needed was to fuse this intellectual material with the poetry practised by 'such as Mr. Pound'. Murray lacked 'creative instinct'.[88] Pound's close friend and fellow poet did not.

Later in 1920, visiting them in the country for the weekend of 18–19 September, Tom told the Woolfs he wanted 'to write a verse play in which the 4 characters of Sweeny act the parts'. It would concentrate, tellingly but revealingly, on 'externals'.[89] Drawing especially on the anthropologically-informed classical scholarship of F. M. Cornford, eventually this would become 'Sweeney Agonistes'. Yet, quite apart from 'Sweeney Agonistes', producing his new, long poem was also part of Tom's plans. That poem, too, might draw on a melange of literature and anthropological lore. Yet, frustratingly, as 1920 drew towards its close, he felt he could not quite bring this idea to fruition. Like Pound, he had grown used to incorporating into his work material lifted from earlier poems. In 1920 he foregrounded such a technique as a plus point. Writing in *The Times Literary Supplement* about the dark Jacobean dramas of Philip Massinger, he contended,

> One of the surest of tests is the way in which a poet borrows. Immature poets imitate; mature poets steal; bad poets deface what they take, and good poets make it into something better, or at least something different. The good poet welds his theft into a whole of feeling which is unique, utterly different from that from which it was torn; the bad poet throws it into something which has no cohesion. A good poet will usually borrow from authors remote in time, or alien in language, or diverse in interest.[90]

Though in this piece, published in late May, Tom had gone on to mention George Chapman's seventeenth-century borrowings from Seneca, and the way Shakespeare and Jacobean dramatist Cyril Tourneur had filched from the French of Montaigne, in effect he was setting out the method that would underlie the still embryonic *Waste Land*. His lecturing and his deep grounding in philosophy let him articulate theories about poetry that nourished his own verse to a degree unusual among poets. So, for instance, using a German word employed by Schopenhauer, he argued that in the best Jacobean drama could be found 'that perpetual slight alteration of language, words perpetually juxtaposed in new and sudden combinations, meanings perpetually *eingeschachtelt* [encased] into meanings, which evidences a very high development of the senses, a development of the

English language which we have perhaps never equalled'. Glissading between dramatic poetry and poems written for private reading, he associated this period in Jacobean drama with the verse of Donne as the culmination of an era when 'the intellect was immediately at the tips of the senses. Sensation became word and the word was sensation.' Again, he saw this process as akin to the formation of a 'chemical compound'.[91] His theory here can appear scientific and detached; the resulting poetry sounds at once pained and pinpoint, musical with echoes that ripple out across eras and cultures, extending the boundaries of language.

Tom had developed a sense of the making of art as arduous. Drawing on Rémy de Gourmont, and on Édouard Dujardin's 1919 *De Stéphane Mallarmé au prophète Ezéchiel: et essai d'une théorie du réalisme symbolique*, he maintained that 'the creation of a work of art is like some other forms of creation, a painful and unpleasant business: it is the sacrifice of the man to the work, it is a kind of death'.[92] For his own labour-intensive poetic toil he would need time. Meanwhile, Dujardin's linking of poetry and religion in the context of discussions about 'la réel' (the real), 'la réalisme symbolique' and 'la bible' (not to mention his connecting Mallarmé with Wagner) nourished Tom's thinking about the poem he wanted to write.[93] When he did compose it, reality and the unreal interpenetrated; the biblical book of Ezekiel, ancient religions and Wagnerian leitmotifs fused. Other topics he wrote about in summer 1920 – Cleopatra, Dante, sex and fertility throughout nature (Tom alludes to de Gourmont's work on 'physiology', *Physique de l'Amour: essai sur l'instinct sexuel* which Pound was about to translate) – would resurface in his forthcoming poem. When he argued in July that 'the critic and the creative artist' were 'frequently . . . the same person', he defined the combination he had striven to become.[94]

In November he published his first article in Thayer's *Dial*. 'The Possibility of a Poetic Drama' shows him still thinking about issues that preoccupied him while watching Murray's *Medea* earlier that year. Many 'poets hanker for the stage'. Tom was conscious the great age of English poetic drama was long past; yet it struck him that, among forms of art, 'the drama is perhaps the most permanent, is capable of greater variation and of expressing more varied types of society, than any other'. Possibly the oddest thing he said in this essay was that 'poetic drama's autopsy was performed as much by Charles Lamb as by any one else'.[95] What he referred to was the way Lamb in his *Specimens of English Dramatic Poets Who Lived about the Time of Shakespeare* had anthologised extracts from plays so that they could be read privately as poems.

Tom would grow increasingly interested in how one might write modern poetic drama; but the poem that he was about to produce would anthologise, in an often Poundian way, extracts from plays and older poems. Like his admired Dante and his brilliant contemporaries Pound and Joyce, Tom 'knew', as he put it that November, 'how to pillage right and left'.[96] Reflecting on Matthew Arnold's contention that the Romantic poets simply 'did not know enough', Tom as a critic knew a vast amount; his ideal was 'to see the best work of our time and the best work of twenty-five hundred years ago with the same eyes'.[97]

Yet his poem would not come. Life filled with other work: not just bank tasks, but moving house and the emotional demands of looking after Vivien, himself and visitors. He wrote very little prose in late 1920, his energies exhausted by the sheer practicalities of living. Harold Peters and several companions arrived in England in mid-October en route to the Mediterranean in an ocean-going yacht. They knew 'no one in London'. Tom tried to entertain them: such Americans in London populate 'Sweeney Agonistes'. All this increased his sense of 'strain'.[98] His prose hints at recurrent thoughts of mortality. He wrote not just of Lamb performing an 'autopsy', but with regard to poetasters advised curtly, 'Kill them off'; his December *Dial* piece, 'The Second-Order Mind', ends with the eerily resonant phrase, 'a monarchy of death'.[99]

He had just seen mortality close-up. While the Eliots were moving flats, Vivien's father, who had helped with legal arrangements, had collapsed suddenly at home on 21 October. At first it looked like food poisoning. The next day, when Tom was called to Compayne Gardens, specialist physicians decided to carry out an emergency operation in the house. They discovered a huge abdominal abscess 'just beginning to break'. Mr Haigh-Wood was within five minutes of death, and the surgeon feared he would not live until morning.[100]

Tom stayed up all night at his father-in-law's house. Vivien was 'on the edge of collapse'.[101] Her brother helped procure medicines. Two live-in nurses assisted with the old man, who hung on with great spirit. Watching him when he lay on the edge of unconsciousness, Tom was moved by the way the elderly painter rallied and, recognising his son-in-law, asked him when *The Sacred Wood* would be published. The doctors stipulated a second operation was necessary. Eventually returning home to make room for the nurses, Vivien waited anxiously at Crawford Mansions. As the invalid lay ill for days, then weeks, Tom felt intense trepidation.

Mail went unposted. Meetings had to be rescheduled. Though he tried to slog on at the bank, in early November he was in bed for several days. It was mid-November before they completed the move to their new flat; but Mr Haigh-Wood's illness dragged on for months. Eventually he regained most of his strength, but recurrent 'fluctuations' left Vivien 'completely exhausted'.[102] Appalled at what she saw as an ongoing 'long losing battle against *horrible* illness, unimaginable pain, doctors' mistakes – obstinacy – stupidity – delays – family's blindness', she told Mary Hutchinson she never went to bed without fear.[103] Each morning she woke struggling to summon up the courage to pick up the telephone in their new flat and make the call to her father's house.[104]

Visiting his father-in-law regularly, Tom kept going by hardening his shell. 'There are times, I think', he wrote to Schiff (whose wife Violet was both a talented musician and an invalid), 'when one must try to seal one's intellect hermetically, to prevent it from being destroyed by circumstances which it cannot mend'.[105] He was impressed that Vivien managed to endure, and he emphasised to his mother that he wanted the insurance policy on his life kept up for his wife's sake.

Forced to cut back on engagements, he did fulfil a commitment to speak at a dinner given by the Poetry Circle of the Lycaeum Club, where he encountered a woman with an interest in Tarot cards. He also dined with the Woolfs. As often, Virginia Woolf was struck by the way Tom bottled things up. She noticed, too, an intensity underlying his armature of propriety. He was 'all caught, pressed, inhibited; but great driving power some where – & my word what concentration of the eye when he argues!'[106] Others, less perceptive, were more hostile. Having been reviewed harshly by Tom, on 4 December Irish essayist Robert Lynd published an attack on *The Sacred Wood* which saw its author as 'Buried Alive'. Reviews of that book were mixed. Some, including those by Murry and Aiken, came from people who knew Tom well, and discerned that his literary theory owed significant debts to Rémy de Gourmont. Other reviewers found 'a dessication of the emotions' and an arrogance or self-righteousness in league with a demanding intelligence.[107] In New York Knopf bought 350 copies of the Methuen edition, giving it a small but effective American circulation.

The Eliots' new flat at 9 Clarence Gate Gardens had been built shortly before the Great War, not far from 221B Baker Street, fictional home of Tom's childhood hero, Sherlock Holmes. After Crawford Mansions, the Clarence Gate Gardens interiors were roomier, with higher ceilings. The apartment had one more room, and was in 'a much better block' in a superior area, a mere stroll from Regent's Park and close to the Francis Holland Church of England School for Girls.[108] On either side of the relatively narrow road were 'very respectable looking' six-storey red-brick blocks with basements. The street was comparatively dark, but its build-ings handsome. To the rear the brickwork was grey and there was a small courtyard with a garden. The frontage was more imposing, with wrought-iron balconies and iron railings. The entrance to the Eliots' block (numbers 1–21) sported substantial brass-handled double doors between twin sets of pillars, leading to an inner stairwell and an elevator. Their flat was 'only one flight up', Tom assured his mother, and 'will do beautifully for you when you come'. Vivien liked it too – efficiently managed, 'quiet, warm, well ventilated'.[109] Here the Eliots might feel happy hosting Tom's family or new acquaintances such as the poet Walter de la Mare. In an attempt to minimise disturbance, they had taken over the flat along with its fittings, but nothing was ever straightforward. The old lady who had lived there previously 'insulted us'. 'Maliciously', Tom complained, she 'had the electricity, gas, and telephone cut off so as to put me to the trouble of putting them on again'.[110]

Adjoining the Eliots' new home was the red-brick Parish Church of St Cyprian. Built in 1903, it was dedicated to the third-century Bishop of Carthage, a Latin author who had been martyred in AD 258 for denying the pagan Roman gods and holding true to his Christian faith. The white and gold interior was beautiful, adorned with a statue of the saint and stained-glass windows showing among other things the martyrdom of St Sebastian. If it seemed odd to be living in twentieth-century London beside a site associated with ancient Carthage, then that is an oddity which *The Waste Land* – swirling from modern London street scenes to the St Augustine of 'To Carthage then I came' – would replicate.[111]

Tom had been 'trying to write a little', he confessed to Schiff on 6 December, but was finding his 'brain quite numb'. Vivien encouraged him to take a break: he should 'have a change' – a brief spell in Paris. Shortly before Christmas he set off for a reinvigorating week. Maurice Haigh-Wood was with him for part of the time, and Tom met old and new French acquaintances, including Fritz Vanderpyl and several writers and painters. For Vivien he bought a small picture by 'one of the best of the modern painters, Raoul Dufy'. Dufy's lightness and brightness might lift her spirits. Tom was delighted to find French intellectuals whom he met knew him by reputation, even if they did not read English. He lodged at the Pension Casaubon, where he had billeted as a student a decade earlier. The Casaubons had died, but their grandson now ran the place. 'If I had not met such a number of new people there', he wrote to his mother, 'Paris would be desolate for me with prewar memories of Jean Verdenal and the others.'[112] His old tutor, Alain-Fournier, too, was dead; but Fournier's brother-in law, Jacques Rivière, now edited *La Nouvelle Revue Française*.

When he got back, Tom found Vivien still worried about her father. Tom was late in sending Thayer the first of the 'London Letters' he was to write for the *Dial*; he also pondered Thayer's confidential invitation to manage, for a substantial fee, an 'English edition' of that magazine, but concluded it would be 'physically impossible' given that he was working in 'an office six days a week' from '9.30 to 5', and did not feel able to resign from the bank.[113] Managing an English *Dial* would do nothing to advance the poem he wanted to write; but the notion of taking charge of a magazine had its attractions. For the moment, however, there were more pressing concerns. Mr Haigh-Wood remained ill. Christmas was difficult, though it brought the customary gifts from America. Turning their minds to Lottie Eliot's proposed visit in the spring, the couple began to think how best to accommodate this mother-in-law whom Vivien had never met.

15

To Lausanne

IN London if Tom gave voice to his cosmopolitanism, sometimes he did so in spite of the place. Having thought recently about *La Nouvelle Revue Française* and a possible English edition of the American *Dial*, he continued to contemplate the editing of magazines, and specifically the one that his friend Wyndham Lewis was about to launch, *Tyro*. Like Lewis, he felt a growing disaffection with London literary reviewing. He complained to Maxwell Bodenheim in January 1921 about 'the placid smile of imbecility which splits the face of contemporary London' and about 'the putrescence of English literature and journalism'. However, he also sniped at Prohibition-era America, saying he wanted to stay in England and see if the English 'can ever be roused to anything like intellectual activity'. To Americans, when he wished, he could take that tone; to English people he usually expressed himself differently. Able to get along with – and quarrel with – writers from both countries, he had 'got used to being a foreigner everywhere, and it would fatigue me to be expected to be anything else'.[1]

Talk of 'fatigue' and 'putrescence' was understandable. Though convalescing, Charles Haigh-Wood continued to be seriously ill. Vivien dreaded making engagements in case either she or her father needed help. She was undergoing a 'course of treatment for her stomach'.[2] Pondering her situation, she bought, she told Mary Hutchinson on 5 January, 'a copy of Tom's book to send to my lover of the past, anonymously'.[3] Vivien, whom Tom's 'social English friends' had nicknamed the 'river girl', kept in the flat a copy of J. Ivo Ball's illustrated volume *Down the Silver Stream of the Thames*, which bore the signature of her former lover, Charles Buckle; its title is an allusion to Edmund Spenser's wedding poem, 'Prothalamion' with its 'silver streaming Thames' and its lyrical refrain, 'Sweet Thames, run softly till I end my song, / Sweet Thames, run softly, for I speak not loud or long'.[4]

Tom used those words in the more sordid context of the dirty, littered modern Thames in the long poem he worked on during 1921. He followed them with words from another Renaissance love poem, Andrew Marvell's 'To His Coy Mistress'. In an article on Marvell published on 31 March, he argued that 'A whole civilization resides in these lines.'[5] Blending a sense of an addled culture with anxieties about a mind gone wrong, Tom added Marvell's words to his own; conscious of modern London's face-splitting 'smile of imbecility', he clearly links sex with thoughts of death,

But at my back in a cold blast I hear
The rattle of the bones, and chuckle spread from ear to ear.[6]

For Vivien to send anonymously her husband's book to her ex-lover was spiteful. It suggests she sought to prove to Buckle, and perhaps to herself, that she had been right to marry Tom. Her championing of her husband's genius gave her a sense of purpose, but their relationship grew more troubled. 'I am alive and well, but very tired', Tom told his mother in a short, mid-January note; Vivien was 'showing signs of breaking up'.[7] His early 1921 piece 'Prose and Verse' begins with talk of the 'disconnected' and 'lifeless', of 'worn nerves' and 'arthritic limbs'.[8] Painfully fatigued herself, Vivien watched Tom come home weary each dinner time, 'more inclined for a quiet evening of reading, and early to bed, than to begin the real business of his life, and sit up late'.[9]

February brought Knopf's publication of *The Sacred Wood*, but the New York edition, which simply added a Knopf title page to Methuen's first-edition pages, and comprised just 365 copies, was small. There were few reviews. In London, far, far away, Tom could feel isolated, even mis-understood. Virginia Woolf saw him in company looking 'pale, marmo-real'. He seemed 'like a chapped office boy on a high stool, with a cold in his head, until he warms a little, which he did. We walked back along the Strand. "The critics say I am learned & cold" he said. "The truth is I am neither." As he said this, I think coldness at least must be a sore point with him.'[10]

At home with Vivien, some evenings he wrote to his mother about arrangements for her visit; or read in its colloquial German the Jewish writer Arthur Schnitzler's 'brilliant' stream-of-consciousness novella about a young man with woman trouble who contemplates suicide, *Leutnant Gustl*.[11] As Tom knew, Schnitzler's notorious 'new play', *Reigen* (*La Ronde*), dealing with 'the most intimate problems of sexual life', had been 'very badly treated' by the Berlin public.[12] Vivien watched him. She had a strong sense of what was 'the real business' of her poet husband's life, but was less certain what was the real business of her own.

'Fearfully run down', she seemed about to contract bronchitis. Mary Hutchinson came to visit. She talked to Tom, while Vivien remained 'shut in her room'.[13] Tom welcomed Mary's conversation, and, sensing 'crisis', turned to Brigit Patmore for advice in early March.[14] Ready to help, Vivien's old friend Lucy Thayer had a flat nearby at 12 Wigmore Street. Herself sometimes unstable, Lucy understood something of the Eliots' problems. She offered them the use of her flat if Tom's mother, brother and sister arrived to occupy Tom and Vivien's apartment. Given Lottie Eliot's age and health, this seemed appropriate: at Clarence Gate Gardens the visiting Eliots could be looked after by Ellen Kellond. Yet moving out of their own home and into Lucy Thayer's flat while their visitors were in town threatened to be stressful for Vivien and Tom.

Nevertheless, convinced they should vacate their own apartment and offer it to their visitors, Tom assured his mother on 6 March, 'Vivien and I have absolutely the same opinion about this.'[15] Perhaps; but Vivien's health grew perilously worse. Invited to dinner on 13 March Tom came 'alone', Virginia Woolf noted in her diary, 'since his wife is in a nursing home, not much to our regret'. She found her visitor, 'Eliot', rather remote: 'Will he become "Tom"?'[16] His cares weighed on him heavily. On 17 March he told Brigit Patmore that his wife had spent four days 'lying in the most dreadful agony with *neuritis* in every nerve, increasingly – arms, hands, legs, feet, back'.[17] Though her father was making a remarkable recovery, having to contemplate the arrival of her formidable mother-in-law did nothing to ease Vivien's ordeals. 'Neuritis', as understood at the time, was a disease involving 'the inflammation of one or more bundles of nerve fibres' and, 'in severe cases' could 'last for months'.[18] Never having seen such a bad case, Vivien's doctors could offer no certain hope. Tom worried his wife might die. She seemed to be losing touch with reality, and he registered her hurt. 'Have you ever been in such incessant and extreme pain that you felt your sanity going', he asked Brigit Patmore on 17 March, 'and that you no longer knew reality from delusion? That's the way she is.'[19]

He had to lead a double, even a multiple, life. He tried to understand and care for Vivien as best he could, which, in turn, exhausted him. Each working day he needed to go to the bank and be professional, accurate, reliable. That he could manage. Routine was helpful, but contributed to a self-protecting aspect of him that Katherine Mansfield called during the spring of 1921 'the bluff'. She found Tom 'a rare, delightful being', even

as she decided that 'the bluff oppresses me'.²⁰ Then there was his public
literary life, much of which he found congenial. Even if there, too, he
bluffed at times, it helped keep him sane, and even let him be witty, as
he was with Virginia Woolf when she shared a taxi with him one March
Sunday night to go to see Congreve's Restoration comedy *Love for Love*.
'Are you as full of vices as I am?' she asked him. 'Full. Riddled with them',
he replied. They chatted briefly about literature; she worried her work
involved depending on 'an illusion'. He told her she didn't really mean
that. She thought she did. Later, after sitting beside him at the theatre,
she confided to her diary that,

> I think one could probably become very intimate with Eliot because
> of our damned self conscious susceptibility: but I plunge more than
> he does: perhaps I could learn him to be a frog. He has the advantage
> of me in laughing out. He laughed at Love for Love: but thinking
> I must write about it I was a little on the stretch.²¹

Laughter released him from strain, but only temporarily. Later in March
Vivien came home from the nursing home to Clarence Gate Gardens, but
remained in bed. Tom explained to Sydney Schiff that on medical advice,
'She has not been allowed to see anyone, except myself, or to write letters.'²²
By the start of April she was a little better. Perhaps she might go to the
country for a month. He thought it would be a year or two before she
recovered.

Outside the flat things were also a struggle. At Lloyds Bank his work
on post-war German debts was challenging but usefully absorbing. In
the sometimes febrile literary world, while keeping on generally good
terms with the Woolfs (though Virginia worried on occasion that 'Eliot
never admired me, damn him'), Tom felt that 'I and Murry have fallen
apart completely.' No longer could he hide his conviction that Murry
was a poor writer: 'verbose', with too facile a love of 'money and being
a public figure'.²³ Vivien's hostility towards Katherine Mansfield, on whom
Murry cheated, exacerbated this disagreement. Surveying his own troubled life, Tom brooded on the Victorian Catholic convert John Henry
Newman's intense spiritual autobiography, *Apologia pro Vita Sua*, and on
the extended poem he so wanted to write. When he could, he applied
his mind not just to the pain of this, but, purposefully, to the technical
challenge. 'We do not like long poems', he opined gloomily. The pained
Gothic imagination of Edgar Allan Poe, familiar to him since his childhood dental ordeals, was in his thoughts at this difficult time. Poe's theory
that 'no poem should be more than 100 lines' haunted him; the issue was

how to sustain intensity.[24] In the spring of 1921 Woolf was discomfited to realise that Tom 'does like Poe'.[25]

Contemplating extended composition in verse, he had noted recently how Conrad Aiken's long poem echoed his own cadences. It also lost intensity, getting far too diffuse; yet maybe it helped Tom. Aiken's *The House of Dust* tried to link an individual psyche to a 'darkened city' of 'towers', bells, loves and 'nightmare streets' where 'spring returns', and 'cards' might 'tell your future'. 'Time is dissolved' in 'dust' as sometimes unfaithful lovers 'Sit and talk' and 'misconstrue' each other ('What shall we talk of?'), and people cry out 'Good-night! Good-night! Good-night!'[26] Aspects of this surely lodged in Tom's consciousness, resurfacing in the long poem he was attempting to work on. Pound's developing 'Cantos' offered another, more helpful model – one, like his own recent verse, increasingly pieced together out of quotations, allusions, snatches. If Tom could get the structure right, a lengthy poem could work: 'No one who is willing to take some trouble about his pleasures complains of the *length* of the Divine Comedy'. He thought it was no bad thing for an extended poem to contain some material 'of ephemeral interest', but 'it should not have been composed as a number of short poems'.[27] This was a problem. For he had several shorter pieces, including 'The Death of the Duchess', that he had been hoarding for years, hoping perhaps they might fit into a larger structure. Like 'The Death of the Duchess', these older poems, allusive yet intimate, were veined with anxieties about sex and death.

Frustratingly, the material would not gel. On 5 February 1921 he showed Lewis 'a new long poem (in 4 parts) which', Lewis told Sydney Schiff, 'will be not only very good, but a new departure for him'.[28] Yet Tom held this work back. For *Tyro* he sent instead a short 'Song to the Opherian'. He got one of the words wrong: he seems to have meant 'orpharion', an instrument like a lute to which Elizabethan love songs (such as those of John Dowland) were sometimes sung. Edited down to thirteen lines, this poem is no sweet love song. With its sense of frustrated eroticism ('I may not kiss or clutch'), its 'blackened river' and 'bed' and 'pendulum in the head' and 'bleeding' and 'tears', it signals physical and psychological angst transmuted into something haunting yet scarcely comprehensible – meaning that refuses to come into shape. This was Tom's compositional problem as he struggled throughout 1921. Unusually, he published 'Song to the Opherian' under a pen-name, 'Gus Krutzsch', echoing the name of his manly footballing St Louis schoolfellow August R. Krutzsch. Doing so may have been a mischievous way of hiding the intimate hurts of 'Wonkypenky' from the public gaze.[29] It hints too at how, as Tom looked forward to his mother's arrival that summer, he was acutely conscious of his American background.

'Gus Krutzsch' (changed from 'Heine Krutzsch') also features in the long American narrative section positioned to open his long poem. As well as revisiting his past, Tom was thinking early in 1921 about writers who could create characters that convincingly incarnated 'myth'. How might one attempt this in a modern era largely 'barren of myths'? Epitomising Englishness, John Bull had been such a myth, but was now 'degenerate'; in film Charlie Chaplin, 'not English, or American, but a universal figure', might be another. Chaplinesque or not, England's theatres and music-hall stars allowed audiences, 'purged of unsatisfied desire', to 'live the myth'.[30] These ideas nourished 'Sweeney Agonistes', the drama of disastrous desires in London that Tom was plotting; more immediately they nurtured what became *The Waste Land*.

Recently returned from Paris, he was spurred, as so often, by the French capital's cosmopolitan culture. The new phenomenon of Dada, which was moving westwards and which that April would produce Man Ray and Marcel Duchamp's *New York Dada*, intrigued him. He thought Dada in Paris 'a diagnosis of a disease of the French mind', even 'a moral criticism', but 'whatever lesson we extract from it will not be directly applicable in London'. This holds open the possibility of indirect applications. Thoughts of Dada led him to Baudelaire, 'a deformed Dante' who had 'intellect *plus* intensity'. Tom wanted just that combination for his extended poem. Further evidence that the work was taking shape lies not least in the quotation which ended his *Tyro* piece, 'The Lesson of Baudelaire'. That quotation from Baudelaire's preface to *Les Fleurs du Mal* would be positioned prominently in Tom's long poem, mounting a disconcerting moral challenge to the reader as ally and hypocrite: '*Vous, hypocrite lecteur . . .*'[31]

In January he composed and reworked the first of his 'London Letters' for the *Dial*. Telling Thayer it was 'the first writing of any kind that I have done for six months', he mentioned, 'It will be several months before I have any verse ready for publication.'[32] As he faced up to his problems, his 'London Letter', which did not appear until April, articulates 'an overwhelming sense of difficulty'. Splenetically, it complains of London-published poetry as 'dull, immature, slight, and bad'. Georgian poet John Drinkwater's verse is 'dull, supremely dull'. 'I do not wish to dwell upon the dulness', Tom writes, but dwell on it he does, lamenting a reading public that 'knows no tradition, and loves staleness'; the 'independent' man is rejected in 'a world of mass-production' characterised by 'Regular Hours, Regular Wages, Regular Pensions, and Regular Ideas'.[33] The great English poet who made much of dullness is Alexander Pope, who ends his satire on literary life, *The Dunciad*, with a mock-apocalypse in which 'Thy hand great Dullness! lets the curtain fall, / And universal Darkness covers all'.[34] Tom singled out 'the last lines of the "Dunciad"' for praise in June.[35] In his prose of early 1921 he imagined several mock apocalypses – from a 'Second Flood' brought on by all this dullness to a 'Last Judgement', supposedly imagined by modern English poets 'who know a little French' and featuring 'Roman candles, Catherine wheels, and inflammable fire-balloons'. In his poetry, too, he turned to Pope.[36]

Probably around this time, though their first composition cannot be dated precisely, he wrote around seventy lines of Popeian couplets about a lady, Fresca (first mentioned in 'Gerontion'), who lies in bed, affectedly 'unwell'. Awaking 'from dreams of love and pleasant rapes', she summons her maid, corresponds with a friend about 'Lady Kleinwurm's party', uses the toilet and has a bath. Connected with prostitution and the 'hearty female stench', Fresca seems a poetaster in a shallow milieu. She has been 'thrilled' into 'hysteric fits' by 'the Russians'. With a dash of misogyny, Tom typed in Popeian accents,

Women grown intellectual grow dull,
And lose the mother wit of natural trull.[37]

This passage concluded with lines that again echo Marvell's 'To his Coy Mistress', with its 'chuckle spread from ear to ear.'

In early 1921 Tom had written of Marvell as a poet from a 'Puritan' background who managed to learn from the rather different tradition of the 'French'.[38] Those words at least as accurately describe himself. As it survives, his typescript entitled 'The Fire Sermon' then changes its verse form. It veers away from Pope towards the sounds of a nightingale, associated in Classical mythology with Tereus's rape of Philomela. The poem may allude to a Renaissance song but Tom's typescript here resembles a Dadaist or other French avant-garde text. Jean Cocteau in *Le Potomak* (1913) had broken up Wagner's *Tristan und Isolde* (a work Tom also plundered) with his

Cor de Tristan se rappelant
Cor
Cor
Cor de Tristan . . .[39]

Tom went even further. Twitteringly, he disintegrated the nightingale's call in a soundscape suspended between Dada and Elizabethan English:

Twit twit twit twit twit twit twit
Tereu tereu
So rudely forc'd
Ter[40]

There then follow descriptions of seedy life in modern London, including an account of a twenty-one-year-old 'clerk' who 'assaults' a typist; her reaction to his sexual attentions is 'indifference'.[41] These several versions of sexual encounters, each mentioning or involving what is or comes close to rape, read as enactments of similar scenes from different eras, functioning rather like reincarnations of some underlying, disturbing myth. Drawn from Tom's reading and, conceivably, from his awareness of 'society' London as well as the seedier goings on around Crawford Mansions, these passages are works of imagination; nor should the 'Fresca' be taken as Vivien. Nevertheless, the pervasive sense of tormented sexuality, the disgust and the horrified fascination with London life do seem to speak, however indirectly, from Tom's problematic experience.

Other poems or part-poems woven into his projected composition do this too. If 'The Death of the Duchess' has links to life with Vivien, then the opening of the surviving typescript of the new poem's first part, 'The Burial of the Dead' (which begins, 'First we had a couple of feelers down at Tom's place') presents an account of a night on the town that calls up Tom's memories of going with Aiken to rough areas of Boston. The 'Tom' of the opening has a wife called 'Jane' (the name Mary Hutchinson had given to a version of herself in her 1917 *Egoist* short story), so he is not Tom Eliot; yet he shares aspects of Tom Eliot's past.[42] The work's second part, initially called 'In the Cage' then retitled 'A Game of Chess', begins with a passage about a woman in a grand interior that alludes to Shakespeare's *Antony and Cleopatra*. Further links to the rape of Philomel precede a transition to a very edgy conversation between a couple, beginning, 'My nerves are bad tonight'. Modulating from jagged conversation into the music of ragtime, this passage seems uncomfortably close to the situation Tom and Vivien found themselves in when the poem was under construction. Vivien, who had a good ear for dialogue, read these lines in typescript and described them as 'W O N D E R F U L'. When the passage concluded with a long, Cockney-accented conversation involving sex and an abortion, she pencilled in the line (which Tom kept, almost unaltered, in his final version), 'What you get married for if you dont want to have children'.[43]

In a poem preoccupied with infertility, childlessness (touched on before in that line of 'Petit Epître', 'Est-ce qu'il n'a pas d'enfants?') is part of both text and subtext.[44] The way these needling Cockney voices are interrupted repeatedly by the call of a pub landlord asking customers to drink up because the bar is closing, 'HURRY UP PLEASE IT'S TIME', may hark back again to the days when the Eliots had lived close to a pub at Crawford Mansions; but, like so much else in the poem, it can point in other directions too. Tom had developed a technique which let even the simplest phrases resonate in several telling ways. 'Splendid' was Vivien's verdict on the conclusion of 'A Game of Chess' whose last line alludes to Ophelia's mad scene in *Hamlet*, 'Good night, ladies, good night, sweet ladies, good night, good night'.[45] Yet in Tom's poem this sounds as if spoken to drinkers leaving the modern tavern. The words may have been encouraged by Laforgue and by the modern urban 'Good-night! Good-night! Good-night!' of Aiken's *House of Dust*, but through placing and allusion Tom gets far more value from his line. Its meaning radiates out in multiple directions, heightening the unsettling intensity.

In his poem it was as if different eras were speaking to one another, scenes being acted and re-enacted across the centuries. During 1921 he read several very different works which also traversed vast temporal domains. One was George Bernard Shaw's Bergsonian drama of evolution, *Back to Methuselah*, which extended from encounters between Adam and Eve in 'B. C. 4004' to a scene imagined 'As Far as Thought Can Reach: A. D. 31,920'.[46] Tom never liked Shaw, but this 'attempt to expose a panorama of human history' interested him later in 1921, even if he denounced as too 'clever' its avoidance of 'things which always have been and always will be the same'.[47] Bravely and challengingly, his own poem confronted such constants. Slightly more to his taste than Shaw was Frederic Manning's *Scenes and Portraits* which he read that summer; though 'derivative', it too voyaged through history, especially religious history, presenting significant encounters from ancient Uruk to the France of Renan: for Tom, fascinated by the history of religions, Manning was 'one of the very best prose writers we have'.[48]

Joyce's *Ulysses*, which he had been devouring for years in serial form in the *Little Review*, was inspirational. However low-key their behaviour at the time, meeting Joyce had been a significant event for both writers. In May Joyce sent Tom manuscripts of the 'Circe', 'Eumaeus' and 'Oxen of the Sun' episodes of *Ulysses*. Pointing out a couple of instances where the novelist had mixed up English and American idioms, Tom told him the work was 'superb', particularly 'the Descent into Hell, which is stupendous'. The material was so good that 'I wish, for my sake, that I had not read it.'[49] That May to Robert McAlmon, an American poet who had just moved to Paris, Tom enthused not just about that city ('still alive') but also about Joyce, a foreigner who could live in the midst of the metropolis yet remain 'independent' within it, and who had found the right 'form' for his art. Later in 1921 Tom described *Ulysses* as 'the greatest work of the age'.[50] He was struck by Joyce's 'marvellous parody of nearly every style in English prose from 1600 to the *Daily Mail*'. Into his own long poem Tom incorporated reworkings of and gestures towards English poetry from many centuries. To appreciate this fully, as he said of Joyce's efforts, 'One needs a considerable knowledge of English literature'; yet to feel the compelling force and reach of the language you need only read it aloud.[51]

Ulysses spurred and confirmed Tom's artistic technique. As he put it, looking back in 1923, the 'method' of structuring a modern work on an ancient narrative (in Joyce's case an account of recent life in Dublin patterned on Homer's *Odyssey*) was no mere 'amusing dodge' to provoke 'disgust' but a new form of 'classicism' that had 'the importance of a scientific discovery'.

> In using the myth, in manipulating a continuous parallel between contemporaneity and antiquity, Mr Joyce is pursuing a method which others must pursue after him. They will not be imitators, any more than the scientist who uses the discoveries of an Einstein in pursuing his own, independent, further investigations. It is simply a way of controlling, of ordering, of giving a shape and a significance to the immense panorama of futility and anarchy which is contemporary history.

Surprisingly, since Yeats's verse had had so little effect on his own, Tom saw the origins of Joyce's method in Yeats's work, and thought it helped make 'the modern world possible for art' – especially for writers like himself who had a keen sense of links between anthropology and literature. 'Psychology (such as it is, and whether our reaction to it be comic or serious), ethnology, and The Golden Bough have concurred to make possible what was impossible even a few years ago. Instead of narrative method, we may now use the mythical method.'[52]

By the time he wrote that, Tom was looking back not only at *Ulysses* but also at his own 'long poem'. Immersed in it, however, he was not nearly so clear about its structure. Ever since drafts and rejected passages of *The Waste Land* resurfaced in the late 1960s, biographers and critics have pored over them. Yet these materials are incomplete. Given the compositional processes of the poem's final part, and what we know of Tom's earlier ways of working, it is extremely likely that, despite the fact that some very early fragments do survive, notes towards a good deal of the poem have simply vanished. Surely the three sections now titled 'The Burial of the Dead', 'A Game of Chess' and 'The Fire Sermon' did not start life as extensive typescripts. The earliest extant version of part four of the poem looks very like a neatly penned fair copy of older materials now lost. Only *The Waste Land*'s fifth section survives in something approaching its full versions – manuscript drafts followed by typescripts. So, while linking the poem's growth to Tom's life in 1920 and 1921 can be illuminating, we shall never know exactly how and when it was formed from start to finish.

Clearly it reflects a sense of crisis that was deeply personal as well as conditioned by post-war society. His reading in older and in recent literature helped give this embodiment, but his poem is frightening because it seems to imply that underneath all words and rituals may lie only arbitrary urges and nothingness. With a good deal of the poem in his mind and, it appears, some of it on paper, he oscillated in spring 1921 between deepening anxiety about life with Vivien as his family's visit approached and a need to seal himself off from the pain of all this in order to concentrate on his work at the bank and on his poem. A sense of how devastated, yet also determined and focused he felt is evident from what begins as a simple letter of thanks to Richard Aldington on 7 April. Aldington had sent flowers to Vivien, and Tom responded to his offer to present more the following week.

Tom encouraged Aldington to send 'kingcups buds' [*sic*] since 'she is very fond of them'.[53] Bright yellow kingcups are still common in the area around Bosham and not least in the Itchenor woods where Vivien and Tom had enjoyed picnics. The sight of the flowers meant something to him as well as to her. He went on to say he would be 'infinitely grateful' if Aldington could help him search for 'a tiny country cottage' which he hoped 'might be just the saving of my wife's health'.[54] For all its practical tone, this letter reveals an underlying mixture of vulnerability, a certain tenderness towards Vivien, and despair and anger: Tom seems to feel another setback could be the last straw. His annoyance is manifest when he contemplates an ongoing miners' strike that threatened to upset daily life. It could continue, he complains, 'for god knows how long'. Potentially, the strike might disrupt communications; though he does not say so explicitly, in those days of coal-powered vessels it had the potential to play havoc with transatlantic travel, and there were fears that a general stoppage was looming. Tom tells Aldington he feels 'contempt' for all political parties and a 'profound hatred for democracy'. He is in the 'blackest gloom'. Though that mood may be in part personal, it gives rise to this shocking, very un-American outburst, then presages a sense of widespread cultural collapse.

> Whatever happens will be another step toward the destruction of 'Europe'. The whole of contemporary politics etc. oppresses me with a continuous physical horror like the feeling of growing madness in one's own brain. It is rather a horror to be sane in the midst of this; it is too dreadful, too huge, for one to have the comforting feeling of superiority. It goes too far for rage.[55]

This is a letter written by a man on the edge. Its author wanted to use as the epigraph for his long poem a quotation from Joseph Conrad's *Heart of Darkness*, detecting at the heart of so-called civilisation only '"The horror! The horror!"'[56]

Yet he managed not to go under. A week later he outlined to his mother further arrangements for her visit, and itemised his ongoing writing and lecturing. The eleven paragraphs in this businesslike letter are uncharacteristically short. Six begin with the word 'I'.[57] His wife is mentioned only in a postscript: she would be disappointed and anxious if Tom's mother did not occupy the Clarence Gate Gardens flat. There is no mention of Vivien's health, though she was still bedridden. On occasion Tom let his own anxieties almost overcome him. At other times, with a determination approaching the inhuman, he sought to suppress them, becoming in his way what *The Waste Land* terms a 'human engine'.[58] He strove to hold on to his identity as a person not defined by illness, and, sometimes mechanically, to present to the world beyond the flat the best impression he could. Vivien, on occasion, struggled to do something similar, but knew she could not always achieve it.

By 22 April she had spent 'eight weeks in bed so far'. Murry, his own wife ill, came over from France to England and managed something of a rapprochement with Tom whom he thought could appear 'disdainful'.[59] Mentioning Vivien's illness, Tom outlined to Murry four books he wanted to write: one on Elizabethan poetry; one that would consider seventeenth- and eighteenth-century poets, including Pope; one containing 'analyses of my favorite poets in French, German, Italian and the Classics'; and a fourth volume on 'the present day'.[60] None of these works would be written. Still, their scope helps explain why around this time the young English Literature lecturer I. A. Richards tried unsuccessfully to persuade Tom to become a Cambridge academic. Tom's mention of these projects seems partly designed to impress the sometimes domineering Murry, who was delivering lectures for the English Literature school at Oxford University, and partly to impress himself.

Around the start of May Vivien felt well enough to go 'to the seaside' to recuperate.[61] Work kept Tom at the bank. Patients with nervous complaints were often advised to spend quiet periods away from home, and he had already made arrangements to take several weeks off when his mother arrived in June. Nonetheless, spending time apart from one another with the prospect of having to reunite again soon to cope with Mrs Eliot's visit further complicated Vivien and Tom's relationship. Around this time he wrote a long leading article on Dryden for *The Times Literary Supplement*, but was discontented with its 'unconnected scraps'.[62] Oddly, he compared Dryden with Baudelaire whose 'violently joined images' he admired. Given his own domestic situation, it is striking Tom quotes a long passage from Dryden's play *Aurungzebe* about 'unchaste wives'. Though presented as 'purple comedy', some of the lines have a darker edge:

Home is the sacred refuge of our life:
Secure from all approaches but a wife.
If thence we fly, the cause admits no doubt:
None but an inmate foe can force us out.
Clamours, our privacies uneasy make;
Birds leave their nests disturbed, and
    Beasts their haunts forsake.[63]

Thinking Dryden's 'best play' *All for Love*, a reworking of the tragic erotic drama of Shakespeare's *Antony and Cleopatra*, Tom, about to vacate his own home, was alert to passages about love gone wrong.[64]

At Lloyds his day job demanded considerable 'thought and strength'. Apologising to John Quinn for not having been in touch because of 'a protracted series of private worries' which robbed him of 'the concentration required for turning out a poem of any length', he explained that the bank 'when I have private anxieties on my mind,' was 'too much'. His mother's impending visit would be 'another anxiety as well as a joy'.[65]

He had hoped to nip over to Paris briefly while Vivien was at the seaside and before his mother arrived. That proved impossible. Perhaps he might go later in the year – ideally, he informed Dorothy Pound on 22 May, 'after I have finished a little poem which I am at present engaged upon'.[66] Little or not, the poem was still unfinished when his mother, brother Henry and sister Marion reached London on 10 June 1921, planning to stay for two months. Tom and Vivien were together again, presenting a united front to the visitors, and showing them how best to manage at Clarence Gate Gardens. Tom attempted to secure separate lodgings for his brother, but Henry ended up sharing Lucy Thayer's flat with Tom and, for a time at least, with Vivien.

Tom also set in motion arrangements for his relations to be received at Garsington. He had told his mother all about Lady Ottoline. Lottie Eliot was 'very excited' at the thought of meeting her.[67] It seems unlikely that Tom's mother had read D. H. Lawrence's *Women in Love*, published in London that June, whose Hermione with her 'horse-face' suggesting 'unenlightened self-esteem' was in part a version of Ottoline Morrell ('to the life' thought Virginia Woolf) and had caused Ottoline, as she made clear to Tom, considerable hurt.[68] This was Mrs Eliot's first trip to England, a country she had read about all her life – the home of classic English literature, and now of her gifted literary son. She was eager to encounter his titled, unusual literary friend in her country manor. Henry, tagging along, was more sceptical.

It was six years since Tom had last met his family. Vivien had been advised by her doctor to remain outside London. Against her specialist's 'express command', she had come to be with her husband. For her, for him and for the visitors, matters were tense. 'These new and yet old relationships involve immense tact and innumerable adjustments', he explained to Aldington. 'One sees lots of things that one never saw before.'[69] The main person Mrs Eliot Senior had never seen before was Vivien. Tom's father had made up his mind without meeting her; Lottie, used to reading between the lines of Vivien's letters, had come to judge for herself. Vivien spent considerable time with her mother-in-law, and one day invited her and Marion Eliot to tea with Osbert and Sacheverell Sitwell. Osbert thought Vivien 'bitterly resented' the visiting matriarch. Vivien gave him the impression that Mrs Eliot had withheld money from Tom because she felt her late husband would not have approved of attempts to 'ease' Tom's financial 'burden'. Yet, Osbert recalled decades later, when eventually he 'met old Mrs. Eliot it was difficult to think any ill of her. She appeared to be a strait-laced, straightforward, conventional, but kindly lady.'[70] Lottie tried. Vivien tried. But by 21 June Tom saw his wife was 'very tired again'. Two days later he was 'very tired' too.[71]

At the end of the month Tom went to see the Ballets Russes perform Stravinsky's daringly dissonant and provocatively danced ballet *Le Sacre du printemps* at the Princes Theatre, Shaftesbury Avenue. He may also have attended the work's Queen's Hall concert performance by an augmented orchestra conducted by Eugene Goossens some days before – an 'extraordinary concatenation of sound'.[72] Certainly he noted that 'on the first night' the music 'was received with wild applause'. Stravinsky was in London. Hailed as 'the greatest success since Picasso', he attended both concert and ballet performances, impressing Tom as he 'took the call many times, small and correctly neat in pince-nez'. 'To me', Tom wrote, 'the music seemed very remarkable'. It had a 'modernity' the accompanying ballet seemed to lack.[73] Premiered in Paris eight years earlier, famously *The Rite of Spring* had caused a riot. Though the London *Times* critic in 1921 could find 'no drama, no story' but only a 'passionless ritual' as the 'Chosen Virgin' (ballerina Lydia Sokolova) danced herself to death, initially surrounded by a 'spasmodic quiver' of other dancers, nonetheless the audience 'roared itself hoarse' in saluting Stravinsky.[74] Attending a '"family house"' performance of the ballet, Tom the City gent used 'the point of an umbrella' to restrain the 'mirth' of people inclined to mock what they saw.[75] This scandalous modern ballet patterned on an ancient pagan fertility ritual reminded him of *Ulysses* as well as of *The Golden Bough*. It confirmed his conviction that a powerful new work of art could draw on an ancient structure – such as that fertility rite which Jessie Weston discerned under-girding Arthurian myths.

His American visitors had different tastes. Soon his strong-spirited mother was keen to make an excursion to the historic, castled English city of Warwick; to behold Shakespeare's Stratford; to visit the Kenilworth made famous by Sir Walter Scott. Tom, who had never been to Warwick, readied himself to accompany her there on 9 July. 'She is terrifyingly energetic for seventy-seven.' Vivien, having had enough, had headed back to Bosham; Lottie Eliot's journal shows she toured this area, too, staying near Itchenor with the Hutchinsons whose cottage had no electricity and very primitive sanitation, but found it 'a nightmare'.[76] Tom's phrasing to Aldington – 'I was just getting my wife away to a place in the country' – suggests Vivien had to be evacuated from London. He hoped she might stay there until the end of July.[77] That was just before his mother was due to leave.

If Mrs Eliot's visit was wearing out Vivien, Tom too felt 'the strain of accommodating myself to people who in many ways are now strangers to me'.[78] And, in the midst of all this, another long-running situation developed. For some time, after the demise of *Art and Letters*, there had been a proposal either to revive it or to start a new quarterly literary journal. Negotiations were now at a particularly delicate stage. Thanks to his expertise, Tom was being lined up as the potential editor. Everything depended on money. The financial backer would be Lady Rothermere, wealthy estranged wife of the publisher of the *Daily Mail*. Lady Rothermere spoke to Thayer in New York. Lady Rothermere spoke to Tom in London. Lady Rothermere contacted other people too. Would the new magazine be linked to the *Dial*? Might it be a reborn *Art and Letters*?

Her Ladyship could be demanding to deal with, and Tom, whose links to Thayer and other editors mattered to him, knew it. 'Exceptional tact' was called for. 'I am sorry to say', he confessed to Ottoline Morrell, '[I] was obliged to call Vivien back from the country to help me out.' Vivien was '*invaluable*'. Still, however, Lady Rothermere held back from placing matters on a definite basis. Vivien, whose own opinion of her Ladyship's plans was that there was 'nothing in the whole business', left London once again, 'worn out', as soon as she could.[79] It had been difficult for her, Tom and Henry to share the Wigmore Street top-floor flat. As the hot July sun beat down through a large skylight, Vivien joked, or half joked, she was 'becoming gradually insane'. She reminded Thayer in a letter that he had once invited her to drown herself with him. 'I am ready at any moment.'[80] Still, once the in-laws had gone, she expected she and Tom might be off to Paris in October.

He was attempting too much: to make his mother, brother and sister happy; to ensure things worked somehow with Vivien; to perform his bank duties; to negotiate about a magazine; to write his 'London Letter' for the *Dial*; and to keep the long poem with which he was struggling still alive in his mind. So far he was just about coping, though it was hard to juggle his family and friends as Lottie Eliot traversed England. If Garsington and Lady Ottoline impressed his mother, who kept a detailed diary of her trip, Henry saw things differently. An intelligent man of finance from Chicago, his tolerance for English rural quaintness was limited; he listed picturesque villages whose names sounded like 'Rotton Eating – Moping Sulky – Ham-on-Rye'. Writing up a mocking account of his visit to aristocratic Garsington with its 'polygamous buttery', and interiors of cobalt 'blue, coral pink, peacock green, dull gold', Henry cast a sceptical eye on the milieu that appeared to enthral his brother. At 'Rotting Wold' he wrote,

> There is a fine gallery of paintings by Picasso, Izzasso, Djingerpop Pfyz, Funiculi-Funicula, and the rest of our little group of intelligentzsia; also a discriminating collection of triptychs, prie-dieu, and moth eaten obscure Florentine Primitives, for Lady Ottoline will tolerate nothing in her collection that is not either hot off the griddle, or petrified with age. Her penchant for Neo-lithic rock drawings and early Senigambiah rattles and teething rings shows how unsullied is her aesh aesthetic [*sic*] taste. The visitor should not pass up the swimming pool, surrounded by what appears to be, at first glance, stone hitching posts in an advance stage of decay, but which prove on close inspection to be art treasures from Hallicarnassus, or

Philippopolis, or somewhere. To appreciate the versatility of our charming hostess, however, one should see her clotting cream, or making cheeses in the buttery, or slaughtering a sheep, in the fold.[81]

Tom loved Henry, and shared aspects of his sense of humour. Yet, working on his own avant-garde poem which juxtaposed the supposedly primitive with the very contemporary, he was now at least as close to Lady Ottoline's milieu as to 2635 Locust Street, St Louis. At times he felt awkward with the people to whom his kinship was strongest. The pull between his mother and his wife was even more difficult. Mrs Eliot, Sr, so loath to let him go, came to feel, she told Henry, that Tom longed for what his family could offer: 'I think the poor boy misses the affection that makes no demands from him, but longs to help him. Vivien loves Tom, and he her, although I think he is afraid of her.'[82] Lottie Eliot had seen a good deal of Vivien, as Tom had hoped; but she remained sceptical. Henry, after living at close quarters with Vivien for several days at Wigmore Street and having corresponded with her for years, was even more so. Discussing Tom's wife after returning to Chicago, Henry wrote to his mother that October,

> Vivien always recites some account of her migraines and malaises in her letters. But I suppose that is natural; it is a relief to talk about one's pains. I do not think she takes proper care of herself, though. I have seen her drink coffee at midnight. I have a feeling that sub-consciously (or unconsciously) she likes the role of invalid; and that, liking as she does to be petted, 'made a fuss over', condoled and consoled, she unconsciously encourages her breakdowns instead of throwing them off by a sort of nervous resistance. It is hard to tell how much is physical and how much mental and uncontrollable by will power; but I think that if she had more of 'the Will to Be Well' she would have less suffering. To acquire this sort of willpower unaided is something like pulling oneself up by one's boot-straps; but I think some strong impulse from outside, some change in her circumstances, might call forth the necessary willpower to be well. She needs something to take her mind off herself; something to absorb her entire attention.[83]

Doing his best with his family, Tom continued wheeling and dealing over the possible new magazine. Having taken time off to entertain his guests, he had to immerse himself in bank business. Where once as head of the new Information Department, he had enjoyed a fine office overlooking the streets of London, now he was underneath them. He called this new workplace 'my cave'.[84] I. A. Richards, who visited him in a Lloyds basement office, described him 'stooping, very like a dark bird in a feeder, over a big table covered with all sorts and sizes of foreign correspondence'. About a foot above Tom's head was a window made of panes of reinforced 'thick, green glass squares' set into the pavement 'on which hammered all but incessantly the heels of the passers-by'. It was a relentlessly oppressive, claustrophobic atmosphere: 'There was just room for two perches beside the table.' Richards thought that the concentrated work required in sorting out the 'highly tangled story' of the materials on that table must have been 'a big, long headache'.[85]

The headache continued. Tom's family left for America on Saturday 20 August. He and Vivien saw them off. 'Stunned', Vivien became very emotional. She fretted afterwards lest her mother-in-law and sister-in-law might have thought she 'behaved like "no lady", and just like a wild animal'. These Americans struck her as oddly 'emotionless'; she felt she had made 'a fearful mess' of getting to know Henry.[86] Her natural vivacity was the opposite of old-school, Boston-trained reserve. It had attracted Tom, but she worried it horrified his family. She saw in them the constricting reserve that so many people detected in Tom. '*Be personal*, you must be personal', she soon urged Henry, 'or else it's no good. Nothing's any good.'[87] 'Polite, formal, even stiff, black-clothed New Englanders' was how Osbert Sitwell remembered Lottie and Marion Eliot.[88] Henry, deeply sympathetic towards his younger brother and knowing what mattered to him, had taken away Tom's old typewriter and replaced it with a brand new one. 'A bloody angel', Vivien called him.[89] He had left her a bunch of roses too.

'Vivien is not well at all', Tom confided to Sydney Schiff, confessing that the 'strain' surrounding his family's departure had left him with a 'reaction' that was 'paralysing'.[90] He wrote to his mother to say how they missed her, how they felt their Clarence Gate Gardens flat had become *her* flat – scarcely a feeling Vivien was likely to welcome. It took them some time to move back in, along with their small cat, 'a very good mouser'.[91] Tom was 'completely exhausted', but while all this was going on, the plan for Lady Rothermere to back the new magazine gathered pace.[92] He committed himself to becoming 'sole responsible editor'. His solicitor drew up a letter of agreement which Her Ladyship signed: she was to provide £600 annually for three years to cover running costs and payment to Tom of at least £100 per annum. He would have 'entire control of the literary contents'.[93] This, at least, was a major success; but in his vulnerable state the responsibility, while exciting, made him 'more worried than anything'.[94]

Sceptical about Lady Rothermere's 'inadequate' largesse, Vivien had her own worries as she underwent further consultations with specialist doctors.[95]

Writing his 'London Letter' that September, Tom recalled Stravinsky's *Rite of Spring* and how it had made a new music through transforming 'the rhythm of the steppes into the scream of the motor horn, the rattle of machinery, the grind of wheels, the beating of iron and steel, the roar of the underground railway, and the other barbaric cries of modern life' which Tom regarded as 'despairing noises'.[96] He was seeking to do something similar in his own long poem, but the adjective 'despairing' revealed his state of mind. Richard Aldington, now permanently separated from his wife the poet H. D., having difficulties with his own mother, and used to dealing with writers' problems, sensed Tom was suffering from nervous exhaustion. To Aldington Tom was 'the one friend I have made since my return' from fighting in the war. The returned soldier wanted to help his struggling ally, and defended Tom against the New England wariness of fellow poet Amy Lowell, telling her that Tom had 'a soundness, a coolness, an urbanity, Ezra never could have. He is quite unprovincial, which is perhaps the highest praise one can give an Anglo-Saxon writer. He is certainly the most attractive critical writer ever produced by America; I for one am extremely grateful to him for living in England and not a little proud that he prefers to.'[97] Aldington invited Tom for a weekend to stay near his home, Malthouse Cottage, in Lower Padworth, on the banks of the Kennet and Avon canal close to Aldermaston station, easily reached by train from London.

While Tom was there around the start of September, Aldington lent him a French book. Tom read it on the train back to London and during bank lunch hours. Jean Epstein's *La Poésie d'aujourd'hui: Un nouvel état d'intelligence* was newly published in Paris. Epstein discussed the fusion of 'L'intelligence et la sensibilité' in modern literature, including the writing of Proust, whom he associated with an 'aristocratie névropathique' (a neurasthenic aristocracy). Modern poets from Baudelaire to Cocteau were associated with 'nervosité', and sometimes with kinds of 'dissociation' that gave their work a 'hermétique', difficult quality. Epstein discussed 'Précision et brièveté' as well as incantatory 'répétition' – qualities Tom had long admired in verse – and the Frenchman linked poetry and science as well as verse and illness. Sometimes poetry had to evade rules of logic and even grammar, making it 'difficile'. Poetry might involve sensing before understanding; as Cocteau had argued, it demanded 'la bataille contre l'inexprimable' (the struggle against the inexpressible). Epstein, who went on to become a film director, linked poetry to 'le cinéma' (rather than to theatre) because of its intimate powers of suggestion; fascinated by the 'esthétique de succession' of 'movies', he argued a poem could be made out of 'une bousculade de détails' (a rush of details). This was an aesthetic of quick transitions and striking metaphors, at once poetic and cinematic. The third part of Epstein's book, mentioning 'magasins des mythes' (stores of myths), linked modern literature and the new poetry of extreme rapidity to a sense of intellectual 'fatigue' at once personal and civilisation-wide. Most attuned to this were people who brought together creativity, intelligence and 'la fatigue nerveuse'.[98]

Having 'enjoyed immensely' his weekend with Aldington, Tom told him he found all this 'most interesting'. He disagreed with some of the conclusions, 'but it is a formidable work to attack, and therefore very tonic'.[99] Just after reading Epstein's book, he wrote to Aldington about feeling 'tired and depressed', making reference to 'neurasthenics like . . . myself'.[100] As so often, illness and creativity seemed bonded for him; and Epstein's book supplied an aesthetic to reinforce the combination. In this same letter he mentioned he had just finished 'an article, unsatisfactory to myself, on the metaphysical poets'. Here he argued that

> It appears likely that poets in our civilization, as it exists at present, must be *difficult*. Our civilization comprehends great variety and complexity, and this variety and complexity, playing upon a refined sensibility, must produce various and complex results. The poet must become more and more comprehensive, more allusive, more indirect, in order to force, to dislocate if necessary, language into his meaning. (A brilliant and extreme statement of this view, with which it is not requisite to associate oneself, is that of M. Jean Epstein, 'La Poésie d'aujourd'hui'.)[101]

Though Tom did not take on board Epstein's theories lock, stock and barrel, he did deploy the psychological term 'dissociation', maintaining that a 'dissociation of sensibility' had set in during the seventeenth century, leading to Romantic poets who 'thought and felt by fits, unbalanced'. As elsewhere, he aligned his favoured English Metaphysical poets, especially Donne, with his cherished French poets, particularly Laforgue. Taking issue with Samuel Johnson who had complained that in Metaphysical verse 'the most heterogeneous ideas are yoked by violence together', he also set out one of the most brilliant descriptions of how poetry is composed.

> When a poet's mind is perfectly equipped for its work, it is constantly amalgamating disparate experience; the ordinary man's experience is chaotic, irregular, fragmentary. The latter falls in love, or reads

Spinoza, and these two experiences have nothing to do with each other, or with the noise of the typewriter or the smell of cooking; in the mind of the poet these experiences are always forming new wholes.[102]

His own long poem carried a strong sense of the 'chaotic, irregular, fragmentary', splicing together various voices, some of them distinctly nervy. For the time being, he had given it the title 'HE DO THE POLICE IN DIFFERENT VOICES',taken from chapter sixteen of Dickens's *Our Mutual Friend* where a boy reading newspaper reports aloud is praised because 'He do the Police in different voices.'[103] Its sonority and resonance unforgettably compelling, Tom's poem depends throughout on intercut voicing and revoicing.

The first two parts, 'The Burial of the Dead' and 'In the Cage', had been typed on his old typewriter, probably in May, during a 'fine hot rainless spring' with its 'crop of murders'.[104] Other shorter poems, including the sexually tormented one entitled in typescript 'Song for the Opherion', were also candidates for possible inclusion. Though most of the long poem's bleak encounters appear heterosexual, he built in allusions to many shades of sexuality, whether (in part three) that of Mr Eugenides – whose name means 'good breeding' and who seems to be gay – or to Tiresias – a man who, the poet Ovid recounts, spent seven years as a woman. In so doing, Tom let his poem speak not just for and from different eras, places and languages, but also (like the work of other modernists including Marcel Duchamp and Man Ray – photographed cross-dressed as Rrose Sélavy in *New York Dada* that April) for and from different sexualities. All are linked by a pervasive sense of torment, infertility, waste. Several poems and fragments would be incorporated, in whole or part, into the larger structure; others would be cut adrift.

Repeatedly that summer, he pondered how to reconcile the wearying raggedness of life with large-scale ordering principles in art. The sometimes jagged, cut-up angularities of 'cubism' were not 'licence, but an attempt to establish order', he wrote in July. To be 'surprising' was 'essential to art: but art has to create a new world, and a new world must have a new structure'. Joyce had succeeded in *Ulysses*; Woolf's best short stories, more 'feminine' and bound up with 'contemplating the feeling rather than the object which has excited it', were often 'remarkable' but 'examples of a process of dissociation'. Tom was writing here for readers of the *Dial*, but also thinking aloud in ways relevant to the bundle of papers, thoughts and feelings he was trying unsuccessfully to finesse into his new poem. 'What is needed of art is a simplification of life into something rich and strange.'¹⁰⁵ Those last words echo a song about drowning in Shakespeare's *Tempest*; Tom alluded to the same song that year in 'Dirge' (about a drowned 'Bleistein' who has, unsettlingly, 'Graves' Disease in a dead jew's eyes') and in untitled lines beginning 'Those are pearls that were his eyes'. Neither piece became part of his long poem. However, another drowned man, 'Phlebas the Phoenician', would feature mesmerically in its chilling fourth part, 'Death by Water'. There drowning brings forgetting of 'profit and loss', and a concluding memento mori invites 'Gentile or Jew' to 'Consider Phlebas, who was once handsome and tall as you'.¹⁰⁶

Classing himself among the 'neurasthenics' by September, Tom was, he told Aldington in confidence, 'seeing a nerve specialist'.¹⁰⁷ Vivien had made the appointment, and accompanied him. The specialist strongly recommended a complete change of scene. Valuing Tom's service, Lloyds Bank granted three months' leave. Friends did what they could. Virginia and Leonard Woolf hosted him at their seventeenth-century country cottage, Monks House, near Lewes in Sussex, for the weekend of 24–25 September. Virginia Woolf enjoyed seeing him, a little 'disappointed to find that I am no longer afraid of him'.¹⁰⁸ Back in London Tom got quotations for printing and publicising his proposed magazine – 'about the size of the *Nouvelle Revue Française*'; but its launch was put on hold.¹⁰⁹ Even from a distance, people who knew him detected something was wrong. Katherine Mansfield wrote to Violet Schiff in October: 'Poor Eliot sounds tired to death. His London letter is all a maze of words. One feels the awful effort behind it – as though he were being tortured. But perhaps thats all wrong and he enjoys writing it. I don't think people ought to be as tired as that, though. It is wrong.'¹¹⁰ To his brother Henry Tom wrote candidly, 'I have been feeling very nervous and shaky lately, and have very little self-control.' This hints at flare-ups of temper, but also depression. He wrote that Vivien needed 'change and stimulus'. His family's visit had been unsettling, but their leaving cut him to the quick: 'Your having been here seems very real', he confided to Henry, 'and your not being here but in Chicago seems as unreal as death'.¹¹¹ He tried to make light of his troubles to his mother, but she worried nonetheless.

Tom's specialist's advice had been to leave immediately for three months, and remain apart from all contacts, resting his mind completely and adhering strictly to a set of rules, which included reading only 'for pleasure, not profit' two hours a day.¹¹² Tom was not so sure. He thought of simply giving up the bank and living off his journalistic wits; but felt that would bring added stresses. With Aldington, who was kind and generous to him, he discussed the idea of writing a book on Wren's London churches; but it would be unremunerative. Still unsure about the specialist's advice, but recognising he must try to get better, he wrote that he had asked Vivien to accompany him to the Kent seaside resort town of Margate 'and stay with me as long as she is willing'.[113] He aimed to spend a month there, after which Lady Rothermere had offered him the use of her Mediterranean villa at La Turbie near Monte Carlo. Vivien would travel with him to France, he hoped, but then go somewhere else 'healthy'.[114] Helping Tom with his voluminous correspondence, she wrote to Thayer to say, 'Tom has had rather a serious breakdown.'[115] Vivien ended her letter by stressing how keen she had been to get out of England for years, and hinted she might come to visit Thayer, who was then in Vienna.

At Margate Vivien and Tom stayed at the 'nice, comfortable', sea-facing Albemarle Hotel in Cliftonville from 15 October.[116] 1920s Margate prided itself as a place where 'Weary men of business are rejuvenated and invigorated by the magical air'; it catered for 'the jaded city dweller, pale and worn' who sought to be 'restored to vigour and activity'.[117] With its chalk cliffs, expansive beaches and many entertainments, the seaside town was a popular summer destination; in 1921 even in late October and early November it boasted entertainments from a performance of Handel's *Messiah* to cinemas showing Charlie Chaplin comedies or romantic dramas such as *Wasted Lives*, *Puppy Love* and *Cupid Hires a Taxi-cab*.[118] From the Eliots' four-storey hotel, one could stride from Cliftonville into town along a walkway at the foot of the cliffs, cutting at low tide across broad sands that in summer were crowded with deckchairs but in winter almost deserted. Tom, 'not unhappy', as Vivien put it on 26 October, kept 'regular hours' and was 'out in this wonderful air nearly all day'.[119] She was going to return to London next day, leaving him at the hotel, but she stayed with him a few days longer, sure he showed 'great improvement already'.[120]

Before she left, Tom, who had been practising 'scales on the mandoline', had decided he needed less 'a nerve man' than 'a specialist in psychological troubles'.[121] Ottoline Morrell had recommended he travel to Lausanne in Switzerland to consult Dr Roger Vittoz, who had treated her as well as helping Aldous Huxley's brother Julian. Tom wrote to Julian Huxley, asking him just 'how brilliant a physician' Vittoz was, particularly 'as a psychologist'.[122] A full recommendation came by return. Vivien agreed Vittoz sounded appropriate. She wrote to Bertrand Russell, saying so, and sending love from them both. She also congratulated the philosopher on becoming a first-time father. Tom joked that if the baby did not have Russell's characteristic pointed ears, nevertheless 'they will sharpen in time'.[123]

He could not quite switch off. He read *The Times Literary Supplement*, and sent in letters to the editor, one of them after noticing correspondence from George Saintsbury about his piece on the Metaphysical poets.

He mailed a postcard to Aldington, then wrote him a short note in which, bluntly, he described the poetry of H. D. as 'stucco'; he added, a couple of weeks later, that he disliked its 'neurotic carnality'.[124] One day around the start of November he walked to the Nayland Rock shelter that overlooks the expansive Margate sands and is close to a memorial to some drowned sailors, one of whom had the unusual surname Crunden – a name familiar from his St Louis childhood. 'Sitting' in one of the individual dark-varnished wooden seats on this covered 'shelter on the front', he wrote 'a rough draft of part III' of his evolving poem, running to 'some fifty lines'.[125]

Some of these presented a confessional speech uttered, apparently, by a woman (like Tom's bank colleague Miss Holt) from Highbury, where he had taught. In his original pencil draft, he first of all had a speaker talk of going 'on the river'. There is recollection of how 'I raised my knees / Stretched on the floor of a perilous canoe'. A lover promises '"a new start"'; but that seems not to have worked out, and 'There were many others'.[126] What survives in the finished poem are the famous lines:

'On Margate Sands.
I can connect
Nothing with nothing.
The broken fingernails of dirty hands.
My people humble people who expect
Nothing.'
      la la[127]

Elsewhere this section juxtaposes the modern, oil-and-tar-polluted Thames with the historic love affair between Queen Elizabeth I and the Earl of Leicester, who sailed on a river barge – 'A gilded shell'.[128] Next come strange fragments of singing, quoted from the Rhine maidens in Wagner's opera *Götterdämmerung* (*The Twilight of the Gods*); then the Margate passage. Later Tom explained this part of his poem as 'The Song of the (three) Thames-daughters'. It is followed by allusions to St Augustine arriving in Carthage (where he encountered 'a cauldron of unholy loves') and to the 'burning' of the Buddha's Fire Sermon. Whatever else is going on here, there are river girls, sex gone wrong and a movement from erotic pain to 'asceticism'.[129] Its fleeting voices sound a poetry of torment.

Tom wired Dr Vittoz in Lausanne. Receiving a favourable response, he prepared to depart via London. Set on this course, he felt more confident; he had already attempted self-diagnosis. 'I am satisfied, since being here', he wrote to Aldington, 'that my "nerves" are a very mild affair, due, not to overwork, but to an *aboulie* and emotional derangement which has been a lifelong affliction'. He may have had difficulties with lack of willpower and emotional problems, but there was 'Nothing wrong with my mind'.[130] He was eager both to show Vivien the new parts of the poem he had been writing and to take the whole lot 'away with me' to Lausanne.[131] On 16 November he saw Mary Hutchinson – a '*great* pleasure'.[132] Then, the following day, a Thursday, he and Vivien set off from London for the Hôtel du Pas-de-Calais, 59 rue des Saints-Pères, Paris.

When he saw them in Paris, Pound thought Tom 'looked not too badly'.[133] In the French capital the Eliots spent several days together, which Vivien found 'very perfect'.[134] Then, at 9.20 on a November evening she saw her husband on to a train as he headed for Switzerland. Suddenly alone on the platform, she felt stunned, as if hit on the head with 'a broomstick'.[135] Though she had decided to visit 'a man' she knew in Cologne (probably her old admirer, Thayer), nonetheless Vivien stayed on in Paris. She saw the Pounds from time to time, and Joyce who struck her as vain and egotistical. 'The man from Cologne' (whose identity she kept secret when mentioning him to Mary Hutchinson) said he would come and stay with her towards the end of December, but it is not clear if he ever did. Thayer's letters show he remained on affectionate terms with Vivien, but also suggest he was wary of becoming entangled with this woman with whom six years earlier he had enjoyed flirting, yet who was now Tom's wife.[136] One of Thayer's purposes in coming to Europe was to undergo analysis with Freud in Vienna; he too had been feeling under strain.

Vivien considered remaining in Paris, if finances allowed; she decided residence there would suit her husband better too, but she felt confused. Sometimes she thought she had 'even forgotten Tom'. At other moments, 'No-one seems at all real to me.'[137] As so often, her own health seemed almost to parallel his; Thayer had sympathised with her in late October about 'nervous breakdowns' that were 'both in the same family'.[138] She was uncertain what the future held. 'About Tom – I *don't know* I don't know', she wrote to Mary Hutchinson, whose company and conversation she missed.[139]

Lausanne throughout the second half of November and December was calm and foggy – so overcast that for much of his stay Tom could not even see the spectacular surrounding mountains. Though he remained mainly in the town itself, in December he visited Berne where he acquired Hermann Hesse's 1920 *Blick ins Chaos: drei Aufsätze* (*A Look into Chaos: Three Essays*), which suggested that at least half of Europe was sliding towards complete disorder. Confirming his own sense of decaying civilisation, the book filled him with 'admiration'.[140] If perception of impending chaos matched his personal breakdown and nourished his evolving long poem, his anxieties were countered by Vittoz's treatment and by Lausanne's comparative tranquillity. Its streets sloping down to the shores of Lac Léman where lake steamers and small boats were moored, this well-heeled place of banks and chocolatiers was quiet after London and Paris. The castle, cathedral, casino, gift shops and cobbled streets attracted appreciative tourists. With 70,000 inhabitants, Lausanne, chief city of Switzerland's Vaud region, was contained but cosmopolitan. Its grandest hotel, the Beau-Rivage Palace at Ouchy, overlooked the Lake with its smart yachts and mountain views: 'un symbol prestigieux' of Lausanne's *bon ton*.[141] If not quite so imposing, Tom's hotel was assuredly elegant. The Hôtel-Pension Ste-Luce, on the corner of the avenue Ste-Luce further up the hill, had high-ceilinged rooms that looked out on to lawns adorned with mature trees and a pale, dinky summer house.[142] Lady Ottoline had recommended it, and the staff told Tom they had put him into what had been her room. Talking French, he was among 'many nationalities, which I always like'.[143] Vittoz's clinic, which formed part of his house, the villa Cimerose in the avenue Linden, was just a short stroll downhill.

Then almost sixty, Dr Roger Henry Melling Vittoz, whom Tom liked 'very much personally', had been born near Lausanne, the son of a history professor resident for a time in England.[144] Trained in Lausanne and Geneva, the doctor had been influenced by Pierre Janet, whose work Tom knew. As well as coining the psychological term 'dissociation', Janet had written about rather Prufrockian problems of the will including 'l'irrésolution' in *Les Obsessions et la psychasthénie*.[145] A kindly, rather formal man, the tall, balding Vittoz soon offered a 'diagnosis' of Tom's problem, which the poet regarded as 'good'.[146] While in Lausanne, Tom used Janet's terminology to describe the condition for which he was being treated as 'psychasthénie', sometimes associated with fatigue and anxiety.[147] Dr Vittoz, he wrote to Ottoline Morrell on 30 November, 'inspires me with confidence' and was 'putting me through the primary exercises very rapidly'.[148]

Tom read the 1921 edition of Vittoz's book, *Traitement des psychonévroses par la rééducation du contrôle cérébral* and marked in his copy a passage concerning '*Aboulie*' (lack of will).[149] Julian Huxley, who had been experiencing problems with 'any attempt to reach a decision, even in trivial matters' a few years earlier when Lady Ottoline had recommended Vittoz to him, recorded in old age a description of the Swiss physician's initial 'exercises':

His method was to propose some simple subject on which to concentrate, such as visualizing a circle or a square, or solving an easy mathematical problem, and to test the validity of my efforts with the side of his hand on my forehead, whereby he claimed that he could feel and estimate the special brain-pulse accompanying genuine concentration. Gradually more complex subjects for concentration were propounded and the exercises became easier to carry out.[150]

Vittoz believed 'insufficient brain control' was at the root of illnesses such as Tom's, which could be brought on by 'sorrow, or excessive worry in work'. The brain had 'two different working centres': 'the conscious or objective' which controlled 'reason, judgment and will'; and 'the unconscious or subjective' which was 'in a general way the source of the ideas and sensations'. Under conditions of 'insufficiency or instability of control' the objective brain grew weak; the balance between the two 'centres' was thrown out of kilter, producing at times 'a whirl of unconnected and uncontrolled ideas'.[151] Strengthening the will let patients regain 'control'. Having written about the need to overcome poetry's 'dissociation of sensibility' some months before encountering Vittoz, Tom had developed an aesthetic that chimed with aspects of this physician's thought. The American poet came, too, from a family whose strict New England ancestry relished a flinty emphasis on self-control. The better he got to know Vittoz, the more convinced he became he had made the right choice.

Vittoz encouraged *'concentration on the idea of calm'*, asking a patient to 'imagine' the 'brain in a state of calm' by focusing on an 'object' that would 'evoke in his mind some idea which will itself produce that feeling'. The physician did not use the term 'objective correlative', but his method accorded with Tom's poetics. An appropriate object to focus on might be a landscape or a piece of music or a 'prayer'. A favourite exercise was to concentrate alternately on 'the mathematical symbol of infinity' and then on the numeral 1.[152] Another thought-exercise involved focusing on a word, then making sure that it was 'rubbed out letter by letter', before applying the same process 'to a sentence'.[153] This sits interestingly alongside the compositional technique of eliminating parts of sentences (and even words) that Tom was essaying already:

To Carthage then I came

Burning burning burning burning
O Lord thou pluckest me out
O Lord thou pluckest

burning[154]

Vittoz's ideas, techniques and treatment functioned as encouragement and confirmation. They followed soon after Tom read in Jean Epstein's book that neurasthenic conditions might heighten creativity.

Not for the first time he managed to write from the heart of his illness at the same time as drawing strength from his cure. Vittoz explained that there might be physiological symptoms of anxiety 'due to insufficient brain control' such as 'excessive excitability which makes the sufferer aware of the slightest noise, and is very frequently a cause of insomnia'.[155] Tom marked that passage in Vittoz's book, and wrote the word 'handwriting' beside a section dealing with how under conditions of 'exhaustion' arising from 'over-tension' often 'the muscles are at first more or less contracted and sometimes painful'.[156] This may relate to problems with his fingers; in a photograph taken with his mother that summer, he is wearing a finger stall.[157] It is impossible to know exactly what he confided to Dr Vittoz, but some months later he wrote of how 'Whenever I get very tired or worried I recognise all the old symptoms ready to appear, with half a chance, and find myself under the continuous strain of trying to suppress a vague but intensely acute horror and apprehension. Perhaps the greatest curse of my life is noise and the associations which imagination immediately suggests with various noises.'[158] Helping patients control their brains through a strengthened will, Vittoz aimed to cure both psychological and physiological symptoms. Tom's long poem filled up with a cacophony of noises: car horns, an out-of-tune church bell, animal cries, shouts, thunderclaps.

For Vittoz 'an uncontrolled idea' was 'like a rudderless vessel'.[159] Concentration brought the mind back into balance, helping it resist *aboulie*. Exercises, such as listening for short spells to a metronome or writing down the figure 1, then speaking it 'mentally' three times with an interval between each time, increased the power of concentration'.[160] So did very deliberate attention to conversation and '*Concentration on the idea of control*'. Several of Vittoz's exercises involved sounds and listening. He stressed the need to avoid the '*cliché*', by which he meant 'bad impressions' which had become 'crystallized in the brain' and so 'always reproduce the same symptom mechanically'.[161] Patients had to understand how to rid themselves of clichés. What poet could disagree with that?

After just over a week of this psychotherapy Tom enthused about how 'at moments I feel more calm than I have for many many years − since childhood − that may be illusory − we shall see'.[162] He listened to the sounds of the Swiss city, noisy when 'children come downhill on scooters over the cobbles', pleasant when a local 'Good orchestra plays "The Love Nest"', a hit from the 1920 Broadway show *Mary*, its tune simple and sentimental to the point of monotony, and its description poignantly remote from Tom's situation.[163] Asking her how she was, he mentioned it to his own close friend Mary Hutchinson in England.

> Just a love nest
> Cozy with charm,
> Just a love nest
> Down on a farm.
> A veranda with some sort of clinging vine,
> Then a kitchen where some rambler roses twine.
> Then a small room,
> Tea set of blue;
> Best of all, room –
> Dream room for two.
> Better than a palace with a gilded dome,
> Is a love nest
> You can call home.[164]

Tom listened as the Lausanne band played, and was very far away from all that.

In an odd way, there was a lot of American culture around him: *Tarzan*, *Les Nuits de New-York* and Charlie Chaplin at Lausanne's several cinemas; Broadway musical tunes in its streets; even in the local newspaper mention of 'tourbillons' (tornados) near the Mississippi.[165] Thinking of his family, he sent a 'Christmas letter'.[166] In lines written in Lausanne, but later dropped from his poem, he wrote of how 'Aeneas' mother, with an altered face, / Appeared once in an unexpected place'. This allusion to a classical mother, Aphrodite, who is recognised by her son as 'a goddess', is compared to the way 'The sweating rabble in the cinema / Can recognise a goddess or a star'.[167] Such fusing of the ancient maternal with the erotic power of the screen 'goddess' is telling. Like other aspects of the poem, it hints how much older mythological patterns underlie modern urban life; but it shows too a rather awkward attempt to reconcile the maternal with the erotic: a challenge for Tom in his life.

While he underwent psychological treatment, material from boyhood came into his head, mixing with his reading and recent sufferings. 'By the waters of Leman I sat down and wept' was part of a passage he added to 'The Fire Sermon', fusing the Old Testament psalmist's 'By the rivers of Babylon, there we sat down, yea, we wept, when we remembered Zion' (Psalm 137:1) with his own situation here beside Lac Léman.[168] As his powers of concentration increased, he turned his attention not so much towards revising the poetry he had brought with him as to writing a fresh, concluding section. Matthew Gold has pointed out that the poet reached a stage where he was 'speaking Vittoz' language' in his correspondence.[169] On 13 December he wrote to his brother Henry, 'The great thing I am trying to learn is how to use all my energy without waste, to be *calm* when there is nothing to be gained by worry, and to concentrate without effort.' He hoped that if he could achieve this, 'I shall place less strain upon Vivien, who has had to do so much *thinking* for me.'[170] A few days later he explained to Sydney Waterlow that he had become aware of 'losing power of concentration and attention, as well as becoming a prey to habitual worry and dread of the future; consequently, wasting far more energy than I used, and wearing myself out continuously. And I *think* I am getting over that.' Tom was also 'trying to finish a poem – about 800 or 1000 lines. *Je ne sais pas si ça tient*. [I do not know if it will work].'[171]

The section that was to conclude his poem presented suffering and breakdown; also instruction involving 'control'. Featuring a voice of authority emanating from a thunderstorm, it was sometimes clear and incantatory, but often a swirling vortex of fragments. The damp of wintry Lausanne and the physician who counselled 'control' do not feature. Instead, presented through hypnotic repetition, the landscape is one of 'sweat', 'sand' and 'dry sterile thunder and no rain'. There, like a halluci-nation, is heard the cry of a bird Tom remembered from boyhood:

> If there were water
> And no rock
> If there were rock
> And also water
> And water
> A spring
> A pool among the rock
> If there were the sound of water only
> Not the cicada, and
> Dry grass singing
> But sound of water over a rock
> Where the hermit thrush sings in the pine trees
> Drip-drop drip-drop drop drop drop
> But there is no water . . .[172]

Pencilled in Lausanne on square-lined paper, these words formed part of what Tom regarded as his poem's finest section. The passage about searching for water in the desert and not finding it but hearing instead, like a vivid acoustic hallucination, the water-dripping song of the bird, communicates a sense of implacable desperation that can be detected equally by young children and by sophisticated older readers. Filled with longing, frustration, a restless search for spiritual meaning, and a fluid, incantatory beauty, it is one of the most haunting passages in poetry.

Tom seems to have written it relatively quickly, and made few changes in revision. 'A moment comes', he wrote in 1922, 'when the thing comes out almost automatically; I think that it is partly the anxiety and desire to express it exactly that form the obstacle; then a moment of self-forgetfulness arrives and releases the inspiration'.[173] That was how some of his finest poetry was written, not least in Margate and Lausanne.

He followed those lines containing the thrush's song with several other passages spliced together, including his pre-1914 one about the Dracula-like figure who 'crawled head downward down a blackened wall'. Soon came another strange acoustic triumph: 'Then spoke the thunder'. Readers hear a simple sound repeated three times

DA

. . .

DA

. . .

DA

. . .

Though articulated in the age of Dada, these monosyllables come from a very ancient fable. Each 'DA' metamorphoses into a Sanskrit word, as happens in the original passage from the *Upanishads* that Tom had read at Harvard. Probably working from memory, he reordered the words. They remain untranslated, enhancing their aural weirdness and the poem's sense of resonating far into distances of time and space. In the original these sounds are uttered in response to urgent requests for guidance from the Lord of Creation, who speaks in the form of thunder. Each time the thunder-word 'DA' is uttered, listeners interpret it differently, and each interpretation is pronounced correct: the first 'DA' in the modern poem becomes '*Datta*' (which means 'give'); the second becomes '*Dayadhvam*' ('sympathise'); the third emerges as '*Damyata*' ('control').[174]

Yet in the poem each of these words of instruction is succeeded by an instance where the guidance has not been accepted, or, with painful consequences, seems to have been followed wrongly. The injunction to 'give' brings mention of 'The awful daring of a moment's surrender' which cannot be retracted and is kept secret; the counsel to 'sympathise' brings an image of being locked solipsistically inside the prison of the self; the culminating advice to 'control' sparks a memory of expertly sailing a boat, but this leads to an apparently vanished erotic opportunity: the mood of the verb in the phrase 'your heart would have responded' suggests a heart that never did so.[175]

Soon control seems lost. A short last verse paragraph brings further breakdown, whether heard in the nursery rhyme 'London Bridge is falling down falling down falling down' or in the swirl of fragments that ensues, bringing 'ruins' and madness. 'O Hieronimo!' Scofield Thayer had written in an unsigned 'Comment' in the May 1921 *Dial*, signalling disapproval of what seemed to him a crazy idea. Thayer was alluding to the figure of Hieronimo in Kyd's Elizabethan drama, *The Spanish Tragedy*, which carried the alternative title of *Hieronymo is Mad Agayne*.[176] Tom's 'Hieronymo's mad againe' glances towards the same play, sometimes regarded as an ancestor of *Hamlet*, and tilts his own poem towards insane breakdown, unless the repetition of the Sanskrit words of guidance and the final 'Shantih shantih shantih' (meaning, Tom later explained, 'The Peace which passeth understanding') can be heard as a closing note of calm.[177]

Written in Lausanne, this latest section of the poem pivots between despair and saving guidance. Over a decade later, Tom told Virginia Woolf, 'he wrote the last verses' of *The Waste Land* 'in a trance – unconsciously', and emphasised that 'he did not like poetry that had no meaning for the ear'.[178] Veering among several languages, its lines usually strike readers more for their sound of chaos and longing, with a hint of final hush in the 'Sh' of the three-times-repeated 'Shantih', than for any sense of benign closure. In the manuscript there was a full stop after the last 'Shantih', but Tom got rid of that punctuation mark when he typed up his draft. Even after he had completed this passage, he was uncertain how his poem should be arranged, and exactly how many sections would constitute the finished work. Writing to his brother on 13 December about how he liked being among people of 'many nationalities', he stated, 'I am certainly well enough to be working on a poem!'[179] The emphatic exclamation mark and the word 'certainly' may signal that actually Tom was not quite sure how recovered or otherwise he was. Nor could he decide the exact length of his poem: '800 or 1000 lines'. He had still not been able to control it completely, to resolve it in its final order. Shortly before leaving Lausanne he told Henry he was about to rejoin Vivien in Paris, and looking forward to socialising there. Tom's phrasing suggests recovery, but not total well-being: 'I am ever so much better, my concentration improves and I am beginning to feel full of energy. I am working at a poem too.'[180]

People have long argued about whether or not the passages following the 'DA' injunctions have biographical significance. In the section about giving, the poet wrote in his early manuscript draft, 'My friend, my friend, beating in my heart, / The awful daring of a moment's surrender'.[181] Since the line above, in which the words 'we brother' seem to have been crossed out, may indicate a male addressee, some detect the presence of Jean Verdenal. Yet the phrasing 'My friend, my friend' echoes a speech in Act IV, scene i, of Dryden's *All for Love,* that play which Tom had so admired earlier in 1921. In it Dolabella, following an interchange about 'constancy', laments how his friend Antony has lost his loving relationship with Cleopatra, whom he thinks unfaithful: 'My friend, my friend, / What endless treasure thou hast thrown away'.[182] This echo of a ruined heterosexual relationship might more readily call to mind the Eliots' troubled marriage. The poem has roots in that relationship which contribute to its power, but it is written so that any autobiographical sources are endlessly refracted. In Tom's terminology, they are made 'impersonal', given a wider, carrying resonance that came to voice the despair of a whole society rather than simply a damaged personal intimacy. That blend of the intimate and the overarching gives the poetry much of its remarkable power, its startling, aching acoustic.

Tom left Lausanne for Paris around New Year 1922, having written a poem like no other in the English language, but its final form remained unresolved. It was still a bundle of papers in his luggage. He was no longer happy with the title 'He Do the Police in Different Voices'. Apparently echoing the title of a poem by Madison Cawein (published in *Poetry* in January 1913), the new title he chose highlights despair, barrenness and his use of Jessie Weston's ideas about how ancient fertility ceremonies underpinned more modern religious and cultural designs. Tom drew on his memories of Weston's book at several points, and not least in the new lines written in Lausanne. These allude to the search for healing (provided, Weston explains, by 'the Doctor'), to the revival of a 'Waste Land', and to the Holy Grail quest with its 'ruined Chapel' often linked to a cemetery.[183] Having read about the Grail quest since boyhood, Tom wrote of 'tumbled graves, about the Chapel' in 'What the Thunder Said'.[184] His poem would be called *The Waste Land.*

16

The Waste Land

A T the start of 1922, when Tom reached Paris, his wife thought him 'much better'.[1] Long-term residence in the French capital, she had decided, was not for her. Nevertheless, after he returned to London on 16 January, Vivien was going to stay on and spend time in Lyons without him.[2] Their relationship remained fraught. Pound, who had recently translated, for New York publisher Boni and Liveright Rémy De Gourmont's *Physique de l'amour* (a sexually explicit work advocating the right to 'leave' monogamy, then 'return at will'), considered having a serious conversation with his friend about sex.[3] Still, Tom seemed happier now 'in the midst of Paris', so Pound decided not to broach the subject.[4] Tom went to see the charismatic, leggy 'Paris Miss' Mistinguett 'at the Casino de Paris'. A vibrant singer-actress, she made him think of music-hall stars he loved, including Marie Lloyd.[5] Explaining to John Quinn in February that Tom had come 'back from his Lausanne specialist looking O.K.', Pound made it clear, however, that he was still 'worried about' him. Might there be a way to release him from the bank, and, ideally, from Vivien? 'Eliot has beautiful manners, wd. adorn any yacht club, etc.' Himself too wildly outspoken ever to adorn a yacht club, Pound was sure Tom 'ought to be private secretary to some rich imbecile . . . failing that you might send over someone to elope, kidnap, or otherwise eliminate Mrs E.'[6]

In Paris Tom (whose own imaginings turned more than once in his work to men who eliminate women) talked with his countryman Pound about books, including ancient Greek drama. The Eliots met Pound's publisher Horace Liveright, who was visiting. They dined with Joyce. Eager for the publishing coup of 1922, the ambitious Liveright was angling to publish *Ulysses* and further work by Pound as well as Tom's new poem. However, Liveright worried that this last seemed too short to make a book, and soon asked if the poet could 'add' more material.[7] Tom spoke with Jacques Rivière and went looking for André Gide; both wanted him to contribute to the *Nouvelle Revue Française*. In the Pounds' small studio apartment at 70 bis, rue Notre-Dame-des-Champs, not far from the Luxembourg Gardens and less than a mile from Tom's old student lodgings, Pound pored over the bundle of papers containing his friend's most recent poetry. Astutely, he opined on 8 January that this new work was only 'in semi-existence'.[8] It looked 'damn good', but needed reshaping. A month or so later he wrote that Tom had arrived with a 'poem (19 pages) in his suit case' and that it had been 'finished up here'.[9] Pound was very much part of that final honing; the bundle had run to more than nineteen pages. Revising and editing continued after Tom returned to London. This process involved both himself and Pound, who scribbled vigorously in blue pencil over Tom's words. They went through the whole thing at least three times each, pretty much halving its length.

Pound's *Poems 1918–21* had just been published by Boni and Liveright. The volume contained the fourth, fifth, sixth and seventh 'Cantos', which Tom had read earlier with fascination. Criss-crossing history and geography, these poems fused Western and Eastern motifs; bookishly, they melded quotations from several languages, mixing lyric moments with passages of direct speech. In compositional technique, they were akin to parts of *The Waste Land*. Used to editing, Pound had been doing more than working on his 'Cantos'. In 1921 he had been looking over and bringing into print another long poem, Jean Hugo's 'The Cape of Good Hope', a one-hundred-and-twenty-eight-page typescript translation of Jean Cocteau's capacious 1918 *Le Cap de Bonne-Espérance*. Pound had subjected it to a 'brushing up' until, he felt, it read as if 'written originally in English'; it had appeared in the Autumn 1921 *Little Review* which Tom had read by November.[10]

Immersed in the Parisian literary scene, Pound had a taste for Cocteau's work. *Le Cap* emanated from the Paris of Dada, Picasso and Stravinsky. With its 'foaming Cumean / shaken Sybil', fragmented verse paragraphs, odd sounds ('ue ue eo ea') and snatches of song, this poem too, while dealing with the modern world of war and air travel, ranged across history.[11] Hints of narrative in it remain only slivers.[12] In suggesting how Tom should revise *The Waste Land*, Pound cut swathes of conventional storytelling: out went the Popeian couplets about Fresca (Pope had done this sort of thing better) and the long depiction of sailing off America's northeast coast. As the drafts were scribbled on and sent back and forth, the poem became more cubist or kaleidoscopic. Pound also approved cutting the account of a Boston night on the town which had opened part one.

Now, after that excision, the work began strikingly with 'April is the cruellest month', and had at its start a focus on 'breeding'. Turning convention on its head, Tom's arresting lines present the renewing fertility of spring as painful, not pleasurable: April brings back a torturing cycle of mingled 'Memory and desire'.[13] The poem develops less through extended narrative than through juxtapositions of striking images. Not without elements of 'story' – the lines about walking through the desert longing for water now stand out all the more – in its episodic structure it has moved closer to French avant-garde verse.

Accepting Pound's brilliant suggestions, Tom remained the author and final shaper of his work. Pound's editing was highly ethical: he cut material, leaving only Tom's best words to stand, but did not interpolate words of his own. He was sharpening, rather than inventing or adding. This editor of genius was vital to *The Waste Land*, as was Vivien who also furthered the poem's honing. Once again, Tom's creative endeavour and illness operated eerily in tandem. As soon as he returned, alone, to London, he was 'in bed with influenza' for at least ten days; and on 20 January, he wrote to Thayer mentioning he would 'shortly have ready a poem of about 450 lines, in four parts', and asking whether the *Dial* might publish it. If so, how much might they pay?[14] Tom seemed minded to cut all the 'Death by Water' section, and wondered if each of his poem's 'four parts' might appear in successive issues of the magazine. At the end of his manuscript he had placed what Pound saw as 'superfluities', including 'Song for the Opherion' and 'Exequy' in which a buried lover's 'suburban tomb' becomes a holy place for ritual sex and suicide.[15] Wisely, Pound advised cutting these. They added nothing, and without them the final 'Shantih shantih shantih' might resonate far more impressively. Pound convinced Tom that from 'April' to 'shantih' had to be how the poem should run.

'Complimenti, you bitch', Pound wrote from Paris on 24 January, protesting himself intensely jealous of what had emerged from Tom's manuscripts. From the rue Notre-Dame-des-Champs came increasingly bawdy verses celebrating how 'Ezra performed the caesarean Operation' of delivering the eventual poem.[16] Towards the end of the month Tom still wondered about using 'Gerontion' as a preface. No, Pound advised. Should all mention of Phlebas be cut? Absolutely not, came the reply from Paris. So the poem became a five-part piece, its fourth section much shorter than the others. Proud of his sometimes bloody interventions, Tom's assertive poetic midwife (who had been reading the work aloud and thought it sounded great) suggested that the epigraph from *Heart of Darkness* about 'horror' might lack *gravitas*. Reluctantly, while considering it 'somewhat elucidative', Tom dropped this. Later, drawing on his undergraduate reading of Petronius and his own darkest fears, he substituted instead the epigraph in Latin and Greek in which the withered Sibyl of Cumae longs 'to die'.[17] Ultimately, using a phrase from Dante, in later editions he would dedicate the poem to Pound, calling him gratefully '*il miglior fabbro*' – the greater craftsman.

Even as he completed *The Waste Land*, Tom was getting ideas for another extended work in verse. Unfinished, unpublished, it would lie for several years. Like *The Waste Land*, 'Sweeney Agonistes' is patterned on anthropological interpretations of literature (in this case Aristophanic ancient Greek comedies) which detected fertility rites undergirding literary forms. In both works sexual fertility has gone wrong. Tom's fragmentary drama would fuse these ideas with jazz-age songs and rhythms. In the wake of their meetings in Paris, he and Pound had been comparing notes on Greek plays, while Tom reread Aristophanes. Pound had odd ideas about human sexuality: he had opined that the 'brain' might well be 'in origin and development, only a sort of great clot of genital fluid'.[18] He liked to see himself as a phallic force to be reckoned with, and suggested to his friend: 'Aristophanes probably depressing, and the native negro phoque melodies of Dixee more calculated to lift the ball-encumbered phallus of man to the proper 8.30, 9.30 or even ten thirty level now counted as the crowning and alarse too often katachrestical summit of human achievement.'[19] Benignly, he wrote to Tom, 'May your erection never grow less', and explained that 'I had intended to speak to you seriously on the subject' in Paris.[20] This suggests that Pound realised *The Waste Land* was bound up profoundly with Tom's sex life; a few days earlier Pound had implied that the poem represented an 'exuding' of 'deformative secretions'.[21] In 'Sweeney Agonistes', however satirically treated, Tom's articulation of sexual torment would continue. The poet who in life had fine yacht-club manners created a drama featuring a man who wants to 'do a girl in'.[22]

Tom and Vivien were reunited in London when she returned to the flat around 25 January to find him still ill with flu. 'V. sends you her love', Tom wrote to Pound just after she was back, adding that she 'says that if she had realised how bloody England is she would not have returned'. He had been feeling 'excessively depressed'.[23] Nevertheless, he donned his dinner jacket on 2 February to dine with Lady Rothermere and Richard Cobden-Sanderson who was to become the publisher of the new magazine he would edit. He also tried to catch up with correspondence. A letter arrived from Thayer, offering $150 for Tom's new poem, sight unseen. Possibly sensing continuing tensions between the Eliots, as St Valentine's Day approached Thayer sent 'Valentinian love to Vivien and yourself!'[24] On 14 February Tom lunched not with Vivien but with Conrad Aiken, telling him he was seeking an American publisher for his new long poem. Aiken recommended the Dunster House Press in Cambridge, Massachusetts, but, though Tom pursued it, this idea came to nothing.

He had begun showing *The Waste Land* to friends, including Aldington. Instead of accepting Thayer's offer (worth about £35), Tom cabled asking for at least £50, but his cable was garbled in transmission. Meanwhile he was writing more prose: London letters for the *Nouvelle Revue Française* and the *Dial* as well as a short piece for Lewis's *Tyro* arguing that 'literature is not primarily a matter of nationality, but of language'. He did not want productions that were only of 'local importance' like most modern writing from England, America and Ireland. He sought work like Joyce's, that had 'not only the tradition but the consciousness of it'.[25] That was what the completed *Waste Land* possessed to an astonishing degree. It sent deep taproots into English-language verse, then went even further, in strong, sustaining contact with other European and non-European traditions.

Yet still he despaired. His *Dial* 'London Letter' for May emphasised 'the particular torpor or deadness which strikes a denizen of London after his return' from an absence of 'three months'. English and American poetry seemed, for the most part, 'conventional and timid'. This *Waste Land* poet who would go on to write 'The Hollow Men' pondered the frightening idea of 'the man who has no core', and detected a lack of true 'moral integrity' in modern poetry. American work, including the 'uninteresting' verse of Robert Frost, had its own 'torpor'.[26] Tom could debate the finer points of Jacobean drama, but his domestic situation was as bleak as ever. His own wife terminally sick, Middleton Murry understood such strains. Spending a weekend in Murry's company during February, Tom was able to set aside their aesthetic differences, replacing them with a sense of shared difficulties. A doctor told Vivien she should go at once to a nursing home. She could not sleep and Tom found it hard to cope with her. She went. Arranging to sublet their flat, he moved back to 12 Wigmore Street, waiting for her to return.

He contacted Pound, who was soon in touch with Scofield Thayer, telling him, 'Eliot has merely gone to pieces again. Abuleia, simply the physical impossibility of correlating his muscles sufficiently to write a letter or get up and move across a room.' This was, Pound opined, 'a pathological state, due to condition of his endocrines'.[27] Reflecting on Tom in late February, Katherine Mansfield decided he was 'attractive' yet 'pathetic': 'He suffers from his feelings of powerlessness. He knows it. He feels weak. It is all disguise. That slow manner, that hesitation, side long glances and so on are *painful*. And the pity is that he is too serious about himself, even a little bit absurd. But its natural; it's the fault of London that. He wants kindly laughing at and setting free.'[28] Mary Hutchinson felt similarly about this man she was so fond of, and 'tried hard to "loosen him up"'.[29] Pound, too, perceived his good friend needed to be emancipated from at least some of his troubles, and strove to buy him time to write without anxiety. Judging the situation desperate, Pound urged Thayer to find a way of getting Tom money – perhaps through a prize offered by the *Dial*, or maybe via a loan or subscription. Around this time Tom substituted that new epigraph to *The Waste Land* ending with those Greek words meaning, 'I want to die'.[30]

He was angry at Thayer, whom he felt was exploiting him. Their history of rivalry complicated friendship: eager for the success of the *Dial*, Thayer had been less than rapturous about Tom's editing a new magazine that might become a competitor. Tired, sometimes thin-skinned, Tom asserted the value of his own poetry in demanding more cash for *The Waste Land*. Drawing on the businessman part of his character, he pulled himself together and wrote to Pound, setting out terms he had agreed for his new, London-based but internationally oriented journal. He solicited Pound (who had turned against England's literary culture) as a contributor, hoping his friend might also attract work from Continental writers including Cocteau. Tom wrote, too, to Valéry Larbaud, asking to publish a lecture on Joyce that Larbaud had delivered in Paris during December. It would form part of the first number of the new 'critical review'.[31] He secured a contribution for the same issue from Hermann Hesse on 'Recent German Poetry', and convinced Sydney Schiff to translate *Blick ins Chaos*.

On 13 March, having moved flats to 12 Wigmore Street and sublet 9 Clarence Gate Gardens until June, Tom described himself (probably accurately) as 'irritable and exhausted'. However, his magazine planning showed he believed he could cope with his problems as before – by throwing himself determinedly into work. Having been edited so effectively by Pound, he became all the more a committed editor, sourcing contributions and composing business letters with consummate aplomb. Sometimes he immured himself in protective editorial reserve; writing a short note to Thayer about Schiff's translation of *Blick ins Chaos*, he signed himself 'Sincerely yours, T. S. Eliot', as if he and Thayer maintained a purely commercial relationship.[32] Yet, better than most people, Tom knew the business of writing. He understood that good authors valued style first, but cared, too, about financial reward.

Having received a garbled telegram apparently indicating Tom wanted at least £856 for his new poem, Thayer sent a frosty but not belligerent reply. Pound was wary of Tom's new magazine; offering £10 per 5,000 words, it was likely to pay less than the *Dial*. Yet he remained concerned about Tom. 'Eliot is at the last gasp', he wrote to William Carlos Williams in America on 18 March.[33] Having been the beneficiary of John Quinn's largesse, Pound had been developing a scheme he called 'Bel Esprit'. Using a subscription model, the aim was to channel money to talented artists – 'captives' needing 'release'. Sending Williams an outline of his idea, he explained that Aldington and he had already pledged £10 each per annum. 'Leisure', Pound contended, was essential to the true artist, but Tom had returned to the 'bank, and is again gone to pieces, physically', along with his 'invalid wife'. Bel Esprit was less a charity than a way to 'restart civil-ization', bolstering artistic excellence.[34] Branches of it might be set up in various European and American locations to support the arts generally. Tom must be its first beneficiary.

Soon Pound publicised this heady scheme in several places. He wrote about it for the *New Age* magazine. He distributed a private circular, making clear the plan had been hatched without Tom's knowledge. He also stated Tom's 'bank work has diminished his output of poetry, and . . . his prose has grown tired'. Pound proclaimed *The Waste Land* a 'series of poems, possibly the finest that the modern movement in English has produced'.[35] This was a big claim for a 'series' that almost no one had read, but several subscribers pledged cash. May Sinclair matched the money committed by Pound and Aldington. As the plan developed, Tom felt increasingly awkward.

Virginia Woolf had suffered frightening bouts of chronic insomnia the previous summer, then a relapse in January. She was still under the weather when she saw Tom in early March. Intelligently and unpatron-isingly nice to her, he made her smile. She found him 'grown supple as an eel; yes, grown positively familiar & jocular & friendly, though retaining I hope some shreds of authority. I mustn't lick all the paint off my Gods.' He told her about his nascent magazine and wanted her to contribute – Leonard Woolf too. Work would be needed by 15 August. Then he discussed his new poem. It would take up about '40 pages' and they agreed the Hogarth Press would publish it 'in the autumn'. Tom does not seem to have shown the Woolfs *The Waste Land* yet. He was hoarding it. 'This is his best work, he says', Woolf wrote in her diary. 'He is pleased with it; takes heart, I think, from the thought of that safe in his desk.' They gossiped, not least about Murry, whom they consid-ered dishonest as a writer, and probably as a man. 'I've ceased even to think about Murry. I've forgotten all about him', Tom maintained. Woolf, a connoisseur of such gossip, had heard from Clive Bell, via Mary Hutchinson, that Tom used 'violet powder to make him look cadaverous'.³⁶ Tom, though he could seem cheerful to Woolf, was run down again: the powder may have been a nod to Baudelaire (a poet who advocated wearing 'make-up'), but it may just have been for a skin complaint.³⁷

His situation grew little better. Moving had been 'hell', and by 16 March Vivien, back from her nursing home, was 'in bed with fever'. Once more he had been 'very tired and depressed'.³⁸ Finding out about Bel Esprit hardly cheered him. If news of it reached the bank, where he was trusted and had just been given a special period of leave, it could be seen as a slur on his employer. Pound, having sounded Tom out about his financial needs, meant well, but a scheme that required thirty guarantors each to pledge £10 per annum sounded unreliable. Also, it could embarrass Tom and his friends. Over the coming months, it did.

By early April he was still keeping *The Waste Land* hidden from the Woolfs. 'My dear Tom', Virginia Woolf wrote to him, slipping in a request to see it.³⁹ No poem arrived. Nor had he arranged for it to be published in book form in America. He had, though, received an offer from Pound's publisher, Liveright, who had been impressed by Tom in Paris. Boni and Liveright remained keen to publish the poem in New York that autumn, but there was a contractual complication: Tom was obliged to offer Knopf two books following the 1920 New York edition of his *Poems*. The American-issued *Sacred Wood* had been the first of these two; now Tom asked if *The Waste Land* might be the second. Oddly, as he had done with Thayer, so with Knopf he expected a decision without the publisher having seen the work. He simply told Knopf that Liveright had offered him $150, and he expressed eagerness to 'get the poem published as soon as possible'.⁴⁰ Given Tom's apparent impatience, Knopf advised him to accept Liveright's offer. So Alfred Knopf lost the opportunity to publish *The Waste Land*, and said simply that he would look forward to Tom's next book of prose.

Vivien's return to England and to her husband brought a deterioration in her health. On 3 April Tom told Lucy Thayer (herself in Europe) that Vivien 'evidently really needs to get away from London and from England for long periods together'.⁴¹ There was no suggestion he might accompany her. Still, he supported her decision to head to Paris in early April. Unfortunately, she fell ill as soon as she got there, returning home with 'a temperature of 100'.⁴² Her doctor advised her 'not to see anyone or talk'. 'Frightfully vexed', she wanted to speak with Mary Hutchinson about 'most *important* matters'.⁴³ Like Vivien, Tom found Mary's company a solace, but his wife's return seems to have coincided more or less with his becoming unwell again too. Awkwardly, the Eliots tried to aid each other, whether that meant their being apart or together. Togetherness could make them both suffer.

To Tom's satisfaction he had recently received from Sylvia Beach, an American in Paris who ran the bookshop Shakespeare & Company, a 'beautiful *broché* [paper-backed] copy of *Ulysses*'.[44] Beach was the European publisher of Joyce's novel and Tom was due to review it for the *Dial*. He produced no '"full dress" review', but eventually submitted his important essay, 'Ulysses, Order, and Myth', which appeared in November 1923. Vehemently he contested Aldington's criticism in the April 1921 *English Review* that *Ulysses* was designed by a 'great undisciplined talent' so as 'to disgust us with mankind'.[45] Regarding Joyce's novel as a masterpiece, Tom hoped that, if his intuition and Pound's comments were accurate, *The Waste Land* might be fit to stand beside it.

The Waste Land was his greatest achievement, but he worried circumstances might conspire against him. Recognising that Vivien had had a particularly 'bad time recovering herself' while she also had a sick husband 'on her hands as well', on 20 April he complained to Sydney Schiff that he felt 'about ready to chuck up literature altogether and retire'.[46] Meanwhile Pound (as he said he had done in Paris in January) was trying to get his friend to send *The Waste Land* to the *Dial*. Pound wanted Thayer to pay handsomely for it.[47] Thayer, however, decided Tom was insulting him, demanding far beyond the going rate for a work he had not even set eyes on. Negotiations stalled.

Complaining of 'incessant illness', but sure they were fit enough to travel and needed a change, Tom asked Ottoline Morrell on 26 April if she could recommend a hotel in Brighton where he and Vivien might recuperate.[48] Feeling a bit stronger, he had gone to the London Coliseum to see Léonide Massine of the Ballets Russes dance – 'more brilliant and beautiful than ever'. Adopting the accents of Bloomsbury, Tom told Mary, 'I (having never been so close before) quite fell in love with him.' Mary had sent news about Massine, and Tom, considering the dancer 'a genius', wanted 'to meet him more than ever'.[49] For the moment, though, he stressed that he and Vivien were trying to get away together for the sake of their health. On 5 May Aldington had told Amy Lowell Tom was 'very ill, will die if he doesn't get proper & complete rest'.[50]

Instead of going to Brighton, the Eliots went to Royal Tunbridge Wells, a historic spa town in Kent about thirty-five miles from London by rail. They stayed at the four-storey, ivy-covered Castle Hotel which faced on to a three-hundred-acre common. During the week Tom commuted daily to London's Cannon Street, but Vivien felt 'very seedy'. Probably sensing his son-in-law would benefit from a break, and doing what he could for the Eliots' marriage, Vivien's father stepped in. Having been at death's door not so long before, the old artist had made a spirited recovery. Now he wanted to treat Tom to a fortnight's Swiss vacation in Lugano from 20 May until 4 June; Tom had two weeks' holiday from the bank. Vivien was trying to decide whether to accompany her husband as far as Paris, or 'go miserably to the seaside in further search of health'.[51] Again, there seemed no suggestion she and Tom would remain together while abroad, though they did plan to go as a couple to visit Garsington in mid-June.

Tunbridge Wells failed to revive them. Repeatedly Tom had postponed a piece on Seneca he was supposed to be writing for *The Times Literary Supplement*. Before heading for Lugano he struggled to construct his *Dial* 'London Letter' for July. Vivien recalled him as 'in a state of collapse – so *ill – he asked me what he should say*'. She made suggestions. He wrote them down, 'not caring'.[52] Though Vivien's memories (penned about six weeks later when she was annoyed) may be coloured by her own circumstances, Tom's 'London Letter' was unusually short. He mocked English politics ('the Liberal is merely a drifting Conservative') and suggested that the University of Oxford should choose as its next professor of poetry 'an American, Professor Irving Babbitt'.[53] It did not.

He was certainly fed up. When the *Chapbook*, where he had published a substantial essay in 1920, sent him a questionnaire about poetry, his answers were honest but dourly monosyllabic:

1.   Do you think poetry is a necessity to modern man?
No.
2.   What in modern life is the particular function of poetry as distinguished from other kinds of literature?
Takes up less space.[54]

Given that he had already written in four hundred and thirty-three lines what Ezra Pound had told him was 'the longest poem in the Englisch langwidge', these answers made sense.[55] They were also shorter than Pound's.

Editing a magazine demands stamina. The Woolfs had allowed Tom to hand-copy a list of about six hundred names and addresses of potential subscribers supplied by the Hogarth Press. He felt too exhausted to type this up before departing for Lugano. Nonetheless, preparations for his journal's first issue were going ahead, necessitating liaison with the publisher, Richard Cobden-Sanderson. Just before leaving, Tom received for his magazine from Leonard Woolf the 'Plan of the Novel, "The Life of a Great Sinner"' by Dostoevsky, which Virginia Woolf had co-translated; Tom also wrote to Knopf, confirming that he would accept

Liveright's offer to bring out *The Waste Land* as a book in the autumn. This would help him secure American copyright, while he might still offer Knopf a future prose volume. Then he set off. While he was in Lugano, Vivien would spend several days relaxing in her old seaside haunts at Eastbourne.

In 1922, for anyone feeling strain and needing somewhere to recuperate, Lugano's Hotel Bristol was an excellent choice, particularly if someone else was paying. When Tom arrived around 22 May, the mountain views across Lake Lugano were breathtaking. The whole region was idyllic: nearby was a settlement called Paradiso. Capital of the Italian-speaking Swiss canton of Ticino, Lugano was home to about 15,000 people. Set on an elevated site, the Bristol, opened two decades earlier, was the city's first Grand Hotel. Extensive grounds sloped down to the waterfront. Guests could ascend from or descend to the lakeside in a private cable car. Transposed from Tunbridge Wells, Tom savoured red 'Barolo' wine, white sparkling 'Asti Spumante', an Italian Swiss lakeside festival and, at night, a display of fireworks.[56] He walked; he boated on the lake; he bathed – all 'good for me'.[57] Yet his father-in-law's gift of this holiday indicated how difficult his marriage was. The Swiss resort would have been the perfect place for a couple; but Charles Haigh-Wood, a loving father who knew his daughter as well as anyone, and who respected Tom, realised his son-in-law had to get away. Despite Lugano's 'American trippers', Tom relished the gift. 'I shd like', he wrote to Lady Ottoline, 'six months of Italy and heat and sunshine, and have never felt quite so lazy and languid.'[58]

He met Hermann Hesse, to whom he had written. Hesse, who had known depression and was deeply interested in Buddhism, had moved in 1919 to the Casa Camuzzi in nearby Montagnola. There he had been writing his Indic novel *Siddhartha*. Like Tom in *The Waste Land*, he sought to fuse perceptions of East and West. After World War I, again like Tom, Hesse had championed the unity of European culture, even if the book Tom so admired, *Blick ins Chaos*, was filled with foreboding. It argued 'the Downfall of Europe is foretold' by Dostoevsky, especially in *The Brothers Karamazov*. 'This downfall', wrote Hesse, 'is a return home to the mother, a turning back to Asia, to the source, to the "*Faustischen Müttern*" and will necessarily lead, like every death on earth, to a new birth'.[59] Encouraged by Tom, Sydney Schiff would publish these words as part of his translation of Hesse in the June *Dial*. Tom's unpublished long poem also had a 'turning back to Asia' in its use of the Buddha's Fire Sermon and in 'What the Thunder Said'. Yet in the newly revised *Waste Land*, even if the wasted, infertile terrain were to be reborn through the coming of the rain invoked in the final section, that would bring only a cyclic return to the poem's hurtful beginning. Whatever Tom and Hesse discussed, both envisaged a gruelling future. However, Tom, meeting a man whose thinking he so admired, was delighted that Hesse would contribute an article on recent German poetry to his new journal. 'Ich erinnere ich mich immer an meinem Besuch bei Ihnen', he wrote: 'I am still full of memories of my visit to you.'[60]

He made another visit, too. Crossing into Italy, he spent a couple of days with his staunch friend Pound who was then in Verona. They spoke at length. Tom found Pound 'delightful', but remained wary of Bel Esprit.[61] Pound's idea was to recruit supporters in New York (including Quinn, who pledged $300), and to have Aldington look after British operations. However uneasy, Tom did not veto this. Pound asked him about his marriage. To Quinn, setting out Tom's problems, Pound wrote in early July, 'Eliot has always been very reserved about his domestic situation, so much so that I thought Mrs. E. had syph; and marvelled that they didn't get a dose of 606 [arsphenamine, a compound used to treat syphilis]. Last time I saw him I got down to brass tacks. And find that the girl really has a long complication of things, tuberculosis in infancy, *supposed* to have been cured.' As Tom outlined Vivien's symptoms, Pound thought the problem was probably pituitary. Later that summer he asked Louis Berman, author of *The Glands Regulating Personality* (1922), to speak to Tom; but Tom made it clear that no one could work out just what Vivien's illness was. 'I find', Pound told Quinn, 'that she has all along behaved very finely [*deleted:* wanted separate establishment, so she shouldn't get on Tom's nerves, and prevent his working], is ready to live by herself if it will help T. to write etc. And in general ready to do anything she can to help his work. He can't simply chuck her in the Thames, even if he were so disposed, which he aint.'[62] Vivien, as ever, believed in Tom's talent; their marriage was hurting them both.

Back in London and feeling refreshed, Tom found that his wife, too, thought her problems might be glandular in origin. Tensions between them continued. Despite having said in May to Ottoline Morrell that visiting Garsington on 16 June 'will suit us very well', Tom now explained that there had 'been a misunderstanding'. He blamed Vivien. 'She knew that I had already told her that I could not leave London for a weekend until she went to Bosham in July.'[63] After keeping Lady Rothermere waiting for most of a year, he felt under pressure to produce his magazine's first issue. If he had more leisure, he explained to Ottoline, he could do all sorts of things; but he had not, and could not. Advised by Lady Ottoline, Vivien had seen a new specialist. He had told her at once, in addition to glandular problems, she had 'poisoning from colitis'. The cure, Tom told Ottoline on 15 June with a degree of resigned annoyance, was 'perfectly new and violent'. For four weeks Vivien was to consume cachets called Ovarian Opocaps containing 'the glands of animals' on a 'purely experimental' basis, in addition to having 'a very strong internal disinfection, and going without food *completely* for two days a week'.[64] Meanwhile, the Eliots were moving back from 12 Wigmore Street into their 9 Clarence Gate Gardens flat.

On weekdays Tom squeezed in lunchtime literary meetings at Ye Olde Cock Tavern, 22 Fleet Street, a characterfully tall narrow building which still exists and boasts associations with a variety of writers. Here he plotted his new magazine. Restless and dissatisfied, he had no sooner moved into Clarence Gate Gardens than he cabled Quinn on 21 June to say he was unhappy about Liveright's *Waste Land* contract. Apologetically, he asked Quinn for help, which was forthcoming immediately. In effect the busy New York lawyer acted as Tom's agent. Over the next few months he negotiated a significantly better deal, then assisted with typescript and proofs. At first Tom had not even told Quinn the title of his new volume; Quinn took it all on trust. When, eventually, he read *The Waste Land* in typescript, he regarded it as 'poems' rather than a poem.[65] 'I thank you from the depth of my heart for your kindness', Tom wrote, and soon made it clear he would present Quinn with the bundle of surviving manuscripts.[66]

Around the same time, perhaps as part of a theatre visit, Mary Hutchinson arranged for Tom to meet Massine. Tom thought this 'very sweet' of her, and, signing his letter 'With love, Tom', told her so. 'Do you think Massine liked me? and would he come and see me, do you think?'[67] His continuing warmth towards Mary and his excitement at meeting Massine reveal eagerness to find distractions from the situation at home. Vivien 'starved' herself as the doctors ordered. One night in late June while she did so, Tom escaped to dinner and an ensuing dance, then headed to the Wigmore Street flat (not yet fully vacated), finishing off there what was left of a bottle of vermouth. He packed up his remaining clothes to move them back to Clarence Gate Gardens. 'Rather fun', he described his evening to Mary, hoping to see her soon.[68]

By 25 June both Vivien and Tom were uneasy about her new treatment. She arranged to see a different Harley Street specialist, and, unsure how to proceed, sent Pound details of her symptoms. These included colitis, temperatures of almost 100°F (37.8C°), exhaustion, insomnia ('this has been going on for eight years'), migraines, and what she called 'Increasing mental incapacity'. That last symptom she explained by saying, 'I have a horror of using my mind and spend most of my time in trying to avoid contact with people or anything that will force me to use my mind.' Though despairing at times, she was determined to try to get well. She confided to Pound that she and Tom planned a week's holiday together in Paris in late September; if she could find 'intelligent doctors', she might go on to Switzerland or Germany. Tom thought there was more to the illness than Vivien had revealed, noting she was '*very* ill and exhausted'.[69]

Rumours spread that his proposed new journal might never appear. While sympathetic to his situation, Lady Rothermere wanted progress. She seemed to favour the title the *London Review*; Tom thought that 'weak'.[70] Supportively, Vivien came to the rescue, proposing that the magazine be called the *Criterion*. Tom liked that idea, and so did Cobden-Sanderson. Lady Rothermere agreed, and preparations for a launch in October gathered pace. Tom experienced the usual editor's problems: some contributors exceeded their word limit, others did not deliver what he expected. He decided the first two parts of *The Waste Land* would appear in issue one, due on 1 October, the rest following in issue two. All going well, early contributors might include Virginia Woolf, Hermann Hesse and Marcel Proust. In a brave but risky move, the quarterly *Criterion* would contain more work by foreign writers than was customary. Tom was gambling his literary reputation and perhaps even the balance of his mind on his new poem and his new periodical together.

Bel Esprit, too, seemed a gamble. The further the proposal advanced, the more awkwardly entangled he felt. Discussing Pound's ideas at length with Aldington, he made clear he appreciated the motives which led his friends to try to buy him out of the bank, but could hardly accept or reject the scheme until it was reasonably certain what his 'income, tenure, and security' might be.[71] 'Precarious' was his word for the planned arrangements; increasingly he believed Bel Esprit smacked of 'slightly undignified charity'.[72] Rodker, one of very few potential backers to have seen *The Waste Land*, had already printed, strictly for private circulation, that circular in which the work was hailed as a triumph of 'the modern movement'.[73] Again, regardless of the outcome of Bel Esprit, this made publication of *The Waste Land* in the *Criterion* and in book form crucial to Tom's entire future.

'It is a risk', Pound admitted with regard to Bel Esprit. 'So is an oil well.'[74] Tom was willing to venture a good deal on his poem and his magazine, but Bel Esprit looked too problematic. Hearteningly, it showed his friends rallying round, yet the way several of its contributors were also producing paid work for the *Criterion* made the network almost strangulatingly incestuous. It was, he explained to Aldington, 'embarrassing and fatiguing to me in spite of the motives, which I appreciate'.[75]

As discussions grew protracted over the summer, Virginia Woolf found people more ready to offer one-off lump sums to Tom himself; some feared Pound might 'drink it all first'. 'Poor Tom', Woolf termed her friend.[76] Lady Ottoline started distributing further forms. There was to be a new committee, on which Aldington and Woolf were to serve, to raise money specifically for an Eliot Fellowship Fund. Mary Hutchinson, Lytton Strachey and others seemed eager to donate. Leonard Woolf was sceptical. Virginia encountered opposition. 'I am told that most people are as badly off as Tom', she wrote to Lady Ottoline on 18 August, 'and as most people have to earn their livings, they don't see why they should bind themselves for ever to earn £10 yearly for some one else'.[77]

Tom's view was that provided he kept his bank position then at least he remained independent of friends' charity. Even if £300 per annum were raised, he would still have to earn a further £300 from time-consuming literary journalism in order to match his current £600 salary. So why should he commit himself to giving up Lloyds Bank? He worried 'everybody concerned' would 'be made ridiculous'.[78] He was distressed, too, lest people think his family wealthy enough to fund him; to Pound he had explained that his mother's circumstances were reduced. In the midst of all, while pursuing his day job as if everything was well, he had to summon up the shrewdness and energy for negotiations involving *Criterion* contributors and would-be contributors – some to be lured in, others headed off; many were his friends or his friends' contacts. Difficult in a different way was coping with Vivien's illness. Largely, he kept that private. As money-raising schemes linked to Bel Esprit took on a life of their own, he seemed unsure whether to deflect them, accept them or try to direct them. How much should he tell his family in America and his in-laws about what was going on? Then always there were his commitments to the *Dial* and to other journals that had asked him for prose; throughout these troubles, he strove to keep faith with his insistent conviction that he was, after all, a poet.

Pressures mounted. He was having advertising circulars for the *Criterion* printed. 'You know that I have no persecution mania', he told Aldington on 13 July, but he was 'quite aware how obnoxious I am to perhaps the larger part of the literary world of London and that there will be a great many jackals swarming about waiting for my bones.' If things fell flat, he would have to accept huge loss of 'prestige and usefulness', and might 'retire to obscurity or Paris like Ezra'.[79] There was nervous jokiness in his phrasing, but it was clear-eyed. He had much to be nervous about.

Aldington took umbrage at Tom's 'London Letter' for July (submitted before he went to Lugano), which implied leading English critics were second-rate. Tom was getting 'bitter and hypercritical'. An American, after all, he did not fully understand the 'very subtle' English 'repulsion for everything which seems to be assuming superiority'. Tom made light of this 'little difficulty', but it rankled.[80] He wrote one more short 'London Letter' for the *Dial,* then, saying he felt he could not maintain an appropriately high standard, suggested they find another correspondent. Over time a 'breach' developed between him and Aldington.[81] Even more, that July, Aldington's reproach angered Vivien. Maintaining that her husband 'always leaves his letters behind for me to read', without Tom's knowledge she informed Aldington his note was 'unkind, and not friendly. It is exactly the letter to upset Tom, and to harden his pride, and to help to precipitate the disasters we all foresee and which you cheerfully say he is asking for.' She told Aldington she was largely responsible for the 'London Letter' which had so annoyed him; that she was behind the title of Tom's new journal – a title Aldington disliked; and Vivien added that, though she had fought to keep Tom in England when they were first married, she hated the place now. 'I hope Tom will soon get out.' Her bleakest words were, 'You know I am ill and an endless drag on him.'[82]

Once again, Vivien remained fiercely loyal to what she saw as her husband's genius. She perceived he was taking a big risk, and wanted him to win. 'He does stand or fall by this review', she wrote with regard to the *Criterion*. 'Each person who gives him a push now gives him a push out of England. And that will be damned England's loss.'[83] Vivien fought from a position of weakness. She saw Tom's temper, his pride, his vulnerability, and wanted to do what she could to help. Yet she also recognised how worn out he could become, and sensed that she could exhaust him. As usual, he hardened his shell to survive. Failure would help neither of them.

When Vivien moved to an 'inconceivably tiny' cottage in Bosham for the summer, Tom weekended there with her, staying in London for the rest of the week. In town on 19 July, he met Dorothy Pound who handed him over 4,000 Italian lira (then worth about £40) from Bel Esprit; as if anticipating the money, Vivien had hired two household helps, 'one in the mornings and one for the evenings'. She thought she and Tom might go and live in Paris after Christmas, if only he left the bank. Having told Aldington a few days before how much she hated England, now, thinking of Bosham, she informed Mary Hutchinson, 'there is no country I like better than English country', and offered the opinion that London was far better than Paris.[84] Tom would try to buy a bungalow near Bosham in mid-September, conscious Vivien now 'hated' leaving the place, but he failed in his attempt.[85]

If his wife could be demandingly unpredictable, Tom could come over as difficult too. Virginia Woolf detected that when she met him with Roger Fry and Clive Bell in London at the end of July. Bell had been full of gossip, but then attempted his 'best behaviour'. Tom, Woolf noted, 'was sardonic, precise, & slightly malevolent, as usual'.[86] He could put on a façade. Pound knew this, and thought him like a possum, an idea that appealed to Tom. The two poets took to refering to each other as 'Rabbit' and 'Possum' – using nicknames from the white Southern writer Joel Chandler Harris's Uncle Remus stories, popular in America from the 1880s onwards. To 'play possum' means to act as if dead, and Harris's characters Brer Rabbit and Brer Possum derived, ultimately, from African American folk-culture. 'What do you think of "The Possum" for a title?' Tom asked Pound, thinking about the emergent *Criterion*.[87]

Pound had suggested Tom 'send Vivien over to Paris' for a rest and for medical advice, but Tom thought she was too ill. Neuralgia, neuritis, eye trouble and colitis were among her sufferings, though it is tempting for twenty-first-century observers to speculate she was afflicted with depression. In accord with early-twentieth-century medical guidance, all her meat was minced three times in a machine; she took vitamins and protein supplements each day, and needed 'the best sealed medical milk'. Tom, who had a bout of neuralgia himself in early August, hoped this newly recommended diet was 'really doing her good'.[88] Maybe they would go to Paris in October, after the *Criterion* was published. Tasks associated with the magazine proliferated: one Tuesday night after work at the bank he wrote at least ten letters. Still, having kept his wife's troubles largely private from Pound for so long, he showed a certain relief in being able to discuss them more freely. Impressed and amused by Pound's assumed expertise in the physiology of love (he had, after all, been translating de Gourmont's book on sex), Tom hailed him as 'student of the Kama-Sutra', wishing him 'Good fucking, brother'.[89]

For different correspondents he adopted different voices. He hired 'a very nice, intelligent, serious Scotch woman', Miss Duff, as a 'shorthand typist'. She came for a few hours 'twice a week' to help cope with the demands of magazine editing. Tom grew used to dictating formal, efficient-sounding letters.[90] Typed up on *Criterion* notepaper, these gave the magazine's address as 9 Clarence Gate Gardens; problematically, there was now little or no boundary between his home life and work. At least the first issue's contents were shaping up, though not quite as the editor had anticipated: as well as *The Waste Land* (now likely to appear entire in the first issue), he now expected to publish pieces by George Saintsbury, May Sinclair, poet-critic T. Sturge Moore, Aldington and several foreign contributions, including the lecture on Joyce by Larbaud and Hesse's article on recent German poetry. The journal's objectives remained lofty. Tom summarised them in a letter to German intellectual E. R. Curtius, to whom he sent *The Sacred Wood*. The 'great aim is to raise the standard of thought and writing in this country by both international and historical comparison. Among English writers I am combining those of the older generation who have any vitality and enterprise, with the more serious of the younger generation, no matter how advanced, for instance Mr Wyndham Lewis and Mr Ezra Pound.'[91] Mr Pound, Mr Lewis and himself were to be the magazine's 'jailbirds'– the resident bad boys.[92] Mostly Tom wanted contributors to represent the *Criterion* as unimpeachably impressive – 'the best people of each generation and type'.[93] His first issue, containing nothing by Pound or Lewis, would open with the irreproachable wisdom of seventy-seven-year-old George Saintsbury, retired Professor of Rhetoric and English Literature at the University of Edinburgh. Pound, who thought Saintsbury 'a meritorious old dodo', soon described Tom's magazine as 'very good' and 'octogenarian'.[94]

At last Tom had sent a typescript of *The Waste Land* to Pound in Paris, so that Pound could show it to his visitor James Sibley Watson, Jr, of the *Dial*. Tom seemed minded to accept a developing offer to have the *Dial* publish it. This deal would bring payment at roughly the usual rate, but there would be an understanding also that the magazine would award him its annual $2,000 prize 'for services to the cause of letters'.[95] Initially, the publisher, James Sibley Watson, found the poem 'disappointing', but after reading it three times he thought it might be 'up to' Tom's 'usual'.[96] Pound had sounded out *Vanity Fair* about possible US publication of *The Waste Land* (a 'series of lyrics'), as it was rumoured that Tom and Thayer had 'split', so that the *Dial* would not publish the work.[97] Nevertheless, by mid-August, in a prickly and necessarily punctilious way, Tom was edging towards agreement with his old classmate's magazine – provided Boni and Liveright did not object to his poem appearing in a journal at almost the same time as they brought it out as a book.[98] The *Dial* and Boni and Liveright came to a mutually beneficial arrangement. Edmund Wilson, then managing editor of *Vanity Fair*, asked Tom for some prose instead. So it was that *The Waste Land* was lined up to be published in London in the October *Criterion,* then in New York in the November *Dial*, then as a slim volume by Boni and Liveright in December. It would be the following year before the poem became a British book.

As August 1922 drew to a close, Tom was rushing to pull together the material for the first issue of his magazine. Let down by a translator, he found himself having to translate Larbaud's lecture, 'The "Ulysses" of James Joyce', and was working against the clock. His mother sent him addresses of possible subscribers at Harvard; she registered that Vivien was ill and in Bosham, and hoped she would 'soon be better'.[99] In London there were setbacks. Cobden-Sanderson's father died on 7 September. Stressed, Tom fidgeted over the magazine's contents. Having overestimated the amount of material he could fit into ninety-six pages, he reverted to his original idea of publishing just '*The Waste Land* I–II' in the first issue, only to change his mind yet again.[100] It seems that, like other people, he was torn between treating *The Waste Land* as a series of poems and as a single work. Overwhelmed with gratitude to Quinn, Tom sent him not only his poem's manuscripts but also the notebook ('Inventions of the March Hare') which he had started in 1909. Quinn accepted the *Waste Land* material 'as a mark of friendship', but insisted on sending Tom $140 for the notebook.[101]

By mid-September Tom was correcting 'excellent' proofs from Boni and Liveright.[102] Manifesting a lasting ability to get over fallings out, he enjoyed having dinner with Murry on the 13th. Neither man had changed his view of the other, but both were keen they should get on. Among other things, each knew 'the worries' of bringing out a literary magazine.[103] Despite delays, it looked as if the *Criterion* would be ready for 15 October. Tom knew Bel Esprit was still under way, but, after a meeting with Virginia Woolf during the time *Criterion* proofs were being corrected, he gave her the distinct impression that he thought Bel Esprit 'impracticable'.[104] Woolf and her husband agreed. Yet the scheme ran on. Vivien believed if the *Criterion* succeeded and money from the Pound-inspired fundraising could be '*guaranteed*', then 'Tom would automatically leave the bank'.[105]

At this juncture Tom felt unable to go over all the ins and outs of his predicament. Vivien was ill again. Galley proofs needed correcting. Advertising for the *Criterion* had to be booked in newspapers and magazines. Further circulars must go to potential subscribers. Lady Rothermere had to be kept happy: details of financial arrangements, about which Tom was scrupulous, must be sent to her at 'Claridges Hotel, Paris'. With these pressures as well as Lloyds Bank to contend with, he felt 'assailed from all sides'. To get through, he 'had to keep his mind off' the whole complex tangle of Bel Esprit 'and concentrate on what I must do from hour to hour'.[106] The first page proofs of the magazine arrived on Saturday 30 September. Going through them on Sunday, Tom posted them back to the printer on Monday. By Tuesday night he had proofed the whole journal a second time – 'extremely satisfactory', though the setting of *The*

Waste Land was proving fiddly.[107] Tom would receive a 'dummy' copy of the magazine a few days later.[108] In the midst of all this his old college room-mate Howard Morris, now 'a very successful Bond Broker in New York' dropped by. They talked finance. Howard expected 'another slump'. Tom bore this in mind when discussing with Henry what to do about income he was now receiving from inherited stock in the St Louis Hydraulic-Press Brick Company. Yet Howard, 'a late Harvard friend of mine', seemed almost from a buried life.[109]

At home Tom maintained a small shrine to that life, at least as far as it included his family. Ancestral pictures hung on the wall. Occasionally disconcerting visitors, these confirmed at once his sense of tradition and his foreignness. Having visited less than a year earlier, his brother Henry had been convinced that 'The strain of going out among people who after all are foreigners to him, and, I believe, always must be to an American – even Henry James never became a complete Englishman – has, I think, been to him pretty heavy.' His brother recalled Tom complaining in 1920 of 'always having to be keyed up, alert to the importance of appearances, always wearing a mask among people'.[110] If Henry (like Lady Rothermere) thought Tom needed simply to relax and rest, he may have been right, but Tom's public and private life afforded less and less respite. His collection of family photographs was a reminder of earlier generations of hard-working, stern-faced Eliots who had simply buckled down and endured; it was also, to a poet who hoped his mother might visit him again, a consolation; and it was an ancestral challenge, a personal criterion against which he measured himself, even as he came to feel further and further removed from much modern United States life.

In the *Criterion*'s first issue Tom was the only American writer. He was also the sole contributor of new verse. Consciously or not, he assembled around *The Waste Land* prose that clearly set it off. Saintsbury's opening essay on 'Dullness' counselled against '"passiveness"' in reading; the elderly professor urged readers to 'extend your knowledge and interests as far as possible' and, if encountering 'a reference or allusion' that seemed difficult, not to condemn it '*without making sure that the fault is not your own*'.[111] This was surely good advice for readers of *The Waste Land*. The second piece was a translation of Dostoevsky's plan for an unfinished novel, a story involving 'horror', 'passionate desire', religion and 'the abyss'; though in September 1922 Virginia Woolf and Tom agreed that Dostoevsky was 'the ruin of English literature', Tom once described his own life as a Dostoevsky novel authored by Middleton Murry.[112] Then, on either side of *The Waste Land* came two items relating to doomed love affairs: the first part of T. Sturge Moore's account of 'The Legend of Tristram and Isolt in Modern Poetry', and May Sinclair's tale 'The Victim', in which a man who suspects his partner of sexual betrayal commits a murder and has to live with the consequences of his knowledge. The first issue continued with Hesse's piece on 'Recent German Poetry', which envisages 'the ruin of the world' and states that '"Dadaism" belongs thereto'; the final article was Larbaud's discussion of 'The "Ulysses" of James Joyce' – the masterpiece Tom came to see as using that 'mythical method' so vital to his own long poem.[113] Editorially, then, he set *The Waste Land* carefully among prose with which it resonated, deftly establishing a reading context that spurred and guided its initial public. He printed his poem without epigraph or dedication. After the concluding words of Sturge Moore's 'Tristram and Isolt' (which Tom had edited so that its first part ended with mention of how 'cut or wired flowers doomed to sterility' compared poorly with 'bloom on thriving plants'), readers turned the page and encountered *The Waste Land* with its opening lines about 'Lilacs' and 'dead land', 'roots' and 'tubers'.[114]

A newly printed *Criterion* went to Lady Rothermere, now in Florence. She was unimpressed. Another early copy went to the *Dial*. Yet even before these were dispatched, Tom's published poem had met with one of its best informed readers. Vivien, who knew 'So much depends on the *Criterion*', felt the poem 'has become a part of me (or I of it) this last year'.[115] Though she had given high praise to the passage about nervous anxiety within a couple's relationship, she had asked Tom to remove the line 'The ivory men make company between us' – perhaps because it was simply too painful.[116] Feeling utterly bonded to the work, it seemed to her 'a terrible thing, somehow, when the time came at last for it to be published'.[117] If *The Waste Land*, with its images of adultery, sex gone wrong and edgy, nervous exchanges, can seem like a pained act of exposure, nonetheless its 'impersonal' allusive technique, its almost infinitely expanding resonances and its arcane use of anthropologically inflected structures prevent it from being reduced to that – and designedly so.

Waiting to see what his poem's public impact might be, in private Tom chastened himself for some of Vivien's health problems, but was hardly to blame for them all. Each partner in the marriage seems to have continued to deploy illness and work to manipulate the other; certainly Vivien had used illness to try to coax Scofield Thayer when Tom first met her. Tom, immuring himself in his labours, could not help but note that Pound had a wife who enjoyed good health, a family who could help her and some prospect of wealth. Vivien, he confided to Pound that November:

has none of these things. Her father's property, such as it is, is practically all tied up in Irish real estate, which he has been trying to sell all his life, has never paid much, now pays less, and can't be got rid of; which will be an encumbrance to her and her brother for the rest of their lives. Finally, at the most optimistic view, she will *never* be strong enough to earn her own living. If I had only myself to consider, I should not bother about guarantees [of financial security] for a moment: I could always earn my own living. But I am responsible toward her in more than the ordinary way. I have made a great many mistakes, which are largely the cause of her present catastrophic state of health, and also it must be remembered that she kept me from returning to America where I should have become a professor and probably never written another line of poetry, so that in that respect she should be endowed.[118]

Vivien's Irish links mean that she too (as well as the Emily Hale whom Tom had heard sing 'Mavourneen') might be hidden behind that reference to the phrase '*Mein Irisch Kind*' (My Irish child) in those lines of *The Waste Land* which he quoted from *Tristan und Isolde* – words of love that lead only to a vision of an expanse both '*Oed' und leer*' (Desolate and empty).[119] Vivien, like Tom, was part of the poem's desolation.

No sooner was the *Criterion* published than its editor set off 'for about a fortnight's rest' in Worthing, a small seaside town about ten miles from Brighton. 'T. is running down again', Vivien worried in November.[120] He was bad tempered, and it showed, though his wife was unlikely to disagree with his splenetic outburst in a letter to Pound (who liked a misogynist rant) that Katherine Mansfield was 'one of the most persistent and thick-skinned toadies and one of the vulgarest women Lady R[othermere] has ever met and is also a sentimental crank'.[121] Vivien was worried that, while initial sales looked promising, Lady Rothermere, whom she disliked, wanted to abort the magazine. Determined to back Tom, Vivien wondered if he might finance the journal using Bel Esprit money and £500 that she could provide but which would 'halve my income'.[122] Pound, wisely, advised the Eliots to save their cash. He would convince Lady Rothermere to hold firm. 'Of course', he wrote to Tom, 'if she says it looks like a corpse, she's right, mon POSSUM, do you expect her to see what is scarce discernible to the naked eye, that it is *supposed* to be PLAYIN' POSSUM'. Perusing the *Criterion*'s drab, sober covers and sometimes worthy essays, Pound had his own reservations. He thought it reeked of 'the Athenaeum Club', niffy with establishment respectability.[123] But about *The Waste Land* he had no doubts.

Nor did Tom. However, the prospect of getting the time he wanted to write more poetry seemed now more remote than ever. He still had thoughts of authoring a book on seventeenth-century literature, building on pieces including his *Times Literary Supplement* essay on Marvell. Yet this was not what he craved to do. 'My dear Ezra, I dont want to write articles for the *Times* or for anything else, I dont want to write articles at all, I dont want to write, no sensible man does who wants to write verse.' Better to edit a magazine than to churn out journalism. Unlike Pound, Tom thought England tolerable. He just wanted to be 'let alone'. He bitched, 'There are only half a dozen men of letters (and no women) worth printing.' His remedy would be to fill up the magazine with people of 'other occupations', such as the donnish anthropologist J. G. Frazer.[124]

Tom wanted to leave the bank. Spending the rest of his career there seemed 'abominable'.[125] Annoyingly, he could not see how to escape in a way that would provide legally credible guarantees 'for my life *or for Vivien's life*'.[126] Bel Esprit had become a torment, tantalising yet unachievable. Then, on 18 November, things suddenly got worse. Tom let Aldington know he had been sent a cutting from the *Liverpool Daily Post and Mercury*; its 'Books and Bookmen' column contained not just a report about Bel Esprit but a 'false story' that two years earlier a collection had raised £800 for Tom who had simply pocketed the cash. 'The joke was that he accepted the gift calmly, and replied: "Thank you all very much; I shall make good use of the money; but I like the bank!"'[127] Furious over this 'libel', Tom, who had been expecting trouble, consulted his solicitor and a more senior barrister. Though he did not sue, he wrote to the newspaper pointing out the untruth of the 'tale' and denying Bel Esprit existed 'with my consent or approval'. If this last assertion was debatable, the poet's sense of injury was not. In a public letter to the *Liverpool Daily Post and Mercury* he stated that 'The circulation of untrue stories of this kind causes me profound astonishment and annoyance and may also do me considerable harm.'[128] In private he felt menaced. An anonymous 'Wellwisher' mailed him a donation of four postage stamps 'to strengthen my poetry until I became poet laureate!'[129] He might have laughed. Instead he felt 'utter exhaustion'.[130]

Vivien's insomnia, his magazine work and other worries meant most nights he slept for 'seldom more than five hours'.[131] He found himself getting back from the bank, then dozing off before dinner. For months in the later part of 1922 Vivien had 'hardly seen anybody'. Impressed by her 'infinite tenacity of purpose' as she stuck to her prescribed 'spartan regimen', Tom saluted her 'persistence and courage'. She ate her dinner in bed, not feeling strong enough to get up. 'If I were not tied to the bank I could have gone abroad with her for a time; as it is she is not only under the strain of her own treatment but the strain of our very tense and always rushed and overworked mode of life.'[132]

On edge when news reached him of the official announcement that he had won the *Dial*'s $2,000 prize, he found his pleasure contaminated by tetchiness. Awkwardly, word of the award had 'leaked out' in advance.[133] Rumours were circulating that the poet of *The Waste Land* was tubercular; that he suffered from epilepsy; that he had tried to kill himself.[134] He feared lest the *Liverpool Daily Post* story was picked up in America too. Life was consumed by 'worry and fatigue'.[135] His brother congratulated him, but Henry was not sure he liked *The Waste Land*. Several reviewers, including Edmund Wilson, were enthusiastic; others simply bemused. Tom told Henry, 'there is a good deal about it that I do not like myself'.[136]

For Boni and Liveright's book-length version he had added notes written during the summer. His first intention was that such annotation would spike the guns of critics tempted to accuse him of plagiarism; showing himself well aware he had used pieces of earlier poems, he would signal clearly the sources his allusive method drew on. However, there was still too little material to fill even a small volume, so, ensuring that *The Waste Land* would be a book rather than a pamphlet, he extended his notes in a way that he later regretted. Readers have been divided as to the helpfulness of these authorial annotations, but for many they have provided useful clues about underlying structural elements. Several comments seem spoof-like: 'I do not know the origin of the ballad from which these lines are taken: it was reported to me from Sydney, Australia.'[127] Their effect has been to fuel an academic industry, reinforcing the poem's rootedness in sometimes recondite literary tradition, sending readers off to the library and away from the poet's biography.

Few readers or hearers, however, fail to detect that the poem contains a pain and a horror by no means 'academic'. If *The Waste Land* has come to be read as articulating Western civilisation's sense of crisis, it can be heard also as a lasting cry, giving voice to a darkness deep in the human psyche. The poem's universality is astonishingly powerful; its resonances seem to expand forever. Yet, while conscious that *The Waste Land* could be read as 'social criticism', Tom remarked over a decade later, 'To me it was only the relief of a personal and wholly insignificant grouse against life; it is just a piece of rhythmical grumbling.'[138] Shifting, spiky, flowing, weird, haunting, its rhythms are what convince its auditors. 'He sang it & chanted it rhythmed it', wrote Virginia Woolf when Tom first read it aloud to her on Sunday 18 June 1922. She and Leonard would publish it from their Hogarth Press in the following year – the first publication of the work in book form outside America – but her first, accurate impression was less of a text than of sound:

> It has great beauty & force; & tensity. What connects it together, I'm not so sure. But he read till he had to rush – letters to write about the London Magazine – & discussion thus was curtailed. One was left, however, with some strong emotion. The Waste Land it is called; & Mary Hutch, who has heard it more quietly, interprets it to be Tom's autobiography – a melancholy one.[139]

'Anguish' was the word Mary Hutchinson settled on to describe the emotional tenor of such numinous verse.[140] His mother recorded of the poem, 'Tom wrote me before it was published that he had put so much of his own life into it.'[141] He had, and Vivien knew her life was in it too. All this helps give the verse its undertow of damage, its longing, its frustrated, ineradicable music.

It was 15 December when *The Waste Land* became an American book. One thousand copies were printed, each stamped with an individual number, published from 105 W. 40th Street, New York. Hard at work assembling the contents for the next few issues of the *Criterion*, Tom opened the small, pale-jacketed volume in his London flat. Slightly heavier than it looked, underneath the dust jacket it was bound in black boards with only the words THE WASTE LAND in gold on the front board. Inside, the poem now carried its Latin and Greek epigraph (though no dedication), and was printed in large type – never more than sixteen lines of poetry per page. Thanks to this generous spacing and to the added prose ballast of the Notes, it managed to fill sixty-four pages. Throughout, the verse carried line numbers (one every ten lines), as if to bind together a work that kept threatening to explode into separate shards. The inside front-jacket flap quoted an early review by Burton Rascoe in the *New York Tribune*, calling *The Waste Land* 'a thing of bitterness and beauty' and, 'perhaps, the finest poem of this generation'. The note on the rear flap began simply, 'T. S. Eliot was born in 1888 in St. Louis, Missouri', then went on to hail him as 'without question the most significant of the younger American writers'. Tom, weary and very far from the city of his birth, looked at the name 'T. S. Eliot' in plain black print on the title page.

It was as if he had never been young.

Abbreviations

Books by T. S. Eliot

CC: *To Criticize the Critic and Other Writings* (London: Faber and Faber, 1965).

CPP: *The Complete Poems and Plays of T. S. Eliot* (London: Faber and Faber, 1969).

Facsimile: *The Waste Land: A Facsimile and Transcript of the Original Drafts including the Annotations of Ezra Pound*, ed. Valerie Eliot (London: Faber and Faber, 1971). Facsimile pages on even-numbered pages, transcriptions on facing pages.

IMH: *Inventions of the March Hare: Poems 1909–1917*, ed. Christopher Ricks (London: Faber and Faber, 1996).

L1: *The Letters of T. S. Eliot, Volume 1: 1898–1922, revised edn*, ed. Valerie Eliot and Hugh Haughton (London: Faber and Faber, 2009).

L2: *The Letters of T. S. Eliot, Volume 2: 1923–1925*, ed. Valerie Eliot and Hugh Haughton (London: Faber and Faber, 2009).

L3: *The Letters of T. S. Eliot, Volume 3: 1926–1927*, ed. Valerie Eliot and John Haffenden (London: Faber and Faber, 2012).

L4: *The Letters of T. S. Eliot, Volume 4: 1928–1929*, ed. Valerie Eliot and John Haffenden (London: Faber and Faber, 2013).

OPP: *On Poetry and Poets* (London: Faber and Faber, 1957).

SE: *Selected Essays*, third enlarged edn (London: Faber and Faber, 1951).

UPUC: T. S. Eliot, *The Use of Poetry and the Use of Criticism*, Second Edition (London: Faber and Faber, 1964).

VMP: *The Varieties of Metaphysical Poetry*, ed. Ronald Schuchard (London: Faber and Faber, 1993).

Individuals

CCE: Charlotte Champe Eliot (TSE's mother)
EP: Ezra Pound
HWE: Henry Ware Eliot (TSE's father)
HWE, Jr: Henry Ware Eliot, Jr (TSE's brother)
TSE: Thomas Stearns Eliot
VE: Vivien Eliot (TSE's first wife)

Institutions

Beinecke: The Beinecke Rare Book and Manuscript Library, Yale University
Hayward Bequest: The Papers of the Hayward Bequest of T. S. Eliot Material, Kings College Archive Centre, Cambridge, England
Houghton: The Houghton Library, Harvard University

Notes

Introduction

1   *CPP*, 16, 37 ('Gerontion'), 78, 69.
2   *CPP*, 89 ('Ash Wednesday').
3   Valerie Eliot, in BBC TV programme, 'Arena: T. S. Eliot', broadcast on 6 June 2009 (these remarks were made first in a 1971 interview).
4   Graham Bruce Fletcher, 'The Silly Songs of T. Stearns Eliot – a Private Memoir Made Public', *Exchanges* (T. S. Eliot Society (UK)), 6.2 (Summer 2013), 7.
5   *SE*, 337 ('In Memoriam').
6   *CPP*, 182 ('East Coker').
7   Ronald Schuchard, 'Valerie Eliot and the State of Eliot Studies', opening address, T. S. Eliot International Summer School, London, 6 July 2013.
8   Valerie Eliot to the present writer, 18 October 1983.
9   TSE, 'American Literature and the American Language', *CC*, 44.
10   Clare Reihill, quoted in Felicity Capon, 'T. S. Eliot's fountain pen replaces Dickens's quill at the Royal Society of Literature', *Daily Telegraph*, 19 March 2013 (accessed online).
11   [TSE], *Fireside*, Number 2 (Houghton MS Am 1635.5 (2)).
12   *L1*, 457.
13   *CPP*, 13.
14   Valerie Eliot to the present writer, 28 June 1983.
15   Sir Herbert Read, 'T. S. E. – A Memoir', in Allen Tate, ed., *T. S. Eliot: The Man and his Work* (London: Chatto and Windus, 1967), 13.
16   *L3*, 208.
17   *The Letters of Ralph Waldo Emerson, Vol. IV*, ed. R. L. Rusk (New York: Columbia University Press, 1939), 338–9.
18   *L4*, 137–8.
19   Clive Bell, 'How Pleasant to know Mr Eliot', in Tambimuttu and Richard March, eds, *T. S. Eliot: A Symposium* (New York: Tambimuttu and Mass, 1965), 16.
20   TSE, quoted by Theodore Spencer, recorded by HWE, Jr, and put into print by Valerie Eliot in *Facsimile*, [1].
21   Virginia Woolf, *The Diary of Virginia Woolf, Volume 2, 1920–24*, ed. Anne Olivier Bell and Andrew McNeillie (Harmondsworth: Penguin, 1981), 178.

Chapter 1 – Tom

1   HWE, Jr, to HWE, 'Saturday June 1st' [1901], (Houghton bMS Am1691(60)); 1 June 1901 was a Saturday.

2   *L1*, xxxvii.

3   *L1*, 222.

4   *L1*, 324.

5   These phrases are quoted from family correspondence in Cynthia Grant Tucker, *No Silent Witness: The Eliot Parsonage Women and their Unitarian World* (New York: Oxford University Press, 2010), 225. Theodora had only 'one pair of limbs'.

6   *L1*, 316.

7   HWE, telegram, to Thomas Lamb Eliot, 26 September 1888 (Houghton bMS Am 2560 (24)).

8   Walter Graeme Eliot, *A Sketch of the Eliot Family* (New York: Press of Livingston Middleditch, 1887), 112.

9   *L4*, 114.

10   Eric Sigg, 'Eliot as a Product of America', in A. David Moody, ed., *The Cambridge Companion to T. S. Eliot* (Cambridge: Cambridge University Press, 1994), 16–17.

11   Walter G. Eliot, *A Sketch*, 109, 110.

12   HWE, 'Reminiscences', quoted in Tucker, *No Silent Witness*, 40.

13   'In Memoriam Henry Ware Eliot', *Washington University Record*, Series I, Vol. XIV, No. 5 (February 1919), 4–5.

14   HWE, Diary (Houghton bMS Am 1691.15(1)).

15   EP to TSE, 24 October 1939 (Beinecke).

16   Walter G. Eliot, *A Sketch*, 110–11.

17   *L1*, 317.

18   *L4*, 640.

19   CCE, *Easter Songs* (Boston: James H. West, [1899]), 6.

20   CCE, Poems scrapbook (Houghton bMS Am2560 (68)), 20 and 23.

21   Ibid., typed loose sheets, 'The Wednesday Club'.

22   *L1*, 143.

23   CCE, Poems scrapbook (Houghton bMS Am2560 (68)), 11.

24   CCE, copyist, Fortunatus' hymn (Houghton bMS Am2560 (67)); CCE, Poems scrapbook, 3.

25   Ibid., 18.

26   Abigail Eliot (TSE's cousin), interviewed for the 1971 BBC film, *The Mysterious Mr Eliot*.

27   HWE, Diary (Houghton bMS Am 1691.15(1)).

28   TSE, '[The poetry of Walt Whitman]' (Houghton bMS Am1691 (34)), 1.

29   TSE, 'Introduction' to Edgar Ansel Mowrer, *This American World* (London: Faber and Gwyer, 1928), xiii.

30   HWE, Jr, account of clock (Hayward Bequest, HB/PH/169).

31   *L4*, 138.

32   *The Letters of Ralph Waldo Emerson, Vol. IV*, ed. R. L. Rusk, (New York: Columbia University Press, 1939), 338–9.

33   TSE, 'American Literature and the American Language', *CC*, 44.

34   Ibid., 48.

35   TSE, quoted in William Turner Levy and Victor Scherle, *Affectionately, T. S. Eliot* (New York: Lippincott, 1968), 135.

36   *L3*, 712.

37   This phrase about CCE's exasperation comes from an 1889 letter from Abigail Cranch Eliot to Etta Eliot, quoted in Tucker, *No Silent Witness*, 45.

38   TSE, 'Address', *From Mary to You*, December 1959, 134.

39   Bertha R. Skinker, 'To Mr T. S. Eliot, on reading "Old Possum's Book of Practical

Cats"', 17 March 1940 (Hayward Bequest HB/L 248).

40   *L3*, 649.

41   *L1*, 223, n. 3.

42   TSE, 'Address', 134.

43   Ibid., 134–5.

44   'Uhrig's Cave' (advertisement) at the back of Harry Brazee Wandell, *The Story of a Great City in a Nutshell: 500 Facts about St Louis* (St Louis, n.p., [1903]).

45   TSE, *Fireside*, issue 1, Houghton (MS Am 1635.5(1)); Joe Hayden, 'There'll Be a Hot Time in the Old Town Tonight', music by Theo A. Metz (New York: Willis Woodward and Company, 1896), n.p.

46   William Howland Kenney, *Jazz on the River* (Chicago: University of Chicago Press, 2005), 97; see also David E. Chinitz, *T. S. Eliot and the Cultural Divide* (Chicago: University of Chicago Press, 2003), 39–40.

47   On Eliot singing this song, see Chinitz, *T. S. Eliot and the Cultural Divide*, 39.

48   'Young Men in Society Go in for Minstrelsy', *St Louis Republic*, 25 November 1900, 43; 'Members of Company C, N. G. M., in Black Face', *St Louis Republic*, 27 April 1901, 2.

49   *L1*, 239.

50   TSE to EP, 11 November 1964 (Beinecke).

51   TSE to Mary Trevelyan, 19 December 1944 (Houghton).

52   TSE to Mary Trevelyan, 2 January 1945 (Houghton).

53   TSE, quoted in Janet Adam Smith, 'Tom Possum and the Roberts Family', in James Olney, ed., *T. S. Eliot: Essays from the 'Southern Review'* (Oxford: Clarendon Press, 1988), 216.

54   TSE, 'Why Mr Russell is a Christian', *Criterion*, 6.2 (August 1927), 179.

55   See, e.g., advertisements for 'Hotels and Summer Resorts', *St Louis Globe-Democrat*, 16 May 1896, 7.

56   TSE, 'Introduction' to Mowrer, *This American World*, xiv.

57   'Rain', *St Louis Globe-Democrat*, 16 May 1896, 13.

58   Advertisement, 'Buffalo Bill's Wild West', *St Louis Globe-Democrat*, 10 May 1896, 7.

59   TSE, 'American Literature and the American Language', *CC*, 44. (The Chief Joseph photograph is now in the Missouri History Museum.)

60   TSE, quoted in John G. Neihardt, 'Of Making Many Books', *St Louis Globe-Democrat*, 5 October 1930 (Houghton bMS Am 2560 (161)).

61   'Wind's Deadly Work', *St Louis Globe-Democrat*, 28 May 1896, 1.

62   On the Church of the Unity, see John Snyder, 'Unitarianism in St Louis', in William Hyde and Howard L. Conard, eds, *Encyclopedia of the History of St Louis*, 4 vols (New York, Louisville and St Louis: Southern History Company, 1899), IV, 2344.

63   This photograph (Houghton bMS Am 2560 (245)), is reproduced as plate 10c in *L1*,

64   'Death and Destruction Everywhere', *St Louis Globe-Democrat*, 29 May 1896, 1.

65   TSE, quoted in Neihardt, 'Of Making Many Books'.

66   Information on Mrs Lockwood comes from online Missouri historical records; from the Dean Putnam Lockwood Papers, Haverford College Library; and from Jayme Stayer's 'T. S. Eliot as a Schoolboy: The Lockwood School, Smith Academy, and Milton Academy', *Twentieth-Century Literature*, 59.4 (Winter 2013), 619–55. I am very grateful to Jayme Stayer (John Carroll University) and Diana Franzusoff Peterson (Haverford College) for their help.

67   Theresa Garrett Eliot (TSE's sister-in-law)'s annotation on ms of HWE, Jr, to HWE, 'Saturday June 1st, [1901] (Houghton bMS Am1691(60)).

68   [TSE], 'Publishers' Preface' to James B. Connolly, *Fishermen of the Banks* (London: Faber and Gwyer, 1928), vii.

69   Bryant F. Tolles, Jr, *Summer by the Seaside: The Architecture of New England Coastal Resort Hotels, 1820–1950* (Lebanon, N.H.: University of New England Press, 2008), 103.

70   *L3*, 642.

71   TSE to John Hayward, 27 December 1939 (Hayward Bequest).

72   Ibid.

73   'School Notes', *Smith Academy Record*, January 1903, 9.

74   'An American Fishing Port', *Lippincott's Magazine*, May 1868, 497.

75   [TSE], 'Publishers' Preface', vii.

76   Ibid.

77   Joseph E. Garland, *The Gloucester Guide* (Gloucester, Mass: Gloucester 350th Anniversary Celebration, Inc., 1973), 130.

78   John Greenleaf Whittier, *Poetical Works* (London: Henry Frowde, 1904), 18 ('The Exiles').

79   Rudyard Kipling, *Captains Courageous: A Story of the Grand Banks* (London: Macmillan, 1897), 213, 119, 120, 121, 122, Gordon W. Thomas, *Life Stories of Great Gloucester Fishing Vessels* (Gloucester, Mass: Gloucester 350th Anniversary Celebration, Inc., 1973), 26–7.

80   On Blackburn, see Mark Kurlansky, *The Last Fish Tale* (London: Jonathan Cape, 2008), 53–6.

81   Thomas, *Fast and Able*, 2.

82   *L1*, 217.

83   [TSE], 'Publishers' Preface', viii, vii.

84   *Facsimile*, 63–9.

85   Whittier, *Poetical Works*, 57 ('The Garrison of Cape Ann').

86   TSE, 'Introduction' to Mowrer, *This American World*, xiv.

87   [TSE], 'Publishers' Preface', vii.

88   These photographs too are in the Hayward Bequest.

89   *L1*, 271.

90   *UPUC*, 78–9.

91   TSE, 'Introduction' to Mowrer, *This American World*, xiv.

92   TSE to EP, '22 October Jahr IV' (Beinecke).

93   *L1*, 1.

94   TSE, 'Introduction' to Mowrer, *This American World*, xiv.

95   CCE and TSE, inscriptions in Frank M. Chapman, *Handbook of Birds of Eastern North America*, sixth edn (New York: D. Appleton, 1902) (Hayward Bequest PP/HB/B, 8).

96   Ibid., 400.

97   *CPP*, 73.

Chapter 2 – Hi, Kid, Let's Dance

1   CCE, Poems scrapbook (Houghton bMS Am2560 (68)), 22.

2   Harry Brazee Wandell, *The Story of a Great City* (St Louis: n.p., [1903]), 26.

3   TSE, 'Sherlock Holmes and his Times', *Criterion*, 8.32 (April 1929), 553.

4   Arthur Conan Doyle, *The Adventures of Sherlock Holmes* (London: George Newnes, 1892), 290.

5   *CPP*, 13; see Robert Crawford, *The Savage and the City in the Work of T. S. Eliot* (Oxford: Clarendon Press, 1987), 11.

6   This quotation comes from James Neal Primm, *Lion of the Valley: St Louis, Missouri, 1764–1980*, third edn (St Louis: Missouri Historical Society, 1998), 340; statistics and other information about nineteenth-century St Louis are also taken from this volume.

7   *CPP*, 13, 27 ('Morning at the Window').

8   *L1*, 202.

9   For more on Etta Eliot and her links to Susan E. Blow, see Cynthia Grant Tucker, *No Silent Witness: The Eliot Parsonage Women and their Unitarian World* (New York: Oxford University Press, 2010).

10   Denton J. Snider, *The St Louis Movement in Philosophy, Literature, Education, Psychology, with Chapters of Autobiography* (St Louis: Sigma Publishing, 1920), 468; 'An Evening with Dante', *St Louis Globe-Democrat*, 18 December 1897, 11.

11   Susan E. Blow, *A Study of Dante* (New York: G. P. Putnam's Sons, 1886), 1.

12   Tucker, *No Silent Witness*, 40; *L1*, 376.

13   This and other quotations from Snyder here are from his article, 'Unitarianism in St Louis', in William Hyde and Howard L. Conard, eds, *Encyclopedia of the History of St Louis*, 4 vols (New York, Louisville and St Louis: Southern History Company, 1899), IV, 2337–42.

14   John Snyder, 'Unitarianism in St Louis', 2337–42.

15   *L3*, 428.

16   Details of the church building (now destroyed) and its windows are taken from US Department of the Interior National Park Service National Register of Historic Places Registration Forms accessed on 15 November 2012 at www.dnr.mo.gov/shpo/docs/moachp/11/ChurchMessiah.pdf and at www.dnr.mo.gov/shpo/nps-nr/80004513.pdf. Phrases from William Greenleaf Eliot's writings are quoted, with Washington University Archives sources, in these documents. (All quotations from the Bible are from King James version.)

17   TSE, 'What is Minor Poetry?', *OPP*, 42.

18   Sir Edwin Arnold, *The Light of Asia or The Great Renunciation* (Chicago: W. B. Conkey Co., 1900), 4, 9, 67, 33, 67.

19   *L2*, 302; *L3*, 228.

20   [TSE], *Fireside*, numbers 11 and 1 (see note 22); on the unusualness of Eliot's early study of French at Smith Academy see John J. Soldo, *The Tempering of T. S. Eliot* (Ann Arbor: UMI Research Press, 1983), 25.

21   Details of Eliot's curriculum in his first year at Smith Academy are given in Soldo, *The Tempering of T. S. Eliot*, 171.

22   All quotations in this chapter come from the collection of *Firesides* and associated material in the Houghton Library (MS Am 1635.5 (1–13)).

23   *CPP 177* ('East Coker'), 171.

24   *L3*, 597.

25   Lewis Carroll, *Sylvie and Bruno* (New York: Macmillan, 1889), 65.

26   [TSE], 'Poet's Corner', *Fireside*, number 1 (Houghton MS Am 1635.5 (1)).

27   [TSE], 'Poet's Corner', *Fireside*, number 6 (Houghton MS Am 1635.5 (6)).

28   [TSE], 'Cook's Corner', *Fireside*, numbers 2 and 3 (Houghton MS Am 1635.5 (2 and 3)).

29   Edward Lear, *The Complete Nonsense and Other Verse* (London: Penguin Books, 2001), 250.

30   Ibid., 428, 392, 250; TSE, *CPP*, 29, 136–7.

31   [TSE], *Fireside*, number 11.

32   'The Only Navigator of the Air', *St Louis Globe-Democrat*, 8 January 1899.

33   See, e.g., the cartoon featuring 'Mrs Stockson Bond' and her husband in *St Louis Globe-Democrat*, 12 February 1899, 13.

34   See entry for 'Prufrock, William', in John W. Leonard, ed., *The Book of St Louisans* (St Louis: St Louis Republic, 1906), 472; Prufrock company notepaper, held in the collection of Missouri History Museum, Library and Research Center, Business Letterhead Collection (collection A1430, Box 36, folder 1); on Mrs Stetson, see 'Women's Clubs', *St Louis Globe-Democrat*, 15 January 1899, n.p.

35   George M. Beard, *American Nervousness* (New York: G. P. Putnam's Sons, 1881), 13.

36   [TSE], *Fireside*, number 4; see also Crawford, *The Savage and the City*, 28–9, and, e.g., *St Louis Globe-Democrat*, 27 January 1899, 10.

37   [TSE], *Fireside*, numbers 4 and 5; for Woodbury's printed advertisement see, e.g., *St Louis Globe-Democrat*, 5 January 1899, 12.

38   This anecdote comes from Mary Trevelyan's unpublished memoir, 'The Pope of

Russell Square'; see Lyndall Gordon, *The Imperfect Life of T. S. Eliot*, rev. edn (London: Virago, 2012), 7.

39 TSE photograph, *c.* 1895? (Houghton bMS Am 2560 (161a)).

40 [TSE], *Fireside*, number 5; for Dr Chase's advertisement see, e.g., *St Louis Globe-Democrat*, 7 January 1899, 10.

41 Steven Matthews, *T. S. Eliot and Early Modern Literature* (Oxford: Oxford University Press, 2013), 1–2; *CCP*, 62.

42 'Theatrical News and Gossip', *St Louis Globe-Democrat*, 1 January 1899, n.p.

43 'A Big Show Week', *St Louis Globe-Democrat*, 9 January 1899, 3.

44 'Worthy to Be Printed in Letters of Gold' (advertisement), *St Louis Globe-Democrat*, 8 January 1899, 26; 'Cyrano de Bergerac', *St Louis Globe-Democrat*, 10 January 1899, 5.

45 *You Told Me You Had Money in the Bank, Coon Song & Chorus . . . written and Composed by Matthews and Bulger* (New York: Rogers Bros. Music Publishing Co., 1899), 1.

46 [TSE], *Fireside*, numbers 1, 11 and 2.

47 'Dramatic News and Gossip', *St Louis Globe-Democrat*, 22 January 1899, n.p.

48 'Exodus of St. Louis Hoboes', *St Louis Globe-Democrat*, 7 January 1898, 9.

49 [TSE], *Fireside*, number 7.

50 TSE, 'The Influence of Landscape upon the Poet', *Daedalus*, Spring 1960, 422.

51 'Hoosiers to the Front', *St Louis Globe-Democrat*, 6 February 1898, 11.

52 'James Whitcomb Riley', *St Louis Globe-Democrat*, 11 February 1898, 9; J. W. Riley, *The Best Loved Poems and Ballads* (New York: Blue Ribbon Books, 1934), 127.

53 George V. Hobart, 'Hiawatha up to Date', *St Louis Globe-Democrat*, 3 May 1896, 41.

54 'The Women's Clubs of St. Louis', *St Louis Globe-Democrat*, 9 January 1898, 42.

55 'At the Theaters', *St Louis Globe-Democrat*, 3 February 1898, 4.

56 'Edna May's Salvation Army Song', *St Louis Republic*, 18 November 1900.

57 Eve Golden, *Anna Held & the Birth of Ziegfeld's Broadway* (Louisville: University Press of Kentucky, 2000), 30, 3.

58 'Theatrical News and Gossip', *St Louis Globe-Democrat*, 26 February 1899, 14.

59 [TSE], *Fireside*, numbers 7, 3 and 6.

60 TSE to John Hayward, 27 December 1939 (Hayward Bequest); the Lionberger House still stands in St Louis; on Isaac Lionberger's moves, see Eric Sandweiss, *St Louis: The Evolution of an Urban Landscape* (Philadelphia: Temple University Press, 2001), 216; on Margaret Lionberger, see 'Personal', *Boston Evening Transcript*, 14 November 1912, 5; also *Harvard College Class of 1911 Second Report* (Cambridge Mass:, Crimson Printing Co., 1915), 16, 68.

61 TSE to John Hayward, 27 December 1939 (Hayward Bequest); the St Louis Bagnalls' money probably came from the Adams-Bagnall Electric Company of Cleveland: see 'Woman Sells Large Estate', *St Louis Republic*, 17 July 1904, n.p.; also 'Alton', *St Louis Republic*, 15 November 1903, 4.

62 'Funeral of W. H. Thornburgh', *St Louis Republic*, 27 August 1900, 10; 'Mrs Florence Thornburgh to Marry W. C. Stribling', *St Louis Republic*, 17 June 1903, 6.

63 TSE to John Hayward, 27 December 1939 (Hayward Bequest).

64 Margaret Shapleigh to John J. Soldo, 31 December 1969, quoted in Soldo, *The Tempering of T. S. Eliot*, 27; see also 'Shapleigh, John Blasdel', in Leonard, *The Book of St. Louisans*, 526.

65 TSE to John Hayward, 27 December 1939 (Hayward Bequest).

66 Ibid.

67 Advertisement, 'Dancing Taught', *St Louis Republic*, 30 September 1903, 13.

68 'Children in Charity Benefit', *St Louis Republic*, 3 May 1902, n.p.; 'Mahler's Matinee', *St Louis Republic*, 19 November 1903, 8.

69 Julius K. Hunter, *Westmoreland and Portland Places: The History and Architecture of America's Premier Private Streets, 1888–1988* (Columbia: University of Missouri Press, 1988), 70.

70   'Society's Christmas Interests', *St Louis Republic*, 25 December 1904, Part I, 8.

71   'Social Leaders to Study Delsarte', *St Louis Republic*, 7 April 1892, 1.

72   François Delsarte, 'Address' to Genevieve Stebbins, *Delsarte System of Expression*, fifth edn (New York: Edgar S. Werner, 1894), xlviii.

73   On Hargadine and McKittrick, see Elizabeth McNulty, *St Louis Then and Now* (San Diego: Thunder Bay Press, 2000), 54; for Otto von Schrader's change of address see address lists prefacing *Transactions of the Academy of Science of St Louis*, vols. VI and VII (St Louis: Nixon-Jones Printing Co., 1894 and 1897).

74   TSE to John Hayward, 27 December 1939 (Hayward Bequest); for information about the Lewis Dozier Mansion, see the entry in the online US National Register of Historic Places; on the Glee Club, see *Fiftieth Annual Graduating Exercises, Smith Academy*, 13 June 1905 (Smith Academy Collection, Washington University Archives).

75   [TSE], *Fireside*, numbers 11, 13, 14 and 7.

76   TSE, 'Prize-Day Address at the Methodist Girls School at Penzance' (Hayward Bequest).

77   [TSE], *Fireside*, numbers 11, 5 and 8.

78   'Up the Paraguay River', *St Louis Globe-Democrat*, 5 February 1899, 4.

79   *CPP*, 109. On these and other passages of Mayne Reid's work which can be connected to Eliot's interests, see Crawford, *The Savage and the City*, 15–26.

80   *L1*, 376.

81   Edward Eggleston, *A History of the United States and its People* (New York: Appleton, 1888), iii.

82   'Smith Academy, Washington University, Semi-Annual Record of Thomas S. Eliot of the First Year Class, Second Term – Session of 1899–1900' (Houghton bMS Am 2560 (95)).

83   'Smith Academy, Washington University, Semi-Annual Record of Thomas Stearns Eliot of the Second Preparatory Class, Second Term – Session of 1898–9' (Houghton bMS Am 2560 (95)).

84   TSE, 'George Washington, A Life' (Hayward Bequest).

85   [TSE], 'George W———', *Fireside*, number 8.

86   'Women's Clubs', *St Louis Republic*, 2 March 1902, 3.

87   See TSE's note to line 253 of that poem (*CPP*, 78).

88   John Williams White, *The First Greek Book* (Boston: Ginn and Co., 1896), 3.

89   See Katharine T. Corbett, *In Her Place: A Guide to St Louis Women's History* (St Louis: Missouri Historical Society Press, 1999), 135.

90   'A Brief Review of Many Celebrated Colleges and Schools of Merit', *St Louis Republic*, 30 August 1902, 8.

91   *A Catalogue of the Officers and Students in Washington University with the Courses of Study for the Academic Year 1895–96* (St Louis: Nixon-Jones Printing Co., 1895), 216; other details about the school are taken from this work.

92   Ibid., 218.

93   Roger Conant Hatch, *Fallen Leaves* (Boston: Four Seasons Company, [1922]), 30.

94   'How to Achieve Success', *St Louis Republic*, 6 December 1903, 2.

95   *Smith Academy Catalogue*, 1899–1900, quoted in Jayme Stayer, 'T. S. Eliot as a Schoolboy: The Lockwood School, Smith Academy, and Milton Academy', *Twentieth-Century Literature*, 59.4 (Winter 2013), .634.

96   'What They "Wanted to Be" When They Grew Up', *St Louis Republic*, 26 August 1900, magazine section; 'Twenty-Five Years' Service is Celebrated', 28 April 1904, 10; 'Curd, Charles Paine', in Leonard, *The Book of St Louisans*, 142; 'C. B. C. May Not Play Washington', *St Louis Republic*, 29 October 1900, 3.

97   Guide to the Percy Boynton Papers, University of Chicago Library; 'Ethical Society Lectures', *St Louis Republic*, 20 October 1900, 6.

98   'School Notes', *Smith Academy Record*, June 1902, 12.

99   Roger Conant Hatch entry in *Harvard Class of 1900, Fourth Report* (Cambridge, Mass:

Crimson Printing Co., 1921), 204; Hatch, *Fallen Leaves*, 11; also Soldo, *The Tempering of T. S. Eliot*, 27.

100 Hatch, *Fallen Leaves*, 30, 18; see also *The School Songs of Smith Academy* (St Louis: Mangan Press, [?1907]), 41.

101 Roger Conant Hatch, entry in *Harvard Class of 1900*, 204.

102 TSE to John Hayward, 21 December 1942 (Hayward Bequest).

103 TSE, 'American Literature and the American Language', *CC*, 45–6; Thomas H. McKittrick and M. Haywood Post quoted in Soldo, *The Tempering of T. S. Eliot*, 26.

104 See, e.g., 'Smith Academy Team Dines', *St Louis Republic*, 10 January 1903, 2; and 'High School 15, Smith Academy 11', *St Louis Republic*, 29 November 1901, 6.

105 Football report, *St Louis Republic*, 22 October 1903, 6; 'Smith Academy Defeated Manual', *St Louis Republic*, Part III, 6; see also 'Klipstein' (photograph), *St Louis Republic*, 6 November 1904, Part IV.

106 *Facsimile*, 4; TSE, 'Song to the Opherian', *Tyro*, 1 ([Spring 1921]), 6.

107 *CPP*, 123.

108 J. Louis Swarts is mentioned in 'School Notes', *Smith Academy Record*, June 1902, 12; Soldo, *The Tempering of T. S. Eliot*, 27.

109 *Fireside*, number 8.

110 *L1*, 482.

Chapter 3 – Schoolings

1 TSE to John Hayward, 27 December 1939 (Hayward Bequest).

2 James E. Sullivan, ed., *Spalding's Official Athletic Almanac for 1905* (New York: American Sports Publishing Co., 1905), 187.

3 *World's Fair Authentic Guide* (St Louis: Official Guide Company, 1904), 26, 74, 75, 141, 143; see also Tatsushi Narita, 'The Young T. S. Eliot and Alien Cultures: His Philippine Interactions', *Review of English Studies*, 45.180 (1994), 523–5.

4 TSE, 'The Man Who Was King', *Smith Academy Record*, 8.6 (June 1905), 2, 1.

5 TSE to John Hayward, 27 December 1939 (Hayward Bequest).

6 Sullivan, *Spalding's Official Athletic Almanac for 1905*, 187; Programme for *Fiftieth Annual Graduating Exercises, Smith Academy*, 13 June 1905 (Washington University Archives).

7 'Smith Academy Graduates Eighteen', *St Louis Republic*, 14 June 1905, 11; entries for Lawrence Tyler Post and Walker Moore Van Riper in *Yale University 1909 5th Year Reunion Book* (New Haven: Yale University, 1914), 206–7 and 256–7; entries for Frederick Clinton Lake, Jr, in Robert Dudley French, ed., *History of the Class of 1910 Yale College* (New Haven: Yale University, 1910), 217, and *History of the Class of Nineteen Hundred and Ten Yale College, Volume 2* (New Haven: Tuttle, Morehouse & Taylor Co., 1917), 191; 'Young Orators of Smith Academy Will Compete for Gold Medal in Annual Contest To-morrow', *St Louis Republic*, 13 April 1905, 2; for Post's 'Class Song', see the programme for the *Fiftieth Annual Graduating Exercises, Smith Academy*. Other information from entries in John W. Leonard, ed., *The Book of St Louisans* (St Louis: St Louis Republic, 1906).

8 Typed sheet, dated February 1905, listing names of those chosen to speak in the Smith Academy Preliminary Speaking Contest (Smith Academy Collection, Washington University Archives).

9 *L1*, 5–6; see also John J. Soldo, *The Tempering of T. S. Eliot* (Ann Arbor: UMI Research Press, 1983), and Jayme Stayer, 'T. S. Eliot as a Schoolboy: The Lockwood School, Smith Academy, and Milton Academy', *Twentieth-Century Literature*, 59. 4 (Winter 2013), 619–656.

10 Robert Herrick and Lindsay Todd Damon, *Composition and Rhetoric for Schools* (Chicago: Scott, Foresman and Company, 1899), 12, 13, 30.

11 TSE, 'Le Morte Darthur', *Spectator*, 23 February 1934, 278; see Sidney Lanier, *The Boy's King Arthur* (New York: Scribner's, 1880), 206, 271; on American Arthurianism,

see Alan Lupack and Barbara Tepa Lupack, *King Arthur in America* (Cambridge: D. S. Brewer, 1999).

12   James Russell Lowell, *The Vision of Sir Launfal and Other Poems*, ed. Mabel Caldwell Willard (Boston: Leach, Shewell, and Sangborn, [1896]), 6.

13   Ibid., 17, 20, 25.

14   See Lupack and Lupack, *King Arthur*, 10, 13.

15   Lowell, *Vision of Sir Launfal*, 111.

16   TSE to Otto H. Schwarz in *St Louis Post-Dispatch*, 16 February 1964, quoted in Soldo, *The Tempering of T. S. Eliot*, 27.

17   'St. Louis Travelers who have made from Ten to Twenty Transatlantic Trips', *St Louis Republic*, 4 October 1903, magazine section, [52]; other information from her October 1921 Certificate of Death at Missouri Board of Health Bureau of Vital Statistics.

18   *A Catalogue of the Officers and Students in Washington University* (St Louis: Nixon-Jones Printing Co., 1895), 212.

19   Smith Academy report for TSE dated 'February 1, 1901' (Houghton bMS Am 2560 (95)).

20   *CPP*, 62.

21   *CPP*, 63 (74–5), 67.

22   Lowell, *Vision of Sir Launfal*, 13.

23   Rudyard Kipling, *A Choice of Kipling's Verse*, ed. and intro. by TSE (London: Faber and Faber, 1941; repr. 1963), 136.

24   [TSE], *Fireside*, numbers 13, 6 and 3.

25   TSE, 'T. S. Eliot: A Personal Anthology' (1947 radio script) (Hayward Bequest).

26   Kipling, *A Choice of Kipling's Verse*, 171, 172, 11, 12; *CPP*, 86.

27   'Columbus Benjamin Gast', and 'Robert McCreery Allen', *Smith Academy Record*, February 1900, 8, 9.

28   'Strain Caused Brain Fever', *St Louis Republic*, 20 April 1901, Part I, 7.

29   Herbert Howarth, *Notes on Some Figures Behind T. S. Eliot* (London: Chatto & Windus, 1965), 28; TSE vetted Howarth's typescript very carefully: see Timothy Materer, 'T. S. Eliot and his Biographical Critics', *Essays in Criticism*, 62.1 (2012), 41–57.

30   *L1*, 4.

31   *L1*, 9.

32   Howarth, *Notes on Some Figures Behind T. S. Eliot*, 23.

33   'Favors Juvenile Court Bill: Mrs. Eliot Declares Good Results Will Follow Its Passage', *St Louis Republic*, 11 February 1903, 3.

34   '"Tombs Angel" has Resigned', *St Louis Republic*, 24 November 1904, 12.

35   *L1*, 4.

36   TSE, Lectures on English 26 (1933) (Houghton), XVIII.

37   Ibid; D. H. Lawrence, *Psychoanalysis and the Unconscious and Fantasia of the Unconscious*, ed. Bruce Steele (Cambridge: Cambridge University Press, 2004), 147, 144–5, 146.

38   *L1*, 420.

39   *A Catalogue of the Officers and Students in Washington University*, 220.

40   *L1*, 41.

41   *L2*, 678.

42   'Doctor Day Goes to Boston', *St Louis Republic*, 5 March 1903, 5.

43   Cynthia Grant Tucker, *No Silent Witness: The Eliot Parsonage Women and their Unitarian World* (New York: Oxford University Press, 2010), 178.

44   Ibid., 178–9 and 226.

45   *L1*, 2.

46   *CPP*, 73, 79.

47   'Easter Services and Sermons in the Churches: Evidences of a Larger Life in Which We Live', *St Louis Republic*, 16 April 1900, 10.

48 'Oratorio "Redemption" to Be Given at Church of the Messiah', *St Louis Republic*, 6 April 1900, 9.

49 'Sermons and Services of the Churches: Peace of Soul that Comes through Endurance', *St Louis Republic*, 8 October 1900, 8.

50 'Sermons and Services: "Death in Life and Life in Death"', *St Louis Republic*, 8 April 1901, 10.

51 *CPP*, 68.

52 'Survival of the Faithful: The Law of Immortality', *St Louis Republic*, 28 April 1902, 10.

53 'Urges Special Building for Religious Exhibit', *St Louis Republic*, 10 June 1901, 1.

54 'St Louis Citizens Meet to Honor "Sage of Concord"', *St Louis Republic*, 26 May 1903, 5.

55 'Sees Encouraging Signs in Unitarian Conference', *St Louis Republic*, 19 October 1903, 10.

56 'Deceit in Small Things Makes for Bad Morals', *St Louis Republic*, 23 November 1903, 10.

57 'Union Club's Lenten Concert at Church of the Messiah', *St Louis Republic*, 27 March 1904, 5.

58 HWE, Jr, TS, Notes on a lecture of TSE (1933) (Houghton Library bMS Am 1691 (134)).

59 Ibid.

60 TSE, 'Ezra Pound', *New English Weekly*, 31 October 1946, 27.

61 TSE, Notes for English 26 Lectures (1933) (Houghton), I.

62 HWE, Jr to Donald Gallup, 25 February 1937 (Houghton bMS Am 1691.6(7)).

63 TSE to Eleanor Hinkley, 7 August 1959 (Houghton bMS Am 2244 (3)).

64 TSE, 'The Art of Poetry I, T. S. Eliot' (interview by Donald Hall), *Paris Review*, 21 (Spring/Summer 1959), 49.

65 TSE, 'Religion and Literature', *SE*, 394.

66 *UPUC*, 33.

67 HWE, Jr, TS, Notes on a lecture of TSE (1933) (Houghton bMS AM 1691 (134))

68 'Coming Events', *St Louis Globe-Democrat*, 20 February 1898, 44; 'In Defense of Le Gallienne', *St Louis Globe-Democrat*, 6 March 1898, 13.

69 *The Rubáiyát of Omar Khayyám*, tr. Edward Fitzgerald (New York: Dodge Publishing Co., 1905), 12, 15, 37, 56, 104, 74, 105.

70 *UPUC*, 33.

71 TSE, 'The Education of Taste', *Athenaeum*, 27 June 1919, 521.

72 Henry S. Pancoast, *An Introduction to English Literature* (New York: Henry Holt, 1894), 382; *L1*, 5.

73 Dante Gabriel Rossetti, *The Collected Works of Dante Gabriel Rossetti*, 2 vols (London: Ellis and Elvey, 1887), I, 232, 233.

74 *CPP*, 28 ('The "Boston Evening Transcript"').

75 *CPP*, 587.

76 Thomas Ingoldsby [R. H. Barham], *The Ingoldsby Legends, or Mirth and Marvels* (London: Richard Bentley, 1864), 93, 99.

77 *CPP*, 587, 588; for HWE, Jr's recollection of the poem, see his notes on TSE's lecture on tradition (Houghton bMS Am 1691 (134a)).

78 *CPP*, 589; *The Ingoldsby Legends*, 91.

79 *CPP*, 14; *The Ingoldsby Legends*, 98.

80 *L1*, 376.

81 Percy Bysshe Shelley, *The Poetical Works of Percy Bysshe Shelley*, ed. Edward Dowden (London: Macmillan, 1895), xi, 558; TSE's copy of Dowden's Shelley is now in the archive at Milton Academy (see Soldo, *The Tempering of T. S. Eliot*, 30).

82 *L1*, 4.

83   *L3*, 568.

84   *L2*, 741.

85   TSE, 'The Man Who Was King', *Smith Academy Record*, 8.6 (June 1905), 2, and 'A Tale of a Whale', *Smith Academy Record*, 8.4 (April 1905), 2:

86   TSE, 'The Man Who Was King', 2, 1; see Robert Crawford, *The Savage and the City in the Work of T. S. Eliot* (Oxford: Clarendon Press, 1987).

87   The poem is dated on the copy of the original draft sent to John Hayward with TSE's letter to John Hayward, 19 August 1943 (Houghton bMS Am 2706 (3)).

88   'St Louis Clubmen Planning Concert Hall', *St Louis Republic*, 26 March 1905, Part II, 8; Roger Conant Hatch, 'Smith Forever', *Smith Academy Record*, 8.2 (February 1905), 7.

89   TSE to John Hayward, 19 August 1943 (Houghton); and 'American Literature and the American Language', *CC*, 45.

90   TSE, *Poems Written in Early Youth*, ed. Valerie Eliot (London: Faber and Faber, 1967), 'Note', 7.

91   TSE, annotated carbon copy of 'If Time and Space, as sages say' (Houghton bMS Am 1691 (128)).

92   *Fiftieth Annual Graduating Exercises* programme.

93   *CC*, 43 ('American Literature and the American Language').

94   *L1*, 3.

95   *L1*, 6.

96   *L1*, 4.

97   *L1*, 4.

98   *L1*, 6.

99   Adam Sherman Hill, *The Principles of Rhetoric*, new edn, revised and enlarged (New York: American Book Company, 1895), 81, 111, 132, 13, 170, 273, 352, vii.

100   *L1*, 6.

101   *L4*, 655.

102   HWE, Jr, to Mr Field, headmaster of Milton Academy, 8 November 1937 (Houghton bMS Am1691.6 (3)).

103   Roger Amory, 'Class History 1906', *The Milton Orange and Blue*, 12.15 (4 July 1906), 120.

104   *CPP*, 226 ('Macavity: the Mystery Cat'); Stayer, 'T. S. Eliot as a Schoolboy', 637.

105   *L2*, 336 (the letters were destroyed by TSE after CCE died).

106   *L1*, 10.

107   Stayer, 'T. S. Eliot as a Schoolboy', 637.

Chapter 4 – A Full-Fledged Harvard Man

1   *L1*, 5, 6.

2   *L1*, 6.

3   *L1*, 6; John J. Soldo, *The Tempering of T. S. Eliot* (Ann Arbor: UMI Research Press, 1983), 49.

4   TSE, 'William James on Immortality', *New Statesman*, 8 September 1917, 547.

5   [HWE, Jr], 'The Freshman's Meditation', from *Harvard Lampoon* (authorship attested on accompanying envelope) (Houghton bMS Am 1691.10 (21)).

6   *Official Guide to Harvard University*, ed. Harvard Memorial Society (Cambridge, Mass: The University, 1907), 142.

7   TSE to Winthrop Sprague Brooks, 18 July 1956 (Houghton bMS Am 1691.4).

8   Advertisements in *Harvard Advocate*, 83 (1907).

9   'Directory of Freshmen', *Harvard Crimson*, 8 October 1906, 6–7; 'Robert Haydock' and 'Constant Wendell' entries in *Harvard College, Class of 1910, Third Report* (Cambridge, Mass: Crimson Printing Co., 1917), 151, 310; there is correspondence

between Constant Wendell and Barrett Wendell in the Barrett Wendell papers (Houghton, Series IV. MS Am 1907.1 (1384)).

10 'The "verdant freshman" has become a College tradition', according to 'Review of First Advocate', *Harvard Crimson*, 28 November 1906.

11 Lucien Price and Richard J. Walsh, 'Goldkoastides', *Harvard Advocate*, 81 (1906), 63.

12 Lucien Price, 'A Fake Play', *Harvard Advocate*, 82. 1 (27 September 1906), 8, 9, 11.

13 E. B. Sheldon, 'The Philosophy of Horatio', *Harvard Advocate*, 82. 1 (27 September 1906), 3, 4.

14 Sidney P. Henshaw, 'Tactics for Teas', *Harvard Advocate*, 82. 1 (27 September 1906), 16; HWE, Jr, 'Endicott and the Janitor', *Harvard Advocate*, 71 (1901), 121.

15 Frederick Garrison Hall, Edward Revere Little and HWE, Jr, *Harvard Celebrities: A Book of Caricatures & Decorative Drawings* (Printed for the Editors by the University Press, Cambridge, U.S.A., [n.d.]), 'Wendell'. HWE, Jr's inscribed copy is in the Houghton Library (bMS Am 2560 (76)).

16 TSE, 'Donne in Our Time', in Theodore Spencer, ed., *A Garland for John Donne* (Cambridge, Mass: Harvard University Press, 1931), 1.

17 *Harvard College, Class of Nineteen Ten, First Report, April 1911* (Cambridge, Mass: Crimson Printing Company, 1911), 32.

18 E. H. Wells to HWE, 4 December 1906 (Harvard University Archives, UAIII 15.88.10).

19 Price and Walsh, 'Goldkoastides', 62.

20 TSE's Harvard courses are listed in Manju Jain, *T. S. Eliot and American Philosophy: The Harvard Years* (Cambridge and New York: Cambridge University Press, 1992), 251–6.

21 Wells to HWE, 4 December 1906.

22 *L1*, 11.

23 HWE, Jr, 'Tillinghast, Stroke Oar', *Harvard Advocate*, 70 (1900–1901), 16 (among copies of HWE, Jr's articles in Houghton bMS Am2560 (75)); *L1*, 10.

24 Leon Magaw Little, carbon copy of piece written on 13 May 1968 for the TSE memorial issue of the *Harvard Advocate* (Houghton bMS Am1691.4 (136)); on TSE's response to the *Crimson* editorial, see Soldo, *The Tempering of T. S. Eliot*, 50.

25 '1910 on College Courses: The Results of the Annual Post-card Canvass', *Harvard Illustrated Monthly*, 11.8 (May 1910), 263–4.

26 *CC*, 80.

27 'Directory of Freshmen', *Harvard Crimson*, 8 October 1906, 6–7.

28 Little, *Harvard Advocate* carbon copy.

29 Gilbert Murray, *A History of Greek Literature* (London: Heinemann, 1897), xv.

30 'Mr. Murray's Lecture on the Iliad', *Harvard Crimson*, 9 May 1907, 6.

31 This inscription, over a small door in the west wall of Memorial Hall, is quoted and translated in *A Guide Book to the Grounds and Buildings of Harvard University* (Cambridge, Mass; The University, 1898), 63.

32 George Herbert Palmer, 'Necessary Limitations of the Elective System', in G. H. Palmer and Alice Freeman Parker, *The Teacher: Essays and Addresses on Education* (New York: Houghton Mifflin, 1908), 250.

33 *Official Guide to Harvard University* (1907), 1, 9.

34 '1910 on College Courses', 262–3, 261.

35 Conrad Aiken, 'King Bolo and Others', *Harvard Advocate*, 100. 3 (Fall 1966), 30.

36 *CPP*, 43 ('Sweeney Erect').

37 R. J. Walsh, 'On the Decoration of College Rooms', in *Selections from the Harvard Advocate, 1906–1916* (Cambridge, Mass: The University Press, 1916), 143. Walsh was in the Class of 1907.

38 Details of the interior of the Union building are drawn from *Official Guide to Harvard University* (1907), 161–3.

39 TSE, 'Donne in Our Time', 1.

40   'Books Added to Union Library', *Harvard Crimson*, 11 December 1906, 1; 'Latest Books in Union Library', *Harvard Crimson*, 26 February 1907, 3.

41   *CPP*, 15.

42   Grover Smith, *T. S. Eliot's Poetry and Plays: A Study in Sources and Meaning*, second edn (Chicago: University of Chicago Press, 1974), 161.

43   Aristophanes, *The Acharnians*, ed. W. W. Merry, fourth edn (Oxford: Clarendon Press, 1893), v.

44   TSE in 'Some Views of Readers' on rear jacket flap of Douglas Young, *The Puddocks: A Verse Play in Scots from the Greek of Aristophanes*, second edn (Makarsbield, Tayport: The Author, 1958).

45   Charles Henry Conrad Wright, *A History of French Literature* (New York: Oxford University Press, 1912), 878, 794, 675, 792, 743, 744, 804, 805.

46   Walsh, 'On the Decoration of College Rooms', 141, 142.

47   T. S. Matthews, *Great Tom: Notes Towards the Definition of T. S. Eliot* (London: Weidenfeld and Nicolson, 1974), 24–5; Matthews reproduces this photograph, then in the possession of Mrs B. J. L. Ainsworth, among the plates following page 108.

48   E. Lloyd Sheldon, 'Undergraduate Literature at Harvard', *Harvard Illustrated Magazine*, 7.6 (March 1906), 111.

49   Howard Morris entry in *Harvard College Class of 1910 Fourth Report* (Cambridge, Mass: Crimson Printing Co., 1921), 267.

50   Little, *Harvard Advocate* carbon copy.

51   Peters gave his address in *The Digamma Club Year Book: 1908* (Harvard University Archives), 20; his parents' names are in the *Harvard College Class of 1910 Fourth Report*, 304; family details from MyTrees.com.

52   'Results of the Interclass Tennis', *Harvard Crimson*, 1 May 1907; 'Progress of Tennis Tournament', *Harvard Crimson*, 3 May 1907.

53   Anthony M. Sammarco, 'Andrew J. Peters, Mayor of Boston', Forest Hills Educational Trust website post, 28 January 2010; several books deal with the background and career of Andrew James Peters, including Francis Russell, *The Knave of Boston* (Boston: Quinlan Press, 1988), 68–84.

54   Information on these friends of TSE is drawn from *The Digamma Club Year Book: 1908* and from their entries in the *Harvard College Class of 1910 Fourth Report*.

55   A contemporary photograph of the Digamma Club appears opposite the title page of *The Digamma Club Year Book: 1908*.

56   James Hoopes, *Van Wyck Brooks: In Search of American Culture* (Amherst: University of Massachusetts Press, 1977), 30.

57   Again, information on these friends of TSE is drawn from *The Digamma Club Year Book: 1908* and from their entries in the *Harvard College Class of 1910 Fourth Report*.

58   Hoopes, *Van Wyck Brooks*, 30.

59   Little, *Harvard Advocate* carbon copy.

60   TSE, 'Ballade of the Fox Dinner', reprinted in Soldo, *The Tempering of T. S. Eliot*, 59–60; information about fellow club members and their addresses comes from *The Digamma Club Year Book: 1908*.

61   Winthrop Sprague Brooks, letter of 14 November 1946 beginning 'My dear Furgeson' (Houghton bMS Am 1691.4 (132)).

62   Ibid.

63   TSE, to Leon Magaw Little, 11 October 1957 (Houghton bMS Am 1691.4).

64   TSE to EP, 7 January 1934 (Beinecke).

65   *IMH* 315, 317.

66   Ibid., 315 ('[Columbo and Bolo verses]').

67   Stanley Cobb, 'Winthrop Sprague Brooks', *Auk*, 82.4 (October 1965), 684.

68   digammaclub.org/

69   D. A. Sargent, 'The Origin and Significance of the Inter-Collegiate Strength Test', *Harvard Illustrated Magazine*, 9.7 (April 1906), 164, 165, 169. See below, p. 165.

70   John Hall Wheelock, *The Last Romantic: A Poet Among Publishers: The Oral Autobiography of John Hall Wheelock*, ed. Matthew Bruccoli with Judith Baughman (Columbia: University of South Carolina Press, 2002), 38.

71   Conrad Aiken, 'King Bolo and Others', in Tambimuttu and Richard Marsh, eds, *T. S. Eliot: A Symposium* (London: Tambimuttu and Mass, 1965), 20.

72   Little, *Harvard Advocate* carbon copy.

73   *IMH*, 318, 316 ('[Columbo and Bolo verses]').

74   Ibid., 315('[Columbo and Bolo verses]').

75   TSE, '[Notes on characters and plots]', n.d. (Houghton bMS Am 1691.14(14)).

76   TSE to Polly Tandy, 4 September 1935 (British Library).

77   *Sandow on Physical Training*, compiled and edited, under Mr Sandow's direction by G. Mercer Adam (New York: J. Selwin Tait and Sons, 1894), 112, 12, 10, 15.

78   Aiken, 'King Bolo and Others', 20.

Chapter 5 – A Rose

1   *CPP*, 596 ('Song', 'when we came home across the hill' (1907)); 591 ('Song', 'If time and space, as sages say' (revised 1905)); 597 ('Before Morning').

2   This anonymous spoof from the December 1908 *Harvard Lampoon* is quoted in John J. Soldo, *The Tempering of T. S. Eliot* (Ann Arbor: UMI Research Press, 1983), 99.

3   Conrad Aiken, 'King Bolo and Others', in Tambimuttu and Richard March, eds, *T. S. Eliot: A Symposium* (New York: Tambimuttu and Mass, 1948), 20; in classical mythology Lamia was a dangerous seductress.

4   *CPP*, 600 ('Song', 'The moonflower opens to the moth'), 598.

5   Their comments are quoted in Soldo, *The Tempering of T. S. Eliot*, 56, but Soldo does not realise that the first set of names are those of *Monthly* editors, and so the phrase 'Gift from the Monthly' that appears above Tinckom-Fernandez's negative comment should be taken literally.

6   Ibid., 102.

7   *CPP*, 600.

8   'Improvements in Holyoke House', *Harvard Crimson*, 3 March 1908; 'Holyoke House Improved', *Harvard Crimson*, 29 September 1908.

9   Fred E. Haynes, 'Amusements', in Robert A. Woods, ed., *The City Wilderness: A Settlement Study* (Boston: Houghton Mifflin, 1898), 180.

10   'Sale of Hotel Caprio', *Boston Evening Transcript*, 10 October 1905.

11   William I. Cole, 'Criminal Tendencies', in Woods, *The City Wilderness*, 159.

12   *Facsimile*, 125.

13   *L4*, 182.

14   H. P., 'The Influence of the Comic Opera', *Harvard Advocate*, 83 (1908), 99.

15   Ibid.

16   TSE, 'Wilkie Collins and Dickens', *SE*, 460; Barbara Meredith Waldinger, 'No Mother to Guide Her', *Theatre Journal*, 54.4 (December 2002), 654.

17   '"Fifty Miles from Boston" Proved Popular', *Evening Tribune* (Providence, RI), 7 April 1908, 17.

18   *Facsimile*, 5, 125.

19   *Facsimile*, 125.

20   'Plays of the New Week', *Boston Evening Transcript*, 8 January 1910.

21   Shef's story, 'The Mongol and the Chinaman', was commended in 'The Advocate', *Harvard Crimson*, 24 February 1897; his 1909 *Harvard Monthly* article on 'The Chinese Classics and Modern Research' was regarded as 'closely reasoned' but lacking in vitality by H. D. Fuller, 'Monthly Reviewed', *Harvard Crimson*, 10 December 1909; Shef's 'Confucianism' appeared in *The Harvard Classics*, Vol. 51 (1914), 451–6.

22   See *L1*, 11, which strongly suggests Tom and Shef had been meeting.

23   W. A. Neilson, 'First Advocate Number', *Harvard Crimson*, 6 November 1907.

24   John Davidson, *The Poems*, ed. Andrew Turnbull, 2 vols (Edinburgh: Scottish Academic Press, 1973), I, 65.
25   Arthur Symons, *The Symbolist Movement in Literature*, second edn (London: Archibald Constable, 1908), 1, 3, 8, 9.
26   Ibid., vi.
27   *CC*, 126–7 (the bracketed translation is mine).
28   *L3*, 768; Symons, *Symbolist Movement*, 17, 20.
29   TSE, 'The Perfect Critic', *Athenaeum*, 9 July 1920, 40.
30   Symons, *Symbolist Movement*, 24, 37, 70, 95, 153.
31   Ibid., 122, 101, 108, 102–3 (the bracketed translation has been supplied by David Kinloch, to whom thanks).
32   TSE, 'Baudelaire and the Symbolists', *Criterion*, January 1930, 357.
33   Symons, *Symbolist Movement*, 109; *CPP*, 601('Nocturne'), 15.
34   Gluyas Williams, quoted in Soldo, *The Tempering of T. S. Eliot*, 53.
35   Haniel Long's 1908–9 diary (Brown University Archives), quoted in ibid., 55.
36   Alan Seeger, *Letters and Diary* (New York: Scribner's, 1917), 184–5.
37   Alan Seeger, *Poems* (New York: Scribner's, 1915), 117; *CPP*, 17.
38   The first, manuscript version of 'The Deserted Garden', dated 1908, is in Houghton bMS Am 1578 (10); revised, the poem appears in Seeger, *Poems*, 10–26.
39   Seeger, *Poems*, 47, 50, 49.
40   TSE, 'Short Reviews', *Egoist*, December 1917, 172.
41   TSE, 'The New Elizabethans and the Old', *Athenaeum*, 4 April 1919, 134.
42   *CPP*, 52; Alan Seeger to Edward Eyre Hunt, 30 July 1909, in M. A. DeWolfe Howe, *Memoirs of the Harvard Dead in the War against Germany* (Cambridge: Harvard University Press, 1920), 111.
43   TSE, 'Short Reviews', 172.
44   *CPP*, 599.
45   Symons, *Symbolist Movement*, 84.
46   Long, diary in Soldo, *The Tempering of T. S. Eliot*, 55–8.
47   This letter is reproduced photographically in 'A Short History of the Signet Society', by Nathan C. Shiverick, which can be found on the Signet Society's website.
48   John Hall Wheelock, *The Last Romantic: A Poet Among Publishers: The Oral Autobiography of John Hall Wheelock*, ed. Matthew Bruccoli with Judith Baughman (Columbia: University of South Carolina Press, 2002), 35–6.
49   Shiverick, 'A Short History of the Signet Society', reproduces the 1910 Annual Dinner menu, and quotes this 'perennial' Signet drinking song.
50   Pierre La Rose, introduction to *The Third Catalogue of the Signet* (Boston: Merrymount Press, 1903), xxiv; Shiverick, 'A Short History of the Signet Society', 1910 menu.
51   Frederick Garrison Hall, Edward Revere Little and HWE, Jr, *Harvard Celebrities: A Book of Caricatures & Decorative Drawings* (Printed for the Editors by the University Press, Cambridge, U. S. A., [n.d.]), 'Pierre'.
52   'Monthly Review by Prof. Schofield', *Harvard Crimson*, 30 October 1909.
53   *L1*, 486.
54   'Review of Current Advocate', *Harvard Crimson*, 15 November 1909.
55   '1910 on College Courses: The Results of the Annual Post-card Canvass', *Harvard Illustrated Monthly*, 11.8 (May 1910), 264, 263.
56   'Prof. Palmer Repeats Library Talk', *Harvard Crimson*, 31 March 1909.
57   George Herbert Palmer, *Self-Cultivation in English* (New York: Houghton Mifflin, 1909), 43, vi; Palmer's views on TSE as reported by R. F. A. Hoernlé in a letter of 11 February 1919 to Ralph Barton Perry (Harvard University Archives), cited in Manju Jain, *T. S. Eliot and American Philosophy: The Harvard Years* (Cambridge and New York: Cambridge University Press, 1992), 34.
58   Palmer, *Self-Cultivation*, 37.

59   Ralph Barton Perry, quoted in Ronald P. Kriss, 'As Student and Teacher, Santayana Left Mark on College', *Harvard Crimson*, 30 September 1952.

60   *VMP*, 49; *L1*, 483.

61   George Santayana, *Interpretations of Poetry and Religion* (New York: Charles Scribner's Sons, 1900), 263.

62   *SE*, 145 ('Hamlet') and 287 ('The Metaphysical Poets').

63   Palmer, *Self-Cultivation*, 43.

64   'Assignment of Rooms for Courses', *Harvard Crimson*, 3 October 1908.

65   Murray Anthony Potter, *Sohrab and Rustum: The Epic Theme of a Combat Between Father and Son, A Study in its Genesis and Use in Literature and Popular Tradition* (London: David Nutt, 1902), 108, 98.

66   William Henry Schofield, *Mythical Bards and the Life of William Wallace* (Cambridge: Harvard University Press, 1920), 53, 54, 224, 225, 233, 265.

67   *L1*, 486.

68   William Henry Schofield, *English Literature from the Norman Conquest to Chaucer* (New York: Macmillan, 1906), 248.

69   John Morgenstern, 'A Figure behind T. S. Eliot: W. H. Schofield', *Notes and Queries*, September 2009, 422.

70   TSE, 'What Dante Means to Me', *CC*, 125.

71   Dante Alighieri, *The Inferno of Dante Alighieri* (London: J. M. Dent and New York: E. P. Dutton, 1900), 16, 17 (Canto II); TSE's copy is in Houghton *AC9.E1464.Zz910t.

72   *L4*, 411.

73   See Herbert Howarth, *Notes on Some Figures Behind T. S. Eliot* (London: Chatto and Windus, 1965), 69.

74   TSE, 'The Latin Tradition', *Times Literary Supplement*, 14 March 1929, 200.

75   E. K. Rand, 'The Latin Literature of the West from the Antonines to Constantine', in S. A. Cook et al., eds, *The Cambridge Ancient History* (Cambridge: Cambridge University Press, 1939), XII, 587.

76   William C. Greene, 'Clifford Herschel Moore', *Proceedings of the American Academy of Arts and Sciences*, 68.13 (December 1933), 649.

77   Pencil ms note stuck to page 5 of TSE's 1804 *Petronii Saturae et Liber Priapeorum* (Hayward Bequest).

78   Ibid., pencil note on p. 76.

79   *CPP*, 61, 59.

80   *CPP*, 59.

Chapter 6 – Secret Knowledge

1   *L4*, 130.

2   Jules Laforgue, *Oeuvres Complètes*, 3 vols (Paris: Société du Mercure de France, 1902–3), I, 58, 90, 123, 82, 100, 76; for translations, see *Poems of Jules Laforgue*, tr. Peter Dale (London: Anvil Press Poetry, 1986), 26, 64, 100, 75, 57, 51.

3   TSE, 'Modern Tendencies in Poetry', *Shama'a*, 1.1 (April 1920), 13.

4   Dale, *Poems of Jules Laforgue*, 261, 64, 273.

5   Laforgue, *Oeuvres Complètes I*, 99; Dale, *Poems of Jules Laforgue*, 72.

6   TSE, 'Reflections on Contemporary Poetry', *Egoist*, July 1919, 39.

7   Dale, *Poems of Jules Laforgue*, 249; I owe the point about the Ether Monument to Carey Karmel (private communication).

8   *CPP* 13; Dale, *Poems of Jules Laforgue*, 371.

9   *L1*, 212.

10   TSE, 'Introduction' to EP, *Selected Poems* (London: Faber and Faber, 1928), viii.

11   Dale, *Poems of Jules Laforgue*, 49; *CPP*, 25.

12   *L2*, 241.

Notes

13 Dale, *Poems of Jules Laforgue*, 323.

14 *L2*, 657.

15 TSE, 'Ezra Pound', *New English Weekly*, 31 October 1946, 27.

16 Laforgue, *Oeuvres Complètes*, III, 163, 201, 210.

17 Ibid., II, 144, 149, 150, 158.

18 Ibid., II, 197.

19 *CPP*, 78, 69.

20 *CPP 66*; TSE, 'Introduction' to EP, *Selected Poems*, viii.

21 TSE, manuscript, 'The Defects of Kipling' (Harvard University Archives (HUG 4298.65)).

22 TSE to John Hayward, 5 January 1942 (Hayward Bequest).

23 Van Wyck Brooks, *The Wine of the Puritans: A Study of Present-Day America* (London: Silley's Ltd, [1908]), 16, 17, 11, 34, 134, 142.

24 TSE, 'The Wine of the Puritans' (review), *Harvard Advocate*, 87.5 (7 May 1909), 80.

25 TSE, 'Gentlemen and Seamen', *Harvard Advocate*, 87.7 (25 May 1909), 115.

26 L. B. R. Briggs, 'Federation Number of the *Advocate*', *Harvard Crimson*, 29 May 1909 (accessed online).

27 TSE, 'Ballade of the Fox Dinner', in John J. Soldo, *The Tempering of T. S. Eliot* (Ann Arbor: UMI Research Press, 1983), 60; TSE, 'The Point of View', *Harvard Advocate*, 87.6 (20 May 1909), 82.

28 See Edward Butscher, *Conrad Aiken: Poet of White Horse Vale* (Athens: University of Georgia Press, 1988), 121–3.

29 Frederick Garrison Hall, Edward Revere Little and HWE, Jr, *Harvard Celebrities: A Book of Caricatures & Decorative Drawings* (Printed for the Editors by the University Press, Cambridge, U. S. A., [n.d.]), 'Pierre'.

30 W. G. Tinckom-Fernandez, 'T. S. Eliot, '10: An Advocate Friendship', *Harvard Advocate*, 125.3 (December 1938), 6.

31 William Allan Neilson, *Essentials of Poetry* (Boston: Houghton Mifflin, 1912), vii, 5, 13, 271, 272.

32 Ibid., advertisement preceding title page.

33 Irving Babbitt, *Literature and the American College: A Defense of the Humanities* (Boston: Houghton Mifflin, 1908), 49, 74, 80, 81, 253, 254, 124, 230.

34 Irving Babbitt, *The Masters of Modern French Criticism* (Boston: Houghton Mifflin, 1912), vii.

35 Ibid., 16.

36 *L3*, 866.

37 See Wisner Payne Kinne, *George Pierce Baker and the American Theatre* (Cambridge, Mass: Harvard University Press, 1954), 137–40.

38 HWE to Thomas Lamb Eliot, 25 March 1910, quoted in Cynthia Tucker, *No Silent Witness: The Eliot Parsonage Women and their Unitarian World* (New York: Oxford University Press, 2010), 225.

39 'Board of Editors', *Harvard Advocate*, 88 (5 October 1909–4 March 1910), verso of title page.

40 See '1910 Class Elections Today', *Harvard Crimson*, 13 December 1909 (accessed digitally).

41 *L1*, 12.

42 *L1*, 11.

43 Ibid.

44 George Santayana, *The Life of Reason, or the Phases of Human Progress, Volume I, Reason in Common Sense* (London: Constable, 1906), 284.

45 TSE to William B. Goodman, 12 October 1961 (Houghton bMS Am 1691.3).

46 TSE, 'Egoists' (review), *Harvard Advocate*, 88.1 (5 October 1909), 16.

47 *L1*, 12.

48 James Huneker, *Egoists: A Book of Supermen* (New York: Scribner's, 1909), 9, 14, 5, 34, 33, 18, 48, 3, 8, 79, 78, 101, 95, 78, 79; *CPP*, 16, 38, 62; TSE, 'Introduction' to Charles Baudelaire, *Intimate Journals*, tr. C. Isherwood (London: Blackamore Press 1930), 7–26.

49 Huneker, *Egoists*, 167, 168, 171, 172, 181, 174, 215.

50 TSE, 'Egoists', 16.

51 Soldo, *The Tempering of T. S. Eliot*, 57.

52 TSE, 'Egoists', 16.

53 James Huneker, *Overtones: A Book of Temperaments* (New York: Scribner's, 1904), 219–24; Huneker, *Egoists*, 196.

54 *L1*, 486; James C. Young, 'Yeats of Petitpas', *New York Times*, 19 February 1922.

55 *CPP* 33; *IMH*, xiv, xxxix, 346; Huneker, *Overtones*, 303.

56 Huneker, *Overtones*, 277; *CPP*, 18.

57 TSE, 'Convictions (Curtain Raiser)', *IMH*, 11.

58 TSE, 'First Caprice in North Cambridge', *Inventions*, 13.

59 TSE, 'Second Caprice in North Cambridge', *IMH*, 15.

60 *IMH*, 15, 111.

61 Soldo, *The Tempering of T. S. Eliot*, 58.

62 *CPP* 602; '"Tristan und Isolde" Again', *New York Times*, 13 March 1909 (accessed online).

63 Huneker, *Overtones*, 327, 328, 330.

64 TSE, *Inventions*, 17 ('Opera').

65 *CPP*, 601.

66 *CPP*, 603.

67 Tinckom-Fernandez, 'T. S. Eliot, '10', 47.

68 TSE's sketches are now in the Harvard Art Museum repository; TSE, Notes on Fine Arts 20 b (Houghton Ms 1691.14 (7)), 2.

69 Karl Baedeker, *London and its Environs* (Leipzig: Dulau & Co., 1908), 168. TSE's annotated copy, Hayward Bequest HB/B/4.

70 TSE, [Notes on Renaissance Painters, Harvard Lecture Notes] (Hayward Bequest (HB/P/3), 5, 7).

71 *L1*, 13.

72 The letters 'abs' underlie some of TSE's 1909–10 grade report (Houghton bMS Am 2560 (96)).

73 *IMH*, 18, 125.

74 'Continuation of Clothing Collection', *Harvard Advocate*, 19 May 1910 (accessed online).

75 TSE's 1909–10 grade report.

76 *L1*, 13.

77 *CPP*, 604.

78 'Harvard's Day Indeed', *Boston Evening Transcript*, 24 June 1910 (clipping) (Houghton bMS Am 2560 (97)); *CPP*, 171.

Chapter 7 – Voyages

1 W. G. Tinckom-Fernandez, 'T. S. Eliot, '10: An Advocate Friendship', *Harvard Advocate*, 125.3 (December 1938), 6.

2 Ibid., 6, 48.

3 TSE, note on a draft of 'The Dry Salvages' (Magdalene College Library, Cambridge), quoted in Helen Gardner, *The Composition of Four Quartets* (London: Faber and Faber, 1978), 120.

4 Leon Magaw Little, carbon copy of piece written on 13 May 1968 for TSE memorial issue of the *Harvard Advocate* (Houghton bMS Am 1691.4 (136)).

5   Leon Magaw Little to TSE, 13 December 1960 (Houghton bMS Am1691.4 (68)).

6   *L1*, 11.

7   Leon Magaw Little to TSE, 16 November 1956 (Houghton bMS Am1691.4 (60)).

8   Leon Magaw Little to TSE, 30 August 1961 (Houghton bMS Am1691.4 (73)).

9   *L1*, plate 21B; the marked resemblance between the man in the photograph and photographs of Harold's brother Andrew J. Peters, mayor of Boston, strengthens this identification.

10 TSE to Leon Magaw Little, 9 August 1961 (Houghton bMS Am1691.4 (20)).

11 TSE to EP, 3 January 1934 (Beinecke).

12 TSE to Leon Magaw Little, 11 August 1956 (Houghton bMS Am1691.4 (7)).

13 Jonesport, Maine 1910 Census, 43, Carver William (accessed online); Jonesport Maine Marriages: 1850–92, 9 May 1886 (accessed online).

14 TSE to Leon Magaw Little, 11 August 1956 (Houghton bMS Am1691.4 (7)).

15 'Cruise of the Lapwing', Fredericksen transcription held by Jonesport Historical Society, Maine. I am deeply grateful to Mr William Plaskon of the Jonesport Historical Society; to Ms Susan M. Sanfilippo, Curator, Pembroke (Maine) Historical Society; to Dr Stephen N. Sanfilippo (editor of *Seasongs*); and to Dr Richard King of Mystic, Connecticut, for their work in tracking down this ballad.

16 TSE to Leon Magaw Little, 7 August 1964, 12 October 1956 and 23 October 1962 (Houghton bMS Am1691.4 (25), (8) and (23)).

17 *CPP*, 39; *Facsimile*, 55, 57, 65, 67, 69, 57.

18 TSE, draft of 'Marina' (Bodleian Library, Oxford Ms Don. C. 23(1)); *CPP*, 109–10.

19 TSE, 'The Art of Poetry I, T. S. Eliot' (interview by Donald Hall), *Paris Review*, 21 (Spring/Summer 1959), 56.

20 Alan Dale, *The Great Wet Way* (New York: Dodd, Mead & Co., 1909), 164–5.

21 TSE, 'What France Means to You', *La France Libre*, 8.44 (15 June 1944), 94.

22 Dale, *The Great Wet Way*, 11, 80, 149, 154, 222, 235, 226–7, 71, 206, 236, 16–17.

23 Karl Baedeker, *London and its Environs* (Leipzig: Dulau & Co., 1908), 168. TSE's annotated copy, Hayward Bequest HB/B/4.

24 *L1*, 30; see also George Watson, 'Quest for a Frenchman', *Sewanee Review*, 84.3 (Summer 1976), 468.

25 *L1*, 18.

26 *L1*, 22.

27 Christian Y. Dupont, 'Chronicling Longfellow's Interest in Dante: Henry Wadsworth Longfellow Dana and Joseph Chesley Mathews', *Dante Studies*, 128 (2010), 193; Douglass Shand-Tucci, *The Crimson Letter: Harvard, Homosexuality, and the Shaping of American Culture* (New York: St Martin's Press, 2003) 129–36.

28 'Prichard, Matthew Stewart', *Dictionary of Art Historians*, http://www.dictionaryofarthistorians.org/prichardm.hym.

29 *L1*, 101.

30 *L3*, 132.

31 Jean Verdenal's casual mention of 'le cubisme' and 'le futurisme' (*L1*, 35) assumes TSE knew about these movements; see also Nancy Duvall Hargrove, *T. S. Eliot's Parisian Year* (Gainesville: University Press of Florida, 2009), 132–43. My account of Eliot's Paris is greatly indebted to this enjoyable book.

32 *L1*, 20; TSE, 'A Commentary', April 1934, 452.

33 *L1*, 21, 31.

34 This description is based on the photograph reproduced as figure 2 in Hargrove, *T. S. Eliot's Parisian Year*, 88. The quotation is from a letter to TSE by Jean Verdenal, *L1*, 36.

35 TSE, 'What France Means to You', 94.

36 *L1*, 15, 14.

37 TSE, 'A Commentary', *Criterion*, 30.52 (April 1934), 452.
38 TSE, 'The Elementary Forms of the Religious Life' (review), *Monist*, 28.1 (January 1918), 159.
39 TSE, 'The Interpretation of Primitive Ritual' (Hayward Bequest, King's/PP/HB/P, 4), 5.
40 TSE, 'Rencontre', *Nouvelle Revue Française*, 12.139 (1 April 1925), 657.
41 TSE, 'A Commentary', 452.
42 *CPP*, 32; TSE, 'The Metaphysical Poets', *SE*, 288.
43 This book list is towards the back of the notes on mystical, anthropological and psychological works in the Houghton Library (MS Am 1691 (129)); TSE's notes are cited from the cards headed 'B. de Montmorand' and 'Janet. Nevroses Vol II); B. de Montmorand, 'Ascétisme et Mysticisme', *Revue philosophique de la France et de l'étranger*, 57 (January–June 1904), 256.
44 Contemporary reviews quoted in Hargrove, *T .S. Eliot's Parisian Year*, 118.
45 Ibid., 115, 117, 121, 151.
46 *L1*, 49.
47 TSE, 'A Commentary', 452.
48 Ibid.
49 TSE, Notes on lectures of Henri Bergson, Paris, 1911 (Houghton bMS Am 1691 (139)), 1, 2, 9.
50 William James, 'The Philosophy of Bergson', *Hibbert Journal*, 7 (1909), 562, 563, 566, 571, 572, 573, 577.
51 TSE, *A Sermon Preached in Magdalene College Chapel* (Cambridge: Cambridge University Press, 1948), n.p.
52 TSE, 'Rencontre', 657.
53 Ibid.
54 TSE, 'A Commentary', 451.
55 TSE, 'What France Means to You', 94.
56 TSE, 1951 conversation with Robert Gibson, recorded in Robert Gibson, *The End of Youth: The Life and Work of Alain-Fournier* (Exeter: Impress Books, 2005), 199; *L1*, 25, note 1.
57 TSE, 'Preface' to Charles-Louis Philippe, *Bubu of Montparnasse*, tr. Laurence Vail (Paris: Crosby Continental Editions, 1932), vii.
58 *IMH*, 43, 111, 176, 43.
59 TSE, 'The Art of Poetry, I, T. S. Eliot', 56.
60 *IMH*, 335; Philippe, *Bubu*, 20; *IMH*, 338; Hargrove, *T. S. Eliot's Parisian Year*, 15–16.
61 *CPP*, 24.
62 *L1*, 82.
63 *IMH*, 37, 314.
64 *IMH*, 338.
65 TSE to John C. Pope, 8 March 1946, quoted in Hargrove, *T. S. Eliot's Parisian Year*, 24.
66 TSE, 'A Commentary', 453.
67 *L1*, 26.
68 TSE, 'Lettre D'Angleterre', *Nouvelle Revue Française*, 21.122 (1 November 1923), 620.
69 See Albert Thibaudet, 'L'esthétique des trois traditions', *Nouvelle Revue Francaise*, March 1913, 355–93.
70 Andre Schlemmer, quoted in Watson, 'Quest for a Frenchman', 469.
71 *L2*, 237.
72 Ibid.
73 TSE, 'Rencontre', 657.
74 *L1*, 25.
75 Information about Jean Verdenal and quotations from his nephew are drawn from Claudio Perinot, 'Jean Verdenal: T. S. Eliot's French Friend', *Annali di ca' Foscari*:

Rivista della Facoltà di Lingue e Letterature Staniere dell'università di Venezia, 35.1–2 (1996), 265–75.

76 *L1*, 20–37; Jean Verdenal to TSE, 26 December 1912 (Houghton bMS Am 1691.6 (15)).
77 VMP, 216; *L1*, 23, 24, 21, 22.
78 *L1*, 35, 34.
79 *L1*, 16.
80 *L1*, 33.
81 *L1*, 34; *CPP*, 16.
82 *L1*, 31; *CPP*, 31.
83 TSE, 'A Commentary', 452.
84 *L1*, 37.
85 *SE*, 255.
86 *L1*, 20.
87 *L1*, 20.
88 *L1*, 17.
89 *IMH*, 18, 116–18.
90 TSE's London Baedeker, 102.
91 *L1*, 18; TSE's Baedeker, [453].
92 TSE's Baedeker, 308, 312, 278.
93 *L1*, 18.
94 *CPP*, 31, 33.
95 *L1*, 16.
96 *L1*, 19.
97 'The Theatres', *Times*, 17 April 1911, 9.
98 *L1*, 17.
99 *L1*, 20.
100 'Eine verkunste Fassade', *Münchner Stadtanzeiger*, 15 July 1911, 2. Information about the Pension Burger and the Munich of the era is drawn largely from *Guide to Munich and Its Environs*, fortieth edn (Munich: A. Bruckmann's Verlag, 1914) and Rainer Metzger, *Munich: Its Golden Age of Art and Culture, 1890–1920* (London: Thames and Hudson, 2009).
101 TSE to John Hayward, 8 February 1940 (Hayward Bequest HB/L 12).
102 Ibid.
103 *IMH*, 43.
104 *CPP*, 13.
105 *L1*, 63.
106 *CPP*, 16–17.
107 IMH, 176.
108 Metzger, *Munich*, 269, 100, 101.
109 *L1*, 25, 32.
110 *IMH*, 312, 311.
111 *L1*, 94.
112 *Guide to Munich and Its Environs*, 70.
113 See George L. K. Morris, '"Marie, Marie, Hold on Tight"', *Partisan Review*, 21.2 (1954), 231–4; and *Facsimile*, 125–6.
114 *CPP*, 61.
115 TSE, 'Notes on Italy' (Houghton bMS Am1691 (131)); *CPP*, 64.
116 Ibid.; the pressed flower is now in a separate envelope in Houghton.
117 TSE, 'Notes on Italy'.
118 *CPP*, 40, 41.
119 TSE, 'Notes on Italy'.
120 Ibid.

121   Ibid.

Chapter 8 – A Philosopher and Actor Falls in Love

1   Conrad Aiken, 'King Bolo and Others', in Tambimuttu and Richard March, eds, *T. S. Eliot: A Symposium* (New York: Tambimuttu and Mass, 1965), 20.
2   *IMH*, 48.
3   See Conrad Aiken, *Selected Letters of Conrad Aiken*, ed. Joseph Killorin (New Haven and London: Yale University Press, 1978), 25, 26.
4   *L1*, 28.
5   TSE's lease for 16 Ash Street (Houghton bMS Am 2560 (101)).
6   *L1*, 163, 61.
7   *L1*, 61.
8   The *Blue Book of Cambridge* (Boston: Boston Suburban Book Co., 1911) gives a good sense of Ash Street and surrounding streets.
9   TSE's rent receipt dated 1 February 1913 (Houghton bMS Am 2560 (100)).
10   *Blue Book of Cambridge*, 49, 51.
11   *L1*, 24.
12   *IMH*, 331, 328; *CPP*. 19.
13   *L1*, 93; *IMH*, 330, 331; *CPP*, 20–21.
14   *L1*, 143.
15   *L1*, 33.
16   TSE, Receipts, 1912–14 (Houghton bMS Am 2560(100)).
17   *L1*, 31, 33.
18   C. R. Lanman, 'Buddhism', in William Allan Neilson, ed., *Lectures on the Harvard Classics* (Vol. 51 of *The Harvard Classics*) (New York: P. F. Collier & Son, 1910), 446, 449.
19   *Facsimile*, 113.
20   C. R. Lanman, Course Records 1892–1926 (Harvard University Archives HUG 4510.48), 72–5.
21   *Facsimile*, 111.
22   *Official Register of Harvard University*, 10.1, Part XVIII (17 June 1913), 69.
23   TSE's Vedanta Society *Catalogue* (Houghton bMS Am 2560 (98)).
24   [TSE], 'What India is Thinking About To-day', *New Statesman*, 18 December 1915, 258. I am grateful to Professor Ronald Schuchard for calling my attention to this recently discovered review.
25   Lanman, Course Records; Dines Andersen, *A Pali Reader . . . Part I* (London: Luzac and Co., 1901), 70–71; for a translation approved by Lanman and by TSE, see Henry Clarke Warren, *Buddhism in Translations* (Cambridge: Harvard University Press, 1896), 151–2.
26   *CPP*, 70.
27   TSE's copy of *Upanishads, The Twenty-Eight* (Bombay: Tukaram Javaji, 1906) is in the Hayward Bequest, King's College, Cambridge (King's/PP/HB/B (29)).
28   Letter inside TSE's copy of *Upanishads*.
29   *CPP*, 80.
30   TSE, notes on Eastern philosophy (Houghton bMS Am1691.14 (12), 1).
31   TSE, Receipts, 1912–14.
32   Ibid.; *CPP*, 80.
33   TSE, Philosophy 12 (notes) (Houghton bMS Am 1691.14 (9)), 1.
34   Ibid., 3, 14.
35   TSE, index-card notes on mystical, anthropological and psychological works (Houghton MS Am 1691.129), notes on G. T. W. Patrick, *Heraclitus*, 2.
36   TSE, Philosophy 12 (notes), 17. TSE wrote down '*pur*' the Greek word for 'fire' and the word '*anathumiasis*' in Greek letters, but for convenience I transliterate them here.

37   *Facsimile*, 110.

38   TSE, Philosophy 12 (notes), 17, 16, 18; *CPP*, 171.

39   TSE, Philosophy 12 (notes), 18.

40   TSE's annotated copy of Benedict de Spinoza, *Opera* (The Hague: Martin Nijhoff, 1895), 111 (Hayward Bequest, King's College, Cambridge (HB/B/27)).

41   Hugo Munsterberg, *Psychotherapy* (1909; repr. New York: Moffat, Yard and Co., 1913), 207.

42   TSE, 'Physiology of Organs of Skin' (notes) (Houghton bMS Am 1691.14 (8)).

43   Aiken, *Selected Letters*, 26.

44   Ibid.

45   TSE, *After Strange Gods: A Primer of Modern Heresy* (London: Faber and Faber, 1933), 40–41.

46   Patanjali, tr. James Haughton Woods, *The Yoga-System of Patanjali: Or the Ancient Hindu Doctrine of Concentration of Mind* (Cambridge: Harvard University Press, 1914), 40, 41; for a fuller reading of such aspects of TSE's thought, see Cleo McNelly Kearns, *T. S. Eliot and Indic Traditions* (Cambridge and New York: Cambridge University Press, 1987).

47   Masaharu Anesaki, *Katam Karaniyam: Lectures, Essays and Studies* (Tokyo: The Herald Press, 1934), 1 (repr. from *Hibbert Journal*, 4.1 (1905)).

48   Masaharu Anesaki, *The Professorship of Japanese Literature and Life at Harvard University* (n.p., [1914]) (Harvard University Archives, HUC 4465.4B), 1, 2; TSE's notes on Eastern philosophy, Philosophy 24A course outline.

49   TSE, notes on Eastern philosophy, 2 (recto and verso).

50   Ibid., 10 (verso).

51   Ibid., 18, 19, 23.

52   Ibid., 46.

53   TSE, Report on the Kantian Categories (Hayward Bequest HB/P/2), 10–11.

54   TSE, 'Philosophy 15 Report on the Relation of Kant's Criticism to Agnosticism' (Hayward Bequest HB/P/2), 1, 4, 9.

55   TSE, manuscript of a paper on Bergson (Houghton bMS Am 1691(132)), 1, 13, 22.

56   Aiken *Selected Letters*, 30.

57   Ibid.

58   TSE, index-card notes on mystical, anthropological and psychological works, notes on James, 1.

59   Ibid., notes on Underhill and Moses.

60   Ibid., notes on Royce.

61   TSE, [Ethics] (Houghton bMS Am 1691.14 (32)), 2.

62   TSE's Harvard College Assistant in Philosophy Miscellany, 1912–14 (Houghton bMS Am 2560 (99)).

63   Philosophy A examination paper for 1913–14 (Houghton bMS Am 2560 (99)).

64   S. W. Cram to TSE, 15 November 1913 (Houghton bMS Am 2560 (99)).

65   Robert F. Rattray, 'Mr. Rabindranath Tagore', *Harvard Crimson*, 8 April 1913 (accessed digitally). Tagore's lecture to the 'Harvard Philosophical Club' is announced in 'What is Going on Today', *Harvard Crimson*, 18 February 1913 (accessed digitally); on TSE's listening to Tagore, see, Rabindranath Tagore, *Selected Letters of Rabindranath Tagore* ed., Krishna Dutta and Andrew Robinson (Cambridge and New York: Cambridge University Press, 1997), 519–20.

66   'What is Going on Today', *Harvard Crimson*, 4 April 1913 (accessed digitally).

67   TSE, [Relation between politics and metaphysics] (Houghton bMS Am 1691 (25)), 2.

68   Ibid., 2.

69   Ibid., 11, 15, 19, 21.

70   Ibid., 23. The quotation is from *Purgatorio*, Canto XVII, 94–6.

71   TSE, *The Sacred Wood* (1920; repr. London: Methuen, 1960), 169, 170 ('Dante').

72   My translation.

73   Aiken, *Selected Letters*, 30.
74   Conrad Aiken, *Earth Triumphant and Other Tales in Verse* (New York: Macmillan, 1914), 197, 211–12, 123, 27–8.
75   Conrad Aiken, *The Clerk's Journal, Being the Diary of a Queer Man: An Undergraduate Poem, together with A Brief Memoir of Harvard, Dean Briggs and T. S. Eliot* (New York: Eakin Press, 1971), 6.
76   Conrad Aiken in *The New York World*, quoted on the rear jacket of TSE, *Poems* (New York: Alfred Knopf, 1929).
77   'Crimson Calendar', *Harvard Crimson*, 7 March 1914 (accessed online); Aiken, *Selected Letters*, 182 (writing in 1931 Aiken dates this incident to 1912, but Boas was at Harvard only in session 1913–14, so 1914 seems more likely).
78   *L1*, 39, 41.
79   *L1*, 42.
80   TSE, '[Degrees of Reality]' (Hayward Bequest King's/PP/HB/P, 5), 1, 13.
81   TSE, [Outline of a paper on the interpretation of primitive ritual] (Hayward Bequest King's/PP/HB/P, 4a and 4b), 1.
82   TSE, [paper on the interpretation of primitive ritual] (Hayward Bequest King's/PP/HB/P, 4b), 5.
83   Ibid., 11, 10.
84   Ibid., 11.
85   J. G. Frazer, *The Dying God* (London: Macmillan, 1911), 266.
86   TSE, [paper on the interpretation of primitive ritual], 13.
87   Russell, quoted in Ray Monk, *Bertrand Russell, The Spirit of Solitude* (London: Jonathan Cape, 1996), 349.
88   *L1*, 61.
89   Bertrand Russell, *Selected Letters of Bertrand Russell, Volume 1: The Private Years, 1884–1914*, ed. Nicholas Griffin (London: Allen Lane, 1992), 500; Russell, quoted in Monk, *Bertrand Russell*, 350.
90   Benjamin Apthorpe Fuller, *The Problem of Evil in Plotinus* (Cambridge: Cambridge University Press, 1912), 85.
91   Russell, *Selected Letters*, I, 507.
92   *CPP*, 31.
93   'Declined the Call', *St Louis Republic*, 18 February 1900, 12.
94   Eleanor Hinkley, note with 'Stunt Show' programme (Houghton bMS Am2560 (101)).
95   Richard W. Hall, 'Recollections of the Cambridge Social Dramatic Club', *Proceedings of the Cambridge Historical Society*, 38 (1959–60) (text supplied digitally by the Society, whose generosity I acknowledge with gratitude).
96   *CPP*, 31.
97   Robert Marshall, *The Second in Command: A Comedy in Four Acts* (London and New York: Samuel French Ltd, 1910), 136.
98   *CPP*, 34 ('La Figlia Che Piange').
99   Henry Arthur Jones, *The Manoeuvres of Jane* (New York and London: Samuel French, 1905), 51.
100   John Hartley Manners, *The House Next Door* (n.p., 1912), 26.
101   Hubert Henry Davis, *A Single Man, A New and Original Comedy in Four Acts* (Boston: Walter H. Baker, and London: Heinemann, 1914), 105.
102   *CPP*, 84, 85 ('The Hollow Men').
103   This quotation and other details of the Cambridge Social Dramatic Club are drawn from Hall, 'Recollections'.
104   TSE to Leon Magaw Little, 7 August 1964 (Houghton bMS Am 1691.14 (25)).
105   Richard S. Kennedy, *Dreams in the Mirror: A Biography of E. E. Cummings* (New York: Liveright, 1994), 86.
106   See *Pound/Cummings: The Correspondence of Ezra Pound and E. E. Cummings,* ed. Barry Ahearn (Ann Arbor: University of Michigan Press, 1996), 182

107 Jerome K. Jerome, *Fanny and the Servant Problem: A Quite Possible Play in Four Acts* (New York and London: Samuel French Ltd, 1909), 56.

108 *L1*, 83.

109 See Berkeley Street School Association Records, Arthur and Elizabeth Schlesinger Library on the History of Women in America (Radcliffe College, Harvard MC 238 (1 and 3)); a 1904 Berkeley Street School photograph that includes Amy de Gozzaldi, Emily Hale, Eleanor Hinkley and friends is at MC349–1f-2.

110 E. E. Cummings to EP, 23 July 1946, EP and Cummings, *Pound/Cummings*, 182.

111 TSE, nn. 111, 112 TSE, Receipts, 1912–14; Pierre Loti, *Le roman d'un enfant* (1890; repr. Montreal: La Bibliothèque électronique du Québec, n.d.), 274 (ch. LXXVII).

112 TSE, Receipts, 1912–14; Leonard Merrick, *The Man Who Understood Women and Other Stories* (Leipzig: Bernhard Tauchnitz, 1908), 7.

113 *CPP*, 18 ('Portrait of a Lady').

114 'Stunt Show' (printed programme) (Houghton bMS Am2560 (101)); reproduced in *L1*, 40.

115 Ibid.

116 Eleanor Hinkley, note with 'Stunt Show' programme (Houghton bMS Am2560 (101)).

117 'Ecstasy' from *Three Songs with Pianoforte Accompaniment* by Mrs H. H. A. Beach (Boston: Arthur P. Schmidt, 1893), 3–5.

118 *A May Morning: Song*, words by Fred E. Weatherly, music by L. Denza (London: Chappell & Co., 1894), 8.

119 This information comes from the authoritative Margaret Ruthven Lang website: http://www.margaretruthvenlang.com (accessed February 2013).

120 Margaret Ruthven Lang, *An Irish Love Song*, Op. 22 (1895) at http://songsofamerica.net/cgi-bin/iowa/song/693.html (accessed February 2013).

121 TSE concert miscellany: printed programmes (Houghton bMS Am2560 (103)).

122 *CPP*, 61–2.

123 *CPP*, 62.

124 See Nancy Duvall Hargrove, *T. S. Eliot's Parisian Year* (Gainesville: University Press of Florida, 2009), 195.

125 John N. Burk, ed., *Philip Hale's Boston Symphony Programme Notes* (New York: Garden City Publishing Co., 1939), vi–vii.

126 TSE concert miscellany: printed programmes.

127 Ibid.

128 Burk, *Philip Hale's Boston Symphony Programme Notes*, 33.

129 TSE, receipts, 1912–14.

130 *Minutes of the Proceedings at the Meetings of the Warden and Tutors of Merton College, Oxford. October 1905–December 1926*, 139 (Merton College Archives).

131 *L1*, xix.

132 Ibid.

133 Ottoline Morrell, quoted in Miranda Seymour, *Ottoline Morrell: Life on the Grand Scale* (London: Hodder and Stoughton, 1992), 390.

134 'T. S. Eliot Letters to Emily Hale, 1930–1956: Finding Aid C0686' (Princeton University Library Manuscripts Division).

135 *L1*, xix.

Chapter 9 – The Oxford Year

1 *IMH*, 82.

2 Conrad Aiken, *Earth Triumphant and Other Tales in Verse* (New York: Macmillan Company, 1914), 15–16.

3 *L1*, 63.

4 *L1*, 43.

5   *L1*, 55.
6   *L1*, 43.
7   *IMH*, 90.
8   *L1*, 47; *Facsimile*, 103.
9   *L1*, 46, 45.
10 *L1*, 48, 45.
11 *L1*, 48.
12 *L1*, 45, 47.
13 *L1*, 51.
14 Robert Burns, *The Best Laid Schemes: Selected Poetry and Prose of Robert Burns*, ed. Robert Crawford and Christopher MacLachlan (Edinburgh: Polygon, 2009), 156.
15 *L1*, 51.
16 *L1*, 49.
17 *L1*, 63.
18 *L1*, 49.
19 Ibid.
20 *L1*, 78.
21 TSE, telegram, to HWE, 3 August 1914 (Houghton bMS Am1691 (76)); not included in *Letters*, this telegram had been misdated to 1918 in the otherwise wonderfully catalogued Houghton Library collection.
22 *L1*, 57.
23 Ibid.
24 *L1*, 59.
25 Karl Baedeker, *London and its Environs* (Leipzig: Dulau & Co., 1908), 168: TSE's annotated copy, Hayward Bequest HB/B/4.
26 *The Rosary*, lyrics by Robert Cameron Rogers, music by Georgia B. Welles (Philadelphia: Morris Music Co., n.d.), 3; *L1*, 59.
27 *IMH*, 343.
28 *L1*, 61, 69.
29 *L1*, 61.
30 *L1*, 61–2, 64.
31 *L1*, 69.
32 Bertrand Russell, *The Autobiography of Bertrand Russell, 1914–1944* (London: Allen and Unwin, 1968), II, 19.
33 TSE, 'The Art of Poetry, I, T. S. Eliot' (interview by Donald Hall), *Paris Review*, 21 (Spring/Summer 1959), 51.
34 EP, 'Vortex. Pound.', *Blast*, 1 (1914), 154.
35 EP, *Selected Letters of Ezra Pound, 1907–1941*, ed. D. D. Paige (London: Faber and Faber, 1992), 40.
36 *L1*, 63.
37 Ibid.
38 *L1*, 64.
39 *L1*, 67.
40 Max Beerbohm, *Zuleika Dobson* (1911; repr. Harmondsworth: Penguin, 1911), 8, 7.
41 Brand Blanshard, 'Eliot at Oxford', in James Olney, ed., *T. S. Eliot: Essays from the 'Southern Review'* (Oxford: Oxford University Press, 1988), 27.
42 *L1*, 70.
43 *L1*, 71.
44 *L1*, 70.
45 Ibid.
46 *L1*, 70, 66.
47 Blanshard, 'Eliot at Oxford', 27.
48 *L1*, 66.

49   Blanshard, 'Eliot at Oxford', 28.
50   *L1*, 67.
51   Minutes of the proceedings at the meetings of the Warden and Tutors of Merton College, Oxford, October 1905–December 1926, 134 and 150 (Merton College Archives).
52   Merton College Debating Society Minute Book, 1902–21 (Merton College Archives, MCR 12.1.21), meetings 695 and 696.
53   *L1*, 85, 86.
54   *L1*, 77.
55   Merton College Debating Society Minute Book, meetings 698 and 699.
56   *L1*, 84.
57   TSE, 'Wyndham Lewis', *Hudson Review*, 10.2 (Summer 1957), 167.
58   *L1*, 85; other information on Ellwood from Bodleian Library L.P. admissions records and entry books for 1914–15.
59   *L1*, 93.
60   N. Levinson, 'Wiener's Life', *Bulletin of the American Mathematical Society*, 72.1, Pt. 2 (1966), 9.
61   *L1*, 85.
62   *L1*, 82.
63   *L1*, 85.
64   *L1*, 82.
65   *L1*, 76.
66   Blanshard, 'Eliot at Oxford', 32.
67   Ibid., 33.
68   [TSE], 'A Commentary', *Criterion*, 3.9 (October 1924), 2.
69   Ibid.
70   *L1*, 92.
71   TSE, [On objects] (Oxford tutorial paper) (Houghton bMS Am 1691.14 (21)).
72   TSE, [Object and point of view] (Oxford tutorial paper) (Houghton bMS Am1691.14 (25)); TSE, 'Professor H. H. Joachim', *Times*, 4 August 1938, 12.
73   *L1*, 65.
74   I am indebted to the late Roger Highfield of Merton College for these details of TSE's Merton library borrowings (letter of 28 February 1983); TSE, 'The Development of Leibniz's Monadism', *Monist*, 26.4 (October 1916), 552, n. 18.
75   TSE, inscription dated '3.x.51' on his 1911 copy of Aristotle's *De Anima Libri III* (Hayward Bequest, King's College, Cambridge, HB/B/2).
76   TSE, [Notes on Aristotle (Oxford, 13 October–3 December 1914)], 13 (Houghton bMS Am 1691.14 (16)).
77   *L1*, 71.
78   *L1*, 74.
79   *L1*, 73, 91.
80   TSE, 'Professor H. H. Joachim', 12.
81   Harold Joachim, reference for TSE, 26 August 1918 (Houghton bMS Am1691(102)).
82   TSE, [On objects].
83   Harold Joachim, *The Nature of Truth* (Oxford: Clarendon Press, 1906), 66.
84   *CPP*, 31 ('Mr. Apollinax').
85   *IMH*, 345.
86   *L1*, 81.
87   *L1*, 75.
88   *L1*, 69.
89   Ibid.
90   *L1*, 83.
91   Merton College Debating Society Minute Book, meeting 700.

92   *L1*, 87, 88.
93   *L1*, 82.
94   *L1*, 87.
95   Norbert Wiener, 'Relativism', *Journal of Philosophy, Psychology and Scientific Methods*, 11.21 (8 October 1914), 562, 564, 565, 566, 568, 567.
96   *SE*, 15 ('Tradition and the Individual Talent').
97   Wiener, 'Relativism', 575.
98   *SE*, 15.
99   Wiener, 'Relativism', 575, 576.
100 TSE, *SE*, 16.
101 Wiener, 'Relativism', 574; Norbert Wiener, 'Ecstasy', *Encyclopedia Americana* (New York and Chicago: Encyclopedia Americana Corporation, 1918), IX, 570.
102 *L1*, 89, 91, 88.
103 *L1*, 79.
104 Norbert Wiener, 'Aesthetics', *Encyclopedia Americana*, I, 199.
105 E. R. Dodds, *Missing Persons: An Autobiography* (Oxford: Clarendon Press, 1977), 40.
106 Ibid.
107 *L1*, 93.
108 Wyndham Lewis, 'Early London Environment', in Tambimuttu and Richard March, eds, *T. S. Eliot: A Symposium* (New York: Tambimuttu and Mass, 1965), 25.
109 See *Oxford English Dictionary* entry for 'bullshit'.
110 *IMH*, 307, 311.
111 Ezra Pound and Wyndham Lewis, *Pound/Lewis: The Letters of Ezra Pound and Wyndham Lewis*, ed. Timothy Materer (London: Faber and Faber, 1985), 8, 9.
112 *L1*, 94.
113 TSE, [Ethics] (Houghton bMS Am 1691.14(32)), 1.
114 *L1*, 97.
115 *L1*, xxvi, 100.
116 TSE, [Ethics], 1.
117 TSE, [Ethics], 2.
118 TSE, [Ethics], 11.
119 Details from Roger Highfield, letter of 28 February 1983.
120 TSE, [Ethics], 11; printed handout headed *OUTLINE OF BOOK VII* inserted at the February 27 section of TSE's [Notes on Aristotle (Oxford, 13 October [1914]–10 June [1915]), 84 (Houghton bMS Am1691.14(17)).
121 *Facsimile*, 95, 97.
122 *Facsimile*, 91, 95, 97. On the dating of the poem by minute examination of its paper, see Lawrence Rainey, *Revisiting 'The Waste Land'* (New Haven and London: Yale University Press, 2005), 13–14, 34, 198.
123 *L1*, 94, 95.
124 *L1*, 99.
125 *L1*, 95.
126 *L1*, 104; EP, *Ezra Pound to his Parents: Letters 1895–1929*, ed. Mary de Rachewiltz, A. David Moody and Joanna Moody (Oxford: Oxford University Press, 2010), 345.
127 *L1*, xix.
128 On the dating of these poems, or at least their transcription around April 1915, see Rainey, *Revisiting 'The Waste Land'*, 198.
129 *L1*, 104.
130 *CPP*, 28.
131 *L1*, 104.
132 *L1*, 95, 97, 96.
133 This sketch is reproduced opposite page 1 of Carole Seymour-Jones, *Painted Shadow: The Life of Vivienne Eliot* (London: Constable and Robinson, 2001).
134 *L1*, 150.

135   *L2*, 740.

136   *L1*, 105.

137   VE to Scofield Thayer, [22 February 1915] (Beinecke YCAL 34 series IV Box 31, folder 812).

138   Virginia Woolf, *The Diary of Virginia Woolf*, Volume 3, ed. Anne Olivier Bell and Andrew McNeillie (London: Hogarth Press, 1980), 15.

139   Seymour-Jones, *Painted Shadow*, 8.

140   Maurice Haigh-Wood, quoted in ibid., 13.

141   Maurice Haigh-Wood, quoted in ibid., 22.

142   VE to Scofield Thayer, [3 March 1915] (Beinecke YCAL 34 series IV Box 31, folder 812).

143   TSE, [Notes on Aristotle], 90, 93, 106, 107, 109, 110.

144   Maurice Haigh-Wood, quoted in Seymour-Jones, *Painted Shadow*, 75.

145   VE to Scofield Thayer, 'Thursday' (Beinecke YCAL 34 series IV Box 31, folder 812). Though the postmark on the envelope containing Vivien's letter is indistinct, it was franked at 12.15 on '3' of a month in 1915.

146   *L1*, 151.

147   Rudyard Kipling, *A Choice of Kipling's Verse*, ed. and intro. by TSE (London: Faber and Faber, 1941; repr. 1963), 108.

148   Envelope accompanying letter from VE to Scofield Thayer dated 'Thursday'; Beinecke Library, Yale University, YCAL 34 series IV Box 31, folder 812; no other Thursday that year falls on the third day of a month.

149   See Manju Jain, *T. S. Eliot and American Philosophy: The Harvard Years* (Cambridge and New York: Cambridge University Press, 1992), 32.

150   *L3*, 885.

151   *L1*, 151.

152   *L1*, xix.

Chapter 10 – V. S. Eliot

1   *IMH*, 383.

2   EP, *Ezra Pound to his Parents: Letters 1895–1929*, ed. Mary de Rachewiltz, A. David Moody and Joanna Moody (Oxford: Oxford University Press, 2010), 351.

3   'Marriages', *Times*, 30 June 1915, 1.

4   'Thomas Stearns Eliot of St. Louis Weds Abroad', *St Louis Globe-Democrat*, 16 July 1915, 1.

5   *L1*, 110.

6   'Thomas Stearns Eliot of St. Louis Weds Abroad', 1.

7   *L3*, 251.

8   *L1*, 114, 113.

9   Inscription on photograph of Henry with Mr and Mrs Harvey (Dorothy Dudley), taken at Chicago in June 1915 (Hayward Bequest (King's/PP/HB/P, 143)).

10   Wyndham Lewis, 'Early London Environment', in Tambimuttu and Richard March, eds, *T. S. Eliot: A Symposium* (New York: Tambimuttu and Mass, 1965), 31.

11   *CC*, 164 ('Ezra Pound: His Metric and Poetry').

12   *L3*, 119.

13   *L1*, 117.

14   *L1*, 116.

15   *L1*, 115.

16   Bertrand Russell to Ottoline Morrell, 10 September 1915 and 13 July 1915, in Bertrand Russell, *The Selected Letters of Bertrand Russell, Volume 2: The Public Years, 1914–1970*, ed. Nicholas Griffin (London: Routledge, 2001), 48, 45.

17   *L1*, 120, 121.

18   *L1*, 120.

19 William Hamilton Fyfe, letter of recommendation for TSE, Oxford, [June 1915] (Houghton bMS Am1691 (81)).

20 *L1*, 119.

21 Theodora Eliot to Charlotte Eliot Smith, 13 August 1926, *L3*, 251.

22 *L1*, 125.

23 *L2*, 124.

24 *L2*, 90.

25 CCE, 'Thomas Stearns Eliot', typed memorandum [*c.* 1921] (Houghton bMS Am2560 (106)).

26 Statement by Theresa Eliot (Mrs HWE, Jr), recalling her husband's account, 28 March 1970 (Houghton bMS Am2560 (105)).

27 *L1*, 121.

28 *L1*, 120.

29 *L1*, 122.

30 Ibid.

31 *L1*, 123.

32 Statement by Theresa Eliot, 28 March 1970.

33 *L1*, 702.

34 Russell, quoted in Ray Monk, *Bertrand Russell: The Spirit of Solitude* (London: Jonathan Cape, 1996), 439.

35 Ottoline Morrell to Bertrand Russell, quoted in ibid., 440.

36 Bertrand Russell, draft letter to Ottoline Morrell, quoted in ibid., 440.

37 *L1*, 125, 126.

38 *L1*, 125.

39 'Royal Grammar School', *South Bucks Free Press, Wycombe, Maidenhead, and Marlow Journal, and South Oxfordshire Gazette*, 27 August 1915, 1.

40 L. J. Ashford and C. M. Haworth, *The History of the Royal Grammar School, High Wycombe, 1562 to 1962* (High Wycombe: Governors of the Royal Grammar School, 1962), 77.

41 *L1*, 131.

42 Ashford and Haworth, *The History of the Royal Grammar School*, 79.

43 'Grand Cinema', *South Bucks Free Press*, 24 September 1915, 7.

44 *L1*, 131.

45 'Recruiting Rally at Wycombe', *South Bucks Free Press*, 8 October 1915, 3.

46 *L1*, 129, 130.

47 *L1*, 144.

48 *L1*, 131.

49 Ibid.

50 Mark Gertler's 1916 Garsington painting is reproduced in William Packer, 'Focus on the strengths of a problematic master', *Times*, 3 November 2012, 113.

51 I am grateful to Rosalind Ingrams for showing me Lady Ottoline's coloured threads, and the house; also to Professor David Bradshaw of Oxford University for guiding me round Garsington with a group in 2012.

52 *CPP*, 62.

53 Bertrand Russell to Ottoline Morrell, [10 September 1915], Russell, *Selected Letters*, 48.

54 Bertrand Russell to Ottoline Morrell, 13 October 1915, quoted in Monk, *Bertrand Russell*, 441.

55 See Monk, *Bertrand Russell*, 444; Russell, *Selected Letters*, 50.

56 VE to Scofield Thayer, 24 October 1915 (Beinecke YCAL 34 series IV, box 31, folder 812).

57 Compton Mackenzie, *Carnival* (New York: Appleton, 1913), 314.

58 VE to Scofield Thayer, 24 October 1915.

59 *L1*, 137.

60 *L1*, 138.
61 TSE, 'The Ultimate Belief' (review), *International Journal of Ethics*, 27.1 (October 1916), 127.
62 *L1*, 166.
63 *L2*, 318.
64 *L1*, 147.
65 Ibid.
66 *L1*, 157, 168.
67 *L1*, 170.
68 TSE, 'Thomas Stearns Eliot', *Harvard College Class of 1910 Fourth Report* (Cambridge, Mass: Crimson Printing Co., 1921), 107.
69 C. A. Evors, *The Story of Highgate School* (London: Chapman and Hall, n.d.), 13, 14; *L1*, 234.
70 T. Hinde, *Highgate School: A History* (London: James and James, 1993), 83, 86. 'Scrape' is thinly spread butter.
71 John Betjeman, *Summoned by Bells* (London: John Murray, 1960), 29.
72 TSE, 'Thomas Stearns Eliot', 107.
73 TSE, 'The Ultimate Belief', 127.
74 Ottoline Morrell, *Ottoline at Garsington: Memoirs of Lady Ottoline Morrell, 1915–1918*, ed. Robert Gathorne-Hardy (London: Faber and Faber, 1974), 96–7.
75 TSE, *Knowledge and Experience in the Philosophy of F. H. Bradley* (London: Faber and Faber, 1964), 23.
76 Ibid., 75.
77 Ibid., 76, 55.
78 *L1*, 153.
79 *L1*, 154.
80 *L1*, 172.
81 EP to John Quinn, 9 March 1916, quoted in *Facsimile*, x.
82 *L1*, 149.
83 Russell, *Selected Letters*, 59.
84 Miranda Seymour, *Ottoline Morrell: Life on the Grand Scale* (London: Hodder and Stoughton, 1992), 256; Morrell, *Ottoline at Garsington*, 101–2.
85 Russell, *Selected Letters*, 59.
86 *L1*, 150.
87 *L1*, 225.
88 *L1*, 207.
89 *L1*, 152, 151.
90 *L1*, 152.
91 *L1*, 156.
92 *L1*, 160.
93 TSE, 'The Development of Leibniz's Monadism', *Monist*, 26.4 (October 1916), 544.
94 TSE, 'Theism and Humanism' (review), *International Journal of Ethics*, 26.2 (January 1916), 285.
95 *Facsimile*, xii.
96 TSE, 'Mr Leacock Serious', *New Statesman*, 29 July 1916, 404; Stephen Leacock, *Essays and Literary Studies* (London: Allen Lane, 1916), 73.
97 TSE, 'Mr Leacock Serious', 73–4.
98 *L1*, 157.
99 *L1*, 164.
100 [TSE/VE], 'The Reef of Stars' (review), *Saturday Westminster Gazette*, 9 December 1916, 20.
101 *L1*, 158.
102 Osbert Sitwell, memoir of TSE, quoted in *L2* 318.
103 *L2*, 705.

104   Enid Faber (10 November 1950), quoted in *L2*, 593.
105   TSE, Concord Academy Address [June 1947] (Houghton bMS Am1691 (46)).
106   *L1*, 159.
107   *L1*, 161.
108   *L1*, 165.
109   *L1*, 156; Monk, *Bertrand Russell*, 469.
110   Betrand Russell, quoted in ibid., 469.
111   Morrell, *Ottoline at Garsington*, 120.
112   Bertrand Russell, quoted in Monk, *Bertrand Russell*, 469.
113   Bertrand Russell, quoted in ibid., 470.
114   Betrand Russell to Ottoline Morrell, 22 August 1916, quoted in ibid., 470.
115   *L1*, 162.
116   Betrand Russell to Ottoline Morrell, 1 September 1916, Russell, *Selected Letters*, 76; see also Monk, *Bertrand Russell*, 471.
117   *L1*, 162.
118   *L1*, xix.
119   *L1*, 165.
120   *L1*, 165, 154.
121   *L1*, 160.
122   [TSE], 'Charles Péguy' (review), *New Statesman*, 7 October 1916, 20.
123   *L1*, 162.
124   Ibid.
125   TSE, 'Conscience and Christ' (review), *International Journal of Ethics*, 27.1 (October 1916), 112.
126   TSE, 'Group Theories of Religion and the Religion of the Individual', *International Journal of Ethics*, 27.1 (October 1916), 117.
127   *IMH*, 83.
128   TSE, *Syllabus of a Course of Six Lectures on Modern French Literature* (Oxford: Frederick Hall, 1916), 5.
129   [TSE], 'An American Critic', *New Statesman*, 24 June 1916, 284.
130   TSE, report on his 1916 Oxford University Extension Lectures, quoted in Ronald Schuchard, *Eliot's Dark Angel* (New York: Oxford University Press, 1999), 31, 32.
131   Valerie Eliot in *L1*, 228.
132   Joint Committee's minutes (19 October 1916), quoted in Schuchard, *Eliot's Dark Angel*, 32.
133   *L1*, 171.
134   Monk, *Bertrand Russell*, 481.
135   Russell, *Selected Letters*, 86; see also Monk, *Betrand Russell*, 482.
136   Russell, *Selected Letters*, 86.
137   *L1*, 169.
138   *L1*, 171.
139   *L1*, 173.
140   Ibid.
141   *L1*, 174.

Chapter 11 – Observations

1   VE to Scofield Thayer, 2 August 1915 (Beinecke YCAL 34, series IV, box 31, folder 812).
2   Bertrand Russell, *Principles of Social Reconstruction* (London: Allen and Unwin, 1916), 173, 174; a description of Russell as 'the ablest' man appeared in a *Nation* review of this book quoted opposite the title page of the 1917 reprint.
3   *CPP*, 31.
4   Ray Monk, *Bertrand Russell: The Spirit of Solitude* (London: Jonathan Cape, 1996), 433.

Notes

5   Bertrand Russell to Constance Malleson (whose stage name was Colette O'Niel), 21 October 1916, Bertrand Russell, *The Selected Letters of Bertrand Russell: The Public Years, 1914–1970*, ed. Nicholas Griffin (London: Routledge, 2001), 482.

6   Monk, *Bertrand Russell*, 511.

7   Russell, *Selected Letters*, 51.

8   Bertrand Russell to Constance Malleson, 30 October 1917, ibid., 129.

9   *CPP*, 47 ('Mélange Adultère de Tout'), 38 ('Gerontion').

10   *CPP*, 38.

11   Matthew 5:27.

12   *L3*, 712.

13   *L2*, 639.

14   *L2*, 627, 628.

15   Lawrence Rainey, *Revisiting 'The Waste Land'* (New Haven: Yale University Press, 2005), 34; Lyndall Gordon, *Eliot's Early Years* (Oxford: Oxford University Press, 1977), 95–97; *Facsimile*, 105, 107.

16   TSE, '"The Duchess of Malfi" at the Lyric: and Poetic Drama', *Art and Letters*, 3.1 (Winter 1919/20), 37.

17   TSE, 'Eeldrop and Appleplex, I', *Little Review*, 4.1 (May 1917), 9.

18   *L1*, 177, 213, 239.

19   *L1*, 177.

20   *L1*, 178.

21   TSE, 'Reflections on *Vers Libre*', *New Statesman*, 3 March 1917, 518, 519.

22   Ibid., 519.

23   EP to James Joyce, 19 April 1917, *IMH*, 291.

24   *Times Literary Supplement* review of *Prufrock and Other Observations*, repr. in *T. S. Eliot: The Contemporary Reviews*, ed. Jewel Spears Brooker (Cambridge and New York: Cambridge University Press, 2004), 6.

25   *CPP*, 13.

26   *L1*, 194.

27   TSE, 'Elements of Folk Psychology', *International Journal of Ethics*, 27.2 (January 1917), 254.

28   *CPP*, 46 ('Le Directeur').

29   *CPP*, 47.

30   I. E. P., White Plains, New York, 'Critical Epilepsy', in 'The Reader Critic', *Little Review*, 4.3 (July 1917), 25; James Joyce, 'The Reader Critic', *Little Review*, 4.2 (June 1917), 26; see also the magazine's front cover.

31   *L1*, 175; Mary Hutchinson, 'T. S. Eliot', short, unpublished, undated biographical sketch in typescript in the possession of Jeremy Hutchinson, who has allowed me to quote from it; another copy is at the Harry Ransom Humanities Research Center, University of Texas at Austin, and is quoted in Carole Seymour-Jones, *Painted Shadow: The Life of Vivienne Eliot* (London: Constable and Robinson, 2001), 243.

32   Jeremy Hutchinson on 'Desert Island Discs', BBC Radio 4, 25 October 2013.

33   Quoted on the caption to Vanessa Bell's 1915 portrait of Mary Hutchinson in the Tate Gallery, London (Tate 01768), available online.

34   Mary Hutchinson to Lytton Strachey, 17 January 1917, quoted in Seymour-Jones, *Painted Shadow*, 204.

35   Clive Bell to Mary Hutchinson, 16 January 1917, quoted in ibid., 203–4.

36   TSE, 'Reflections on *Vers Libre*', 518.

37   Clive Bell to Mary Hutchinson, 8 April 1917, quoted in Seymour-Jones, *Painted Shadow*, 204–5; *CPP*, 29.

38   Maurice Haigh-Wood (1980), quoted in Seymour-Jones, *Painted Shadow*, 205.

39   Jeremy Hutchinson on 'Desert Island Discs', and letter to the present writer, 10 November 2013.

40   My interview with Jeremy Hutchinson, 3 December 2013.
41   Mary Hutchinson, 'T. S. Eliot', holograph memoir in the possession of her son, Jeremy Hutchinson (quoted with his permission).
42   Ibid.
43   Mary Hutchinson, 'T. S. Eliot', short, unpublished, undated biographical sketch in typescript.
44   Mary Hutchinson, 'T. S. Eliot', holograph memoir.
45   *CPP*, 74.
46   Mary Hutchinson, 'T. S. Eliot', holograph memoir.
47   *L3*, 712.
48   Mary Hutchinson, 'T. S. Eliot', holograph memoir.
49   Russell, *Principles of Social Reconstruction*, 164, 165.
50   *L1*, 180.
51   *L1*, 188.
52   *CPP*, 47; *L1*, 182.
53   *L1*, 180.
54   *L1*, 195.
55   *L1*, 182.
56   *L1*, 185.
57   *CPP*, 63, 62, 77.
58   *L1*, 219; *CPP*, 46 ('Le Directeur').
59   Karl Baedeker, *London and its Environs* (Leipzig: Dulau & Co., 1908), 124. TSE's annotated copy, Hayward Bequest HB/B/4.
60   *L1*, 219.
61   TSE, 'London Letter', *Dial*, 70.6 (June 1921), 691.
62   Benefactors' Board, St Magnus Martyr, Lower Thames Street, London.
63   Memorial tablet ('rest[ore]d Xmas 1889'), vestibule, St Magnus Martyr.
64   *CPP*, 69.
65   Ibid.
66   *L1*, 186.
67   John Ruskin, *The Works of John Ruskin, XVII*, ed. E. T. Cook and Alexander Wedderburn (London: George Allen, 1905), 432.
68   *L1*, 195.
69   *L1*, 185.
70   *L1*, 188.
71   Ibid.
72   *L1*, 189.
73   *L1*, 198; see also Vivien Whelpton, *Richard Aldington: Poet, Soldier and Lover, 1911–1929* (Cambridge: Lutterworth Press, 2014), 125, 150.
74   EP to John Quinn, 11 April 1917, quoted in *Facsimile*, xii.
75   *L1*, 192.
76   *L1*, 197.
77   *T. S. Eliot: The Contemporary Reviews*, ed. Brooker , 16.
78   Ibid., 16, 6, 4, 5, 13.
79   *L1*, 199.
80   Ibid.
81   *L1*, 205.
82   *L1*, 371; George Simmers, 'T. S. Eliot's Letter to "The Nation"' and 'Eliot, Corridors and T. E. Hulme' on the Great War Fiction website at http://greatwarfiction.wordpress.com (accessed March 2013); *IMH*, 93.
83   *L1*, 203.
84   Katherine Mansfield, *The Collected Letters of Katherine Mansfield, Volume V: 1922–1923*, ed. Vincent O'Sullivan and Margaret Scott (Oxford: Oxford University Press, 2008), 256.

85	Katherine Mansfield to Ottoline Morrell, ?24 June 1917, Katherine Mansfield, *The Collected Letters, Volume I; 1903–1917*, ed. Vincent O'Sullivan and Margaret Scott (Oxford: Clarendon Press, 1984), 312.
86	*L1*, 205.
87	*L1*, 206.
88	VE to Scofield Thayer, 1 July 1917 (Beinecke YCAL 34, series IV, box 31, folder 812).
89	Ibid.
90	Aldous Huxley to Ottoline Morrell, 21 June 1917, in Ottoline Morrell, *Ottoline at Garsington: Memoirs of Lady Ottoline Morrell, 1915–1918*, ed. Robert Gathorne-Hardy (London: Faber and Faber, 1974), 207.
91	[TSE], 'M. Bourget's Last Novel', *New Statesman*, 25 August 1917, 500.
92	*CPP*, 48.
93	TSE, 'Reflections on Contemporary Poetry, [II]' *Egoist*, 4.9 (October 1917), 133, 134.
94	*CPP*, 48; *IMH*, 292.
95	*IMH*, 86.
96	*CPP*, 49.
97	*CPP*, 44, 45.
98	*IMH*, 365.
99	*L1*, 210.
100	*CPP*, 51.
101	*IMH*, 87; F. O. Matthiessen made the Ruskin connection: see B. C. Southam, *A Student's Guide to the Selected Poems of T. S. Eliot*, fifth edn (London: Faber and Faber, 1990), 76.
102	*IMH*, 87; translation by Alice Crawford.
103	*L1*, 210, 211.
104	TSE, 'The Letters of J. B. Yeats', *Egoist*, 4.6 (July 1917), 89.
105	TSE, *Ezra Pound: His Metric and Poetry*, CC, 164, 166, 177.
106	EP, 'Vers Libre and Arnold Dolmetsch', *Egoist*, 4.6 (July 1917), 90.
107	TSE, 'Reflections on Contemporary Poetry, I', *Egoist*, 4.8 (September 1917), 119.
108	*L1*, 221.
109	According to Hugh Kenner, cited in Humphrey Carpenter, *A Serious Character: The Life of Ezra Pound* (London: Faber and Faber, 1988), 264.
110	Alfred A. Knopf to John Quinn, 17 August 1917, quoted in *Facsimile*, xii.
111	*CPP*, 51; Edwin Lester Arnold, *The Wonderful Adventures of Phra the Phoenician*, with an introduction by Sir Edwin Arnold (New York: A. L. Burt, [1890]), 4.
112	*L1*, 222; *CPP*, 45 ('A Cooking Egg').
113	*L1*, 214.
114	Mary Hutchinson, 'War', *Egoist*, December 1917, 171.
115	*L1*, 220.
116	*L1*, 223.
117	*L1*, 221.
118	Ibid.
119	*L1*, 222.
120	Bertrand Russell to Constance Malleson, 16 October 1917, Russell, *Selected Letters*, 127–8.
121	*L1*, 227; 225, 227.
122	Bertrand Russell to Constance Malleson, 30 October 1917, Russell, *Selected Letters*, 129.
123	*L1*, 228.
124	Bertrand Russell to Constance Malleson, 30 October 1917, quoted in Monk, *Bertrand Russell*, 511.
125	Bertrand Russell to Constance Malleson, 7 November 1917, quoted in ibid., 514.
126	Bertrand Russell to Constance Malleson, 13 November 1917, quoted in ibid.

127 Bertrand Russell to Constance Malleson, 14 November 1917, quoted in ibid.
128 *L1*, 234, 235.
129 *L1*, 239.
130 Bertrand Russell to Constance Malleson, 1 January 1918, quoted in Monk, *Bertrand Russell*, 515.
131 *L1*, 241.
132 *CPP*, 49.
133 *L1*, 244.
134 *L1*, 231.
135 *L1*, 246.
136 *L1*, 234.
137 *L1*, 239.
138 [TSE], 'Correspondence', *Egoist*, 4.11 (December 1917), 165.
139 *L1*, 242.
140 Ibid.
141 *L1*, 240.
142 *L1*, 242.
143 *L1*, 240.
144 *L1*, 244.
145 *L1*, 240.

Chapter 12 – American

1 *L1*, 245.
2 TSE, 'Turgenev', *Egoist*, 4.11 (December 1917), 167.
3 Advertisement, 'The May–June Poetry Review', *Times*, 1 May 1917, 8.
4 [TSE], 'Short Reviews', *Egoist*, 4.11 (December 1917), 173.
5 [TSE], 'Short Reviews', *Egoist*, 5.1 (January 1918), 10.
6 TSE, 'In Memory of Henry James', ibid., 1.
7 Ibid., 2.
8 Frank Norris, *The Pit: A Story of Chicago* (1903; repr. New York: Doubleday, 1920), 288.
9 TSE, 'In Memory of Henry James', 2.
10 TSE, 'Disjecta Membra', *Egoist*, 5.4 (April 1918), 55.
11 TSE, 'Reflections on Contemporary Poetry', *Egoist*, 4.10 (November 1917), 151.
12 [TSE], 'A Contemporary Thomist', *New Statesman*, 29 December 1917, 312.
13 TSE, 'Recent British Periodical Literature in Ethics', *International Journal of Ethics*, 38.2 (January 1918), 274.
14 *L2*, 124.
15 TSE, 'Recent British Periodical Literature in Ethics', 276, 277.
16 [TSE], 'The Elementary Forms of the Religious Life' (review), *Monist*, 28.1 (January 1918), 158, 159.
17 [TSE], 'Elements of Folk Psychology' (review), *Monist*, 28.1 (January 1918), 160.
18 See Edward Butscher, *Conrad Aiken: Poet of White Horse Vale* (Athens: University of Georgia Press, 1988), 129.
19 [TSE], 'New Philosophers', *New Statesman*, 13 July 1918, 296.
20 Edwin B. Holt, *The Freudian Wish and its Place in Ethics* (New York: Henry Holt, 1915), 10, 105, 45; *IMH*, 54; *CPP*, 32.
21 TSE, 'Literature and the American Courts', *Egoist*, 5.3 (March 1918), 39.
22 Bertrand Russell to Constance Malleson, 6 January 1918, quoted in Carole Seymour-Jones, *Painted Shadow: The Life of Vivienne Eliot* (London: Constable and Robinson, 2001), 191.
23 Ray Monk, *Bertrand Russell: The Spirit of Solitude* (London: Jonathan Cape, 1996), 521.
24 Bertrand Russell, 'The German Peace Offer', *Tribunal*, 3 January 1918, quoted in Monk, *Bertrand Russell*, 520.

Notes

25   TSE, 'Style and Thought', *Nation*, 23 March 1918, 769.
26   *L1*, 251.
27   'Announcements', *Egoist*, 5.3 (March 1918), 47.
28   *L1*, 269.
29   Ibid.
30   Apteryx [TSE], 'Verse Pleasant and Unpleasant', *Egoist*, 5.3 (March 1918), 44.
31   *L1*, 254.
32   *L1*, 252.
33   *L1*, 253.
34   *L1*, 255.
35   *L1*, 256.
36   *L1*, 262, 258.
37   *L1*, 260.
38   Ronald Schuchard, *Eliot's Dark Angel: Intersections of Life and Art* (New York: Oxford University Press, 1999), 93.
39   *CPP*, 56–7.
40   *CPP*, 42–3, 54–5; Lawrence Rainey, *Revisiting 'The Waste Land'* (New Haven and London: Yale University Press, 2005), 198–9.
41   *IMH*, 383.
42   [TSE], 'Correspondence', *Egoist*, 5.3 (March 1918), 47.
43   TSE, 'London Letter', *Dial*, December 1922, 661.
44   *L1*, 259; [TSE ('Apteryx')], 'Professional, Or . . .', *Egoist*, 5.4 (April 1918), 61.
45   William Thackeray, *Vanity Fair* (1848; repr. Harmondsworth: Penguin, 1979), 622 (chapter 53).
46   [TSE ('Apteryx')], 'Professional, Or . . .', 61.
47   *L1*, 266.
48   Jerome K. Jerome, *Three Men in a Boat* (New York: Henry Holt, 1890), 190.
49   'The Troops at Marlow, The Military Regatta', *South Bucks Free Press, Wycombe, Maidenhead, and Marlow Journal, and South Oxfordshire Gazette*, 29 June 1917, 3; Jerome, *Three Men in a Boat*, 190.
50   *L1*, 272.
51   See photograph 259 in Hayward Bequest, King's/PP/HB/P, 259.
52   *Marlow Directory and Almanac 1915* (Marlow: Welbourne & Simpson, 1915), 35.
53   *L1*, 266.
54   *L1*, 262.
55   *L1*, 266; TSE, 'The Hawthorne Aspect', *Little Review*, 5.4 (August 1918), 47.
56   TSE, 'The Hawthorne Aspect', 48, 49, 50, 53.
57   *L1*, 266.
58   Ibid.
59   Aldous Huxley, *Letters of Aldous Huxley*, ed. Grover Smith (London: Chatto and Windus, 1969), 156.
60   *L1*, 267.
61   T. S. Apteryx [TSE], 'Observations', *Egoist*, 5.5 (May 1918), 69, 70.
62   *CPP* 40–41; [TSE], 'Contemporanea', *Egoist*, 5.6 (June–July 1918), 84.
63   TSE, 'Tarr', *Egoist*, 5.8 (September 1918), 106.
64   [TSE], 'Contemporanea', *Egoist*, 84.
65   Ibid.
66   [TSE], 'Short Notices', *Egoist*, 5.5 (May 1918), 75.
67   Sacheverell Sitwell, *Egoist*, 5.5 (May 1918), 70.
68   *L1*, 271.
69   Ibid.
70   *IMH*, 383.
71   *L1*, 268, 269.

463

72   Harold Peters entry in *Harvard Class of 1910, Fourth Report* (Cambridge, Mass: Crimson Printing Company, 1921), 304.
73   *L1*, 273.
74   *L1*, 272.
75   *L1*, 269.
76   *L1*, 274.
77   *L1*, 279, 283.
78   'Registration Card' for Thomas Stearns Eliot, 19 August 1918, US National Archives and Records Administration, accessed online in March 2013 at www.archives.gov/atlanta/wwi-draft/eliot.html
79   *L1*, 276.
80   *L1*, 277.
81   *L1*, 279.
82   *L1*, 280.
83   Charles W. Eliot, letter 'To Whom It May Concern', 27 August 1918 (carbon) (Houghton bMS Am1691 (103)).
84   *L1*, 288.
85   Ibid.
86   *L1*, 289, 286.
87   *L1*, 290.
88   *L1*, 297.
89   *L1*, 300.
90   *L1*, 295.
91   *L1*, 291.
92   *L1*, 297.
93   *L1*, 285.
94   Virginia Woolf, *The Diary of Virginia Woolf, Volume 1: 1915–1919*, ed. Anne Olivier Bell (London: Hogarth Press, 1977), 210, n.34.
95   Virginia Woolf, *The Question of Things Happening: The Letters of Virginia Woolf, Volume II: 1912–1922*, ed. Nigel Nicolson (London: Hogarth Press, 1976), 295, 296.
96   Woolf, *Diary*, I, 218–19.
97   TSE, 'Studies in Contemporary Criticism, I', *Egoist*, 5.9 (October 1918), 114.
98   Woolf, *Diary*, I, 219.
99   Ibid., 223.
100   'Not Here, O Apollo', *Times Literary Supplement*, 12 June 1919, repr. in *T. S. Eliot: The Contemporary Reviews*, ed. Jewel Spears Brooker (Cambridge and New York: Cambridge University Press, 2004), 21.
101   'Is This Poetry?', *Athenaeum*, 20 June 1919, repr. in *T. S. Eliot: The Contemporary Reviews*, ed. Brooker, 22.
102   TSE, 'A Note on Ezra Pound', *To-day*, 5.19 (September 1918), 4, 5, 6.
103   TSE, 'Studies in Contemporary Criticism, I', 113.
104   'Is This Poetry?', 22.
105   *L1*, 303.
106   *L1*, 304.
107   *L1*, 306.
108   *L1*, 310.
109   *L1*, 309.
110   TSE, 'Studies in Contemporary Criticism, II', *Egoist*, 5.10 (November–December 1918), 132.
111   Ibid.
112   'President Wilson's Message Home', *Times*, 27 December 1918, 7.
113   *L1*, 311, 312.
114   *L1*, 312.

115   *L1*, 404, 405.
116   *L1*, 314.

Chapter 13 – Old Man

1   VE, Diary for 1919, entries for 8, 9, 10 January (Bodleian Library, MS Eng. Misc. f532); *L1*, 317, 316

2   'In Memoriam Henry Ware Eliot', *Washington University Record*, Series I, 14.5 (February 1919), 3, 4.

3   *L1*, 316.

4   *L1*, 315.

5   *L1*, 316.

6   *L1*, 317.

7   *L1*, 323.

8   *L1*, 319.

9   VE, Diary for 1919, entry for 9 January; Carole Seymour-Jones, *Painted Shadow: The Life of Vivienne Eliot* (London: Constable and Robinson, 2001), 11; *The Medical Directory 1919* (London: J & A Churchill, 1919), 336.

10   *L1*, 320.

11   Seymour-Jones, *Painted Shadow*, 223.

12   Betrand Russell to TSE, 19 March 1919, quoted in ibid., 225.

13   This academic correspondence is quoted from Manju Jain, *T. S. Eliot and American Philosophy: The Harvard Years* (Cambridge and New York: Cambridge University Press, 1992), 34, 35.

14   *L1*, 323.

15   *IMH*, 349; Dante Alighieri, *The Inferno of Dante Alighieri* (London: J. M. Dent and New York: E. P. Dutton, 1900), 379 (Canto XXXIII, 122). See *CPP*, 37–9.

16   *IMH*, 349–51.

17   *L1*, 380.

18   *IMH*, 352, 350.

19   [TSE], 'The New Elizabethans and the Old', *Athenaeum*, 4 April 1919, 135; TSE, 'A Sceptical Patrician', *Athenaeum*, 23 May 1919, 361; *L1*, 342.

20   *L1*, 343.

21   *L1*, 328.

22   VE, Diary for 1919, entry for 2 March.

23   Ibid., entry for 3 March.

24   *L1*, 338.

25   *L1*, 340.

26   *L1*, 331.

27   TSE, 'American Literature', *Athenaeum*, 25 April 1919, 237.

28   TSE, 'A Romantic Patrician', *Athenaeum*, 2 May 1919, 266–7.

29   TSE, 'Kipling Redivivus', *Athenaeum*, 9 May 1919, 298.

30   *L1*, 342.

31   TSE, 'Kipling Redivivus' (letter), *Athenaeum*, 16 May 1919, 344.

32   *L1*, 345.

33   *L1*, 381.

34   *L1*, 332; Brigit Patmore, *My Friends When Young* (London: Heinemann, 1968), 87.

35   *L1*, 334.

36   *L1*, 337.

37   Virgina Woolf, *The Diary of Virginia Woolf, Volume 1: 1915–1919*, ed. Anne Olivier Bell (London: Hogarth Press, 1977), 235, 262, 265.

38   Virgina Woolf, *The Question of Things Happening: The Letters of Virginia Woolf, Volume II: 1912–1922*, ed. Nigel Nicolson (London: Hogarth Press, 1976), 344.

39   *L1*, 345.
40   Woolf, *The Question of Things Happening*, 350.
41   Ibid., 355.
42   TSE, 'Beyle and Balzac', *Athenaeum*, 30 May 1919, 392, 393.
43   TSE, 'Criticism in England', *Athenaeum*, 13 June 1919, 457.
44   *L1*, 338.
45   *L1*, 338–9.
46   *L1*, 343.
47   Lytton Strachey, quoted in *L1*, 352.
48   Lytton Strachey to TSE, 13 February and 20 July 1920 (Houghton bMS Am1432 (136 and 138)); see also *L1*, 388, 445, 477.
49   *L1*, 347.
50   *L1*, 358.
51   *IMH*, 350.
52   Ottoline Morrell, *Ottoline at Garsington: Memoirs of Lady Ottoline Morrell, 1915–1918*, ed. Robert Gathorne-Hardy (London: Faber and Faber, 1974), 120.
53   *L1*, 350.
54   *L1*, 365.
55   *L1*, 349.
56   *L1*, 358, 359.
57   *L1*, 356.
58   *L1*, 342.
59   *L1*, 353.
60   *L1*, 357.
61   *L1*, 365.
62   VE, Diary for 1919, entries for 21, 22 June.
63   *L1*, 366.
64   *L1*, 367.
65   VE, Diary for 1919, entry for 21 June.
66   *L1*, 368.
67   *L1*, 370.
68   Ibid.
69   TSE, 'The Education of Taste', *Athenaeum*, 27 June 1919, 520.
70   TSE, 'Reflections on Contemporary Poetry, [IV]', *Egoist*, 6.3 (July 1919), 39.
71   *L1*, 367.
72   TSE, 'Reflections on Contemporary Poetry, [IV]', 39.
73   *L1*, 411.
74   *L1*, 423.
75   TSE, 'Reflections on Contemporary Poetry, [IV]', 39, 40.
76   Ibid., 39.
77   Ibid.; Conrad Aiken, *The Charnel Rose* (Boston: Four Seas Company, 1918), 12, 13, 19, 29, 30, 42, 43.
78   TSE, 'Reflections on Contemporary Poetry, [IV]', 40.
79   *L1*, 375, 399.
80   *L1*, 378.
81   *L1*, 381, 379.
82   *L1*, 376.
83   *L1*, 379; VE, Diary for 1919, entries for 12, 13 July.
84   VE, Diary for 1919, entry for 20 July.
85   Ibid., entry for 22 July; *L1*, 399.
86   *L1*, 381.
87   VE, Diary for 1919, entry for 21 July; *The Medical Directory 1919*, 377.
88   *L1*, 388, 386.
89   *L1*, 382.

90 *L1*, 384.
91 TSE, 'A Foreign Mind', *Athenaeum*, 4 July 1919, 553.
92 TSE, 'The Romantic Generation if it Existed', *Athenaeum*, 18 July 1919, 616, 617.
93 TSE, 'Was There a Scottish Literature?', *Athenaeum*, 1 August 1919, 680, 681.
94 Ibid., 681.
95 TSE, 'Reflections on Contemporary Poetry, [IV]', 39; TSE, 'Whether Rostand Had Something about Him', *Athenaeum*, 25 July 1919, 665; TSE, 'Some Notes on the Blank Verse of Christopher Marlowe', *Art and Letters*, 2.4 (Autumn, 1919), 198.
96 *L1*, 378, 387.
97 TSE, 'Tradition and the Individual Talent, [I]', *Egoist*, 6.4 (September 1919), 55.
98 Ibid.
99 TSE, 'The Old Comedy', *Athenaeum*, 11 June 1920, 761.
100 'Tradition and the Individual Talent, [I]', 55.
101 TSE, 'Humanist, Artist, and Scientist', *Athenaeum*, 10 October 1919, 1015.
102 TSE, 'Tradition and the Individual Talent, [I]', 55.
103 *L1*, 387.
104 *L1*, 392.
105 *L1*, 393.
106 EP, *Collected Shorter Poems* (London: Faber and Faber, 1968), 172.
107 *L1*, 393.
108 *L1*, 407.
109 *L1*, 388.
110 *L1*, 407.
111 EP to Dorothy Pound, August 1919, quoted in Humphrey Carpenter, *A Serious Character: The Life of Ezra Pound* (London: Faber and Faber, 1988), 349.
112 EP, Canto XXIX, quoted in A. D. Moody, *Ezra Pound: Poet, Volume 1* (Oxford: Oxford University Press, 2007), 360, 361.
113 VE, Diary for 1919, entry for 31 August.
114 Ibid.
115 Ibid., entry for 5 September.
116 Ibid., entry for 7 September.
117 *L1*, 394.
118 Richard Aldington, *Life for Life's Sake: A Book of Reminiscences* (New York: Viking Press, 1941), 260.
119 *L1*, 395.
120 TSE, 'Hamlet and his Problems', *Athenaeum*, 26 September 1919, 941, 940.
121 TSE, 'Swinburne and the Elizabethans', *Athenaeum*, 19 September 1919, 909, 910.
122 TSE, 'Hamlet and his Problems', 941.
123 Ibid.
124 Ibid.
125 [TSE], 'Murmuring of Innumerable Bees', *Athenaeum*, 3 October 1919, 972.
126 TSE, 'The Preacher as Artist', *Athenaeum*, 28 November 1919, 1252.
127 [TSE], 'Murmuring of Innumerable Bees', 972.
128 *L1*, 426.
129 *L1*, 406; VE, Diary for 1919, entries for 26–30 September.
130 *L1*, 401.
131 *L1*, 405.
132 TSE, 'Humanist, Artist, and Scientist', 1014.
133 *L1*, 404.
134 *L1*, 415.
135 TSE, 'War-paint and Feathers, *Athenaeum*, 17 October 1919, 1036.
136 TSE, 'The Method of Mr. Pound', *Athenaeum*, 24 October 1919, 1065.
137 Ibid.
138 EP, *Quia Pauper Amavi* (London: Egoist Press, 1919), 19.

139   TSE, 'The Method of Mr. Pound', 1066.
140   VE, Diary for 1919, entry for 8 October.
141   TSE, 'Our Inaccessible Heritage', *Athenaeum*, 24 October 1919, 1076.
142   For information about TSE's London Library membership application, I am grateful to Mark Storey of the London Library.
143   TSE, 'The Preacher as Artist', 1253.
144   TSE, 'Tradition and the Individual Talent, II', *Egoist*, 6.5 (December 1919), 72.
145   *L2*, 627.
146   TSE, 'Tradition and the Individual Talent, II', 73.
147   TSE, 'The Old Comedy', 761.
148   TSE, 'The Comedy of Humours', *Athenaeum*, 14 November 1919, 1180.
149   TSE, 'Tradition and the Individual Talent, II', 72.
150   VE, Diary for 1919, entry for 19 November.
151   TSE, 'The Local Flavour', *Athenaeum*, 12 December 1919, 1332.
152   *L1*, 420.
153   [TSE], 'Ben Jonson', *Times Literary Supplement*, 13 November 1919, 637; *Purgatorio*, XXI.
154   [TSE], 'Ben Jonson', 637, 638.
155   EP, *Collected Shorter Poems*, 208.
156   *L1*, 425.
157   *L1*, 421.
158   *L1*, 424.
159   *L1*, 423.
160   *L1*, 426.
161   VE, Diary for 1919, entry for 25 December.
162   *L1*, 424, 425.
163   VE, Diary for 1919, entry for 26 December.
164   Ibid., entries for 30 and 31 December.

Chapter 14 - Professional

1   'Public Appointments' and 'Appointments Vacant', *Times*, 6 January 1920, 3.
2   *L1*, 485.
3   TSE, 'Modern Tendencies in Poetry', *Shama'a*, 1.1 (April 1920), 11.
4   *L1*, 444.
5   TSE, 'John Maynard Keynes', *New English Weekly*, 16 May 1946, 47.
6   John Maynard Keynes, *The Economic Consequences of the Peace* (New York: Harcourt, Brace and Howe, 1920), 3, 5, 6, 279, 297.
7   TSE to John Hayward, 29 November 1939 (Hayward Bequest).
8   Michael Hickling, 'Return from the Island of the Saints', *Yorkshire Post*, 20 April 2013, 8 (I am grateful to Mark Webster for calling this to my attention); *CPP*, 68.
9   *L1*, 453.
10   *L1*, 435.
11   A. David Moody, *Ezra Pound: Poet, Volume I* (Oxford: Oxford University Press, 2007), 390; *L1*, 464.
12   *L1*, 435.
13   *L1*, 436.
14   *L1*, 447.
15   Ibid.
16   TSE, 'The Naked Man', *Athenaeum*, 13 February 1920, 208; TSE, 'Swinburne', *Athenaeum*, 16 January 1920, 72; [TSE], 'Correspondence: The Phoenix Society', *Athenaeum*, 27 February 1920, 285.
17   TSE, 'The Perfect Critic, II', *Athenaeum*, 23 July 1920, 103.
18   *L1*, 463.

19   TSE, 'Swinburne', 72.

20   *CPP*, 171.

21   TSE, 'The Naked Man', 208.

22   VE, Diary for 1919, entry for 4 January 1920 (Bodleian Library, MS. Eng. Misc. f532).

23   *L1*, 458.

24   *L1*, 451.

25   *L1*, 450, 475.

26   *L1*, 481.

27   *L1*, 460.

28   TSE, 'A Brief Treatise on the Criticism of Poetry', *Chapbook*, 2:9 (March 1920), 9.

29   Dante, *The Divine Comedy, II, Purgatorio*, tr. John D. Sinclair (New York: Oxford University Press, 1980), 342, 343; TSE, 'The Method of Mr. Pound', *Athenaeum*, 24 October 1919, 1065; *CPP*, 75, 59.

30   [TSE] 'Murmuring of Innumerable Bees', *Athenaeum*, 3 October 1919, 972; TSE, 'The Poetic Drama', *Athenaeum*, 14 May 1920, 635.

31   Katherine Mansfield, *The Collected Letters of Katherine Mansfield, Volume IV: 1920–1921*, ed. Vincent O'Sullivan and Margaret Scott, 1996), 11; *L1*, 473.

32   *The Question of Things Happening: The Letters of Virginia Woolf, Volume II: 1912–1922*, ed. Nigel Nicolson (London: Hogarth Press, 1976), 437.

33   *L1*, 475–6.

34   *L1*, 464.

35   Ibid.

36   *L1*, 474, 501.

37   [Garnet Smith], 'Romance and Religion', *Times Literary Supplement*, 27 May 1920, 330.

38   TSE, inscription in his copy of Jessie L. Weston, *From Ritual to Romance* (Cambridge: Cambridge University Press, 1920) (Houghton *AC9.El464.R920w).

39   *L1*, 476.

40   *L1*, 479, 482.

41   *L1*, 468.

42   *L1*, 472.

43   Ibid.

44   *L1*, 477.

45   Ibid.

46   *L1*, 478.

47   Ibid.

48   *L1*, 483.

49   *L1*, 489.

50   *L1*, 495.

51   *L1*, 493.

52   Wyndham Lewis, *Blasting and Bombadiering*, second edn (Berkeley: University of California Press, 1967), 270.

53   *L1*, 655.

54   Lewis, *Blasting & Bombadiering* (London: Eyre and Spottiswoode, 1937), 276.

55   *L1*, 494.

56   Ibid; TSE, 'Wyndham Lewis', *Hudson Review*, 10.2 (Summer 1957), 169.

57   *L1*, 497; Wyndham Lewis, 'Early London Environment', in Tambimuttu and Richard March, eds, *T. S. Eliot: A Symposium* (New York: Tambimuttu and Mass), 30.

58   TSE, 'Wyndham Lewis', 168.

59   *L1*, 492.

60   See Hayward Bequest photographs 268 and 273 and captions; *L1*, 498.

61   *L1*, 492.

62   *L1*, 493.

63 *L2*, 185.

64 *L1*, 493.

65 Peter Ackroyd, *T. S. Eliot* (London: Hamish Hamilton, 1984), 62.

66 TSE to John Hayward, 29 November 1939 (Hayward Bequest).

67 Virginia Woolf, *The Diary of Virginia Woolf, Volume 2: 1920–24*, ed. Anne Olivier Bell and Andrew McNeillie (London: Penguin, 1981), 67–8.

68 Richard Aldington, letter to Amy Lowell, 17 June 1920, quoted in Vivien Whelpton, *Richard Aldington: Poet, Soldier and Lover* (Cambridge: Lutterworth Press, 2013), 243; Katherine Mansfield, *The Collected Letters of Katherine Mansfield, Volume IV: 1920–1921*, ed. Vincent O'Sullivan and Margaret Scott (Oxford: Clarendon Press, 1996), 47.

69 *L1*, 488.

70 *L1*, 496.

71 Ibid.

72 *L1*, 491.

73 *L1*, 498.

74 *L1*, 501.

75 *L1*, 499, 500.

76 *L1*, 499.

77 *L1*, 504.

78 *L1*, 499.

79 *L1*, 502.

80 Ibid.

81 Ibid.

82 *L1*, 511.

83 Jeremy Hutchinson, 'Desert Island Discs', on BBC Radio 4, 25 October 2013.

84 *L1*, 508.

85 *L1*, 515.

86 *L1*, 510.

87 TSE, 'Euripides and Gilbert Murray: A Performance at the Holborn Empire', *Art and Letters*, 3.2 (Spring 1920), 38–43.

88 Ibid., 43.

89 Woolf, *Diary*, 2, 68.

90 [TSE], 'Philip Massinger', *Times Literary Supplement*, 27 May 1920, 325.

91 Ibid., 325, 326.

92 TSE, 'Artists and Men of Genius' (letter), *Athenaeum*, 25 June 1920, 842.

93 Edouard Dujardin, *De Stéphane Mallarmé au prophete Ezèchiel: et essai d'une théorie du réalisme symbolique* (Paris: Mercure de France, 1919), 32–75.

94 TSE, 'The Perfect Critic, II', 104.

95 TSE, 'The Possibility of a Poetic Drama', *Dial*, 69.5 (December 1920), 441, 442, 443.

96 Ibid., 443.

97 TSE, 'The Second-Order Mind', *Dial*, 69.6 (December 1920), 586, 589.

98 *L1*, 517.

99 TSE, 'The Second-Order Mind', 586, 589.

100 *L1*, 514.

101 *L1*, 511.

102 *L1*, 521.

103 *L1*, 520.

104 Ibid.

105 *L1*, 521.

106 Woolf, *Diary*, 2, 77.

107 *T. S. Eliot: The Contemporary Reviews*, ed. Jewel Spears Brooker (Cambridge and New York: Cambridge University Press, 2004), 66.

108 *L1*, 515.

109 *L1*, 538.

110	*L1*, 515.
111	*CPP*, 70.
112	*L1*, 536.
113	*L1*, 531, 529.

Chapter 15 – To Lausanne

1	*L1*, 532.
2	*L1*, 541.
3	*L1*, 534.
4	Stephen Spender, *Eliot* (Glasgow: Fontana, 1975), 49; list of TSE library books in VE's scrap book (Bodleian Library MS. Eng. Let. b. 20); see Edmund Spenser, *Poetical Works*, ed. J.C. Smith and E. De Selincourt (Oxford: University Press, 1912), 601 ('Prothalamion'); *CPP*, 67.
5	[TSE], 'Andrew Marvell', *Times Literary Supplement*, 31 March 1921, 201.
6	*CPP*, 67.
7	*L1*, 534.
8	TSE, 'Prose and Verse', *Chapbook*, 22 (April 1921), 3.
9	*L1*, 538.
10	Virginia Woolf, *The Diary of Virginia Woolf, Volume 2, 1920–24*, ed. Anne Olivier Bell and Andrew McNeillie (Harmondsworth: Penguin, 1981), 91.
11	*L1*, 542.
12	'A Forbidden Play', *Times*, 15 February 1921, 9; *L1*, 542.
13	*L1*, 540.
14	*L1*, 542.
15	*L1*, 544.
16	Woolf, *The Diary of Virginia Woolf*, 2, 100.
17	*L1*, 546.
18	*Encyclopedia Britannica* (1911), entry for 'Neuritis'.
19	*L1*, 546.
20	Katherine Mansfield, *The Collected Letters of Katherine Mansfield, Volume IV: 1920–1921* (Oxford: Oxford University Press, 1996), 201.
21	Woolf, *The Diary of Virginia Woolf*, 2, 103, 104.
22	*L1*, 548.
23	Virginia Woolf, *The Question of Things Happening: The Letters of Virginia Woolf, Volume II: 1912–1922*, ed. Nigel Nicolson and Joanne Trautmann (London: Hogarth Press, 1976), 472; *L1*, 536.
24	TSE, 'Prose and Verse', 5.
25	Woolf, *The Question of Things Happening*, 467.
26	Conrad Aiken, *The House of Dust* (Boston: Four Seasons Company, 1920), 12, 20, 42, 134, 38, 48, 86, 96, 140.
27	TSE, 'Prose and Verse', 5.
28	Wyndham Lewis to Sydney Schiff, 7 February 1921 (British Library, MS add. 52919).
29	TSE, 'Song to the Opherian', *Tyro*, 1 ([Spring 1921]), 6.
30	TSE, 'The Romantic Englishman, the Comic Spirit, and the Function of Criticism', *Tyro*, 1 ([Spring 1921]), 4.
31	TSE, 'The Lesson of Baudelaire', *Tyro*, 1 ([Spring 1921]), 4; *CPP*, 63.
32	*L1*, 539.
33	TSE, 'London Letter', *Dial,* 70.4 (April 1921), 448, 449, 450, 451.
34	Alexander Pope, *The Poems of Alexander Pope*, ed. John Butt (London: Methuen, 1965), 425.
35	[TSE], 'John Dryden', *Times Literary Supplement*, 9 June 1921, 361.
36	TSE, 'London Letter' (April 1921), 451; TSE, 'The Lesson of Baudelaire', 4.
37	*Facsimile*, 23, 27.

38   TSE, 'Andrew Marvell', 201.

39   Jean Cocteau, *Oeuvres romanesques complètes* (Paris: Editions Gallimard, 2006), 217.

40   *Facsimile*, 31.

41   *Facsimile*, 27, 33, 35.

42   *Facsimile*, 54.

43   *Facsimile*, 11, 15.

44   *IMH*, 87.

45   *Facsimile*, 15.

46   Bernard Shaw, *Back to Methuselah: A Metabiological Pentateuch* (Harmondsworth: Penguin, 1939), v, vi.

47   TSE, 'London Letter', *Dial*, 71.4 (October 1921), 49.

48   *L1*, 569.

49   *L1*, 561, 562.

50   Woolf, *The Question of Things Happening*, 49.

51   *L1*, 563, 564.

52   TSE, 'Ulysses, Order and Myth', *Dial*, 75.5 (November 1923), 480, 481, 482, 483.

53   *L1*, 549.

54   *L1*, 550.

55   Ibid.

56   *Facsimile*, 3.

57   *L1*, 551.

58   *CPP*, 68.

59   *L1*, 553.

60   *L1*, 553–4.

61   *L1*, 556.

62   *L1*, 568.

63   TSE, 'John Dryden', 362.

64   Ibid.

65   *L1*, 556–7.

66   *L1*, 564.

67   *L1*, 567.

68   D. H. Lawrence, *Women in Love* (1921; repr. Harmondsworth: Penguin, 1979), 328; Woolf, *The Question of Things Happening*, 475.

69   *L1*, 568.

70   Osbert Sitwell, unpublished memoir, 19 February 1950, Harry Ransom Humanities Research Center, University of Texas at Austin, quoted in Carole Seymour-Jones, *Painted Shadow: The Life of Vivienne Eliot* (London: Constable and Robinson, 2001), 274.

71   *L1*, 567, 568.

72   'Contemporary Music', *Times*, 8 June 1921, 10.

73   TSE, 'London Letter,' *Dial*, 71.4 (October 1921), 452.

74   'Le Sacre du Printemps', *Times*, 28 June 1921, 8.

75   TSE, 'A Commentary', *Criterion*, 3.9 (October 1924), 5.

76   *L1*, 569; *L2*, 90.

77   *L1*, 569.

78   Ibid.

79   *L1*, 570, 571.

80   *L1*, 571, 572.

81   HWE, Jr, 'Picturesque Mumps' (typescript dated 1921), (Houghton bMS Am 1691.10 (20)).

82   *L1*, 575.

83   *L1*, 597.

84   *L1*, 573.

85 I. A. Richards, 'On TSE', in Allen Tate, ed., *T. S. Eliot: The Man and his Work* (London: Chatto and Windus, 1967), 4.

86 *L1*, 576.

87 *L1*, 577.

88 Sitwell, memoir, quoted in Seymour-Jones, *Painted Shadow*, 274.

89 *L1*, 576.

90 *L1*, 578.

91 *L1*, 590.

92 *L1*, 579.

93 *L1*, 578, 579.

94 *L1*, 578.

95 *L1*, 592.

96 TSE, 'London Letter', (October 1921), 453.

97 Richard Aldington, letter to Amy Lowell, 7 April 1921, quoted in Vivien Whelpton, *Richard Aldington: Poet, Soldier and Lover* (Cambridge: Lutterworth Press, 2014), 243.

98 Jean Epstein, *La Poésie d'aujourd'hui: Un nouvel état d'intelligence* (Paris: Editions de la Sirène, 1921), 60, 58, 61, 64, 73, 127, 97, 113, 169, 173, 182, 181, 189.

99 *L1*, 580.

100 *L1*, 581.

101 TSE, 'The Metaphysical Poets', *Times Literary Supplement*, 20 October 1921, 670.

102 Ibid., 669.

103 *Facsimile*, 5.

104 *Facsimile*, 5–21; TSE, 'London Letter', *Dial*, 71.2 (August 1921), 213; on the May datings, see Lawrence Raincy, *Revisiting 'The Waste Land'* (New Haven and London: Yale University Press, 2005), 17–21.

105 TSE, 'London letter' (August 1921), 215, 214, 216, 217.

106 *Facsimile*, 121, 123, 61.

107 *L1*, 582.

108 Woolf, *The Diary of Virginia Woolf*, 2, 140.

109 *L1*, 583.

110 Mansfield, *The Collected Letters of Katherine Mansfield, Volume IV*, 303.

111 *L1*, 584, 585.

112 *L1*, 592.

113 *L1*, 590.

114 Ibid.

115 *L1*, 592.

116 *L1*, 593.

117 *Margate Official Guide* (Margate: Borough of Margate Publicity Committee, 1929), 1.

118 'Entertainments, Cinemas, etc.', *Isle of Thanet Gazette and Thanet Times*, 29 October 1921, 1.

119 *L1*, 593.

120 *L1*, 594.

121 *L1*, 601, 594.

122 *L1*, 594.

123 *L1*, 599.

124 *L1*, 601, 606.

125 *L1*, 601–2.

126 *Facsimile*, 51, 53.

127 *CPP*, 70.

128 Ibid.

129 *CPP*, 78, 79.

130 *L1* 603.

131 *L1*, 606.

132   *L1*, 607.

133   *L1*, 616.

134   *L1*, 619.

135   *L1*, 618.

136   *L1*, 619.

137   *L1*, 618.

138   Scofield Thayer to VE, 20 October 1921 (carbon) (Beinecke YCAL MSS 34 Box 1, Folder 813).

139   *L1*, 619.

140   *L1*, 646.

141   Jean Charles Biaudet, *Histoire de Lausanne* (Lausanne: Editions Payot, 1982), 360; several other details in my account of Lausanne during TSE's stay are taken from November and December 1921 issues of the *Feuille d'Avis de Lausanne et Résumé des Nouvelles* available digitally through the Swiss National Library.

142   The hotel is now demolished but can be seen in an old postcard, 'Lausanne – Hôtel-Pension Ste-Luce', published in Lausanne by G. Vaney Burnier.

143   *L1*, 614.

144   *L1*, 608; biographical details about Roger Vittoz are drawn from Pierre Téqui, ed., *Notes et Pensées: Angoisse ou Contrôle*, revised edn (Paris: Téqui, 1992).

145   Pierre Janet, *Les Obsessions et la psychasthénie* (Paris: Félix Alcan, 1903), 336.

146   *L1*, 608.

147   *L1*, 609.

148   *L1*, 608.

149   *L1*, 594.

150   Julian Huxley, *Memories* (London: Allen and Unwin, 1970), 124.

151   Roger Vittoz, *Treatment of Neurasthenia by Means of Brain Control*, tr. H. B. Brooke, second edn (London: Longmans, Green & Co., 1913), viii, 13, 1, 5, 7.

152   Ibid., 67, 59.

153   Ibid., 75.

154   *Facsimile*, 53.

155   Vittoz, *Treatment of Neurasthenia*, 27.

156   *L1*, 594; Vittoz, *Treatment of Neurasthenia*, 37.

157   *L1*, plate 30.

158   *L1*, 750.

159   Vittoz, *Treatment of Neurasthenia*, 54.

160   Ibid., 62.

161   Ibid., 68, 96.

162   *L1*, 608–9.

163   *L1*, 609.

164   *L1*; 'The Love Nest', Otto Harbach (lyrics) and Louis A Hirsch, (New York: Victoria Publishing Company, 1920), 2.

165   'Conditions aux Etats-Unis', *Feuille d'Avis de Lausanne et Résumé des Nouvelles*, 27 décembre 1921, 20.

166   *L1*, 614.

167   *Facsimile*, 29.

168   *Facsimile*, 25; *CPP*, 67.

169   Matthew K. Gold, 'The Expert Hand and the Obedient Heart: Dr. Vittoz, T. S. Eliot, and the Therapeutic Possibilities of *The Waste Land*', *Journal of Modern Literature*, 23.3/4 (Summer, 2000), 533.

170   *L1*, 614.

171   *L1*, 617.

172   *Facsimile*, 71, 73; *CPP*, 71, 73.

173   *L1*, 725–6.

174   *CPP*, 73, 74, 80.

175	*CPP*, 74.
176	*L1*, 563.
177	*CPP*, 74–5, 80.
178	Virginia Woolf, *The Diary of Virginia Woolf, Volume 4: 1931–35*, ed. Anne Olivier Bell, assisted by Andrew McNeillie (London: Penguin, 1983), 288.
179	*Facsimile*, 81, 89; *L1*, 614.
180	*L1*, 620.
181	*Facsimile*, 77.
182	Edmund Gosse, ed., *Restoration Plays from Dryden to Farquhar* (London: J. M. Dent, 1912), 55, 57.
183	Jessie L. Weston, *From Ritual to Romance* (Cambridge: Cambridge University Press, 1920), 96, 167.
184	*Facsimile*, 77.

Chapter 16 – *The Waste Land*

1	*L1*, 622.
2	Ibid.
3	Rémy de Gourmont, *The Natural Philosophy of Love*, tr. EP (New York: Boni and Liveright, 1922), 156.
4	*L1*, 631.
5	TSE, 'London Letter', *Dial*, 72.5 (May 1922), 513.
6	EP, *The Selected Letters of Ezra Pound to John Quinn 1915–1924* (Durham, NC: Duke University Press, 1921), 206.
7	See Lawrence Rainey, *Revisiting 'The Waste Land'* (New Haven and London: Yale University Press, 2005), 76.
8	EP, *Ezra Pound to his Parents: Letters 1895–1929*, ed. Mary de Rachewiltz, A. David Moody and Joanna Moody (Oxford: Oxford University Press, 2010), 493.
9	EP, *Selected Letters of Ezra Pound to John Quinn*, 206.
10	EP, *Pound/The Little Review: The Letters of Ezra Pound to Margaret Anderson* (London: Faber and Faber, 1988), 266, 270; *L1*, 606.
11	Jean Cocteau, 'The Cape of Good Hope', tr. Jean Hugo, *Little Review*, 8.1 (Autumn 1921), 51, 57.
12	Ibid.
13	*CPP*, 61.
14	*L1*, 623.
15	*L1*, 625; *Facsimile*, 101.
16	*L1*, 626.
17	*L1*, 629; *CPP*, 59.
18	EP, 'Translator's Postscript', in de Gourmont, *The Natural Philosophy of Love*, 206.
19	*L1*, 630.
20	*L1*, 630, 631.
21	*L1*, 626.
22	*CPP*, 124.
23	*L1*, 629.
24	*L1*, 632.
25	TSE, 'The Three Provincialities', *Tyro*, 2 ([Spring 1922]), 12, 13.
26	TSE, 'London Letter' (May 1922), 510, 512, 513.
27	*L1*, 640.
28	Katherine Mansfield, *The Collected Letters of Katherine Mansfield, Volume V: 1922–1923*, ed. Vincent O'Sullivan and Margaret Scott (Oxford: Oxford University Press, 2008), 75.
29	Jeremy Hutchinson to the present writer, 10 November 2013.
30	*Facsimile*, 3; *CPP*, 59.
31	*L1*, 655.

32 *L1*, 654.

33 EP, *Selected Letters of Ezra Pound 1907–1941*, ed. D. D. Paige (London: Faber and Faber, 1982), 172.

34 Ibid., 172, 173.

35 *L1*, 649.

36 Virginia Woolf, *The Diary of Virginia Woolf, Vol. 2, 1920–24*, ed. Anne Olivier Bell and Andrew McNeillie ((Harmondsworth: Penguin, 1981), 170, 171.

37 Jeffrey Meyers, 'T. S. Eliot's Green Face Powder: A Mystery Solved', *Yeats Eliot Review*, 28.3/4 (2011), 34.

38 *L1*, 652.

39 Virginia Woolf, *The Question of Things Happening: The Letters of Virginia Woolf, Volume II: 1912–1922*, ed. Nigel Nicolson (London: Hogarth Press, 1976), 521.

40 *L1*, 656.

41 *L1*, 657.

42 *L1*, 661.

43 Ibid.

44 *L1*, 658.

45 TSE, 'Ulysses, Order, and Myth', *Dial*, 75.5 (November 1923), 481 (quoting Aldington).

46 *L1*, 663.

47 *L1*, 664.

48 *L1*, 666.

49 *L1*, 667.

50 *Richard Aldington: An Autobiography in Letters*, ed. Norman T. Gates (Philadelphia: Penn State University Press, 1992), 67.

51 *L1*, 668.

52 *L1*, 701.

53 TSE, 'London Letter', *Dial*, 73.1 (July 1922), 96.

54 TSE, 'Answers to the Three Questions', *Chapbook*, 27 (July 1922), 8.

55 *L1*, 626.

56 *L1*, 674.

57 *L1*, 676.

58 *L1*, 675.

59 Herman Hesse, 'The Brothers Karamazov – The Downfall of Europe', tr. Stephen Hudson, *Dial*, 72.6 (June 1922), 607.

60 *L1*, 675.

61 *L1*, 687.

62 EP, *Selected Letters of Ezra Pound to John Quinn*, 210–11.

63 *L1*, 668, 678.

64 *L1*, 679.

65 *L1*, 714.

66 *L1*, 681.

67 *L1*, 680, 681.

68 *L1*, 680.

69 *L1*, 684.

70 *L1*, 685.

71 *L1*, 688.

72 Ibid.

73 EP, *Selected Letters of Ezra Pound*, 175.

74 Ibid.

75 *L1*, 688.

76 Woolf, *The Question of Things Happening*, 544.

77 Ibid., 548.

78 *L1*, 691.

79	*L1*, 699.
80	*L1*, 708.
81	*L1*, 745.
82	*L1*, 701, 702.
83	*L1*, 702.
84	*L1*, 706.
85	*L1*, 745.
86	Woolf, *The Diary of Virginia Woolf*, 2, 187.
87	*L1*, 708.
88	Ibid.
89	*L1*, 693, 709.
90	*L1*, 718; *L2*, 3.
91	*L1*, 710.
92	*L1*, 712.
93	*L1*, 750.
94	*L1*, 780; EP, *Ezra Pound to his Parents: Letters 1895–1929*, ed. Mary de Rachewiltz, A. David Moody and Joanna Moody (Oxford: Oxford University Press, 2010), 505.
95	*L1*, 742.
96	*L1*, 721.
97	John Peale Bishop to Edmund Wilson, 5 August 1922, quoted in Rainey, *Revisiting 'The Waste Land'*, 74.
98	*L1*, 723.
99	*L1*, 733.
100	*L1*, 743, 747.
101	*L1*, 748.
102	*L1*, 746.
103	*L1*, 756.
104	*L1*, 751.
105	*L1*, 768.
106	*L1*, 752, 754.
107	*L1*, 756.
108	*L1*, 758.
109	*L1*, 759.
110	*L1*, 613.
111	George Saintsbury, 'Dullness', *Criterion*, 1.1 (October 1922), 15.
112	F. M. Dostoevsky, 'Plan of a Novel, "The Life of a Great Sinner"', *Criterion*, 1.1 (October 1922), 16, 17, 19; Woolf, *The Diary of Virginia Woolf*, 2, 203.
113	Hermann Hesse, 'Recent German Poetry', *Criterion*, 1.1 (October 1922), 90; TSE, 'Ulysses, Order, and Myth', 483.
114	T. Sturge Moore, 'The Story of Tristram and Isolt in Modern Poetry', *Criterion*, 1.1 (October 1922), 49.
115	*L1*, 768, 765.
116	*Facsimile*, 11, 13, 127.
117	*L1*, 765.
118	*L1*, 788.
119	*CPP*, 62.
120	*L1*, 770.
121	*L1*, 775.
122	*L1*, 770, 771.
123	*L1*, 772.
124	*L1*, 776.
125	*L1*, 788.
126	*L1*, 789.
127	*L1*, 790.

128   *L1*, 794.
129   *L1*, 800.
130   *L1*, 801.
131   *L1*, 796.
132   *L1*, 816.
133   *L1*, 796.
134   See John Peale Bishop's letter to Edmund Wilson, 3 November 1922, quoted in Rainey, *Revisiting 'The Waste Land'*, 104.
135   *L1*, 798.
136   *L1*, 803.
137   *CPP*, 77.
138   *Facsimile*, 1.
139   Woolf, *The Diary of Virginia Woolf*, 2, 178.
140   Mary Hutchinson, 'T. S. Eliot', short, unpublished, undated biographical sketch in typescript, holograph emendation, in the possession of her son Jeremy Hutchinson (quoted with his permission).
141   *L2*, 124.

Index

T. S. Eliot is referred to as TSE throughout.

Abbey, Edward Austin 61
Abbott, Jacob 53, 56
Ackroyd, Peter 4, 357
Action Française, L' 153
Adams, Henry 12, 315
Adams, John 12
Adams, John Quincy 12
Aiken, Conrad: at Harvard with TSE 100,
    102–103, 115, 129, 131, 165, 169, 192; TSE
    confides in over sexual anxiety 150, 160,
    204, 208, 213; reads 'The Love Song of
    J. Alfred Prufrock' 165, 173; recognises
    TSE's poetic genius 184–5; advises TSE
    to visit Ezra Pound in London 207;
    interest in Freudian ideas 293, 326; TSE's
    disdain for 352; cancels holiday with
    TSE 353; reviews *The Sacred Wood* 364;
    recommends publisher for *The Waste
    Land* 403–404; poetry of 107, 184, 201,
    255, 327, 336, 360, 365, 371, 375
Alain-Fournier, Henri 146, 150–51, 153–4
Aldington, Richard: assistant editor at the
    Egoist magazine 235; serves in the Great
    War 275; admires TSE's editorial skills
    328–9; unimpressed by TSE's beard 334;
    war experience 342; on TSE 358; sends
    flowers to Vivien 377; TSE's friendship
    with 380, 381, 385–6, 388, 390; TSE
    shows *The Waste Land* to 404; and
    Pound's 'Bel Esprit' scheme 406, 411,
    413–14; on James Joyce's *Ulysses* 408;
    breach with TSE 415

Amory, Roger 77, 78
Anesaki, Masaharu 175
Armstrong, Martin 207
Arnison, George Wright 241
Arnold, Edwin, *The Light of Asia* 41
Arnold, Edwin Lester 283
Arnold, Matthew 363
Art and Letters (journal) 346, 353, 360
Athenaeum (journal) 308–309, 316, 318, 335,
    338, 346, 349, 350
Augustine, St 180, 365, 390

Babbitt, Irving 86, 130–31, 132, 168, 257
Bagnall, Effie 50
Baker, George Pierce 131
Bakewell, Charles Montague 176–7, 180
Balfour, Arthur 177
Ballets Russes 149, 322, 380, 408
Barrie, J. M. 51, 190, 195, 208
Baudelaire, Charles 46, 90, 108, 132, 133,
    372, 379, 407
Beach, Sylvia 408
Beerbohm, Max 208
Beethoven, Ludwig van 198
'Bel Esprit' (Ezra Pound's subscription
    scheme) 406, 407, 411, 413, 418, 421, 422
Bell, Clive 243, 267, 278, 284, 307, 323, 406,
    416
Bell, Vanessa 235, 267
Belvalkar, Shripad Krishna 169–70
Bennett, Arnold 273, 287, 304
Bergson, Henri 130, 145–6, 164, 166–7; TSE

attends his lectures in Paris 149–50, 154; TSE becomes sceptical about 177–8, 183; TSE lectures on 256

Betjeman, John 247

Blake, William 346–7

Blanshard, Percy 210, 211, 213–14

Blast (journal) 202, 207, 222, 234, 235, 237, 242

Blood, Charlotte (TSE's grandmother) 20

Blood, Thomas Heywood 33

Bloomsbury group 244, 253, 268, 306, 319, 326, 347–8, 350, 408

Blow, Susan E. 38

Boas, George 185

Bodenheim, Max 57, 352, 367

Bomberg, David 212

Boni and Liveright (publishers) 295, 349, 400, 401, 407, 412, 417, 418, 423

Bosham, West Sussex 253–5, 268–9, 281, 284, 303, 324, 334, 377, 415

Bosschère, Jean de 279, 301

Boston, Massachusetts 81, 93, 105–106, 109, 114, 124, 135, 138, 160, 166, 167, 179, 182, 185, 189–90, 194–9, 245, 300, 317, 329

Boynton, Percy H. 56

Bradley, F. H. 177, 218, 222, 294; *Appearance and Reality* 7, 214; *Essays on Truth and Reality* 214; TSE's PhD thesis on 220, 248

Brett, Dorothy 243, 247, 248

Briggs, LeBaron Russell 76, 82, 84, 114, 128

Brokmeyer, Henry C. 38

Brooks, Van Wyck 94, 107, 127–8, 134

Brooks, Winthrop Sprague, 'Nick' 95, 97

Browning, Elizabeth Barrett 248

Browning, Robert 69, 123, 137, 339

Buckle, Charles 227, 367–8

Buddha's Fire Sermon 170, 273, 336, 341, 390, 410

Buddhism 122, 174–5, 220, 410

Bulmer, John Legge 209, 211, 217

Burns, Robert 204

Butler-Thwing, Francis Wendell 210, 227

Byron, George Gordon, Lord 60, 71, 291

Cahiers de la Quinzaine, Les (journal) 151

Cambridge, England 3, 86, 222–3

Cambridge, Massachusetts 3, 76, 87–8, 93, 111, 117, 129, 135, 138, 166, 170, 188, 195, 199, 217, 316, 359; Social Dramatic Club 189–94

Cannan, Gilbert 243, 253, 298

Carrington, Dora 247, 248

Carroll, Caroline J. 166

Carroll, Lewis 43

Catholic Anthology (1915) 225, 277

Cawein, Madison 399

Channing, William Ellery 16

Chapbook (journal) 346, 409

Chase, George Henry 89, 115

Child, Harrison Bird 77, 155

Churchill, Winston (American writer) 55–6

Claudel, Paul 153

Clutton Brock, Arthur 245

Cobb, Richard 76, 79

Cobden-Sanderson, Richard 336, 403, 409, 413, 418

Cocteau, Jean 149, 373, 385, 401, 405

Colefax, Lady Sibyl 287

Collingwood, R. G. 215

Common Sense (newspaper) 294

Connolly, James B. 32

Conrad, Joseph 74, 301, 317, 347, 353, 378

Copeland, Charles Townsend 113, 114, 126–7

Cornford, F. M. 360, 361

Costello, Harry Todd 181, 185

Criterion (journal): proposal for 381–2; TSE commits to being editor 384; TSE solicits work for 405, 406; given name by Vivien Eliot 413, 415; TSE's anxiety over 414; first issue 416–20

Croonenbergh, Charles 37

Culpin, Karl 211, 213, 217, 258, 277, 341

Cummings, E. E. 184, 192, 350

Cunard, Lady Nancy 303, 305, 343

Curd, Charles P. 55–6, 60, 62, 63, 76

Cushing, Colonel Charles 33

Dada (art movement) 330, 372, 373, 401

Dale, Alan 144–5

Dana, Henry Wadsworth Longfellow 145–6

D'Annunzio, Gabriele 149, 204

Dante 38, 111, 118–19, 146–7, 151, 173

Davidson, John 105, 107

Davidson, Thomas 38

Davis, Hubert Henry 191

Dawes, Samuel 16

Day, Reverend John William 67–8

de la Mare, Walter 365

Debussy, Claude, *Le Martyre de Saint Sébastien* 148–9

Delacroix, Henri 178

Delsarte, François 52

Demos, Raphael 188, 294

Deussen, Paul Jakob 170

Dial (journal) 303, 346, 387, 398, 405, 414; TSE article 'The Possibility of a Poetic Drama' 352; TSE article 'The Second-Order Mind' 353; TSE article 'Ulysses, Order, and Myth' 408; TSE wins the magazine's $2,000 prize 423; TSE's 'London Letters' in 365–6, 372, 404, 409, 415; TSE's negotiations to publish *The Waste Land* in 402, 403–404, 408, 417

Dickens, Charles 20, 53, 54, 330, 387

Diels, Hermann Alexander 171–2

Dismorr, Jessica 212

Dodds, Eric 221

Dolmetsch, Arnold 221

Donne, John 75, 82–3, 325, 336, 340, 362, 386

Dostoevsky, Fyodor 153, 319, 409, 410, 419

Dowden, Edward 72–3

Dozier, Lewis 52

Drinkwater, John 382

Dryden, John 379, 399

Duchamp, Marcel 387

Dudley, Dorothy 235

Dudley, Helen 235

Duncan, Isadora 52

Dunne, Annie (TSE's nanny) 21, 24, 27, 28

Durkheim, Émile 147, 186, 188, 193

East Coker, Somerset 12

Egoist (journal) 207, 235, 281, 282, 285, 288, 293, 298, 301, 302, 306, 325, 329; TSE becomes assistant editor of 275; Pound publishes 'Drunken Helots and Mr Eliot' in 276; plan to publish Joyce's *Ulysses* in serial form 295, 327; special issue memorialising Henry James 290–91; publishes 'Tradition and the Individual Talent' 327, 330, 334; demise of 336

Egoist Press 275, 295, 323, 336, 338, 346

Elgar, Edward 68–9

Eliot, Abigail Adams (TSE's grandmother) 17

Eliot, Abigail (TSE's cousin) 16, 29, 354

Eliot, Ada (TSE's sister) 11, 64, 67, 82, 106

Eliot, Andrew (ancestor) 12

Eliot, Reverend Andrew (ancestor) 20

Eliot, Charles William (Harvard President) 6, 79, 305, 329

Eliot, Charlotte Champe, 'Lottie' (TSE's mother): death of daughter Theodora 12; birth of TSE 12; interests and education 13, 38; family background 20, 36, 74; poetry of 14–16; religious inclinations 14–16, 39; and TSE's childhood 28; writes biography of William Greenleaf Eliot 17; anxiety for TSE's health and social life 64, 75–6; and St Louis World's Fair (1904) 68; on TSE's education 79; reaction to TSE's marriage 238; wish for TSE to have an academic career 249, 250; visit to England 348, 378, 379–84

Eliot, Charlotte (TSE's sister) 11, 28, 52, 66

Eliot, Christopher Rhodes (TSE's uncle) 66, 67

Eliot, Etta (TSE's aunt) 38

Eliot, Frederick (TSE's cousin) 29, 40, 66, 106, 131

Eliot, George 298

Eliot, Henry (TSE's brother): and TSE's childhood 11, 19, 28; takes family photographs 24, 33; and *Student Life* magazine 42; taste for Tin Pan Alley 47; on family's conservatism 65; remembers TSE reading Milton as a child 69; at Harvard 79–80, 82; partial deafness due to childhood illness 138; announces TSE's marriage to the St Louis press 234; sympathetic to TSE over marriage 234–5; TSE's correspondence with 246, 314, 324, 348, 359, 388, 396, 398; financial support for TSE 255, 259, 304, 318; sends family photographs to TSE 289; visit to England 379–80, 382–4, 419; on Garsington 382–3; on Vivien's ill-health 383; congratulates TSE on *The Waste Land* 423

Eliot, Henry Ware, 'Hal' (TSE's father): family background 12; literary and artistic background 13–14; brick company 14, 37; pride in his ancestry

16–17; house in Gloucester, Massachusetts 33; interest in natural science 34; attitude to sex education 65; and St Louis World's Fair (1904) 68; and TSE's education 83; Ezra Pound writes to regarding TSE's career 233–4; reaction to TSE's marriage 233–4, 238; concern for TSE after marriage 242; dislike of TSE's move to England 255; financial support of TSE 259, 263, 296, 310–11; helps TSE try to enrol for military service 304–305; dislike of Vivien 311; pride in TSE 311; death 312

Eliot, Margaret (TSE's sister) 11

Eliot, Marion (TSE's sister) 11, 33, 195, 379

Eliot, Martha (TSE's cousin) 29

Eliot, Mary (TSE's aunt) 66

Eliot, Samuel A. 190

Eliot, Theodora (TSE's niece): *see* Smith, Theodora Eliot

Eliot, Thomas Lamb (TSE's uncle) 12, 14, 40, 74

Eliot, Thomas Stearns:

Childhood and education: birth and immediate family 11–12; family background 12–18, 20–21, 33–4; family home 17–20, 23; plays in the girls' school playground 18–19; relationships with girls 29, 50–51; relationships with other children 23, 29; experiences cyclone in St Louis 25–7; attends Mrs Lockwood's school 27–8; summers in Gloucester, Massachusetts 28–34; sense of American history 16–17, 33–4; early literary tastes 6, 37, 52–4, 60–63, 69–75; attends Smith Academy 42, 53–8, 59–62, 65, 71–3; 'becomes' T. S. Eliot 42; produces *Fireside* (first surviving literary work) 42–50, 53, 54, 57, 63; earliest surviving verses 43; interest in actresses 49–50; attends Jacob Mahler's Dancing Academy 51–2; writes *George Washington, A Life* 54; visits Camp Maple Hill, Quebec 66–7; published in the *Smith Academy Record* 71–5; attends Milton Academy, Massachusetts 75–8; arrival at Harvard 79–83; academic study at

Harvard 82–91, 115–21, 126–34, 136–8, 168–81; poor academic performance at Harvard 83–4, 90–91; takes up rowing 84; Harvard friendships 84–5, 91–3, 95–7, 102–3, 105, 107, 110–11; membership of the Digamma/Fox Club at Harvard 93–7; 'Columbo' and 'Bolo' poems 95–100; body-building at Harvard 99–100; published in the *Harvard Advocate* 101–104, 111–12, 115, 123, 136; parodied in the *Harvard Lampoon* 102; reads Arthur Symons' *The Symbolist Movement in Literature* 107–10; first reads Laforgue 109–10; interest in French literature at Harvard 108–10, 122–6, 134–5; is invited to join the Signet Society 112–14; election to the Stylus club 114; influence of Irving Babbitt 130–31; hospitalised with scarlet fever 138; recites graduation 'Ode' 138–9; graduates from Harvard 138–9; sails round Mount Desert Rock, Gloucester, Massachusetts 140–44; brief visit to London (1910) 145; year abroad in Paris (1910–11) 144–57; encounters Cubism and Futurism in Paris 146; friendship with Jean Verdenal 154–7; travels in France (1910–11) 157; visit to London (1911) 157–8; completes 'The Love Song of J. Alfred Prufrock' in Munich (1911) 159–63; visits Italy (1911) 163–4; returns to Harvard for doctoral study 165; interest in Buddhism and Eastern thought 168–71, 174–6, 181; studies Sanskrit, Pali and Indic Philology at Harvard 168–71, 174–5; attends lectures by Masaharu Anesaki at Harvard 175–6; attends lectures by Rabindranath Tagore at Harvard 181; paper to the Philosophy Club on Walter Lippmann's *A Preface to Politics* 181–3; President of the Harvard Philosophical Club 185; appointed Sheldon Fellow in Philosophy at Harvard 185–6; paper on the science of religion (1913) 186–8; meets

Bertrand Russell at Harvard 188–9; acts with the Cambridge Social Dramatic Club 189–93; relationship with Emily Hale 194–200

Residence in England: curtailed visit to Germany (1914) 202–206; arrives in England from Germany (1914) 206–208; meets Bertrand Russell in London 207; meets Ezra Pound in London 207–208; goes up to Merton College, Oxford 208–11; spends Christmas 1914 in London 212–13; visits Swanage, Dorset (1914) 213–14; fails to meet F. H. Bradley at Merton College 214; studies philosophy with Harold Joachim 214–16; takes up rowing at Oxford 217; doctoral thesis on F. H. Bradley 220, 248–9, 250; reads 'The Love Song of J. Alfred Prufrock' to the 'Coterie' (Oxford poetry-reading group) 221; gives talk to 'Heretics' in Cambridge, England 222–3; meets Wyndham Lewis 221–2; first publication of his poems in a book (*Catholic Anthology*, 1915) 224–5; meets Vivien Haigh-Wood 225–6; resigns from teaching post at Harvard 230; marries Vivien Haigh-Wood 230–31; uses the name Stearns-Eliot 232–3; literary and artistic introductions by Ezra Pound 235; adjusts to married life 236; takes on teaching post at Royal Grammar School, High Wycombe 237; visits America after his marriage 237–9; 'honeymoon' in Eastbourne 239, 240; dependency on Bertrand Russell 240–41, 242, 245, 254; teaching post at Royal Grammar School, High Wycombe 241–2; mixes with the Bloomsbury set 244, 267–8, 309–10; teaching post at Highgate Junior School 245, 247, 258; meets Lady Ottoline Morrell 247–8; cancels visit to America for his doctoral presentation 249–50; moves into flat in Crawford Mansions 250; visits Garsington 249–50; publishes articles in the *Monist* 251; review writing

240, 242, 246, 251–2, 255, 348–50; rents house in Bosham, West Sussex 253–4; takes on evening lecturing posts 256–7; publishes *Prufrock and Other Observations* 261, 265, 275, 276, 277–8, 283; difficulties in his relationship with Vivien 262–3; rents Senhurst Farm jointly with Bertrand Russell 281, 285; friendship with Ezra Pound 264, 416; relationship with Mary Hutchinson 267–70, 327–8; takes position at Lloyds Bank, London 270–71; becomes assistant editor at the *Egoist* 275; writes poetry in French 279; writes booklet on Ezra Pound's poetry 282–3; rents house in Marlow jointly with Bertrand Russell 287; tries to enrol for military service 290, 303–305; visits Bertrand Russell in prison 294; edits Pound's poetry 295; relationship with Vivien 298–9, 336–7, 347, 354–7, 377, 383, 400, 407–408; meets Virginia Woolf 307; death of father 312–13; physical collapse and begins writing 'Gerontion' 314; owns a dog 317, 334; publishes *Poems* with the Hogarth Press (1919) 319; holiday in France with Ezra Pound (1919) 332–4; grows a beard 334; *Ara Vos Prec* published by John Rodker (1920) 337; subscribes to the London Library 339; visits Paris with Vivien (1920) 348; rivalry with Ezra Pound 349; visits France with Wyndham Lewis 354–5; meets James Joyce in Paris 354–5, 400; moves to flat in Clarence Gate Gardens 364; relationship with Virginia Woolf 319, 357–8, 368, 370–71, 406; uses pen-name 'Gus Krutzsch' 371; begins composition of *The Waste Land* 373–5; visit of his mother, brother and sister to England 379–84; sees Stravinsky's *Rite of Spring* 380–81; approached to be editor of *Criterion* 381–2, 384; sees a nerve specialist 388; takes break in Margate for his health 389–90; writes rough draft of Part III of *The Waste Land* in

Margate 390; travels to Lausanne for
treatment with Dr Vittoz 391–6;
continues composition of *The Waste
Land* in Lausanne 395–9; completes
The Waste Land and dedicates it to
Ezra Pound 401–403; moves to
Wigmore Street 405; reported to use
violet powder on his skin 406–407;
takes break in Royal Tunbridge Wells
for his health 408; treated to vacation
in Lugano, Switzerland by father-
in-law 409–11; accused of profiting
unfairly from 'Bel Esprit' scheme
422; awarded *Dial*'s $2,000 prize 423;
reads *The Waste Land* to Virginia
Woolf 423
Character and characteristics: anxiety about
masculinity 45, 98–100; anxiety
about sexuality 152, 204, 212–13, 224,
280–81; appearance 45, 102, 210, 222,
357–8; childhood anxieties about the
body 46, 57; critical judgements of
others 318; editorial astuteness 295,
308; interest in natural science 34–5;
interest in ragtime and music hall 2,
21–2, 47, 105–106, 298, 410; language
proficiency 172, 271, 303, 344; love of
childish jokes 1–2; musical tastes
198–9; nostalgia for America 289,
296, 302, 309; plays chess 34, 169,
255, 321; punctiliousness 358; self-
consciousness about ears 2, 45, 51;
sexual gaucheness 2, 3, 82, 154, 160;
sexuality 326–7; shyness 20, 57, 78,
81, 85, 98, 102, 192, 210, 214; speaking
voice/speech 168, 296–7, 307
Health: assessed for military service
303–4; breathing and nasal problems
342–3; headaches and sciatica 309–10;
hernia and wearing of a truss 8,
23–4, 64, 285, 356; links between
illness and creativity 159, 314, 376,
384, 402; lung problems 37–8; minor
ailments 276, 328, 351, 402; mother's
anxiety for 75; 'nervous sexual
attacks' 162, 223, 234; nervous strain
288–9; neuralgia 416; 'neurasthenic'
388–9; operation on his nose 359;
rheumatism 281; scarlet fever 138;

suffers from 'cerebral anaemia' in
Munich 159; treatment by Dr Vittoz
for nervous problems 380–84; weight
loss 300
Literary influences: Aiken, Conrad 381,
385; Andrewes, Lancelot 315, 336;
Aristophanes 86, 89; Arthurian myths
and the Grail quest 53, 61, 71, 118,
282, 351, 399; Augustine, St 180;
Baudelaire, Charles 108, 372;
Bhagavad Gita 169; Browning, Robert
69, 123; Burns, Robert 204; Byron,
George Gordon, Lord 60, 71;
Carroll, Lewis 43; Cocteau, Jean 383;
Conan Doyle, Arthur 37; Conrad,
Joseph 74; Dante 111, 118–19, 156–7,
161, 183–4, 362; Davidson, John 107;
Dickens, Charles 387; Donne, John
82–3, 325, 336, 340; Dryden, John
399; Fitzgerald, Edward 69–71;
French Symbolists 107–109, 135;
Gautier, Théophile 280; Goldsmith,
Oliver 54, 190; Gourmont, Rémy de
364; Hawthorne, Nathaniel 28–9;
Heraclitus 171–2; *The Ingoldsby
Legends* 71–2; James, Henry 129, 134,
135; Jonson, Ben 74, 342; Joyce,
James 385–6; Keats, John 75;
Khayyám, Omar 69, 70; Kipling,
Rudyard 31, 61, 63, 73, 127; Kyd,
Thomas 398; La Rochefoucauld,
François de 60; Laforgue, Jules 7,
109–10, 122–6, 135, 136, 152, 266, 325,
385; Lear, Edward 44, 74;
Longfellow, Henry Wadsworth 54;
Lowell, James Russell 61; Mallarmé,
Stéphane 362; Malory, Sir Thomas
61; Marvell, Andrew 368, 373;
Maurras, Charles 153; Milton, John
69; Nerval, Gérard de 108–99; Ovid
62; Petronius 120–21; Philippe,
Charles-Louis 151–2; Poe, Edgar
Allan 45–6, 60; Pope, Alexander 60,
373; Pound, Ezra 371; Reid, Mayne
53; Renaissance drama 53–4, 82, 99,
126, 131, 330, 361–2, 398; Rossetti,
Dante Gabriel 71; Shakespeare,
William 60, 62, 103, 374, 375, 388;
Shelley, Percy Bysshe 72–3, 347;

Spenser, Edmund 63, 367–8; Stendhal
320; Stevenson, Robert Louis 61, 73;
Stoker, Bram 169; Swinburne,
Algernon Charles 103; Tennyson,
Alfred, Lord 61, 103; *Upanishads* 170,
397; Verlaine, Paul 135; Virgil 62;
Wagner, Richard 373; Webster, John
263; Xenophon 62
Religious influences: early reading about
non-Christian religion 41; fascination
with martyrdom 26, 147, 158–9, 183,
213–14; interest in Buddhism and
Eastern thought 168–71, 174–6, 220;
interest in Catholicism 24, 292;
interest in mysticism 178, 220;
Puritan family influence 18; religious
anxiety 333; and scepticism 177,
256–7; Unitarian background 12, 17,
24, 38–41, 68, 221
Views and comments: on academic life 217;
admiration for Ezra Pound's poetry
338–9; anti-Semitism 4, 8, 57–8, 163,
284, 297, 315, 352; on being
American in England 324, 367; on
Bertrand Russell 294; on Browning
69, 137; on the composition of
poetry 386–7; on Cubism 387; on
difficulty in poetry 386; on the
English 274; on English literary life
367; on English women 224, 226;
francophilia 42, 50, 111, 131, 132, 133,
134–5; on Henry James 291–2; on his
early commitment to poetry 73; on
his literary success 317, 320–21; on his
marriage 262; on his New England
ancestry 128; on his responsibility
towards Vivien 421; on his sense of
displacement 9; on the influence of
his grandfather 17–18; on James
Joyce's *Ulysses* 387; on Katherine
Mansfield 421; on marriage 236, 252;
on national cultural identity 319–20;
and Norbert Wiener's 'Relativism'
218–20, 222; on Paris 144; on
studying Indian philosophy 174; on
Virginia Woolf 387; on war 207; on
writing *The Waste Land* 398
Poetic works: see separate entries for 'The
Love Song of J. Alfred Prufrock' and

The Waste Land; 'Ballade pour la
grosse Lulu' (1911) 161, 165, 222; 'The
Boston Evening Transcript' 225, 308;
'Burbank with a Baedeker: Bleistein
with a Cigar' 163, 301; 'The
Confidential Clerk' 261;
'Conversation Galante' 134–5, 255; 'A
Cooking Egg' 280; 'Dans le
Restaurant' 280, 283; 'The Death of
Saint Narcissus' 223–4; 'The Death
of the Duchess' 262–3, 371; 'Eeldrop
and Appleplex' (short story) 263;
'Entretien dans un parc' 165; *Four
Quartets* 139, 172; 'Gerontion' 69,
219–320, 236, 261, 302, 314–15, 321,
324, 332, 333, 336, 340; 'The
Hippopotamus' 280, 287–8, 292, 308;
'The Hollow Men' 191; 'Hysteria'
293; 'Interlude in London' (1911) 157;
'La Figlia Che Piange' 255; 'Le
Spectateur' (later retitled 'Le
Directeur') 308; 'The Love Song of
St Sebastian' 203–5; 'Lune de Miel'
279, 308; 'Marina' 32, 143–4;
'Mélange Adultère de Tout' 266–7,
270, 308; 'Morning at the Window'
206, 255; 'Mr Apollinax' 190, 216,
255, 260; 'Mr Eliot's Sunday
Morning Service' 297, 308; *Murder in
the Cathedral* 272; 'Nocturne' (1909)
136; 'Ode on Independence Day, July
4th 1918' 232, 298, 302; 'Opera' (1909)
136; 'Petit Epître' 280–81, 374;
'Portrait of a Lady' 166; 'Preludes'
152, 222; 'Reflections on *Vers Libre*'
(essay) 264–6; 'Rhapsody on a Windy
Night' 125, 152, 222; 'Song to the
Opherian' 371; 'Spleen' 136;
'Suppressed Complex' 224, 293;
'Sweeney Agonistes' 45, 57, 69, 74,
87, 89, 361, 372, 403; 'Sweeney
Among the Nightingales' 297, 301,
308; 'Sweeney Erect' 297; 'Tristan
Corbière' 282; 'The Triumph of
Bullshit' 222; 'Whispers of
Immortality' 280, 308
*Prose works: Ezra Pound: His Metric and
Poetry* (1918) 282–3, 349; 'The Lesson
of Baudelaire' 372; 'London Letters'

(written for *Dial* magazine) 372, 385,
404, 409, 415; *The Sacred Wood* 183,
323, 331, 351, 353, 359, 364, 368, 407;
Selected Essays (1932) 275; 'Tradition
and the Individual Talent' 147, 293,
309, 327, 330–32, 334, 338, 340, 341,
344; 'Ulysses, Order, and Myth' 408
Eliot, Valerie (*née* Fletcher) 1, 3–5, 200
Eliot, Vivien (*née* Haigh-Wood):
characteristics and background 225–6,
270, 284, 415–16; engagement with
Charles Buckle 227; relationship with
Scofield Thayer 227–30, 244–5, 250,
278, 283–4, 389, 391; meets TSE 225;
marries TSE 230; belief in TSE's
literary genius 230–31, 368, 415;
persuades TSE to stay in England
238–9; 'honeymoon' in Eastbourne
240; relationship with Bertrand
Russell 237, 239–40, 244, 244–5, 249,
258, 259, 260–62, 285–7, 313, 321,
411; takes dance lessons 244, 347;
fears for TSE joining up 275–6, 304;
corresponds with TSE's mother 286,
288, 296; attempts career as an actress
296; spends time in a nursing home
369–70; unwillingness to travel to
America 247–8, 309, 404; and *The
Waste Land* 374, 402, 420; meets
TSE's mother 380; makes
appointment for TSE with nerve
specialist 388; proposes name for
Criterion 413; Aldous Huxley on 279,
300; Bertrand Russell on 236–7; Lady
Ottoline Morrell on 245–7, 253–4;
Virginia Woolf on 319
Ill-health: childhood tuberculosis 252,
411; colitis 411–12, 416; dental work
300, 309; doctors unable to diagnose
411; exhaustion, insomnia, mental
strain 412–13; eye problems 300, 416;
falls ill immediately after marriage
232; fever 407–9; laryngitis 271;
manipulative use of 229, 239, 420;
migraines 328, 337; mood swings as a
girl 227; nervous complaints 313, 334,
355–6, 391; neuralgia 253, 416;
physically undeveloped 252;
rheumatism 253; treatments for 407,
411–12, 416, 422–3; TSE blames
himself for 411, 420; TSE's mother
gives advice on 264; Aldous Huxley
on 300; Henry Eliot on 383
Eliot, William Greenleaf (TSE's grandfather)
13, 14, 17–18, 39, 40–41, 68
Elkin Matthews (publisher) 275
Ellmann, Richard 4
Ellwood, Charles Abraham 212
Emerson, Ralph Waldo 8, 15–16, 38, 68
English Review (journal) 235, 276
Epstein, Jacob 224
Epstein, Jean, *La Poésie d'aujourd'hui* 385–6,
394
Etchells, Frederick 212
Eucken, Rudolf Christoph 203

Fabian Society 38
Fauchois, René 153
Finck, Hermann 158
Fitzgerald, Edward, *Rubáiyát of Omar
Khayyám* 69–71
Flaubert, Gustave 134
Fletcher, Graham Bruce 1
Fletcher, John Gould 235
Flint, F. S. 235
Fokine, Mikhail 149
Forbes, Edward Waldo 136, 146
Ford, Ford Madox (Ford Hermann Hueffer)
235
France, Anatole 147
Franke, Kuno 69–70
Frazer, J. G. 118, 331, 422; *The Golden Bough*
187–8, 215, 351, 386
Freud, Sigmund 293
Frost, Robert 414
Fry, Roger 145, 253, 273, 306, 319, 426
Fuller, Benjamin Apthorpe 156, 189

Gardner, Isabella Stewart 114, 145, 236
Garsington, Oxfordshire 242–3, 278, 293,
321, 328, 344, 353, 382, 411
Gaudier-Brzeska, Henri 224
George V, King of England 310–11
Gertler, Mark 243, 248, 284, 353
Gide, André 153, 401
Gilbert, Charles 80, 93
Gloucester, Massachusetts 6, 24, 28–34, 134,
140, 143, 238, 273, 278, 302

Goethe, Johann Wolfgang von 203
Gold, Matthew 396
Goldsmith, Oliver 54, 190
Goossens, Eugene 380
Gordon, Lyndall 4, 262
Gosse, Sir Edmund 287
Gourmont, Rémy de 332, 341, 362, 364
Gozzaldi, Amy de 189–90, 192–3, 194, 213,
    217
Grant, Duncan 343
Graves, Robert 287
Griffin, Nicholas 260

Haigh-Wood, Charles 227, 271, 275, 363–4,
    367, 409, 410
Haigh-Wood, Maurice 227, 228, 232, 236,
    268, 278, 365; war experiences 256, 277
Haigh-Wood, Vivien: see Eliot, Vivien (née
    Haigh-Wood)
Hale, Edward Everett 190
Hale, Emily: background and upbringing
    189–90; in the Cambridge Social
    Dramatic Club 192; TSE falls in love
    with 8, 193–200; writes to TSE 210; TSE
    sends roses to 213, 347; TSE still in love
    with when he marries Vivien 255; TSE
    asks Eleanor Hinkley for news of 254–5;
    TSE writes to 322
Hall, Dick 192
Hallowell, Robert Canby 124
Happich family 202, 205
Hargrove, Nancy 148
Harris, W. T. 38
Harvard University 79–82, 86–9; Fogg
    Museum 136; Harvard faculty 86,
    115–16; Harvard Union 88–9
Hatch, Roger Conant 56, 60, 74
Hawthorne, Nathaniel 12, 28–9, 42, 300
H. D. (Hilda Doolittle) 235, 275, 385, 390
Held, Anna 50
Heraclitus 171–2, 188
Herbert, George 115
Hesse, Hermann 405, 410, 413, 420
Hinkley, Barbara 29
Hinkley, Eleanor (TSE's cousin): summers
    in Gloucester, Massachusetts with TSE
    29; neighbour of TSE in Cambridge,
    Massachusetts 82, 166, 189–90; interest in
    drama 131, 190, 192, 195–6; introduces

TSE to Emily Hale 194; TSE's
    correspondence with 157–8, 202, 208,
    209, 211, 212, 217, 221, 223, 224, 226, 254,
    280, 322
Hocking, William Ernest 185
Hoernlé, R. F. A. 185, 250, 314
Hogarth Press 306, 319, 406, 424
Holt, Edwin B. 293
Homer, Winslow 30
Horne, Edward Hastings 242–3
Horne, John Van 169
Hosmer, James Kendall 38
Howarth, Herbert 120
Hueffer, Ford Hermann: see Ford, Ford
    Madox
Hugo, Jean 401
Hulme, T. E. 228, 256, 277
Hume, David 150, 177
Huneker, James 133–6
Hunt, Edward Eyre 104, 114, 131, 138
Huntington, E. V. 179
Husserl, Edmund 203
Hutchinson, Barbara 268, 359
Hutchinson, Jack 267, 270, 304, 305
Hutchinson, Jeremy 268, 359
Hutchinson, Mary: at Bosham, West Sussex
    253, 324, 334; relationship with Clive Bell
    267–8, 284; relationship with TSE 9,
    267–70, 316, 319, 322, 323, 327–8, 330, 359,
    369, 391, 395, 405, 406, 412; admires
    Prufrock and Other Observations 278;
    friendship with Vivien Eliot 284, 285, 287,
    288, 354, 358, 364, 367, 407; TSE publishes
    short story by 284, 374; supplies TSE's
    address to Virginia Woolf 307; sexuality
    326; on TSE 405; and Ezra Pound's 'Bel
    Esprit' scheme 414; on *The Waste Land* 424
Huxley, Aldous 221, 243, 278, 284, 312, 350,
    353, 357; on Vivien Eliot 279, 300
Huxley, Julian 243, 389, 392–3
Huxley, Juliette 243
Huysmans, Joris-Karl 133–4, 222

Imagism 235, 282, 307
Inge, W. R. 178
International Journal of Ethics 240, 242, 251

James, Henry 29, 61, 129, 134, 290–92, 296,
    300, 301, 331

James, William 38, 86, 113, 150, 172, 178, 220
Janet, Pierre 148, 152, 220, 392
Jepson, Edgar 276, 359
Jerome, Jerome K. 299
Joachim, Harold 177, 214–16, 223, 228
Johnston, J. A. H. 247
Jones, David 43
Jones, Jane 50
Jones, Stephen 20–21, 47
Jonson, Ben 74, 99, 131, 342
Joplin, Scott 22
Jourdain, Philip 250–51
Journal of Speculative Philosophy 38
Joyce, James 172, 267, 276, 292; TSE's
    admiration for 301, 307, 309, 339, 408;
    meets TSE in Paris 354–5, 375; TSE on
    376; *A Portrait of the Artist as a Young
    Man* 207, 275, 295; *Ulysses* 10, 295, 301,
    327, 338, 375–6, 387, 400, 408
Julius, Anthony 4

Kant, Immanuel 176–7
Kaufmann, Julia Juvet 62
Keith, Elmer 166
Kelly, E. H. 247
Keynes, John Maynard 342, 344–5
King, Henry 46
King, Willie 303
Kingsley, Charles 42
Kipling, Rudyard 31, 56, 61, 63, 73, 127, 229
Kite, Thomas Brown 169
Kittredge, George Lyman 113
Knopf, Alfred A. (publisher): publishes
    TSE's booklet on Ezra Pound 282; turns
    down *Prufrock and Other Observations* 283;
    turns down book of prose criticism 306,
    313; publishes *Poems* (1920) 336, 340, 341,
    350; publishes *The Sacred Wood* 364, 368;
    turns down opportunity to publish *The
    Waste Land* 407, 409–10
Kyd, Thomas, *The Spanish Tragedy* 398

La Rochefoucauld, François de 60
La Rose, Pierre 114, 129
Laforgue, Jules 6, 7, 108, 109–10, 122–6, 152,
    157
Lake, Frederick Clinton 60, 75
Lambert, Gerard 59
Langfeld, Herbert Sidney 173

Lanman, Charles Rockwell 115, 168, 170,
    309
Larbaud, Valéry 405, 418, 420
Larisch, Marie 162
Lawrence, D. H. 64–5, 222, 243
Lear, Edward 44
Léautaud, Paul, *Poètes d'Aujourd'hui* 122, 133
Lesourd, Homer W. 77
Lévy-Bruhl, Lucien 147–8, 186
Lewis, Wyndham: and *Blast* magazine 207;
    first impression of TSE 221–2;
    unwillingness to publish 'offensive'
    material 222; exhibits in the Second
    London Group Exhibition (1915) 224;
    TSE socialises with in London 235, 315;
    planned New York Vorticist exhibition
    249; serves in the First World War 256;
    sexually explicit story published in the
    Little Review 293, 295; TSE's admiration
    for 301–302, 307, 417; TSE arranges
    contribution to the *Athenaeum* 346; and
    Tyro magazine 353, 367; meets James
    Joyce in Paris with TSE 354; holidays in
    France with TSE 354–5; TSE's friendship
    with 355, 359–60; TSE shows *The Waste
    Land* to 371
Lionberger, Isaac H. 50
Lionberger, Margaret 50
Lippi, Fillippo 136–7
Lippman, Walter 181, 182–3
Literary World (journal) 276
Little, Clarence 142
Little, Leon Magaw 85, 93–4, 97, 141–2
Little Review (Chicago journal) 263, 267, 293,
    295, 301, 327, 375, 401
Liveright, Horace 400–401, 407, 410, 412
Liverpool Daily Post and Mercury 422
Lloyd, Marie 158, 400
Lloyd George, David 337
Lockwood, Ellen Dean 27–8
Loeb, James 89
Loisy, Alfred 149
London Library 339
Long, Haniel 104, 111, 112, 114, 131, 134, 135
Longfellow, Henry Wadsworth 40, 48, 54
Loti, Pierre 194
'Love Song of J. Alfred Prufrock, The':
    TSE completes while in Munich
    (1911) 159–62; TSE shows to Conrad

Aiken 165, 173; TSE reads aloud to the 'Coterie' (Oxford poetry reading group) 221; published in *Poetry* magazine (1915) 233, 234; published in *Prufrock and Other Observations* 261, 275, 275–6; read aloud by Katherine Mansfield 278;

Themes and influences: anxieties about masculinity 7, 99–100; Arthur Symons and Laforgue 110; Charles-Louis Philippe's *Bubu de Montparnasse* 151; criticism of James Huneker 133; fog imagery in 37; influence of Laforgue 124–5; *The Ingoldsby Legends* 72; 'Interlude in London' 157; Jean Verdenal 156; name taken from St Louis Prufrock Furniture Co. 44; Oscar Wilde's *Salomé* 89; 'Pervigilium Veneris' 120; poetic form 69, 265–6; Seeger's translation of Dante's *Inferno* 111; sense of age 1; title anticipated by Longfellow's 'The Courtship of Miles Standish' 54; TSE's study of Italian art 137, 207–8

Lovejoy, A. O. 68
Lowell, Abbott Lawrence 83
Lowell, Amy 201, 292, 385, 408
Lowell, James Russell 12, 61
Lugano, Switzerland 409, 410
Lynd, Robert 320, 364

MacAvity, Ronald A. 77
MacCarthy, Molly 247, 248
MacDiarmid, Hugh 172
Mackenzie, Compton 244
MacVeagh, Rogers 114, 131
Mahler, Jacob 51–2
Mallarmé, Stéphane 109, 248
Malleson, Lady Constance 258, 260, 284, 287, 293–4
Malleson, Miles 284
Malory, Sir Thomas, *Morte d'Arthur* 61
'Mama Lou' (Letitia Lula Agatha Fontaine) 22
Man Ray 387
Manchester Guardian 251
Manning, Frederic 375
Mansfield, Katherine 306, 315, 319; reads 'The Love Song of J. Alfred Prufrock' aloud at Garsington 278; ill-health 316,

335; on TSE 358, 369–70, 388, 404–5; dislike of Vivien 350; Vivien's dislike for 370; TSE criticises to Ezra Pound 421
Marburg, Germany 202–203
Marc, Franz 161
Marsden, Dora 275, 327
Marvell, Andrew 373
Massine, Léonide 408, 412
Matisse, Henri 145
Matthews, Steven 46
Matthews, T. S. 92
Maurras, Charles 153, 154
McAlmon, Robert 375
McCarthy, Desmond 253, 308
McKittrick, Thomas ('Tom Kick') 18, 19, 27, 56
McLennan, John Ferguson 118
McVeagh, Lincoln 346
Melville, Henry 12
Merrick, Leonard 194–5
Merton College, Oxford 208–99
Methuen, Sir Algernon 323, 346, 359
Meyerstein, E. H. W. 221
Miller, James E. 4
Milton, John, *Samson Agonistes* 69
Milton Academy, Massachusetts 75–8
Moffatt, Adeleine 166, 212
Monist (journal) 251
Monk, Ray 244, 260
Monro, Harold 207, 346
Monroe, Harriet 201, 207, 208, 233
Montmorand, Maxime Bernier de 148
Moore, Clifford Herschel 220
Moore, Marianne 301
Moore, T. Sturge 419
More, Paul Elmer 89, 257
Morgenstern, John 118
Morrell, Lady Ottoline 236, 244, 266, 279, 293, 328, 345, 408, 411; TSE meets in London 247; depicted by D. H. Lawrence in *Women in Love* 243, 380; encourages publication of TSE's poetry 255; and Garsington 242–3; Henry Eliot on 382–3; and plans to raise an Eliot Fellowship Fund 414; recommends Dr Vittoz to TSE 389, 392; on TSE 249–50; and Vivien Eliot 240, 253–4, 321–2, 353
Morrell, Philip 242–3, 247
Morris, Howard 77, 80, 91–3, 140, 419

Moses, Josiah 179
Münsterberg, Hugo 113, 172–3
Murisier, Ernest 178
Murray, Gilbert 86–7, 117, 360
Murry, John Middleton 315, 319, 346, 351,
    404, 418, 419; appointed editor of the
    Athenaeum 316; arranges reviews of TSE's
    work 350; asks TSE to review his own
    play in the *Athenaeum* 349–50;
    commissions work from TSE in the
    Athenaeum 318, 335; falls out with TSE
    370, 378, 406; receives copy of *Prufrock
    and Other Observations* 278; reviews *The
    Sacred Wood* 364
Myers, L. H. 299

Nation (journal) 306
Neilson, William Allan 129–30
Nerval, Gérard de 108–9
New Statesman (journal) 251, 255, 264
New York Tribune 424
Newman, John Henry 68–9, 370
Norris, Frank 291
Nouvelle Revue Française 150–51, 153, 165,
    167, 365, 401, 404

Ohler, William Richard 138–9
Omega Club 273
Oxford, England 208–59

Palgrave, Francis Turner, *Golden Treasury*
    62–3
Palmer, Ella M. 166
Palmer, George Herbert 61, 115–17, 138, 171,
    314
Paris, France 146–7
Parker, Charles Pomeroy 89
Parker, George 80
Patanjali, *Sutras* 175
Pater, Walter 111
Patmore, Brigit 318, 321, 322, 323, 379
Patrick, G. T. W. 171
Péguy, Charles 153, 255–6
Perinot, Claudio 154
Perkins, Joyce Carroll 190
Perry, Ralph Barton 185
Peters, Harold 93, 97, 99, 141–2, 144,
    302–303, 323–4, 363
Petronius 120–21

Philippe, Charles-Louis 151–2, 154, 167
Poe, Edgar Allan 45–6, 370–71
Poetry (Chicago journal) 207, 208, 235, 247,
    255, 265, 282; publishes 'The Love Song
    of J. Alfred Prufrock' 233, 234
Poetry Bookshop, London 207, 226
Poetry Review (journal) 290
Pope, Alexander 372–3
Post, Lawrence Tyler 60, 75
Post, Levi Arnold 169
Potter, Anthony Murray 117–18
Pound, Dorothy (*née* Shakespear) 207, 275,
    333, 359, 415
Pound, Ezra: TSE first encounters poetry of
    136; secretary to W. B. Yeats 207;
    meets and is impressed by TSE in
    London 207–208; introduces TSE to
    literary and artistic figures 221, 235,
    243; encourages publication of TSE's
    poetry 222, 224–5, 251, 255, 267,
    275–6, 283; TSE sends poems to 224;
    on TSE's marriage 232; writes to
    TSE's father 233–4; friendship with
    TSE 264, 416; foreign editor of the
    Little Review 267, 282; publishes
    Catholic Anthology 277; encourages
    TSE's imitation of French poets 280;
    TSE reads Pound's poems before
    publication 295; TSE's belief in 301;
    TSE shows 'Gerontion' to 315;
    holiday in France with TSE (1919)
    333–4; publishes *Quia Pauper Amavi*
    338; works for the New York *Dial*
    346; wish for TSE to leave banking
    352–3, 400; proofreads *The Sacred
    Wood* 359; sees Eliots in Paris 391;
    recognition of TSE's marriage
    difficulties 400; translates Rémy de
    Gourmont's *Physique de l'amour* 400;
    editorial contribution to *The Waste
    Land* 10, 401–403; envy of TSE's
    accomplishment in *The Waste Land*
    402; TSE dedicates *The Waste Land* to
    349, 403; on TSE's health 404;
    develops 'Bel Esprit' subscription
    scheme to fund artists 406, 407, 411,
    413–14; on Vivien's ill-health 411;
    gives TSE nickname 'Possum' 416; on
    the *Criterion* 421

Poetry of: 'Cantos' 339, 371, 401;
  'Homage to Sextus Propertius' 339;
  'Hugh Selwyn Mauberley' 342, 349,
  350; *Poems 1918–21* 401
Powel, Thomas 114
Powell, Harford 104
Power, Father G. D. 24
Prichard, Matthew 145, 155
Proust, Marcel 354, 413

Quarterly Review (journal) 276
Quinn, John 134, 293, 346, 379, 400, 406;
  support for publication of TSE's poetry
  in America 283, 295–6, 306, 313, 336;
  negotiates publication of *The Waste Land*
  412, 418; and Pound's 'Bel Esprit' scheme
  411

Rainey, Lawrence 262, 297
Rand, Edward Kennard 120
Rascoe, Burton 424
Rattray, Robert 181
Read, Herbert 350
Reed, John Silas 104
Reed, Nathan 16
Reid, Mayne 53
Revere, Paul 16
Richards, I. A. 378, 384
Richmond, Bruce 334
Ricks, Christopher 4, 157, 166
Riley, James Whitcomb 48–9
Rivière, Jacques 146, 150–51, 365, 401
Robbins, Elizabeth 299
Roberts, William 212
Robey, George 158
Robinson, John 77, 91
Rodker, John 306, 323, 337, 346, 350, 413
Rossetti, Dante Gabriel 71
Rostand, Edmond, *Cyrano de Bergerac* 47
Rothermere, Mary Lilian Share
  Harmsworth, Viscountess (Lady
  Rothermere) 381–2, 384, 389, 403, 411,
  413, 418, 420, 421
Royce, Josiah 38, 86, 113, 114, 179, 182, 185,
  186, 250
Rubenstein, Ida 149
Ruskin, John 273–4
Russell, Bertrand: as visiting professor at
  Harvard 86, 182, 188; impressions of

TSE as a Harvard student 188–9; TSE
  meets in London 207; TSE's poem 'Mr
  Apollinax' inspired by 189, 216; hosts
  TSE in Cambridge, England 222–3;
  relationship with Lady Ottoline Morrell
  236, 240, 244, 249, 253–4, 322; on TSE
  and Vivien 236–7, 244; relationship with
  Vivien Eliot 237, 238, 240–41, 243–4,
  244–5, 258, 260–62, 285–7, 293, 312, 318,
  322; makes over investments to TSE 242;
  introduces TSE to literary and artistic
  circles 242–3; introduces TSE to Lady
  Ottoline Morrell 247–8; takes TSE to
  Garsington 249–50; encouragement of
  TSE's academic work 250; sacked from
  Trinity College, Cambridge for anti-war
  activities 253; encourages publication of
  TSE's poetry 255; relationship with Lady
  Constance Malleson 258, 284, 285, 286,
  293, 294; as benefactor of TSE 263, 285,
  287; publishes *Principles of Social
  Reconstruction* 270; imprisoned for
  anti-war activities 294
Ryan, Charles Hills 60

Saintsbury, George 389, 419
Sand, George 62
Sands, Ethel 237
Sanger, Dora 248
Santayana, George 114, 116–17, 132–3, 189,
  220, 223
Saturday Westminster Gazette 252
Saunders, Helen 212
Schiff, Sydney 299, 315, 324, 328, 343, 346,
  358, 359, 405, 408, 409
Schiff, Violet 299, 315, 324, 328, 343
Schleiermacher, Friedrich 15
Schmidt, Karl 179
Schnitzler, Arthur 378
Schofield, William Henry 117, 118
Schrader, Atreus Hargadine von 52, 93
Schuchard, Ronald 4, 297
Secker, Martin 323
Seeger, Alan 110–11, 131, 134, 290–91
Seymour-Jones, Carole 227, 313
Shakespeare, William 74
Shapleigh, Margaret 51
Shaw, George Bernard 375
Sheffield, Alfred D. 67, 77, 106, 168, 296

Sheldon, Edward 201

Shelley, Percy Bysshe 72–3, 347

Sigg, Eric 12

Simmers, George 277

Sinclair, May 276, 299, 406, 420

Sitwell, Edith 287

Sitwell, Osbert 287, 295, 303, 343, 346, 350, 380, 384

Sitwell, Sacheverell 302, 324, 380

Smith, George Lawrence 66

Smith, Grover 89

Smith, J. A. 215

Smith, Rose (TSE's aunt) 17

Smith, Theodora Eliot (TSE's niece) 66, 147, 234

Snider, Denton J. 38

Snyder, Reverend John 39–40, 41, 57

Soldo, John 60, 79

Spenser, Edmund 367

Spinoza 172

Squire, J. C. 346

St Louis, Missouri: cultural influences on TSE 2, 5–6, 21–3, 48; cyclone, May 1896 24–7; Eliot family home in 11, 17, 19; fogs 37; press announcement of TSE's marriage 234; St Louis Philosophical Society 38; World's Fair (1904) 59, 68

Starbuck, E. D. 215, 220

Stayer, Jayme 60, 77, 78

Stearns, Thomas (TSE's grandfather) 20, 33

Stevenson, Robert Louis 61, 73

Stewart, J. A. 221

Stimpson, Mary 166

Strachey, Lytton 243, 267–8, 318, 321, 326, 350, 414

Stravinsky, Igor, *The Rite of Spring* 10, 380–81, 385

Swanage, Dorset 213–14

Swinburne, Algernon Charles 103, 203

Symbolism 108

Symes, Lillia 230, 339

Symons, Arthur 105; *The Symbolist Movement in Literature* 107–10, 112

Synge, J. M. 240

Teasdale, Sara 27

Tennyson, Alfred, Lord 61, 103

Thayer, Lucy 227, 228, 230, 369, 407

Thayer, Scofield: TSE meets at Milton Academy 77; at Oxford with TSE 210; relationship with Vivien 225–30, 382, 389, 391; corresponds with Vivien 237, 244–5, 250; unhappy about Vivien's marriage to TSE 239; edits *Dial* magazine 302–303, 346, 372, 398; arranges reviews of TSE's work 350; invites TSE to edit an English *Dial* 365–6; rivalry with TSE 405; negotiates publication of *The Waste Land* in *Dial* 403–404, 408, 417

Thornburgh, Edwine 51, 52

Times Literary Supplement 276, 308, 334, 337, 339, 342, 351, 361, 379, 389, 409, 422

Tinckom-Fernandez, William George 84–5, 104, 107, 114, 129, 131, 136, 140

Tree, Iris 343

Twain, Mark, *Huckleberry Finn* 24

Tylor, E. B. 187

Tyro (journal) 353, 367, 371, 404

Underhill, Evelyn 178–9, 181, 220

Van Bever, Adolphe, *Poètes d'Aujourd'hui* 133, 222

Van Ness, Ann 206, 217

Van Riper, Walker Moore 60

Vanderpyl, Fritz 354, 365

Vandervelde, Lalla 287

Vanity Fair (magazine) 417

Verdenal, Jean Jules 146, 153, 154–7, 161, 165, 167–8, 245, 256, 261

Villon, François 188

Virgil 156–7

Vittoz, Dr Roger Henry Melling 389, 390, 392–4

Vorticism 202, 207, 224, 225, 235, 242, 302

Wadsworth, Edward 212, 224, 235, 256, 302, 323

Wagner, Richard 135–6, 161; *Tristan und Isolde* 198, 373

Waste Land, The: TSE's resolution to write 'long poem' 343; early lines written while still at Harvard 168–9; composition of 9–10, 341, 373–7, 387–8, 390, 393, 395–9, 401–403; TSE discusses with Mary Hutchinson 268–9; TSE shows Wyndham Lewis material for 371; epigraph for 378, 402–403, 405; Ezra Pound assists in editing 401-402; dedication to Ezra Pound 349, 403; TSE negotiates publication in *Dial* magazine 402, 403–405, 408, 417; first publication 416–24; TSE reads aloud to Virginia Woolf 10, 423; reception of 423–4

Themes, images and influences: Conrad Aiken 327; St Augustine 180; Buddhism 168, 175, 410; comic opera 106; and 'The Death of the Duchess' 263; 'Geronition' as possible prelude to 315; TSE's experience of sailing at Gloucester, Massachusetts 32, 143, 162-3; Oliver Goldsmith 54, 190; the hermit thrush 35, 67; Huneker's *Egoists: A Book of Supermen* 133; Aldous Huxley's Crome Yellow 243; 'hyacinth girl' episode 269; imagery from TSE's London working life 271-3, 345; imagery from Weston's *From Ritual to Romance* 53, 351-2, 399; different languages in 271; literary tradition in 330, 342; James Russell Lowell's *A Vision of Sir Launfal* 61; Andrew Marvell 368; Maurras's *L'Avenir de l'Intelligence* 153; Gérard de Nerval 108-9; Ovid 62; philosophical influences 176, 183; poetic form 339-40; religion and ritual 187; Shakespeare 62, 126; Edmund Spenser 63, 367-8; thunder in 27; figure of Tiresias 1, 118; title 387, 399; the *Upanishads* 170; Wagner 126; John Webster 62-3.

Waterlow, Sydney 197, 251, 343, 346, 350, 396

Watson, George 154

Watson, James Sibley 417

Waugh, Arthur 276

Weaver, Harriet Shaw 275, 294–5, 327

Wedekind, Frank 161

Wendell, Barrett 82, 86

Westermarck, Edward 118, 223

Westminster Gazette 251

Weston, Jessie L. 117, 381; *From Ritual to Romance* 118, 351–2, 399

Whait, John Robert 238, 342–3

Wharton, Edith 291

Wheelock, John Hall 104, 107, 113

White, John Williams 54

Whittier, John Greenleaf 12, 31, 32

Wiener, Norbert 179, 181, 212, 218–20, 222

Wiggins, Kate Douglas 29

Wilde, Oscar 89

Williams, William Carlos 276, 406

Wilm, E. C. 177

Wilson, Edmund 417, 423

Wilson, Woodrow 274, 306, 310–11

Woods, James Haughton 169–72, 174, 175, 215, 216, 225, 238, 250, 309, 313–4, 320

Woolf, Leonard 244, 306, 350, 359, 388, 406, 409, 414, 423–4

Woolf, Virginia: and the Bloomsbury set 244, 350; meets TSE and publishes *Poems* (1919) 306–308; on TSE 307–308, 357–8, 364, 368, 369, 406, 416; friendship with TSE 9, 319, 370–71; sexuality 326; hosts TSE at Monks House 388; agrees publication of *The Waste Land* by the Hogarth Press 406; contributes to the first edition of the *Criterion* 409, 413; and schemes to provide funds for TSE 414, 418; TSE reads *The Waste Land* to 10, 423

Wright, Charles Henry Conrad 90

Yeats, Jack Butler 134, 281

Yeats, W. B. 181, 207, 208, 273

CONTENTS

Introduction v

1. It's Not Him, It's You!
The Common Denominator 1
OK, So It's Me. Now What? 5
The Secret to My Success. 10

2. Sales: What It Is and Why It Works
The Truth About Sales 17
The Dreaded Telemarketers of Dating 19
Emotions vs. Logic 24
Are You Playing Games? 28

3. The Product: You
Know Your Product 35
Love Your Product 41
Packaging Your Product 47
Attracting Attention to Your Product 53

4. Finding Him
Prospecting 59
SEE Factors 68
Icebreakers 73
Filling the Funnel 77

5. Getting Him Interested

Recognizing Buying Signs 87
The KISS Principle 98
End at the Height of Impulse 105
Indifference 114
Nonverbal Communication—What You Can't Hear 127
Using Jones Effect 133

6. Keeping Him Interested

Hold Back Your Bullets 141
Whatever You Do, Don't Cut to the Close 152
Taking Control 162
Don't Sweeten the Deal 173

7. Closing the Deal

Never Assume 181
What Motivates Him to Marry 187
Sense of Urgency 198
The Silent No 206
Buyer's Remorse 215

8. Maintaining the Right Mentality

Don't Drink and Date 227
The Waiting Game 239
No Means Next 245
Practicing in Game-like Conditions 250
Index 255

INTRODUCTION

Like most women out there, my girlfriends and I have struggled with dating. Let's face it, at some point, we've all been dumped, stood up, cheated on, or left stranded in limbo. Many of us have failed to take our relationships beyond a casual hook-up. And get a guy to commit? Forget about it. You may as well be asking them to cut off their right leg.

Like many of you, I blamed men for all my dating problems. If only he had a better past, a better mother, or a better ex-girlfriend, I would not still be single. But after so many "It's not you, it's me" speeches, I began to wonder. Maybe the guy wasn't at fault. Maybe there was a reason I was hearing the same excuses over and over. Maybe it really was me.

Then everything changed. The change did not take place overnight. It was gradual. As a matter of fact, I was not even aware of it. Dating was the last thing on my mind. I was just trying to start my career in sales. I wanted to become a top-notch saleswoman. And I did it. I became very successful. And with my success in sales came success on the dating scene. Was there a correlation? Not a conscious one. However, as I found out quickly, when you become a good saleswoman, it gets into your blood. It permeates most everything you do. You change. The sales persona began to seep into my relationships, and suddenly men were eating out of my hand. It was amazing, and I didn't even realize why it was happening.

I wrote this book because my days of rejection are now in the

past. I have discovered what all of us have been doing wrong, and I can teach women how to start doing it right. No, I'm not a psychologist. I'm an entrepreneur. Sales is my forte. My job is to get people interested, and keep them that way until they make a commitment. It doesn't matter what the product is—the strategy is always the same, and the strategy always works. I know how to make a product as attractive as possible to a prospective buyer. I know how to plan; I know how to prospect. I can tell when customers are losing interest, and I know how to turn them around.

The bottom line? My career is based on getting the results that I want. It has become clear to me why women do not get the results that they want: they don't know how to employ the techniques that all salesmen routinely use. To put it bluntly, women just do not know how to sell themselves.

In every relationship a sale is made. Either you sell him on a commitment, or he sells you on why he doesn't want one. It may not sound romantic, but it's the truth. And it's the reason that you are still single. The good news is your luck is about to change. You don't have to have a job in sales to turn your love life around. This book will give you the strategies you need to get the guy you want.

You too can learn how to apply the tricks of a saleswoman's trade to selling your most important product: you. I'm going to teach you how to find him, meet him, get him interested, and keep him that way. Gone are the days of waiting and wondering what to do next. You are now the one who is in control. You are the one who makes all the moves. You are the one who can close the deal. All of the techniques that make me successful in business can and will make you successful at dating.

IT'S NOT HIM, IT'S YOU!

The Common Denominator

Several years ago I was sitting in a café in Georgetown having breakfast with my best friend, Adison. She had dragged me out of bed that morning to talk about her most recent relationship, which, like many before, was headed downhill fast. Before I could even order a cup of coffee, she declared that her latest would-be-boyfriend, Gavin, was an asshole. She then proceeded to give me the play-by-play of their relationship with her usual enthusiasm.

"He never calls when he says he will. He acts like he likes me one minute, but then I don't hear from him for days. I am just so fed up with men and their games!"

I listened, as good friends do, as Adison vented her

frustrations. She rambled on about Gavin's commitment phobia; how his hot and cold behavior drove her up the wall; and how the next time she saw him, she was going to give him a piece of her mind. But somewhere between the words jerk and player, I realized that this most recent relationship disaster sounded a lot like her last one. In fact, when I thought about it, it seemed like getting dumped was becoming a pattern for her.

As Adison was about to call this guy an asshole for the tenth time, it hit me: maybe it wasn't such a coincidence that all the guys she dated turned out to be jerks. Maybe there was an actual reason for it. It did seem a little odd that all the guys she liked drove her crazy and eventually ended up MIA, especially since each relationship started out so differently. Yet somehow she kept getting the same result. I realized I knew what was happening. There was only one common denominator in all of Adison's relationships, and it wasn't the men.

"Adison," I said. "Do you ever think maybe it's not him, it's you?"

Adison's jaw dropped. As soon as the words left my mouth, I cringed and waited for her reaction. I was supposed to be her friend. I was supposed to be on her side. I was supposed to call this guy a selfish bastard, not bruise her already damaged ego. In fact, I was just about to recant my statement when she said, "Really? You think I'm making him act this way?"

Up until that moment I truly believed that Adison and I had

just been picking the wrong guys. Whenever our relationships got rocky, we would blame the guy for being insensitive, unavailable, or just plain shady. We truly believed that most men were frogs and we were going to have to kiss a lot of them to find our prince. But now I had seen the light. Men weren't the cause of all our headaches, we were. If a guy didn't act exactly the way we wanted him to, we would freak out, overreact, and drive him away.

Take Adison's new relationship for example. This guy, Gavin, did like her. There was definitely a mutual attraction when they began dating. However, Adison started assuming that they were in a relationship after only a couple of weeks, whereas Gavin was still testing the waters. She switched into full girlfriend mode before Gavin had really decided how he felt about her. So when she started coming on strong, calling a lot and making all-weekend plans with him, he started to back off.

This, of course, drove Adison crazy. And the crazier she got, the more she pressured him. The more she pressured him, the less he wanted to see her. She became angry and critical whenever they were together and accused Gavin of being immature for wanting to spend more time with his friends instead of hanging out with her. On the flip side, Gavin was becoming more and more convinced that Adison was trying to control him. For God's sake, they had only been dating for a month! Eventually Gavin stopped returning her calls all together, leaving Adison in

relationship limbo, wondering what had happened.

Adison and I spent the next hour dissecting all of our previous relationships. In almost every instance, we realized that the guys we had thought were jerks were really not so bad after all. We just blamed them for the fact that the relationships had gone awry. We had come up with every excuse in the book for why they behaved badly, when really, we just didn't know how to act with a guy we liked. It didn't matter that Adison was a smart, pretty girl. The way she behaved completely turned guys off. What an epiphany! I had to laugh at all the crazy mistakes we had made throughout the years. Looking back, I wondered how I could have been so oblivious.

Suddenly, Adison became panic stricken.

"Ohmigod, Jess, do you know what this means?" She shrieked. "I have been dumped three times in the last year, and I am now realizing it's because of something *I'm* doing. *I'm* turning guys off. All this time I thought I was just dating the wrong kind of guy. It never occurred to me that I might be bad at dating. Now what am I supposed to do?"

Good question. At the time, I didn't have the answer. I just knew that this problem wasn't unique to Adison and me. All of my friends were suffering from their own dating dilemmas as well. The more I thought about it, the more I was certain. It wasn't the guys that were making our lives miserable. It was us!

OK, So It's Me. Now What?

Years later I was in Las Vegas with my good friend Lana. We were attending a conference to promote her latest children's video. After a couple hours of standing on our feet, we decided to take a break and get some lunch. We found a restaurant in the casino and quickly grabbed a seat. A few minutes later, two guys sat down at the table right next to us. The one on my side was extremely cute, and I couldn't help but overhear his conversation. He had just closed a huge deal. One of the networks had agreed to fund his TV pilot. After a couple of minutes I realized "cute guy" kept glancing my way. After the fifth or sixth time, I finally decided to catch his eye. He smiled at me, and I leaned over to him and said, "You guys sound like you're celebrating."

Ten minutes later we were engrossed in conversation.

Twenty minutes later "cute guy'" asked for my number.

I could go into more details about how the weekend unfolded. How "cute guy" (his name was Daniel) showed up at the club we were at that night. He bought us drinks, held my hand, and kept telling me how adorable I was. But the particulars of that evening are trivial. After all, lots of boys and girls meet and party in Vegas. The crazy part was what happened the next morning. As I went downstairs to check out, Daniel was waiting for me in the lobby. He begged and pleaded with

me to stay another night. He even offered to pay for another room at his hotel. When it became clear I wasn't going to be convinced, he reluctantly let me go. But not before telling me that I was the most amazing woman he's ever met and making me promise I would see him again.

When Lana and I jumped in a cab to the airport, she looked at me with amazement and said, "How is it that every guy falls in love with you?"

I had to laugh.

"No seriously," she continued. "When I was single I had guys hit on me, but they didn't fall all over themselves the way they do for you. It took weeks, usually months, to get them to commit. I feel like that guy would have reserved the Chapel o' Love tomorrow if you had let him. How do you do it?"

It was at that moment that I realized I had to write this book. I had a secret, and it was time to share it.

The Girl I Used to Be

As I said before, I wasn't always so successful with men. Even after my "It's not him, it's you" epiphany years earlier, I still had my share of dating disasters.

In college, I had an on-and-off relationship with a guy named Shawn. I really liked him, and when we started dating again my junior year, I thought we were finally on the same page. I asked him to my sorority formal which happened to

fall on my twenty-first birthday. I was very excited that I would be spending such a big night with a guy I really liked. On top of that, all my friends would be there to celebrate. However, two days before my birthday he called to tell me he couldn't go with me anymore. The girl he *really* liked had just asked him to go to her formal on the same night. I was devastated. I felt rejected. I never wanted to see him again. Unfortunately he lived next door.

Another time I fell hard for a Sigma Chi who lived upstairs from me. He would come over all the time and we'd eat, watch TV, and make out. We never defined our relationship, but since we hung out so much, I figured there was no need. He was my boyfriend, as far as I was concerned. Then one day I overheard a couple girls on the quad talking about him. I listened in and learned that he had been pining away for one of their cheerleader friends who finally decided to go out with him. The next time I saw him he was holding hands with C-H-R-I-S-S-Y from the squad.

Then there was Danny. I dated Danny for eleven months. I call that time period the Crash of '99. I was head over heels for him. Funny thing was, at first he chased me. He wanted to take me out and I kept turning him down. He called and pursued relentlessly. Eventually I caved in and went out with him. After seeing him a few times after that, I was hooked. The tables were turned, and now I was the one pining after him while he scheduled me in between rounds of golf. My entire week

revolved around Danny. If he wanted to hang out, I dropped everything and ran over. I never knew when I was going to see him again, so I took every chance I got. I stopped making plans with friends because I didn't want to be somewhere that I couldn't leave in case he called. It was a disastrous relationship. I was absolutely powerless, and I didn't know how to regain control. So eventually after many tears, I finally left Danny. He had a new girlfriend three days after we broke up.

So as you can see, I've had my fair share of sob stories. Realizing that I didn't know how to date was only the beginning. I knew that I had a problem—I just didn't know how to fix it.

Luckily, after college I stumbled upon the formula for dating success. I had figured out how to get a guy interested, keep control, and get him to commit. My love life took off, and guys who had never noticed me before were falling all over themselves to ask me out. Whereas before, I couldn't catch the eye of the captain of the chess team, I was now dating celebrities and professional athletes. I was even pursued by one of *Fortune's 40 Richest Men Under 40*. Guys were telling me they were in love with me after only a matter of weeks, and all of my boyfriends were discussing marriage. It was crazy, but it felt great. I couldn't believe the change. I was the same person I had always been, but now I was getting the response I had always wanted.

Since I discovered this secret, I have not been dumped,

stood up, cheated on, or left in limbo wondering where I stood. I have had men go to great lengths to get my number and they have all asked for a commitment without me having to say one word. But the best part of all is that I no longer have to settle for the guys that just want me. I can pick any guy I want, and I know I can make him want me right back.

So what's my secret? How do I do it? It's all laid out right here in this book. And what exactly is the difference between this book and all those others out there? Simple. This book is not based on opinion or secondhand advice. It will not just help you understand men and why they do the things they do. What good is having that information if you don't know how to use it? No, this book is different. It will teach you exactly how to gain control of your love life and make you effective in dating, regardless of who you are or what you look like.

Now be prepared. This book presents some rather unorthodox advice. But that's a good thing. How many other dating books have you read that have done absolutely nothing for you? This book is different. It won't be like *The Rules*. It does not contain flimsy outdated advice my mother's mother gave me. And it's not like *He's Just Not That Into You,* because honestly, by the time you're done reading this book, he will be. No longer will you sit around with your girlfriends analyzing text messages and waiting for phone calls. You want to land a boyfriend? You want to get married? Well, you can. I am going to show you how to use proven techniques to get any guy you want.

The Secret to My Success

After graduating from college, I had no idea what I was going to do with the rest of my life. Flipping through the *The Washington Post* one day, I saw an ad for a sales job at a local marketing firm. I had never done any sales before, and frankly, the thought conjured up visions of used car dealers. But time was slipping by, and my funds were dwindling, so I went on an interview. I was immediately sent out into the field on a ride along with an established female sales rep. She was my age, sharp, pretty, and had a phenomenal attitude. As we pulled up to an office park in Bethesda, Maryland, I asked her who we were going to see. She replied, "I have no idea. I never set appointments."

Now I was completely curious. She was going to walk in, unannounced, and try to meet with the business owner? How was she going to do that? I watched her as she walked into the first business cold—without calling first, without a contact name—and within minutes was meeting with the man in charge. I was amazed at how she approached her potential customers with no warning and soon had them eating out of her hand. She closed three customers that day. None of them knew we were coming, but they all signed a contract before we left. She made it seem so easy to get people to do what she wanted. At times she even made them think it was their idea. By the

end of the day she had made three hundred dollars in commissions. She was so confident, so in control, so powerful. I was sold. I wanted to learn everything she knew.

After I got the job, I immediately began training. It was all so foreign to me—I felt like a fish out of water. But I was amazed at all that I was learning, and the more I practiced my sales techniques, the more comfortable and natural they became. After a few weeks, I was closing my own deals, and after only a few months I noticed a big change in my attitude. I felt more confident, more secure, more logical. It wasn't that I had just learned to sell a product. I now knew how to get people interested in what I had to say. I knew the best way to get them to like me. I knew how to get them to do what I wanted.

Then one night after work, I decided to meet up with a guy I had just started seeing. I liked him, but I didn't know how much he liked me. Prior to working in sales, I was always nervous before I went out with someone new. But this time was different. I wasn't worried about what he was going to say or how I would respond. I felt totally at ease and completely sure of myself.

Suddenly it hit me.

All the sales techniques that I had learned were applicable to dating! In fact, dating itself was nothing more than a big fat sale. Salespeople don't just sell products; first and foremost, they sell themselves. There was no difference between

winning over a customer and winning over a man. The same strategy applied. Every time I went on a date, all I was doing was trying to sell myself. However, until I landed my job and learned the art of selling, I'd been doing it all wrong. That evening, armed with my new techniques, it wasn't long before my date was putty in my hands.

Shortly after I discovered this secret, I was on the phone with one of my very best friends, Dave, who has been in medical sales for the last ten years. Dave is married, but still likes to flirt with women when he's out on the town with the guys. He told me about some girls he and his friends had met that Saturday night. In particular, he couldn't believe how persistently two of them were pursuing him after only an hour.

"I don't know what it is, but women just fall in love with me," he said, laughing. "By the end of the night these girls were saying things like, 'Dave, you've got such a great personality. I have never met anyone like you. You're so genuine. I wish you weren't married.' My brother actually got pretty pissed because he really liked one of them, but she was all over me!"

"So you're saying this happens to you a lot?" I asked.

"All the time. I recently had to change barbers, because the chick that used to cut my hair kept coming on to me. It must be because I'm married," he said.

"Why do you say that?" I asked. "Did all this start happening right after you tied the knot?"

Dave thought for a second. "Hmmm, no, I guess not,

because even my wife teases that I used to be a player. The night I met her I was actually hooking up with one of her friends. So even before I got married, I had this strange power over women."

I couldn't help but laugh at his comment. Dave had no shortage of ego.

"It's not a strange power, dummy! It's because you're in sales."

Dave was immediately skeptical. "Sales? No, that's not it."

"Okay, then, you tell me. When did you get this 'power'? Did you have it in high school or college?" I asked.

"Well, no. Now that you mention it, girls never liked me in school. I had one girlfriend in college, and I'm not even sure she liked me."

"So would you say you mysteriously got this power around the same time you landed your first job in sales?"

Dave was quiet for a few seconds, and then, as if a light bulb went off in his head, he said, "Wow! Maybe you're right. After I got in sales, my dating life did make a complete one-eighty. I never realized that before, but it's exactly what happened."

"Of course it is. The same thing happened to me," I said.

"It makes total sense now that I think about it," he said. "We spend all day trying to convince people that we have a great product that they should buy. We have to get them interested and keep them interested. We have to make them want to commit to us without seeming pushy or annoying. You're right. It's not a power at all. It's sales."

Dave and I started thinking about all of our friends and their dating habits. It made total sense. Most of our friends have never sold a thing. And, not surprisingly, those same friends were awful at dating. But the few friends we did have in sales were not just slightly better at dating— they were great at it.

Start Strong, Finish Strong

There are a lot of smart, funny, beautiful women out there who continually get dumped not because of *who* they are, but because of *what* they do. The truth is that it doesn't matter how great of a person you are. You could have a double MBA, be a concert pianist, and have legs up to your ears. If you say or do the wrong thing in the beginning stages of dating, you are impacting a man's perception of you. And his perception (as far as he's concerned) is reality. If you've ever wondered how a guy didn't see how fabulous you are, it's because you showed him desperation, neediness, excessive emotional attachment, or a variety of other negatives that will ultimately, in his mind, override your good qualities. You have to learn to present yourself appropriately so that doesn't happen. That is why it's imperative to learn how to sell yourself.

I know what you must be thinking. There is no way you can sell someone on loving you. And you're right. You can't use sales to manipulate someone into loving you. But what you can do is make sure you keep seeing the guy long enough for

him to get to know who you really are.

Most women I know say or do something early in the relationship that ruins their chances of ever being taken seriously. Even if the relationship carries on for months, or even years, the fact that they didn't handle themselves well in the beginning often dooms the relationship. The beginning, when the ground rules are being established, is a critical time in any relationship because it ultimately determines the direction the relationship will take. To finish strong, you have to start strong. It's what most women have missed, and salespeople have learned: a rewarding relationship, just like a sale, begins at hello.

Where You Lose Him

Like I said before, when relationships don't work out, most women blame commitment-phobic men, bad hair days—you name it. But those are just excuses. Women never want to admit that they did something wrong. God forbid! Then they would have to accept the blame for their relationship gone awry.

But salespeople know if they lose a deal, it's because *they* did something wrong. *No one else!* Sure, you will hear some of them complain that the customer was too difficult or the territory was too tough, but ultimately those, too, are just excuses. A good salesperson knows that all success and failure

come from within. A deal can be won or lost at any point, and relationships are no different. What does this mean? It means that at any point in a relationship you can lose his interest. Some women lose him after sex. Some lose him on date three. And some women, whether they know it or not, lose him at hello.

If you aren't having any luck in the dating department, whether your obstacle is attracting men, holding on to them, or getting them to commit, your luck is about to change. Just as salespeople know it's never the customer, or the territory, women must understand that our dating success depends on us alone. If we aren't getting the results that we want, we are doing something wrong. We must find out what that something is and we must change it. This isn't rocket science—it's just sales. And this book will teach you the tricks of the trade so that you will never lose him again.

SALES: WHAT IT IS AND WHY IT WORKS

The Truth About Sales

When I first began discussing the correlation between dating and sales, many of my friends had a hard time accepting the idea because of the stigma behind it. They equated sales to being pushy and forceful. They thought it was a lowly profession comprised of used cars and vacuum cleaners. Now they know that just isn't the case. Professional sales positions are highly competitive and incredibly hard to break in to. The compensation is so great now that many salespeople can make more money than doctors and lawyers.

Good salesmanship is not persuading someone by way of force. It's a series of techniques. It's body language. It's reading people and timing things well. It's a strategy that

when planned and executed correctly, will give you the highest possible chance to get the results you want. Selling is an invaluable talent that can land you a job in any industry. Now, it can even land you a man.

You may be worried that you are in over your head. You've never had a sales job, and, quite frankly, you don't know if you could sell a loaf of bread to a starving man. But the truth is you already use sales in your everyday life. From the moment you wake up and decide what outfit is most likely to impress your boss, until later that night when you convince your girlfriends where to eat dinner, you are constantly engaging in sales. Whenever you go on an interview, you are selling yourself to an employer. Whenever you try to get a better deal on a car or a house, meet new people, or make new friends, you are drawing on the same set of skills that sales entails. Some people are naturally good at sales, while other people really need to work to master the techniques. The good news is you don't have to become a superstar salesperson in order to change your love life. In sales, a little goes a long way. You only need to improve your ability to sell by a small amount in order to get huge results.

Don't worry if you are a little intimidated. Everyone is afraid of what they don't know or don't understand. Don't tell yourself that this stuff isn't for you and that you just don't work that way. These techniques aren't for one type of person. They are for everyone. If it feels strange at first, it's only

because you are stepping out of your comfort zone, which always takes some getting used to. But the more you learn and practice, the more natural it will feel.

The Dreaded Telemarketers of Dating

While you're learning these techniques, you will find the answers to questions you had about previous relationships. Questions like: *Why do guys like it when you play hard to get? Why can't I call him? Why is it when I don't care about a guy he's all over me, but when I do care, it never works out?*

But before we dive in, we need to clarify something. As I said before there are a lot of misperceptions about sales out there. I have friends that *think* they know how to "sell" a guy on a relationship, but have missed the mark completely. These women are like the telemarketers of dating. They bother men with their constant calling, bad timing, and annoying inability to take no for an answer. They subscribe to old adages like, "persistence ends resistance," and so believe, if they just don't give up, they will wear a guy down.

My friend Steve was dating a cute redhead named Sydney. They met at a charity event and hit it off right away. From the very beginning they spent a lot of time together. After just a week, she was already sleeping at his house. Although Steve

really liked Sydney, he wasn't quite sure if he was in love. After three months and much contemplation, he decided he needed some time apart to see how he really felt. One night, he told Sydney he really cared about her, but wasn't sure if he was ready for a serious commitment. Of course, upon hearing this, Sydney was distraught. She did not want to lose Steve and was willing to do whatever was necessary to get him to stay.

"I love you!" she declared. "I haven't said it before, because I was afraid to. But I do, I love you. I know that we belong together. Think of how much we have in common. We need to talk about this. Spending time apart won't solve anything. We can work through this. Just give it another chance. You won't find anyone else that will love you as much I do!"

Sydney spent the next three hours trying to convince Steve they were right for each other, and while Steve felt bad about what she was saying, it didn't really change the way he felt about her. Sydney was trying to sell herself, but she was going about it in exactly the wrong way. Steve told me later that the best thing she could have done was give him space. He felt Sydney was becoming too dependent and wondered if she was really the tough, strong, smart woman he initially fell for. If she had understood good sales techniques, she would have known how to handle this situation, and when Steve had this talk with her, his feelings may have changed. But instead, she begged and pleaded with him, which made her seem desper-

ate. Sydney left Steve's apartment that night and never saw him again.

You can never convince someone to date you, let alone love you, by telling them how much you need or love them. It would be like trying to sell a car by saying, "Hey, I would really love you to buy this car. You don't know what your commission means to me. I've never felt this way about a customer. No one will appreciate your down payment more than I will. I just really need you to buy it. If you don't, I don't know what I will do." Well, that's a convincing argument if I ever heard one. By saying these things, you may make the guy feel guilty or sorry for you, and once in a while, he may even give in and take you back. But it won't make him *want* to be with you. And that's the whole trick to dating successfully. It's not about getting guys to *do what you want*—it's about getting them to want you. Then they'll happily give you what you need. You will never convince a man to love you by letting him know how much you love him. That's not sales, that's begging. And it just doesn't work.

Need another example of bad selling? I've definitely got one.

When I first told my cousin Nicole that I was writing this book, she laughed.

"I've done that before!" She said. "I used to sell advertising for a local paper during college. I've tried using sales to date and it just doesn't work."

Curious, I asked, "Well, what exactly have you tried?"

"Well, take Adam for instance. He's a bartender I met when I was out one night with the girls. I thought he was cute, so I was really persistent in getting his number—just the way you are with sales. He said he was in a relationship at first, but after a few hours of flirting with him, he finally gave me his number. We went out a few times, and I totally fell in love with him. But he was so hesitant to commit. We got in a big argument about it, and he told me not to call him anymore. But, in sales you don't take no for an answer. So I called him. He didn't call me back, so I called him again. Anyway, when I never got a call back I thought about what I would do if a customer didn't call me back—I would go visit them at their place of business. So I went back to the bar and asked him why he hadn't returned my calls. I tried to tell him he was missing out on a good thing, but he looked at me like I was a complete psycho and told me to lose his number. So you see, sales just doesn't work."

I tried to explain to my cousin that what she was doing wasn't sales—it was stalking. Sales is not simply being persistent until someone gives in to you. My cousin's strategy was to bulldoze over this guy. Just like the previous example, she didn't try to get him to *want* her, she tried to force him to *do what she wanted.* There's a big difference.

Okay, last story and then I promise to move on. My friend Ray met a girl on an Internet dating site. She looked attractive and seemed sweet in her profile, so he asked her to meet him

for drinks one night. Well, the girl spent the whole night trying to "sell herself." She told Ray she gave great massages, and loved to cook in her underwear. She also told Ray that she was the total package, and he should take her off the market before someone else did. That form of self-promotion is not sales. Telling a guy that you're a catch isn't going to convince him that you are one. He's got to see it in time—for himself. It's your job to make him see it, but telling him outright isn't the way to do it.

Sales is an art form that takes time to master. But once you do, you will see how it can absolutely change your life. There are very few products that can sell themselves without the help of a salesperson. If you had the most beautiful house on the block in the best location and next to the best school, you still would have trouble selling it without a realtor. You would need someone who could find you potential buyers, show them the house, point out its good features, and negotiate a great deal for you. Without that realtor, your house could sit on the market for months without a bite, and you could ultimately settle for a price less than what you wanted.

You are that house. You can either keep dating your way, hoping that someday the perfect guy will stumble upon your house by happenstance, or you can stop dreaming and realize you need to learn to become your own realtor.

Remember, you can't come across as needy or desperate for a sale, and you can't be pushy or overly aggressive. None of

those things will entice a person to buy from you, and in dating, the same rules apply. Realize that sales is not something you should learn; it's something you must learn. Your dating success depends on it!

Emotions vs. Logic

Understandably, women often rely on their emotions in order to make decisions about dating. We hate that little anxious feeling in the pit of our stomach, and we won't rest easy until something is done about it. Yes, we know we should probably wait for him to call us, but we really want to talk to him. So we pick up the phone and make the call ourselves. Unfortunately, going with these gut feelings can be very dangerous. When you are dating someone you really like, it's easy to make emotional, rather than rational, decisions. Your heart overrides your head. Now that you've called him, you feel better, but what about him? What kind of message did you send by calling? Even though you made a decision that felt right to you, it may have terrible repercussions.

Take my friend Sarah, for instance. She was head over heels for Brody. They had been seeing each other for only a few weeks but got serious very fast. Sarah knew she was in love and was dying to tell Brody how she felt. All her friends

thought it was just too soon to say it, and she should wait for him to say it first. But Sarah didn't care. She said her heart was telling her to do it, and she would explode if she held it in any longer. Against all advice from her friends, she proceeded to tell Brody she loved him. To her surprise, he did not say it back. Their relationship continued for a couple more months after that, but Brody eventually broke up with her. Sarah was devastated. Since the relationship felt so right to her, she could not believe that Brody did not feel the same.

Sarah's emotions had clouded her judgment. Because it *felt* right to drop the L-bomb, Sarah went ahead and did it. Looking back, she wonders how she could have been so rash. Obviously, Brody liked her, but she scared him off by telling him she loved him too soon. Instead of thinking logically about where she and Brody were in the relationship and acting accordingly, she acted based on how she felt. In this case, being honest and up front completely backfired on her. Had she understood sales and how to implement sales techniques, she would not have made such a blunder, and she and Brody may have had a chance.

One Strike, You're Out

Have you ever gone out with a guy a couple times, had great chemistry, thought you could really have something with him, and then never heard from him again? Unfortunately, this happens all the time. You are left in dating limbo wondering why

he dropped off the face of the Earth when everything seemed to be going so well. Well sure—it's theoretically possible that some external complication did prevent him from returning your call. Maybe he was suddenly shipped off to Iraq, or his mom was run over by a Mack Truck. Things like that do happen. Just not very often.

More than likely, you screwed up. Somewhere in the course of dating you made an emotional decision that felt right to you but turned him off. Just like Sarah and Brody. She made one bad move, and he dumped her. Granted, this was the granddaddy of all bad moves, but sometimes all it takes is something small and seemingly insignificant to cause a bad reaction. You may think it's okay to call or text just this one time, but that one time could be one too many. You need to be extra cognizant of what you are doing with a guy so that you don't ruin your chances. In this game, it takes just one strike and you're out.

I'm sure you can think of tons of examples of when a guy did or said something that completely turned you off. It only took one thing, one word, one look, and you were done. Are you really surprised that men are the same way?

Most women try to validate why they do something they know they shouldn't be doing. My best friend Adison knows she shouldn't call a guy the morning after she sees him, but she always comes up with some excuse to pick up the phone and do it anyway. I've heard everything from, "He left his

watch here" to "I forgot to thank him for dinner, and I don't want him to think I'm rude."

She's not fooling anyone. The bottom line is she's dying to hear his voice. She wants to talk to him so she finds an excuse to validate her decision. She tries to rationalize why she's doing it, but the real reason is emotionally driven. I, on the other hand, have no emotional ties to this guy so I can tell her with a clear head, "Do not call him! You just saw him last night." Of course, she never listens. No matter what logical advice I give her, her emotions won't let her accept it. Her stomach tells her she won't feel better until she makes the call. So instead of listening to logic, she listens to her emotions. Then she's completely blindsided when the guy loses interest.

Winning the War Against Your Emotions

There is a reason they say hindsight is twenty-twenty. When you look back on your past relationships you can clearly see what went wrong because you are no longer emotional about them. *Emotion clouds logic.* Making a good, sound decision becomes extremely difficult when you're emotional. That being said there is only one way to win the war with your emotions: you must understand and formulate your dating strategy *before* you become involved with someone. It's the only way. If you try and plan your course of action during the dating process, your emotions will tempt you, and you will

fumble and ultimately lose the game. So it's important that you learn and understand these techniques prior to dating someone. However, if you are already involved, you can still rescue your current relationship. You will just have to work harder to stay on track and keep your emotions at bay.

Are You Playing Games?

My friend Carey doesn't play games. She doesn't believe she has to. Whenever she meets a new guy, she makes a point of telling them that she is not a game player. Her approach is to be completely open with her thoughts and feelings, so there is no confusion or miscommunication. Yet, she can't seem to hold on to a man. Guys always tell her that they just aren't ready for a serious relationship. She says it's because she has bad timing. One day when we were out to lunch, she looked at me so frustrated and said, "I just don't get this new trend. All the men around here are just not in the mood to settle down with one girl. It's driving me insane. It's like marriage isn't cool anymore and guys want to be bachelors for the rest of their lives."

I decided I had to tell her what was really going on, since she obviously didn't have a clue. I told her that if she is constantly getting the same reaction from guys, then it is she, not they, who is the problem.

At first Carey didn't believe me. She swore that it was not her fault. "I'm young and in great shape," she said. "I have a great job, and I'm fun to be with. There's no way it's me."

I tried to explain to Carey that she was right. She was young and beautiful. It's not that she wasn't a catch. The problem was that she was doing something that deterred men from wanting a relationship with her. In order to get a different result with men, she would have to figure out what she was doing that was turning them off, and then change it.

I've known Carey for years, and she'll be the first one to tell you that men are her primary focus. Carey will always dump her friends for a night out with a guy. Whenever she meets someone she likes, she cuts off all ties to the outside world, and the guy becomes her top priority. She falls hard and fast, and wants to spend every minute with the guy she's dating.

"You don't think guys can sense that you're rearranging your life for them?" I asked. "It seems obvious to me that your overeager nature is what's making men back away from you. I know you want to spend time with someone you like, but dropping everything to go out with him when he calls is too extreme, especially in the beginning. I know it's what you want to do, but it isn't always what's smart."

"But I don't want to play games!" She pouted. "If I meet some-one I like and he wants to spend the whole weekend with me, why should I pretend I have other things going on? I just want to do what I feel like and not have to play these dumb games!"

"I know it's not what you *want* to do, Carey. But unfortunately it's what you are going to *have* to do," I explained.

The most common complaint I hear from women is that they don't want to play games. They are too old to play games, too tired, too mature, too pretty, and too smart. Doing what they *feel* like seems natural, and dating strategically sounds too orchestrated. What they want is to meet someone, be honest about their feelings, and have someone like them for who they are. It sounds good in theory. But unfortunately, you can't do that. Whether you like it or not, relationships just don't work that way, especially in the beginning.

Carey's problem was that because she was immediately making the guy her number one priority, men perceived her to be needy and lacking a life of her own. If she continued to do what she felt like doing (and not play any games) she would continue to hear the same response from men. After all, the definition of insanity is doing the same thing over and over and expecting to get a different result. If Carey wanted to get guys to act differently toward her, then she would have to start acting differently toward them. The next time she started to date a guy she would have to restrain herself from seeing him too much. She and I both knew this was going to take a serious amount of discipline, but no one said it was going to be easy. Carey might never be able to change how she *wanted* to act with a guy, but she could change her behavior.

Is that playing a game? Does that mean she's not being who

she really is? You can think of it that way if you like. I prefer to think of it as having a strategy to get what you want. Carey could continue to act on her feelings, but the greatest indicator of future events is the past. And her past was pretty lonely.

It's Not a Game—It's a Strategy

You need a strategy to get anywhere in life. If you wanted to start a business you would need a business strategy. If you wanted to lose weight, you would have a diet strategy. If you wanted to get your finances in order, buy a new house, land a new job, you would need a strategy! So why is dating any different? You want a man, you need a strategy. You would never say something like "I want to find a new job but I am not going to think too much about it. I am going to let the chips fall where they may. I will go with the flow on the interview and let whatever happens happen." Who does that? Yet this is what most women do when they are dating. They expect love to just happen. Like the movies. A man will see them across a crowded room, be awestruck by their beauty, and court them with flowers, candy, and the occasional love poem. A logical plan just doesn't fit into their romance. Well, wake up! This is real life and not a chick flick. In real life you have to be smart and savvy to get what you want.

Ladies, your patterns are making you succeed or fail with guys. I know you are tired of the games and just want to tell a

guy who you are and what you're looking for. Well, after being in sales for many years I completely understand. Sometimes I get tired, too. But does that mean I can just sit down with a customer and put my naked intentions on the table, and say, "You know, sir, I'm tired of pounding the pavement. I'm tired of meeting with different people and trying to make a sale. I am looking for a good customer who will repeatedly buy from me. I could spend the next hour trying to sell you my product but I don't want to play games here. I just want to know, are you going to buy from me or what?" Can you imagine?

I am not asking you to change your morals, values, personality, or sense of humor. I don't want you to change who you are. I just want you to change how you date. That will require a strategy, and that strategy will require discipline—discipline to not always do what you want, but instead, to do what is smart. If you've always been one of those girls who hates playing games, let's be brutally honest for a minute. Girls that say they don't play games either:

1. Don't know how to play,
2. Are too lazy to play, or
3. Don't have enough discipline to play.

Well, before you go any further in this book, make a decision. Are you going to keep making excuses or are you going to start getting results? You can't do both. You have to pick

one. Are you willing to stop getting hung up on the whole "game playing" thing and start accepting that you need a strategy to get the guy you want? You haven't had success so far, so something's got to change. That something is you.

Decide right now that you are up for the challenge, and I will show you how to find him, get him interested, and close the deal. It's all in your power. You just have to learn how. The rest of this book will teach you all the secrets of the sales world. Starting with learning the basics of the most important product you will ever sell—Yourself!

THE PRODUCT: YOU

Know Your Product

When I landed my medical sales job, I had zero medical experience. I had been in sales my whole life, but the industry was completely new to me. I didn't know anything about hospitals, let alone the cardiac monitors I was selling. But I was always a firm believer that a good salesperson can sell anything. So even if I didn't know the product that well, I could still get by.

After being at my new job for only a few months, I thought I was ready to take my first big client meeting alone. My boss always came with me before, but this time he had a scheduling conflict and couldn't make it. I told him it was no problem because I could handle the meeting on my own.

When I arrived at the hospital I was excited. If my meeting went well, and the client liked our equipment, I was going to make a huge commission. I started setting up the table as the hospital staff began to trickle in.

I began my demonstration by thanking everyone for attending and started going through my pitch. I felt good. It flowed. People were paying attention and nodding in agreement. The usually stoic director of nursing was actually smiling. The head doctor was, too. I thought I had nailed it. But then something happened that I wasn't prepared for.

The staff started asking questions.

I don't know about you, but before that day, I had never heard of ST Analysis. I didn't know how to answer when the director of nursing questioned if the 12-lead report was derived or diagnostic. And when the CEO wanted to know what bandwidth the telemetry system ran on, I wanted to crawl under a rock. Just as foreign as this is sounding to you now, they might as well have been speaking Chinese to me back then.

I lost the deal. I left that hospital wondering how I could have been so unprepared. When I told my boss what happened, I expected him to be furious with me. Instead, he said, "I hope you learned a good lesson today. I know you are great at sales, and I know you are great with people. But those things don't matter if you don't know your product. If you don't know your product, Jess, you'll never survive here."

He was right. I didn't know my product well enough to sell it. I tried to make up answers and skirt around issues. At one point I just agreed with one of the doctors when he said he thought our monitors ran on a 608 frequency. I had no idea what he or I was talking about. And let me tell you, everyone in that room knew it.

It is imperative to know your product in sales. Can you imagine going into a meeting and not knowing how to answer questions about what you are selling? Sadly, it's not that unbelievable. There are many salespeople who try to win deals using 100 percent personality and zero product knowledge. I know because I've tried it. But eventually not knowing how to answer simple questions about your product will leave your customers confused and frustrated, and will ultimately drive them into the arms of the competition.

In the dating arena, you are your product, and I am astounded by how many women out there don't really know themselves. One of the biggest compliments I get from men is that I really know who I am. Regardless of whether they agree with my opinion or not, they love that I have one. I know my product from the inside out.

My friend Kayla is the worst dater. I love her to death, but she can't get past two dates with a guy. She hasn't had a long-term relationship since high school. Kayla's biggest problem is that she doesn't really know who she is. She hasn't yet figured out the kind of person that makes her Kayla. If you

asked her if she was a Democrat or Republican, she would say
she's not into politics. If you tried to discuss religion, she
would tell you she just loves God. If you asked her what
restaurant she wanted to go to for dinner, she would say she's
up for anything you want. She hardly has an opinion about
anything. I remember one date asked her, "What do you think
about the war in Iraq?" To this she replied, "I try not to." Yes,
she knew there was a war going on, but that only proved she
hadn't been living in a closet for the last few years. She had no
opinion on the subject. She thought she was being easygoing
by staying neutral, but instead she came off looking like she
wasn't smart enough to form her own opinion. Men find her
boring because she cannot carry on an interesting conversation. She reminds me of the princess Eddie Murphy was
betrothed to in *Coming to America*. He tried to get to know her
by asking her what she liked, and she kept responding with
"Whatever you like." And as we all know, the entire movie is
based on him chasing a sassy go-getter from the Bronx so he
wouldn't have to marry the annoyingly passive princess.

I know it's an unusual concept to grasp. Most people never
stop to think about who they really are. But seriously, how can
you expect someone to get to know you if you don't even
know yourself. You may be able to fake it for a while, but
believe me, you will eventually be found out. No one wants to
date a Stepford wife, so you better start doing some soul-
searching and figure out what makes you you. You need to be

able to answer questions like, *What are your goals in life? What motivates you? Are you passionate about music, politics, or sports? What makes you happy? What really drives you nuts? What would you be doing if you could do anything?*

If you can't answer these questions off the top of your head, now is the time to really think about them. If you find yourself starting sentences with, "I don't know, I guess I like...," or "Gee, I haven't really thought about that...," make the time to think about them now.

How Interesting Are You?

If you are one of the many women out there that only likes talking about shopping, celebrity gossip, and your coworkers' love lives, how do you expect a man to really get to know you? You may know what Gwyneth Paltrow named her two kids or how many times JLo's been married, but that's not going to show a guy how intelligent and funny you are. You need to have more to talk about.

Think of yourself like a cable TV package. Do you only have basic cable or do you have the deluxe service? I don't have to tell you that if your package only has E! or Bravo, a guy will not stay tuned in for long. Guys want a little variety. They may start out watching ESPN, then switch to Discovery, and finally finish the night off with Comedy Central. I'm not saying you have to fake interest or knowledge in any of these

areas. What I am saying is that you need to have a broader range of interest. Venture into unknown territory and try to expand your horizons. The more channels you have, the more likely you will find a guy that has some of the same "stations" as you do. That will give you more things to discuss and thus connect on.

I've never been one of those girls who has tried to learn about sports in order to relate to guys, so I am not going to tell you to go out and research his favorite team or learn all the rules of the game in order to impress him. I think forcing yourself to take interest in something that you don't give a hoot about is pointless. If you are not truly interested in something, you will struggle to understand and retain information about it. However, if you open your mind to exploring new things, you will inevitably find more interests and have a greater chance of finding a guy that shares them.

Get to know your most important product—you. If you don't know your product, you will find yourself constantly struggling to sell yourself. Whether it's expanding your interests or gaining more knowledge for those you already have, figure out what makes you the person you are. Because if you don't know, you will continually lose your customers.

Love Your Product

After the disaster with my first sales meeting, I was sent to New Jersey for follow-up training. All the new sales reps were crammed into a little room and given a chance to ask questions. Most inquiries were regarding standard product knowledge. However, one newbie decided to ask something rather unorthodox. His sales were down, and we all knew that something had been plaguing him since the day he was hired. Whatever it was, he kept to himself, but it was severely impacting his performance. He sat quietly for the entire training, hoping someone else would ask his question for him. When it was apparent that no one was having the same problem, he slowly raised his hand and asked it.

"How do you become successful at selling a product that you don't really like?" he asked sheepishly.

The rest of us sat in silence. How would the teacher answer that? What kind of advice would he give? And what did he think of this rep that basically just announced that he thought our product sucked?

The teacher smiled, walked closer, and put his hand on the rep. "How do you become successful at selling a product you really don't like?" The teacher repeated. "The answer is simple. You don't."

You would think with all the different techniques a salesperson

has, liking the product wouldn't be a huge roadblock. Well, I'm here to tell you that if you don't like your product, you haven't hit a roadblock. You've hit a dead end.

In dating, you are the product. If you don't like the product and you aren't confident in it, you cannot possibly be successful at selling it. There is a direct correlation between how much you like your product and how much someone else will like it. You will never get anyone to love something you, yourself, do not love.

My friend Ebony doesn't like herself very much. She doesn't eat right or exercise, and she smokes and drinks quite frequently. She complains that she's not in very good shape and that her skin is starting to wrinkle. She is so unhappy with her lifestyle that she beats herself up about it constantly. In short, Ebony does not love herself. When she goes on dates, this poor self-image comes shining through. If a guy is nice to her and actually treats her well, she doesn't like him. Why? Because subconsciously she thinks, *How can this guy possibly like me so much? He must not be very smart. He must be even more worthless than I am.* On the flip side, if she meets a guy who treats her like garbage, she loves him! Why? Because he can see who she really is . . . a woman undeserving of love. He must be smart. He must be worthy. She chases him and tries to get him to love her. But it doesn't work. You can't get someone to love you until you completely love yourself.

Be Confident in Your Product

When you love your product, you automatically become confident in it. Confidence is the outward expression of an internal feeling about yourself. If you feel good about yourself it permeates your being and is visible to those around you. People see that you are confident and just like a magic mirror, they reflect that feeling back to you. They agree with your level of self-worth. However, if you do not feel good about yourself, they see that as well, and the mirror reflects those feelings tenfold.

Back in college I was very insecure about my small chest. I thought I had the body of a fourteen-year-old boy and no guy could possibly like it. I went out with my friends to parties and watched as they all got hit on. I remember standing there, wishing that I had bigger boobs so someone would talk to me. Then one day I told my mother that I wanted to get implants. She looked at me like I was crazy and said, "Honey, it's your head and not your chest that needs fixing."

She was right. It wasn't my flat chest that was keeping me down. It was my insecurity. The more I dwelled on the negative, the more people felt my negativity. The magic mirror was working overtime. The more I convinced myself that no one could find me attractive, the more people agreed with me. I didn't love my product, and therefore, no one else did either.

I decided I had to stop focusing on what I didn't like about

myself and start focusing on what I did like. I forgot about my boobs and decided I liked my long legs. Wherever I went, I told myself I had the best legs out there. I told myself this over and over. Eventually I began to love my legs, and the rest of my body. Soon I was walking taller and acting more confidently. Once I started loving myself, and believing I was a pretty girl, the guys started noticing me.

If you are insecure about your height, your weight, a particular body part, or even something that is internal, men will be able to sense it. It's lack of confidence that holds women back and nothing else. You know yourself best, and if you are not confident, men may start to wonder if there is something about you that they don't see yet. Maybe you are a needy person? Maybe you have a sixth toe? Why on Earth would a seemingly attractive woman not be confident? You actually will invoke in him the feeling that you are not as great as you seem to be. Why else would you be so insecure? Most of the time men never even notice what it is we are so self-conscious about. They do, however, notice the insecurity we exude because of it.

Confidence Is Contagious

When you are out with a guy, be aware that confidence (or lack there of) is contagious. During the course of the evening he may ask you questions that you might not like answering.

Maybe he will ask where you live, and it's at home with your parents. Maybe he will ask if you work out, and until last week you thought Gold's was the name of a popular jewelry store. You can answer these questions with a scrunched face and a worried look, and your date will immediately feel your insecurity, or you can answer these questions with confidence. Look him in the eye. Don't flinch. Give it to him straight. If he sees you have no problem with yourself, he won't either.

When I was in high school, I drove an old 1987 Chrysler New Yorker. It was a boxy car that looked like it belonged to a grandfather rather than a sixteen-year-old. I was terribly embarrassed to drive it to school for fear of being teased. Then I realized if I just acted like my car was cool, other kids would too. Whenever someone jokingly said, "Nice car, Jess" I just responded with a confident, "Thanks! I love it." At first they were taken aback, but then they actually started to agree with me. I could fit all my friends in the car *and* it had all leather interior. Pretty soon, I had everyone believing that the New Yorker was totally cool.

Once You Know Yourself, Be Yourself

There is no better advice from Socrates than "Know thyself." But once you do know yourself, you need to be yourself. You've got interests. You've got likes and dislikes. You have to be confident and comfortable enough in your own skin so as

not to cater to a man. Some girls are afraid to voice their opinions because they don't want to "rock the boat." They are so afraid of the guy not liking them that they would rather stay quiet about things that they don't agree with. But men don't want to date a mindless bimbo without an opinion of her own. If there is one thing worse than a woman who doesn't know herself, it's one who's afraid to be herself.

My father dated a woman who was so afraid to offend him that she never voiced her opinion about anything. She thought if she ever disagreed with what he said, he wouldn't like her. For instance, my father is a diehard Democrat and she was a known Republican. Yet whenever they got together and my father started talking politics she kept her mouth shut. He'd argue a point, and she would just smile and agree with him. Even after a year she was still afraid to speak her mind for fear of offending him. She didn't stick up for her needs in other areas as well. She was never particularly fond of motorcycle riding; in fact, you could almost say she hated it. Yet every weekend she'd smile and get on the back of Dad's bike for a three-hour ride. She figured she was making him happy by always doing the things he wanted to do. But eventually my dad dumped her and told the family that he couldn't stand to be with someone who didn't know how to stand up for her beliefs, even if they were contradictory to his own.

Men aren't offended by differences in opinions. Just because you don't agree with a guy doesn't mean you aren't a

likable person. One of my boyfriends used to love the fact that I had such a different perspective from him. He said it was one of the sexiest things about me, and it showed how confident and smart I was.

Don't be afraid to be you. If you don't like something, you can and should say so. You have to figure out if you are compatible, and you can't possibly do that by pretending to be something you know you are not.

Just remember: you cannot expect anyone to like you more than you like yourself. So if you do not love your product yet, it will not matter how many sales techniques you learn. You will not be able to close the deal. Focus on your strong points. A salesperson never enters a meeting thinking about the chinks in his armor. He thinks of all the positive things about his product. He answers even the toughest questions with confidence. He truly believes he's got the best thing out there! And if you truly believe you are the best thing out there too, men will agree with you.

Packaging Your Product

My first job out of college was anything but glamorous. I went door-to-door, cold-calling on small businesses, trying to make a thirty-dollar sale. Everyday, I was out in the field,

pounding the pavement, come rain, sleet, snow, or ungodly heat. The summer of 2000 was one of the worst. I remember returning to the office at the end of each day with my mascara running down my face, thanks to the humidity. I finally decided I had to start dressing weather-appropriately. For the following three months I lived in a black skirt and a gray halter top. It was the bare minimum I could get away with at the office. It wasn't exactly a professional look, but it did attract attention from the male reps, which got me quite a few free lunches.

In September, my boss announced that she would be hiring someone for an assistant manager position and was specifically looking to promote from within. I was excited since I knew there was no one with a better record than me. I had trained half of the office, was the highest producing rep, and knew how the business worked.

However, three weeks later my boss was interviewing several different candidates and had not yet approached me. I was perplexed. How could she ignore the obvious? I decided I had to find out.

After everyone had gone home one night, I waited around to talk to her. I was nervous, but I was also completely baffled by being overlooked. When I brought the issue to her attention she seemed surprised. She told me that it looked to her like I was completely happy where I was. Her perception of me was that I was a hard worker and a good producer, but really liked

being the "blonde with the nice legs." It was the first time that statement felt like an insult. She told me the assistant she was looking for was serious and respected. She didn't want a manager other employees flirted with. She needed someone people looked up to, and while they didn't look down on me, they did sometimes try to look down my shirt.

I went home that night upset. I desperately wanted the promotion but honestly believed all hope was lost. I plopped down on my couch and flipped on *Working Girl,* one of my favorite movies. I grabbed a bag of peanut M&M's to ease the pain. Just as I was about to slip into a sugar-induced coma, Melanie Griffith told Joan Cusack, "If you want to be taken seriously, you need serious hair." It was at that moment I realized what I needed to do.

Over the weekend I chopped off my hair. Instead of the long blonde locks I had been sporting, I now had a neat bob. I also bought two new suits. I ditched my open-toed shoes and traded in my hoop earrings. I decided I was going to start dressing for the job I wanted, not the job I had.

Everyone in the office was impressed with the transformation, especially my boss. The new look gave me a whole new attitude. I was more confident and serious, and everyone treated me with more respect. By the end of the year, my boss announced that she had found her assistant manager. I was officially promoted shortly thereafter.

Dress for the Part You Want

Clothes do not just make the man. They make the woman, too. How you dress communicates a lot about you. First impressions are made from how you look. With that in mind, remember that if you want to get noticed, be taken seriously, and eventually get married, you need to communicate that with the way you dress.

When my friends and I were in college, we used to go clubbing a lot. Wednesday through Sunday we were out on the town having the time of our lives. We would buy fun clubbing clothes every week so we always had something new to wear. We loved our mini-skirts and midriffs. Didn't matter if it was twenty degrees outside, we'd dress like it was the middle of August. We danced with a lot of guys and got a lot of numbers, but we were never taken out to dinner, never called at a decent hour, and never treated with very much respect. We dressed like party girls, and we were treated like party girls. No one took us seriously.

It wasn't until much later in life that I realized that how I was dressing was severely impacting men's perception of me. I was a single girl, but I didn't want to be. I wanted to be someone's girlfriend. I was dressing proactively to get attention and get noticed. It was working but not in the right way. I was dressing for the part I had, not the part I wanted.

I have nothing against skimpy attire. If you got it and want

to flaunt it, be my guest. But know the kind of perception you are giving men. You definitely want to be treated with respect, and a bad first impression is hard to recover from. It's a mistake to think all attention is good attention. If a man notices you because your cleavage is starring him in the face, he will be less interested in where you went to school and more interested in what cup size you are. However, on the flip side, not putting enough effort into your appearance can impact your dating life as well.

Men Judge Books by Their Covers

Men are visual. When I say that, I don't mean that they don't understand something unless you paint a picture for them. I mean they are visually turned on or off by what they see. Women are different. Attraction can grow for us. But men know in three seconds if they find you attractive or not. And unfortunately what a woman thinks is attractive is usually very different from what a man thinks is attractive.

There may be things women will often overlook in a guy, but that men cannot get past. It seems shallow, but it's the reality. Sure there are men who don't place as much importance on appearance, but they are not the majority.

The good news is that most appearance issues are fixable. You just have to admit they need fixing and then put in the work to fix them. Telling yourself you are too tired to put on

any makeup or you are too busy to go to the gym will only hurt one person—you. Don't make excuses for a shoddy appearance. If you want to attract a guy, you have to stop doing what's easy and start doing what's right. If it means getting up an extra half-hour before work to straighten your hair, do it! Stop pretending it doesn't matter. It does. No matter how great a product you have, poor packaging can destroy its salability. Men absolutely judge books by their covers, so you need to make yours as spectacular and eye-catching as it can be.

Faye, one of my oldest friends, did not know how to dress well. She is an attractive girl, but it was sometimes hard to tell. She loved her comfy sweaters and often wore baggy, high-rise jeans. She thought it took too much effort to wear a skirt or high heels. She wanted a man to love her for her mind and didn't want to go through the hassle of making herself up. Besides that, she thought women who wore makeup looked like hookers. Whenever we went out, whether it was on the town or to the grocery store, I got all the attention, because I was the one that looked like a lady. She, on the other hand, looked like she had just rolled out of bed.

A few years ago, Faye started putting a little more stock into her appearance. Instead of the usually bulky sweaters, she started wearing form-fitting shirts and nice fitting pants. I almost died when she came out one night wearing a skirt. Men immediately took notice. She seemed much more approachable and feminine. Two years ago she met her husband, and now is pregnant with their first son.

If you want to land a man, you have to dress for the occasion. Faye was a single woman who wanted to find someone but didn't want to dress for the part. She was ultraconservative with her hair, clothes, and makeup, which made men perceive her as homely and unattractive. When she realized she would have to dress for the part she wanted, she got the part she was looking for.

If you want to attract a man, you have to be willing to dress to do so. It sounds like a fine line to walk, but it's really very simple. Remember that less isn't necessarily more when it comes to clothes, ladies. Guys don't have to be able to see your boobs to know you've got them. But also make sure that you are making yourself as attractive as possible. Put effort in to your appearance. Men are visual. You want to give them something nice to look at, while still leaving something to the imagination!

Attracting Attention to Your Product

My first trip to Los Angeles was an eye-opening experience. The sunny West Coast city was so different from the conservative D.C. area. The streets were crowded; the restaurants were filled with trendy people; and the women, my god, the women. The women in L.A. were drop dead gorgeous. Wherever you went you saw one beautiful woman after

another. Every time I saw one, it conjured up those old boob-job feelings. But after spending a few weeks there I realized why all women in L.A. look like Barbie dolls. They are all trying to keep up with each other.

By nature, women are competitive with other women. The ones in L.A. have an even harder task than most, and try relentlessly to get noticed over other girls. They spend their money on the best clothes, jewelry, hair stylist, and yoga instructors. However, as beautiful as they are, they still have difficulty attracting men. They complain about never meeting anyone, just like women everywhere else.

After thinking long and hard about it, I realized that although most women in L.A. are extremely beautiful, most look the same. They invested all their time, energy, and money into trying to edge out the competition, but it wasn't working.

It gave me an idea for a little experiment.

I went out with my friend Lana one night, to a bar filled with girls that could be contestants from *America's Next Top Model*. I decided instead of trying to look as good as they did, I would apply a standard sales technique often used when trying to stand out amongst heavy competition. I would separate myself from the pack, not by trying to look better than everyone else, but by looking as *different* as possible. I wore my favorite jeans, a cute T-shirt, and an Army hat. Although that may not sound like a special outfit, at this particular nightclub, I would be the only one looking sporty. Most of the women

would be wearing dresses, and none of them would be wearing a hat.

On my way to the bar, twenty-five feet from the entrance, I was stopped five times by men either telling me how cute I looked or commenting on my hat. Lana and I decided to hit the dance floor after grabbing our first drink. As we danced, I noticed a group of handsome guys sitting in the V.I.P. section. They apparently noticed us as well, since one of the guys kept waving and motioning for us to come over. He asked if we wanted to join his party. We, of course, said yes, and proceeded through the golden gates of the V.I.P. section. All the guys went nuts about my hat. I felt a little bad for Lana, who wasn't getting very much attention, but it just proved my point that making yourself different is what will attract the most attention.

Lana and I agreed that the night had been successful. I decided that I was going to proceed with the experiment back home. Whenever I went out I decided to wear something different, something eye-catching that would draw attention to me. Sometimes I wore a hat; sometimes I wore my hair in two braids. I went to my high school reunion in jeans and a funky shirt while everyone else there was wearing a black dress. When it got warm out, I started wearing shorts with heels instead of a dress—anything I could find to set myself apart from the crowd. I tried on headscarves, jewelry, and funky belts. Sometimes I would dress up if I knew everyone else

would be dressing down, or I would dress down when everyone else was dressing up. There was no right or wrong. All that mattered was looking different.

Repeat Your Best Outfits

Whenever Adison goes running, she wears her Yankee cap. She usually stops for coffee when she is done working out, and someone almost always comments on her hat. Knowing this, I told her she should incorporate the hat into her daily wardrobe.

You need a couple of staple outfits that are sure to get you noticed. The great thing about trying to be different is that you not only get noticed because you stand out, you also have a conversation starter. Men love when you give them a reason to come talk to you. It takes the pressure off of them for coming up with something to say.

I have five outfits that are always sure to get me noticed. I wear them a lot. My girlfriends will call and ask me what I am wearing that evening, and I will tell them "Outfit number four." It doesn't matter if they have seen it a hundred times before, they aren't the ones whose attention I am trying to grab.

If you know that certain things in your wardrobe drum up a lot of attention, then wear them often! Don't buy new clothes that will only make you blend in. Try new styles that are a little unusual and see what kind of reaction you get. If you

notice another female while you are out, ask yourself why you noticed her and then copy what she is doing. I once noticed a girl running in front of my apartment because she was wearing a hot pink running suit. Now I own one as well.

Different Is Sexy

It has become the standard for women to emulate each other. We see celebrities on TV and want to look like them. We follow trends in fashion or hair, and try to replicate an image. But you have to be careful that you don't end up blending in with your surroundings. Looking like everyone else won't attract attention to your product.

Millions of girls dream of being supermodels, but few ever actually fulfill that dream. Cindy Crawford is one the world's most popular and beautiful. However, Cindy did not always see herself that way. Growing up, she was very self-conscious about her mole, and contemplated getting it removed. Her first modeling pictures were actually airbrushed to hide the mole, and many thought she would never make it big with a mark on her face.

But they were wrong. That mole separated Cindy from the thousands of girls aspiring to be supermodels. The mole became her trademark and took her to the top. That mole is now a sex symbol that is revered and imitated by girls around the world. It just proves that different can be sexy. Very, *very* sexy!

Don't shy away from something that makes you different. Embrace it. My sister is blind as a bat, but instead of getting contacts, she got glasses. They make her stand out and seem very sophisticated and sexy. Fitting in and looking like everyone else is boring. You want to be different. Doesn't matter if it's because of some characteristic that isn't normally classified as attractive. Justin Timberlake was once quoted as saying, "I have a big nose, but I rock it!" Usually big noses are not a symbol of sexy, but last time I checked, JT was the one bringing it back.

There will always be someone out there who is prettier or thinner than you. So trying to be the best looking, most beautiful girl on the planet is a lost cause. I'm not saying you don't need to be the best looking, most attractive you that you can be. I'm just telling you that in order to stand out, you don't have to be more attractive than everyone else. Find a style that you can make your own. You definitely don't have to fit some supermodel mold. Just accentuate the unique person you are, and you will attract the attention you deserve.

FINDING HIM

Prospecting

By the time I finished my first full year in medical device sales I had achieved 120 percent of my quota. This shocked a lot of people. My assigned target of 2.1 million in revenue hadn't been met by the previous sales rep for years, and no one thought a young girl with no prior medical experience was going to do any better. When I attended the national sales meeting I was congratulated by my coworkers (who all happened to be men). When the commotion finally settled down, I decided to relax by the pool with my good friend Lou. Lou had been a medical sales rep for over six years. This year, likc the last year, he had just missed his quota. As we sat by the pool talking numbers, I wondered how it was that I outsold him by almost

a million dollars. Here he was, a seasoned rep that knew the product better and had stronger relationships with his customers. Yet, he was beaten by a young rookie that had no prior medical experience. Lou and I talked almost every day, so I knew he was a hard worker. He seemed to get up earlier and work later than I did. And he was always in a hospital or at least driving to one, so I knew he wasn't sitting at home. So how in the world had I closed more deals than he did?

Before I even got the question out of my mouth, Lou was already answering it.

"Prospecting," he said. "I hate it. I don't do it. I may go to hospitals everyday, but they are hospitals that have already bought from me, or hospitals where I know people really well. I never go to new hospitals and look for new business. I hate introducing myself to new people and asking if they need anything. I just want them to call me. I don't like stepping out of my comfort zone."

I thought about what Lou was saying, and it made perfect sense. Unlike him, I prospected every week. I would spend days at a hospital that didn't have my equipment, introducing myself and making new contacts. I was always trying to find new business whereas he was just maintaining what he already had. That reason alone is why I outsold Lou.

Prospecting is a necessary and essential part of my success in sales. However, it's also one of the most important factors in dating.

My sister Lisa and I could be twins. We're the same height, weight, and thanks to our favorite boxed color treatment, we now have the same hair color. We also have very similar personalities and senses of humor. However, after we broke up with our boyfriends last year, Lisa started going on ten times as many dates as I did. She had a date at least twice a week, whereas I was lucky if I had one date a month. What was the reason? She went prospecting. Lisa dedicated two nights a week for looking for potential guys. She would attend happy hours, work functions, and restaurant openings. Not only that, Lisa also made sure to try new places. She hardly ever went to the same place twice, unless she found it to be a good place to fish for men. Meanwhile, I was going out to the same bars and clubs with my friends. Just like Lou, I did what was easy, instead of what was smart. My philosophy was, let's go where we have fun and if something comes up, great. If not, that's okay. And that's a fine attitude to have, but it's not conducive to finding a man.

If you are ready to have a relationship, and would like to get married in the next three to five years, it's time to get serious and put some more effort into prospecting. I hate to tell you this, but fate won't deposit a boyfriend on your doorstep anymore than it will sell my equipment for me. If I want to make quota, I have to get out there and make it happen. I have to meet new people, introduce myself, and show them what I've got. If you really want a relationship, you are going to have to

do the same thing. I know it's uncomfortable to put yourself out there—believe me, prospecting is not my favorite thing either. But if you want to find The One, you have to accept the fact that you will need to put some time and effort into looking for him.

My friend Linda hates going out. She would much rather rent movies or cook dinner for her friends. She had a boyfriend for five years, but it didn't work out, and now she is thirty-seven years old and still searching for the right guy. The problem is, she doesn't really search. She just complains about never meeting anyone.

One day I said to her, "Linda, where do you think you are going to meet someone? In your stairwell? You never go out and put yourself in a situation where you could meet anyone. He's not going to come knocking on your door, you know. You have to take matters into your own hands. You have to force yourself to get out more."

"But why should I?" she complained. "I went out all last year and never met anyone. All the guys around here are mindless and boring. I'm not going to find anyone intellectually stimulating in a bar. So why go out at all? I'm happier at home."

"Just because you didn't find anyone last year does not mean you won't find anyone this year. You have to keep going. In sales we have a saying: *Every no brings you closer to a yes.* If you always went to the same bars and saw the same people,

of course you didn't find anyone. You never went anywhere new, so you never met anyone new. If you really think all the men around here aren't worth your time, then by all means, go ahead and stay home. But please don't complain about it. It won't help you find a guy, and it won't change your situation."

Linda knew I was right. If she wanted to get married, she would have to start creating opportunities to meet men. Like many women, she was holding on to the old adage that love would strike when she least expected it, and it was seriously hurting her chances.

The idea that we don't have to do anything and the man of our dreams will find us is just not realistic. If that's how you think, you need to put down the Danielle Steel novel and come back to earth. Men and women these days are extremely busy with life, career, and friends. If you don't put the effort into looking for your future husband, you very well may never find him. I know that is scary to hear, but it's true.

If Linda wanted to change her luck, she was going to have to change her methods. When I asked her what her schedule for the week was like, she would tell me she had lots of plans, but none of them were prospecting opportunities. She would go to her sister's house for dinner one night, to the movies with a friend another, and then to an all-female Pilates class the next. She was doing activities that were filling her time, but there was no way she was going to meet anyone with a schedule like that.

Think about your week right now. What are your plans? Are they conducive to prospecting? Or will you be sitting somewhere that will give you very little opportunity to meet someone? If the answer is yes, then you need to modify your agenda.

How to Prospect

The smart way to prospect is to go where the most opportunity is. For example, when I go to a large hospital, there are more people to contact than at a small hospital. So I better my chances at finding a new customer. Likewise, there are more guys at a driving range than there are at the mall. Instead of hanging out at your girlfriend's house, go to sports bars and pool halls. Coffee shops are also becoming a good place to meet men. You have to be creative and think to yourself, *If I were a guy, where would I be?* I have met a couple of very cute boys at my local dog park. The funny part about that is that I don't own a dog. But I walk there with a girlfriend and when a guy asks which dog is mine, I tell him that I am thinking about buying one and I am just checking out my options. They are more than happy to tell me about how great their dog is, and before I know it they are asking for my number.

Prospecting Events

Every weekend there is something going on in your particular city that will bring out the boys. You just have to search for it. Contrary to popular belief, I think meeting guys at bars and clubs is totally possible because the sole reason they are there in the first place is to meet girls. The mentality that you can't meet a good guy at a bar is just not true. Guys that are out in the bar scene are sociable, have lots of friends, and are open to making new ones. They wouldn't be there otherwise. Yes, you may have to sort through a few duds, but there are good candidates out there too.

There are certain places and events that you can bank on for good prospecting. For example, bar crawls are fantastic opportunities for prospecting. The last time I went to a bar crawl I met two very quality guys. One was a UVA graduate and the other was a marathon runner. As for events, last St. Patrick's Day was a feast for my girlfriends and me. Every man in Washington, D.C., was out and about from ten in the morning until ten at night.

Get Creative

Besides seeking out guy-friendly places, you can also change up your daily routine. Go to different grocery stores, switch gyms, try a different church. I switched hairdressers

and ended up dating the owner of a very trendy salon. It's not just about going where you think the guys are, although that is definitely a good strategy. It's also about putting yourself in different places at different times. Change up your daily routine and see what happens. I used to go to the same grocery store every Saturday morning, until one day my friend met a guy at Whole Foods. She told me that Monday nights at Whole Foods is a prospecting bonanza! Every guy in our city shops there, and for some reason, they go on Monday nights. Guess where I shop now?

Make sure you don't get stuck in a rut with your daily routine. Don't always go to the same Starbucks. If you belong to a health club, try another location. Get creative about where you look for men. You may find one right in your own backyard.

The Law of Averages

One thing to remember about prospecting is that even the best saleswoman doesn't find new business every day. Sometimes, we don't make a breakthrough for weeks, or even months. I can remember prospecting different hospitals all summer without a bite. It seemed like I was never going to find a new customer. But then, all of the sudden, I hit the jackpot and found a hospital that was building a whole new wing. Those three months of prospecting paid off considerably.

The Internet is a great place to increase your law of

averages, especially if you are like Linda and would rather not leave the comfort of your own home. It's one of the best places to prospect because a bar can only fit a finite amount of people, whereas online sites are filled with numerous men. Your chances of meeting the right guy are quadrupled by the use of the Internet. The old stigma of online dating has just about disappeared. If you're still hesitant about joining a dating site, then you can use less specific networking sites. I have personally met some great guys through Facebook. Being on the site doesn't necessarily mean you are looking for a relationship, so you (and your potential dates) may be a little less squeamish about logging on. Just be smart and careful about meeting people you don't know. Don't put out too much personal information right away and always tell a friend who you are meeting and where you are going.

Just remember, your future husband doesn't know where you live, so you have to get out there and make your presence known. Sitting at home and doing nothing may be what's easier, but it won't get you what you want. Don't get discouraged if you have been prospecting for months and haven't met anyone. It will take time. You will not find someone you like every time you go out. That is a certainty. But if you keep prospecting you will eventually find him. It's the law of averages—a numbers game. Every no *will* bring you closer to a yes. And the more times you go out, the better your chances.

SEE Factors

When I went to the Sundance Film Festival last year, my girlfriends and I made it our mission to find cute guys. We got dressed in our cutest winter gear and went out every night prepared to party and prospect. One of the girls in the crew, Leah, was attracting far more men than the rest of us. She was getting two and three phone numbers every night, while the rest of us just watched in awe. After our third night there, one of the other girls announced that Leah was a guy magnet! She just had "It"—that unexplainable quality that men love. Even though the rest of us were equally as attractive, guys naturally flocked to her.

But I knew that wasn't it. Leah was doing something that the rest of us weren't. She was doing something so simple, that even as my friends watched her, they still didn't see it. She was using her SEE Factor.

What Is SEE?

Some women would rather jump off a bridge than approach a man. We have been taught to let him come to us. Or as *The Rules* would instruct: smile at the room and look like you are having a good time with your friends. Don't make eye contact. Make it seem like you are hard to get, so that you don't seem needy. He needs to come over and get your attention so that

you keep the element of "the chase" going, right?

Wrong.

Guys need a sign that you are willing and interested to talk. Walking over to a girl and starting a conversation is very scary. Most guys would feel more comfortable addressing Congress. Knowing that, you need to give him an indication that he won't be immediately rejected. In sales we use something called the SEE Factor. We use it when approaching someone for the first time. SEE stands for three things. **Smile. Eye-contact. Energy.** When I walk into the office of someone I have never met, I smile, make eye contact, and exude good energy. This puts the person at ease immediately. Applying the same method to dating is simple. When you see a guy you think you might be interested in, walk by him, smile, look him right in the eye, and let him sense your good energy.

I know—easier said than done, right? The reality is you have most likely never done this before, and it will take several times to get comfortable with it. But in order to get what you want in life, you will eventually have to try new things. So, you may as well start now.

I watched Leah when we went out and saw how she used her SEE Factor. The rest of the girls huddled together and didn't make eye contact with anyone. Leah would walk around the room smiling, looking men in the eye and exuding a very positive and friendly energy.

Leah knows how to prospect. She makes twenty trips to the

bathroom (the long way around the bar) so that she can continually see and be seen. She isn't afraid to make eye contact and smile. That is what makes her a guy magnet. If the other girls had not been isolating themselves and made more of an effort, they would have gotten the same results.

I am not asking you to do much here. Just think of how hard guys have it. They actually have to think of something to say. Then they have to stand there, wait for you to accept them, and engage them in conversation or reject them and send them on their way. You don't have to worry about any of that. You walk by the guy, smile, give him a good "one Mississippi, two Mississippi" eye lock, and keep walking. The energy part of the SEE Factor is your prospecting attitude. You want to exude good energy, which means being confident and positive. Guys don't want to talk to chicks that are in bad moods, having a lousy time, or feeling bad about themselves, and believe me they can tell.

Now what will happen when you use your SEE Factor while prospecting? The same thing that happened to Leah. Guys will flock to you. Have you ever seen the movie *Swingers*? Vince Vaughn and his friends are at a Hollywood party. Vaughn spots a hot girl smoking a cigar at the other end of the room and says to his friend, "Is she looking at me?"

His friend glances over at the girl who is engrossed in conversation, paying no attention to Vince and replies, "No."

A few seconds pass, and Vince asks again, "What about now? Is she looking now?"

His friend glances over at the girl again and replies, "No, dude, she's not looking at you. Will you quit asking me if she's looking at you? She hasn't looked at you . . . wait, she just looked."

With that, Vince's character shakes his friend's hand and makes his move over to girl. That's all he's waiting for, ladies. All you need to do is give him the SEE and he'll make the next move. Guaranteed.

Preparing to Use SEE

An important thing to remember is that if you are not looking your best, you won't feel comfortable using the SEE Factor. Girls dress to impress when they are going out on the town, but what if you are just making a stop at the quickie mart? What if you see a cute guy in the check-out line? If you typically leave the house afraid of bumping into someone you know, then you need to put more effort into your appearance. Remember you can meet a guy *anywhere*. So you have to be prepared.

I once ran to Kinko's to pick up some business cards, and I didn't do my hair or put on any makeup that day. I was tired, so I threw on a pair of sweats and an old T-shirt. When I got there I was the only one in the store, until an extremely good-looking guy walked in. I wanted to smile at him, but I felt like I wasn't looking my best. So I didn't, and I missed my opportunity.

I know on Sunday morning it's annoying to shower and dress up just to go out and run errands, but it's something that you have to do. If you are only looking good on Friday nights when you hit the town, then you only have one chance in the entire week to meet anyone. I, on the other hand, make sure I look good everyday. Everyday is a prospecting day for me. So my chances are seven times greater than yours.

If you are prospecting outside, maybe jogging or at the park, I strongly recommend losing the sunglasses. There is no way you can appropriately execute the SEE Factor while wearing them. Besides that, no man will ever approach a woman with sunglasses because it puts up a huge wall between you. They have no idea what you are thinking with them on. Are you looking his way? Did you notice him when you walked by? Do you seem like a friendly person? Who knows? You are wearing huge glasses the size of Texas. He can't see your eyes— he's not coming over.

Practice the SEE Factor. I guarantee that a lot of guys would like to approach you, but their fear of rejection keeps their feet planted where they are. There is nothing sexier than a woman who is confident in herself, and looking a man in the eye conveys complete confidence. If you get nervous, just remind yourself that all you are doing is smiling at someone. How is that bad? It may take some getting used to, but I guarantee if you use your SEE Factor, you will be approached.

Icebreakers

Every Thursday night, I meet up with two of my girlfriends for happy hour. We always pick a new place with great specials on food and drinks. Usually we all arrive around five-thirty to get prime seating, but one Thursday, I was running late. When I arrived, my friends were both sitting at the bar, not talking to anyone and looking rather bored.

"Hi, girls." I said. "Anything happening?"

"No," one of my friends replied. "But there is a really cute guy over there that I have been eyeing all night."

"Well, let's talk to him," I said.

"What? No!" my friend insisted. "We can't talk to him first."

"Sure we can," I told her. "That's how I met my last two boyfriends."

I waited until the guy made his way closer to us. I pretended that I was playing with my phone and walked over in his direction. When I looked up he was looking right at me.

"Do you have the time?" I said, still holding my phone, which, by the way, had the time clearly displayed.

"Sure. It's ten-thirty," he replied smiling.

"Great. Thank you," I said, returning to the girls.

Five minutes later the guy came over and talked to us for the rest of the night. Unfortunately for my friend, he asked for my

number instead of hers. Just goes to show you, guys do like it when you initiate the conversation.

If you see someone you want to meet, you must do something about it. Can you imagine if, as a salesperson, I had the attitude that I wasn't going to approach customers first, that they had to come to me? I'd be out of a job pretty fast.

Most women do not want to make the first move. In fact, most other books will tell you not to make the first move because you will come off as too aggressive or desperate. The truth is it is totally fine to approach a man . . . if you know how to do it. Most of the guys that I've dated, I've approached first. The problem isn't that talking to a man first may ruin your chances; it's what you are *saying* to that man that may ruin them.

So what do you say when you're making the first move? The trick to starting a conversation is to use an Icebreaker, a small remark or question that can be directed toward just about anyone—something that seems spur-of-the-moment, unintentional, and casual. I would never walk up to a guy and say something like, "Hi, my name is Jess. What's your name?" That looks like I am trying to meet him. I want to make it look like meeting him is almost accidental.

When you use an Icebreaker, you cannot possible feel rejected if he has a girlfriend in the bathroom or, even possibly, a boyfriend who is getting him a drink. You were just asking for the time, not hitting on him for goodness sakes! Using an Icebreaker will also keep a guy from sensing your agenda

right away. There is nothing more of a turnoff to a guy than a girl who is out hunting for a serious relationship. You don't want him to think you are prospecting for a husband, even if that is exactly what you are doing.

The great thing about Icebreakers is that you can use the same one over and over. You don't need to come up with a different one every time you go out. The guys will never know.

Last year my friends and I went to Oktoberfest determined to meet new people.

We decided that when we saw a guy we wanted to talk to, we would stop him and say, "Hey, don't you go to my gym?" The guy would say no, but he almost always engaged in conversation after that. With the six of us prospecting, we probably asked fifty guys this question. It was fun and we all got several numbers from doing it.

Try and think of some standard Icebreakers so that when you come across a guy you want to meet, you don't struggle to find something to say. It's a good idea to think of Icebreakers ahead of time, otherwise your nerves will get the best of you and you may end up missing your chance. Some Icebreakers that are good to have in your back pocket are:

Do you know if there is a wait for a table?
Can you take a picture of my friends and me?
Do you know what the happy hour specials are?
Where did you get that shirt/hat/pair of sunglasses?

That drink looks good, what is it?

Didn't you go to my high school?

You can use the above Icebreakers at any bar, club, or restaurant. If you are someplace like a grocery store, you can follow a guy to the wine or produce section and ask him if he knows how to pick a good pinot or avocado. Usually, this is all it takes for you to open the lines of communication. The guy will take over from there.

Don't worry. It can be the lamest Icebreaker on Earth, and it won't matter. I have a friend who is an aesthetician, and she loves to break the ice by asking men if they have ever been waxed! I'm not kidding. Say anything and he'll take it from there. Guys love it when women make the first moves in these situations. I know, because I have asked them. Not once has a guy told me he would rather do the approaching. Remember you aren't asking him out, you are just being friendly and sociable. There is a big difference.

Be aware of situations that you can break into and make contact. Armed with these tactics, you can start talking to any guy you find while prospecting and as long as you keep it casual, you will get the result you are looking for.

Filling the Funnel

When my mother recently got involved in real estate, she was very excited. She bought every book, went to every lecture, and committed herself to giving this new venture 100 percent. After a couple of months she found her first clients, a newly married couple. She was eager to sell them a house and focused all her time and energy on this one deal. But after several weeks of searching for that perfect fit, her clients suddenly dropped her. As you can imagine, my mom was pretty upset, but she decided to move on and find another client as quickly as possible. She found a couple that needed to relocate to Virginia by the end of the month. She was once again excited by the possibilities, and this time she was certain she would see results much faster.

But a month later the couple called to tell her they had changed their mind about relocating and would not need her anymore. Once again, she was depressed. It took her a couple days to get back on the horse this time and to begin to look for another client. After a month she still hadn't found anyone. At lunch one day she expressed her disappointment to me.

"I have been at this for almost nine months," she said. "And I am just not seeing any progress. I find clients, I work really hard to help them find a good fit, but ultimately something happens, and it doesn't work out. Now I have to start all over

from scratch, and it's really disappointing."

I could sympathize with my mom's frustration. Every sales-person has been in her shoes at some point. However, the good ones have learned what to do to avoid having to start all over again when they lose a sale—they fill the funnel.

I told my mom her main problem was that she only focused on one client at a time, so when that one client fell through, it left her back at square one. Good salespeople don't put all their eggs in one basket; they fill the funnel with lots of sales, knowing that some will not work out. Never let the funnel dry up. It's a cardinal rule. You must keep prospecting so that you have enough business to lose a few deals and still be okay. Once my mom started juggling a few deals at a time, her sales picked up, and she was making money.

Most of my friends date the way my mom started out sell-ing houses. One prospect at a time. My friend Laurel, who is unmarried at forty-two, once told me that the biggest mistake she ever made was focusing all her efforts on one man.

"If I could go back and do it all over again" Laurel said, "I would have kept my options open at all times. Whenever I was dating someone and another guy would express interest, I would always say, 'Thanks, but I have a boyfriend,' even if I had only started seeing the guy. Looking back on it now I wish I had given those guys a chance. I wish I had gone out to din-ner with them once at the very least."

When most of my friends find a guy they like, they immediately

cut off all other prospects the minute they start dating him. They tell me they want to see where the relationship will go and they want to focus all their attention on this one guy, hoping he will be the one. To me that sounds risky. Why would you cut off other men when you aren't even sure if this one is going to work out?

Some women do this subconsciously. They don't realize that they close all doors when they start dating someone new. But they do. They don't leave themselves open for other opportunities to come along. Other women simply think they cannot date more than one man at a time. In fact, I know women that think it just flat out wrong to date multiple guys. But why? Why is it wrong? Unless the man thinks that you are dating exclusively (and in the beginning stages they definitely don't), I see no problem.

My friend Anne had been dating Charlie for two months. She liked him a lot, but wasn't sure where the relationship was going yet. They were spending almost every night together and for all intents and purposes, she called him her boyfriend, even though they'd never actually agreed that their relationship was exclusive. One night a mutual friend of Anne's and mine had a birthday party and Charlie couldn't attend due to his long work schedule. When Anne walked through the door she was almost knocked off her feet. There was a very tall and very handsome man talking with the birthday boy. Anne immediately wanted to know who he was.

His name was Victorio. He was twenty-eight and adorable.

Anne spent almost the entire evening talking to him. At the end of the night Victorio asked Anne for her business card, but she hadn't brought any with her. He asked how he was supposed to call her if she didn't give him her number. Anne just smiled. She wasn't sure what to say. She wanted to give him her number, but she was already dating Charlie. She decided it wouldn't be right even though she and Charlie had never really talked about being exclusive with each other.

Eight months later, Anne was still seeing Charlie but they still hadn't defined their relationship. One night she finally got up the nerve to tell Charlie how she felt and ask if there was a future for them. Charlie said he wasn't sure. He knew that he wasn't ready for anything serious and really didn't want to talk about it any further. Of course this completely shocked Anne. Here she had been spending all her time with Charlie and he wasn't sure if she was the one? They broke up shortly after that, and Anne tried desperately to reconnect with Victorio. However, he was already seriously dating someone else. Anne should have been filling her funnel all along, instead of presuming she and Charlie were a couple with a future.

When I date someone new, I just assume he is seeing other people like I am. We don't have any conversations about our relationship in the beginning. Why should we? We hardly know each other. Until the guy has the "relationship talk" with me (and not the other way around), I see no reason to cut off

other would-be-suitors. Later in the book you will learn how to get him to want to have that conversation, but for now you should just concentrate on filling that funnel!

Dating with a Net

Hopefully, you will only be married once. You are looking for just one guy in a sea of many. It's up to you how quickly (or slowly) it takes you to find him. If you only date one guy at a time, then it will take you a lot longer than if you fill your funnel. It's really the only way to date. I am not saying you should cheat on your wonderful boyfriend and continue to juggle other men on the side. Not at all. I'm saying don't cross your fingers and hope that the guy you've been dating for three weeks will be the one to work out. Salespeople don't stop prospecting when they come across one opportunity to make a sale. They work on closing deals and continue filling the funnel at the same time. That way if one deal falls through, they still have another one in the funnel to move on to. You have to date the same way or you could be wasting a lot of your time like Anne did with Charlie.

When Anne finally realized she needed to fill the funnel, she took it very slowly. She usually dated two guys. Sometimes she was really into one of them, and the other became a backup guy. But until she heard the words, "I love you, I want to be with you and only you," she continued to fill the funnel. She

dated backup guy on the days she didn't see the guy she was really into. This prevented her from doing stupid things with the guy she really liked—like seeing him too much, or placing too much importance on him early in the relationship. If things didn't work out with the guy she was really into, her backup guy cushioned the blow. She also didn't have that "I have to start all over" feeling because she was still dating someone she enjoyed spending time with. If backup guy tried to get serious with her, she was open and honest about her feelings and intentions with him. If he was okay with it, they continued to see each other, and if he wasn't, they would part ways.

Another reason filling your funnel is such a smart idea is that it keeps you from getting emotionally attached too soon. Most of my girlfriends meet a guy, and after one date they proclaim that they have found Mr. Right. They are completely swept off their feet by someone who's still a complete stranger. But, nonetheless, they are daydreaming, waiting by the phone and analyzing every second of their last date. My best friend Adison was this way. She was dying to find a boyfriend. So whenever she met someone who showed interest in her, she immediately focused all her time and energy on him.

That's exactly what happened when she found Gavin. She was prospecting the pages of MySpace and she stumbled upon his profile. He was very cute and after a few short e-sessions, they decided to meet at a restaurant near her house. Dinner was fun, and afterward Adison asked Gavin to come back to

her place. They continued to have a good time, and Gavin didn't leave until 3 AM.

She called me the following morning and proclaimed her love for her new beau.

"He's so cute and sweet. I just love him. I can't wait to see him again. I hope he calls tonight. I want to take him to my company party on Friday and then to your barbeque on Saturday. I think I'm going to call him and ask him tomorrow if he doesn't call me by tonight."

Adison called him the next day and the day after. They saw each other without a hitch for a couple of weeks. Adison didn't go out with any other guys because she was so into Gavin. She believed that they had something special and she was in it for the long haul. But then suddenly Gavin started to pull away. He didn't always answer Adison's calls and he didn't come over as much. When he did come over she never wanted him to leave because she didn't know when she was going to see him again.

One day at lunch she was telling me how she was checking his page on MySpace and she discovered several pictures of him posted with the same girl.

"I think he's seeing this girl Rachel. I don't know what to do. I texted him last night to come over, but he said he was at his parents' house. So I drove over to his house, and his car was outside. He lied to me. I don't know if I should text him and tell him he's a jerk or if I should call him and talk to him about it."

I looked at her like she had three heads. "Adison, you don't do anything. He never said he wanted a relationship with you. He never said you were his girlfriend. You just started acting like you were together. You should have continued to go out with other guys while you were seeing him."

Adison agreed I was right. But it was too late. She had lost Gavin and now her funnel was dry. She was back at square one, and she was not happy about it.

This is not an uncommon scenario. It happens to a lot of women. The smart ones learn from it and decide not to let it happen again. The rest of them continue on this path and wonder, "Why does this keep happening to me?"

If Adison had a couple of guys calling her, this story may have turned out differently. Instead of wasting time driving by Gavin's house, waiting for his calls, and checking his profile on MySpace, she could have been out with someone else. Even if she really only liked Gavin, if she was out with other guys, she wouldn't be home obsessing about him. On top of that, Gavin would have sensed that Adison was busy doing other things and may have kept pursuing her. But she put all her eggs in Gavin's basket, and when he ultimately stopped calling her, she was left completely alone, devastated, and had to start all over again.

To sum it all up, filling the funnel works for several reasons:

1. **You don't get too attached too soon.** If you are out with other people then you are not sitting at home thinking

about Mr. One-and-Only. You can drive yourself crazy by obsessing about a man, and when you see him again, he'll know you've been pining after him. Believe me, guys aren't dumb. They know.

2. **You won't be a complete wreck if he dumps you.** Because you have a couple of different men to date, your confidence won't be shattered if the relationship doesn't pan out. Of course, the initial breakup will still sting, but your ego will be intact because you have other men lusting after you.

3. **Your odds are better.** The more men you date, the more likely you are to find The One. Think about it, you can either date one man every six months and then in five years you will have dated ten guys. Or you can date ten guys in one year and in five years you will have dated fifty guys! The more guys you date, the closer you get to finding The One.

When I started filling the funnel, a lot of the guys were fine with not knowing what I was doing when I wasn't with them . . . at first. But after a while they began to wonder. Then they began to ask. Then they began to worry. And when a guy worries, that is a good sign for you. (This is also when the Jones Effect kicks in, which you will learn about later on.)

So remember ladies, fill the funnel. It's the only way to find the man of your dreams, and it will help you keep him once you do.

Getting Him Interested

Recognizing Buying Signs

The Washington Marriott was packed. After a long day at the National Anesthesia Convention, my boss and I decided to grab a drink and a bite to eat at the downstairs bar. Finding a table would have been difficult but Paul, the rep from Boston, had already grabbed a table and was waiting for us to join him.

I had just met Paul for the first time the week before. He was British, and cute, with messy brown hair and big blue eyes. Over the last few days at the convention we struck up an immediate friendship. I liked him. I really liked him. But I had heard from someone that he was already in a relationship. After a couple of drinks we all started to relax and I started turning on the charm. I was dying to find out if he really had

a girlfriend. I was dying to know how serious it was. And most importantly, I was dying to know what he thought about me. As we sat there talking about how many conventions we had all been to in the last year, I realized I was far from finding out the answers.

Just when I thought we were going to be talking shop all night, my boss lent me a helping hand and asked me how I was handling my recent breakup. Suddenly all attention turned to me and my newly single status.

"We weren't really that compatible," I said. "He was a great guy but in the end it was for the best," I said, trying to seem caring yet over it at the same time. My boss gave me a pat on the back. "Well, don't worry, there's a lot of fish in the sea," he said. "I'm sure you'll find someone you like."

My boss then excused himself to the restroom, and Paul and I were left alone. At that moment I finally got the signal I had been waiting for. Paul turned to me and said, "So what kind of guy do you like, Jess?"

That was it. Game over. He liked me. He might as well have said, "So, Jess, you're a cute girl that I would like to know better. Do you think I'm your type?"

An hour later we were kissing in the lobby.

People in general won't just come out and tell you their level of interest. You have to learn to read their Buying Signs. Buying Signs are those little subtle indicators that tell you when you are piquing someone's interest. When Paul asked

me what kind of guy I liked, it told me that he was interested to see if he would fit into that category. Why else would he ask? Asking that particular question was a safe way to find out if I would be interested. There was no way he would have flat out asked if I liked him. Face that kind of rejection? No way.

Lots of my girlfriends don't know how to read a man's Buying Signs and they end up chasing guys that are either moderately interested or not that interested at all. They ignore the clear signs, or in this case, lack thereof, and instead of learning how to get the guy more interested, they simply throw themselves at him—killing the small amount of interest he had left. Just a word to the wise, as a salesperson, molesting a customer to get them to buy has never worked for me, and it certainly won't work for you.

Don't Ignore the Signs

Learning how to read Buying Signs will save you a huge headache and maybe even a bit of humiliation. When I was a freshman in college I was gaga over Zach Palamino. He was a few years older than I was, and every time I ran into him on campus I started to hyperventilate. One night at a frat party my friend grabbed him and made him dance with me. I was over the moon. He was slightly intoxicated, but I didn't care. I spent the rest of the night talking to him and he even walked me to my car and asked for my number.

After that night, I saw him a few times on campus. He would always stop and talk to me, but never said anything about going out. He never called either. I was plagued with distress. Why would he ask for my number and then not call? Why wasn't he asking me out?

One night I decided to take matters into my own hands. So I called him. He answered the phone and talked to me for roughly three minutes. Then he said his roommate needed to use the phone and he would call me back. He never did.

Looking back on it now, I realized that Zach started out only moderately interested, and the actions I took from there made him even less interested. When I saw him on campus I went out of my way to run into him. I ended every conversation mentioning that he should call me. I even had a friend talk to him for me. Pathetic, I know. One night while drinking at a local bar, I told him how hot I thought he was and tried to kiss him. At the time I saw nothing wrong with my actions. I told myself he was just shy and I needed to be more aggressive. Now when I think about it, my face gets redder than a tomato. How could I have been so oblivious? How did I not read the signs?

The truth is I didn't want to read the signs. I wanted to ignore them! I was so crazy about Zach that accepting he may not like me was something I couldn't face. And because he never verbally said he was not interested, I continued to believe he was. He danced with me one night at a party and walked me to my car so I thought it was love. Wouldn't you?

READER/CUSTOMER CARE SURVEY

We care about your opinions! Please take a moment to fill out our online Reader Survey at **http://survey.hcibooks.com.**
As a **"THANK YOU"** you will receive a **VALUABLE INSTANT COUPON** towards future book purchases
as well as a **SPECIAL GIFT** available only online! Or, you may mail this card back to us.

(PLEASE PRINT IN ALL CAPS)

First Name		MI.		Last Name	

Address			City	

State		Zip		Email	

1. Gender
- ☐ Female   ☐ Male

2. Age
- ☐ 8 or younger
- ☐ 9-12   ☐ 13-16
- ☐ 17-20   ☐ 21-30
- ☐ 31+

3. Did you receive this book as a gift?
- ☐ Yes   ☐ No

4. Annual Household Income
- ☐ under $25,000
- ☐ $25,000 - $34,999
- ☐ $35,000 - $49,999
- ☐ $50,000 - $74,999
- ☐ over $75,000

5. What are the ages of the children living in your house?
- ☐ 0 - 14   ☐ 15+

6. Marital Status
- ☐ Single
- ☐ Married
- ☐ Divorced
- ☐ Widowed

7. How did you find out about the book?
(please choose one)
- ☐ Recommendation
- ☐ Store Display
- ☐ Online
- ☐ Catalog/Mailing
- ☐ Interview/Review

8. Where do you usually buy books?
(please choose one)
- ☐ Bookstore
- ☐ Online
- ☐ Book Club/Mail Order
- ☐ Price Club (Sam's Club, Costco's, etc.)
- ☐ Retail Store (Target, Wal-Mart, etc.)

9. What subject do you enjoy reading about the most?
(please choose one)
- ☐ Parenting/Family
- ☐ Relationships
- ☐ Recovery/Addictions
- ☐ Health/Nutrition
- ☐ Christianity
- ☐ Spirituality/Inspiration
- ☐ Business Self-help
- ☐ Women's Issues
- ☐ Sports

10. What attracts you most to a book?
(please choose one)
- ☐ Title
- ☐ Cover Design
- ☐ Author
- ☐ Content

HEFG

TAPE IN MIDDLE; DO NOT STAPLE

BUSINESS REPLY MAIL
FIRST-CLASS MAIL PERMIT NO 45 DEERFIELD BEACH, FL

POSTAGE WILL BE PAID BY ADDRESSEE

Health Communications, Inc.
3201 SW 15th Street
Deerfield Beach FL 33442-9875

FOLD HERE

Comments

The Gray Area

Guys will never flat out tell you just how interested they are. You have to figure out their level of interest on your own. I was always under the impression that a man's feelings were black and white. He either liked me or he didn't. It wasn't until much later that I realized there was a huge gray area. I remember nearly losing my mind trying to figure out Zach. Some people call it mixed messages when a guy asks for your number, but then doesn't call. Or he calls you, but not regularly. He may be all over you one night, but not the next. It's up to you to understand and interpret these signs. He's not going to spell it out for you—but I will. You are in the gray area and these are not mixed messages. These are clear signs of moderate to low interest.

Learning to Read

One day as I was checking my profile on MySpace, I got a friend request from an extremely handsome Orlando Bloom look-alike. I was totally surprised and excited as I read over his profile. He was a young doctor who seemed to have a great sense of humor. I decided to post a comment on his page saying thanks for the friend request. I waited a couple of days to check to see if he would respond. To my disappointment he didn't. I decided to let it go, after all what could I really do at this point? A couple months went by and I had almost

forgotten about my Orlando. But as I was checking my profile on my birthday, I realized he had sent me another comment. I was elated and rejuvenated. He was definitely digging me, or so I thought. I gave it a day, posted a comment back, and waited for a response. Nothing. No reply. I was perplexed. I wanted to meet this guy. He seemed so interesting, not to mention gorgeous. All my friends urged me to e-mail and ask him out. They kept reminding me that he was the one who found me and initiated contact. I went back and forth about what to do. I knew what they were saying was true, but I also knew that his Buying Signs were telling me he was only moderately interested, if that. Being persistent would not heighten his level of interest. So against my friends' advice I decided to go with what my head was telling me. I didn't write him again.

The following week I decided to go to a restaurant opening in Chinatown. As I walked toward the mass of people swarming the entrance, I saw the same dark curly hair that was driving me to insanity. It was him. My Orlando. He was in line waiting to get in. I walked right up to the door, avoiding the line, and strolled right by him. As I stood by the bar talking to friends, I eagerly waited for him to walk through the door. After what seemed like hours, he finally did. But he was not alone. On his arm was a tall brunette he clearly knew very well. As he leaned on the bar to order drinks, she stuck his hand deep into his back pocket. *Girlfriend,* I thought. *Definitely the girlfriend.*

I was very glad that I didn't continue to e-mail Orlando. He

was less than moderately interested, like I originally thought. He had a girlfriend and they could have been in a fight when he contacted me. There was a little interest there, but not a significant amount. Continuing contact with him would have been the wrong thing to do. He was clearly into his relationship and the only thing to do was wait. Maybe they would break up, maybe they wouldn't. But I had done my part. E-mailing him again was not going to get him more interested. I was glad I read his Buying Signs and acted accordingly, instead of continuing to pursue him.

Unfortunately most of the time you aren't going to find out what's happening on the other side like I did. You are going to have to read the signs and determine for yourself what his interest level is. I was lucky enough to get a sneak peek, but that doesn't happen very often. You have to be smart enough to read the signs and act accordingly. I could have easily kept e-mailing Orlando, thinking he was interested, but it would have backfired on me. He had a girlfriend, and the ball was not in my court. I would have seemed overeager, and it would have scared him. Now that I had stopped e-mailing him, if he and his girlfriend ever broke up, there would still be a chance.

The Initial Signs of Interest

Gauging a man's interest in you is pretty simple, as there are definitely standard buying signs that every man uses. The first

is the look. If a man is interested in meeting you, you will catch his eye. It's the same thing that happens when you walk through the mall. If you see a dress or a pair of shoes you like, what do you do? You stop and look. Some men try not to make it obvious, others are rather overt about it. Needless to say, when someone is interested in buying, they first stop and look.

The second sign of interest is questioning. When a customer is interested in a product, they ask a lot of questions. They want to know as much as they can about that product in the little time they have. Think about when you try on a dress at the mall. If you like it, you ask questions like, *How much is it? Does it come in my size? Are there any other colors?* Men are no different. They will ask you questions about yourself if they are interested. Just like Paul asking what kind of guys I like. If a man is interested he will want to know who you are, what you do, where you live, and anything else he can think of.

The third sign is change in attitude and mannerisms. When a customer is interested in buying, he may suddenly change his tone of voice, attitude, or posture. He may become friendlier or chattier. When a man is interested in a woman, he will do exactly the same thing. Once I noticed a guy walking a very cute puppy in front of my local coffee shop. A girl who wanted to pet his dog stopped him. He stood there with his sunglasses on, hands in his pockets, only talking when the girl asked a question. She tried petting the pup for a minute but had a hard time because it was jumping around. As soon as she left,

another girl walked by and noticed the dog. The guy smiled at her, took his hands out of his pockets and removed his sunglasses (change of mannerisms). The girl asked him about the dog as she petted it, and the guy picked up the dog so she could get a better look. Then he started asking her questions (change in attitude).

The fourth and final sign of interest is probably the most obvious. When a customer is interested they basically tell you before you can even ask. They make closing statements like, "That sounds good," or "This seems to fit what I need." A man won't say those things exactly, or at least let's hope not, but he will say things that reference seeing you again. I once met a guy at my gym who asked me where I usually went running. When I told him the specific trail, he said he often runs there too and we should run it together sometime. That is a closing statement. If he doesn't come out and ask you for a date on the first meeting, you should not be discouraged. Listen for other closing statements that tell you he wants to see you again.

The Signs of Low to Moderate Interest

After you've met and maybe even gone on a few dates, it will be a lot easier to tell what his interest level is. If he calls you a lot, sends you texts everyday, tries constantly to see you, he's very interested. Anything less than that is moderate to not-that-interested. Doesn't matter what the extenuating

circumstances are. A stressful job, a heavy travel schedule, a recent breakup, they are all just excuses. If he's not sending you a clear signal of high interest, it's because he's not that interested . . . at least not yet. You can certainly change his level, but you have to first be honest with yourself and realize that you may be more into him than he is into you.

If you don't hear from a man for days and making plans only happens on his terms, read the signs. Moderate interest. If you only hang out with his friends, at his house and doing what he wants, again, moderate interest. If he only calls you when he's out, drunk, and late at night . . . do I really need to tell you what that means?

There's no such thing as mixed messages. The signs are very clear. The only problem is with you, the interpreter. It can be tough to face the fact that the man you are pining after may not be as interested in you as you want. But if you make excuses for his wishy-washy behavior, you are only kidding yourself. Everyone else, including your friends, knows exactly what's happening, even if they don't tell you.

Starting High, but Ending Low

Unfortunately just because someone expresses initial interest doesn't mean you're guaranteed to close them. Sometimes customers start off extremely interested in my product, but somewhere in the sales process, their interest wanes. The

worst part about that is that they'll sometimes continue to act interested just to be nice. Sometimes they just want free pens, and sometimes they want me to take them to lunch. There are several reasons why an uninterested customer will string me along, so I have to look for signs that indicate the customer is serious about buying from me.

After you've been dating a while, you have to be careful a guy doesn't do the same thing to you. You have to continue to read his signs throughout your entire courtship. Remember, just because he initially asked for your number or told you how the room lit up when you walked in doesn't mean he's in love with you.

Adison often makes the mistake of assuming when a guy asks for her number he is totally smitten with her and therefore she can act any way she wants. She throws her sales strategy out the window and ignores all other signs. She figures he made the first move, so she has the upper hand. She doesn't think twice about anything she says or does. Then when the guy breaks off the relationship she's left baffled. "He asked for my number!" she cries. "He chased me!" She just doesn't seem to grasp the concept that just because a man's interest starts out high doesn't mean it will stay that way. A man's interest is like the weather. It can drop from high to low overnight.

It's important to read a man's buying signs, whether they be sky high or valley low. Your actions can effectuate his level of interest, so don't despair if the outlook seems gloomy at the

moment. It is very possible to turn him around. But first you have to read and accept the signs, so that you know where you stand. Learn the signs of someone really liking you. Learn the signs when someone only moderately likes you. And most importantly, learn the signs of when someone doesn't really like you but because you are readily available, they use you when they want to. Don't make excuses for rotten behavior. If a man is truly interested and is thinking about a serious relationship with you, there will be clear signs telling you so. If he's not there yet, don't worry. The rest of this book is going to teach you how to get him interested and keep him that way.

The KISS Principle

My good friend Aidan relies heavily on blind dates. He's a smart but quiet guy who doesn't go out much, and prefers to be set up through friends. He figures they know his likes and dislikes, so having them choose his dates for him should be a safe bet. However, the last date he went on had him really doubting his friends' ability.

The night got off to a great start when Aidan's date walked in exactly the way she had been described. She was a cute brunette with a curvaceous figure and a dazzling smile. *Jackpot!* he thought to himself. He was instantly pleased and ready for an

enjoyable evening. Unfortunately not long after they ordered their first drinks, the good start came to a screeching halt.

She asked Aidan what he did for a living.

"I own a wine store," he said

"Oh my god, really?" she exclaimed. "I love wine. I have been to a lot of the vineyards in the area. I use to be a waitress at this restaurant on Capitol Hill, and they wanted the staff to be familiar with all the wines so we could accurately describe them to the patrons. There were so many wines that it was hard for everyone to remember them all, but I must have a nose for wine because I could just smell the wine and know exactly what was in it. Everyone thought it was amazing actually."

Aidan raised his brow, "Well, that's cool."

"Do you like sports?" the girl asked.

"Uh, I do. I'm not as into them as I used to be, but I do follow my favorite teams," Aidan said.

"Oh, me too! I mean, I do like sports, like football and soccer are okay, but I'm not married to them. I can sit down and watch them with my boyfriend if that's what he wants to do, but I don't have to be in front of the TV every Monday night for the Skins' game. It's something that I can take or leave myself. I actually played field hockey when I was in high school, so I am pretty athletic. The year I was the co-captain we won the regional championship. Gosh, that was so long ago, now that I think about it . . ."

Again Aidan raised his brow, then looked down at his watch.

After forty-five minutes passed, he finally told the girl that he forgot to lock the back door at the store and had to go. She hugged him goodbye and told him she had fun. He lied and said the same thing.

When Aidan called me the next day, I asked him about the date. He only had one thing to say.

"She talked too much. We're not going out again."

"Oh? What was it she was talking about exactly?" I asked.

"Mainly herself," he replied. "She started off pretty good. She seemed interested in getting to know me, but then whenever I answered her questions, she would immediately come up with a story that related back to her. It got very annoying."

"Well, she was probably trying to show you that you and she have a lot in common. She just went about it the wrong way."

"Maybe, but at this point I don't care what her intention was. I'm not putting myself through that again," Aidan said firmly. "She was just agreeing with everything I said anyway. The conversation was not interesting at all. It's too bad because she was very attractive and I would have gone out with her again. Oh well, on to the next."

Aidan's date started out doing the right thing. She asked questions. At first she seemed genuinely interested in Aidan. But as soon as he answered her question, she would jump in and ramble on and on about her own stories, always turning the conversation back to herself. Many girls I know do the same thing. They go on dates and talk way too much. It's a

disease known as "verbal vomit." There is no faster way to kill a potential relationship than to verbal vomit on your date. You may think you are keeping the conversation going by telling your funny and agreeable stories, but you will just come off looking like a motor mouth.

KISS Your Date

People often think that salespeople are great talkers. But it's not the talking that makes them great. Just the opposite. The real secret is that salespeople are great listeners. Whenever I visit with customers, I make sure that they are the ones doing most of the talking. My rule is they talk 75 percent of the time and I talk 25 percent of the time. The last thing I want to do is to monopolize the conversation and bore the customer. I know that people love to talk, and they lose interest fast when they are just sitting there listening to my pitch. I have to engage them, just like you have to engage your dates. Men especially have short attention spans. After a few minutes of listening to you, you have to let him talk. If you drone on, he will lose interest in what you are saying and then lose interest in you. Remember, we have two ears and one mouth for a reason!

It's more important to listen to your date than it is to try and relate to everything he's saying. When you are out with a guy, the best thing you can do is to ask him questions about himself. You can always keep the conversation going with

questions. When he answers, listen to him, and when it's your turn to talk, use the same principle salespeople have been using for years: the KISS principle. It stands for keep it short and simple. Using KISS will help keep you from babbling. It's the only cure for verbal vomit.

When I first started to date Kyle, my boyfriend of two years, he worked on air for a popular local morning radio show. Because he was a well-known personality in the D.C. area, young attractive girls were constantly chasing after him. The last few he dated were a lot younger than I was, so I knew dating me would be a big change for him. We went to a comedy show in Baltimore on our first date. The drive took an hour both ways, but the conversation never stalled because I continually asked Kyle questions about himself, his family, his career, his aspirations. Whenever he asked me a question, I would KISS the answer, and then turn the attention back to him. By the time we returned home that night, Kyle turned to me and said, "You are the most interesting person I have ever met. I just love talking to you!"

It's funny—when you let someone else do the talking, you are the one that seems interesting.

Verbal Vomit with a Headache

Because women are such emotional creatures, it's often hard for us to keep what we're thinking from coming out of

our mouth. If we are nervous, we say we are nervous. If we can't believe a guy asked us out, we'll actually tell him we can't believe he asked us out. Unfortunately it's not always a good idea to disclose all the thoughts dancing around in our heads. Just because you are thinking it doesn't mean you should be talking about it. Especially on a first date.

There are certain things that shouldn't be discussed when you are starting to get to know someone. For instance, you shouldn't discuss personal problems that you aren't exactly over yet. When you complain about a bad situation at home, work, or anywhere else, you could end up giving your date something I call Verbal Vomit with a twist of headache.

My good friend Isabel just went through the hardest year of her life. She had bought a second condo as an investment property even though her gut was telling her she couldn't afford it. After a few months of trying to rent it without success, she decided to put it up for sale. The real estate agent she hired assured her they would get a good deal for it, but as the months progressed she had to keep lowering the price. Finally after having it on the market almost a year, she went into foreclosure.

I've never seen my poor friend such a wreck. Of course, she bounced back, but it took a toll on her emotionally. When she started dating again she was still mentally exhausted from the experience. She said she had a migraine every day that year, and she let her dates know it, too. If a guy brought up anything relating to the housing industry, Isabel would unload all her

frustration right on his plate. She would tell him how angry she was and how she wanted to strangle her agent. She complained about not being able to eat or sleep and thought she may need therapy due to the whole ordeal. A couple of times, Isabel even ended up crying about it. Her dates sat there not knowing exactly what to say and feeling very uncomfortable.

In the beginning, you really should keep the personal strife in your life private. I know women who talk about their abusive father, eating disorders, pregnancy scares, medication they take, health problems they've had, and a million other things that are meant for a therapist, not a first date. If you really want to scare a man off then go ahead and air all your dirty laundry. But if you want to keep seeing a guy, learn to keep the personal things to yourself for the time being. When he tells you he had the flu and couldn't leave the house for a week, don't tell him about the year you couldn't get out of bed because of your clinical depression. Instead, just keep the focus on him. Continue to ask him questions about himself, and be sure to KISS all your answers.

Don't Kiss and Tell—Kiss and Listen

When you are excited about someone, it's easy to ramble. You are making a connection and bursting to tell him all the things you're thinking. But what makes a person like you has less to do with what you say and more to do with how you

make them feel. People like to feel that they are being heard. They like to feel like their voice matters. Keep that in mind when you are on your dates. Making a good impression isn't tough, if you know how to listen.

Verbal Vomit comes in many forms. Some women are just chatty. Some are afraid of the awkward silence. Some think that the only way for a guy to realize how great they are is to just flat out tell him, "Hey, I'm great." Whatever form it comes in doesn't really matter. All that does matter is keeping it under control. Sit back, relax, and remember if you don't KISS your date, you *will* kill it.

End at the Height of Impulse

When my friend Anne moved to San Francisco, she didn't know a soul. I admired her strength to pick up and move three thousand miles from home, but I also worried about how she would meet people and regain her social life. After only being out west a few months, she decided to join Match.com. It seemed like the best way to meet guys and get back on the social scene. She posted her profile and began receiving e-mails immediately. After sorting through a slew of messages, she decided to make a date with Patrick, a sous-chef from Los Angeles. He was tall, dark, and handsome with a

seemingly good sense of humor. They decided to meet on a Friday night and get a couple drinks. Now remember, as I tell you this story, Anne and Patrick had never met before. In fact, they hadn't even spoken on the phone.

When Anne walked in and saw Patrick she was immediately pleased. He was exactly what his profile had stated—yummy! Patrick was excited to meet Anne, too. He thought she was gorgeous. The first encounter was a success. They got a few drinks and the night began.

After their third round, Patrick suggested they get some dinner. They left the bar and headed to a nice restaurant on the bay. Dinner was delicious and Anne and Patrick were engrossed in conversation for the next three hours. They decided to then go for a walk on the beach. Patrick picked up some champagne and glasses, and they headed out for a midnight picnic. By now Patrick and Anne had been drinking for hours and inhibitions were long gone. They started making out on the beach, and Anne eventually ended up at Patrick's where they continued to make out until six in the morning.

The next day Anne was beaming. It was the perfect first date. She was extremely excited and even called to tell me about it. Just as she was in the middle of the story, her other line beeped. "It's him!" she squealed. "Let me call you right back." She clicked over and didn't call me back for two days.

Those two days she didn't call back she spent with Patrick. Basically their first date started Friday and didn't end until

Sunday. The following week Patrick called and asked to see her again. She accepted, of course, and spent that entire weekend with him, too. At some point during their weekend slumber party, they consummated their relationship. Her rationale? She felt like she knew him after spending so much time with him, even if it was only in the span of two weeks. Things were going exactly the way she wanted. She was happy.

Then came the third week, which also became known as the final week. That's when things got rocky. I won't bore you with the mundane details but by week three the happy couple was no longer a couple, and Anne was calling me crying and cursing his name. I tried to console her, but eventually I had to tell her that she had done something terribly wrong. She spent way too much time with Patrick in the beginning of the relationship. If it was going so well, she should have pulled back a little more. She shouldn't have said yes every time he asked her out, and she should have cut the dates shorter. Every time she went out with Patrick they spent at least twelve hours together! It was relationship overkill.

Saying No

Even though Patrick kept pursuing Anne and asking her out, she shouldn't have always accepted. Just because a guy asks you a question doesn't mean you are required to come back with an affirmative answer. It's perfectly fine to turn a guy

down. "No" is not a dirty word in dating. It is vitally important not to overdo it by seeing each other too much in the first
few weeks. Even if you are totally falling in love, in the very
beginning you have to keep a guy wanting more. You do this
by leaving him when things are at their most exciting. It's
called Ending at the Height of Impulse. You want to end the
date at the appropriate time so that the guy is still thinking
about you when you're gone.

All Good Things Must Come to an End, Quickly

You've seen it before, and it always works. It's why soap
operas end at the most exciting point of the show. It's why *Sex
and the City* ended after only six short seasons. Why George
Costanza exited every meeting after a great joke. You always
want to leave on a high note. Similarly, you have to leave a
man wanting more, and you can't do that if you never leave.
You will have to restrain yourself from spending too much
time with a guy in the very beginning.

I know this is hard to do. When you meet a guy you actually like, and you are feeling good about how things are going,
the last thing you want to do is go home. But it truly is the only
way to keep him coming back. I don't care if you found your
soul mate and he's different from all the other guys. Don't let
your heart confuse you. If you spend too much time with him
right away, he can and will get burned out.

The Danger of Losing Impulse

When I was a brand new sales rep selling phone service, I walked into a lawyer's office in a small town in southern Virginia. I asked for the head attorney that made all the decisions for the office. I was surprised when they immediately took me back to see him.

His name was Sully. He was a great big man with a great big laugh. He shook my hand and told me to have a seat. He was more than willing to hear what I had to say. I was excited as I gave him my spiel. I knew this deal was in the bag from the buying signs he was giving me. Sully broke out the phone bill and we started going over it. He was impressed at how much money I could save him. He kept nodding his head yes and told me that the deal sounded great. Right there—that is the Height of Impulse. That is when I should have ended the conversation, pulled out the contract, and closed the deal.

But instead I kept talking. I was enjoying sitting there, building a relationship with him. We got off the subject a couple of times, talking mainly about his kids and his love of fishing. At one point, we even stepped out of the office so that Sully could get in a quick smoke. Eventually I glanced at the clock and realized I had been there for almost two-and-a-half hours. Usually these visits only took about forty-five minutes, tops. I couldn't waste anymore time. Just as I was about to break out my pen and have Sully put his signature on the deal, he looked at his watch.

"I have to run, Jessica. This deal sounds good, but I just need to think about it a little bit longer. Come back next month and see me. We'll talk then."

I was crushed. But it was my fault. Had I just closed him when he was at the Height of Impulse, I would have made the sale. But instead I just kept sitting there, talking, letting his impulse drop. When I finally tried to close him, he was no longer excited about the offer. He was just drained from talking for two hours.

If you want to turn a new relationship into a long-term one, you are going to have to make Ending at the Height of Impulse a religious practice. Until a guy tells me that he is crazy about me, and I get all the right buying signs from him, I will never spend more than a few hours with him. Doesn't matter how much I like him and how hard it is to leave him, I will do it. I will do it because I know it's the only way to get what I want.

It's so easy to get wrapped up in what you are doing when you are having a great time. But you have to be able to make the logical decisions we talked about earlier. If you really like a guy you are going to have to discipline yourself to leave him when he is the most excited about you.

After Anne got over Patrick, she got back on Match.com. She understood what she had done wrong and swore on a stack of Bibles she wouldn't do it again. Her next date was with Cyrus, a mortgage broker who had also moved out west from D.C. He and Anne planned to meet for coffee. Since it

was their first meeting, I advised her to keep it short and simple, no matter how well it was going.

Two hours into the date Anne thought about her promise. But just as she was getting ready to thank Cyrus for a good time, he asked her if she wanted to get some dinner with him. She didn't want to say no, mostly because she was having such a good time, but also because she didn't want to be rude. What if she turned him down and he became discouraged? What if he never asked her out again? So instead of going home like she should have, she went out to dinner.

Three hours later Anne and Cyrus were drunk, half-naked, and back at his place. They fooled around until two in the morning. Anne didn't want to repeat the Patrick situation, so she sobered up and drove home instead of sleeping over. But by then, she had already sealed her fate. Cyrus saw her two more times and then never called again.

Keeping Your Promise

I know it's difficult to End at the Height of Impulse, so here's what I suggest. Before you go on a date, make a promise to yourself that you are not going to stay past a certain time. If it's a first date, say goodnight at ten or eleven. If you happen to be on an Internet date, I would limit yourself to only one hour, or two cups of coffee. It's always better to leave earlier than later, especially when you are just meeting someone

for the first time. As the relationship progresses, keep setting time limits and make sure you do it before you get there and start having a good time.

Once, I was dating a high profile attorney who was also labeled an eternal bachelor. He was a night owl and loved to stay out until the wee hours of the morning. On our third date he took me out to dinner and wanted to stop by a local hot spot where his friends were partying. I had already planned to leave him no later than midnight, so when the clock struck twelve, I told him I was catching a cab home. He, of course, was stunned to hear this. How could I leave in the middle of a party? He begged me not to go. He said he would have his driver take me home anytime I wanted. I told him I had to get up early and couldn't stay any later. With that, I turned and slipped out the back door.

I was having a great time, but I had a long-term goal. I wanted the bachelor to fall head over heels for me. And in order to do that I needed to make sure he kept wanting me even after I left. And he did. He never understood why I always left him around midnight. He started calling me Cinderella and asked if he bought me some really expensive Jimmy Choo's would I stay out longer? He called me constantly and even consulted my friends about our relationship. Of course the more he pressured, the less interested I became. But nonetheless, the technique worked, and he was smitten.

The Impulse Killer

Perhaps the easiest and most fatal trap to fall into is spending the night. You can't possibly End at the Height of Impulse if you spend the night with your date. Now, if he's your boyfriend who you have been seeing for several months, that's one thing. But even then, you still shouldn't spend every night at his place. Some of my friends spend the night with a guy after only two or three dates, and that is a total impulse killer.

When I was dating the trendy salon owner, I often had to remind myself to End at the Height of Impulse. He asked me over to his house to watch *Entourage* one night. It was only the third time we had ever hung out and he tried to get me to stay over. When I told him no and then actually left, he was floored . . . but in a good way. He called me later and told me that I was the only girl to ever decline an invitation to sleep over. So not only did I End at the Height of Impulse, I did something that made me *different* from all the other girls.

It is much too hard to resist the urge to sleep over if you haven't already made the promise to yourself that you are going home. Don't do what most girls do. They tell themselves they will make a decision later in the evening after seeing how they feel. The problem is that it always feels good! It never feels like you should go home. But that is exactly the point when you should put your shoes on and skedaddle.

It's vital to a salesperson's success to know when to close a

customer. Close too late and they get bored and start to wish you would just leave. There is a reason the saying goes *timing is everything* and not *timing is most things.* Timing really is everything, and it is within your control. Even if he is singing your praises, you have to resist the urge to stay. If he is begging you not to leave, that just means you are doing the right thing. Don't deviate from the strategy! If you can discipline yourself to go when the going gets hot, you will see just how hot a guy gets going!

Indifference

Ever wonder why so many married women say, "When I met my husband, I wasn't even interested in him." Or, "I would have never noticed my husband, but he chased me down and made me go out with him." It's funny to hear stories like that, but it's also very telling.

When my friend Julie was single she was trying desperately to date her future husband's best friend. It was a classic triangle. George, her husband, was in love with her, and she was in love with his best friend Layne. Julie wasn't interested in George, but she liked him a lot as a friend. They would have lunch, go shopping, or just hang out and talk. George could see how smart, funny, and wonderful Julie was because she

wasn't trying to date him. She didn't come on strong and hang on his every word. She didn't rush to answer his every text. She wasn't worried if she had to decline an invitation, and wasn't afraid to say no to him. She was indifferent. She liked hanging out with him but she didn't feel like she was going to die if she didn't see him. And because she didn't have romantic feelings for him, she never got mad at him for not calling on time or going out with other girls. That natural indifference was what enabled George to see Julie for who she really was, and allowed him to fall in love with her.

Now if you ask Layne, he will tell you he saw a very different girl in Julie. This girl was not indifferent. Quite the opposite. She always seemed to pop up wherever he was and constantly vied for his attention. If there was ever an opportunity to hang out with him, she made sure she was there. She tried everything she could think of to get Layne to like her. But it didn't work. Layne perceived Julie as clingy and flat-out annoying and thus was never able to see the good qualities George did. After many months of cat and mouse, George finally convinced Julie to give up on Layne and give him a chance. After dating for two years, Julie decided she would never find someone that loved her more than George, so she married him.

Women often end up marrying men they aren't initially interested in because they are naturally indifferent with them in the early stages. They are essentially able to be themselves

instead of googly-eyed teenagers, high on emotion. They don't show the guy their deep-rooted feelings early on, simply because they don't have any! But you don't have to marry the guy who wears you down. You can learn how to close the deal with the guy you like right away.

Neediness

Before we talk about how and why it's important to be indifferent with the guy you really like, we need to understand why you may have such a difficult time doing it. The answer can be summed up in one word: neediness. If you are needy, you cannot possibly be indifferent. Neediness is, without a doubt, the most unattractive quality a woman can display.

What exactly is neediness? It is obvious to the most casual observer but often not to a needy woman. Ask yourself these questions. Have you ever been afraid to confront your boyfriend? Do you always do what he wants to do? Are you available at the drop of a hat? Is it okay that he never says how he feels about you, or tells you he loves you? Do you compromise on the things that you want the most? If you do these things, you could very well be needy. A great example is my friend Evelyn. After telling me for years that she wanted to get married she decided that she really didn't want to when her boyfriend told her living together was the same thing, minus the hassle. That is what I call needy.

Most needy women don't even realize that they are needy. Never have any of my needy friends admitted to me that they need a relationship to be happy, but their actions prove the contrary. They can start off strong, but somewhere in the dating process they lose their independence. The indifferent attitude suddenly dissipates, and they become desperate for the guy to like them.

The first thing you have to do is ask yourself if you are needy. You can't solve a problem if you can't admit you have one in the first place. Most women believe that because they have good jobs and make their own money that they are independent, and therefore, are certainly not needy. But neediness has nothing to do with financial instability. It is an emotional insecurity that women often mistakenly think can be fixed by a relationship.

So how can you tell if you are one of the needy ones? Well, there are several phrases women use that are codes for neediness. If you have ever said one the following phrases, either out loud or to yourself, you may be a needy girl.

"I think if I were married or had a boyfriend, I would be happier."
"I just don't like being single."
"I am a 'relationship person.' I just like being in a relationship."
"I fall in love very easily."

While these are some examples of things that women will say, more often than not, it's what they do that pegs them as

needy. If you are the kind of person that is never *not* in a serious relationship, then you could be needy. I have friends that "relationship hop," meaning when they detect that their serious relationship is on the decline, they immediately run out and find another serious relationship to jump into. They don't want to date casually or fill the funnel because they like the security that comes with a long-term boyfriend. Relationship hoppers get seriously involved very quickly. They move at the speed of light, taking the relationship from zero to sixty in a matter of weeks. Most hoppers think it's a good sign if the relationship moves this fast, but the reality is that they have now committed themselves to a man they hardly know. As the relationship progresses, the hopper may realize the guy is not exactly what she thought he was, but she can't bring herself to end things and go back to being single. She may not have the relationship she wants, but at least she has a relationship.

Most everyone will admit that they prefer being in a relationship. At some point in their life, everyone dreams of finding true love. So hoping to find the man of your dreams does not necessarily mean that you are needy. The difference between people with a healthy understanding of relationships and needy people is that needy people are willing to compromise and rationalize a subpar relationship because they would rather not be alone. They may tell themselves that it's their fault that things aren't going well. They are too critical or nitpicky. They often become the unhappiest of people because

they are not in the right relationship, and it is not fulfilling their real needs. These are all signs of neediness, and if they sound familiar to you, it may be time to accept it and start dealing with it.

It's very important to understand that a relationship is not a solution to a problem. Many women think they would be happy if they were married or at least seriously involved with someone. Inevitably, these women find out what true *unhappiness* really is. Instead of being single and alone, five years later, they end up divorced, with a two-year-old, no job, and single again. A relationship based on neediness does not solve problems; it compounds them. Believe me, marriage will only make your problems worse. Unfortunately I am not your therapist. I cannot be the one to help solve whatever issues need resolution. What I can do though, is tell you how to act so that you don't seem needy and end up scaring off a great guy, or worse, locking yourself into a bad relationship.

The Most Powerful Tool You Have

There is an old sales story about indifference. Back in the late eighties, two computer salesmen from competing companies went to a large technology convention. They set their booths up across from each other and prepared themselves for a busy day. The convention was packed with people. Many wandered by and glanced at the salesmen's displays, but no

one stopped to ask any questions. Back then, hardly anyone owned a computer and no one thought they could afford it. Finally after a long day of no prospects, the convention ended. Both salesmen were disappointed. Not a single person stopped by either of their booths.

Just as they started to pack up, two women approached the first salesperson's booth. At long last, a potential buyer! The salesperson was so excited. After a long day of standing on his feet, he had an opportunity to make a sale. He thought about how much he needed the money, and he eagerly made his presentation. He told the ladies that they wouldn't regret purchasing his product. Satisfaction was guaranteed! When they said they were going to think about it, the salesperson became even more desperate. He didn't want to lose his only prospect of the day. He began to reiterate the value of his computer and how much he would appreciate their business.

But his enthusiasm didn't convince them. The ladies thanked the first salesperson and walked away from his booth. The second salesperson had watched all of this transpire and knew this was his chance. The women walked over to his booth, but instead of dropping everything and giving them a lively welcome, he continued packing up his display. He politely told the ladies he wished they had gotten there earlier because he would have had time to go over his fabulous product. But he had another appointment early the next day and had to get home to prepare. Upon hearing this, the ladies

became even more interested. This man didn't need their business. He has customers buying from him all the time. His product must be good. They begged him to go over his presentation for them.

After the salesperson made his pitch, the ladies seemed interested. They asked questions and debated on price. The salesperson knew that he just needed to tip them over the fence. He looked at both of them and said, "Look, ladies, this is a great computer. It's going to give you just what you need. But my time is precious, so if you want to buy it— that's great. If not, I am going to have to finish packing up now."

He looked them both dead in the eye and said nothing. The women looked at each other and then back at the salesperson.

"We'll take it," they said.

Never Let Him See You Sweat

As bad as a salesperson needs to make a sale, we cannot show that to the customer. We have to make customers want our product, and that won't happen if they sense we need them to buy it. We know that customers are evaluating our product and if they perceive us as being anxious for a sale, they will start having second thoughts. They will wonder, *Why is this person so eager for me to buy? Is it because no one else has? Am I the only person who has shown interest? Why is this salesperson so needy?*

If a man perceives you as anxious for a relationship or just generally overly interested in him in the very beginning, he will wonder the same thing. The only way to combat neediness is to act indifferent. Just like the second salesperson, you too have to convey the take-it-or-leave-it attitude. You must have the mentality that if this person doesn't buy it, someone else surely will because your product is just that good. When a customer (or a man) sees that, the product instantly becomes more attractive.

The trick is to keep your indifference at the most crucial times. When the second salesperson saw that the ladies were still undecided, he knew they could have gone either way. He was smart though. Instead of acting out of desperation, he fought back his need for the sale and poured on more indifference. He never let the women see him sweat.

There will be times when you will feel the urge to act out of neediness, too. Things may not be going in your favor and your natural reaction may be to hold on even tighter, or worse, beg to get your way. I can remember dating a guy who always wanted to go away with his friends on the weekends. For the first month of dating, he would take off Saturday morning and not come home until Sunday night. Even though I hated it and wanted to beg him not to go, I knew the best thing to do was to act indifferent. I pretended that I didn't really care if he stayed or went. I had other plans myself. After the fourth weekend trip he asked me if I wanted to go away with them. I

said no, but that he should go if he wanted. Well, he didn't go away that time, or any time after. Begging him to stay would have never paid off, but practicing indifference certainly did. Remember, you can never convince someone to want you by saying how much you need them. No matter what, you must keep your indifference. You can never let him see you sweat.

Not Too Hot, Not Too Cold, but Just Right

Terri and Kim were two friends I counseled last summer. They both had trouble keeping men interested. Their relationships never lasted more than a few weeks. The funny thing was they both took the complete opposite approach with men. Terri was afraid that men wouldn't like her if she didn't seem totally interested in them. She told me point blank, "I'm afraid if I don't give a guy 100 percent of my attention, he will think I'm not interested and then he won't be interested. I feel like I need to show a guy how much I like him because that is what I would want him to do."

On the other hand, Kim always acted completely disinterested in men. She would play hard to get and would often get mad at them for little things in an effort to keep them in pursuit. But the opposite of love is not hate (it's indifference), and her tactics started wearing guys thin. Eventually they grew tired of her cold, hard exterior and chalked her up as bitchy.

Kim and Terri didn't realize it but they were both ruining

their own chances for a relationship. Terri was too hot, showing too much affection from the very start and Kim was too cold, acting completely disinterested and snobbish. Instead of sitting at opposite ends of the spectrum, they both needed to move toward the middle.

You want to convey to a man is that you like him, yes, but if the relationship doesn't happen, so what? You'll move on and be just fine. That is what indifference truly is. Not too hot, not too cold, just right.

Seeming Indifferent

Seeming indifferent may be difficult at first, but the more you practice, the better you will become at doing it. There are some phrases that you need to lose from your vocabulary in order to sound indifferent. These are a few of them:

"Why haven't you called me?"
"Where were you last night?"
"What are we?"
"How do you feel about me?"
"I think we should talk about us/our relationship."

All the above phrases can easily be replaced with more indifferent sounding language such as:

"I've been so busy. What have you been up to lately?"

"I was out so late last night I don't even know when I got home.
 What about you?"
"You're a pretty cool guy. If you're lucky I may go out with you
again." [said with a smile]

You should also try incorporating phrases like "no big deal"
and "either way."

But even more important than what you say is how you say
it. You have to give the *impression* that you really are indifferent . . . at least for a little while. Freaking out over little things
and questioning a man to death is not being indifferent. You
obviously care a whole lot if you are accusing him of checking out the waitress on your third date. You have to be cool,
calm, and relaxed in order to seem indifferent. Anything less
than that shows too much emotion too soon. Think of it like
playing poker. You may have a full house, but if you let
everyone at the table know it, you are going to lose. You need
a good poker face. That way you can get what you want and
take home the jackpot.

Don't tell a guy that you are doing any of these things on
purpose. Sometimes women get nervous and actually confess
the reason they are playing it cool. That's like announcing that
you are about to bluff in the middle of a game. Don't tell him
what's really going on when you use any of these techniques.
You want him to think it's because you are still on the fence
about him and he needs to win you over. You don't want to tell

him it's because you read this book. If you tell him you are doing all these things on purpose, with an agenda, he really will think you are playing a game.

Launching Your Relationship

If you only learn one lesson from this book, let this be it. It's by far the most important to understand and utilize. For a relationship to go from casual to serious, both involved people have to feel the same way about each other at exactly the same time. So if you give off the vibe you are ready for a relationship before he does, you will be making a very risky move. Think of it like launching a spaceship where the pilot and the navigator have to turn their keys at precisely the same moment. Because most people don't fall in love at the exact same moment, many relationships fail to launch because one person arrives early to the ship and jams in a key, while the other person is still in route to the launch pad. Don't be that eager person. You will ultimately scare the guy off by showing him how you feel before he does. It may be what you want to do, but I promise you will end up alone waiting on the tarmac. The best thing to do is to remain indifferent—or at least pretend to be. If you feel yourself on the road to the launch pad, pull over into the cell phone waiting area!

Nonverbal Communication— What You Can't Hear

Ask any salesperson and they will tell you that 90 percent of communication is nonverbal. When I sit down with customers, I listen to what they tell me, but I am also paying very close attention to their body language. I have met with customers who have told me that they love my product. However, their body language tells me that they aren't really sold yet. Maybe they have their arms crossed, maybe they won't look me in the eye, maybe it's just the expression on their face. There are so many nonverbal clues that are dead giveaways to what a person is really thinking. It is much more important to read those signs because people often cater what they say, but they can't fake body language. Body language will always give you the true story.

The Not-so-Cozy Couple

While my friend, Elsa, and I were at dinner, I noticed a couple sitting to our right. The girl was a very cute blonde, and the guy was a preppy Zack Morris–type. Their body language could not have been more different. He was sitting back with his one arm perched on the back of the chair. His other arm rested comfortably in front of him. He seemed distracted and

was constantly looking around the room at people nearby. The girl, on the other hand, was fixated on the guy. She was leaning over most of the table to hold his hand. She rubbed his arm lovingly, while he scratched at a spot on his shirt. I turned to Elsa to point them out.

"See that couple over there?" I motioned. "See how the girl is so much more interested than he is?"

Elsa glanced over. "Wow! She's practically climbing over the table to hold his hand. Meanwhile, he is just relaxing back in his chair, not looking terribly impressed with her."

Just as we were wrapping up the conversation the guy turned toward us and said, "You girls want to share what you've been saying about us for the last ten minutes?"

My face must have turned beet red. I was totally caught off guard, but worst of all, what was I going to say? Oh, I was just noticing how your girlfriend is totally in love with you, but you seem to be more interested in the stain on your tie?

"Oh, um . . . I am writing a book, and I usually observe couples," I blurted out. "I like to guess by their body language what their relationship is like."

The girl sat up in her chair. She hadn't noticed at all that we had been talking about them. "Oh how fun! What did you notice about us?"

"Well . . . " I stammered. "I noticed that you guys must have been in a relationship for a very long time."

"We have!" she exclaimed. "I just moved here a few months

ago from Texas to be with him. It was a surprise."

I could tell by the look on the guy's face, it wasn't a good surprise.

"Well, that's great. Long distance is hard. I'm sure he's glad to have you as a roommate now," I said jokingly.

"Actually, we don't live together, yet," the girl said, seeming embarrassed. "But I think that's going to change soon. Right, honey?"

The guy sat up and loosened his tie. "Well, uh. I think we need to talk about that actually."

The girl looked at him as if he had just insulted her mother.

"What do you mean, we need to talk about that? I thought we settled that. I move fifteen hundred miles to be closer to you, and you still want to have distance between us?"

I quickly grabbed the check and paid the bill. Elsa and I couldn't get out of there fast enough. I had just triggered a fight, and it wasn't going to be pretty. Poor girl.

Maybe if she had listened to his body language, she would have seen it coming. But it was clear. She wasn't aware of nonverbals. Not his, and not her own.

Mirror Theory

I know it's hard to always keep your body language in check. You have to think about so many other things while dating that you can go nuts thinking about them all at once.

But you have to be aware of what you are telling a guy while you are out with him—even when what you're saying is not coming out of your mouth.

One night while out with the girls, I met a very attractive guy. His name was Kevin, and he was classic tall, dark, and handsome. Just from the look of him, I knew that he could have his pick of women. He asked for my number that night and we set up a date for the following week.

I met Kevin for drinks at a hotel bar in Dupont Circle. We had only discussed having drinks, which was fine with me. I didn't want to be stuck having dinner if the date didn't go well, and I knew he felt the same way. When I walked in and saw him, I was immediately excited. He was a lot cuter than I remembered, and I remembered him being pretty cute. But, because of this, I reminded myself that a lot of other women found him attractive, too, so I knew I had to play it cool. I wasn't concerned about saying the right things, but I knew that I had to watch my body language. It was rare for me to be so initially attracted to someone I hardly knew, and I didn't want to blow the date before it even got started.

I remembered an old trick I used during meetings with clients. It's called the Mirror Theory. If I wanted a customer to be completely comfortable, especially in a high-pressure setting, I would mirror their body language. However they were sitting or standing, I would mirror. If they were talking fast or slow, I would mirror. Whatever nonverbals they were giving

me, I would give right back. In dating, using the Mirror Theory prevents you from coming on too strong and seeming more interested than he is. It also prevents you from coming off too cold, which a lot of girls also do because they are so afraid of being transparent. The Mirror Theory will have your body language just right.

When Kevin and I were sitting at the bar, he had his whole body turned toward me. I mirrored that and sat with my whole body turned toward him. When he sat back, I sat back. When he leaned in, I leaned in. After sitting at the bar for an hour, he asked me if we could continue our date over dinner.

We walked to a sushi place nearby, and Kevin grabbed my hand. I made a joke about him being a fast mover. He dropped my hand and looked disappointed. I laughed and told him he could hold my hand, I didn't mind. Then I gave him a flirty smile, and he picked my hand back up again.

At dinner I continued to use the Mirror Theory. When he was smiling, I was smiling. When he was serious, I was serious. Halfway through our meal, he stopped mid-sentence and told me something that validated every move I had made up to that point.

"I have to admit, I am a little intimidated by you," he said. "Most of the girls I go out with, I can tell within minutes that they are totally into me. But you, I can't tell just how much you like me yet. That's odd for me."

"How can you tell when other girls are into you?" I asked.

"Well, they sort of hang on my every word. They giggle a

little too much. They think every thing I say is funny, even when it's not. They look at me like they are dying for me to kiss them. I don't get any of that from you. I feel like you are smarter than the average bear. Like I said, it is a little intimidating, but I am totally up for the challenge. In fact, I find it extremely refreshing."

Kevin had no clue that all I had been doing that night was mirroring his every move. All he knew was he wanted to see me again.

Listen to What He Says, Hear How He Sounds

Using the Mirror Theory is a safe way to keep yourself in check throughout your date. But don't just watch his body language, pay attention to his tone of voice as well. Maybe you didn't *tell* him how you think he walks on water, but the *sound* of your voice did. Contrary to popular belief, a guy would rather you talk in your normal voice. Sounding like Paris Hilton and putting on a "baby voice" is actually unattractive and could give a guy the impression you aren't that smart. Besides, most of the time people use that voice to talk to babies and animals. This is a man, not a Shar-Pei. You want to come off confident, smart, and sophisticated. You don't want to talk like a two-year old. Some women talk like this on purpose but others don't even realize they are doing it.

Other things to keep in mind? The expression on his face. Is

his body leaning toward you or away? Smile and laugh when he does. Try not to beam at him. You don't have to have a constant grin on your face for him to think you are having a good time.

Watch him, mirror his body language, and you will be just fine. Remember, he may not feel the way you do yet, so it's better to play it cool. If the Mirror Theory starts really working for you and he starts coming on strong, be careful. You don't want to mirror *everything* he does.

Using Jones Effect

When I was nineteen, I was head over heels for my best friend Elliot. He and I worked together promoting various nightclubs. For years I pined away for him while he romanced other women. They came and went, but I remained a constant. Always by his side, always there when he needed me. I thought of myself like his girlfriend; he thought of me like a little sister. I was always careful not to flirt with men around him. I didn't want him to think I was unavailable in case he suddenly decided he was in love and couldn't live without me.

After years of patiently waiting, I decided I'd had enough. My prayers had fallen on deaf ears, and Elliot was never going to come around. As hard as it was to accept, I knew I would have to

move on. While Elliot was away on summer break, I met Philip. Philip was an intolerably good-looking French-American who absolutely adored me. Wherever we went, women would comment on my delicious piece of arm candy. And while I certainly had an affinity for Philip, I still harbored feelings for Elliot.

The night Elliot returned from summer vacation, he threw a party at our club. Usually I would show up with girlfriends, but this time I brought Phillip with me. As I approached the front door, Elliot greeted me with a huge bear hug. "Hi, gorgeous!" he exclaimed. "How have you been?"

He hadn't yet realized I came with the Abercrombie & Fitch model standing to my right. Suddenly I lost my nerve and wanted to push Philip into the bushes so I wouldn't have to explain him. But before I could find a shrub big enough to hide him, Philip extended his hand.

"Hi, you must be Elliot. I'm Philip."

Elliot went from excitement to confusion. He shook Philip's hand and then looked at me askance.

"Well, seems like you've been busy while I was away," he said.

I didn't know what to say, so I shrugged. Elliot looked at me for a minute and then lifted the velvet rope for Philip and me.

"I'll see you guys inside," he said.

Philip and I settled into a booth with some friends. Elliot came over a couple times to say hello, and each time Philip seemed to take his cue and kiss me. I could tell Elliot was a little weirded-out by the whole thing. Never in the two years

that I knew him had he seen me with another guy. I was dying to run after him and scream, "I don't like Philip! I'm sorry! Let's go back to the way it used to be!" But then I remembered, the way it used to be wasn't any better than this. I ordered another drink, wishing I were twenty-one so I could dull the pain with something stronger than a Shirley Temple.

At the end of the night we all stood outside. Philip was tired and wanted to go home. I told him I would catch a ride with someone else since I wanted to go to the after-hours party. As he leaned in to kiss me, I saw Elliot watching from the corner of my eye.

As soon as Philip left, Elliot grabbed me.

"You're staying out?" he asked.

"Yeah, if that's okay?" I said puzzled.

Elliot smiled and took my hand. He yelled to one of the guys, "Hey, man, let's go to that club, Red. Jess and I will meet you there."

Elliot held my hand as we walked to the car, something he had never done before. He opened my door to let me in. I turned to thank him and suddenly before I knew what was even happening, he was kissing me! Elliot and I were kissing! Right there in the parking lot. I couldn't believe it. He pulled backed, looked deep into my eyes, and then said, "You're not serious with that guy are you?"

That was the night I learned about Jones Effect.

What Is Jones Effect?

Jones Effect is the highly proven theory that you want what other people have. That is why you will often hear salespeople say, "Everyone is buying one of these. In fact, I sold one to your neighbor yesterday." We know if you think other people are buying it, you will want to buy it, too.

Why is Jones Effect so effective in convincing people they like something? Why do we need social proof that others feel the way we do? Simply put, we as people believe if someone else likes what we like, it validates it as good.

Remember that old eighties movie *Can't Buy Me Love?* Patrick Dempsey played Ronald Miller, a geeky high school student who mowed lawns and had a crush on the captain of the cheerleaders. He was such a social outcast that he sat in the visiting section at football games. Not only did girls not like him, they didn't even acknowledge his existence.

Then came his brilliant idea! Ronald, who had always dreamed of being popular, gave up his plan to buy a telescope and instead paid popular girl Cindy Mancini $1,000 to go out with him. Cindy doubted Ronald's popularity plan and scoffed, "Just going out with me is not going to make you popular." To which Ronald replied, "Well, I have a thousand dollars that says it will."

He was right. One month later, Cindy and Ronald annulled their fake relationship and Ronald was the hottest item on the

school's menu. Every girl wanted to date the guy that had gone from geek to chic. Ronald put his money on Jones Effect and the gamble paid off!

Jones Effect is so powerful it can take even the most unlikely product and turn it into a bestseller. Ronald was a social leper until Cindy came along. But with her approval, the entire student body had a change of heart.

The Misconception of Jones Effect

Most of my friends have never heard of Jones Effect. And if they have, they don't know how to use it. Most women have at least one Elliot story. It's funny looking back on it. All along I was afraid for Elliot to see me with another guy. Even having him see me talk to one for too long made me nervous. But in the end, that is exactly what he needed to see. He needed to see someone else want me. As soon as he did, he took immediate action.

I think many women feel the way I did. We don't want the guy we like to think we're into (or out with) someone else because he may get discouraged and give up on us. But that is honestly a misconception. He won't see it as you liking someone else (although if he does, it's not always a bad thing to make him worry). All he sees is someone else wanting you. And that is a good thing. Other men should want you. You are a desirable woman who men would kill to be with and he

needs to know that. Seeing you talk to another man will not deter him from pursuing you. On the contrary, it will only fuel the fire.

Keep Him Jonesing

When you begin dating someone, it's perfectly fine for him to think you are out with other men. It's okay to talk about your male friends, because he should know that they exist. You are too cute and funny to not have any men in your life. Don't feel the need to always explain where you are and who you are with. You want him to question if you have another date. If he says something to you about it, you can always come back with, "I didn't realize we were only dating each other exclusively. I'm sorry, do we need to talk about it?"

When you first start dating someone you want it to be pretty obvious that other men find you attractive. You should talk to and be friendly with men around you. As the relationship progresses you can tone it down, but you don't want to let it go completely. Men are competitive by nature, and they like feeling as if they are fighting other guys for you.

Jones Effect = Attractive

Think about how many times you have been affected by Jones Effect. When you find out a guy has a girlfriend or see

a ring on his finger, don't you automatically find him slightly more attractive? Of course you do. Because someone else has him. He is wanted by someone else. I'm not saying you should steal someone else's boyfriend. All I am saying is if you have absolutely no one wanting you, what does that say? Don't hide the fact that you have guy friends. You don't have to ignore other guys at a party. Don't be afraid to let him see you interact or talk with members of the opposite sex. Unless he's very insecure, it will not prevent him from liking you. Don't be obvious about it, but don't hide it either.

But Be Warned . . .

Now a word of caution: Jones Effect must be used with kid gloves. You don't want to overdo it. There are women who go overboard with their use of Jones Effect. I have a friend who flirts like crazy with other guys when she's out with her boyfriend. She loves to make him jealous. Every time they go out together she starts flirting with the waiter, the bartender, the man in line for the restroom, and anyone else she comes in contact with. She will grab their hands, arms, and even their legs. I've seen her sit on a random guy's lap in an effort to get a rise out of her boyfriend. He knows what she is doing and it creates a lot of drama between them. That's not using Jones Effect, that's abusing it.

Don't drop too many names when it comes to Jones Effect

either. If you are always talking about your friend Mike who likes you, or your coworker Bob who calls you too much, you will be perceived as boastful and arrogant. It's definitely a fine line to walk, so you have to be careful. Used wisely, Jones Effect can be a good tool. Used foolishly, it can be deadly.

6

KEEPING HIM INTERESTED

Hold Back Your Bullets

I'll never forget the first woman to ever cry in my office. Her name was Amelia. She was a tiny blonde with a big personality. Her blue eyes, which were usually filled with excitement and enthusiasm, were now flooded with tears and runny mascara. As she sat in front of me trying to find her words, I remember thinking she looked more like a woman who had just lost her boyfriend instead of a sale.

But that's why she was sobbing so profusely. She had been pounding the pavement for weeks, trying to find new customers. Ten different business owners had invited her to sit down and give them her pitch, but as time progressed she was unable to close any of them.

"I just don't understand it," she cried. "None of the other reps had as many deals in their funnel. Yet, they were able to close at least two or three, and I couldn't close any of mine. I feel so stupid. I don't think I can work here anymore."

Although she was being a bit dramatic, she was right. Having ten deals in her funnel was unusual. Most of the other reps didn't have nearly that good of a prospecting rate. She was able to get customers interested, but somewhere in the course of the sale, she was losing their interest. She knew it, and that's why she felt so bad.

"Hey, you have gotten through the toughest part. Finding the business and getting the person interested to hear what you have to say is what takes the most effort. You just need to figure out what you are doing that is losing the customers' interest. Tell me exactly what you said to each person and we'll figure it out together."

Though her sniffles, Amelia recounted the last few weeks for me. When she was asked to sit down and give her pitch for the first time, she immediately told the customer about the trial caller ID we were offering. I had always taught the sales force not to lead with that but rather keep it in their back pocket as an incentive to push the customer over the fence. But Amelia's nerves probably got the best of her so she led with it. Then she told the customer how much money they could save with our program, along with how they would be able to get online billing.

"Did they ask about online billing?" I questioned her.

"No, but I figured it was just another great part of the deal and they should know about it."

As I listened to her finish the story I realized Amelia's problem. She was so afraid that the customer would lose interest and kick her out of their office at any moment that she told them about all the perks of the offer right up front, instead of pacing the conversation and dishing them out accordingly.

"Amelia," I said. "Has anyone told you the Bullet Theory?"

"Um. No," she replied.

"Very simply put, you have to hold back your bullets. Online billing is a bullet. The trial caller ID is a bullet. All the perks of signing a contract with you are bullets. You only have a handful, and if you throw all of them out right away, you are going to be left with no ammunition for the rest of the conversation. The sales process can take weeks, even months, and you have to keep the customer interested all the way to the close. So you have to divvy out your bullets little by little. That way, you continue to keep them interested. You threw out all your bullets on the first meeting, so by the second or third time you went back, your customer started to lose interest, and you had no bullets left."

Amelia realized what she was doing wrong. She tried to fix it, but she was never able to hold back her bullets. She was too worried the customer would lose interest. She continued to throw out her bullets in the very beginning of her pitch, and

ultimately she had to find another job.

When dating, women sometimes have the same problem as Amelia. They throw out all their bullets right away, too. In dating, bullets are a woman's valuables, such as kissing, making out, and the biggest bullet of all, sex. Some women think if they don't throw out theses bullets right away, a guy actually won't like them. But, as Amelia quickly learned, if you throw out all your bullets right away, you have nothing left to keep a man's interest.

Emptying Your Gun

My friend Camille introduced me to one of her coworkers Sylvia. Sylvia was having major boy problems and Camille wanted me to talk with her. Sylvia was a thirty-five-year-old attractive and successful attorney, but she hadn't had a serious relationship in years. I got an opportunity to talk to Sylvia alone one night at a dinner party.

"Tell me about the last two guys you were interested in," I said to her.

"Well, first there was Josh. I met Josh at a Halloween party given by a friend of mine. I had seen him around, but we had never really talked before. We struck up a conversation that lasted most of the night. He asked for my number and we went out that weekend."

"Okay, so how did the first date go?"

"It went alright. He came over and we were going to go out

to dinner but instead we ordered in and watched a movie. Well, we didn't really watch the movie. But I still had a good time."

"So you guys made out all night?"

"Yeah, you could say that." She laughed.

"Did you have sex?" I asked.

"No, but we came very close a couple times."

"Okay, what happened after that night?"

"We went out again. We went to a party and then back to his place . . . and uh, that time we had sex," she said with an embarrassed laugh.

"Hmmm, okay. So you went on two dates before becoming intimate?"

"Yeah. We saw each other for about two weeks after that and everything was fine. Then he had to go out of town for work. I didn't hear from him when he came back, so I called him. He didn't pick up, so I left a message on his machine. I don't know what happened, but that was two weeks ago now, and he still hasn't returned my call."

"So you never heard from him again?" I said.

"No."

I wanted to tell Sylvia what she did wrong in that situation, but I wanted to see if she was a habitual offender, so I asked her to tell me about the second guy, too.

"Last weekend I went to this concert in the park by my house and I saw this really hot guy. I smiled at him, and he

came right over. We hung out the rest of the night and had a blast. He was definitely one of the coolest guys I have met in a long time. Anyway, I must have been drinking more than I should have because we ended up back at my place. Anyway, long story short, we did not have sex but we did spend hours making out. Finally we both fell asleep."

"So what happened the next day? Did you have breakfast together? Or did he leave right when you guys woke up?" I asked

Sylvia's eyes dropped to her feet. "When I woke up, he was gone. He didn't leave a note or a number."

It was clear. She was a habitual offender. The crime: misuse of a firearm.

I had to explain to Sylvia the Bullet Theory. She was great at meeting guys and getting them interested, but she was losing them because she was emptying her gun on the first couple of dates. She spent too much time with them and became intimate with them way too soon. Even though she didn't have sex with the second guy, the fact that she almost did told him all it would take would be one more date.

"Sylvia, your affection and your body are all precious things. You don't even really know these guys that well and you are giving all your valuables away within the first few dates. They don't have to do any work to get them either. You have to hold these bullets back so that you keep the guy interested."

"Okay, maybe I screwed up with Josh, but the 'concert in

the park guy' I didn't sleep with," she interjected. "Isn't that what's really the most important thing here? You aren't sup-posed to have sex on the first date, and I did not do that."

"No, you didn't. But believe me, he knew that it wasn't going to be long before you gave in," I told her. "Look, the concert guy didn't call you because based on how you acted the first night, he knew he was going to get you into bed quickly. He either didn't want to sleep with a girl that had been around the block, or he figured the reward of sleeping with you wasn't worth the risk of you becoming emotionally attached. There aren't a lot of girls who sleep with men and don't want something more from them. So most guys, believe it or not, would rather turn down sex than do it and then have to spend weeks shaking an emotionally attached girl off their tail."

Sylvia looked dumbfounded. How was all this so obvious to me and news to her?

Unfortunately, most girls suffer the same consequences of throwing out all their bullets. In Sylvia's case, she had wanted someone to like her so badly, that she jumped all over a guy when he showed a little bit of interest. She needed to learn to keep her gun locked and loaded in order to keep her dates coming back for more.

Building Anticipation

When I was a kid, my favorite time of year was right before Christmas. My parents would put up a big tree and my sister and I would decorate it with dozens of colorful ornaments. We'd sing carols and make cookies. All of our family would visit, and each would bring a present that we were instructed to put under the tree. As the days passed and Christmas neared, the presents began to pile up. My sister and I would shake and rattle them with glee, wondering what was inside. We begged our mother to let us open just one, but she firmly told us, no. We had to wait until Christmas day.

On Christmas Eve we couldn't sleep. We tossed and turned in our beds, wishing it was morning so we could run downstairs and tear into our presents. Then at 7 AM we'd burst into our parents' room, jumping on the bed, pleading with them to wake up and let Christmas day begin. We'd open our gifts and spend days under the tree playing. I remember taking all my presents to bed and sleeping with them for a week.

That is how I remember the holidays. Notice I did not mention what I got each year. Frankly, I can't remember any of the presents I received as a kid. But I do remember the wonderfully agonizing feeling of anticipation. It went on for weeks and it filled our house with excitement. It wasn't the presents that made it so thrilling. It was the *waiting* to open them that did it.

You have to think of yourself as a present under the tree. You want a guy to be so anxious and eager to open you up, he can hardly stand it. You want to build anticipation within him, and you cannot do it if you throw out your bullets right away. Imagine if my mother gave in every time my sister and I begged to open a gift before Christmas. Then the anticipation would only last for moments instead of for weeks. The excitement would never build, and we'd not cherish the gift as much. If you meet a guy, and within a few dates (or worse, a few hours) he gets what he wants from you, he won't cherish you either.

There is a direct correlation between waiting for something and cherishing it once you have it. The longer you wait, the more you want it and the happier you are when you get it. Knowing this basic principle, you should understand why it is in your best interest to hold back your bullets. Not just the sex bullet— all of them. The longer a guy waits, the better.

Do Bullets Expire?

But eventually you have to throw out all your bullets, right? Isn't there a point that a guy will lose interest if things aren't progressing physically? Don't bullets have an expiration point? The answer is no. They aren't like a carton of milk. Bullets don't go bad. When you hold back your bullets you are conveying the message that you really respect yourself. When

you throw them out right away you are saying that you don't. Respect is contagious just like confidence. If you respect yourself, others will respect you. If you don't respect yourself, don't expect anyone else to either. If a guy pressures you, especially for sex, then you really need to question what his motive is for seeing you. If he tells you that sex is really important to him and he cannot see you anymore if you two aren't having it, then dump him. He's clearly after one thing.

Personally, I rarely kiss on a first date. Sometimes, I don't even kiss on the second or third. Sounds crazy, right? But it's holding back this bullet that puts me in a whole other category from other women. If I hold back the kissing bullet, I am subsequently holding back several other bullets, too. If I am not kissing him, I am not making out with him, and certainly not having sex. That one bullet helps me hold back a lot of the other ones.

When I told Sylvia this she looked at me like I was out of my mind. She couldn't hold back for one hour, let alone one full date.

"Doesn't the guy think you are weird? Doesn't he think you aren't interested?" she asked.

"Nope. I act flirty. I hug. I kiss on the cheek, and I smile. If they go in for a real kiss, I just say, 'I'm sorry, I'm just not ready to kiss you, yet.' If they ask when I will kiss them, I tell them that I really don't know. I have to build the desire to kiss someone. It may take one date, it may take four. But the

honest truth is, most guys don't even ask why I am not kissing them."

Sylvia was amazed. "I feel like I have to kiss them or they will lose interest and move on to someone else."

"And that is the exact opposite of what will happen." I told her.

A good salesperson knows how to use her bullets. If you throw them out too soon, you can jeopardize the sale. Likewise, if you throw out yours too soon, you can jeopardize your relationship. You have to keep your gun loaded at all times, even if you are dying to fire it off. I know there will also be times that your hormones will be raging and holding back won't be easy. But it is what is necessary! If you don't want a long-term relationship with a guy, go ahead and sleep with him after two dates. Just understand that men don't respect or seriously date women they have sex with so soon. He may stick around a little while if you are lucky, but even if you get a relationship out of him I guarantee it won't be the one you want. In the back of his head he will always think you sleep around. It won't matter if you tell him that you don't typically do that sort of thing and he's the only one you have ever done this with. All he will hear is the Charlie Brown schoolteacher: "Womp womp, womp womp." What you say is always can-celled out by what you do.

So when exactly is it appropriate to throw out your bullets? There isn't a set time line. It really depends on when you feel

he wants something more from you than just a good time. You have to feel comfortable with the relationship as it is. Don't think that if you have sex with a guy, you will get closer to him and thus get him even more interested. That's a complete fallacy. If he's only moderately interested in you, sex is not going to be the tipping point. There are many things you will learn in this book that will help you build interest, and sex is not one of them.

Whatever You Do, Don't Cut to the Close

All of my single friends complain about the same thing. If they are in their twenties I hear, "I want a boyfriend." If they are in their thirties I hear, "I want to get married." Getting involved in a serious relationship seems to always be in the forefront of their minds. Never do they say, "I want to meet someone who seems right for me, date him, and see if we are compatible." No, when they meet a guy, their brain goes straight to relationship mode. Forget casually dating him. They want to find a way to get him into a relationship as quick as possible.

Women are always looking to close the deal, even if there

isn't a deal on the table yet. As a salesperson, I think about closing deals, too. But only when I have one to be closed. If I don't have a sale that I have been working on for a while, I am not concentrating on the close, I am concentrating on finding business. Then, after I find the business, I am concentrating on getting the customer interested and building a good relationship. After all of that, then and only then, do I focus on the final stages of the sale. This is the cycle. It does me no good to worry about how I am going to close a deal before I even find a prospect.

When it comes to dating, most women don't think that way. They obsess about a marriage when they aren't even dating someone. So when they do find a prospect, they try to close on a commitment almost immediately, and that is always a recipe for disaster.

After dating a workaholic named P.J. for almost a year, my very good friend, Isabel, realized that he was never going to want to get married or have children. She was angry for wasting so much of her time on him and now having to start all over again. So when she started dating Harrison, she did not want to waste one second of her time if he didn't want to get married and start a family either. After they had been dating a few weeks, she decided to casually ask him one night if he saw marriage and children in his future. Harrison said he definitely wanted to get married and have kids someday. Of course, upon hearing this, Isabel was delighted. She told him she had

always wanted children, too, and was glad they had the same goals. She also asked him about his upbringing and religious beliefs, just to be sure they were in alignment as well.

I spoke to Isabel shortly after she had this discussion with Harrison. She said it was so nice to finally find someone that was on her level and wanted the same things. She thought Harrison was a good candidate and could see them having a very bright future.

Unfortunately, their relationship did not last long after that conversation. Harrison told her a few weeks later that he just didn't have time for a serious relationship. He told her he thought she was a great person but couldn't commit at this point of his life. Isabel was completely dumbfounded. How could he tell her one minute that he wanted a family, and the next minute tell her he didn't even want to commit to being a boyfriend?

Isabel had made a classic mistake. She had tried to cut to the close. I know women are worried about wasting their time with a man who doesn't want to get married, but that doesn't mean you can forgo the dating cycle and cut right to the close. For some reason, as soon as a woman decides she likes a man, she wants to know his intentions. It doesn't matter if she has only been seeing the guy for three weeks; she wants to define the relationship. Why? Because the thought of not knowing where "this" is going is absolute torture. Women say to me all the time, "I just want to know where I stand. If he is never planning on getting married, I need to know, because I am not just here for a good time."

Yes, ladies, I do understand your intentions, but they are counterproductive to what you are trying to do. In the beginning, a man is just getting to know you and seeing if he even likes you. He can't tell you his intentions, because frankly, he doesn't know what they are yet. If you cut to the close at this point, you are basically pressuring him to make a decision about something he knows nothing about. You are telling him, "Hey, buddy, don't even think about taking me out again unless you think you want to marry me."

You may not think you are pressuring him by asking these questions, but you are. Asking a guy whether he wants to get married on the first few dates would be like me meeting a client for the very first time and trying to close him right after introducing myself. Can you imagine if I sat down with a new customer and said, "Hi, my name is Jess, and I am looking to sell this product. But before I even waste my time telling you all about it, I need to know if you are ever going to buy it. If you don't think you are going to purchase it sometime in the near future, I won't waste my breath. So tell me right now are you going to buy it or not."

I would never sell a thing that way. I have to have a good relationship with a customer and have them seriously interested in my product before I can even start to ask those closing questions. How would they know if they are going to buy my product? They don't know anything about it yet. Just like in dating, you can't go out with a guy on a first date and say

you are looking to get married, have kids, buy a house, and call it a day. It will never work. In fact, it will make men run.

Isabel thought because she so casually asked P.J. about marriage and didn't say she wanted to specifically marry him, bringing up the subject would not be a big deal. She could not have been more wrong. Don't ever announce that your next goal in life is to get married. Don't ask a man what his marriage plans are either. That kind of talk is meant for people who are already involved in a serious relationship. If you ask a guy early on in the relationship if he wants to get married someday, he is going to think you are going to try and marry him. When a guy hears you want a serious relationship of any kind, it doesn't matter if you don't say with whom—he's going to assume you mean him. He's the one sitting across the table from you. He's the one you're dating. Who else could you be talking about?

It's not always good to tell a guy what you're really thinking. If you're interested in someone and want to know if marriage is high on his priority list, asking him point blank is not the way to find out. It's too scary, and it turns guys off. How would you feel if a guy told you what he really wanted on a first date? I imagine it would sound something like, "You know, I just really want to have sex sometime soon. If a woman isn't seriously interested in sex, then I really don't want to waste my time. Can you see yourself doing it in the next few days, weeks, or months from now? I am only inter-

ested in dating women who are going to want to have sex in the very near future."

Now, tell me that's a turn-on for you, and if so, you can keep on having your early marriage talks.

Creating Skepticism

Back when I was a sales trainer, I was asked to ride in the field one day with a brand-new sales rep who was having difficulty closing deals. Joe was a former football player who injured himself and was now looking for another career. He told me he wanted to get into sales because he wanted to control his income and get paid what he was worth. Unfortunately, so far, it wasn't working out for him.

"I don't know what it is, Jess. Maybe I am just not cut out for this. People don't want to buy from me. I think they are intimidated by me."

"Well, Joe, that's why I'm here." I said. "I'm just going to listen today and see if I can determine what you may need to do differently. Usually it's just a matter of tweaking your game. Don't throw in the towel yet."

We walked into a law office, and I let Joe take the reins. Behind the front desk two ladies were chatting away, getting little work done. *Perfect,* I thought. I knew they were sociable people, and they weren't busy at the moment. Joe kicked off his pitch.

"Hi, how are you doing today, ladies? My name is Joe, and yes, I am a sales rep. But don't worry; I'm not going to sell you something you don't need. I promise you're going to love it. I'm here on behalf of your local phone carrier. We have some new rates, and for only twenty-nine ninety-nine a month, you can get our deluxe package. Do you have a current phone bill I could look at and show you what I'm talking about?"

At that point I couldn't watch the Titanic sink. I walked out of the business, knowing Joe would be right behind me. Seconds later the door flew open and Joe stormed out. "That's it. I quit. They wouldn't even let me see a phone bill. I couldn't even get through my pitch. How is it that everyone else on the team can sign up three to four people a day and I haven't signed up one person this week?"

"Joe," I said. "The answer is very simple. It's not that you're intimidating, or that you just aren't cut out for this. You just turned them off before you got started. The first thing you said in there is 'Hi, I'm a salesperson, and for only twenty-nine ninety-nine, I can sell you this.' Joe, people are automatically skeptical of salespeople trying to sell them something they don't need. The first thing you did was announce that you were selling something, and then you told them the price before even explaining the product. You created skepticism, which caused them to put up a wall in defense. In sales, you want the customer to get excited about the product and then you tell them

how much it costs. It doesn't work the other way around."

"But, Jess, don't they already know I'm a salesperson when I walk in the door? And twenty-nine ninety-nine is a good deal. I am just trying to cut to the chase and get down to business. Besides, I say it very casually so they don't feel pressured."

"Yes, and you see how well it's working for you," I said.

Price Before Product?

You never want to tell a customer up front that you are about to sell them something, and you never tell them the price in the beginning of a conversation. Even though $29.99 is a good deal, customers don't know that until you've explained what they are getting for that price. Price is to be discussed at the end of the sales cycle, not the very beginning. You never want to tell someone how much something costs before they have actually seen it and understand its worth.

Women who talk marriage too soon are breaking that same rule and making the close much more difficult for themselves. You can't talk about marriage until a guy knows your product— you—and understands the value of it. Talking marriage on the first couple of dates is like discussing price on the first meeting.

People are always a little skeptical that a salesperson is only interested in making money off them. However, once we gain their trust, they will ultimately be fine with buying from us.

Women are in the same boat. There are lots of men out there who are known to be skeptical of women. They are skeptical that we are all just out to land a husband to take care of us. Your job is to prove them wrong. You have to get this wonderful man to trust that you aren't like all the other women out there. You aren't looking to get married; you are looking for someone with whom you're compatible. Will it lead to marriage? Hopefully. But the best thing to do is not talk about these thoughts. Not in the beginning anyway. You want to reduce skepticism, not create more.

I told Joe not to announce that he was a salesperson and to wait until the close to discuss the price. I told him to walk in and start out with something light and fun. There is no need to restate the obvious. Yes, he is a salesperson, but the customer doesn't need to be reminded of that.

Joe went to the next business. Instead of walking in and giving his usual pitch, he smiled at the lady at the front desk and broke the ice first. They chatted for a bit, he made a couple of jokes, and a few minutes later she was rummaging through her desk looking for an old phone bill. After that, he had no problem closing the deal.

Don't Ask, He'll Tell

When I started dating James, a professional tennis player, I knew that he had many women trying to land him. He dated

models and actresses who constantly tried to lock him down. When he met me, he was surprised that I never once asked about his feelings or what the expectations of the relationship were. After we had been dating for a couple months, he finally asked me one night where I thought the relationship was going. I couldn't help but smile on the inside. The ball was now in my court. Would I return the serve? Absolutely not. I decided I was keeping the damn thing for as long as I could. I told James I was having a great time with him, but that I wasn't sure if I was ready to have the "relationship talk" quite yet. I wish I could have taken a picture of his face. It was like I was speaking a foreign language. He just didn't understand.

After that, I was pursued hard.

James finally told me that he loved me, and we dated for several months. Ultimately I ended things with him because he got too serious! Today we are really good friends. Ironically, he always says to me, "I wonder if the reason I fell so hard for you was because you never pressured me into a relationship. I wonder if you had been like every other girl and tried to tie me down, would I have been as into you?"

I know the answer. Had I said I wanted a relationship right away, James would have never fallen for me.

Sorry, ladies, but you just can't rush this one. Getting a guy to commit to a relationship doesn't happen over night. In my industry, it usually takes six to eight months to close a deal. It is a long and delicately planned process from the time I meet

a customer to the time I close the deal. I can't reveal my ultimate intentions right away, and neither can you. Don't worry about him not taking you seriously. It is obvious that I am trying to sell my equipment when I sit down with customers, just like it's obvious that you are trying to find a meaningful relationship when you go on dates. I'm not going to remind my customer that the primary reason I'm meeting with them is to sell them something. That would be ludicrous. No. I tell them I am there because I can help them. I am there because I care about their business. I am there because I was in the area and wanted to see what they were doing for lunch. I am not there because I need them to hurry up and buy. When the time comes to close your deal, asking him won't be an issue. What he says about marriage before dating you is irrelevant. So in the meantime, don't shoot yourself in the foot by cutting to the close.

Taking Control

I was sitting at a hotel bar in Chicago having a glass of wine when Isabel called. She was packing for our trip to Miami that weekend and getting excited about leaving town for a few days. But that wasn't all she was excited about. She was excited to see Doug, her new love interest who lived in South

Beach. Doug and Isabel had been dating for a little over a month now, and she was starting to develop deep feelings for him. This weekend was supposed to be girls only, but it was clear that Isabel was going to break that rule. She wanted to spend as much time with Doug as she could.

"So what's your plan?" I asked. "Are you going to hang out with the girls or are you planning to stay with Doug the whole weekend?"

Isabel laughed. "You know me too well," she said. "I promise I will hang out with you girls. I just really miss him and want to see him as much as I can."

"I understand," I said. "So are you ditching us at the airport or will you at least make it out to dinner with us on Friday?"

Isabel hesitated for a moment. "Um, I'm not sure. I kind of want to get down there, feel things out, and then make a decision."

I was a little puzzled. If Isabel was so excited to see her boyfriend, why hadn't she made plans with him already?

"What do you mean?" I questioned. "You just said you want to spend as much time with him as possible. Now you want to get down there and see what's what?"

I should have known by the sound of her voice that something wasn't right.

"I do want to see him. I want to see him badly," she said. "But the thing is, the last time I was down there he said he thought we were moving a little fast. He said he had such a great time that it kind of scared him. So I'm not sure what to

do at this point. I did talk to him yesterday, and he asked me what I was going to do when I got here. I told him I wasn't quite sure yet, because what else could I say? I have to wait until he asks me to get together. I certainly can't pressure him about letting me stay at his place. But once he sees me, I'm sure he'll ask me to."

As she was telling me the story, I knew what was happening. Doug was losing interest in my friend. He had come on strong in the beginning, but now his feelings were starting to fade. As an impartial bystander, I could clearly see what her next move should be. I wanted to say to her, "Isabel, just tell him that you are staying with your friends and that if he wants to see you, you'll be at the Shore Club. Why are you waiting around for him to make the decision? You are giving him all the control!"

But sometimes it's hard to say that to a friend, and I knew she wouldn't do it anyway. She liked Doug too much and there was no way she was going to take matters into her own hands like that, even though it was the smart thing to do.

"Here's my plan," she started. "I'm thinking we'll get there on Friday, and I will hang out by the pool in the afternoon with the girls. Doug knows when I am getting down there, so he'll probably call then. I'll most likely meet up with him for dinner, and then I'm sure he'll want me to come back to his place."

I didn't know what to say to my friend. The situation didn't

sound good to me. If Doug really wanted to see her, he would have already made plans with her. Now she was left hanging in limbo, waiting for him to make the next move.

"OK, Isabel, do whatever you want to do. Personally, I think you should make your own plan for the weekend. Then tell Doug what you'll be doing, instead of waiting around for him to make up his mind."

Isabel laughed. "How can I do that? The plan I want is to spend the whole weekend with him. Now that he's told me he's scared about his feelings, I can't push him. I can only wait until he's ready to see me."

"True, you can't make plans with him. But you can make plans with us. Take some control. Tell him that you're going to be hanging out with the girls all weekend. Tell him if he really wants to see you, you may be able to do dinner Friday night, but he needs to tell you right now, otherwise you are going out with the girls. Then you won't have to sit around waiting and wondering whether or not you'll see him. He'll have one choice, and if he really wants to see you, he'll take it."

Isabel thought for a second. "But I don't want to only see him on Friday. I want to spend the whole weekend with him. If I say that I could be limiting my time with him. Also I feel like asking him to decide right now is too demanding. He may still be freaked out about things. No, I think it's best if I just wait for him to call and see what he says."

I gave up after that.

The thing I used to hate the most about dating was the fact that I had no control. I was always told to let the guy make the move. Let him call you, let him ask you out, let him try and kiss you. So where did that leave me? It left me waiting. Just like Isabel. Waiting for him to call all the shots and be 100 percent in control. I don't have to tell you how horrible it feels to be powerless in a relationship. Isabel was going through the same thing. Doug thought they were moving too fast, and she was left in limbo waiting for him to decide if and when he wanted to see her.

In Isabel's situation, she could have easily taken control by telling Doug she could only really see him on Friday because the rest of the weekend she wanted to spend with her girlfriends. That is taking control. Even though it's not exactly what she wanted to do, it was the only good move to make. Doing this would allow her to gain some ground back, put her in a less vulnerable position, and enable her to see how much Doug really liked her. If he came to see her or tried to convince her to stay with him, she would know more about how he really felt. But even more importantly, she would be the one making the moves. And that would put her back on equal playing ground.

Of course the problem that Isabel (and most women) had is that doing this would mean making a move that is completely opposite of what she wanted. She wanted to spend the whole weekend with Doug. She was hoping that eventually he would

make plans with her. To make her own plans meant she would risk not seeing him at all, and she wasn't strong enough to do that. So instead, she kept biding her time and waiting it out. And you know what? When we arrived in Miami on Friday she stared at her phone all day and complained repeatedly about him not calling. Where was he? What was he doing? Why hasn't he called yet? Eventually he did call her that night. It was around nine-thirty and she ran to meet him. We didn't see her again until we boarded the plane on Monday. Seemingly she got what she wanted—the entire weekend with Doug. However, the minute we got back to D.C., Doug sent her an e-mail telling her he just didn't think it was working out.

I can't fault her too much, because I used to be the same way. I would like a guy and instead of taking control, I would just do nothing and wait to see what he would do, hoping it would work out the way I wanted. Luckily, throughout the years I realized how counterproductive that was. I always thought it was risky to take matters into my own hands. Then I realized it was much more dangerous to do nothing. Doing nothing gave the guy the upper hand. It gave him the power to make all decisions. And when a guy has all the power and makes all the decisions, he will undoubtedly lose interest. Luckily, I realized that I could easily take control of my relationships, and it actually worked better than I could have ever imagined. I could learn to make my own moves, without seeming overaggressive. It took a while to learn how to do it,

but once I did, I became more confident, more powerful, and thus more desirable to the opposite sex.

An Easy Way to Take Control

I once dated a man on *Fortune* magazine's "40 Richest Men under 40" list. He was CEO of one of the largest companies in the D.C. metro area. I can't disclose his real name, but we will call him John. I met John at Café Milano. I walked into the restaurant with a few girlfriends and almost instantly we were approached by one of John's friends. He asked if we would like to join them for dinner. We accepted and walked over to the table. John instantly rose to his feet and offered me the chair next to him. I knew who he was, and I knew his reputation. He was a playboy—thirty-nine, unmarried, and always with a trophy on his arm. After a few drinks I gave my friends the signal to leave and we started to get up. John immediately broke out his Blackberry and told me to give him my number so we could get on the list at his next party. So I gave it to him.

The next day at lunch, as I was retelling the details of my evening to my mother, my phone beeped. It was a text message from John. He said it was very nice meeting me last night, and he wanted to invite me to a pool party that afternoon. I was, of course, very excited to hear from him, but I knew that I couldn't just drop everything to attend his little soiree. If I really were indifferent, I wouldn't change my plans

at the last moment. For a second I picked up the phone to text John back to thank him and tell him I couldn't make it when a light bulb suddenly went off in my head. Why did I have to text back right now? Why couldn't I keep the ball in my court for a little longer? I put the phone down and decided I would do something I had never done before. I would not return his text until the next day.

John looked at his phone all day that day. He told me later that he had a good time at the party but kept checking his Blackberry wondering when I was going to text him back. As the night progressed, he said he began to question if he was ever going to hear from me.

The next day, I woke up early with a knot in my stomach. Had I made the right move? Did I wait too long to text back? What if he was mad and thought I was blowing him off? I reached for my phone to send him a text and at that very moment it rang. It was John! Only this time he wasn't texting, he was actually calling!

I decided not answering my phone was working. For twenty-four hours now, I had all the control in the relationship, and it felt great. So when John called me that morning, I let it go to voicemail. Sounds risky, doesn't it? But when I finally did call him back later that afternoon, he was absolutely ecstatic. I was flirty with him, and I thanked him for inviting me to his party. I apologized for not being able to make it but I did not apologize for not calling sooner. I didn't give him a

reason as to why I waited so long because I wanted him to think that I had other things going on. Nevertheless, he immediately asked me what my weekend plans were and when he could take me out to dinner. Instead of replying with my usual, "Anytime!" I told John I'd have to get back to him later in the week after I looked at my schedule.

That Saturday we had our first date. I was picked up in John's personal limo and we had dinner at the best steak house in D.C. We chatted, drank wine, made jokes, and had a good time. When we got back into the limo after dinner he asked if I would like to see his place. I knew if I went upstairs I wouldn't be able to resist kissing him. So I coyly smiled and told him maybe another time.

The next day John called me to tell me he had a great time. At least that is what he told my answering machine. He said he wanted to take me out again to a concert next weekend. I was definitely excited, but I knew I had to stick with what was working for me. I waited another day to call him back. This time when I did, John made a comment about never being able to get a hold of me. He said, "I didn't know you were such a busy girl. I am going to have to start booking time with you weeks in advance! Maybe you should get a secretary."

I just laughed, but inside I knew my new strategy was working like a charm.

John and I dated for six weeks, and in that time period he never once was able to reach me by phone or text message. He

always left me a voicemail and had to wait for me to return his call. I had never felt more in control of a relationship and it was fantastic. When I finally decided to end it with John, he confided in a mutual friend that he really liked me and that I was the only girl that he really liked in a very, very long time.

Men are used to being the ones who are in control of the phone calls. When I first meet a guy and give him my number, I definitely want him to call, but I don't want to sit by the phone waiting for him to decide when to call me. That gives him all the power. He gets to decide when to make contact and I have to have my phone charged and ready. If I immediately answer when he calls or texts, then it's obvious I am sitting around waiting for him. If he's a smart guy, he won't call that often to ensure that when he does, I'll pick up the phone.

Some of my friends are so relieved when a man calls them that they can't answer their phone fast enough. Sometimes the guy doesn't even have to leave a message, and they will still call him back! Ladies, c'mon! If a guy doesn't leave you a message and you call him back, what is that telling him? He can sense how desperate and available you are by how often and eagerly you respond. He has so much control that he only has to do the bare minimum, and you come running. No, if he doesn't have the courtesy to leave a message, then you don't have the courtesy to call him back. End of story.

Instant Gratification Can Screw You

Most girls only worry about gratifying themselves in the moment. Isabel, for instance, got what she wanted in the short run—an entire weekend with Doug. But she ended up jeopardizing what she could have had in the long run—a serious relationship. Had she just tried taking control, she probably wouldn't have gotten dumped after the weekend. She may not have seen Doug while she was in town that time, but she would have at least seen him again. Now the relationship was completely over.

Look, I know that the hard part about taking control is that usually it means making a move in the opposite direction. You want so badly to do what makes you feel good in the moment, but in a lot of cases, that can hurt you. Especially, if the guy is losing interest, like Doug. That is when it is vital to take control. I know it seems risky to make your own moves, but what is even more risky is handing over all your power. Just remember, when it comes to guys, the most dangerous thing you can do is nothing.

Keep Control, Keep Interest

If you want to take your relationship from start to finish, you are going to have to stop being a passenger, and get in the driver's seat. I myself used to be in your shoes. I can remember waiting all day for a phone call only to have the guy finally

contact me late at night, telling me where to meet him and his friends. I would then have to convince my girlfriends to change our plans. There were plenty of times when I dated guys and wondered what the status of our relationship was. I worried about when I would see them again. I felt like I had to always go along with their plans. It was unsettling to be so out of control, but it was no one's fault but my own. I let the guy make all the moves and then jumped to meet him when he did. I did this partly out of the desire to see him and partly because I was afraid he'd be mad if I didn't.

You have a choice. You can sit around and wait, or you can have a life of your own. If you don't make any weekend plans because you want to be ready to see him when he beckons you, just know that he is very aware that he's got you. I know you think you are playing it safe when you do nothing, but you are really making the riskiest move of all. If it hasn't happened already, you will one day wake up and realize that your agenda is no longer your own. You both are working for one person's happiness, and that person isn't you.

Don't Sweeten the Deal

A new emergency room was being built in the tiny town of Summersville, West Virginia. I had been visiting the facility

for months, and finally they were ready to evaluate my equipment. I brought in a brand-new cardiac monitor for the nurses to use for a few weeks, hoping that they would fall in love with it and realize they couldn't live without it. As I was setting up the equipment, I noticed that all the nurses were gathered around a table in the back of the room. I walked over to see what the commotion was about and saw two huge boxes with the words Cheesecake Factory written on top. Suddenly I felt a pang of nervousness. There wasn't a Cheesecake Factory within 300 miles. It could only mean one thing. I quickly scanned the room looking for what I feared. Suddenly I saw it, there in the corner. An eighteen-inch flat-panel Philips monitor. My competition had beaten me here . . . and they had bought cheesecake.

The topic of conversation that day was not about which monitor the staff liked better. It was about the yummy dessert the oh-so-thoughtful Philips rep had brought them. In a town where a fancy dinner was a night out at Applebee's, the cake from the dessert mecca had the tiny country hospital talking. I was screwed, I thought. My company didn't allow gifts of any sort. I was going to have to do my best to sell the nurses without the help of sugar.

I followed up a week later with the facility. I knew they were going to be deciding soon on which vendor to go with, so I would really have to do my best to convince them they wanted me. I entered the usually busy ER and found only one

nurse at the front desk. I was about to ask her if everyone had called in sick, when I saw an empty box of Krispy Kremes sitting on the table. As I glanced over to the snack room, I saw all the nurses smiling, laughing, and eating doughnuts.

For the next few weeks I continued to fight a losing battle. The Philips rep was constantly invited back to meet with other staff members, while I had to fight just to get a twenty-minute appointment. On every visit, at least one staff member referenced the doughnuts. One nurse even declared in my presence that she "loved when the Philips rep came to visit!" I got back to my hotel room the last night I was in town and logged onto my e-mail. I was going to have to tell my boss that it wasn't looking good. But just as I signed in, I noticed I had an e-mail from the hospital's director of nursing. She wanted me to come back tomorrow at 7:30 AM to talk. I was curious as to what this meant. I set my alarm and went to bed wondering.

The next day I was at the hospital right on time. I walked into the director's office, and she saw me right away.

"Hi, Jess. Thanks for coming back on such short notice. We have been dragging our feet on buying our new monitors but we had a meeting late last night and all the nurses agreed that your monitor is the one we want."

"Oh!" I said, a bit too surprised. "That's fantastic."

The director laughed. "You seemed surprised?"

A bit embarrassed, I felt the need to come clean. "Well, after the Philips rep had brought so many treats for the staff, I

was a little worried. They seem to really like the cheesecake and doughnuts," I laughed.

"Oh they did. They talked about it more than the monitors," she admitted. "But it didn't make us like his monitor. If anything it actually had the reverse effect. We wondered why he didn't talk about the monitor like you did. All he did was bring us food. Every time we saw him, he had something else to give us. It was almost as if he needed to persuade us with dessert because his product wasn't as good as yours."

I shook my head in agreement. "Yes, I was thinking the same thing. That's why I didn't bring any cake myself."

I think she knew I was lying.

That was the day I learned you don't have to sweeten the deal. You can't hide your product behind gifts and favors, hoping that will win a customer over. The Philips rep was hoping to do that, but in the end, he didn't earn the staff's trust and respect; he was merely used for his Krispy Kreme connections.

Some women believe the way to a man's heart is through his stomach, his laundry, and other tokens of appreciation. But gifts will not make a man like you. In fact, excessive gift giving will only cheapen you and make it seem like your product is not good enough to stand on its own either.

One of Adison's biggest dating problems is that she gives too much too soon. When she starts seeing someone, she wants them to like her so much that she does lots of thoughtful things for them thinking it will win them over.

When she started seeing Tony, a real estate developer, she immediately went into her normal routine. He picked her up for their first date and took her to a very nice Italian restaurant. They had great conversation and at the end of dinner she told him she had a gift for him. She knew that Tony smoked so she bought him a sterling silver Zippo lighter with his initials engraved on the side. Tony thanked her for the present and told her he would call her soon to go out again.

When she hadn't heard from him in a week, Adison got nervous. When Tony finally did call she was so relieved she thought she needed to do something nice for him. So when he asked if he could take her to his favorite Greek restaurant, she told him she would cook dinner for him instead. He, of course, wasn't going to turn that down. She prepared a three-course meal while he watched the Virginia Tech game on her couch.

For the next few weeks, Adison continued on this track. She would do little things at first, like pick up Tony's dry cleaning and give him neck massages after a stressful workday. If his apartment was messy, she would surprise him by cleaning it while he was out for his morning jog. As time went on, the favors and gifts got more extravagant. She took his car to the garage, his dog to the groomer, and when his plasma TV broke, she bought him a new one.

For a while, Tony took full advantage. They dated for several months, until one day, he met a hard-nosed business-woman with a no-nonsense attitude. Rebecca was quick-witted

and vivacious. She wouldn't give Tony the time of day, let alone a Zippo lighter. He pursued her relentlessly (while still dating my friend) and when she finally gave in, he proposed within a few months. Adison was devastated and didn't understand how he could leave her. She had done everything for him, and this was how he treated her? How could he leave after all that she had given him? She didn't realize you can't win men over with Zippo lighters, home-cooked meals, or plasma TVs.

When you are already in a committed relationship, gifts and favors are seen as thoughtful (but even then you have to be careful that you aren't the one doing all the giving). However, if you think you can close the deal by continually giving gifts and doing favors, you are sorely mistaken. I'm going to give it to you straight here. If you can't just "be you" and feel you have to sweeten the deal of being with you, you are in for a rude awakening. Gifts and favors won't make a man love you. Doesn't matter how many nice things you do. A great product doesn't need extra incentives. In fact, when too many incentives are thrown in, it often makes people think twice about what they are buying.

Tony could see that was what Adison was doing, and even though it was nice to have a new TV and home-cooked meals, it didn't make him love her. Instead he began to use her and ultimately lost respect for her. The more Adison gave, the more he took. When Tony finally met a woman whose product

could stand on its own, he was instantly enamored. Rebecca had enough confidence that she didn't need to sweeten the deal.

The Danger of Giving Too Much

Be careful when giving gifts and doing favors. There is such a thing as overkill. When a man brings me flowers every week and continually tries to give gifts, it makes me very suspicious. I begin to wonder if he has anything else to offer. A smart, good-looking, confident guy shouldn't need flowers and chocolates to win a woman over. All he really needs to do is be himself. And think about this: if a guy kept giving you presents, wouldn't you start to take advantage? And whether you know it or not, taking advantage of someone indicates how little you respect them. So if you are trying to earn someone's love (which works in tandem with respect), gift giving is not the way to go.

The truth is, if you are going to bend over backwards for a guy and continue to always give, give, give, then you are just asking for him to take, take, take. One day you will wake up and find that you are treated more like a personal assistant than a girlfriend. You will find yourself running all the errands and doing all the dirty work while he kicks back on the coach after his long workday. The bottom line: if you find yourself continually doing things for a man, you really need to look at

the deeper issue here. You aren't totally sold on your own product yet. Don't even think about the close. You need to go back to the beginning of this book and start over.

CLOSING THE DEAL

Never Assume

After two years in real estate, my mom was about to close the biggest deal in her career. She had been working on selling a million-dollar house in Old Town Alexandria, and she had finally found a prospective buyer who was ready to make an offer. She invited me over for a celebratory dinner that evening.

"I'm just so excited!" my mother exclaimed. "After all my hard work, it's finally happened!"

"That's great mom! Where's the contract? Let's see it!" I said anxiously.

"Oh, he hasn't given it to me yet. He's going to fax it over next week after he meets with his accountant and lawyer," she

said pouring herself another glass of champagne.

My mood immediately changed. "He hasn't signed yet?"

"Well, no, but he's already said he's going to take it. We've met several times; he's verbally told me he wants it, so the paperwork is just a technicality."

"Mom," I started carefully. "Let me tell you one thing I have learned in sales. Never assume anything. Until you have that contract signed and in your hand, you haven't closed the deal."

But my mom didn't want to listen. She was too busy dancing around the living room with her bottle of bubbly.

Two weeks later the deal still hadn't closed. But Mom wasn't stressing; she was absolutely certain that the paperwork was coming in any day. She decided to go on vacation to reward herself for all her hard work.

After almost a month had gone by, I stopped by my mom's house to see her. When I walked in, she was furiously cleaning her kitchen and hardly noticed me standing in the doorway.

"Mom? What's going on?" I asked. She only cleaned that vigorously when she was upset.

"I lost the deal," she said. "The buyer called me last night and said he got cold feet. I'm just so aggravated right now, I could scream. How could he tell me that he's going to take the property and then back out?" she said, looking for something she hadn't bleached yet.

"Well, I hate to say I warned you, but until you have something in writing, you really can't count on it."

"I know, but he said all he had to do was go over some things with his lawyer and accountant and the deal was done."

"Yes, but so many things could have happened between then and now. You can't assume that everything will fall into place just because you want it to. I know you were getting all the right signals, but until the deal is signed, sealed, and delivered, you haven't closed it and you can't stop working at it."

Unfortunately my mom had learned the hard way that assuming the sale is dangerous. I have had many customers give me all the right signals, too. I've even had them tell me without a shadow of a doubt that they will buy from me. But I've also had those same people back out at the last minute. That's why I never assume a deal is closed until I have the contract in my hand.

Assuming anything can be quite dangerous. There are many women out there spending their time with men they assume they will end up marrying. The signs are there: they are calling them, sleeping with them, maybe even living with them. But until a man has told you that you are the one, puts that ring on your finger, and says his "I do's," you shouldn't assume anything.

I finally thought Adison had found the right guy. Ben had his own software company, was smart, hard working, and very attentive. They hit it off right away, and Adison knew she was

in love. She was dying to tell Ben how she felt but knew that she shouldn't be the first one to say it. So she held it in. Six months into the relationship they had their first big "relationship talk." Adison thought this would be it. He was going to tell her he loved her. She sat and listened as Ben struggled with the words. Finally he got to his point.

"I just think it's silly for us to have two places. You are here all the time. You go home once a week to pick up the mail and get more clothes. We are just wasting money paying two rents. I think it's better if you just move in here," Ben stated.

Adison was shocked. Not at all what she was expecting. Maybe a little more than what she was expecting. She just wanted an "I love you," and instead she got "Move in with me." *Well,* she thought, *he must love me. He wouldn't have me move in otherwise.*

She moved in. And for a while things were great. Six months later she still hadn't heard those three little words from Ben. But she did hear four other words: "Let's buy a house." Again, she thought he must love her or he wouldn't be doing these things. He was obviously scared to say "I love you" or maybe just bad at expressing his feelings. What's more important anyway? Saying how you feel or showing it? So they bought a house.

After living in their new home for a year, Ben told her one night that he really wanted to have a baby. Now Adison was completely thrown off. She hadn't gotten an "I love you" or

"Will you marry me," but Ben wanted her to have his child? She couldn't hold it in any longer. She had to say what she had been suppressing all this time.

"I love you," she declared. "I moved in with you, bought this house with you, all because I thought we were going to get married. But you have skipped over all the important parts of a relationship. You skipped the 'I love you' and now you are skipping the 'Will you marry me?' Why can't you say these things to me? It's obvious that you want them, I know I wouldn't be here if you didn't, so I want to hear you say it. You are going to have to start telling me how you feel instead of just having me read the signs. I want you to say you love me and want to marry me."

Ben didn't know what to say. At first he got angry. He tried to blame Adison for overreacting and being too emotional. But then he got very quiet and finally told Adison how he truly felt.

"Of course I want you here. I want you in my life and I want you to have my children. I just don't think marriage is for me, though. I am totally happy the way things are, and I see no reason to change them."

Adison felt like she was punched in the stomach. She finally realized why Ben hadn't said he loved her. It wasn't because he didn't know how to say it. It was because he just didn't feel it. He loved having her around. He loved having her to hold at night. He loved having someone to eat dinner with and take on

vacations. But he wasn't truly in love with her, and he didn't want to commit to her. She had just assumed all along that he did.

I tried to tell Adison once that she shouldn't assume Ben loved her. But she didn't want to listen. After she moved in and they started to house hunt, I told her not to assume it meant he was going to marry her. But she didn't want to listen to that either. Finally after two years she realized what Ben really wanted. He wanted her to live with him and raise his kids without either of them having to commit to each other.

Assuming how a man feels is very dangerous. Sometimes you may be right in your assumptions, but if you are wrong, the effects can be devastating. If Adison had told Ben that she was only going to move in with him *if and when* they were engaged, she would have avoided the mess she was now in.

Doesn't matter what stage of a relationship you are in—two weeks, two months, two years. You should never assume how a man feels about you. If he loves you, he will tell you. If you are his girlfriend, he will tell you. If he wants to marry you, he will tell you. If he doesn't tell you, it's a big red flag that you *should* worry about. Don't try to rationalize his behavior. Don't assume he isn't giving you what you want because he's had a bad past, a bad mother, or a bad ex-girlfriend. People do what they want to do. Likewise, they don't do what they don't want to do. It's just that simple. So when he says he can't do something or doesn't know how, it really means he just doesn't want to.

If you learn not to assume in your relationships, you will save yourself a lots of problems and heartache. People have different motivations for getting involved in relationships, and some of them don't have anything to do with love. A man can be lonely and just want a companion. He can live and spend time with someone he has no intention of settling down with. Scary, I know. But just look around, it happens to people everyday. It's happened to your friends and people in your family. So you have to ask yourself if it's happening to you. It's not a pleasant fact to face, but you must. You don't want to waste your time with someone who ultimately won't give you what you want. Remember: just because he is dating you, sleeping with you, or even living with you doesn't mean you should just kick back, relax, and wait for the proposal. Until he's down on one knee, ready to make it official, don't assume anything.

What Motivates Him to Marry

Jeffery and Camille have been dating for six years. They are both thirty-five years old. For the last three years Camille has been pressuring Jeffery to get married. She has brought it up several times and has become increasingly frustrated with the situation. As we were working out one day, I asked her how

long she would wait for Jeffery before she came to her wit's end and moved on.

"I told Jeffery that if we weren't engaged by December then I was leaving," she said. "I told him if he couldn't make a decision by then, I wasn't going to wait around any longer."

"Well, December is only two months away. I guess you'll have your answer soon," I said.

Camille laughed nervously. "Actually, that's what I said last year. The deadline was last December, not this one."

As I listened to Camille it became very clear. She would never leave Jeff. She gave him a deadline but never followed through on it. She wasn't going to leave, and the worse part was Jeff knew it. I wanted to be a good friend and support her, but at the same time I wanted to grab her and say, "He won't propose if he doesn't feel like he has to or he will lose you! Right now he knows that you aren't going anywhere."

It amazes me that women haven't fully accepted this concept. But if a man knows he's got you and has no fear of losing you, then he has no real motivation to marry you.

The number one rule in sales and negotiation is to be willing to walk away. If a customer knows that I will ultimately cave to their wishes and give them whatever they want, they have all the power and I will always lose. There must be a fear that at some point I will walk away if I don't get what I need as well. This is called Fear of Loss (FOL). Fear of Loss is something you will have to use throughout your entire rela-

tionship. You have to be willing to walk away, and he has to know it.

Jeff was not fearful of losing Camille. For the last five years he has felt extremely secure about their relationship. He knew he wasn't going to lose her, so he knew he could keep putting her off. She might get angry and frustrated every so often, but in the end, he knew that would pass and she would still be there. So why marry her? Camille was in a terrible situation. Because she made it obvious that she would never leave, her only recourse was to nag Jeff to marry her. Unfortunately nagging him wasn't going to get him to want to marry her. The most that it could ever do was annoy him so much that he'd finally say, "Fine! I'll marry you." But who wants a proposal like that?

The Number One Motivator

If you didn't know this already, fear is the most motivating factor in the human experience, and FOL is what ultimately drives men to marriage. Think about it. If a man knows he has your heart and soul, knows you would never stray, knows you would bear his children, and doesn't have to put your name on his checkbook, *why would he*? Taking a wife is like making a capital purchase. Unless you make more money than he does, he knows he will be sharing his hard-earned money with you. And if for some reason things don't work out in the long run,

he runs the risk of you taking half of his income. It doesn't sound romantic, I know. But this is something men worry about.

However, when a man meets a woman who knocks his socks off, a woman he's *afraid he might lose* if he doesn't treat her right, then he can't wait to get her down that aisle! He won't want to risk losing her to anyone else. He'll pay any price to have her because the thought of her being with another man drives him absolutely bonkers. He won't rest until he has closed the deal.

Think that sounds crazy? Most women are motivated to get married by Fear of Loss, too. Only it's not in the same way. I have girlfriends who are desperately trying to get married because they feel they are getting too old and they are afraid of losing their chance to land a husband. They are afraid if they don't get married right now they will lose their youthful looks and no man will ever show interest again. So when they reach a certain age, some women just marry whomever crosses their path. Whether or not it's the right guy is irrelevant. They are so afraid of losing their opportunity to wed, they marry whomever. Now that is what I think is crazy!

Fear of Loss vs. Sense of Gain

I have used Fear of Loss (FOL) many times in business. When I was starting my own company I had to hire a sales

staff, and I had to do it fast. I packed in a hundred interviews one week in the hopes of finding great candidates for my team. To my disappointment, I found only one that really stood out above the rest. His name was Greg. He was a graduate of Harvard, young, ambitious, and above all, he had the attitude I was looking for. I wanted him on my team. I knew he would be a tremendous asset. The only problem was he had interviews with three other big companies the following week, and I was just a tiny business trying to stay afloat. I was fearful of losing him if he went on the other interviews. But what could I do? Try to convince him that we were the best company out there? Tell him how much I needed him and how he would never find another boss as good as me? Beg him to forget the other interviews and shove a W-2 in his hand? He might have been flattered by it, but it wouldn't have made him want to work for me. No, none of that would work. The only thing I could do was use FOL.

I told Greg that I had to fill the position by Monday. I told him that I really liked him, but another equally qualified candidate was ready to start the very next day. I looked him straight in the eye and said, "Greg, if you can start Monday, you've got the job. If you still need time to think about it, I am going to have to go with the other candidate."

Now, of course, this was risky, but so was letting him go on his other interviews. I had to go out on a limb.

Greg shifted around uncomfortably in his chair. He let out

a big sigh and shook his head. Just when I thought I might
have made a mistake, he said, "OK, I can start Monday"

Greg later told me that he really didn't have any other interviews. He only told me that to make him seem more desirable.
How funny to think he was using FOL on me! I told him it
worked.

For some reason, women think if we promise a man the
world we will get him to love us and then marry us. I have
seen my friends bend over backwards for guys in an effort to
get them to propose. You must understand this: listing all he
has to gain by marrying you won't make him marry you. What
does work is the attitude that you aren't sticking around if the
situation is not going in the right direction. You have to have
the will and ability to leave. Then, when things are not going
well, you have to actually do it. I know it can be risky. But
sometimes you have to leave someone in order to get someone
to appreciate and respect you. I know your fear is that you will
end up leaving and he won't come after you. But, if he
doesn't, then he didn't really love you in the first place, and
you are essentially holding on to something that won't make
you truly happy.

Creating Fear of Loss

So how do you create FOL? No, you don't threaten to leave
every week. You don't want to become a ticking time bomb

that reminds him you could explode at any moment. If you are in a situation like Camille, you will eventually have to pack your stuff and make a move. But that's the worst-case scenario.

The best way to avoid being forced to make that kind of move is not living with the guy before you are officially engaged. If you are with him 100 percent of the time and he knows you aren't going home with anyone else, he really has nothing to worry about. He already knows you belong to him so there isn't any incentive for him to make it official. He's not gaining anything he doesn't already have. Don't let yourself get to this point. Ask Camille—it's not a fun situation to be in. You need to combat this by being proactive instead of reactive. Instead of waiting until the end of the relationship to use FOL, the best thing to do is to use it right in the beginning. In the beginning you've automatically got FOL because the guy doesn't have you yet. Now all you have to do is keep it.

Keeping FOL

My friend Micha played it just right. She had dated a series of men, but none seemed to really float her boat. Then she met Brian. Brian was a little older, extremely successful, and looked like Pierce Brosnan. She was a smitten kitten. I had never seen Micha, my business confidant and former boss, in such a giddy state. She once told me if things didn't work out with Brian, she would turn into a puddle, which is something so un-Micha-like to say.

Brian was smitten as well, and one night after only a few weeks of dating he told Micha he was falling in love with her. He said he had never felt this way about anyone, which, of course, propelled Micha over the proverbial moon. She wanted to shout to the heavens that she felt the same way, but did she do it? Absolutely not! Micha is a saleswoman and a logical, strategic thinker. She knew he needed to fear losing her. She told him she was flattered. She said she was enjoying spending time with him and felt very close to him. She did not tell him she was in love, too, even though she really was.

When I asked her why she held back, she said it was too soon to say it. She was ecstatic that Brian had professed his feelings, but she had to make sure they were deep-rooted feelings that would lead to marriage.

"I'm in for the long haul," she said to me one night on the phone. "He needs to be pining away for me. I want him to sweat. I want him to be crazy nuts for me and fear losing me to someone else. So, even though I want to start naming our unborn children, I am going to hold back."

Brian asked Micha to move in with him. But she declined his offer. She told him that she couldn't live with anyone she wasn't at least engaged to.

"It just wouldn't feel right," she said with a smile, then went away for the weekend with her girlfriends, leaving Brian to stew for the next three days.

When she returned, she found Brian on the beach waiting

for her. He had set up a picnic on the beach to ask her to marry him. That was three years ago. Today, Micha and Brian live in a huge house in Santa Monica, and they just welcomed their second son.

Micha is no fool. She knew that she had to play a little FOL to really get Brian to make a move. A man can tell you he loves you, tell you he is crazy for you, and then turn around a month later and leave you in the dust. If that hasn't happened to you, it's happened to someone you know. Just because a man professes his feelings fast and furiously doesn't mean he's going to end up popping the question. It doesn't even guarantee he'll be around next week. Do not throw caution to the wind when you hear those three little words. Do not, I repeat, do not rest on your laurels just because a man says he's in love.

Throwing Away FOL

Let's look at how my friend Beth handled a similar situation. She was in love with Rudy from almost the minute she shook hands with him. Rudy was tall, dark, and handsome, and basically swept her off her feet. After only a few weeks he told her he had never felt this way about anyone, and he felt that he was falling in love with her. Overjoyed at hearing this, Beth told Rudy she was falling for him, too. They began spending all their free time together and were soon acting like

an old married couple, after only dating for a month. Beth started slowly moving into Rudy's house, leaving clothes and toiletries each time she was over. She would talk about where they would spend the holidays that year and where they would go on their next vacation. Then one day, almost out of the blue, Rudy told Beth he needed some space. He told her he wasn't sure if he was ready for all this and needed time to think. Beth was blindsided. She didn't understand what had happened. Just months ago he was professing his undying love, and today he was breaking up with her?

It was obvious Rudy began to feel stifled. He told Beth he loved her, but once he got her so quickly and completely, he decided he didn't really want her. The FOL he once felt before was gone, and now he was left feeling trapped.

Rudy and Beth have been broken up for a while now, and Rudy is dating someone else. It may have worked out for the two of them if Beth had taken it slowly. When Rudy confessed his feelings she should have told him she was flattered and having a good time with him. She should have kept the FOL a little longer to ensure his feelings were real. Instead, she let Rudy have her completely, and it destroyed any FOL, as well as any chance she had for marriage.

We All Make This Mistake . . . Just Learn from It

We are all giddy schoolgirls in the early stages of the relationship, and it's wonderful when the guy seems totally smitten with us. He says he loves us, and so we reciprocate. We immediately get comfortable and open up about our feelings. Now the guy knows he's got us. A couple months later he is singing a different tune. He falls off the face of the Earth, or worse, starts pulling back little by little (the slow death is always worse to me), leaving us to wonder what happened. Well, I will tell you what happened: we met him half way. When he told us he was falling in love we saw that as a green light to "let 'er rip!" We opened up completely and basically announced "I'm all yours." That is where most of us make our biggest mistake.

You don't have to disclose your feelings just because he has. In the beginning especially, you have to keep that FOL for as long as possible. He can't know he's totally got you. It is easy to get caught up in a whirlwind romance, but you have to keep your head out of the clouds and make sound decisions if you want to take a relationship all the way to the altar. Don't get carried away if a guy falls head over heels in love with you. Know that you are on the right track. Remember, as long as a guy is not 100 percent sure of how you feel about him, he will be afraid he could lose you at any moment, and that fear of loss will keep him begging for more.

I'm happy to report that Camille and Jeffery are now engaged. After six years of begging and pleading she finally decided she was fed up and told Jeffery she was leaving. She said it was obvious he would never marry her and she was ready to find someone who would. Jeff knew she meant it this time. Suddenly, he wasn't so complacent. Fearing he was really going to lose Camille, he high-tailed it to the nearest Tiffany & Co. and purchased a two-carat princess cut diamond. They are getting married later this year. Jeff never thought she would ever leave him, but once he was afraid of losing her, he moved to action. Fear of loss gets them every time.

Sense of Urgency

A few months after my mother began dating my stepfather, Tim, she told him that she was thinking of moving to Florida. Her sister lives in West Palm Beach, and my grandparents are not far from there either. Tim didn't think much of it at first. They were just dating after all. But as Tim began to fall for my mom, she turned up the heat on the subject. One night she said to Tim, who at fifty-one had never been married, that she had found a condo in Wellington, Florida, and she was going to be moving at the end of the year.

Tim was shocked. "Are you really leaving at the end of the year?"

My mom just shrugged her shoulders and said, "Well, my kids are grown up and away at school. The rest of my family is down south and I really have nothing else keeping me here," she said as nonchalantly as possible.

She and Tim went to dinner that night. My mother chatted on about other things, but Tim kept thinking about what she had said. At the end of the night, he kissed my mom and drove home. The next time he saw her, he proposed.

No one knows how to date strategically better than my mom. She is a born salesperson and has taught me a lot of what I know. Tim, like many guys, was happy playing the field. He had dated many women in his lifetime and was very content not being married. Then he met my mother. Unlike all the other women, she knew how to get him to propose. She knew how to pressure him without him feeling pressured. She used one of the oldest sales tactics there is. She created a Sense of Urgency.

What Is Sense of Urgency?

I know you have seen it on QVC—that little timer in the corner that says there are only five emerald bracelets left! You must buy them before the clock runs out or you miss your chance! That little timer is creating a Sense of Urgency

(SOU). If the clock weren't ticking, no one would rush to order. You may see a product you like, but without SOU, you could take your time and mull it over. There would be no pressure to make a decision, so you may never make one. Without Sense of Urgency, QVC would be out of business.

When you are dating someone you absolutely need to create SOU, especially if you want to take the relationship all the way. If you don't think your time is precious, then expect it to be treated that way. My mother knew how to create a Sense of Urgency, and because of it, Tim proposed after only a year. But just like Fear of Loss, you can't only use Sense of Urgency when closing the deal; you must use it in the beginning, middle, and end of your courtship.

Sense of Urgency from the Start

I love being friends with Isabel because she is so easygoing and flexible. Anytime I call her, she's ready to do something. But that quality is often her downfall with men. When a guy calls, she is always open to do something. If she has a previous engagement, she'll rearrange it to free up her schedule. The men she dates are aware of this, so they don't feel any urgency to see her, call her, and finally, commit to her.

I've tried to explain to Isabel that if she's always "on-call," a man will become less urgent about seeing her. Why would he be urgent? She will conform to his schedule. He can call at

his leisure. Her time is irrelevant.

If you begin dating a guy and you let him see you at a moment's notice, you are setting a standard that will become the norm. After you have been dating awhile, he will become comfortable calling you at the last minute, changing plans on you, and even stalling on making a serious commitment. You have to create a SOU from the very beginning in order to set the precedent. Your time is valuable, and you have to be the first to treat it that way.

How to Create SOU

When I ran my sales company, I was continually looking for new recruits every week. I had my receptionist screen applicants and book interviews. She was never to ask the candidate when they could come in for an interview because that would make our schedule look wide open. The perception would be that no one was interested in our position, and there would be no urgency to get the job. So I taught the receptionist to give candidates two choices. She would say, "Well, it looks like we only have two openings this week. Tuesday morning or Thursday afternoon. Which one works better for you?" The candidate would then have to fit into our schedule, which they always did. And not only did no one ever cancel, no one was ever late. People hung up thinking that we must be a great place to work, and the position must be highly

competitive if those are the only two time slots open.

Create the sense of urgency using the same strategy. When you start dating someone, give him two choices of when to see you. But be smart about it. Don't tell him you are free either Friday night or Saturday night. Make at least one of the nights a weeknight. Usually when I start dating someone I give them two weeknights to choose from. I want them to think getting a weekend with me is tough!

Your ultimate goal is to have the man asking when you are available. If he is repeatedly telling you when he is available, you aren't creating enough urgency. When a guy calls me, the first question out of his mouth is "When can I see you?" And my answer is always, "The only night I have open is Thursday. I could possibly do Sunday if that doesn't work." A man will never call me and throw out a day to hang out. I'm always the one who picks the date.

You can gauge how valuable he thinks your time is by how he asks you out. If he is booking you way in advance, that is a great sign. However if he calls you at 6 PM to ask what you are doing for dinner that night, watch out. You are totally working on his time, not yours.

Using SOU to Close

Hopefully, by now, you realize that love is not a fairy tale. The man of your dreams is not going to miraculously appear

one day, sweep you off your feet, and beg you to marry him. If you have a friend that had a courtship like that, I want to talk to her! The fact of the matter is you have just as much work to do as the man when it comes to marriage. Men need to be nudged down the aisle. The only women that haven't had to pressure their boyfriends to marry them are the women that really didn't want to marry them in the first place. Remember my friend Julie? Often she tells people about how George surprised her and begged her to marry him. What she fails to tell them is how she didn't want anything to do with George in the beginning and he had to wear her down to even go out with him. So in those instances, SOU won't be necessary.

But for the rest of us who have found a guy we like and want to close the deal with, we are going to have to learn how to create that SOU. The surprise proposal is not going to happen if we sit back and keep our fingers crossed.

There is a right way to close with urgency and a wrong way. It's vital to learn which is which, because you will ultimately need to use a little in order to get that ring on your finger. Bad urgency is asking repeatedly "When are we going to get married?" or "I have to have kids by the time I'm thirty, so we need to do this now." Bad urgency is throwing out ultimatums and making demands. The kind of urgency you need to apply is indirect, covert, and circuitous. He must feel as if the pressure is not coming from your need to get married. No. Like my stepfather Tim will tell you, the urgency he felt was coming

from the state of Florida, not from my mother. Never once did my mom tell Tim she wanted to get married. But he knew that proposing was the only way to keep her from moving at the end of the year.

When you close with urgency, the first and most important step you must take is to make a timetable in your head. Not the timetable stating how old you have to be when you get married. For the love of Pete, throw that timetable out! This is different. You need to ask yourself how long you would date someone before deciding he is the one. How long do you need to be certain? A year? Two years? Then ask yourself how long *will* you date someone before making it official? They are two very different questions. But you must have answers to both. Why? Because, if you don't create urgency in yourself first, you won't ever be able to create urgency with him. Once you are involved in a relationship it is very easy to let time slip away from you. You don't want to waste ten years with a man who is never going to marry you.

My mom's friend Dora has no sense of urgency. She has been dating the same man for twelve years. She nags him every so often to get married, but he knows he really doesn't have to. He knows because she actually tells him. After every nag she says, "I don't want to push you, I want you to ask when you are ready." So basically her boyfriend has no real urgency to marry her. The clock's not ticking, so he's not popping the question. They will date until she actually does something to get him to

propose. If she does nothing, he will never do it.

If you have decided you have found the right guy *and* you want to marry him, you need to decide how long you are willing to wait for him to propose. It doesn't matter what the length of time that you set is. As long as you set it and it's on your terms. Once you decide on the timetable, you have to stick to it. If you think four years is long enough for him to decide and that deadline has past, you have to go. Sticking around and giving him another year isn't going to do anything except make you angry. When a man keeps you past your expiration date, the relationship will start to curdle. Every woman has a deadline in her head whether she acknowledges it or not. Most of my girlfriends end up staying way past their deadlines, and they end up in one of two places: either the relationship ends or they end up practically twisting the guy's arm to get him down the aisle. By then he has made her wait so long that when the wedding finally comes, it's not a momentous occasion. It's just a relief he finally gave in.

You can easily avoid the above scenario. Once you decide on your timetable, do not share it with him. It won't do any good to tell him you will only date him for three years. The only thing that's important is for you to realize a time will come for you to fish or cut bait. Once you accept that from yourself as well as expect it from another person, you will get what you want. But it must be something you truly believe. Your expectations will be heard loud and clear without you

having to say a word. Most people don't realize how powerful their thoughts are. If you think your boyfriend should propose and you know you will ultimately find someone else if he doesn't, he will sense that from you. On the other hand, if you have the "wait and see" attitude, he will sense that, too, and I guarantee that you will be doing a lot more waiting than seeing. Don't let yourself be convinced that staying the course is ever a good idea. The longer you just wait and see, the longer you will just wait.

The Silent No

After leaving my job to write this book, I thought I had said goodbye to medical sales for good. Until I got a call from an aggressive recruiter named Christina. Christina was well known in the medical community for having the inside scoop on the hot sales jobs. She left me a message one day about a "phenomenal opportunity" with one of the leading bed and stretcher companies.

"Jess, it's Christina! Look here, I have a phenomenal opportunity with Stryker Medical. The reps are making a killing, the territory is doing 100 percent over quota, and the rep in D.C. was just promoted to management. This is a golden ticket! You have to call me back as soon as possible!"

It did sound enticing, but I had mentally moved on from medical into other things. I decided not to call her back.

The next day I had another message on my machine from Christina.

"Jess, look girl, this opportunity is going to go fast! The rep last year became 'Rep of the Year.' What does that tell you? This is the dream medical job. Not a lot of prospecting, tons of repeat business, and a great company culture. Call me!"

After her second message I decided it couldn't hurt to call her back.

I found myself on an interview a week later. Christina called me Sunday night to go over some questions the manager would ask. On my way to the interview, Christina called again to make sure I was there on time and knew where I was going. I met with the territory manager for an hour and instantly established a great rapport. He asked me to come back for a second interview that Thursday, but unfortunately I was going to be out of town. He told me not to worry; he would have Christina call me when I got back in town to set up another meeting.

When I drove home that day, Christina called to see how the interview went. I told her it went so well that the manager asked me to come back for a second interview that Thursday. She was ecstatic. Apparently this manager never secures a second interview on the spot. I knew she really wanted to place me in the position because the payoff would be huge for her.

We hung up the phone and she told me she'd call me after the weekend.

When I got back in town on Monday, I expected to have a phone call from Christina. The rules of recruiting etiquette are rather concrete. You always go through the recruiter. You don't talk directly to the company manager until after the third interview. But as I listened to my voicemail, I received no such call from Christina.

The following day I decided to send Christina an e-mail. I told her I was very interested in the position and wanted to know if she had spoken to the manager about my interview. I sent it off and waited for a response.

After no response by Wednesday, I realized what was happening. I was getting the Silent No. Christina had called me every day until I left town, and now she had literally fallen off the planet. The reason was simple, she didn't have any good news, and so she just didn't call me back. It's a classic sales move. Recruiters, and pretty much everyone else in the world, hate being the bearers of bad news. So when all you get is silence, you are really getting a "No."

It wasn't too much of a shock to me because when someone decides that they are not going to buy from me, they avoid me like the plague. Christina practically stalked me to get me on the interview, and then after she had found out I wasn't getting the job, she disappeared. She had obviously talked to the manager, and even though he had originally asked me to meet with him again, some-

thing had changed in the meantime. He either met a stronger candidate, or just decided that I was not a good fit for the position. Doesn't matter really what the reason was. I wasn't getting the job.

There are times in dating, that you too will receive the Silent No. When a guy suddenly decides he doesn't want to see you anymore, he may stop calling you as much, hoping you will get the hint. He may start getting busier and seeing you less because he doesn't want to have to spell it out. What is a guy really going to say anyway? "Hey I was sitting here thinking about the last few weeks with you, and I realized that I really don't like you that much." Could you say that to someone? No, and neither can he.

The problem is that a lot of girls don't realize that a guy is trying to end the relationship with them. They really believe him when he says he is busy or isn't able to go out this weekend. We start changing our behavior to be accommodating for him. If he stops calling us, we start calling him. If he stops coming to our place, we go to his. If he stops taking us out, we become content just sitting around his house. In essence, we make it impossibly hard for a guy to break it off with us.

My friend Willow had been dating Peter for almost six months. They lived in the same neighborhood and therefore could easily see each other. Things were going very well for a while, but then all of a sudden Peter's behavior began to change. He started to pull away. He wouldn't call or come by as much, and when Willow called him, he wouldn't always

pick up the phone. This went on for weeks. Willow didn't know it yet, but she was getting the Silent No. When she confronted Peter about his change in behavior, he told her he was just stressed at work (a classic excuse). When she pressed the issue, wanting to talk more about it, he told her to stop pressuring him and stormed off.

The relationship continued, and Willow thought Peter's moodiness would pass. She thought if he were stressed about his rigid schedule, she would do her best to be more accommodating. She offered to make Peter dinner at her house during the week so when he came home from work he didn't have to cook. But it didn't seem to alleviate anything. Peter would come by and eat, but he wouldn't engage in much conversation. Usually he ended up going straight to bed. He would still sleep at Willow's house but stopped wanting to have sex, which of course he blamed on being tired from the day. Willow tried to be understanding, but the longer the relationship continued like this, the more upset she became. She called me frantically one night, looking for some advice.

"Willow, it sounds like you are getting the Silent No," I told her. "He doesn't know how to tell you he doesn't want to date anymore."

Willow had a hard time believing it, since Peter hadn't stopped seeing her completely. "Every Friday night he still comes over to watch a movie and fall asleep with me. Why would he do that if he didn't want to date me?" she asked.

"Boredom? Habit? Guilt? It's the easy thing to do? He'd rather hang out with you than go out to a bar?" I said.

Willow, of course, didn't like any of my answers.

Peter's actions continued to vacillate. One minute he was affectionate and attentive, the next he was moody and evasive. Sometimes he would come over and hang out, and sometimes he couldn't be found for days. Willow tried her best to be accommodating for Peter. But after months of trying, the situation didn't improve. The only thing that Willow knew for sure was that this wasn't the Peter she had been dating for the last six months. Eventually she told him she didn't think the relationship was going anywhere and that they may need a break. He told her that was probably a good idea.

After they broke up, a friend told Willow that Peter was dating someone on the side while he was still seeing her.

You have to listen to a man's actions instead of his words because a lot of time the no is silent. A girl can go on forever trying to please a guy who has already decided she isn't the one. It's a confusing predicament, I'll admit. We feel that if a guy doesn't like us he will absolutely make a clean break. Why would he stick around and let us torture ourselves? Just realize that a guy can keep a girl around even if he doesn't have strong feelings for her. Why?

1. **He's a coward.** It's easier just to keep seeing you then to tell you the relationship isn't going anywhere. He doesn't

want to hurt your feelings, and God forbid if you cry or kill yourself over him. (Yes, men have egos like that.)

2. **He's bored.** He likes you but not enough to be exclusive with you. What if someone he really likes comes along? He will hang out with you because you keep him busy on the lonely nights.

3. **He's insecure.** You validate that he is a good-looking, worthy guy. He'd rather have somebody than be completely alone.

4. **He's using you.** He calls when he needs something, and it's on his terms. He doesn't even have to convince you to do what he wants, you are happy to do it.

Don't fall victim to the Silent No. A man is never going to tell you, "Hey this has been great, but after dating for the last few months I realize that I don't really like you as much as I thought I did. You have a great body, which was what initially attracted me to you, but after getting to know you, I realize that I could never marry you. You are too high-strung, and I don't get your sense of humor. I wish you the best of luck, and I know that you will find the man you are looking for one day. I am just not him."

A man is never going to tell you that, and even if he did, would you really want to hear it? I honestly would rather not know the gory details. I'd rather hear the Silent No.

The Excuses

A lot of times the no is silent, but it is sometimes cushioned with an excuse. Some of the favorites are "I'm not sure I can handle my job *and* being in a relationship right now," or "My last girlfriend really scarred me and it's making me fearful of getting close to anyone." But these aren't the only examples. I've heard everything from "I'm a commitment-phobe" to "I just don't ever want to get married."

The problem is that when a guy says something like that, we think we can help solve his problem. If he is overworked and stressed, we think making a relationship easier will change his mind. We just have to be more understanding.

Likewise, if a guy says he's had a bad past relationship, we think convincing him that his ex was just a bad apple will make him realize we are not like her at all and thus, feel comfortable enough to make a commitment again.

But counseling him on his issues and trying to change his mind won't do any good because these are not the real reasons he doesn't want to commit to you. He just can't bring himself to tell you that. The simple truth is that no one likes to be the bearer of bad news. It's just as painful to tell someone you want to break up as it is to hear it.

When my father finally decided to end his relationship with the woman who couldn't be herself, he was struggling with how to tell her it was over. He knew he wasn't in love and had

already started chatting online with other women. After much contemplating he decided to break up with her via e-mail. In the e-mail he stated that his previously failed marriages had made him commitment-phobic. He told the woman that he really cared about her and thought she was a wonderful person, but was not prepared to commit to a monogamous relationship with her or anyone else.

With a severe case of anxiety, my father sent the e-mail. Not two minutes later, the phone rang. It was her. She had gotten the e-mail and wanted to talk.

They met for lunch that very day. The woman showed up in tears, with the e-mail printout in her hand. My father agonized while she went through the e-mail line by line, debating each point he had made. At the end of the conversation she begged him to see a therapist with her. She truly believed if she could just get him some help for his commitment issues, she could save their relationship. My father, feeling trapped and horribly guilty for causing her pain, actually agreed to the therapy!

When I saw my father later that day he was in shambles. He just wanted to make a clean break so he could date other women, but instead he was going to couple's counseling! I had to laugh. I told my dad maybe he should be honest and tell the woman that he wasn't in love with her. My father shuddered at the thought and said, "I'd rather cut off my own arm than tell her that."

Don't make a guy spell it out for you. Be smart enough to know the specific reason he's giving you means absolutely

nothing. The bottom line is, he is breaking up with you. You are probably not going to get the true story from him, so don't waste your time trying to solve the lame excuse he came up with. If he truly loved you and wanted to be with you, he would be. End of story.

There is no such thing as a commitment-phobe. It's a fairy tale character, made up by some guy who was too chicken to tell his girlfriend he didn't really love her anymore. Somehow the fairy tale got passed down from generation to generation, and it has now stuck. It's a great fallback for guys but can drive a woman out of her mind. It's definitely hard to hear the truth, but you can save yourself a lot of time if you just understand and accept that men don't want to hurt your feelings by telling you they don't want you. It's easier and less painful for them to blame themselves. Don't be fooled by thinking you can change him. He doesn't need changing. He will probably fall in love and have kids like most men in the world. It's just not going to be with you.

Buyer's Remorse

Maggie was in love with Sam from the moment she spotted him sitting at the bar in McCormick & Schmidt's. Not only was he the most handsome man she had ever seen in real life,

he was popular and well liked by everyone. When Sam asked her to dinner, she felt like she had struck gold. How lucky she was that such a handsome and charismatic man was into her. She couldn't believe her good fortune.

Sam wined and dined Maggie for the first several months of their courtship. Every weekend they would hit the town, going to the best parties and mingling with D.C.'s social elite. Most nights, they would end up having late night drinks at McCormick & Schmidt's, the place where they first met and fell in love. Maggie was happy. She knew Sam was The One.

As the relationship progressed, Maggie started to settle down. She didn't want to go out as much and enjoyed staying home, renting movies, and cooking dinner. Sam on the other hand, wasn't keen on the idea at all. He thought if he stayed home, he'd be missing something. It killed him not to be the life of the party, but it *destroyed* him to miss the party altogether.

After almost two years of dating, Maggie became distraught. In spite of all his partying, she still loved Sam and wanted to marry him. She just didn't know how to change his wild ways. Desperate, she sought me out for help.

"We've been dating for two years now and I know he is the one." Maggie said. "I just don't know how to get him to settle down and get married."

Knowing Maggie and Sam's relationship, I could clearly see a few problems that needed fixing. I also knew, as great of a guy as Sam was, he was not really the one for Maggie. What

was I to do? Fix her problem, or tell her she needed to find someone else? I decided I would do both, and let her decide.

"Maggie, you and Sam don't go two days without fighting. He's told you that you are too critical of his behavior. He knows you want to change him, but this is who he is. If you really want to marry him, for one month don't nag him about anything. Even if he doesn't come home until three in the morning, keep your mouth shut."

"That's going to be tough," she admitted.

"I know, but if you do it you will notice a change."

So for one month Maggie kept her opinionated mouth shut. She didn't nag Sam about hanging out at bars and going out with his friends. After the month passed, Maggie came back to see to me.

"It worked!" she exclaimed. "He said just the other day that we are getting along much better these days. He said he thinks we are finally on the same page!"

I tried to smile. "I guess as long as you can keep accepting him for who he is then you both will be fine."

"But how do I get him to propose?" she said in a whisper.

"That's easy. You said he wants you to move in with him, right? Tell him you just can't do it unless you are engaged. Then make yourself a little less available for the next few weeks. He'll start to get the message," I told her.

"Okay! I can do that!" she said getting up from the table.

I grabbed her arm before she could run off. "But I have to

warn you of something, Maggie," I said in a very serious tone.

"What?" she asked sitting back in her seat.

"See that empty bar stool over there?" I said.

Maggie turned and looked.

"If you marry Sam, that is where you will be sitting for the rest of your life. If you are happy knowing you will always be chasing him in and out of bars, then go ahead and marry him."

Maggie thought for a second. Then she stood up, shook my hand, and thanked me for my help.

She and Sam were married six months later.

The wedding was the happiest day of Maggie's life. She had finally got what she had always wanted. Unfortunately the minute they got back from the honeymoon, Sam immediately took off to McCormick & Schmidt's and was now staying out even later than before. Maggie had to call the bar so often looking for Sam that she had their number on speed dial.

Over the next seven years, Maggie and Sam struggled to get along. He continued to party and she continued to throw fits about it. She'd scream and cry; he'd yell and storm out. Every year was worse than the last. Maggie tried to bring up having a baby a few times, but since Sam wasn't home long enough to have a real conversation about it, she eventually dropped the subject.

On her forty-third birthday Maggie left Sam. She showed up at my house crying one night with her suitcase.

"I left him," she said. "I just couldn't do it anymore."

I told her I was sorry. I knew they would end up divorcing, but I still felt bad for my friend.

"I should have listened to you," she cried. "You said I would be sitting on that bar stool, and you were right. Now I have wasted ten years with him. I'm forty-three, and I don't think I'll ever have children."

Unfortunately I had tried to tell Maggie she shouldn't marry Sam, but she didn't want to listen. She loved him and wasn't going to rest until she had him. So she took my advice, formed her strategy, and closed the deal. Now she was sobbing in my living room suffering from the worst kind of buyer's remorse.

Buyer Beware

I can tell you how to find a guy. I can tell you how to meet him, get him interested, and finally close the deal. But the one thing that this book is not going to tell you is if he is the right one for you. That is something you will have to decide for yourself. These techniques are powerful. Remember that they are proven to work. So you have to make sure you are using them with the right person. Otherwise you could easily end up marrying the wrong guy and end up suffering from buyer's remorse yourself.

Jody wanted to get married so badly, it's all she ever talked about. She had every detail planned out, from the bridesmaids' dresses to the honeymoon destination. All she was missing

was her groom. So, of course, when she started dating Vincent, he didn't stand a chance.

Vincent knew how desperately Jody wanted to get married. He would often tease her about it and at one point even told her that he had bought a ring but hadn't decided he was going to give it to her. After four years of dating, Jody was nearing the brink of insanity. One day while at lunch she broke down and started crying out of sheer frustration.

"I have been waiting my whole life to get married! Vincent knows how important it is to me and yet he keeps stringing me along, telling me he's not convinced we're ready. I feel totally powerless. What do you think I should do?"

"Jody, the answer is simple," I said. "You need to play hard-ball with him. He has no incentive to marry you. You are basically married right now, just without the paperwork."

Jody nodded in agreement. "I can see that. So what should I do about it?" she asked.

"For one month, I don't want you to talk to or see Vincent. Tell him that you have grown tired of waiting for him to make up his mind, so you've made up yours instead. Then, don't answer the phone, and don't let him come over. If you do that for one month, he will give you that ring," I told her.

As hard as it was, Jody followed my advice. She didn't see or talk to Vincent for thirty days. He tried calling her at home and at work numerous times, but she stayed strong. He tried dropping by in person, but she instructed her doorman to turn him away.

Then, exactly twenty-nine days later, Vincent sent Jody an e-mail asking her to join him for a very special dinner where he would ask her a very special question. She accepted the offer and was delighted when Vincent proposed that night.

When I saw her two months later, she was elated.

"Look at my ring! Isn't it gorgeous? I just can't believe it's finally happening! I can't wait to get married!" Jody said overjoyed.

"I am so happy for you," I told her. "So are you getting married in that chapel you told me about?" I asked.

"No, actually Vincent doesn't want a big wedding, so we are going to go to Mexico and get married there instead," she said.

"Oh, well, are you still going to Nepal for your honeymoon?" I asked.

"No, Vincent thinks we should just stay a few days in Mexico to save ourselves the money. He really wants to put a swimming pool in the back of the house, so if we combine the honeymoon and the wedding, we can do that."

"Oh. Well, that will be nice," I said. "I didn't think you wanted a swimming pool since you've always said they're a safety hazard for children."

Jody bit her lip. "Well, I do think that, but Vincent doesn't want kids so I guess it's not going to be a problem anymore," she said.

"Hmm . . . sounds like Vincent is getting everything he wants. No big wedding, no honeymoon in Nepal, and now, no

kids. I'm just wondering, Jody, are you getting anything you want?"

Jody looked at me and shrugged. She was so determined to get married that she was willing to give up all of her other dreams to do so. She left our lunch quietly, but I could see her mind was racing with a thousand thoughts.

Jody and Vincent got married in Mexico and installed their swimming pool. Almost immediately after the ceremony Jody began to regret her decision. Vincent was never flexible and only wanted to do what he wanted to do. Jody's wants and needs were often ignored or downplayed. Everything they did was for Vincent's benefit, never hers. Five years into the marriage, Jody finally decided to leave him. She had thought marriage was what she always wanted. But she was wrong. Being married to Vincent made her see that marriage itself is just a piece of paper. What she really wanted was a strong loving relationship, which, from the very start, she never had with Vincent.

When she told Vincent she was leaving, he took her house key and threw all her things on the lawn. He made her give back her ring, which we later found out, he gave to his next girlfriend.

Be very cautious, ladies. I know that many of you have dreamed of your wedding day, but just remember that day will come and go. The man you are marrying, however, will be there forever. Marriage itself isn't a goal to be striving for. Marriage

itself won't make you feel happy and complete. Jody made the mistake of thinking it would, so she married Vincent. But she quickly learned just how wrong she was for thinking that.

People will give many reasons as to why marriages fail. I, for one, think the most common reason is because most people marry the wrong person in the first place. They have other motives for wanting to get married. They don't want to be alone, they want security, they are tired of dating, or they feel pressured. Then they reason their way into thinking the person they are with is right for them. Regardless of the reason for doing so, if you marry the wrong person, you have a long and arduous road ahead of you, and buyer's remorse is practically a given.

To me, no amount of money can compare to the value of happiness. When you get married you are basically paying the highest price possible because you are putting your happiness in the other person's hands. If you have the right partner, it's worth it. You are giving him all of you, and in return you are getting all of him. But when you have the wrong partner it is certain disaster. You often give everything and get very little in return. You start to wonder if you have made the right decision and end up very angry and remorseful.

Women often think that marriage will complete their lives, and in essence, make them happy. But the constitution of marriage is like a mixing bowl. People make the mistake of thinking that if they can just get the bowl, they will automatically get a

cake. They don't realize that what you put into it is what you are going to get out of it. If you have the right ingredients, you will come out with a cake. But if you have the wrong ones, all you will get is a bucket of mess. The bowl itself doesn't matter.

Vincent and Jody did not have the right ingredients in their relationship, so the marriage didn't work. She was able to get Vincent to commit by using the techniques in this book, but the techniques won't make him a loving, kind person if he isn't one to begin with. If the guy is wrong for you (or just a complete jerk), you have to be smart enough to see it. In both examples, my friends wanted to marry men who were obviously not a good fit. One was a party boy, more concerned with drinking and socializing than having a relationship. The other was a selfish, greedy man who threw tantrums if he didn't get his way.

Quality Customers

In sales we have what we call quality customers. They are the people who we know will absolutely benefit from buying our product. They are easy to deal with and make repeat orders, but most importantly, our product fits their needs. Unfortunately there are some salespeople only concerned with making the sale itself. It doesn't matter to them if the customer is a good fit or not. They just want to make their commission, so even if someone is not a good fit, they will continue to sell

them if they can. This is dangerous because there is a good chance the customer will experience buyer's remorse to some extent. They didn't buy the right product, but the salesperson was so convincing they purchased it anyway. After the deal is closed, they will call the salesperson with questions because they don't like or don't understand a particular feature. They get frustrated when they realize the product isn't exactly what they wanted. Finally they will end up complaining to everyone they know and eventually hating the product. Then, after all that is said and done, do you know what happens next? They end up making life miserable for the person who sold it to them in the first place.

Because you have learned how to close the deal on any man you want, you also must be careful that you don't close the wrong person. You have to be sure that you, too, are dealing with a quality customer—someone whose needs are met by your product, and not someone you just think you can close the deal on. Otherwise you will suffer from buyer's remorse that will last for years and years. If you end up in a remorseful relationship, your partner is likely to be feeling the same thing. You probably know the old saying *Buyer, beware,* but in this case, it's the *seller* who has to be careful.

Maintaining the Right Mentality

Don't Drink and Date

The best salesperson who ever worked for me was a twenty-five-year-old named Erin. Erin was a petite blonde with a personality that could fill a small auditorium. When she was hired, I knew she would be a high producer, but I had no idea that a third of my sales would come from this one little girl.

Every day Erin would return from the field with a stack of contracts. She outsold every other rep in the office by a mile. Some were extremely jealous of her ability. Others idolized her and wondered what her secret was. I, obviously, loved the girl. She boosted my sales and propelled me into a whole new tax bracket.

After Erin had been working for me for a few months, I started becoming friends with her, and one night she invited

me out to a party being thrown by her boyfriend. When I arrived, I found Erin at the bar, smoking, laughing, and doing shots. I was a little surprised at first to see her downing hard liquor. I told myself it was her boyfriend's birthday and she was just celebrating. *Really, really* celebrating.

The next time I went out with Erin, she was celebrating again. But this time, it wasn't anyone's birthday. In fact, we were out with a bunch of coworkers at happy hour. She ordered several drinks and then eventually moved to shots. By the end of the night she was so drunk that she passed out in the bathroom upstairs.

I was conflicted. Here was this superstar salesperson who almost certainly had a drinking problem. I didn't know how serious it was, and I wasn't sure what to do. Then something happened that forced me to make a decision.

Since Erin was the rock star of the office, I often made an example of her. Two very important clients were coming into town and wanted to ride in the field with one of my reps. I saw no problem letting Erin handle that task—after all, they would be working during the day and nowhere near a bar. But as luck would have it a huge snowstorm hit Boston that day and Erin was stuck three hours from the office with the two clients. I told her to find a hotel for the night. Their safety was first and foremost. I told her to take them out to dinner and be a pleasant, gracious, and *sober* host.

I worried a little that night, but there wasn't much I could

do. The next day Erin made her way back to the office with the clients. When she walked through the door, I knew my worst fear had come true. Erin had a huge welt on her face that stretched from the top of her forehead down to her eye.

"What happened?" I asked in horror.

"Oh, I fell," she answered quickly.

"You fell?"

"Yeah, I fell. I dropped a piece of gum and when I went to reach down and pick it up, I fell."

Judging from the placement of the wound, I knew Erin was drunk when it happened. No one falls directly on their fore-head when attempting to pick up gum.

"So you tried to pick up gum, and did a face dive into the pavement?"

Erin smiled sheepishly. "You make it seem so much worse than it is. I'm just a klutz. I fell," she said picking up her bag and inching toward my door.

"Don't you go anywhere. Go hang out in the back room until I come get you," I told her.

I asked the two clients to sit down with me. They confirmed what I had suspected. They had gone out to dinner, and Erin started drinking. She drank so much that she was slurring her words, dancing on her chair, and even tried to kiss one of them. I was mortified.

I had very high hopes for Erin. She was a phenomenal sales-person, and I had hoped to promote her into management at the

end of the year. My goal was to open another office and have her pioneer it. Now, not only was I not promoting her, I was going to have to fire her and somehow get her to seek help.

When Erin was terminated, it shocked the rest of the office. Most of them never even knew why I let her go. Those that did couldn't believe how stupid she was for jeopardizing her job like that. How could she take out two clients and behave so badly? Didn't she realize she was representing the whole office? Didn't she realize how important it was to make a good impression?

As crazy as it sounds, everyone I know has at some point made the same mistake as Erin. They may not have endangered their jobs by drinking with clients, but I know many women have jeopardized their relationships by drinking on dates.

Drinking While Prospecting

My girlfriend Melinda is a hopeless case. She is a thirty-nine-year-old train wreck. She wants more than anything to find a husband, yet she continuously sabotages her own chances at getting one. Every time we go out together prospecting, Melinda drinks too much. She tells me going out to a bar is unbearable without a cocktail or two. Usually she meets a guy early in the night, while she's still semi-sober. They talk, joke, and generally seem to like each other. If

Melinda were smart, she would give the guy her number, end at the height of impulse, and take herself home. But she's not smart. So instead she keeps drinking, goes home with the guy, has sex, and never hears from him again.

I continually tell Melinda she needs to stop getting drunk. Does she listen? No. It's not because she can't stand going to bars without drinking; it's because she's insecure and afraid of rejection. As far as she's concerned, the alcohol transforms her. When she's drunk she becomes the hottest woman on Earth. Unfortunately, she becomes the most promiscuous woman on Earth as well.

When you are prospecting, you must be careful not to sabotage your own chances at finding someone. If you are out at a bar or club, it's easy to lose count of how many drinks you've had. Melinda never plans on getting drunk. However, when she gets there it's a different story. She gets caught up in the moment. She meets a guy, likes how she is feeling, and doesn't want to lose it. He keeps offering to buy another round, and she can't refuse. Before she knows what's happening, she's making out with the guy in the middle of the club as the rest of us watch, shaking our heads.

This has become a very destructive pattern for my friend. She is a phenomenal prospector, but she doesn't have the discipline needed to close the deal. For years I've watched her do what feels good and seen her make the same mistake over and over. Unfortunately she's not the only woman who does this

sort of thing. There are lots of women out there who don't realize how drinking skews their judgment. They wake up the next day wondering why the fabulous guy they had so much fun with last night didn't ask for their number.

Drinking on a First Date

The only thing that's worse than getting drunk while prospecting is getting drunk on a first date. My friend Katherine is stunningly beautiful. Not only that, she's sweet, funny, and has a lucrative job selling private airplanes. She's very busy during the week and even on the weekends, so she uses Match.com to prospect for men. She usually sets up her dates in the evening, instead of doing coffee or lunch. I thought this was fine, until I realized why she was doing this. Katherine needs to drink on her dates. She is nervous about meeting men she doesn't know and needs something to take the edge off, which is not a horrible thing by any means. I agree that it is nerve-wracking to meet someone you don't know for the very first time, and having a glass of wine is usually pretty harmless as long as you are twenty-one and not driving.

But one day when I was at lunch with Katherine, I realized something. She had met ten guys on Match.com within the last couple of months, and not one meeting resulted in a second date. I thought it was very strange given the fact that

Katherine is such a catch, as well as a professional salesperson. She should know the do's and don'ts of getting a man interested. So why hadn't any of her first dates come back for seconds? I had her tell me exactly what happened on each of her dates to see if I could figure out what the problem was.

As she relived each encounter for me, nothing she said seemed out of the ordinary. She said she would meet for drinks, usually get some dinner, maybe grab another drink afterwards, and then go home. She didn't talk about her dreams of four kids and a mini-van, and she didn't unload any personal problems. Everything she told me seemed completely fine.

Then a few weeks later, I was at Barnes & Noble, and I ran into a guy I used to know in college. We got to talking, and he told me he had been trying online dating. I asked how it was going, and he told me for the most part it was great. The only bad date he had was with a super attractive girl who sold airplanes. Of course I almost choked on my latte when he told me that. There aren't many people in that industry, so I had to ask what her name was. He said it was Katherine.

He told me that the date started off great. They met at a martini bar in the city and had a couple drinks. He was really attracted to her at first. They went to dinner at a little French bistro and Katherine ordered another drink. It was shortly after that when the date started to go sour.

"Jess, it's such a shame," he started. "After a couple of drinks she starts swearing like a sailor. It's the most unattractive

thing. She is such a beautiful girl, but after a couple of drinks she started dropping F-bombs. And it wasn't just one or two; it was every other word! I think she even swore at the waiter."

"Oh my goodness," I said. "That's terrible. You must have felt so embarrassed."

"I did, but the worst part was I thought I could actually like her. When I saw her I was immediately attracted to her. Then she opened her mouth and showed me her class. I can't date a girl with a mouth like that. It's such a turnoff."

I thanked my friend for telling me the story and rushed home to call Katherine.

She didn't realize she was doing it and she wasn't a classless person, but whenever she had too much to drink, Katherine became a potty-mouth.

Sometimes drinking not only causes you to lose your inhibitions, it can also make you do or say certain things that just aren't appropriate on a first date. Katherine knows how to close the deal with guys. She understands the strategy and how to execute it. But with each drink she has, the strategy becomes less important and harder to stick to. She says what's on her mind, and she says it with . . . um . . . conviction? She's enjoying herself and doesn't want to worry about what the future may bring. Of course, this is why the future hasn't brought her anything at all.

Ladies, I know when you go on a date you may be a little nervous. I know that having a drink or two can take the edge

off, and like I said before, I see nothing wrong with it. The problem is that some women don't know their limits. They think the date is going well because they are having a good time, and if they are having a good time, then the guy must be, too. But alcohol can give you a false sense of confidence, and it makes it impossible to think logically.

The Drunk Dial

Perhaps the most dangerous and most common of all dating pitfalls is the dreaded drunk dial. No good can ever come from the drunk dial. It can cause sudden, instant, and otherwise immediate death of a relationship.

Case in point: my friend Jenny met Jeremy at a bar one night. They were both there for a happy hour thrown by a mutual friend. They struck up a conversation and ended up flirting with each other throughout the night. Jeremy told Jenny she was cute and fun to hang out with but didn't ask for her number.

The following week Jenny ran into Jeremy again. This time, at a going-away party. They hung out together for most of the night, and when the party wound down, they decided to continue the good time at a local pub.

At the end of the night, Jeremy still hadn't asked for Jenny's number. But he did tell her about a barbeque that weekend being thrown by one of their mutual friends. She told him she

would come and bring some girlfriends with her.

At the barbeque, Jenny and Jeremy got very flirty and even made out in her car at the end of the night. He finally asked for Jenny's number and told her he would like to go out to dinner sometime during the week. Jenny suggested Wednesday, and Jeremy agreed.

Wednesday rolled around, and Jeremy texted Jenny. The text said he had gotten invited by a friend to a Nationals game and couldn't make dinner. He said he would call later in the week to reschedule. Jenny was disappointed. She felt blown off, especially after kissing him at the barbeque. She decided to go out with her girlfriends that night and ease the pain with some sake bombs.

Jenny told all her friends about Jeremy. She told them they had kissed that weekend, and then he blew her off for dinner in a text message. They were all angry and told Jenny he was a jerk. They told her not to let him treat her like that and to ask him what the hell was going on with the two of them. Why did he wait so long for her number? Why did he kiss her and diss her? What were they doing anyway? Dating? Just messing around? They told her she needed to find out.

At two-thirty in the morning, Jenny reached for her phone. Totally wasted from the night of sake bombs, she dialed Jeremy's number. He answered. The conversation went something like this:

"Hey, it's Jenny. What are you doing?"

"Huh? I'm sleeping. It's two-thirty, and I have work tomorrow."

"Oh, well, how was the game? Was it worth ditching me for dinner?"

"Uh, it was good. I'm sorry about that. I did want to go to dinner, but the tickets were behind home plate. I was planning to make it up to you this weekend."

"Well, I think that was a total asshole thing to do if you ask me. What are we doing anyway? What are we? Are we dating or are we just going to be friends that mess around? Cause I am not like that. I need to be treated with respect."

"Uh, okay."

'Okay?' That's all you have to say for yourself? What are you trying to do here, Jeremy? What exactly is it that you want from me?"

"Well, right now I want you to let me go back to sleep."

"Oh fine. Go to sleep, just know that you are on thin ice, buddy."

And with that Jenny hung up.

The next day Jenny hardly remembered the conversation. She got to work and logged on to her computer. Not feeling that well already, she checked her e-mail and saw Jeremy had sent her a message. He said he was sorry for making her upset. He also told her he was not looking for a relationship, and that he really didn't appreciate the 2 AM phone call. He told her he thought she was a nice girl and he wished her the best of luck in the future.

The Sobering Truth

Jenny totally blew it. If she had read the signs she would have seen that Jeremy had moderate interest in her. Knowing that, she should have acted more indifferently, held back the make-out bullet, and used more of a sense of urgency. She should *not* have gotten drunk, called him up, and asked point blank what his intentions were. That took Jeremy's interest from moderate to nonexistent.

The drunk dial is dangerous because in one fell swoop, you can ruin your chances with someone. Alcohol and cell phones are a toxic combination. For some reason when women get drunk they love to pick up the phone and dial the one they love. Unfortunately they don't realize that getting too drunk always leads to vomiting . . . verbal vomiting, that is.

In order to really be able to follow the techniques in this book, you will have to take alcohol out of the equation. If you are the kind of person who can't just have one drink, then no matter what you have learned from reading this, you will not be able to land your man. Just like emotion clouds logic, so do martinis. There is no way you will be able to think logically and strategically if you are intoxicated.

Don't feel bad. Lots of women have this problem. I have girlfriends who know how to close the deal but still drink too much and ruin their chances. They wake up the following day fully aware of what they did wrong, and yet they will go out

the next night and do it all over again. You are definitely not alone if this sounds like you. Now you just have to recognize that it is a problem and discipline yourself to change it. Drinking and dating is very common and very dangerous. You will not be able to use your head if you are doing it. If you know you cannot limit your alcohol intake, the best advice I can give you is to make your dates during the day. Do coffee or lunch. Maybe try an activity like rock-climbing or hiking. If you are doing some activity other than just standing or sitting around, you will likely not feel the urge to drink. Besides, there aren't many places to get beer on the way up a mountain.

Be smart: don't drink and date. You could ruin your chances of hitting it off with a great guy if you do. You need to keep your head straight and your mind clear. If you know of a girlfriend who also has this problem, it is your responsibility to warn her as well. Friends don't let friends drink and date, either.

The Waiting Game

When I saw my ex-boyfriend Kyle at a fundraiser for missing children, I knew instantly that I wanted him back. He looked great. He had been working out, grew his hair, and was sporting a five o'clock shadow. But it was more than just the

appearance that reeled me back in. After talking to him for twenty minutes, I remembered what a great guy he was, and how silly our breakup had been. I hesitantly left the event, hoping that he would call me.

I got home that evening and physically wrestled with my phone. I wanted to talk to my ex, but I knew that the ball was in his court. He would have to call me. I had to resist. I called everyone in my phone book to avoid dialing his number. I talked to my mom until I fell asleep on the couch. But as hard as it was, I went to bed that night without giving in to my impulses.

Monday morning I got up and went to work. I logged onto my computer to check my e-mail, and lo and behold, there was an e-mail from him. Thank God I hadn't given in! The waiting game paid off. As difficult as it was, I made the right move and a week later Kyle and I got back together.

I know I said that prospecting was the worst part of being a salesperson. Well, I lied. The worst part is the waiting game—the period of time when you can do absolutely nothing but wait for the other person to make a move. That is the worst part by far.

Luckily I only had to wait a weekend to hear from my ex. But sometimes the waiting game goes on for weeks and even months. It's a tough thing to do because the situation is completely out of your control. It's not fun, but here's why it's necessary that you don't give in.

The worst salesperson I ever met worked in my office in Texas. He was notorious for screwing up his own deals. He

would find a customer who was interested, but ultimately he would foul it up somehow.

One of his customers was a busy doctor. The salesperson wanted to switch the doctor's phone carrier, but the doctor wanted to wait and see his next phone bill first. The salesperson knew the doctor was interested and didn't want to let the sale slip away, so he created a sense of urgency and told the doctor he could give him an even better long-distance rate if he signed up by the end of the week. The doctor toiled a few minutes thinking about it. Just before he could answer, a nurse popped her head in and needed the doctor for a minute. He excused himself and told the salesperson he would be right back.

Alone with his thoughts, the salesperson started to worry that he had pressured the doctor too much. What if he came back and said that he'd passed on the deal all together because he couldn't make a decision that soon? He did say he needed to see his next phone bill. What if he needed until the end of the month to get that bill and decide? When the doctor returned, the now freaked-out salesperson jumped up and said he could give him until the end of the month to make a decision. When the doctor heard that, he was surprised and caught off guard. He told the rep he was going to buy today, but if he had more time to decide, he would think about it further and wait until then.

Had the salesperson just played the waiting game and stuck to his first offer, he would have closed the deal that very day. He had created urgency in the doctor, but then got nervous and

recanted. He didn't have the discipline or the confidence needed to wait and see what the doctor was going to say, and he lost the deal because of it.

Women sometimes get the same itch. They drive themselves bananas while sitting around waiting for a phone call. They climb walls waiting for their latest strategy to play out. They want answers and they want them ten minutes ago. Understand that sometimes you will be in a situation where you really can't and shouldn't do anything but wait. Think of it like a game of chess. You make a move, and then you have to wait until the other player makes his. You cannot get impatient. He may make his move right away, or it may take him a while. But you cannot make another move until he does.

Don't Sweat the Techniques

Paige was dating a guy she really liked. Tyler was a tall, charismatic guy with sparkling blue eyes. Everyone he came in contact with liked him instantly. Paige had a lot of competition. The two had been dating for several weeks, and Paige was really starting to fall for him. Problem was that Tyler wasn't exactly acting like he was in love. He would call her, but it was sporadic. He would take her out once a week, but on other days, she never knew where he was. She felt totally powerless and out of control. So one day I told her she needed to change her course of action. Next time Tyler called and asked

her out, she needed to tell him she was busy. She needed to create a little sense of urgency and have him feel a little fear of loss. Paige was terrified to do this. What if he felt rejected and never called again? I convinced her that this was the best course of action and what she'd been doing all along by being so available was even riskier than what I was suggesting.

When Tyler called, I sat there and coached Paige on what to say. She declined his offer to take her out on Saturday. She told him she had other plans and maybe they could go out some other time. With that, she hung up.

A couple days went by, and Paige was an emotional wreck. She walked around like a zombie. She continually asked me if I was sure the strategy would work. I told her that it would, but in the off chance it didn't, it meant Tyler didn't really like her anyway. She continued for the next few days to wrestle with her feelings. Then just as she was about to reach the brink of insanity, Tyler called. He told Paige how much he missed her and needed to see her. This, according to Paige, was something he had never said before. She was elated. The waiting game had paid off.

Like most girls, Paige was terrified to make her own strategic moves. She was worried about the consequences of her actions. In essence, she was happier not knowing how Tyler really felt about her because she would rather have a small piece of him than none of him at all. She worried that making this move would tell her what she feared—that he didn't really

like her. She would actually rather lie to herself and keep seeing him, then get the truth and have to stop.

Sometimes it may be scary to use the tactics you have learned. If a guy truly doesn't care about you and is at the point of using you at his leisure, then the tactics honestly may not work. But do you really want to be with someone who feels that way about you? These techniques are designed to get you what you want, but they are also designed to get you answers about a man's real feelings. Just remember, after every strategic move, you are going to have to play a little waiting game. Don't freak out. Be confident in your logical decision-making. Trust in the techniques that have been proven to work for centuries. Don't make a move and then make the mistake of counteracting it. Sometimes all you can do is wait. It may be agonizing, but you have to do it.

What to Do While You Wait

I have friends who play the waiting game literally by sitting around and waiting. They log into their e-mail every five minutes and stare at their phone to make sure it's still getting service. They can't do anything except talk and obsess about their relationship, which blows the entire situation out of proportion. Here's a good piece of advice. When you are playing the waiting game, don't just sit around and wait! Keep yourself occupied. Go out with friends, go see a movie, read a book. The

waiting game can be unbearable as it is, so if you are really just sitting around and waiting, you can and will drive yourself crazy.

No Means Next

I was waiting at our usual coffee shop for Isabel. She had called me in a panic, on the verge of an emotional meltdown. She had just finished having another explosive fight with Mark, her boyfriend of almost one year. When she walked through the door she looked worn-out and exhausted. I had a double shot of espresso waiting for her.

"What happened now?" I asked gently.

Isabel wrapped her hands around the espresso so tightly, I thought she was going to crush the cup. I could tell she was at the end of her rope.

"Things had been going so well since we got back together. I thought this time it was really going to be different," she lamented. "And now I feel like I screwed everything up."

"You? You screwed everything up? How did you do that?" I said utterly confused. Isabel was a classic people pleaser, so it was unimaginable that she would do something to cause conflict.

"Yes, me. Last night was my cousin's engagement party. Of

course Mark agreed to go with me, and he seemed fine about it. But when we got to the party, Harrison was there. I wasn't going to tell Mark that we dated, but I guess when Harrison came over to say hello, Mark could tell. After that he completely lost it and left the party."

I was even more confused now. "I don't understand. You only dated Harrison for a couple of weeks. It's not like you ran into your ex-fiance. And even if you did, how is that your fault? Sounds like Mark's overreacting to me."

"Well, I promised Mark that if ever we were somewhere that a former boyfriend could possibly show up, I would tell him. Once we ran into my ex, P.J., and Mark felt so uncomfortable he made me promise I would prevent that from happening again if I could. I guess I knew Harrison would be there, but I didn't think to tell him."

"So he left the party and then what happened?" I asked.

"I don't know. Mark never came home last night. I don't know where he went." She started to sob.

"Isabel, aren't you tired? Haven't you had enough of this? I know you love Mark, but this has been the most volatile year you've ever had. You've broken up three times. I know you want to make this relationship work, but by now, don't you realize it's just not going to?"

Isabel wiped her eyes. No matter how hard she tried, the relationship was constantly turbulent. I knew that she didn't want to hear it, but it sounded like it was time to move on. In

sales, we have a saying for a situations like this: No means Next. Sometimes no matter how hard you work on making a sale, it just won't close for whatever reason. Isabel and Mark had broken up and gotten back together numerous times. It was clear that this relationship wasn't going to result in marriage. This was a No. And she needed to move onto the Next.

You can waste a lot of time on a No. I remember when I first started in sales I would spend days in a customer's office, trying to convince him or her to buy from me. Often I would go back to see the same person who had callously turned me down the week earlier, in an effort to change their mind. I spent an exorbitant amount of time with people that just weren't going to buy from me. Then I realized that my time was much better spent moving on to find someone that would.

In sales, we believe you should take three No's and then leave. If you hear No once, then it could be you haven't done a good job getting the customer's attention and you need to change your approach. If you hear No for the second time, you may need to provide more information or figure out another angle to take. But if you hear No for the third time, then believe it to be a true No. After the third No, you are wasting your time with someone.

Isabel was definitely wasting her time. She and Mark had broken up three times that year. She wanted to keep trying to make it work, but at this point it made more sense to move on and find someone who suited her better.

Sometimes it doesn't matter how good a salesperson you are. Some customers just aren't meant to be sold. It has nothing to do with the product, the presentation, or anything else in your control. You won't be able to sell 100 percent of the people 100 percent of the time. So the best thing to do is move on when you get to that point. Continuing to try after so many breakups was only exhausting Isabel and damaging her self-esteem. She thought if she kept working at the relationship, it would pan out in the end. Don't make the mistake of thinking *everything* is within your control. Some things are not and you have to accept that.

Dealing with Rejection

The word No can be hard to handle. When I first heard No from people, it really affected me. I took it very personally. I wondered what was wrong with me? Why didn't this person like me? But then I realized that No didn't mean that I sucked. It didn't mean I had failed and it didn't mean I did anything wrong. No did not mean that I was being rejected.

It's normal to feel rejected when a relationship doesn't work out. Even if you are the one who ultimately ends it, you can still feel rejected. But you have to have the mentality that it is not personal. I know right now you are thinking, *how in the world can it not be personal?* Well, you have to stop thinking that a man not wanting you is a reflection of how good of a person you are. It's not. If your relationship doesn't work out,

it's because it wasn't meant to work out. You were meant for someone else. He was meant for someone else. You are both good people who just aren't good together. That's the mentality you must have.

Anne once dated a guy that started out as a friend. He had liked her for years and finally convinced her to give him a shot. They dated for six months, and he was totally over the moon. But after the crazy infatuation subsided, he started to really look at Anne as a life partner, and wondered if she was the right fit for him. They had very different belief systems and very different goals for the future. So even though this guy was crazy in love with Anne, he broke up with her. Of course Anne felt completely rejected. How could this guy love her for five years, finally get her, and then dump her? What she didn't understand was that he wasn't rejecting Anne as a person. He truly had feelings for her. He just didn't think that in the long run they were right for each other. He needed someone that wanted to stay home, cook dinner, and raise kids. The only thing Anne ever wanted to make for dinner was reservations. Stay home and raise children? That's what nannies are for! So even though he really liked Anne as a person, he had to let her go. It was as rough on him as it was on her.

When a relationship doesn't work out, most women feel they did something wrong and just weren't good enough to keep a guy's interest. But that isn't what it means. You have to realize that not being good as a couple doesn't mean you aren't good on your own.

Whenever a relationship doesn't work out for Isabel she worries she will never meet anyone ever again. But within months she is always dating someone else. I know that this is a constant worry for most of my friends, but that is not a good reason to stay in a dead-end relationship. As long as you go back to prospecting, you will find another potential customer. It's inevitable. So don't fret about letting someone go because you fear you will never meet someone else. You will. You just need to go back to the basics. Prospect, fill your funnel, and keep a positive attitude. You are in control here. So if you want to meet someone else, you will. I promise.

Practicing in Game-like Conditions

Adison had just finished reading the rough draft of this book and couldn't contain her excitement. She finally realized what she had been doing wrong, and now had an action plan on how to do it right. After taking a year-long hiatus from dating, she was ready to get back out there and put what she learned to good use. She told all her girlfriends about the techniques, and they decided to practice amongst themselves. They took turns walking by and giving each other the SEE factor. They practiced their icebreakers, and they would mirror each other's body language. They were all confident and

assertive. They felt good. Enough of the dress rehearsal. They were ready for opening night!

They decided to go to a very well-known bar in downtown San Francisco. After ordering their drinks, they all huddled together nervously trying to build up the courage to approach someone. Adison spotted a very attractive man at the bar. Her friends urged her to walk by him and give him the SEE. Hesitantly, she began moving in his direction. But as she got closer, her heart started racing. Her palms got sweaty, and she wondered what the hell she was doing. The guy turned his head and glanced at her, and almost out of instinct, she looked away. She high-tailed it back to her friends and cried "I can't do it!"

After that, the rest of her friends were terrified as well.

I flew to San Francisco the following week, and Adison told me her horror story. I just laughed. I told her that it was obviously going to be hard to transition from passive to assertive when it comes to meeting men. She had trained herself to look away when a guy noticed her, so of course it would take some getting use to. She explained that she had been practicing with her girlfriends, and they had gotten pretty good at the techniques. But when she got to the bar, she lost all confidence and couldn't do it. I told her that was to be expected because practicing with her girlfriends wasn't going to prepare her for the real thing. What she needed to do was practice in game-like conditions.

Get in the Game

What exactly is a game-like condition? Well, let's say you are a basketball player. Would it make sense to shoot hoops everyday all by yourself? Probably not. When game time comes you wouldn't be able to make the shot because you wouldn't be used to someone trying to block you. So instead of practicing alone, it makes more sense to practice like you are in a game. Have someone try to block while you shoot so that you get the feel of what it will be like when it's time to really play. That's practicing in game-like conditions.

Adison was not successful in the field because she was practicing with women. Not only that, but they were women she knew well and was comfortable with. The anxiety of prospecting comes from approaching someone you don't know. So how could she possibly get a true feel for it, when she was rehearsing with her friends?

I took Adison out that night. We didn't go to a bar. We didn't even go to a restaurant. We just walked the streets of downtown San Francisco. The city was bustling and there were guys everywhere. I told her to just start smiling and making eye contact with any guy that walked by. Didn't matter how young, old, cute, or not so cute he was. The point was just to practice with men that she didn't know. We walked for blocks and blocks. Every time we passed a guy she made up some excuse why she wasn't able to do it. Either he wasn't

looking or he was looking too much. He was too far away, or he was too close for comfort.

After walking around for an hour we started our trek home. I told her that if she couldn't do it on the street with a guy she wasn't interested in, she would never be able to do it when she really needed to. Just then we passed a hole-in-the-wall bar with an outside patio. There was one waiter sitting at a table, smoking a cigarette on his break. This was it, I told her. This was her very last chance. It was like watching a movie in slow motion. Adison took a deep breath and peeled her eyes off the ground. The guy exhaled a long and billowy cloud of smoke. She looked at him. He caught her eye. We had contact! Now all that had to happen was for Adison to smile an enthusiastic and confident smile. Could she do it? She had come this far, but I wasn't sure. A baby cried in the distance. It seemed like an eternity had passed. Then I saw it. The sides of her mouth began to curl. She was doing it. She was smiling! Upon see-ing this, the waiter sat up in his chair, grinned from ear to ear and waved hello. Success! I turned to give Adison a pat on the back, but she was already around the corner, breathing into her doggy bag trying to catch her breath.

When you have conditioned yourself to avoid other people's eye contact, then it will be a bit uncomfortable to use SEE . . . at first. But the more you practice in game-like conditions, the easier it will become. Start out like Adison, smiling at people as you walk by them on the street. Practice on women if it

helps you warm up. Do it whenever you are out of your house. It doesn't matter where you are or who you look at. No one shies away from a friendly smile. The more you practice, the easier it will be for you to do. Then when you spot that handsome man across the room, you won't hesitate for a second. You will know what to do and you will get what you want.

As for the other techniques in the book, you must take the same advice. Don't wait for Mr. Perfect to come along and then start using the Mirror Theory. Practice it on a Mr. OK-For-Now or Mr. Nice-But-Not-Really-My-Type. Try using Sense of Urgency on your backup guy. You won't feel as much pressure if you practice with men you aren't seriously interested in; however, you will get a feel for how to use the techniques and how men will react to them. Then when it's really game time, you won't question yourself. You will be confident in everything you say and do.

Remember that your love life is within your control. You can make it happen. No more sitting around and complaining you don't have a boyfriend and will never get married. Get up and go after what you want. Now that you have a road map to maneuver your way there, you won't get lost . . . and you certainly won't lose him. Take control and remember that no one can love you more than you love yourself.

Good luck and happy prospecting!

INDEX

alcohol, 90, 105–106, 111, 146, 227–239
anticipation, 148–149. *see also* waiting
appearance. *see also* clothes
  confidence in, 43–44
  looking different, 54–58
  looking good, 51–58, 71–72
  looking sexy, 47–49, 57–58
  professional, 47–53
  sunglasses, 72
assumptions, danger in, 181–187
attitude
  appearance and, 49
  energy and, 70
  indifference, 114–116, 119–126
  positive, 10–11
  as sign of interest, 94–95
attraction
  body language, 127–133
  buying signs, 87–90, 91–93
  chemistry, 5–6
  Jones Effect and, 85, 133–140
  looking different, 54–58
  looking good, 51–58
  looking sexy, 47–49, 57–58

baby voice, 132
backup guys, 81–82, 254
behavior. *see also* sex; timing
  alcohol and, 90, 105–106, 111, 146,
    227–239
  impulsive, 105–106, 111
  justifying, 26–27
  needy, 19–21, 29–31, 116–119
  proactive vs. reactive, 193
  self-defeating patterns, 2–4, 230–232
  self-promotion (over), 22–23
  sleeping over, 113–114
  stalking, 21–22
  verbal vomit, 102–105, 235–238
body language, 127–133
breaking up
  excuse making, 213–215
  moving on, 245–248
  Silent "No," 209–211
Bullet Theory, 143, 146
bullets
  overview, 141–152
  anticipation, 148–149
  kissing, 150–151
  making out, 144–146, 150

  sex, 144–147
  timing, 149–152
buyer's remorse
  overview, 215–225
  choices, 224–225
  partners, 219–224
buying signs. *see also* interest levels
  interpreting, 91–93
  men's, 91–98
  reading, 87–90

Can't Buy Me Love (film), 136–137
chemistry, 5–6
closing
  at Height of Impulse, 109–112
  in relationships, 152–162
  in sales, 141–144, 181–183
  Sense of Urgency (SOU), 202–206
  statements, 95, 113–114, 116
  timing, 160–162
clothes
  overview, 47–58
  looking different, 54–58
  looking good, 51–58, 71–72
  looking sexy, 47–49, 57–58
Coming to America (film), 38
commitment
  assumptions about, 183–187
  forcing, 153
  by men, 161–162
  phobia, 2, 15, 213–215
commitment phobia, 2, 15, 213–215
communication
  about commitment, 183–187
  body language, 127–133
  conversation, 73–76, 99–102
  drunk dial, 235–238
  eye contact, 68–69, 72, 93–94
  KISS principle, 98–105
  listening, 101–105, 132–133
  mixed messages, 91, 96
  nonverbal, 127–132
  by phone, 168–171, 235–238
  Silent "No," 206–212
  text messages, 168–171
  tone of voice, 132
  verbal vomit, 102–105, 235–238
competition, 54–56
control. *see also* timing
  overview, 162–173

control. *see also* timing (*cont'd*)
  maintaining, 168–173
  relinquishing, 162–168
  self-control, 111–112
  waiting game, 242–244
conversation. *see also* communication
  dominating, 99–102
  Icebreakers, 73–76
  listening, 101–105, 132–133
Cusack, Joan, 49

dating. *see also* drinking and dating;
    online dating
  casual, 118
  disasters, 6–8
  exclusive, 78–80
  formula for success, 8–16
  multiple partners, 78–80
  over-availability, 162–167, 200–201
  strategies, 59–67
decision-making
  emotional vs. logical, 24–28, 110
  Fear of Loss (FOL) and, 188–198
  power of, 167–168
  Sense of Urgency (SOU) and, 198–
    206
Dempsey, Patrick, 136–137
drinking and dating
  overview, 227–239
  behavior, 105–106, 111, 146, 232–
    237
  drunk dial, 235–238
  patterns, 230–232
  self-sabotage, 227–235
drunk dial, 235–238

emotions
  in decision-making, 24–28, 110
  verbal vomit and, 102–105, 235–238
energy, 69–70. *see also* attitude; SEE
    Factor
excuses, 213–215
eye contact, 68–69, 72, 93–94. *see also*
    SEE Factor

Facebook, 67
Fear of Loss (FOL), 188–198
funnel filling, 77–85, 118, 142

game playing, 26–33, 124–126
game-like conditions, 250–254
giving, trap of, 173–180
gratification, instant, 168–171
Griffith, Melanie, 49
guy magnets, 68–71

Height of Impulse
  overview, 105–114
  ending at, 107–108, 113–114
  loss of impulse, 109–111
  saying "No," 107–108
  self-control, 111–112
  timing, 113–114
He's Just Not That Into You (Behrendt,
    Tuccillo), 9

Icebreakers, 73–76, 250
indifference, 114–116, 119–126
insecurity, 43–44
instant gratification, 168–171
interest levels
  overview, 91–98
  attitude/mannerisms, 94–95
  gauging, 97–98
  low, 95–96
  moderate, 92–96, 95–96
  questioning, 94
Internet dating. *see* online dating

Jones Effect, 85, 133–140

KISS principle, 98–105
kissing, 144–146, 150–151

L-bomb, 20, 25, 185–186, 197
listening, 101–105, 132–133
living together, 193–196, 217
logic, 24–28, 110
long-term relationships, 110, 151, 194–
    195

making out, 144–146, 150

marriage
  changing him, 215–219
  commitment to, 215–224
  Fear of Loss (FOL) and, 192–198
  as goal, 61–62, 187–196
  motivation, 187–190
  obsessing about, 152–157
  pressuring for, 152–157, 159
  Sense of Urgency (SOU) and, 198–206
  timetables, 204–206
  wrong partners, 215–225
Match.com, 105, 110, 232
men
  attention spans, 101
  backup guys, 81–82, 254
  buying signs, 91–98
  commitment phobia, 15, 213–215
  commitments from, 161–162, 183–187
  as competitive, 138
  fear of rejection, 69, 70, 72, 89
  marriage and, 152–157, 188–196
  respect from, 50–51, 151, 176–180, 192
  signs of interest, 93–98
  as skeptical of women, 159
  as visual, 51–53
Mirror Theory, 129–132
mirroring, 129–132, 250
mixed messages, 91, 96
moving on, 245–248
Murphy, Eddie, 38
MySpace, 82, 83, 84, 91–92

neediness, 19–21, 29–31, 116–119
"No"
  breaking up and, 209–211
  moving on and, 245–248
  rejection and, 248–250
  saying, 107–108
  Silent "No," 206–212
  three "Nos," 247

online dating
  Facebook, 67
  Match.com, 105, 110, 232
  MySpace, 82, 83, 84, 91–92
  opportunities, 66–67

over-availability, 162–167, 200–201

phone communication, 168–171, 235–238
prospecting. see also appearance; attraction; online dating
  bar crawls, 65
  being available, 54–58
  drinking while, 230–232
  funnel filling and, 77–85, 80–82
  game-like conditions, 250–254
  places to go, 64–66
  strategy, 64–66
  techniques, 59–62, 64–66

rejection
  coping with, 248–250
  men's fear of, 69, 70, 72, 89
"relationship talk," 80–81, 161, 184
relationships. see also commitment; marriage
  buyer's remorse, 215–225
  control in, 162–173
  failure to launch, 126
  "hopping," 118
  long-term, 110, 151, 194–195
  patterns in, 2–4, 19–21
  "relationship talk," 80–81, 161, 184
  self-worth as key, 35–40, 41–43, 149–151
  seller's remorse, 215–224
  timetables, 204–206
  wrong partners, 215–225
respect
  self-respect, 149–151
  winning, 50–51, 151, 176–180, 192
Rules, The (Shamoon, Fein), 9

sales techniques
  overview, 17–19
  Fear of Loss (FOL), 188–198
  perfecting, 23–24
  prospecting, 59–62, 64–66
  Sense of Urgency (SOU), 198–206
SEE Factors
  overview, 68–72
  energy, 69–70

SEE Factors *(cont'd)*
 eye contact, 68–69, 72
 guy magnets and, 68–71
 practicing, 250–254
 smiling, 68–70
self-confidence, 43–49, 72
self-discipline, 109–111
self-knowledge, 35–40
self-love, 41–44, 47, 254
self-respect, 149–151
self-sabotage, 227–235
Sense of Urgency (SOU), 198–206, 241
sex. *see also* drinking and dating
 kissing, 144–146, 150–151
 making out, 144–147, 150
 timing, 113–114, 151–152, 156–157,
  162–167
Silent "No"
 overview, 206–212
 acknowledging, 211–212
 excuses, 213–215
 lack of contact, 206–209
skepticism, 157–160
smiling, 68–70. *see also* SEE Factor
strategy
 in dating, 59–67
 Fear of Loss (FOL), 188–198
 Icebreakers, 73–76
 importance of, 31–33
 indifference, 114–116, 119–126
 prospecting, 59–67
 in sales, 17–19
 Sense of Urgency (SOU), 198–206
 timing and, 109–114, 160–162
sunglasses, 72
Swingers (film), 70–71

talking. *see also* conversation

"relationship talk," 80–81, 161, 184
 tone of voice, 132
 verbal vomit, 99–105
text messages, 168–171
Timberlake, Justin, 58
timetables, 204–206
timing. *see also* Height of Impulse
 sex, 113–114, 144–147, 151–152,
  162–167
 strategy, 109–114, 160–162
 timetables, 204–206
turnoffs. *see also* drinking and dating
 drunk dial, 235–238
 husband hunting, 74–75
 neediness, 19–21, 29–31, 116–119
 verbal vomit, 99–105, 235–238

ultimatums, 188, 192, 203. *see also* Fear
 of Loss (FOL); Sense of
 Urgency (SOU)

Vaughn, Vince, 70–71
verbal vomit
 into awkward silence, 104–105
 disease of, 99–105
 drunk dial, 235–238
 of personal problems, 102–105
voice, tone of, 132

waiting
 anticipation, 148–149
 for him to call, 82, 162–167
 for sex, 151–152, 162–167
 waiting game, 239–245
waiting game, 239–245
Working Girl (film), 49

Understanding Child Sexual Abuse

Understanding Health and Sickness Series
Miriam Bloom, Ph.D.
General Editor

Understanding
Child Sexual Abuse

Edward L. Rowan, M.D.

University Press of Mississippi
Jackson

www.upress.state.ms.us

The University Press of Mississippi is a member of the Association of American University Presses.

Copyright © 2006 by University Press of Mississippi
Manufactured in the United States of America

First edition 2006

∞

Illustrations by Alan Estridge

Library of Congress Cataloging-in-Publication Data

Rowan, Edward L.
    Understanding child sexual abuse / Edward L. Rowan.— 1st ed.
        p. cm. — (Understanding health and sickness series)
    Includes bibliographical references and index.
    ISBN 1-57806-806-1 (cloth : alk. paper) — ISBN 1-57806-807-X
(pbk. : alk. paper)
    1. Child sexual abuse. 2. Child sexual abuse—Treatment. I. Title.
II. Series.
    RC560.C56R69   2006
    362.76—dc22   2005018087

British Library Cataloging-in-Publication Data available

Contents

Introduction vii

1. Who Becomes an Abuser? 3

2. Who Is at Risk? 19

3. What Are the Effects of Abuse? 29

4. Treating the Survivor 43

5. Treating the Abuser 57

6. Prevention 67

7. The Search for Answers 77

Appendices

A. State Sex Offender Registry Sites 85

B. Publications 90

C. The Internet 92

Glossary 94

Index 101

Introduction

There are two sides to every story. The issue of child
sexual abuse is no exception. In this book I will explore the
dynamics, effects, and treatment options available to both the
children and the adults involved. Broadly speaking, child
sexual abuse refers to sex forced on a child by an older person.
With a few exceptions, the objective is the sex itself. Power
and humiliation are the objectives of rape and the sexual
assaults common in prisons and military organizations, and
they are not part of this discussion.

The language we use to describe what happens between
participants in a sexual experience has a built-in bias. The
terms *sexual abuse, sexual molestation,* and *child rape* have a
negative connotation, as do *victim* and *survivor. Predator,
perpetrator, molester, rapist, child abuser, deviant,* and *pedophile*
are also negative terms. Language bias influences the way
information is processed and it is difficult to feel positive
about any of these terms. Despite this, I will retain those
terms because of their pervasive use in the scientific and lay
literature.

The people who work with clinical populations of damaged
victims and survivors are justifiably angry at those who caused
the damage. They also seem to believe that adults who have sex
with children are using them as substitutes for the adults they are
incompetent to have or to hold. They believe that such people
deserve no sympathy and should be despised. For many in the
larger Judeo-Christian perspective, the only justification for
sexual activity is procreation within the sanctity of marriage. The
sentimental image that children are innocents to be cherished
provides additional justification for despising the child abuser.

University of Hamburg, Germany, psychologist Gunter
Schmidt believes that the negative view about sex with children
relates not to the sex itself but to the evolution of what he calls
"consensual morality." If two people of equal power knowingly
and willingly agree to do something sexual, then it is acceptable.
Conservatives do not believe that children can mutually consent
and liberals focus on the perceived power imbalance, so that
adults who have sex with children have no supporters except
each other.

One complicating factor here is that we live in a society where
children are sexualized in the media. Advertisements for jeans are
only one example of young girls in provocative poses. Does
anyone really believe that a beauty contest for four-year-olds
where the contestants have teased hair and makeup and sing "I
Wanna Make Love to You" is all about college scholarships?
Where is the outrage when children are exploited in that way?

Another factor is the growing body of research that indicates
that while adult-child sex is legally and morally wrong, it is not
inevitably harmful. To assume that it is always problematic helps
create "victims" where there may be none and, in the extreme,
creates "abusers" where there may be none either.

Clinicians who work with offenders see this world differently.
They know that there are many reasons why adults have sex with
children. They strive to understand how each individual comes
to behave in the ways that he or she does and, if possible, to
tailor a treatment program for that person. Their objective is to
stop repetitive behavior so that other children will be safe if and
when the perpetrator returns to society.

In this volume we look first at the men and women who
become abusers. We consider the bases for their sexual arousal by
children, their emotional bonds with children, their lack of adult
opportunities, and the factors that cause them to lose control
over their sexual urges. We look at particular groups such as

priests and incest offenders and at organizations that promote sex with children.

Determination of the true incidence and prevalence of child sexual abuse, discussed in chapter 2, is difficult because of the wide variability in sampling techniques. Clinical and legal samples are not representative of the population as a whole. The true incidence of problems that result from the sexual contact is generally overestimated. In some cases, problems can be created by therapeutic interventions themselves.

For some individuals, the effects of sexual victimization are devastating and often manifest as post-traumatic stress disorder. Chapter 3 examines the great deal of work now being done in an effort to understand the neurobiological correlates of this disorder. Childhood abuse can also damage trust, self-confidence, faith, and the capacity for intimacy later on. There is some evidence that maladaptive personality styles may also be the result of early sexual abuse.

The treatment of survivors follows that for post-traumatic stress disorder: recognize the trauma, control the response to it, and integrate it into life experience. Chapter 4 will consider the recovered memory controversy and particular treatments including psychotherapy, sex therapy, cognitive behavioral therapy, and eye movement desensitization and reprocessing.

A number of sophisticated programs for the treatment of sex offenders are discussed in chapter 5. Most of them attempt to change arousal patterns and build skills for better adult relationships and community integration. There is not a great deal of evidence that they actually change the recidivism rate. Those individuals most likely to reoffend before treatment are still likely to reoffend after it.

The prevention of child sexual abuse, an elusive goal, is examined in chapter 6. Most programs address "stranger danger" despite the fact that the vast majority of offenders are known to

their victims. Organizations such as the Catholic Church and Boy Scouts of America have developed preventive measures to protect both the children and the adults in their programs. Sex offender registries are now required in every state; their value, however, is limited.

Chapter 7 discusses groundbreaking work in the neurobiology of trauma responses that may help to determine which factors are associated with increased vulnerability or increased resilience to traumatic events. Some of this work applies to offenders as well. Brain imaging to determine which areas are activated or deactivated and genetic studies of various neurotransmitters are part of this research.

In thirty years of work with both victims and offenders, I have seen both sides of the story. I hope that this volume will enable the reader to develop a real understanding of the multiple meanings of child sexual abuse.

Understanding Child Sexual Abuse

1. Who Becomes an Abuser?

Each of us is the product of a lifelong series of sexual turn-ons and turn-offs, some reinforced and practiced, some banished from conscious thought, and some resisted every day. Sigmund Freud used the expression *polymorphous perverse* to describe the primitive sexual urges in all of us. Our natural and normal sexual urges become associated with what is happening in the world around us and, in terms of simple behavioral conditioning, events become paired with those sexual urges and become interpreted as sexual turn-ons. Given the right circumstances, any man or woman might become aroused by men, women, children, multiple partners, or animals. Humiliation, power, bondage, or special or specific objects or items of clothing may also become a source of arousal. Potentially then, we might all have "deviant" arousal patterns; most of us, however, choose not to act on them.

Sexual arousal becomes a problem when it leads to the involvement of an unwilling participant. Looking at a centerfold is different from peeking through a window at an unwilling neighbor. Being aroused by underwear is different from stealing that underwear from an unattended laundry basket. A couple may choose to tie one or the other partner to the bed as part of their lovemaking, but that is different from binding an unwilling victim.

Sexual assault is very broadly defined as unwanted sexual contact with another person. Sexual assault on a child, or child molestation, is more narrowly defined but the definition varies from one legal jurisdiction to another. The bottom line is that a child cannot knowingly or willingly consent to a sexual

relationship with a more powerful, older person. Depending on the jurisdiction, to be charged with molestation, the older person must be at least sixteen or eighteen and at least three or five years older than the child. This acknowledges that sexual experimentation between younger peers does exist but that sexual contact between a child and an adult man or woman is wrong. However, violation of a social norm does not inevitably equate with harm to the child.

Not all child sexual abusers are pedophiles. The Diagnostic and Statistical Manual of the American Psychiatric Association, 4th Edition (DSM IV), defines *pedophilia* as one of the *paraphilias* or recurrent and intense sexual urges and sexually arousing fantasies under "deviant" circumstances. Here, *deviant* refers to nonhuman objects of desire, suffering or humiliation by the person or partner, or involvement of children or other non-consenting persons. Pedophiles are aroused by and fantasize almost exclusively about prepubescent children. *Ephebophile* is a term used to describe people who are aroused by pubescent or early adolescent children. Individuals who have sex with children without the exclusive urge and/or fantasy would not technically, then, be pedophiles or ephebophiles. A true pedophile or ephebophile, on the other hand, might have urges and fantasies about sex with children and never act on them. Two alleged examples of this are the respected nineteenth-century British academicians Charles Dodgson (Lewis Carroll) and Sir James Barrie. Both apparently fantasized exclusively about children but sublimated those urges into writing about Alice in Wonderland and Peter Pan, respectively.

Seen from this perspective, "child sexual abuse" is a social construct. Our society believes that sexual contact between adults and children is wrong. It does not matter that the ancient Greeks waxed poetic about men having sex with boys

or that in some cultures children were introduced to sexual behavior by designated relatives. It does not matter that child prostitutes approach men in the streets. It does not matter that children are naturally curious about sexuality. It does not matter that the abuser can rationalize or blame the victim, saying, for example, that the child asked for it, it was educational, or the devil made him do it. No such rationale is valid in this social context. What does matter is that sex with children is an abuse of power. There are, however, a number of studies of boys who initiated sex with adults and felt that they possessed the power in the relationship. Despite this perception, the adult would have been criminally liable if discovered.

Historically there have been a number of attempts to classify and understand the people who have sex with children. Nicholas Groth, a psychologist with the Connecticut Department of Corrections, differentiated between so-called fixated and regressed pedophiles. According to his theory, some people never mature and the objects of their sexual desire remain the same as when they were children themselves. They never grow to develop a sexual interest in adults and their arousal is arrested or fixated on young children. Others have "normal" adult sexual relationships but various stressors might cause them to return or regress to an earlier immature sexual interest in children. By our definition, this group might not even be considered true pedophiles. Both patterns occur and the difference is important because there is hope for controlling future bad behavior in the latter group. Another theory holds that there is a special dynamic in incestuous families and that this form of sexual behavior is different from sexual assault by strangers. One erroneous belief is that an interest in children is part of a homosexual orientation. Some people believe that there might be a genetic predisposition or other physical explanation for attraction to

children. No single formulation is helpful in understanding why some adults have sex with some children. Both men and women may be abusers and they may be so for different reasons.

In the 1980s Sharon Araji and David Finkelhor at the University of New Hampshire developed a comprehensive model to explain the dynamics of child sexual abuse. After reviewing many studies, they determined that significant variables in the behavior pattern formed four clusters: sexual arousal, emotional congruence, blockage, and disinhibition. Their elegant system has not been widely adopted because many child advocates mistakenly believe that it shifts the blame to the victim. This is only one example of how clinicians who come to the area of child sexual abuse as child advocates see the world differently from those who try to understand the perpetrator.

The Araji-Finkelhor model postulates that elements from each of the four clusters must be present for sexual abuse of children to occur.

Sexual arousal. Not everyone finds children sexually attractive or even believes that children can be sexual objects. Those who do have often had sexual experiences when they were children themselves and have grown up in a family or culture that condoned the view of children as sexual objects. This so-called cycle of abuse is not inevitable and is actually less common than might be assumed. The majority of child victims do not become abusers, but some do. Sexual behavior itself is not necessarily arousing. An object or behavior becomes arousing when it is associated with the positive experience of pleasure. The most common pleasure in this context is orgasm, and the most common way to achieve orgasm is through masturbation. Masturbation is a completely normal activity known to almost everyone. Few of us masturbate with

an empty mind, and the fantasies that routinely and reliably turn us on have been reinforced, sometimes hundreds of times, by a pleasurable orgasm. For most of us, the fantasy objects mature as we do, but if the recurrent fantasy object is an idealized child rather than an idealized young adult centerfold, then the person who has such a fantasy might be at increased risk for acting on it. Studies that monitor sexual arousal have shown that many adolescents and adults respond positively to pictures of children as well as adults. The potential for sexual arousal to children is greater than we might imagine, but few people collect pornographic images of children and even fewer produce them for sexual gratification.

When the United States Supreme Court was asked in 1964 to define pornography, Justice Potter Stewart famously replied, "I shall not today attempt to define [it] . . . but I know it when I see it." Pornographic material is that which appeals to one's prurient interest, but not everyone's prurient interest is the same. In 1970 the U.S. Commission on Pornography found the material itself to be harmless. Looking at pictures does not cause deviant behavior; those individuals with deviant arousal seek appropriate pictures. The reason that there is a wide range of material available in any commercial sex shop is that pornography is an individual preference associated with individual arousal patterns. A man turned on by garter belts and high heels would probably not be turned on by animal images. A pedophile would have no interest in images of adults having intercourse unless, perhaps, a woman had small breasts and shaved her pubic hair or a man had shaved his body hair. When high-quality commercial pornography is not available, many individuals will produce their own images. This is especially true for pedophiles, as child pornography is illegal. Many normal adults will be sexually aroused by a variety of stimuli, including images of children.

Many deviant adults will respond to a range of stimuli as well, but pedophiles appear to be an exception—their primary interest is children. Child pornography is illegal and does not appeal to everyone; therefore, the possession or collection of such material seems to be a reliable indicator of a persistent and acknowledged arousal pattern. It is important to understand that, for those who do find children sexually arousing, this arousal feels perfectly natural and they wonder how people could be aroused in any other way. They may realize that others do not approve, but this does not make the urge any less compelling. A classic literary example of this is Vladimir Nabokov's Professor Humbert Humbert, whose loving descriptions and driven pursuit of his "nymphet" Lolita serve to act out his fixated preadolescent fantasies about a girl named Annabel.

Emotional congruence. Most of us no longer identify emotionally with children or try to relate to them as equals. For some, however, it is more comforting and satisfying to act like a child or to be with children. The most obvious explanations for this are developmental delays and immaturity, but those with chronic low self-esteem and lack of self-confidence are simply more comfortable relating to children than to adults. These are not adults who coach or teach children how to play a game; these are adults who join in the game as peers.

Blockage. Some adults who are sexually attracted to children do have a committed relationship with another adult. Most do not, and for many of those who do, sex is not part of that relationship. A man may fail to be turned on because adults are not sexually arousing; he may feel inadequate as an adult partner because of erectile dysfunction or premature or delayed ejaculation. His partner may be sexually unavailable because of physical or emotional absence or disability, sexual dysfunction such as problems with arousal, pain, or orgasm,

or a conflict in the relationship. Failure to establish an adult relationship may be the result of choice or the consequence of inadequate social skills to establish and maintain one. In some cases, a person is unable to maintain an intimate bond with another adult. This inability to bond may be due to circumstances where the first interactions with caregivers were characterized by neglect, rejection, physical abuse, or perceived abandonment and the child failed to attach to those important people. When the child felt bad for whatever reason, there was no one available for support. These individuals grow up without positive relationships in their lives and without the capacity to develop close bonds with others. Some abusers maintain a sexually appropriate adult relationship for show and continue to seek sexual gratification from children.

Disinhibition. The fourth factor simply means that the desire to have sex with children is not controlled or inhibited. There can be many reasons for this. Cultural or family rules may not prohibit and may even encourage sexual contact between children and adults so that the need to avoid such behavior is not internalized. If bonding with an infant is a powerful inhibitor of future sexual abuse, then fathers who are absent or stepfathers or mothers' boyfriends who have no early relationship with the child are more at risk to abuse that child later in life. Some individuals may take advantage of opportunities for sexual behavior with children because of poor impulse control. A severe mental illness manifest as delusional thinking or memory impairment may override previously well-established boundaries. Drug and/or alcohol intoxication may result in short-term suspension of boundaries, as may acutely stressful situations such as death, divorce, or job loss. Obviously, more than one of these conditions can occur at the same time.

Within the framework of these dynamics, there are many paths to becoming a sexual abuser. One perpetrator who has achieved exceptional notoriety of late has been the "pedophile priest." The John Jay College of Criminal Justice study of all priests in the country was reported to the United States Conference of Catholic Bishops in February 2004. The investigators found that approximately four percent of priests had sexually abused a minor child in the last fifty years. Most of the men had graduated from seminary before 1979. At that time young boys were encouraged to retreat from society to a community of similar young men who were indoctrinated with the idea that sexual activity was the original sin. Their sexual identity became "fixed" at the time they left the outside world. When they finally returned to society, they were sexual twelve-year-olds in the bodies of adult priests. The priestly culture of celibacy made no provision for adult sexual relationships and the objects of their sexual interest were children. When a priest did offend, he was usually reassigned and protected by the hierarchy so that, on average, it was twenty-five years before the abuse was reported.

A. W. Richard Sipe, a psychotherapist and former priest, has worked extensively with abusive priests. He attributes much of the problem of abuse to what he calls the "homosocial" secret world of the priesthood—a sexually immature, all-male culture of power and reward. Often inadequately prepared in the higher meaning of celibacy, young priests are left to struggle alone with their preadolescent and adolescent sexual conflicts. According to Sipe, some later abusive behavior by these priests may be attributed to their own adolescent experimentation, some to the culture of abuse in some seminaries, and some to the inherently "evil" ones who choose the vocation for the powerful role of "Father" and easy access to children. Priests are trusted and so have easy access to children.

Other predatory abusers have to work harder to be close to them. They may supervise youth groups or coach youth sports. But they still have to isolate potential victims. Most discover tricks that work for them and evolve into modi operandi. First, they must identify potential victims and test them for vulnerability.

Children gather around when someone takes a puppy to the park. A "steady ender" who always holds the end of the rope and never wants to jump is always welcome on the playground. Kids feel special when an adult wants to play catch or ride bikes with them. A relationship can develop in an Internet chat room where some adults try to pass as children while others openly solicit sex. Once a child has shown interest, the predator begins to test the limits of invasion of personal space. He does this in such a way that he can deny the true intention. "Sorry, I didn't mean to touch you." If the child does not resist then there are invitations for a ride home, or ice cream, or special time together to isolate the child from others and create an opportunity for the sexual approach. The adult characterizes the child as special but, paradoxically, as someone who would never be believed if a parent were told. The perpetrator often rationalizes his behavior in terms of education for the child or as a response to a child's need for closeness. Molesters often believe that children initiate sexual contact and consent to it.

Youth groups such as Boy Scouts, Boys' Clubs, and Big Brothers are often the targets of pedophiles. The boys are there and access is easy. Parents are not always involved in these programs and it is relatively easy to isolate vulnerable boys—especially in a tent on a campout far from observation. Boys looking for role models instead meet predators. Common approaches to lure boys into intimate relationships include massage, initiation rites, pornography, and alcohol.

For many years, the Boy Scouts in particular played down the problem. Their priority was damage control and the avoidance of bad publicity and the potential loss of members. When they learned of abuse, local Scouters asked the perpetrator to resign but usually failed to report the abuse to the police. For decades, the national office of the Boy Scouts of America maintained a confidential file of men who should not be allowed in the program; however, reports to that file from the field were haphazard and, according to freelance journalist Patrick Boyle, the man in charge of those files never read them anyway. Abusers would simply move to another area and rejoin the program.

In the late 1980s a series of high profile lawsuits allowed the public to see the confidential files. By then this file contained the names of nearly two thousand men who should not be allowed to rejoin. Only then did the Scouts take steps to educate their membership about the potential danger within their ranks.

One group of molesters without an access problem is the one that abuses children within the family. *Intrafamilial sexual abuse* is a better term than incest because authority and trust within a household are more important factors than the biological relationship between the individuals concerned. The dynamics of sexual acting-out within families are as varied as the dynamics of any other form of child sexual abuse. One important factor appears to be the failure to develop the nurturing, protective bond thought to be characteristic of parents. Male abusers are often absent and fail to bond with the child when it is an infant. They also feel incredibly entitled to control their households. Sexual abuse of a child is often part of a pervasive pattern of physical and sexual abuse in the home, often in the context of intoxication. Wives are beaten and sexually abused. Pets are tortured. Children who intervene

often meet the same fate, but they might even without intervening. If a mother is absent, a child or series of children may be forced to take on maternal duties, including that of sexual partner. It is striking how often mothers appear to be unaware that a child or succession of children is being abused. Abusers often blame the child as deserving of punishment because they are bad or promiscuous. Pledges to secrecy and threats of retribution for disclosure are nearly universal.

Springfield, Massachusetts, psychologist Denise Gelinas has described an intrafamilial pattern she calls the "parentified child": a child, usually the oldest daughter, functioning in a maternal role. This pattern may carry on for generations. Mother marries a dependent, immature man who needs to be taken care of. When she has children of her own and childcare becomes physically and emotionally exhausting, she withdraws from her husband. He feels angry, abandoned, and incapable of supporting her. As they withdraw from each other, he escalates his demand for nurturance. The situation worsens with each new child in the family.

Mother then turns to the oldest child for support and assistance in meeting the family's needs. She withdraws more from her husband, who now seeks nurturance from the parentified daughter. This is especially true if the father is not confident enough or feels restrained from developing relationships outside the family. The demand may escalate if the father suffers a loss of support or self-esteem such as the death of a parent, loss of a job, personal injury, or birth of yet another child. At first the daughter will try to meet his emotional needs: she asks about his day, listens, and tries to comfort him. If he then shows poor judgment, impulsivity, or an enhanced sense of entitlement, and especially if alcohol is a factor, the relationship may proceed to physical intimacy as well. The father confuses sexual contact with nurturance.

The daughter keeps her secret from the mother because she is responsible for mother's well-being as well as father's. Guilt, low self-esteem, and lost childhood are the consequences. The pattern becomes internalized and she may well choose a husband who is dependent, exploitive, and abusive—just like her father. Her daughter may then fall into the same role and the pattern will continue for generations.

There are common elements in these patterns even though the paths to the sexual abuse of children differ. The abuser first acknowledges children as sexual objects, either in their own right or as substitutes for adults, and then makes an emotional connection with the child to satisfy his own unmet needs. He typically lacks a meaningful adult sexual relationship and fails to develop a social conscience that says that sex with children is wrong, or an intervening variable causes previously good judgment to be temporarily or permanently suspended.

When women molest children, the dynamics are different. The definition of a pedophile as one in whom "the act or fantasy of engaging in sexual activity with prepubescent children as the preferred or exclusive method of achieving sexual excitement" rarely applies. In fact, there are essentially no reports in the literature of women who meet that definition. There are reports of female teachers having sexual relationships with male students, but none of those women have been examined by a mental health professional who then wrote up the case and determined that they were true pedophiles. Several years ago, my colleagues and I looked at the records of nine women who were evaluated for child sexual abuse. The other 591 records in the sample, or 98.5 percent of the accused, were men. The most striking feature was that most of the women offended in the company of a dominant male partner who instigated the abuse. They also tended to display

significant emotional or intellectual impairment that interfered with nurturing and bonding behavior and suspended their judgment about what was appropriate contact with their children.

The cycle of abuse is not a universal phenomenon. Every abused child does not go on to become an abusive adult. Only one-third of male offenders report having been victims themselves. A 2001 British study followed abused boys into adulthood and identified only twelve percent who became abusers. These individuals often had a history of family violence, maternal neglect, and abuse by a woman as well. Abusing others is most common among adolescent males and females for whom abuse is either a model of interaction with younger children or a way to master their own sense of being out of control. Abusing women rarely report a personal history of abuse.

Most adults who are sexually attracted to children have internalized the societal prohibition of such behavior and do not act on that attraction. Others want to overturn that prohibition. The North American Man-Boy Love Association (NAMBLA) puts itself forward as an advocacy group for a misunderstood minority group like gays or transsexuals. Their website states that their mission is to "end oppression of men and boys who have mutually consensual relationships."

It is instructive to quote from NAMBLA material: "Boys often approach sex with great interest and enthusiasm, so that consensual sexual experiences are not harmful. . . . Once sexual experiences have become known to others, secondary harm to youngsters can be induced by inappropriate reactions of parents, police, social workers, lawyers and other adults, where no apparent harm results from the sexual contact itself. . . . If people are not taught to despise their bodies and fear sex, if their sexual choices are not forced upon them by others, and

if they are not subjected to harsh or stigmatizing reactions to their sexual choices and experiences, they will not be harmed by having sex, regardless of how old or young they are or with whom they have sex." The site goes on with glowing testimonials from boys who thought that sex with men was a wonderful, positive experience. At one time, the site recommended that members join the Boy Scouts for easy access to children. There is also a so-called Women's Auxiliary of NAMBLA that supports consensual relationships between women and girls.

Proponents of adult-child sex often point out that such relationships have been perfectly acceptable at some times and in some cultures. Until the late nineteenth century, the age of consent in England was ten. Current Dutch law gives twelve as the age of consent for sex. There have been several societies where adult-child sex was seen not as gratifying adult desires but as beneficial to the child. Early explorers noted that the receipt of adult semen was believed to facilitate growth and development among the Siwans of North Africa, Aranda of Australia, Marquesans, Tahitians, and Etoro and Kaluli of New Guinea. Child brides have been given in ancient China and elsewhere to solidify political and social alliances. The ultimate goal was that the bride produce a child; however, the timing for that was apparently left up to the husband. In Cameroun, sex with a child is seen not as sexual abuse but as a property crime and is punished by having to make a payment to the child's family. When they reach puberty, young girls are frequently given in marriage in polygamous sects in the western United States, some Muslim sects, and some gypsy tribes. Western culture, however, finds adult-child sex unacceptable.

Sex with children is still legal, or at least not actively discouraged, in some parts of the world. Child prostitutes usually come from the poorest class of a society and may be

homeless and drug-dependent. Some are sold by their parents or kidnapped, and selling sex becomes an economic necessity for them. A prostitute in Thailand makes twenty-five times as much as she would in most other occupations.

An estimated half million prostitutes in Thailand are under age 16, 40 percent younger than eleven. There are nearly as many in India, where an even higher percentage is younger. With around sixty thousand child prostitutes, the Philippines is a distant third in Southeast Asia. Most of these prostitutes are girls, but in Sri Lanka an estimated thirty thousand boys are in the trade. Brazil leads South America in child prostitution with perhaps as many as half a million children, both boys and girls, selling sex. The practice also appears to be growing in Colombia and Benin.

Because child prostitution may be culturally acceptable in these areas (e.g., 75 percent of Thai males have paid for sex with a prostitute) it has become the attraction for what has come to be known as "sex tourism." At one time, joining a tour group to Bangkok to have sex with kids was no more difficult than going to Orlando to see Mickey and Goofy. For those patrons the desire for a virginal, disease-free child partner was as much a fantasy as Peter Pan. United States government outrage over the practice has caused some of these countries to be less hospitable to sex-seeking tourists, but for economic reasons the practice is not likely to go away.

It is probably not necessary for a pedophile to travel to South America or Southeast Asia for sex with a child. A 2003 Norwegian survey of all the adolescents in school in Oslo reported that 1.4 percent had sold sex. More boys than girls were sellers and more than half had done so more than ten times. The researchers suggested that the rate among adolescents who were no longer in school might be much higher, as the sellers still in school also acknowledged problems with

delinquent behavior and the use of alcohol and drugs. These problems are more frequent in dropouts. It is quite likely that every city in the United States has a group of such children—homeless, drug-dependent, and selling sex in order to survive.

Proponents of adult-child sex often argue that children desire sexual self-determination. While it is true that children have always experimented and rehearsed sexual behaviors with peers, this is not the same as exploitation by adults. Children neither develop the same sexual scripts nor recognize the same sexual meanings as adults. To them, a kiss is just a kiss.

2. Who Is at Risk?

In child sexual abuse, the more powerful adult takes advantage of the weakness he sees in the child. Being an altar server for an abusive priest, attending a day care center run by an abusive operator, playing for a pedophile Little League coach, or hugging a too-friendly uncle are all activities that put children at a higher risk of abuse; however, not all children in such circumstances become victims. A strong sense of right and wrong, self-confidence, and a willingness to resist and then to report inappropriate behavior all protect against abuse. These same characteristics may also lessen the traumatic response if abuse does occur. Children who lack these attributes are at risk.

No child asks to be sexually abused. Many are. Determining the exact incidence of child sexual abuse is difficult, but surveys have generally found that 10 to 15 percent of American men and 15 to 25 percent of American women were exposed to at least one unwanted sexual experience as children. There appears to be no difference in incidence based on ethnic background. Rates of abuse among African Americans, Hispanic Americans, and Native Americans are the same as those for non-Hispanic white Americans, although individuals, families, and cultural groups may process the experience differently. These differences would be a fruitful area for research.

In 1974 the Child Abuse Prevention and Treatment Act made reporting mandatory in all states. The requirement to report suspected abuse applies to health-care workers, school personnel, childcare providers, social workers, law enforcement officers, and mental health professionals; some states include film processors, emergency medical technicians, and firefighters.

Eighteen states require any person who suspects abuse to report it. Reporting overrides all privileged and confidential communications except those between attorney and client. Clergy privilege (formerly known as priest-penitent privilege) takes many confusing forms. Most states exempt information obtained in confession from mandatory reporting, but they may or may not except "spiritual advice" or the even more vague "communication made in a professional capacity." Fifteen states (Alabama, Alaska, Arkansas, Georgia, Hawaii, Iowa, Kansas, New York, Ohio, South Carolina, South Dakota, Vermont, Virginia, Washington, and Wisconsin) had no obligation for clergy to report abuse in 2003.

"Were you sexually abused as a child?" A survey question like this one elicits a variety of responses, depending upon a number of factors including exactly how the question is phrased, who asks it, and who answers it. The range of activities included in "child sexual abuse" is the first variable. Sometimes the surveyor provides a specific list of sexual activities, but respondents often must decide the definition for themselves. Normal sexual experimentation before age twelve and consensual sexual activity between peers should be excluded. One survey's "sexual experience" might include seductive speech, verbal solicitation, sexual talk, or exposure to a "flasher." Another's "sexual contact" might include kissing or fondling. Fondling may or may not include non-genital touch. Some people do not consider oral or anal contact as real sex. Others do not consider that sex has occurred without penetration. The wide variety of definitions does not minimize the potential impact of any of these behaviors on the victim, as all may have lasting consequences; however, variable definitions make it difficult to compare studies and to determine the true incidence of abusive behavior.

Information gathered in a face-to-face interview where there is clarification and followup in the context of a dialogue differs from that gathered on an anonymous questionnaire. Individuals may give a negative response to a general question but provide a more positive response when asked a specific question. Male and female interviewers are given different responses to the same question. The life experiences of under-graduate students in introductory psychology courses are different from those of the general public. Surveys of patients in a community mental-health center or hospital emergency room provide more positive responses to questions about sexual abuse. Patients in a sexual-dysfunction clinic acknowledge the highest rates of abuse of all.

Remote events are more difficult to recall than recent ones. A complicating factor is the demonstrated inconsistency in adolescent reporting of any sexual behavior. In one study of 217 adolescents in a STD (sexually transmitted disease) clinic, eighty-one reported a history of sexual abuse on their initial interview but only fifty-four answered the same questions positively seven months later. Stress at the time of response and a changing relationship to the questioner are possible explanations for the variable responses, but the responses vary nonetheless.

Younger children who report sexual abuse may be even more inconsistent in their narratives. They may be more sug-gestible when interviewed by poorly trained investigators. They may also be more easily caught up in the mass hysteria of accusations of alleged preschool or day-care sexual abuse. The use of anatomically correct dolls was once considered an essential part of such interviews; however, playing with such dolls is not part of the average child's experience and curiosity about the dolls may contaminate the fact-finding interview.

They are no longer in common use. Hysterical reports of escalating sexual abuse culminating in satanic rituals and murder should be particularly suspect. The FBI has never documented a case of ritualistic satanic child sexual abuse and murder in the United States. Accusations that arise as part of custody disputes must be taken seriously, but also considered in context. Shortcomings in survey and interview methodology must not detract from the fact that millions of children in the U.S. experience sexual contact with adults each year.

One of the better recent statistical studies was done by sociologist Edward Laumann and his colleagues at the University of Chicago in the early 1990s. They studied a representative sample of the general population of the United States and found that 12 percent of males and 17 percent of females had been "sexually touched when children." They specifically excluded non-touching behaviors such as exhibitionism and restricted the definition of "contacts" to those by persons older than fourteen with persons younger than twelve. All age groups reported the same percentage of sexual touch, suggesting that there has been no change in the actual rate of child sexual abuse over the years. Girls were most often touched by men and more often by adult men than by adolescents. Their most vulnerable age range was seven to ten. Boys were more likely to be touched by adolescent females, followed in frequency by adolescent males and then by adult males. Boys tended to be older than girls when victimized and were more likely to have had vaginal intercourse with female abusers than girls were with male abusers. Approximately 70 percent of both men and women reported that they were victims of a single abuser, even though there may have been many instances of abuse. Victims knew the vast majority of abusers as family friends or relatives; only 4 to 7 percent of child sexual abusers were strangers.

By contrast, a similar study done in Britain at the same time was seriously flawed. The surveyors did not ask about masturbation because it was "embarrassing." They did not ask about childhood sexual experience and eliminated any data about "first intercourse" prior to age thirteen because it was "inappropriate to the task." The resulting compilation of sexual behavior in Britain was not useful for comparison.

Gelinas noted that intrafamilial abuse is usually initiated when the child is between the ages of four and nine. Younger children are more compliant and may believe that what is happening to them is really just affection or training. They are also more susceptible to threats and bribes. Abusers exploit the child's loyalty, need for affection, desire to please, and trust. Before the age of eleven or twelve the sexual behavior is usually limited to fondling or oral-genital contact. Vaginal insertion is difficult with a prepubescent girl. Anal insertion does happen.

The abusive behavior in Gelinas's sample was limited to a single incident in 17 percent of cases, lasted less than six months in 24 percent, six to twelve months in 19 percent, one to five years in 31 percent, and more than five years in 9 percent. Gelinas noted that the abuse usually ended at age fourteen or fifteen when the victim realized that such behavior was wrong and was able to spend more time away from home. More force would have been required to continue the abuse and the perpetrators were not prepared to apply it.

Child sexual abuse may result in psychopathology in some individuals, but it does not follow that every incident of abuse produces a psychological disorder. Many studies have been done to survey healthy populations and determine how many people in the sample had sexual experiences as children and how many developed psychological problems. In July 1998 Bruce Rind at Temple University and colleagues wrote an article entitled "A meta-analytic examination of assumed properties

of child sexual abuse among college samples" in the *Psychological Bulletin*, a publication of the American Psychological Association (APA). A meta-analysis is not new research but a method of employing common statistics to compare and compile data from previously published studies. These psychologists tried to test the premise that in a population with a history of child sexual abuse, this exposure would cause intense psychological harm on a widespread basis for both sexes. They examined fifty-nine studies with a combined sample size of nearly sixteen thousand college students, both male and female. Fourteen percent of the men and 27 percent of the women reported a history of child sexual abuse. They looked for correlations of the incidence of child sexual abuse with eighteen symptom clusters, including eating disorders, depression, anxiety, dissociation, sexual adjustment, and somatization, and found that the frequency of problems in the abused group was not different from that in the group that had not been abused. They factored in severity of abuse, factored out adverse family situations such as family violence, conflict, and lack of support, and still found no correlation. When the sexual contact had been experienced as consensual, a significant percentage of respondents (11 percent of the women and 37 percent of the men) thought the experience was positive. Similar percentages reported their response as neutral. Women forced into an incestuous relationship did have more distress, but this was often temporary. The group concluded that while child sexual abuse was morally and legally wrong and obviously devastating to some individuals, it was not inherently and inevitably harmful. They then went on to make what would be a very controversial suggestion: Do not label every single incident as abuse; call it by the value-neutral term "adult-child sex" unless it results in problems. These findings were consistent with research that found that the vast majority

of adults exposed to trauma do not develop post-traumatic stress disorder.

The report that every incident of "abuse" did not cause irreparable harm was met with skepticism by some people, including individuals who accused Rind and the APA of praising pedophilia. The situation was further exacerbated when NAMBLA praised the article on its website. Under intense pressure including the first-ever Congressional resolution condemning a scientific study, the APA apologized for publishing the paper. Irate member psychologists then accused the APA of abandoning good social science in favor of political appeasement. Ultimately, the APA retracted the retraction, but the firestorm has yet to subside. Critics also continue to argue that the college student subjects of the studies had not yet had enough life experiences to precipitate pathological symptoms; however, no lifetime studies have ever been done.

In 2003 meta-analysis made a repeat appearance in the *Psychological Bulletin*. Emily Ozer and colleagues at the University of California–San Francisco analyzed sixty-eight published reports looking for predictors of post-traumatic stress disorder in individuals exposed to stressful events. They found that intense negative emotions such as fear, helplessness, horror, guilt or shame, or a dissociative experience at the time of the trauma were associated with later psychopathology. Although child sexual abuse as a stressful event was not included as one of the factors in this study, the findings appear relevant.

Statistical profiles may be helpful in clarifying population patterns, but they say little or nothing about individual children at risk. The major risk factor for a child to become a victim of sexual abuse is to grow up in a family or neighborhood with an abuser in it.

The family setting most conducive to sexual abuse is one in which the male authority figure has absolute control. As

previously noted, such control is often manifested by physical abuse and threats as well as emotional and sexual abuse. The rules are unpredictable and punishment for violation of them is harsh. Children are isolated from peers and threatened with terrible consequences if they reveal anything. In such a setting, children become passive and compliant and may develop a strong attachment to the abuser in an attempt to ward off attacks. It is not unusual for an older sibling to assume a powerful, sexually dominating role. The same pattern may occur in institutional settings. Low power, low status, and physically or developmentally "different" individuals in boarding schools, camps, and similar settings as well as in families may more easily become victims.

When a friend, neighbor, or extended family member is the abuser, that individual usually follows the expected modus operandi. That adult assesses potential victims for vulnerability, and the child who appears isolated or needy or particularly passive is approached first. A child with an absent parent might be at higher risk of such an approach from a trusted or respected adult but, statistically, the vast majority of victims come from intact families. The abuser first tests the potential victim with seemingly accidental touches in order to gauge the response. If the child welcomes the attention or responds passively, then the contact will increase. Such contact may occur in such a way that the abuser may continue to frame it as innocent or accidental and the victim may question his own judgment about the appropriateness of the touching. The abuser may then introduce sexual talk or pornography into the relationship and a curious, needy, or passive child may continue to go along. Eventually the abuser will find a way to be alone with the child and act out the adult's own sexual desires. A similar pattern of need and curiosity will cause

children to agree to meet someone with whom they have chatted on the Internet, or to go off with a stranger.

Some pedophiles are avid users of the Internet. Pornographic pictures of children are available through file-sharing or for a price. These may be useful in developing fantasies for arousal or masturbation. Many pedophiles find validation for their interests on pedophile-oriented websites. In addition to networking with other pedophiles for files, leads, and mutual reinforcement, some use the Internet to actively seek victims. They frequent chatrooms used by children of the age and sex they prefer and gather information about particular participants. Anonymity may embolden some children and help overcome inhibitions about personal contact. Once a potential victim is identified, the pedophile may take a trust-based approach and try to build a relationship that may eventually lead to a meeting, or may solicit sex directly. Rendezvous sites are generally in neutral territory such as a motel near the child's home. The pedophile may believe that this kind of approach will avoid detection and apprehension—and they may be correct, as long as the child with whom the potential abuser exchanges sexually explicit e-mails is not an undercover police officer.

Statistical profiles of perpetrators are notoriously unreliable. The number of convictions for sexual offenses is not a good measure of their actual incidence. Most offenses go undetected, and others are plea-bargained to different, nonsexual crimes such as criminal threatening or assault. Clinical and legal samples are not representative of the population as a whole. In 1985, psychiatrist Gene Abel and colleagues published information about a unique group of offenders. These New York City men were invited to volunteer for participation in a program in which they would remain anonymous and

their crimes would not be reported. They were asked to list all the sexual contacts they had ever had with children. This study could not be done today because of the requirements for mandatory reporting. Heterosexual pedophiles (not incest perpetrators) averaged 120 "completed or attempted molestations" up to that point in their lives. Homosexual pedophiles averaged 205 separate victims. Some have argued that these men were lying to impress the clinicians. However, a 1990 New Hampshire State Prison survey included incest perpetrators and the average number of lifetime victims was twenty. Three percent acknowledged more than 100 victims. In general, priests tend to have fewer victims, but some number them in the hundreds as well. Potentially, one man can do a great deal of damage, and a few molesters can put a large number of children at risk for future difficulties.

3. What Are the Effects of Abuse?

Survivors of rape, child sexual abuse, domestic abuse, natural disaster, terrorism, hostage-taking, and war—all situations in which a person is rendered helpless by overwhelming forces—may show the characteristic manifestations of post-traumatic stress disorder (PTSD).

The American Psychiatric Association's Diagnostic and Statistical Manual (DSM IV) identifies three clusters of symptoms that characterize PTSD: persistent reexperience of the traumatic event, persistent avoidance of stimuli associated with that trauma and numbing of general responsiveness, and persistent symptoms of increased agitation. Reexperience may be manifest as recurrent and intrusive recollections or flashbacks of the event, recurrent distressing dreams of the event, and psychological or physiological distress when exposed to internal or external cues that resemble an aspect of the traumatic event. Avoidance and numbing are seen as efforts to avoid thinking, feeling, or talking about the trauma, to avoid activities, people, or places associated with the traumatic event, and to be unable to recall certain aspects of that event. The traumatized individual shows decreased interest in significant activities, feels detached from others, and has a restricted range of affective responses and the sense of a foreshortened future. Increased arousal takes the form of difficulty in falling or staying asleep, irritability and outbursts of anger, difficulty in concentrating, hypervigilance, and an exaggerated startle response.

A diagnosis of complex post-traumatic stress disorder proposed for DSM V emphasizes that chronic abuse and abuse in childhood result in additional symptoms. These include difficulty with regulation of emotion, dissociative symptoms, and somatization or related physical complaints. Such individuals experience a damaged sense of self, chronic guilt and shame, feelings of ineffectiveness, and a chronic sense of despair and helplessness. They may idealize the perpetrator, have difficulty in establishing and maintaining trusting relationships, and display a tendency to be revictimized or to victimize others.

Harvard psychiatrist Judith Herman, M.D., summed this up by noting that such traumatic events may produce profound and lasting changes in physiologic arousal, emotion, cognition, and memory as well as in the integration of all these functions. Survivors are "disconnected from the present" and continue to react to life experiences as if they were anticipating, experiencing, or responding to the earlier trauma.

The nature and severity of symptoms may vary depending upon the age at which the trauma occurred. Younger children with fewer defenses and underdeveloped coping strategies are more susceptible to negative aftereffects and may even show significant impairment in personality development. More frequent or severe abuse, especially the trauma of penetration, sadistic abuse for the arousal of the perpetrator, extended time of abuse, a close relationship to the abuser, and the experience of multiple abusers may all increase the negative impact.

Study of the neurobiology of post-traumatic stress disorder is still in its infancy, but animal studies and limited human studies suggest that it is a discrete illness with specific physical manifestations. The human body responds and adapts to stressful events. The nervous and endocrine systems play a key role in this.

First, we need to review basic neuroanatomy. The central nervous system consists of the brain and spinal cord. The

Figure 3.1 Cross-section of Brain

peripheral nervous system carries incoming sensory input and outgoing motor responses to the rest of the body. The autonomic nervous system serves internal organs and has cells within the central nervous system. The autonomic nervous system has two parts: the sympathetic nervous system responds when the body needs to react with "fight or flight," and the parasympathetic nervous system takes over during periods of rest and restoration. The brain consists of three parts: the most primitive innermost layer, the brain stem, is responsible for basic functions such as heart rate and respiration; the central limbic system regulates affect and emotion; and the outer neocortex governs thought and language.

The neuroendocrine system sends chemical messages (hormones or neurotransmitters) to start or stop responses. The hypothalamus in the brain stem controls the endocrine glands via the pituitary gland. In response to pituitary regulation, the

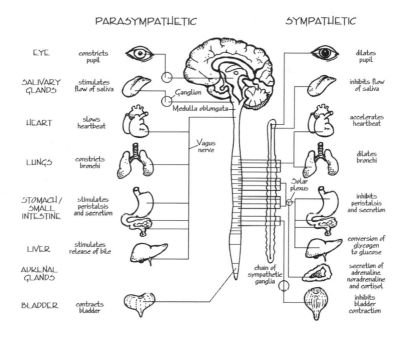

Figure 3.2 Autonomic Nervous System

adrenal medulla (inner part) secretes the catecholamines adrenalin (epinephrine) and noradrenalin (norepinephrine) and the adrenal cortex (outer part) releases cortisol, a gluco-corticoid. The locus coeruleus (literally, "blue place") in the brain stem and sympathetic fibers themselves also produce catecholamines. Serotonin is also a catecholamine and neuro-transmitter whose role is uncertain in the stress response but appears to modulate the norepinephrine effect.

The catecholamines stimulate the sympathetic nervous system to increase heart rate, blood pressure, oxygen con-sumption, and blood sugar, all of which mobilize the body for action. The glucocorticoid cortisol elevates metabolism and blood sugar but also exerts negative feedback on the

hypothalamus and pituitary so that a high level of cortisol closes the loop and shuts off the mobilization of
catecholamines.

When a potentially stressful event occurs, the neocortex
interprets and coordinates incoming stimuli and plans a response. This input is filtered by the hippocampus and amygdala. They are located in the medial temporal lobe, but are
directly connected to the limbic system via the Papez circuit.
The hippocampus receives the motor and sensory input and
puts it into historical context. It provides relational memory
and also determines if information should be stored in long-
term memory or be forgotten. The amygdala assigns emotional significance to the input. The amygdala also contains
many opiate and benzodiazepine receptors which, if blocked,
can interfere with the conditioned emotional response. If
assessment determines that "fight or flight" is indicated, the
locus coeruleus releases catecholamines, the adrenal glands are
stimulated via the hypothalamic-pituitary axis to release both
catecholamines and glucocorticoids, and the body is activated
to respond.

In most people, the stressful event ends and all these
processes return to homeostatic, or balanced, baseline function. This is not true for individuals with post-traumatic stress
disorder. Their systems continue to be sensitive to external
stimuli and they are in a state of permanent alert, prepared for
further attack. Atlanta researcher J. Douglas Bremmer, M.D.,
has reported changes associated with this condition in the
hypothalamic-pituitary-adrenal (HPA) axis and noradrenergic
systems as well as in benzodiazepine, opiate, dopaminergic
and various neuropeptide systems that modulate function in
the hippocampus, amygdala, and prefrontal cortex of the
brain. Neuroimaging studies have shown that post-traumatic
stress disorder is associated with a decrease in hippocampal

volume. (It is not currently known if the hippocampus actually shrinks or if individuals susceptible to PTSD have smaller hippocampi to begin with. Neuroimaging studies have not been done on pre-morbid, asymptomatic individuals.) Without feedback about past experience and current context, the amygdala has exaggerated activation and attaches additional emotional significance to the incoming stimuli. Catecholamines are mobilized and full sympathetic arousal occurs. In individuals with post-traumatic stress disorder, cortisol is also mobilized but is quickly metabolized and does not reach a level sufficient to turn off catecholamine production. This state of hyperarousal causes hypervigilance and increased startle responses. Activation of the amygdala is associated with activity in the visual cortex that may be the basis for flashbacks and nightmares. One small aspect of the original trauma—a look, a sound, a smell, or a feeling—may trigger the whole memory picture along with all the negative emotional responses that accompanied the original event.

Boston psychiatrist Bessel Van der Kolk postulates that the extreme arousal associated with trauma floods the brain with neurotransmitters, "stamping in" vivid sensory memories of the event. These events may take the form of fragmented images that, when stimulated by present emotion, produce a vivid "reliving" of the past trauma in the present. The emotional memory system is housed in the amygdala and operates independently of cortical control. The system operates in a rapid response mode and this hypervigilance may produce sustained fear. These responses become automatic and beyond conscious control.

The overall effects may be so powerful and painful that the survivor becomes overwhelmed and cannot deal with them. Detachment, numbness, and passivity may extend to a complete denial of reality. It is not uncommon for a victim of

abuse to describe the sensation of being outside the body, sometimes floating in the air, and dispassionately observing what is going on. Some theorists believe that depersonalization may progress to somatization disorder (formerly called hysteria), borderline personality disorder, and dissociative identity disorder (formerly called multiple personality disorder). The sense of disconnection may be so great that the survivor resorts to self-injury to feel something—anything. Paradoxically, the sight of one's own blood may be soothing and experienced without pain. The survivor is ultimately unable to integrate the multiple levels of response and finally assigns them to different selves rather than acknowledging that they are part of the same complex emotional reaction. Identity may be fragmented, but the individual is able to survive and to present a superficially normal façade to the world.

The world does not feel like a safe place for the sexually abused child and adult survivor. Basic trust is shattered. This is especially true when the perpetrator is a member of the family. The victim is often isolated from friends and other family members and has to deal with an often unpredictable abuser. The child may think, "Will they be angry, or drunk, or act as if I were special?" When other supposedly caring family members passively ignore—or worse, actively enable the abuse—basic trust is eroded even further. This can be devastating to potential future relationships, especially to sexual relationships. Intimacy and sexuality are often split. A survivor may want closeness but fear sexual contact and avoid both.

Debra Kalmuss, Ph.D., from the Columbia School of Public Health, defines *sexual health* as the ability to "derive pleasure from and make decisions about one's sexual and reproductive behavior and identity in a manner that respects one's own sexual rights and desires as well as those of others."

For someone on whom sex was first imposed on terms dictated by another more powerful person and not associated with pleasure, sexual health may be an unrealized dream. Sexual dysfunctions including low desire, inability to experience orgasm, vaginal muscle spasm (vaginismus), and painful intercourse are common. Sexual behavior is learned, and imposed sex is not a positive experience.

University of Nevada–Reno psychologists Leah Leonard and Victoria Follette have suggested two theories to explain the relationship between child sexual abuse and sexual dysfunction. One is experiential avoidance, a process that includes an unwillingness to reexperience painful thoughts, feelings, and memories associated with the experience of sexual abuse. The other is emotional avoidance, a process where sexual intimacy is associated with emotional pain. Both must be addressed as part of the therapeutic process.

Unwanted sexual activity may result in physical trauma, bleeding, infections, vaginal discharge, itching, urinary tract infections, abdominal pain, or pregnancy. Some clinicians have suggested that early sexual activity causes an increase in sex hormone levels, hypersexuality, and early puberty. Statistics do confirm that survivors of child sexual abuse engage in consensual sexual activity at an earlier age than do their non-abused peers. They are also less likely to use barrier forms of contraception such as condoms and are therefore more at risk of contacting sexually transmitted diseases including HIV/AIDS. They have more partners, more pregnancies, and more abortions and are more likely to be victimized in the future. Some survivors may prostitute themselves in order to have more control over who has access to their bodies and to make their partners pay for it.

Self-doubt as a result of early victimization is common. The child asks, "What did I do to deserve this?" The

perpetrator often tells a female child that she is bad or just like mother and does indeed deserve the abuse. The confusion is compounded if there is any erotic aspect to the abuse, such as involuntary sexual arousal. Rewards from the abuser in the form of treats or privileges also lead to conflicting emotions. Negative feelings may make the survivor more susceptible to self-medication with drugs or alcohol, or the negativity may be converted to physical symptoms requiring relief by prescription medication. Self-identification as a "victim" or "damaged goods" may result in low self-esteem and create a pattern of self-destructive behavior.

Overall, the victims, and then the survivors, lose faith in what is supposed to be the natural order where children are cherished and protected, and where they are safe in the family and community. For them the world becomes unjust.

Young children who are abused may not express themselves verbally, but may demonstrate disorganized or agitated behavior as well as highly sexualized play, inappropriate sexual knowledge, or sexually aggressive behavior. They may act out in their play what they are unable to verbalize. They may have nightmares, but these may not be specifically sexually oriented. They may regress developmentally and wet the bed, suck their fingers, or bang their heads. If the perpetrator was a stranger, the child may demonstrate separation anxiety. All are warning signs of possible abuse. Symptoms of trauma or infection would have few other explanations. Undeveloped psychological defenses and intellectual abilities make it difficult for these victims to understand that they are not responsible, and basic issues in trust and gender identity may be compromised.

Adolescents have multiple developmental tasks to accomplish. They must become independent of parental control, achieve mature sexual expression, develop the capacity for

intimacy and understand how it differs from sexuality, choose an adult role, and crystallize their personal value systems. Sexual abuse complicates each of these tasks. If the abuser was a parent, the conflicting feelings of attachment and hostility must be worked through or else there is great potential for future negative relationships and revictimization. Mature sexual expression gives way to aversion to sexual behavior, sexual identity confusion, and sexual dysfunction. Promiscuity—the seemingly opposite behavior—is also common. For girls, a history of sexual abuse is associated with increased teen pregnancy. Such a pregnancy is often accompanied by stress, substance abuse, and the birth of small, poorly developed babies. Teenage girls who sexually abuse younger children are likely to report a history of sexual abuse themselves. The capacity for intimacy is compromised by an inability to trust others. Adult role choices may be limited as the perception that the world is a safe place is shattered. Self-image may include worthlessness, shame, and guilt.

Any issues unresolved in adolescence will carry over into adulthood, and the resulting behavior patterns become harder to change. The intimate invasion of personal space leaves many survivors with an inability to trust other people to be close to them. The bodily invasion also seems to predispose survivors to focus on somatic responses and to develop a wide range of physical complaints. Not surprisingly, the complaints often involve lower abdominal or pelvic pain, bladder dysfunction, irritable bowel syndrome, premenstrual dysphoria, painful menstruation, chronic fatigue syndrome, and headache. It is also not surprising that women with these complaints are reluctant to seek gynecological services including Pap tests for cervical cancer screening. When they do see a physician, the often vague nature of the complaints results in a disproportionate number of surgical procedures. They may also avoid dental care.

A recent Australian study has shown that, among a group of adult women treated for depression, those with a history of child sexual abuse showed more deliberate self-harm and were more likely to have been recent victims of violence than were their depressed peers. Long-term physical consequences of abuse can become manifest in a great many ways.

According to Gelinas, low self-esteem and guilt are characteristic of the grown-up parentalized female child. These women had no rights as children and feel that they have no rights as adults. They blame themselves for being victimized and do not believe that they deserve better. (Interestingly, abused younger sisters of the parentalized child show all the traumatic effects but not the low self-esteem and guilt. They know they were not responsible.)

These women have problems with parenting; it is difficult for them to balance discipline and affection, especially after their children start to talk and make demands. Children learn to use guilt and feel entitled to have their demands met. Husbands are still needy. Often the new mother's parents continue to make demands on her as well. As she tries to deal with all these demands, she feels progressively more inadequate and withdraws. She may then begin to lean on her oldest daughter, and the cycle continues.

Such a woman may lead a life of quiet desperation until some external event triggers symptoms; promotion or selection for a position that presumes a level of competence she doesn't feel or her daughter reaching the age at which she was abused are examples. She may not demonstrate classic post-traumatic stress disorder but a disguised presentation such as chronic depression, impulsive acting out, or confusion. These women will not spontaneously report their history of abuse, and may not even realize that there is a cause-and-effect relationship. They will disclose if asked.

Progression of the psychological effects of child sexual abuse is associated with particular personality disorders. "Association" is the operative word here because, although a large number of people with these disorders report a history of child sexual abuse, many abused individuals do not develop those patterns of behavior.

Depersonalization, dissociation, and dysphoria are key elements of PTSD and are characteristic of somatization disorder, borderline personality disorder, and dissociative identity disorder as well. A person will not show all these disorders at once or sequentially, but will settle into one pattern over time.

To meet the DSM IV criteria for somatization disorder, a person must have had multiple physical symptoms beginning before age thirty and lasting a number of years. These must include pain symptoms in at least four different sites or functions, two different gastrointestinal complaints, one sexual or reproductive symptom other than pain, and one pseudoneurological symptom, none of which can be explained by a known medical condition such as an arthritic joint, an ulcer, a uterine tumor, or nerve damage.

People with borderline personality disorder have problems with relationships, self-image, affect, and impulse control. They may do anything to avoid perceived abandonment, have intense and unstable interpersonal relationships, struggle with poor self-image, feel chronically empty, demonstrate inappropriate and intense anger, and they may dissociate. Many of these symptoms are carried over from the relationship between victim and abuser.

Individuals with dissociative identity disorder take this defense to an extreme. They have two or more distinct personality states with different and enduring patterns of perceiving, relating to, and thinking about the environment and themselves. These different identities recurrently control that

person's behavior, and things that happen to one identity may not be accessible to the memory of another. A history of a helpless child leaving conscious memory behind in the face of overwhelming force seems very relevant.

While the physical, sexual, and psychological consequences of child sexual abuse are generally the same for boys and girls, boys may deal with them differently. First, a boy is less likely to report abuse. If the perpetrator is female, he may not want to acknowledge that he was overpowered or controlled by a woman. He may also feel that the experience of having sex with an older woman is positive, but his subsequent behavior might indicate that this is not the case. If the perpetrator is male, the child may feel shame, embarrassment, a sense of emasculation, or the fear of being labeled as gay by others. Male anger may be expressed in acts of aggression or criminal behavior. While abused males show the same patterns of reckless and dysfunctional sexual behavior as abused females, they are more susceptible to sexual identity confusion. This is particularly so for prepubescent victims. There seems to be a statistical association between the experience of child sexual abuse and adult male homosexuality. The operative word again is association. Boys who are most attractive to male perpetrators may show effeminate behavior, lack secondary sex characteristics such as facial and pubic hair and a deepening voice, and have no peer support or strong male figures with whom to identify. These factors may contribute to a homosexual identity formation without the complicating factor of sexual abuse, but the experience of sexual activity with an older male may serve to crystallize such an identity. The same does not appear to be true for postpubescent males who may already have identified themselves as committed heterosexuals. No information is available about sexual identity distortion in girls who are abused by older women.

The effects of child sexual abuse on parenting behavior are variable. The boundary violations of abuse could result in survivors exhibiting a range of punitive, permissive, or overprotective behaviors toward their own children. They may reject or mimic their own parents' model of the parent-child relationship.

4. Treating the Survivor

If the worst effects of child sexual abuse are best described in terms of post-traumatic stress disorder, the best treatment approaches should follow that same paradigm. For those traumatized individuals who continue to show symptoms months or years after being abused, formal psychotherapy may offer the best chance for a better life. In general terms, the survivor (no longer a victim) must recognize the trauma, control responses to it, and integrate it into the life experience.

In her classic 1992 book *Trauma and Recovery*, Dr. Judith Herman discussed three stages of recovery from any traumatic experience: safety, remembrance and mourning, and reconnection. It is important to remember that the recovery process is not always a straight-line progression; overlap and falling back are common. Recovery cannot begin until the trauma is identified, acknowledged, and, particularly in the case of child sexual abuse, ended. Herman stresses the importance of a supporting and trusting relationship with the therapist as critical for the recovery process to take place. Telling the truth and establishing clear boundaries are integral parts of the therapeutic relationship.

Safety requires that the actual threat of danger is over and that the abuse has ended. For the abused child, this means an end to the relationship with the abuser and social support for the termination of that relationship. For the adult survivor, it means that society assigns responsibility to the abuser and harm to the victim. To restore a sense of order and justice, the perpetrator should be held legally responsible in terms of both punishment and restitution. Unfortunately, the justice system

and courts do not always provide that, and the adversarial nature of the proceedings is not always a positive experience for survivors and may even lead to additional trauma. Victim advocates in the prosecutor's office and with the police can be particularly helpful in preparing and supporting survivors in dealing with a system seemingly designed to be traumatic. Cross-examination of a witness, particularly a child, can be brutal.

In addition to control of the environment, control of the body, both physical and psychological, is an integral part of safety. It is helpful at the outset for the clinician to educate the patient as to what the usual aftereffects of abuse may be. Symptoms such as hyperarousal, insomnia, or depression must be addressed specifically and directly. An overstimulated sympathetic nervous system needs to be calmed. If relaxation techniques such as biofeedback, meditation, yoga, strenuous exercise, or progressive relaxation are not effective in calming stress, then a range of medication is available to target anxiety, insomnia, depression, or other overwhelming symptoms.

Historically, physicians have prescribed sedation with alcohol, opiates, or barbiturates to deal with such symptoms; patients have also used these substances for self-medication. The results are poor because medication dependency and abuse often follow. Once it was determined that increased sympathetic arousal and increased catecholamine activity in the brain were responsible for much of the clinical picture, it became possible to utilize more specific pharmacological agents. Specific serotonin reuptake inhibitors (SSRIs), for example, reduce catecholamine levels and are now the treatment of choice. In controlled studies, SSRIs paroxetine (Paxil), sertraline (Zoloft), and fluoxetine (Prozac) produce moderate but statistically significant decreases in reexperiencing, intrusive hyperarousal, and numbing symptoms. Beta

blockers such as propanolol (Inderal) and clonidine (Catapres) reduce sympathetic outflow from the central nervous system and block intrusive symptoms, especially flashbacks and nightmares.

Anticonvulsant mood stabilizers such as carbamazepine (Tegretol) reduce flashbacks and angry outbursts by blocking nerve potentiation. In severe cases, low doses of the new so-called second generation antipsychotic medications such as risperidone (Risperdal) may calm the most disturbed patients. The mechanism of action of these drugs is unknown but they are antagonists at dopamine and serotonin receptor sites. Benzodiazepine tranquilizers such as diazepam (Valium) and lorazepam (Ativan) are usually not helpful. These drugs may eliminate the symptoms temporarily, but in doing so may actually interfere with the resolution of distress and increase depression. They do not deal with the cause of the distress, only with the manifestations. Their use also raises the risk of dependence and abuse.

A few studies have been done, mostly with SSRIs, where medication was used to augment psychotherapy. Results from the combined approach are generally better than those with either one alone.

A person cannot engage in psychotherapy if the level of distress is high and the symptoms overwhelming; however, it is possible to begin the healing process by recognizing, naming, and charting the circumstances that produce symptoms and the responses to them. One can then develop plans to ensure safety and reduce distress. Some don't even require a therapist for implementation. For example, if heightened tension and insomnia are associated with the onset of darkness, then a nightlight may provide some sense of security. If panic attacks follow a walk past a perpetrator's house, then a different route home from school or a companion might be helpful.

If depression routinely follows family visits, then such visits should be modified or eliminated. Clearly it is necessary for family members and caregivers to understand and support this process so that they do not amplify the stress or even cause additional trauma to the person trying to recover. Once patterns are identified and modifications in place, the survivor has some control and responsibility for identifying the situations, behavior, or places that trigger symptomatic responses. The person then ceases to be a helpless victim, and is, instead, an active survivor.

Herman calls the second stage of recovery remembrance and mourning. Here the traumatic story is told and acknowledged to be a part of the survivor's life history. Grief for that which is lost—childhood, trust, or family—is expressed and the strong internal core of the self is validated and empowered to move on. This is the stage where psychotherapy is most helpful and it must occur in the context of a trusting therapeutic relationship.

There are often many therapists to choose from. It is always appropriate to ask a potential therapist about training, credentials, therapeutic approach, and experience with survivors of child sexual abuse. Special qualifications such as experience working with children, certification in sex therapy, or the ability to prescribe medication may be considered. It is more important to work with an experienced and trusted clinician than to take whomever the insurance panel provides. Good therapy is a solid investment in future happiness.

There is always some degree of transference in any therapeutic setting. The patient will transfer some feeling about people from the past onto the therapist. Working with those feelings is part of the therapeutic process. However, some feelings can be a barrier to treatment. If the therapist were consciously or unconsciously identified with the abuser, an

enabler, an unsupportive grandparent, an aggressive police detective, or anyone else from the patient's past, that would affect the therapeutic relationship. It is essential that the patient always feel safe enough to be truthful. Similarly, the therapist may have a similar range of feelings toward the patient. This is countertransference. Seeing a patient as a whiner or as incompetent or as in need of rescue can all be problematic. Both parties in the therapeutic relationship must agree to the treatment contract: the goals, the process of achieving those goals, and the boundaries of therapy. A therapist who overidentifies with the patient as victim (especially if the therapist has a similar history of abuse), sympathizes with the perpetrator, experiences "witness guilt" or secondary trauma by listening to the patient's story, wants to rescue the patient, or considers or even experiences boundary violations in some other way should talk this through with a colleague or supervisor. The therapist is also bound to uphold his part of the treatment contract. Any therapist who works with survivors will be stressed by their histories and their pain and will need to deal with that stress response.

Experts agree that "telling the story" and coming to terms with it are essential to recovery. We know that repression is probably the most common defense mechanism used in dealing with trauma. The bad memories are pushed out of conscious awareness but continue to influence behavior. The therapist's role is to help the client deal with the past in an open-minded and supportive manner but not to direct the memory process.

Survivors are particularly adept at reading their therapists. They learned that careful attention to their abuser's statements, moods, and emotions was essential to survival and they transfer those observation skills to the therapeutic relationship. Experienced in altered states of consciousness, they

may be extremely suggestible. It is therefore essential that the therapist not have preconceived notions about the origin of symptoms, as the client may pick these up. This is the basis for the repressed and recovered memory controversy.

In 1988 Ellen Bass and Laura Davis published *The Courage to Heal: A Guide for Women Survivors of Child Sexual Abuse.* They offered advice on coming to terms with known abuse but also observed that "if you are unable to remember any specific instances like the ones mentioned above but have a feeling that something abusive has happened to you, it probably did." Some therapists took this further and suggested to clients that their presenting symptoms were certainly due to child sexual abuse and then pressed them to recall the memories they had repressed. They used techniques such as hypnosis, age regression, guided fantasy, and dream interpretation. Some clients did recover memories including those of abuse in infancy. In 1991 *People* magazine published articles by comedienne Roseanne Barr Arnold and former Miss America Marilyn van Derbur detailing the memories of child sexual abuse that they had recovered. This helped open the gate, and, in pursuit of punishment and restitution, a number of civil and criminal suits were filed against alleged perpetrators as a result of recovered memories.

In a seminal article in the May 1993 *American Psychologist,* Dr. Elizabeth Loftus, then at the University of Washington and now at the University of California–Irvine, questioned "the reality of repressed memory." She pointed out that child sexual abuse was actually remembered vividly by most who reported it and that cognitive memory patterns probably did not exist before age three. Early sexual abuse provided a simple explanation for whatever problem brought the patient to therapy and this explanation was often reinforced by the therapist or by a peer group of survivors. Although these patients

honestly believed that their "recovered" memories were true, Loftus pointed to many studies, including thirty years of her own research, that showed that false memories could be implanted with leading questions, suggestions, and false feedback. The subject would not only insist that the memory was real, but would also add details. Newspaper and magazine articles, reports by other victims, and suggestions may have been incorporated into the memories of a client's own "abuse." The memories were honest but false. This "false memory syndrome" was used to counter the recovered memory claim. Loftus has expressed the fear that false claims would only serve to trivialize the experiences of true victims.

As one might suppose, these divergent points of view were often argued in court with expert testimony on both sides. Judicial bodies tried to make legal sense out of conflicting claims and then issued guidelines. One representative decision was that of the New Hampshire Supreme Court in *State v. Hungerford*. Joel Hungerford's daughter had recovered memories of incest in therapy and had filed criminal charges against him. In ruling against the admission of these recovered memories, the justices wrote that the state must demonstrate "that the reasoning or methodology underlying the testimony is scientifically valid; and that it is capable of empirical testing and can properly be applied to the facts at issue." They found that it was not. They also questioned the percentage of recovered memories known to be false and noted the importance of the age of the witness at the time of the assault or assaults, the length of time between the event and the recovered memory, the presence or absence of verifiable corroborative evidence, and the circumstances of the recovery of the memory. The final point referred specifically to therapy whose purpose was to recover memory. The justices were particularly critical of therapists who ordinarily seek hidden memories, believe that

many problems stem from sexual abuse, and validate allegations of abuse that do arise. As a result of this decision, Hungerford sued his daughter's therapist for damages. The suit was apparently settled out of court.

Washington, D.C., psychologist Christine Courtois developed practice guidelines for therapists of adult clients who do not initially disclose child sexual abuse. The therapist should obtain a good psychosocial history and personality assessment but not uncritically accept or confirm suspicions without corroborating evidence. The clinician should remain neutral, avoid leading questions, and remember that normal childhood memory is spotty. No symptom or set of symptoms is due exclusively to child sexual abuse and other possibilities must be considered. The clinician should keep accurate records, preface possible allegations with "the client reported" or similar words, and seek supervision for all such cases. Hypnosis is generally inappropriate, as is referral to an incest survivors group, if the client does not have conscious memory of abuse. Both have the potential for increased suggestibility. General support groups may be helpful. The therapist should not propose family confrontations or lawsuits, but should be supportive if these do occur.

The goal of treatment at this stage is to achieve an intellectual or cognitive understanding of the abuse, accept it emotionally, and change behavioral responses accordingly. Traditional individual or group psychotherapy is primarily an intellectual exercise. This therapy provides support, empathy, and the opportunity to explore the meaning of the event in the context of life experience and the inner sense of the self. The client works through and integrates the trauma so that there is no further need for maladaptive defenses.

In more active behavioral treatment, the goal is to recondition the response to trauma in order to promote change.

Through the process of *collaborative empiricism* the cognitive behavioral therapist helps the client attach the proper emotional responses to the cognitive triggers and find alternative behavioral responses to them. In *Stress and Trauma,* University of Missouri psychologist Patricia Resick describes several of the behavioral techniques that are combined with cognitive processing. In stress inoculation training, the client gradually approaches the fear-producing stimuli and extinguishes the unwanted response. The first skill taught in this and other behavioral approaches is relaxation training. In progressive muscle relaxation, the client focuses on each major muscle group of the body in turn by first tightening the muscles to help identify them and then relaxing them. The client develops a relaxing mental image to accompany the physical relaxation. With practice, the client should ultimately be able to visualize that special image, breathe out, and let go of all bodily tension. Cognitively, the client practices thought stopping. When a negative thought comes to mind, the person literally says or thinks, "Stop!", focuses on the current reality, and considers alternative ways to deal with the situation. At other times, the client practices covert rehearsal by imagining potentially fearful situations and alternative responses. The final step is to apply all of these techniques—relaxation, thought stopping, and alternative responses—in day-to-day circumstances to engage in the feared behaviors or situations. Successful engagement should be positively reinforced by acknowledgment of that success.

Exposure-based treatment may be either strictly in the imagination (covert) or done in the real world (overt). In systematic desensitization, the therapist and client together create a hierarchy of fears. In a relaxed state, the client imagines a situation briefly and repetitively and then relaxes as soon as a fear or anxiety is experienced. By backing off and then

approaching again, the client should be able to advance through the hierarchy. The well-rehearsed relaxed response should then be transferable to the real world. In "flooding," the client combines relaxation with the experience of prolonged, real exposure to fear-producing cues. Distress should decrease with each subsequent exposure as the client realizes that nothing bad has happened as a result of that exposure.

These behavioral techniques are combined with cognitive processing. This goes beyond the raw emotional response to the trauma and explores the distorted thinking that has resulted. False beliefs such as "I brought it on myself" or "I should have stopped him" need to be addressed as well.

Trauma-focused cognitive behavioral therapy is particularly helpful for children. One study compared child-centered therapy where abused children talked about trauma at their own pace with trauma-focused cognitive behavioral therapy. In addition to the first group's trying to make sense of the experience and identify more effective future responses, a second group of abused children was encouraged to confront increasingly detailed and distressing abuse-related reminders and memories. This was done in a way that was comfortable for each child. Choosing a method of exposure such as imagery, doll play, drawing, reading, letter writing, poetry, or singing gave each child more sense of control. The children kept journals and discussed them with their non-abusing caregivers. The second group did twice as well as the first at resolving symptoms including depression, behavioral problems, and feelings of shame.

For the therapist dealing with a trauma survivor who was a parentalized child, it is important to remember that despite the abuse, parental loyalty is still strong. The suggestion of early, direct confrontation with the abuser may drive the client away. It is more productive to focus on the illegitimacy

of the behavior, its exploitive nature, and the responsibility of the abuser. It is not productive to stress the illegality of the behavior; the survivor may still be protective of abusive parents, and prosecution is impossible anyway if the statute of limitations has expired. Once the survivor is engaged in therapy, it may then be possible to deal more effectively with parents who may still be making demands on the child whom they abused. It is not helpful to blame a mother for initiating the process if she was a victim of abuse herself.

It is important to continue to address physiological disturbances of post-traumatic stress that interfere with the ability to engage in therapy. While some clinicians would address specific symptoms such as anxiety, insomnia, nightmares, flashbacks, eating disorders, headaches, pelvic pain, or chronic fatigue pharmacologically, others would consider them all to be manifestations of post-traumatic neurobiological deregulation and seek to address them more generally.

One such general approach is called eye movement desensitization and reprocessing, or EMDR. This treatment format was developed by Francine Shapiro, Ph.D., and first published in 1989. Shapiro believes that traumatic experiences leave unprocessed perceptions and that these may be resolved through the accelerated information processing that is EMDR. The clinical protocol involves eight stages that include history taking, client preparation, target assessment, desensitization, installation, body scan, closure, and reevaluation of treatment effects. The therapy itself has no empirical basis other than the observation that the stage of rapid eye movement (REM) sleep is associated with vivid dreams but physical relaxation. More intense negative emotion is correlated with more rapid eye movement. The client is encouraged to visualize the targeted image, rehearse positive thoughts, monitor physical distress and follow the therapist's finger as it

moves across the visual field twice per second for twenty-four repetitions. The client then relaxes and scores the episode. It is important to be able to quantify both the intensity of the image and the degree of distress. A ten-point scale, often in terms of how full a container might be, is used. The client learns to pair a positive statement with the negative image, such as "It hurt but I survived." Over repeated exposure, high-scoring negative images accompanied by positive statements should produce lower scores in disturbance, or more relaxation. The process provides a rapid learning experience where new skills and adaptive behaviors replace dysfunctional ones. The patient is no longer stuck in old patterns and is now able to work through the feeling process.

Proponents hypothesize that the positive and negative aspects of right and left brain function become synchronized and negative cognitions become associated with positive emotions. EMDR practitioners acknowledge that their therapy does not work for everyone, but they believe it can be an effective tool in the therapeutic arsenal. Critics argue that it is simply a new twist on systematic desensitization through repeated exposure. Controlled studies have also suggested that the lateral eye movements are not necessary for improvement; benefits may be an example of client suggestibility.

Other treatment approaches, such as acupuncture and bodywork to free up "muscle memories," have been suggested; anecdotal evidence exists of success with some people, but these approaches have not been subjected to rigorous evaluation.

When a person loses a part of himself, even a negative part such as a dysfunctional behavior, there is grief work to be done. Something has been lost, even if the inner self has been healed. Neurophysiologic symptoms are gone, but so are general fantasies of basic trust, idealized good parents, and a happy childhood. All must be mourned and put to rest.

A person must also accept that it may be too late to get even in terms of punishment or compensation. Anger at parents, school, church, social service agencies, police, or whoever else did not protect and defend the victim is understandable but counterproductive.

Herman's third stage of recovery is reconnection. Here the recovering survivor achieves a different view of the world and his or her place in it. There is now a future to look forward to. Reconnection with other people begins, but sexual intimacy is often the most difficult part of connection to achieve. Most survivors need a patient partner and often a good sex therapist to gradually regain or find the level of trust that will enable them to enjoy sexual desire and orgasm. A certified sex therapist has many hours of training and supervision and is recognized as such by the American Association of Sex Educators, Counselors, and Therapists. The therapist must not push the client into the more traditional sex therapy exercises such as massage because that will only increase resistance. Oregon social worker Wendy Maltz has suggested a number of touch exercises that may be more appropriate for resistant survivors. These include touching a variety of sensual objects in a basket, clapping hands with the partner, writing letters on the partner's back with a finger, creating a safe "nest" for calm nonsexual touch and having a clear system of signals for controlling touch. In these exercises, the survivor feels safe, has time to deal with associated negative images, and maintains emotional intimacy as sexual stimulation increases.

A survivor might seek personal empowerment through training in self-defense, sport, or a wilderness experience where danger is faced and overcome and survival acknowledged. Confrontation of offending or collaborating family members might be carefully considered, but only in the context of empowerment and not with an expectation of remorse

or apology. Desecration of a grave may offer some sense of closure but obviously is not going to affect a deceased perpetrator.

Survivor groups can provide mutual support and engage in the mission of making the public more aware of child sexual abuse and its aftereffects. A support group can also be extremely helpful in dealing with regressions that inevitably occur.

Recovery is never truly complete; seemingly unrelated events are stressful and may revive old feelings and symptoms that had been successfully resolved. Changes in physical health and interpersonal relationships are part of life. Uterine cancer, death of a parent, or birth of a child are obvious stressors—but so are promotions, children starting school, and the death of a pet. Stress happens and must be conquered again and again.

Post-traumatic growth is a relatively recent concept. University of North Carolina psychologists Richard Tedeschi and Lawrence Calhoun have reported positive changes that may result from trauma. These include improved relation-ships, new possibilities for one's life, a greater appreciation for life, and a greater sense of personal strength and spiritual development. Survivors may be more vulnerable, but they are also more sure of their own capacity to survive and prevail. They acknowledge that life circumstances have changed; they are able to adapt and are more emotionally engaged and attuned to existential and spiritual matters. This positive con-cept does not minimize the impact of trauma but provides hope for a better life ahead.

5. Treating the Abuser

"Lock him up and throw away the key." "Castrate him." The former punishment for sexual offenders is practiced in "three strikes and you're out" jurisdictions after a third conviction; the latter is practiced in some Eastern European countries. One takes away access to potential victims; the other takes away desire for sex and the ability to perform. The vast majority of sexual abusers experience neither life in prison nor castration, but society demands that something be done to ensure public safety. Courts order that perpetrators be treated and sometimes even order that they be declared "cured" or "safe" before they can be released. Sex-offender treatment programs respond to that demand. Most operate on a solid theoretical base, but the question remains: do they make any difference?

In 1985 psychiatrist Gene Abel, then at Columbia University, outlined a treatment approach that encompassed five strategies: correct cognitive distortions, provide sex education, promote social skills, decrease deviant arousal, and increase nondeviant arousal. All treatment programs include these strategies, although not necessarily in those terms or with equal emphasis.

Sex offenders often see the world through different eyes. Sex-starved nine-year-old girls jump out of the bushes to attack unsuspecting men; men who touch young boys provide them with an education about how the body works; kids consent to have sex with adults; no harm comes from touching or being touched; daughters should submit to fathers' demands. All these beliefs are wrong, but offenders believe them to be true. Such distorted views must be addressed.

As a group, sex offenders may know less about sex than most people do. They may avoid adult sexual relationships for fear of appearing inadequate or they may really be inadequate. They may often be unaware of the dangers of unprotected sex and not consider the possibility of sexually transmitted diseases or unwanted pregnancy, especially with activity other than vaginal penetration. They may have a lot to learn.

Offenders tend to lack appropriate social skills. They may know how to tempt or threaten a child but are unable to approach an adult to establish a relationship that could potentially become a sexual one. More important, they lack the tools to deal effectively with strong emotions such as anger or a need for comfort and support. They have not been socialized appropriately and need such training.

Deviant arousal patterns need to be extinguished, but first they need to be identified. Certain stimuli, emotions, or circumstances are associated with episodes of abuse. A pornographic video, intoxication, and access are simple examples; however, the scenario preceding sexual acting-out is usually more complex. If there is confirmed arousal to inappropriate stimuli, measures may need to be taken to extinguish it. Potentially, these measures can be quite punitive.

The strategy most difficult to implement is increasing arousal to nondeviant stimuli. A man aroused by the sight of a scantily clad adult of the opposite sex would have a hard time being reconditioned to arousal by being urinated on, viewing a corpse, or whipping someone. Similarly, a man turned on by a prepubescent boy would have difficulty being reconditioned to arousal by the sight of a scantily clad woman. An individual may not be able to change an arousal pattern but can learn not to act on the inappropriate desire it evokes.

Treatment programs employ these strategies in different ways. Almost all occur in a correctional setting after the

abuser has been caught, convicted, and sentenced. Rarely does an individual volunteer that he is abusing a child or children, because that is a reportable offense in all jurisdictions. Such an admission is most probably a call for help and should be taken seriously. While some therapists feel that they can counsel sex offenders one-on-one, they are susceptible to lies, half-truths, and distortions and may be overly invested in seeing themselves as successful. The most effective treatment venue is the therapeutic community with its emphasis on group inter-action. No one understands an offender's con games better than another offender.

A therapeutic community is a highly structured environment where people work together to help themselves and each other. Punishment and privileges are determined by group consensus and peer pressure is important in fostering change. A program typically lasts for several months, with multiple opportunities to observe the progress of other offenders in the program.

Most programs have selective criteria for admission. These generally include a commitment to long-term treatment, adjustment within the institution, absence of severe psy-chopathology, recognition of the severity of the problem, and, most important, full and open admission that everything the victim said and for which he was convicted was true. Denial is cause for exclusion—even though there is no objective evidence that such denial has any bearing on the treatment outcome or recidivism rate. It may make the therapist and especially the prosecutor feel better if the prisoner acknowl-edges guilt, but the incest perpetrator who denies that he pen-etrated his daughter may still have a better prognosis than the serial pedophile who cheerfully admits raping twenty boys.

Prisoners are usually highly motivated to seek therapy. It may be a requirement for early release. Child molesters are on

the lowest rung of the prisoner hierarchy and are often abused themselves in a general prison population. Failure to be selected for treatment means longer and harder time.

The first step in most programs is a treatment contract where the offender agrees to abide by the rules and makes a commitment to behavioral change. Failure to progress in treatment or infractions of institutional or unit rules will result in termination. A psychosocial history and psychological assessment will be completed. At this time, two physiologic measures may be introduced: the polygraph and the penile plethysmograph. The polygraph, or lie detector, does not really detect lies. It detects fear by measuring the physiologic reactions associated with autonomic nervous system arousal. These are increased heart rate, rapid breathing, and sweating of the palms. The measure is used primarily to assess the level of internal response to the denial of guilt in specific offenses and in assessing the validity of the overall history of offenses.

The penile plethysmograph, or phallometer or "peter meter," directly measures penile tumescence (erection) with a strain gauge in response to a range of visual and auditory stimuli. Arousal to standardized slides of a variety of subjects, male and female, young and old, in sexual situations portraying degrees of force and seduction are compared with responses to pictures of consensual sexual activity between adults and neutral controls such as landscapes. Results are helpful in confirming or denying the true objects of arousal, and serial testing can monitor progress within the program. Neither the polygraph nor the plethysmograph has enough validity to be used in court, but they can be helpful in the treatment process once concerns about informed consent and self-incrimination have been resolved.

The first treatment phase focuses on group process and individual awareness as to why the offense occurred. A review

of the four factors and a determination of how they apply to each offender are common. The effects of abuse are made clear with videos and discussions about trauma and often with confrontation by adult survivors of abuse who tell about their own life experiences. Specific groups may address issues peculiar to offenders who were themselves abused as children or who need particular help with acquiring social skills. Self-help groups such as Alcoholics Anonymous or Narcotics Anonymous may also be appropriate, as may Sex Addicts Anonymous. Offenders engage in discussion groups based on relevant books such as *Out of the Shadows* by Patrick Carnes or the sex-offender workbook series developed by William Pithers. The "sex addict" model espoused here must not be allowed to serve as a rationalization for bad behavior, but must rather be a format for behavioral change. Dr. John Bancroft at the Kinsey Institute has cautioned that terms like "sexual addiction" and "compulsive sexual behavior" are misleading because out-of-control sexual behavior has multiple causes. It is often associated with short-term mood disturbance, and the problem of clinical depression should be addressed in these cases.

Specific pharmacologic interventions may occur at this time. The anticonvulsant carbamazepine (Tegretol) may reduce impulsivity. A long-acting benzodiazepine tranquilizer such as clonazepam (Klonopin) may be used to reduce chronic anxiety. There is a high rate of depression among offenders and studies have shown this to be a comorbid condition rather than the result of incarceration. Appropriate antidepressant therapy may be indicated. As noted, the concept of "sexual compulsivity" is a controversial one; however, if there is a driven element to the sexual behavior, medications such as specific serotonin reuptake inhibitors (Prozac, Zoloft, or Paxil) may be helpful. Studies have shown that increasing

central serotonin levels does reduce a high sex drive in rats
and mice. As is the case with survivors, it is difficult to engage
offenders in the treatment process as long as they remain
focused on symptoms. Relief of these symptoms promotes
that engagement.

The second phase is a continuation of the first augmented
by specific group therapy experiences such as anger management, self-esteem development, stress management, or sex
education and awareness. Individual work may target specific
patterns of arousal. The offender may be asked to keep a "fantasy diary" to monitor his sexual thoughts. Various behavioral
techniques are then utilized to extinguish deviant fantasies.
Covert sensitization is an internal mental process that pairs a
deviant sexual fantasy with an image such as arrest or public
humiliation. Aversive conditioning pairs the fantasy with an
actual noxious stimulus. Rotten meat and ammonia seem to
be favorites, but electric shock has also been employed.
Ideally, the diary should document a decreasing frequency of
potentially troublesome fantasies and the plethysmograph
should confirm this.

A somewhat more controversial technique is known as
masturbatory satiation. The individual is asked to masturbate
quickly to orgasm and then to continue to masturbate for
twenty or thirty minutes to his favorite deviant fantasy.
Normally, there is a refractory period after one orgasm before
a man can have another. Trying to satisfy the fantasy with a
nonresponsive penis should extinguish the power of the fantasy. One potential problem with this technique is that, in a
young, multi-orgasmic man, it might actually reinforce that
fantasy. Another problem is keeping the individual on track
with his fantasy. This is best done by ongoing tape recording
of fantasies in each practice session. Someone must then monitor the tapes to ensure compliance.

Masturbation is also suggested as a way to increase nondeviant arousal. A positive scenario involving consenting adults is developed and rehearsed. The individual then masturbates to orgasm with that scenario in mind. That should also be monitored carefully by audiotape, as there is a good deal of room for deception in reporting the actual content of the fantasy.

When behavioral treatment fails, medication may be introduced. Medroxyprogesterone acetate (Depo-Provera) and Cyproterone acetate (not currently approved for use in the United States) are anti-androgens; they lower testosterone levels by inhibiting gonadotropin secretion. The result is "chemical castration," as testosterone is required for both sexual arousal and sexual performance. Men with very low testosterone levels have no desire for sex and no erections. Use of these medications interferes with the monitoring of arousal patterns, and the effect lasts only as long as the medication is used because these drugs do not affect the body's ability to synthesize new testosterone.

Family therapy may also be introduced at this phase. Family members may participate in separate groups in order to understand offender dynamics, learn to protect children, and provide mutual support. Couples therapy may help improve communication or address specific family dynamics or sexual dysfunctions.

In the third phase of treatment, the offender continues his own work and may mentor new arrivals in the therapeutic community and lead some of the self-help groups. Emphasis turns to healthy relationships and relapse prevention. The individual must recognize the thoughts, feelings, and situations that contribute to offending behaviors and learn how to intervene at the earliest possible point in his cycle. He does this by rehearsing alternative, more socially appropriate responses.

At the conclusion of this treatment phase the abuser should accept full responsibility for his behavior, be able to recite the cycle of thoughts, feelings, and behaviors that precede offenses, be able to quickly control the deviant urges, and recognize the need for ongoing treatment in the general prison population or in the community at large.

The prediction of success or failure at the end of a treatment program is an inexact science. Abusers inevitably report themselves cured and promise never to offend again. Therapists try to be more objective, but each has an unconscious tendency to believe that his success rate is better than anyone else's. Belief in success probably helps prevent burnout in dealing with this extremely difficult population. Ongoing training and support is essential for any therapist who works with such a high-risk group.

A number of scales have been developed to try to make an objective assessment of potential dangerousness. These range from simple questionnaires to extensive computer-scored assessments. The least valid are those that include offender self-evaluation; after any treatment program, an offender will know what responses are socially desirable and answer accordingly. From an actuarial perspective, history is an excellent predictor of future offenses. Recidivism is most associated with offenders who have had a male victim, a younger victim, multiple victims, and extrafamilial victims. Sadistic sexual behavior in the past, pro-offending attitudes, and a lack of intimate relationships are also associated with re-offending. The single best predictor is continued arousal to children as measured by the penile plethysmograph. Sophisticated offenders can fake interest in other subjects because no one else really knows what they are fantasizing to the picture on the screen; however, continued arousal after completion of a treatment program is not a positive outcome. The final report

should be as objective as possible, and success is always conditional. If the thoughts, feelings, or circumstances that trigger an offense are no longer controlled, the danger of an inappropriate sexual response is greater.

As previously noted, the treatment model has a solid theoretical base but the question remains: does treatment work? The short answer is, probably not. The rate of re-offending for treated and untreated groups seems to be about the same. The man who fondled a particular child when intoxicated will probably not re-offend if he stays sober, access to that child has been terminated, and he does not want to repeat the prison experience. He may now understand everything about the dynamics of his behavior, but this person was not going to re-offend anyway. On the other hand, the serial pedophile may learn to say all the right things during the treatment program but not change his behavior.

A 2004 Canadian study compared the recidivism rate of 321 untreated offenders with that of 403 who had undergone treatment over a twelve-year period. One in five in each group re-offended. Twenty percent does seem to be the generally acknowledged rate of recidivism for sex offenders. Considering that completion of a sex-offender treatment program may take years off a prison sentence, treatment may actually increase the risk to the public by releasing offenders too early.

Despite the depressing statistics, it is unlikely that programs will change anytime soon. Prosecutors and defense attorneys want them to exist. If the accused could not plea-bargain for treatment, there would be even more trials in an already overburdened court system. Sex-offender treatment is a growth industry; many therapists and institutions have a vested interest in its continuation. Sex-offender treatment is not the only modality of unproven value to enjoy popular support (Drug Abuse Resistance Education and abstinence-only sex education

come immediately to mind). Perhaps those third-strike and Eastern European courts have the solution after all. The recidivism rate for those serving life sentences is zero and between 1 and 10 percent for those who have been castrated.

Realistically, then, it is extremely difficult to alter the arousal patterns of a pedophile. Of the four factors identified by the Finkelhor group, sexual arousal and emotional congruence are products of early childhood experience and are part of who the person is. By addressing issues of blockage and disinhibition, the therapist may modulate the response to sexual desire; however, because circumstances change, there are no guarantees to future control of acting-out behavior. As Boyle quotes one man on completion of a correctional treatment program: "I wasn't convinced it was wrong; I was convinced I shouldn't do it." This man, and others like him, should never be alone with a child again.

6. Prevention

Primary prevention is the ideal result of any intervention in a pathological process. The preventive model of public health was developed with reference to infectious diseases and is most easily applied to them. In primary prevention, a healthy person does not contract the disease. Immunization against smallpox and mosquito control to eliminate yellow fever are examples of primary prevention. In secondary prevention, a person may be asymptomatic but have disease risk factors or preclinical disease. Pap smears for cervical cancer, PSA screening for prostate cancer, and weight control and smoking cessation where there is a strong family history of heart disease are all measures that allow early intervention should an existing disease be discovered, and then allow time for effective treatment. Tertiary preventive measures take place after a person shows signs or symptoms of illness but before secondary problems have occurred. Debriding a wound to prevent gangrene or treating AIDS to prevent a viral or fungal superinfection accomplish this.

The preventive model is more difficult to apply to post-traumatic stress disorders, including those caused by childhood sexual abuse. In an ideal world, trauma would be eliminated. If children were made aware of the danger and internalized such devices as "recognize, resist, and report" or "say 'no' and tell someone" when confronted with a high-risk situation, those measures would prevent the trauma and, by extension, prevent post-traumatic stress disorder. If researchers could study resilient survivors and determine whether they possess teachable skills, then the teaching of those skills could

prevent disorder from occurring after a traumatic experience. It is impossible to identify potential offenders before they decide to offend. Society cannot lock up everyone who fits the profile of a pedophile or incest perpetrator. Locking up repeat offenders who might abuse children, who would then grow up to abuse other children, could be considered primary prevention for that second generation of offenders. At this point in time there is no way to inoculate against child sexual abuse.

Secondary prevention is also difficult. A registry of known sex offenders might be considered helpful for families with children at risk in order to identify potential assailants and therefore avoid abuse. People are generally healthy before a traumatic event so there is no preclinical sign like an abnormal Pap smear to encourage early intervention; however, knowing the characteristics of those most likely to develop symptoms of PTSD after trauma might encourage such intervention. Debriefing or talking through a traumatic experience may be marginally helpful after mass disasters, but is not applicable to child sexual abuse. Some clinicians might argue that recovering memories of abuse and dealing with them after a person comes to therapy for nonspecific symptoms such as depression or weight gain would represent secondary prevention, but that intervention is controversial at best. Similarly, it is difficult to identify individuals who are at high risk of offending and encourage them to resist the urges. Addressing disinhibiting factors, such as alcohol and drug consumption or stress in individuals with other factors that might lead to child sexual abuse, would be preventive. One group trying to reach potential offenders is called Stop It Now. This group has hotlines in several cities. An individual who feels the urge to offend can call in and be referred to appropriate services to prevent his acting out. One drawback to this approach is that the hotline is legally obligated to

report offenses that have already occurred. Another example of early intervention is the police "sting" operation where an officer poses as a child on the Internet. When the potential perpetrator tries to meet the "child," he is arrested. Communications leading up to such an arrest must be carefully documented in order to avoid a defense of entrapment.

Psychotherapists provide tertiary interventions. A client presents with symptoms of post-traumatic stress and seeks relief from further deterioration or new symptoms. Identified abusers may seek interventions that will prevent future episodes or worse consequences.

Some interventions may serve to facilitate more than one level of prevention. Incarceration (primary) or treatment (tertiary) of an offender may spare a person at risk (secondary) from committing further abuses.

Despite the fact that fewer than 10 percent of child molesters are unknown to their victims, the principal focus of most abuse prevention efforts is the recognition of "stranger danger." A typical set of rules to teach a child is posted on the California Attorney General's website: "Stay away from people who call you near their car; If someone tries to take you away, yell 'This person is not my father (or mother)' and scream; If you get lost in a store, find another mom with children or go to the checkout counter; Don't keep secrets from your parents; No one should touch you in parts covered by your bathing suit and you shouldn't be asked to touch anyone there either; Don't let anyone take your picture without permission from your parents or teacher."

The most important advice, however, is for parents to "help protect your child by establishing a home environment where your child feels safe to tell you anything, without fear of shame, ridicule, or punishment." This advice is echoed by the New Hampshire Coalition Against Domestic and Sexual

Violence: "Make sure your child knows that their body is their own and no one should do anything to it that makes them feel uncomfortable, sad, or bad. They have a right to say 'no' if someone tries to touch them and not keep it a secret. If a secret makes a child feel sad, bad, or afraid, it is a secret they should not keep."

This is good advice and obviously applicable in situations where the potential or actual abuser is not a stranger; however, it is not advice that is readily available. If one thought that recognition and prevention of sexual abuse were a job for the schools, one would be mistaken. Although there certainly are exceptions, teachers, as a rule, do not talk about sex or sexual abuse. They are not trained to do so, are uncomfortable with the subject, and think it is a parental responsibility. Parents don't want teachers to talk about sex, are not trained to do so themselves, and are uncomfortable with the subject. Many teachers have a standard response to tough questions: "That's a very good question but you should ask your parents when you get home. We need to get on with the lesson for today." Chances are, that will be the end of the query.

Two organizations do have active programs in sexual abuse prevention. Such programs are aimed at protecting children, adults, and the organizations themselves. The Catholic Church and the Boy Scouts of America have much to be concerned about in this regard; both face multiple lawsuits for failure to protect children.

The Catholic Church now requires all adults, including volunteers, who work with children to take youth protection training. One commonly used program is "Protecting God's Children." Formal classroom training is followed by required online testing. After completing the program, a person should recognize the warning signs that an adult may wish to perpetrate abuse, know how to control who has access to children,

know how to monitor programs that involve children, be aware of changes in childhood behavior that may signal abuse, and know the procedures for communicating concern to the appropriate authority.

The program warns participants to pay particular attention to adults who prefer to spend time and form friendships with children, try to spend time with them alone, touch too much, give special gifts, and have a "favorite" child or children. These individuals bend the rules with children and discourage other adults from participating. They may use inappropriate language, tell dirty jokes, and show pornography to children.

When hiring or recruiting adults who are to have access to children, supervisors should check references and previous employers, obtain criminal background checks, and stress zero tolerance for unsafe behavior. Some dioceses exclude individuals with speeding tickets or other moving motor vehicle violations as potentially dangerous. Programs should be monitored so that adults can always be observed if not overheard when with children. Any secluded areas or unused rooms should be secured. More than one adult should always be involved in a program; parental visits and spot checks by supervisors are encouraged.

Persons responsible for the care of children should know these children well enough that any sudden changes in behavior, personal care, or relationships would be recognized. Concerns about suspicious or inappropriate behavior by either children or adults should be reported within the church chain of command and to the appropriate civil authority.

The Church has also prepared materials for parents and urges them to start early in identifying "teachable moments" to talk to their children about sex and sexual abuse so that the children will then be comfortable in talking to the parents

about inappropriate touches or bad feelings about secrets. Children should rehearse saying "no" in these circumstances and know how to contact a safe person at these times.

An audiovisual part of the training does point out that priests, too, can abuse children. That warning is not included in the written handouts. The Church does appear committed to removing abusive priests from the ministry and did remove about seven hundred in the two years 2002 and 2003. Part of that commitment is also due to multimillion-dollar settlements with victims. These have resulted in curtailment of other services, closing of parishes, and, in at least three cases, bankruptcy of a diocese.

The Boy Scouts of America (BSA) also has a course in Youth Protection that is required of all summer camp staff and adult volunteers. Concern about harm caused to children by abuse, the effect of abuse on the reputation of the BSA in terms of membership and community support, millions of dollars in settlements, and the subsequent effect on the BSA's liability insurance program are all factors in this requirement. Escalating insurance premiums effect programs and have resulted in liability surcharges on the annual registration fees of both individuals and units. New volunteers are now required to undergo criminal background checks and names are checked against the confidential file.

The program content of Boy Scout training is similar to that of Church training. The Scouts have also produced the videos *It Happened to Me* for six- to nine-year-olds and *A Time to Tell* for eleven- to thirteen-year-olds to educate youth about sexual abuse. Examples of abusers on the videos include a cousin, a neighbor, and a coach, but not a Scout leader. The Scouts suggest that young boys should see the video with their parents. As an alternative, they recommend that parents

review the videos before they are shown to boys because it is important for parents to be supportive, not to blame the child, and to clearly assign responsibility to the perpetrator. BSA policy now requires that two adults always be present at any Scout activity and that an adult not be alone with a child, especially on camping trips. All incidents and suspicions should be reported to Boy Scout authorities.

The current *Boy Scout Handbook* now contains a section on sexual abuse. "You do not have to let people touch you in ways you find uncomfortable. If you are ever asked to do something you know is wrong, you have the right to refuse." It goes on to stress the "three R's" of Recognize, Resist, and Report. The handbook also includes a tear-out parents' supplement that cites a few more statistics about sexual abuse, lists some possible warning signs, and encourages parents to keep talking to their children. The BSA has yet to address the problem that those individuals who work closely with the boys are generally recruited by the parents of those boys. Busy parents are unlikely to check the references of a potential volunteer and that screening is left to the formal registration process.

In 1994, seven-year-old Megan Kanka of Hamilton Township, New Jersey, was raped and murdered by a man who had recently moved in across the street. Jesse Timmendequas had two prior convictions for child molestation but the Kanka family was unaware of his history. As a result of this tragedy, in 1996 Congress passed and President Clinton signed "Megan's Law," requiring each state to develop and make available to the public a registry of known sex offenders in the community. The legislation gave states discretion in establishing criteria for disclosure but compelled them to make the information public. The New Jersey criteria are

typical for registration of "sex offenders and offenders who commit predatory acts upon children." A person convicted (adult), adjudicated delinquent (juvenile), or found not guilty by reason of insanity in the commission of a sex offense is required to register with the Office of the Attorney General when he is released, moves into the state, or changes addresses within the state. New Jersey recognized three levels of risk and notification: 1) the local police, 2) local police plus schools and religious and youth organizations, and 3) the general public. An offender can petition to terminate his registration after fifteen years without incident.

Every state now has some version of Megan's Law. Access to the Sex Offender Registry varies widely. In some states the public must visit the local police station to look at the list or call a specific hotline, which may not be toll-free. Other states post some or all names and addresses of registrants on the Internet. These laws have been challenged on a number of points, but in 2002 the United States Supreme Court handed down two decisions that affirmed their existence. In *Smith v. Doe,* an Alaska case, the Court ruled that "ex-post facto" registration was not "double jeopardy" and did not extend a sentence that had already been completed because registration was "non-punitive." Since the registry stated that known offenders were not supposed to be harassed in the community, they were not being punished. In *Connecticut Department of Public Safety v. Doe,* the Court ruled that registration is not a deprivation of liberty and that an individual assessment of current danger is not necessary prior to registration.

In August 2004, Massachusetts became the forty-third state to post the names, addresses, and photos of registered offenders on the Internet. Such posting is limited to so-called Level 3 offenders where "danger to the public is high and the individual is likely to reoffend." In ruling on the challenge that

posting this information would make the identified individuals subject to vigilante justice, solicitation by pornographers and other sex offenders, and complicate rehabilitation and reintegration into society, the Massachusetts Supreme Judicial Court ruled that "this is not a utopian society" and the posting served to protect society at large.

Critics continue to point out that since the vast majority of offenders are already known to the family, these lists serve no useful purpose. Even advocates of posting agree that only the most potentially dangerous offenders should be listed because there would otherwise be a flood of information. There are 18,000 registered offenders in Massachusetts alone, but only 975 names were initially posted on the Internet. The controversy will continue as some states seek to add workplace information to the name, address, and photo already posted. Some people see a sort of poetic justice in the fact that pedophiles who solicited sex on the Internet may now find their own photo posted there. They may even be able to register as a sex offender online. The major limitation to any form of listing, however, is that a concerned parent must check repeatedly to see if someone on the list might have recently moved into the neighborhood.

In addition to posting names and addresses, Massachusetts will also use global positioning systems (GPS) and electronic bracelets to track sex offenders still on probation or parole. The GPS device will enable authorities to locate the offender within ten yards of his position and will also signal if it has been removed. Proponents argue that such tracking will not only make the public safer, but will protect the offender from suspicion should an incident occur in his neighborhood. Proposals to extend the monitoring program to those offenders who have completed court supervision would certainly be subject to constitutional challenge.

While primary prevention remains the goal, it is currently an elusive one. Early intervention and effective treatment remain the best hope for protecting children, decreasing disability, and maintaining personal freedom. Researchers continue to pursue earlier and earlier markers of deviation and vulnerability in the hope that they might someday make a true breakthrough in preventive medicine.

7. The Search for Answers

Women who have been sexually abused as children are more likely to breast-feed their own children than are women who were not abused. Pedophiles are more likely to report head trauma before age thirteen than are all people in the general population. What is the significance, if any, of these observations? One man who fantasizes exclusively about preadolescent boys has no contact with them but writes a story about a boy who never grows up. Another volunteers to be a Little League coach in order to be in a position to maneuver boys to his home. How are they different? One child who has sexual contact with an adult is psychologically devastated, another shrugs it off, and a third thinks it was a wonderful experience. How can there be such a wide range of reactions? Research interest in the aftereffects of adult-child sex has increased dramatically in recent years, but questions remain in every aspect of this problem area.

The scope of the problem is the first concern. Standardization of the definition of child sexual abuse would be a good first step. Age, age differential, type of contact, and perceived harm are all important variables. Studies of people in therapy or in prison have selection bias and are not representative of the population as a whole. When the general population is surveyed, the methodology is not standardized. Critical data on racial and ethnic groups with regard to incidence and personal and community aftereffects are woefully inadequate. This is true for the United States and for other countries as well. Are there particular demographic or personal or community dynamics associated with seemingly high-risk groups

such as Catholic priests? The duty to report child abuse limits the ability of researchers to obtain honest historical data. It is impossible to identify the so-called non-contact pedophiles who are aroused by children but do not act out. They are a group that requires further study.

Memory is another concern. The battle between "repressed memory" advocates and "false memory" advocates continues unabated. While "false memory" researchers design studies that new "memories" can, in fact, be implanted, the "repressed memory" group continues to pile up anecdotal evidence that their clients are recovering memories of the true past. It may not be good science, but it is somehow comforting to have an explanation for a problem.

The treatment of both victims and perpetrators is fraught with potential ethical dilemmas. It is sometimes difficult to establish that patients or inmates have given truly informed consent when therapeutic intervention is recommended. A complete and documented explanation of potential risks and benefits is often irrelevant to someone wanting to get better or get out. There is also another ethical dilemma in withholding therapy that has been shown to be beneficial. There are not many randomly assigned, double-blind crossover studies in the pharmacologic treatment of post-traumatic stress disorder. "Control" subjects on a waiting list must ultimately be offered treatment.

For Survivors

With regard to psychotherapeutic interventions, there are a limited number of outcome studies; those that have been done usually have only a three- or six-month followup. Long-term followup is a time-consuming and expensive process,

but it must be done in order to determine, for example, if psychotherapy, cognitive behavioral therapy, or EMDR produces long-lasting results. If all are equally beneficial in the short term because of the positive relationship with a therapist of any of these orientations, then what is the basis for choosing one treatment over another? What results should clients and insurers demand for their healthcare dollar?

Not everyone who is traumatized develops pathological symptoms. It is important to understand why some people are resilient to stress and others thrive on it. Dr. George Bonanno, a psychologist at Columbia University, has done research and written extensively on resilience to trauma. Although most of his work has been done with adults, his conclusions may be applicable to children as well. Bonanno notes first that resilience is different from recovery. Although resilient people may show transient responses to trauma, they maintain a stable equilibrium throughout and enjoy some protective factors that favor the development of positive outcomes and healthy personality characteristics.

Resilience is common and healthy and it comes in many forms. Bonanno calls these hardiness, self-enhancement, repressive coping, and positive emotion and laughter. While some of these are not generally viewed as positive attributes, they aid in adapting to trauma.

Hardy individuals are committed to finding a meaningful purpose in life, believe that one can influence his or her surroundings and the outcome of events, and believe that one can learn and grow from both positive and negative experiences. These people are not as threatened by traumatic situations, their distress is minimal, and they are more confident in seeking support.

While self-enhancement might be considered negative in some social contexts, a positive opinion of oneself, even to the

point of narcissism, is helpful in the face of threat. Those who use repression as a coping mechanism routinely avoid unpleasant thoughts, emotions, and memories. This strategy may cause problems in some social situations but is adaptive in the context of trauma. Individuals who have a positive attitude, show gratitude and a genuine interest in the world, and love and frequently laugh fare better in dealing with stress. They believe that they can learn from it and grow.

These characteristics were found in adults. For children who have yet to develop a fixed personality style and coping mechanisms, a mix of factors including genetic predisposition, family interaction, and community support should be considered as well. There are many potential areas of research in understanding how all these factors are interrelated.

Psychiatrist David Charney at the National Institute of Mental Health has done extensive research in the psychobiological mechanisms of resilience and vulnerability. If people with post-traumatic stress disorder show an increase in brain norepinepherine and serotonin, decrease in hippocampal size, failed activation of the anterior cingulate cortex, and decreased serum cortisol levels, it might follow that resilient people show just the opposite findings. Animal and a few human studies have confirmed some of these hypotheses, but this is still a very new area of research.

The brain must be able to adapt to acute stress and then return to baseline function or homeostasis. If that base-line changes to a different set point, then the person will be more or less vulnerable to the next stressful episode. The resilient person quickly returns to or may not even leave the preexisting baseline level of response. Researchers have suggested many possible mechanisms to explain this. Perhaps there is a genetic difference in catecholamine or cortisol receptor density or receptor sensitivity. A person with fewer or less

sensitive receptors would not be as vulnerable to the stress response. Conversely, more benzodiazepine receptors would facilitate calming.

Charney has suggested that the *allostatic load* may be important. The allostatic load is the cumulative physiologic burden borne by the body from attempts to adapt to stressors and the strains of life. Contributing to the load are eleven known neurochemical, neuropeptide, and hormonal mediators of the stress response (cortisol, dehydroandrosterone [DHEA], corticotropin-releasing hormone [CRH], locus coeruleus-norepinephrine system, neuropeptide Y, galanin, dopamine, serotonin, benzodiazepine receptors, testosterone, and estrogen). Individual levels or variable ratios and interactions may favor resilience or vulnerability.

A similar profile might be developed for psychological risk factors. These would include intelligence, effective self-regulation of emotions and attachment behaviors, positive self-concept, optimism, altruism, a capacity to convert traumatic helplessness into learned helpfulness, and an active coping style in confronting a stressor. To the extent that these traits can be learned or conditioned, that process would involve neural pathways. Brain-scanning techniques such as positron emission tomography (PET) can map function, and magnetic resonance imaging (MRI) the structures, of the brain. Neural circuits for reward, the conditioning and extinction of fear, and the formation of social attachments are most probably located in the amygdala. In resilient individuals, specific incoming stimuli are either not overgeneralized or are quickly extinguished. Reactivated memories are returned to long-term storage, a process that requires protein binding. Extinction—the repeated exposure to a stimulus without response—is facilitated, perhaps by more receptor sites. Cooperative social relationships are easier to forge. If specific

neuronal pathways for these learning processes can be identi-fied, specific genetic mechanisms in response to stress may be mapped and specific interventions developed. This work clearly confounds the notion of a mind-body dichotomy as more and more biological correlates of behavior are discovered.

For Abusers

More genetic, hormonal, and structural work has been done with regard to susceptibility or resistance to stress disorders than to susceptibility or resistance to paraphilic disorders. Neuroimaging studies for differential arousal patterns would be of interest, as would hormonal and genetic studies.

It has been suggested that birth order may play a role in the development of pedophilia. This argument by analogy is based on the observation that, statistically, a subset of male homosexuals tends to have older brothers. The proposed mechanism is called maternal immunoreactivity. This would be similar to Rh and ABO blood group incompatibilities. In some pregnant women, the fetus provokes a maternal immune response so that maternal antibodies cross the placenta and affect the fetus. If the mother develops antibodies about some facet of maleness in the fetus, that response would increase with each subsequent male pregnancy. The maternal antibod-ies somehow disrupt neurohormonal development crucial for sexual differentiation of the fetal brain, and the male has female-type sexual preferences. If gender sexual preference can be disrupted in this way, why could age sexual preference not be disrupted in the same manner? Pedophiles should there-fore, statistically, show a preponderance of men with older

brothers. Some studies have shown this to be true. Disruptions leading to both homosexuality and pedophilia could independently occur in the same individual, but only in a small number of cases. Maternal immunoreactivity is likely to be just one of several factors contributing to sexual arousal to the young.

Several studies have reported an association, in men, between self-reported head injury before age thirteen and later pedophilic behavior. This could mean that subtle brain damage after birth increases the risk of pedophilia or that an as yet unknown neurodevelopmental problem before birth increases the risk of both accident-proneness and pedophilia. The correlation is not robust. Similarly, there are suggestions that pedophiles have a lower than expected level of intelligence, that they have a strong tendency to be left-handed, and that the first appearance of pedophilic behavior in an adult is associated with a temporal lobe disorder and/or an increased prolactin level. Large population studies with neuroimaging and sophisticated neuropsychological testing will be necessary to determine if these are, in fact, risk factors.

While developmental factors do seem to be more important than biological ones in the etiology of pedophilia, there may still be underlying neurophysiologic conditions that contribute to sexual arousal to children. Not every man exposed to the factors associated with such arousal becomes a pedophile. Some as yet unknown physiologic mechanism may make some individuals more susceptible or may even prevent the emergence of sexually abusive behavior in others.

Much work is yet to be done to understand both sides of the adult-child sexual experience. The ability to put aside prejudice and to be open to scientific inquiry is a prerequisite for any such work. Only in this way can we learn to

be of help to those who are truly traumatized by the sexual experience rather than create additional "victims" with our own reactions and unhelpful interventions. We can work to identify and isolate those who will always present a danger to children—but also to identify and treat those who can be rehabilitated and become productive members of society.

Appendix A

State Sex Offender Registry Sites

These sites contain or have links to the relevant statutes and definitions.

Alabama
www.dps.state.al.us/public/abi/system/so

Alaska
www.dps.state.ak.us/nSorcr/asp

Arizona
www.az.gov/webapp/offender/main.do

Arkansas
www.acic.org/Registration/04-registered-sex-offenders.htm

California
www.caag.state.ca.us/megan

Colorado
www.sor.state.co.us/default.asp

Only serious offenders are online. Other requests go to local police departments.

Connecticut
www.state.ct.us/dps/Sex_Offender_Registry.htm

Delaware
www.state.de.us/dsp/sexoff/index.htm

District of Columbia
www.mpdc.dc.gov/serv/sor/sor.shtm

Florida
www3.fdle.state.fl.us/Sexual_Predators

Georgia
www.state.ga.us/gbi/disclaim.html

Hawaii
www.pahoehoe.ehawaii.gov/sexoff

Idaho
www.isp.state.id.us/identification/sex_offender/predator

Illinois
www.isp.state.il.us/sor/frames.htm

Indiana
www.state.in.us/serv/cji_sor

Iowa
www.iowasexoffender.com

Kansas
www.accesskansas.org/kbi/ro.shtml

Kentucky
kspsor.state.ky.us

Louisiana
www.lasocpr.lsp.org/socpr

Maine
www.informe.org/sor

Maryland
www.dpscs.state.md.us/onlineservs/sor

Massachusetts
www.mass.gov/sorb/community.htm

Michigan
www.mipsor.state.mi.us

Minnesota
www.doc.state.mn.us/level3/Search.asp

Mississippi
www.sor.mdps.state.ms.us

Missouri
www.mshp.dps.missouri.gov/MSHPWeb/PatrolDivision/
  CRID/SOR/SORPage.html

Montana
svor.doj.state.mt.us

Nebraska
www.nsp.state.ne.us/sor

Nevada
www.nvrepository.state.nv.us/Sexoffender.htm
Local police determine who may have access to this list.

New Hampshire
www.oit.nh.gov/nsor

New Jersey
www.njsp.org/info/reg_sexoffend.html

New Mexico
www.nmsexoffender.dps.state.nm.us

New York
criminaljustice.state.ny.us/nsor/index.htm

North Carolina
sbi.jus.state.nc.us/DOJHAHT/SOR/default.htm

North Dakota
www.ndsexoffender.com

Ohio
www.esorn.ag.state.oh.us/Secured/p1.aspx

Oklahoma
www.doc.state.ok.us/DOCS/offender_info.htm
Department of Corrections lists "habitual and aggravated" sex
  offenders.

Oregon
Oregon does not maintain an online registry. Call State Police
  for information.

Pennsylvania
www.psp.state.pa.us/psp/cwp/view.asp?a=3&q=150335

Puerto Rico
Puerto Rico does not maintain an online registry.

Rhode Island
Rhode Island does not maintain an online registry. RIS
  Chapter 11-37.1 describes the registration process.

South Carolina
www.sled.state.sc.us/SLED

South Dakota
dci.sd.gov/administration/id/sexoffender/index.asp

Tennessee
www.ticic.state.tn.us

Texas
records.txdps.state.tx.us/sosearch.cfm

Utah
www.udc.state.ut.us/asp-bin/sexoffendersearchform.asp

Vermont
www.dps.state.vt.us/cjs/s_registry.htm

Virginia
sex-offender.vsp.state.va.us/Static/cool-ICE

Washington
Washington does not maintain an online registry, but some
counties do. Release of information is at the discretion of
the local police.

West Virginia
www.wvstatepolice.com/sexoff

Wisconsin
offender.doc.state.wi.us/public/search/search.jsp

Wyoming
attorneygeneral.state.wy.us/dci/so/so_registration.html

Appendix B

Publications

Allgeier, E. R. & Allgeier, A. R. *Sexual Interactions*, 5th edition. Boston, Houghton Mifflin Co. 2000. A basic college textbook about human sexuality with a good section on sexual abuse.

American Psychiatric Association. *Diagnostic and Statistical Manual of Mental Disorders*, 4th edition. Washington, DC. 1994. Includes specific criteria for the diagnosis of each condition.

Bass, E. & Davis, L. *The Courage to Heal.* New York, Harper Collins. 1988. The book that started the repressed memory controversy.

Boyle, P. *Scouts Honor: Sexual Abuse in America's Most Trusted Institution.* Rocklin, CA, Prima Publishing. 1994. Sexual abuse in Scouting as told by participants.

Bremner, J. D. *Does Stress Damage the Brain? Understanding Trauma-Related Disorders from a Neurological Perspective.* New York, W. W. Norton & Co. 2002. Focus on damage to the hippocampus.

Carr, C. *The Alienist.* New York, Random House. 1994. A fictionalized account of child prostitution in New York City in 1896.

Courtois, C. *Recollections of Sexual Abuse: Treatment Principles and Guidelines.* New York, W. W. Norton & Co. 1999. Evolving standards of practice in working with those who may have been abused.

Follette, V. M., Ruzek, J. J. & Abueg, F. R. (eds.). *Cognitive-Behavioral Therapies for Trauma.* New York, Guilford. 1998. Description of various techniques by experts in each.

Friedman, M. J., Charney, D. S. & Deutch, A. Y. (eds.). *Neurological and Clinical Consequences of Stress: From Normal Adaptation to Post-Traumatic Stress Disorder.* Philadelphia, Lippincott. 1995. A collection of relevant studies.

Herman, J. *Trauma and Recovery.* New York, Basic Books. 1992. The classic description of the recovery process.

Laumann, E. O., Gagnon, J. H., Michael, R. T. & Michaels, S. *The Social Organization of Sexuality: Sexual Practices in the United States.* Chicago, University of Chicago Press. 1994. The most extensive field study done in the United States.

Loftus, E. & Ketcham, K. *The Myth of Repressed Memory: False Memories and Allegations of Sexual Abuse.* New York, St. Martin's Griffin. 1996. An expert in memory looks at the controversy.

Resick, P. A. *Stress and Trauma.* Philadelphia, Taylor and Francis. 2001. An excellent treatment resource.

Shapiro, F. *Eye Movement Desensitization and Reprocessing: Basic Principles, Protocols, and Procedures.* New York, Guilford. 1995. A description of this therapeutic approach by its founder.

Sipe, A. W. R. *Celibacy in Crisis.* New York, Brunner-Routledge. 2003. A look at the sexual behavior of Catholic priests.

Van der Kolk, B. A., McFarlane, A. C. & Weisarth, L. (eds.). *Traumatic Stress: The Effects of Overwhelming Experience on Mind, Body, and Society.* New York, Guilford. 1996. Includes several relevant chapters.

Appendix C

The Internet

Stop It Now!
www.stopitnow.com
Sponsors a helpline for abusers, 888-PREVENT

Sex Addicts Anonymous
www.sexaa.org
Twelve-step program with over 500 meetings around the world, 800-477-8191

Sexuality Education and Information Council of the United States (SIECUS)
www.siecus.org
Fact sheets and annotated bibliographies about sexual abuse.

American Association of Sex Educators, Counselors, and Therapists (AASECT)
www.aasect.org
Includes listing of certified sex therapists.

National Center for the Prosecution of Child Abuse
www.ndaa-apri.org/apri/programs/ncpca/ncpca_home.html
Trains prosecutors with reference to all relevant state statues.

VIRTUS
www.virtusonline.org
Produces and updates the Protecting God's Children program for the Catholic Church.

PubMed
www.ncbi.nlm.nih.gov
National Library of Medicine search service with over eleven
million resources.

Open-Mind
www.open-mind.org
Includes an online Survivors Forum.

Survivors Network of Those Abused by Priests
www.snapnetwork.org
For self-help, education, and prevention with fifty support
groups nationwide.

New Hampshire Coalition Against Domestic and Sexual
Violence
www.nhcadsv.org
A representative state group stressing service to victims, education, and accountability.

California Attorney General www.caag.state.ca.us/
childabuse
Guidelines for protection as well as legal remedies.

Computer Retrieval of Information on Scientific Projects
www.crisp.cit.nih.gov
Information about all grant projects currently funded by the
National Institutes of Health. Search for "child sexual abuse."

MedLinePlus
www.medlineplus.gov
Online medical encyclopedia and dictionary.

Glossary

Addiction   Psychological or physiological dependence on a substance or practice that is beyond voluntary control.

Adrenal glands   A pair of small glands that sit upon the kidneys and produce cortisol in the outer layer (adrenal cortex) and adrenalin in the central area (adrenal medulla).

Adrenalin (Epinephrine)   A catecholamine secreted by the adrenal medulla and by neurons in the central nervous system. It increases the rate and strength of the heartbeat and dilates small arteries within muscle tissue.

Amygdala   A cluster of specialized nerve cells deep in each hemisphere that plays an important role in emotions.

Autonomic nervous system   That part of the nervous system that innervates smooth muscle, cardiac muscle, and gland cells. It has two divisions: the sympathetic increases activity and the parasympathetic promotes rest and restoration.

Aversive conditioning   Techniques that pair a painful, noxious, or otherwise unwelcome stimulus with particular thoughts or behaviors in order to extinguish them.

Biofeedback   Technique where changes in unconscious or involuntary body functions are made perceptible to the senses in order to modulate them by conscious mental control.

Brain stem   Portion of the central nervous system that connects spinal cord with brain and contains many nerve cells that regulate primitive brain function.

Castration   Removal of the testicles or ovaries.

Catecholamine   A class of neurotransmitters that includes epinephrine, norepinephrine, and L-dopa.

Celibacy   Complete sexual abstinence.

Cerebellum   Part of the brain that coordinates muscle tone, posture, and eye and hand movements based on sensory information received from other parts of the brain.

Cerebral cortex   Outer layer and major portion of the brain; contains nerve cells for speech, motor activity, sensory reception, emotion, and cognitive functions.

Cognition   The mental activities associated with thinking, learning, and memory.

Cognitive behavioral therapy   Form of therapy that combines verbal communication and behavioral techniques in order to affect change.

Comorbidity   The coexistence of two or more unrelated disease processes.

Cortisol   Hormone produced by the adrenal cortex that affects the metabolism of glucose, protein, and fat; often increases in response to stress.

Countertransference   Therapist's responses to a client based on the therapist's past experiences or response to the patient's transference.

Covert sensitization   A behavioral technique using imagination alone to affect change.

Debriefing   Talking about a traumatic experience immediately after it occurs.

Depersonalization   A state in which one loses the feeling of one's own identity.

Desensitization   The reduction or elimination of reactions to a specific stimulus.

Deviation   A departure from an accepted norm, role, or rule.

Dissociation   An unconscious separation of one group of mental processes from the others.

Dyspareunia   The occurrence of pain on the part of the woman during sexual intercourse.

Dysphoria   A feeling of unpleasantness or discomfort.

EMDR (Eye movement desensitization and reprocessing)   A therapeutic technique where rapid eye movement is paired with repeated traumatic images and positive affirmations.

Enabler   A person who tacitly supports or ignores negative behavior in another, thereby allowing or encouraging it to continue.

Endocrine glands   The glands in the body that secrete hormones which affect the function of other parts of the body.

Ephebophilia   A paraphilia in which there is sexual attraction to postpubescent youths.

Extinction   The progressive decrease in the frequency of a response that is no longer positively reinforced.

Fixation   A firm attachment to a particular person or object from an earlier period of one's development.

Flooding   A behavioral technique in which clients immerse themselves in their most anxiety-producing situations.

Galvanic skin response (GSR)   The measurement of variation in skin conductance due to sympathetically driven increase in perspiration.

Global Positioning System (GPS)   A system that pinpoints geographic location via satellite tracking.

Hippocampus   The seahorse-shaped structure in the cerebral cortex that is part of the limbic system; connects with brain stem nuclei as well.

Hormone   A chemical substance formed in one organ of the body and carried in the blood to alter the function of another organ.

Hypnosis   An induced trancelike state during which the subject is highly suggestible.

Hypothalamus   Part of the brain stem composed of multiple nerve centers; coordinates and controls body functions such as eating, sleeping, and sexual behavior, maintains

body temperature and chemical balance, and regulates many hormones.

Incest   Sexual relations between persons closely related by blood.

Limbic system   An interrelated circuit of deep brain structures involved in emotion, behavior, autonomic function, and smell.

Locus coeruleus   A cell cluster in the wall of the fourth ventricle of the brain whose norepinephrine-containing axons have wide distribution in the cerebellum, hypothalamus, and cerebral cortex.

Magnetic resonance imaging (MRI)   A method of body scanning that can be used to detect abnormalities of structure within the brain.

Masturbation   The self-stimulation of the genitals for erotic pleasure and orgasm.

Meta-analysis   The process of using statistical methods to combine the results of different studies.

Neurobiology   The biology of the nervous system.

Neuroimaging   Techniques used to visualize the function or anatomy of the central nervous system.

Neurotransmitter   A chemical that functions within the nervous system as part of the process of transmitting information from one neuron to the next.

Noradrenalin (norepinephrine)   A catecholamine that serves as the primary neurotransmitter within the sympathetic nervous system.

Pap test   A cervical smear examined for abnormal cells, named for Dr. George Papanicolaou.

Paraphilia   A condition of compulsive responsivity to and obligatory dependence on an unusual and socially unacceptable external stimulus or internal fantasy for sexual arousal.

Pedophilia   A paraphilia in which there is sexual attraction to prepubescent youths.

Penile plethysmograph   A device to measure changes in the volume of the penis.

Pituitary   A gland on the underside of the brain that produces neurohormones which assist in the regulation of hormone production by other glands.

Plea-bargain   A legal maneuver where the designated offense and punishment are agreed upon by the prosecution and defense in order to avoid or end a trial.

Polygraph   An instrument to measure changes in respiration, blood pressure, and galvanic skin response (GSR) while the subject is being questioned about emotionally charged topics.

Pornography   Sexually explicit material designed for arousal.

Positron emission tomography (PET)   A method of body scanning using mildly radioactive compounds to yield images of activity level.

Post-traumatic stress disorder (PTSD)   The reexperience of trauma, avoidance of associated stimuli, and increased agitation following a traumatic incident.

Prostate-specific antigen (PSA)   A substance that induces a state of sensitivity; elevated in diseases of the prostate.

Psychopathology   A general term for mental and behavioral disorders.

Psychotherapy   The treatment of mental distress through verbal communication.

Puberty   The phase of life, usually in adolescence, where reproductive fertility and physical changes consistent with sexual maturity begin.

Rapid eye movement (REM)   The stage of sleep where the eyes move rapidly beneath closed lids, the body does not move, and dreaming occurs.

Recidivism A relapse to a previous behavior pattern.

Regression The return to a more primitive mode of behavior.

Repression The active process of keeping memories out of conscious awareness.

Resilience The ability to recover from or adjust easily to a traumatic experience.

Separation anxiety A developmental stage (usually between eight and fourteen months of age) during which a child experiences anxiety when separated from the primary caregiver (usually the mother).

Serotonin A monoamine that serves as a neurotransmitter in the central nervous system.

Somatization The process by which psychological needs are expressed as physical symptoms.

Testosterone The most potent androgenic hormone, formed mostly in the testes.

Therapeutic community A milieu where patients and staff together make important decisions about community life.

Transference The projection of feelings, thoughts, and wishes onto the therapist as representative of a person from the patient's past.

Vaginismus Painful spasm of the vagina.

Ventricle One of a system of communicating cavities within the brain.

Index

Abel, Gene, 27, 57
Allostatic load, 81
American Psychological Association, 24, 25
Amygdala, 33, 34, 81
Anatomically correct dolls, 21
Anticonvulsants
  in post-traumatic stress disorder, 45
  in sex offender treatment, 61

Benzodiazepines
  in post-traumatic stress disorder, 45
  in sex offender treatment, 61
Borderline personality disorder, 40
Boy Scout Handbook, 73
Boy Scouts of America
  preventive programs, 72
  and sexual abuse, 12
Brain anatomy, 31
Bremmer, J. Douglas, 33

Catecholamines, 32
Catholic Church
  pedophile priests, 10
  preventive programs, 70
"Chemical castration," 63
Child Abuse Prevention and Treatment
  Act (1974), 19
Child Sexual Abuse
  effect on adolescents, 37
  effect on adults, 38
  effect on boys, 41
  effect on young children, 37
  incidence, 19, 22
  sequelae, 24
  and sexual dysfunction, 36
  therapist guidelines, 50
  treatments, 51
Clergy privilege, 20
Cognitive behavioral therapy
  in child sexual abuse, 51
  in sex offender treatment, 62

Cortisol, in post-traumatic stress disorder, 34
Countertransference, 47
Courage to Heal, The, 48

Depression
  in child sexual abuse, 39
  in sex offender treatment, 61
Depersonalization, 35
Dissociative identity disorder, 40

Ephibophilia, 4
Eye Movement Desensitization and
  Reprocessing, 53

"False memory syndrome," 49
Freud, Sigmund, 3

Global Positioning System, 75

Herman, Judith, 30, 43
Hippocampus, 33

Internet
  Sex Offender Registry, 74
  utilization by offenders, 27
  utilization by police, 69
Interviewing, 21
Intrafamilial sexual abuse
  definition of, 12
  family patterns, 25
  incidence, 23

Loftus, Elizabeth, 48
Lolita, 8

Masturbation, 6; in sex offender
  treatment, 63
Masturbatory satiation, 62
Maternal immunoreactivity, 82
"Megan's Law," 73

North American Man-Boy Love
Association, 15, 25

Paraphilia, 4
"Parentified female child"
    as an adult, 39
    evolution of, 13
    treatment of, 52
Pedophilia
    definition of, 4
    fixated, 5
    regressed, 5
Penile plethysmograph, 60, 64
Pituitary gland, 31
Polygraph, 60
Pornography
    child, 8
    definition of, 7
Post-traumatic growth, 56
Post-traumatic stress disorder
    definition, 29
    medication in, 44
    prevention, 67
    treatment, 43
Priest, pedophile, 10
Prostitution, child, 16
Psychotherapy, in post-traumatic
    stress disorder, 45, 69
Public Safety v. Doe, 74

"Repressed memory," 48
Resilience
    in child sexual abuse, 79
    and psychobiology, 80

"Sex addict," 61
Sex offender
    female, 14
    modus operandi, 11, 26
    recidivism, 64, 65
    treatment programs, 59
Sex Offender Registry, 74
Sex therapist, 55
Sexual arousal, in pedophilia, 6
Sexual assault, 3
Sexual dysfunction, 36
Smith v. Doe, 74
Somatization disorder, 40
Specific serotonin reuptake
    inhibitors, 44
State v. Hungerford, 49
Stop It Now, 68
"Stranger danger" rules, 69

Therapeutic community, 59, 63
Transference, 46

van der Kolk, Bessel, 34

Understanding Health and Sickness Series
Miriam Bloom, Ph.D., General Editor

Also in this series

Addiction • Alzheimer's Disease • Anemia • Asthma • Breast Cancer
Genetics • Childhood Obesity • Chronic Pain • Colon Cancer •
Cosmetic Laser Surgery • Crohn Disease and Ulcerative Colitis •
Cystic Fibrosis • Dental Health • Depression • Hepatitis • Herpes •
Mental Retardation • Migraine and Other Headaches • Multiple
Sclerosis • Panic and Other Anxiety Disorders • Sickle Cell Disease •
Stuttering